Origins and Development of Musical Instruments

Jeremy Montagu

THE SCARECROW PRESS, INC.
Lanham, Maryland • Toronto • Plymouth, UK
2007

SCARECROW PRESS, INC.

Published in the United States of America
by Scarecrow Press, Inc.
A wholly owned subsidiary of
The Rowman & Littlefield Publishing Group, Inc.
4501 Forbes Boulevard, Suite 200, Lanham, Maryland 20706
www.scarecrowpress.com

Estover Road
Plymouth PL6 7PY
United Kingdom

British Library Cataloguing in Publication Information Available

Library of Congress Cataloging-in-Publication Data

Montagu, Jeremy.
  Origins and development of musical instruments / Jeremy Montagu.
    p. cm.
  Includes bibliographical references (p.   ) and index.
  ISBN-13: 978-0-8108-5657-8 (hardback : alk. paper)
  ISBN-10: 0-8108-5657-3 (hardback : alk. paper)
  1. Musical instruments—History. I. Title.

ML460.M76 2007
784.1909—dc22
                                        2007016987

In memoriam
Gwen
26.4.1923–12.1.2003
Proverbs 31:10–31

~

Contents

List of Illustrations   vii
Acknowledgments   xi
Explanations and Definitions   xiii
Abbreviations   xvii
Maps   xix

1 Origins   1
Musical Sound   2
Voices   3
Lithophones   6
Percussion Bars   9
Bells and Gongs   14
Rattles   18
Interlude A: Instruments of Protection   24

2 Drums   27
Trouble with Tension   27
Drums   28
Tubular Drums   29
Interlude B: Musicians   41

3 Flutes and Recorders   44
Monotone   44
Whistling in the Wind   45
Vessel Flutes   50
Penny Whistles and Recorders   52
Transverse Flutes   59
Harmonic Flutes   65
Interlude C: The Medieval Renaissance and the First Industrial Revolution   70

4 Reeds   73
Straws in the Wind   73
Oboes and Bassoons   80
Clarinets and Other Single Reeds   85
Free Reeds   94
Interlude D: The Ideal Accompaniment   100

5 "Brass" Instruments: Trumpets and Horns — 103
Interlude E: The Second Industrial Revolution — 116

6 String Instruments — 125
From Bows to Lyres, Harps, and Lutes — 125
Lyres — 128
Harps — 132
Zithers — 140
Stringed Keyboards — 145
Plucked Lutes — 152
Bowed Lutes aka Fiddles — 161
Interlude F: Messengers — 180

7 Pipe Organs — 188
Interlude G: Symbiosis — 194

8 Electrophones — 202
Interlude H: Newly Created, Recognized, or Discovered Instruments — 205

Afterword: Archaeology and Other -ologies — 209
  Classification of Instruments — 210
  Scales and Music — 214
  The Sounds of Science — 217
Bibliography — 225
Index of Instruments and Accessories — 235
Index of Places and Peoples — 245
General Index — 249
About the Author — 257

Illustrations

Figure 0.1	The harmonic series	xiv
Figure 1.1	Bull-roarers and buzzers	4
Figure 1.2	Friction drums	5
Figure 1.3	Kazoos	7
Figure 1.4	Rock gong	8
Figure 1.5	Chinese stone chimes	9
Figure 1.6	Percussion bars	10
Figure 1.7	Timbila	11
Figure 1.8	Balo, Ghana	12
Figure 1.9	Renaissance xylophone	12
Figure 1.10	Sansas, mbiras, and kalimbas	13
Figure 1.11	Iron cattle bells	15
Figure 1.12	Resting bells	17
Figure 1.13	Roman cymbal player	17
Figure 1.14	Jingles and sistra	19
Figure 1.15	Vessel rattles	20
Figure 1.16	Leg rattles	21
Figure A.1	Cog rattles or ratchets	25
Figure A.2	Clappers, etc.	26
Figure 2.1	Frame drums	29
Figure 2.2	Goblet and hourglass drums	30
Figure 2.3	*Ese* drums	31
Figure 2.4	New Guinea drums	32

Figure 2.5	Pair of *tablā* with accessories	33
Figure 2.6	*Naggāra*, paired kettledrums	34
Figure 2.7	Medieval nakers, c. 1330	35
Figure 2.8	Machine timpani	36
Figure 2.9	Renaissance timpani and side drums	37
Figure 2.10	Bronze drum	39
Figure 3.1	Panpipes	46
Figure 3.2	End- and notch-blown flutes	47
Figure 3.3	Whistles, some with one or two fingerholes	49
Figure 3.4	Vessel flutes	51
Figure 3.5	Ocarinas	52
Figure 3.6	External- and tongue-duct flutes	53
Figure 3.7	Early Renaissance recorders	55
Figure 3.8	Later Renaissance recorders	55
Figure 3.9	Flageolets	57
Figure 3.10	Flutes with constricted foot, each with a second to show the foot	58
Figure 3.11	Asian transverse flutes	60
Figure 3.12	Renaissance transverse flutes	61
Figure 3.13	Transverse flutes	63
Figure 3.14	Scale for harmonic flute	65
Figure 3.15	Harmonic flutes	66
Figure C.1	Early medieval instruments	71
Figure 4.1	Some reeds for woodwinds	74
Figure 4.2	Cylindrical shawms or Silk Road *auloi*	76
Figure 4.3	Exotic shawms	77
Figure 4.4	*Ghaita* fork	78
Figure 4.5	European shawms	79
Figure 4.6	English two-key oboes, c. 1800	81
Figure 4.7	Keyed oboes	82
Figure 4.8	English horns	83
Figure 4.9	Bassoons	84
Figure 4.10	Reed squawkers	86
Figure 4.11	Single-reed pipes	87
Figure 4.12	Geminate pipes	88

Figure 4.13	Hornpipes	89
Figure 4.14	Side-blown reed pipes	89
Figure 4.15	Modern *chalumeaux*	91
Figure 4.16	Boxwood clarinets	92
Figure 4.17	German-system clarinets, from Müller to Oehler	93
Figure 4.18	Belgian- and French-system clarinets, from Albert to Boehm	94
Figure 4.19	Mouth organs and free-reed horns	95
Figure 4.20	Accordions etc. and harmonicas	97
Figure 5.1	Horns and conchs	104
Figure 5.2	Moroccan *nafir*	107
Figure 5.3	Renaissance brass instruments	108
Figure 5.4	Slide and natural trumpets	110
Figure 5.5	Fingerhole horns	111
Figure 5.6	Tibetan and neighboring trumpets	113
Figure 5.7	Oceanic and other trumpets	114
Figure E.1	Keyed flutes	118
Figure E.2	Valves for brass instruments	120
Figure 6.1	Harps and pluriarc	126
Figure 6.2	Greek lyres	129
Figure 6.3	Lyres	130
Figure 6.4	Bowed lyres	132
Figure 6.5	Arched harp	132
Figure 6.6	African bow harps	133
Figure 6.7	Neolithic harper	134
Figure 6.8	King David harper, c. 1270	135
Figure 6.9	Nadermann single-action harp	137
Figure 6.10	Erard double-action harp	138
Figure 6.11	Stick, bar, raft, and tube zithers	140
Figure 6.12	Tube, box, and trough zithers	142
Figure 6.13	Box zithers	143
Figure 6.14	Clavichord	145
Figure 6.15	Harpsichord	147
Figure 6.16	Virginals, muselaar, and spinet	147
Figure 6.17	Square piano	150

Figure 6.18   Modern grand piano   151

Figure 6.19   Half-spiked lutes   153

Figure 6.20   Saz types   154

Figure 6.21   Sitar   155

Figure 6.22   Lute body types   157

Figure 6.23   Family of lutes   158

Figure 6.24   Flat-backed lutes   160

Figure 6.25   Alto lute and theorbo   161

Figure 6.26   Fiddle bow frogs   162

Figure 6.27   Spike fiddles   164

Figure 6.28   Solid-bodied fiddles   165

Figure 6.29   Polish and Mexican fiddles   166

Figure 6.30   Medieval fiddle   167

Figure 6.31   Violins in profile   168

Figure 6.32   *Viole da Gamba*   171

Figure 6.33   *Tromba marina*   173

Figure 6.34   Symphony   173

Figure 6.35   Hurdy-gurdies and other instruments   174

Figure 6.36   Buskers' fiddles   175

Figure F.1   Talking drums   182

Figure F.2   African forged iron bells   183

Figure F.3   African side-blown horns   184

Figure 7.1   Portative organ   189

Figure 7.2   Organ   190

Figure 7.3   Modern organ   191

Figure 7.4   Barrel organ   193

Figure G.1   Musical bows   195

Figure G.2   Blown and plucked free reeds   197

Figure G.3   Idioglot trumps   198

Figure G.4   Heteroglot trumps   199

Figure H.1   Plucked drums   207

Figure AW.1   Harmonics from which to make a musical scale 215

~

Acknowledgments

First in date, to a Belgian professor whose name I never learned but who had the kindness to show a British Army sergeant around the Institut Fouad Premier de Musique Arabe (I hope that after nearly 60 years I have remembered the 1940s name aright) and to give me an introduction to Dr. Hans Hickmann, who was then living in Cairo. Then to Eric Halfpenny and Reginald Morley-Pegge, who introduced me to the history of our own instruments and to the Galpin Society. And then to Dr. Otto W. Samson of the Horniman Museum in London, who stirred the enthusiasm of his temporary curator of musical instruments once again into those of the rest of the world. He encouraged me to become a Fellow of the Royal Anthropological Institute, where I was generously welcomed by Anthony Christie, Klaus Wachsmann, and many of my elders and betters, and where I soon became secretary of the Ethnomusicology Panel, whose members such as Nazir Ali Jairazbhoy, David Rycroft, Raymond Clausen, John Okell, and others generously expanded my knowledge of instruments and music through their fieldwork and enriched my collection of instruments, iconography, and recordings.

Much of what one learns, one learns from one's mentors, colleagues, friends, and sources, more than I have space or, shamefacedly, memory to record, though in all four of those categories I cannot sufficiently thank James Blades, Dr. Laurence Picken, and Tony Bingham for all their kindnesses. Then once, and if, one becomes an academic (for which I have to thank R. Thurston Dart, Stanley Glasser, James Wyly, Philip Bate, and London University, Grinnell College, Iowa, and Oxford University), one learns continually from one's students, one of whom, Dr. Lynda Sayce, has been more than generous with her time in reading this book for clarity. For any remaining confusions and obscurities, I can only blame my obduracy in stubbornly adhering to my original text. For encouragement in writing this book and others, I am deeply indebted to Bruce Phillips. For the care and skill shown in editing this text, I am most grateful to Jessica McCleary and Jack Brostrom of Scarecrow Press.

Above all, I honor the patience and encouragement of my late wife, to whose memory this book is dedicated, indeed a woman of valor and of worth immeasurably above rubies.

~

Explanations and Definitions

With a generous but limited number of illustrations, it seems sensible to give priority to the lesser known. On the basis that we all know what the instruments of our modern orchestras, bands, and groups look like, I have chosen to use more pictures of those exotic and older instruments that are less familiar to us all. I have also included references to many books where more illustrations will be found, though realizing that in many cases it is only the larger libraries that will stock them. However, the various national systems of interlibrary loans are a great resource, as is the World Wide Web.

In the captions to the figures, a Roman numeral followed by Arabic numerals (e.g., V 162) is the catalogue number of that instrument in my own collection, one volume of which Scarecrow Press has published so far. The Roman numeral refers to the volume (I to XIII, so far) and the Arabic numerals to the page.

An even greater resource is the world's museums, and all the instruments described here, and many more for which there was no space, will be found within their walls. Historical and ethnographic (folk or folklore, in whatever language equivalents) museums are the treasure houses of every civilization and culture. Art galleries, museums, and ancient churches often have on their walls paintings and carvings that tell us much about the older instruments of our own traditions. Entrance, where it is not free, costs everywhere less than the cheapest meal.

The following definitions are provided for terms that we shall meet frequently in these pages.

For Wind Instruments

The *proximal* (nearer) or upper end is always that closest to the player's mouth and the *distal* (farther) or lower end is that which is farthest. Where the instrument has a flared or wider termination at the distal end, it is often referred to as the *bell*. The words *top* and *bottom*, on the other hand, refer to the normal physical positions, so that the top of a bassoon or a tuba is the bell and, in conformity with the above definition, the "lower" end.

The interior of a wind instrument is the *bore*. When the diameter of the bore, once established below the mouth, embouchure, or reed-well, remains much the same until just before any terminal expansion into a bell, irrespective of minor constrictions or chambers due to the nature of its material or to modifications for improved tuning (also called *intonation*), the bore is referred to as *cylindrical*, whether or not it is geometrically a cylinder. When the diameter expands, whether more or less evenly or in steps, it is often referred to as *conical*, or somewhat more correctly as *conoidal*, despite its lack of resemblance to a true cone. If the bore contracts in diameter, as for example with the recorder, it is referred to as *inversely conical*. There are better, and more accurate, terms available, such as *expanding* or *widening*, and *contracting* or *narrowing*, that are also used here, but since each trade or discipline has its own accepted or conventional jargon, these less accurate terms continue to be used.

For String Instruments with a Body and Neck

The "upper" end is the peg box or peg head and finial, or its equivalent where ligatures, for example, are used instead of tuning pegs.

The *treble* and *bass* sides of an instrument, or its parts such as the feet of the bridge, are those to which the treble (higher pitched) or bass (lower pitched) strings are nearest.

For both winds and strings, *north* and *south* are along the instrument, north always at the "upper" end, and *east* and *west*, like right and left, across it.

With Brass Instruments

We shall encounter the vagaries of terminology from one country to another of treble, alto, tenor, and bass. We shall try to obviate the confusion by adopting the organ-builders' use of feet to indicate pitch. The speaking length of the diapason pipe sounding the C on the second ledger line below the bass stave was around eight feet, and so that became known as the 8' (or eight-foot) C. Because most wind and string instruments sound an octave higher if one halves their length (this is a rule of thumb rather than engineer's precision), the next C up (c) is the 4', and middle C (c') the 2'. Brass instruments in our music are most commonly built in B-flat, one note lower than C and thus a few inches longer. Our standard modern trumpet and cornet would be about 4'6" long if unwound, and that B-flat is therefore the 4'6". The tenor trombone is an octave lower at 9', and the intervening size of the alto trombone, the English tenor horn, the German althorn, the American alto, and so forth, is the 6'6" E-flat. The normal French horn is in 12' F, with the double horn also having a 9' B-flat side, though F-alto horns are also made at 6' F, and even piccolo horns in 4'6" B-flat—the same length as, and sounding very like, a flugelhorn. With so much potential confusion, the use of feet and inches may prove helpful.

The Prefixes Idio- and Hetero-

These will turn up in a number of places here. *Idio-* comes from Greek and means "self" or "same"; *hetero-* is also Greek and means "other." So *idioglot*, when applied to a reed or tongue (Greek *glotta*) means one that is cut from the body of the instrument or its mouthpiece, whereas *heteroglot* means that it is a separate slip of cane or metal that has been tied on or otherwise attached. *Idiochord* is a string that has been cut from the surface of the instru-

ment and remains attached at each end, whereas *hetero-chord* is a separate string attached, for example, as we do a guitar string. And an *idiophone* is an instrument that sounds of itself without the need for skin, string, or air—what Anthony Baines called the "hard percussion," though by no means all are in fact percussed.[1]

The Names of the Musical Notes

While we shall sometimes write them out as we did above with B-flat and E-flat, we shall more often use the conventional musical signs: ♯ for sharp, the semitone or black note above the note name, placed to its right on the piano; ♭ for flat, the semitone below it or to its left; and ♮ for natural to cancel either of those and revert to the plain note name.

When we need to specify a particular pitch, we use here the conventional notation of C for the C below the bass stave (the lowest note in figure 0.1—the C below that would be C' or CC) with similar capitals for each note up to B; c and similar letters for the next octave; c' for middle C and the following notes; c" for the next octave; and c‴ for the next, the highest note in figure 0.1.

Overtones

These are all those sounds of the tonal spectrum that form an envelope to provide a recognizable characteristic to the sound of every note on every instrument. It is the overtones that allow us to distinguish a clarinet's note from an oboe's. Depending on the physical and acoustic nature of an instrument, overtones may be harmonic or inharmonic. Thus harmonics are always overtones, but overtones need not be members of the harmonic series. With some instruments, the overtones, usually close to members of the harmonic series, can be sounded as individual notes, for example, on many of our brass instruments. The harmonic series goes beyond the realm of audibility to infinity. The first sixteen of the series, enough for most purposes (though some eighteenth-century brass players had to rise to the twenty-fourth), are shown in figure 0.1.

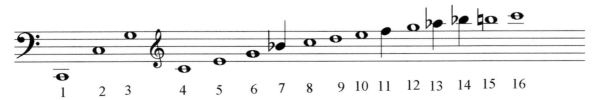

Figure 0.1. The Harmonic Series

Resultants

When two notes are sounded that are both exactly in-tune members of the harmonic series, they will combine to produce resultants, both a combination and a difference. Thus if one were to play simultaneously a fourth harmonic and a sixth harmonic (c' and g' in the figure 0.1 series), one would hear a chord including those two notes plus the low c, the second harmonic ($6 - 4 = 2$) and the e″, the tenth harmonic ($6 + 4 = 10$). This, for example, is how horn players can produce chords, as Weber required in his *Concertino* and Ethel Smythe in her *Concerto for Violin and Horn*—by playing one note and humming the other.

Diatonic and Chromatic

A *chromatic* scale is one in which every note is present, both the white and the black notes on the piano, for example, C, C♯, D, D♯, and so on. A *diatonic* scale is one in which only the notes of any particular key are present: in C major, just the white notes on the piano from C to C.

Archaeological Terminology and Geological Eras

Definitions for these will be found in the afterword, "Archaeology and Other -ologies," where they can be ignored or even excised by those with whose beliefs they conflict.

Note

1. Anthony Baines, *European and American Musical Instruments* (London: B. T. Batsford, 1966).

Abbreviations

Short titles (omitting the subtitles and curtailing the lengthier titles) are used in the notes to save space, and full publication details for books are also omitted there; full titles and publisher data will be found in the bibliography. The notes are deliberately copious to enable further research from a book that, while attempting to cover the origin and development of the musical instruments of the world, inevitably leaves out many details.

In both the bibliography and notes, the following abbreviations are used for those journals or other series that are frequently cited and for some well-known publishers who have produced many books in our field (this list reappears at the beginning of the bibliography).

CNRS	Centre National de la Recherche Scientifique
CUP	Cambridge University Press
DVfM	Deutscher Verlag für Musik
EM	*Early Music*
FoMRHIQ	*Fellowship of Makers & Researchers of Historical Instruments Quarterly*
GSJ	*Galpin Society Journal*
JAMIS	*Journal of the American Musical Instrument Society*
JIFMC	*Journal of the International Folk Music Council*
JIJHS	*Journal of the International Jew's Harp Society*
OUP	Oxford University Press
SIMP	*Studia instrumentorum musicae popularis*
YUP	Yale University Press

Maps

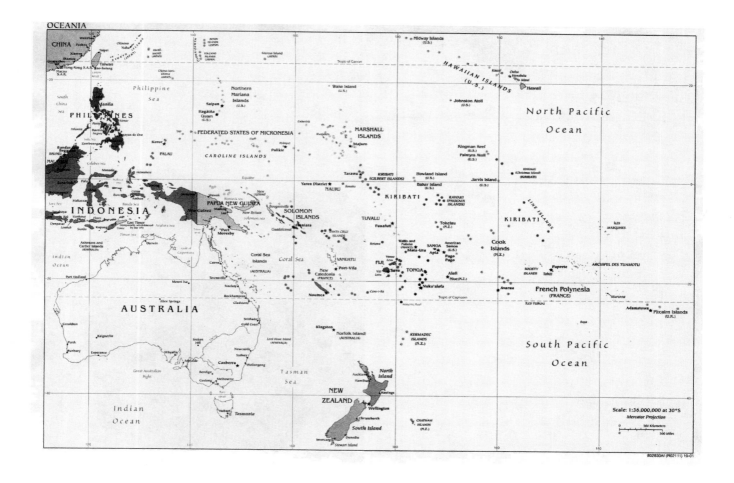

AFRICA

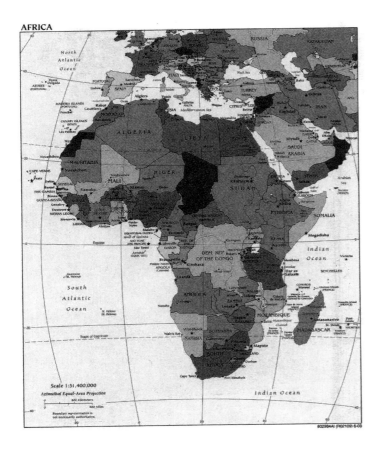

Asia

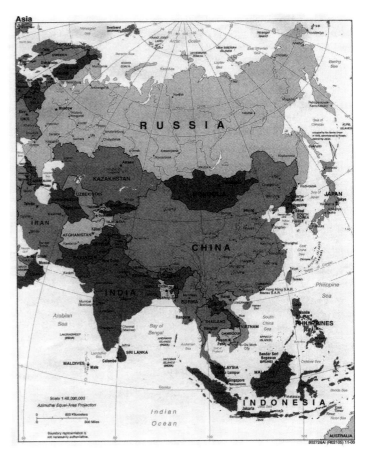

Europe

Latin America

~

CHAPTER ONE

Origins

No musical instrument can be created without purpose, although preexisting objects can be adopted or adapted for the purpose of making music. Before an instrument can even be envisaged, there must be the concept of sound and the desire to create sound. And so before we begin to consider the origins and development of musical instruments, we must first look to that sound that we call music.

Our search begins far away in time. Not perhaps so far away as the music of the spheres, but certainly to the times before mankind became human, for song is inherent in nature—song in the sense of the vocalization or other creation of sound combined with the inflection of pitch or frequency. Dance, too, is inherent in nature in the sense of movement combined with regular or repetitive rhythm.[1]

When either of these became a conscious part of human development is a question impossible to answer, but, on the basis of what we know of the behavior of the animal kingdom, one has to say that it was probably from the earliest time that hominids stood upright. Certainly fellow primates have been seen dancing (or so we would say were they human) and accompanying the dance with movements that make more noise than is necessary for locomotion.[2]

The progression from clapping paws, or hands, to the use of a pair of sticks or a couple of stones is the origin of musical instruments. When did this take place? One could say with some confidence "before the Paleolithic Age" for it could well have been precisely this act that led to the earliest phase of the Paleolithic or, as it used to be called, the Eolithic, the Dawn of the Stone Age.[3] As stones are clashed together, they are liable to crack, to split, even to shatter. The sharp fragments that fell could have been the first tools.

Whether this scenario is true, or whether stone tools came before instruments, no one will ever know. If tools came first, then two flint knappers, chipping within earshot of each other, could have been the first musicians to produce rhythmic counterpoint as they interlocked their rhythms. Smiths and workers who use pestles and mortars do this over much of the world to this day. Many other such theories are equally possible, but it remains likely that musical instruments began with the concussive sounds of two objects struck together.[4]

These are instruments that are still in use. We use wooden sticks as the *claves* of Latin American dance music, and in Australia they accompany the didjeridu (see figure A.2). Wooden shells are used as castanets, similar objects of metal are used as cymbals, and all of these we shall see in more detail as we proceed.

Many of these are used to accompany the dance, and the two most powerful influences on mankind, which may have led to music and to instruments, are dance and ritual. Dance, as we noted above, is inherent in nature, and we see such movements, apparently instinctive, in the youngest of our own children. Why it happens is a matter for studies other than this. Why an impulse toward religion or ritual is almost equally instinctive is again beyond our field, but we must accept that it exists,[5] accept that it is often expressed in dance, and accept that it is often, even normally, accompanied by sound and by song and chant, and that those sounds are what we can call "music."

How, then, do we define *music*? That is something on which there is no general agreement. For me it is *sound*: without sound, there can be no music—even though there can be no music without silence. Music is sound that is *generated deliberately*; casual and accidental sounds are not musical, although, as we shall see, they are often created by objects that we call "musical instruments."[6] Furthermore, music is sound that is generated deliberately *to create emotion*. What that emotion may be is irrelevant. It can be pleasure (it usually is today, especially if the creator expects to earn a living from doing it), but it can also be fear, even terror, certainly awe; very often it is intended to impel movement.

From this, it follows that any object that is used to produce such sound can be called a musical instrument. These are not confined to those tools that we use to create the music of our concert halls, theaters, dance halls, and other places where we hear music today, but all the sound makers, even noisemakers, that extend and derive from them. The old-fashioned motor-vehicle horns, those with a rubber bulb, the hooters with which our children enjoy making sounds revolting to our ears, these have the same reeds as our church organs and so cannot be ignored here (see figure 4.1). The ratchets whirled by football enthusiasts, which indubitably reveal our jubilation when our team has scored a goal and so express an emotion, and which are used also by children to scare birds from crops, these appear from time to time on our concert platforms, and more frequently in our music halls (see figure A.1). Anything with which people make sounds generated deliberately to create emotion is grist for our mill, all the more so when we mill that grist with deliberate rhythms.

Musical Sound

Sound is created with an instrument by setting up vibrations in a string, a column of air, a skin, or solid matter.

String instruments or *chordophones* are plucked (e.g., guitars), bowed (e.g., violins), or struck (e.g., hammered dulcimers). The pitch of the note produced depends upon the length, thickness, mass, and tension of the string. To sound a higher note, one can decrease the length, thickness, or mass or increase the tension—or alter all four. For example, the strings of a guitar are the same length and at similar tension, but vary in thickness and mass, and thus each can be tuned to a different pitch. Higher notes can be played by pressing a string to the fingerboard, leaving a shorter length free to vibrate.

Wind instruments or *aerophones* are played by blowing in various ways:

- across a hole onto a sharp edge (whistles and flutes)
- between two flexible blades (double reeds such as oboes and bassoons)
- between a flexible blade and a rigid mouthpiece (single reeds such as clarinets and saxophones)
- between buzzing lips acting like reeds (brass instruments such as trumpets and horns—the material of which the instrument is made is irrelevant, and "brass" remains a useful term, more familiar than "lip-reeds")
- past a flexible blade in a rigid slot (free reeds such as mouth organs and accordions)

The first three types are known as *woodwinds* and the fourth as *brass*, and the pitch they produce depends on the length and shape of their bore, which controls their overtones (see Explanations and Definitions). On a brass instrument, these overtones can be played by varying the tension of the lips and the air speed; on a woodwind, the first few can be played in the same way. On many modern brass instruments, the notes between these overtones are played by the use of valves, or on the trombone with a slide, thereby adding extra lengths of tubing and thus lowering the pitch. On woodwind instruments and some brass, the scale starts on the lowest note of this series; as holes are opened, one after the other, the sounding length of the tube shortens, so raising the pitch. When the top hole is reached, all are covered again and the player blows harder, producing the next overtone, and opens the holes in sequence again. With some free reeds, the pitch depends solely on the length and mass of the reed, but others behave like the other woodwinds.

Drums or *membranophones* have a skin stretched across a frame and can be struck or rubbed. They may have an open frame (frame drums, such as the tambourine), another skin across the bottom of the frame (tubular drums, e.g., a side drum), or have a closed body (kettle drums, e.g., timpani). The shape and material of the frame affect the tone, while the diameter, thickness, mass, and tension of the skin control the pitch.

The instruments of solid matter, that is, the *idiophones* (e.g., xylophone, triangle, cymbal, etc.), can be struck, rubbed, scraped, or plucked. Any shape and any resonant material can be used. The pitch depends on the nature, volume, density, rigidity, mass, size, and shape of the material.

One further word of introduction. We shall use frequently in these pages such phrases as "in our culture" or "in our music." They are used in place of the meaningless terms "Western music," "European orchestras," and so forth. Possible alternatives are "international culture" and "international music," for "our" music has become international. We cannot talk of "Western" music when "our" sort of music is played worldwide; the Tokyo Philharmonic, for example, is eastern relative to Berlin, but western from Los Angeles. Nor can we legitimately speak of "European" when, for example, since the seventeenth century (even since the sixteenth, south of the Rio Grande), "our" music has been composed and played in the Americas. When saying *our*, I write as someone brought up in England and trained as a musician first in America and then in England, but it implies no value judgment—all musics are music. It is only because "Western" and "European" are without meaning in this context that we must have available *some* word to distinguish between "ours" and that of people brought up and trained in different musics from mine.

Voices

There are a few instruments that have their own voice. Most instruments need to be played, but these need merely to be moved or stroked, and of themselves they will speak. One of our great frustrations in all studies of ancient times is to wonder how anybody could have discovered that doing something would produce a beneficial or useful result. Some actions and their results are obvious enough—pick and eat a fruit from a tree and the result is either pleasant or unpleasant and perhaps fatal. But how did someone discover that tying a string through a hole in the end of a piece of wood or bone, or around the end, and swinging it around their head on the end of the string, would produce a sound? This is an elaborate process: it must be swung in a circle and it must spin on its axis. The wrong cord, the wrong shape, the wrong size, even the wrong surfaces of the piece of wood or bone render it ineffective. It is difficult to conceive of the action that might accidentally have led to this discovery. And yet the use of the bull-roarer is widespread around the world—even, so far as we know, a universal that no culture, no people, has been without at some stage in its development.[7]

The bull-roarer is commonly an elongated oval in shape, sometimes described as fish shape, though rectangular and other shapes are also seen (see figure 1.1). Often one or both faces are carved with decorative patterns, and it has been suggested that it spins better if one face is flatter than the other, or more deeply carved, so as to present greater or lesser resistance to the air than the other face, although the large number whose two faces appear to be identical suggests that this may be unnecessary. What is certain is that the sound is produced in this way and that both rotary motions are necessary, suggesting that some of the sound is due to the passage of the string and the bull-roarer through the air, and some to the per-

turbation of the air as the bull-roarer spins. The sound varies according to the size of the bull-roarer, the length of the string, and the speed of rotation. Larger roarers, slower rotation, and longer strings produce a low muttering sound, threatening like distant thunder—hence one of its names, the "thunder stick," and its association, as the *rhombos*, with Zeus, the ancient Greek god of thunder. Smaller bull-roarers, rotating faster, bellow like a bull, hence the common name in English, while bull-roarers that are even smaller and faster scream like a demon.[8]

It is not surprising that the bull-roarer was so widely used as a ritual instrument, a spirit voice, one that in many areas was secret and known only to initiates. Nobody, unless initiated and shown, could imagine that so simple an object could produce such a sound. So it was used in the Dionysian mysteries in ancient Greece, and as the voice of an ancestor, a spirit, a god, in the initiation rites of cultures in New Guinea, Australia, Africa, and South America. It was also used in Paleolithic times in Europe, for examples have been found in Magdalenean sites in the Dordogne of southern France, at Laugerie-Basse and elsewhere.[9] It must surely be of equal or greater antiquity elsewhere—our knowledge of the Stone Ages is badly skewed by the accidents of where archaeological work has been done and discoveries made. The fact that the caves of central and southern France have been well explored is not evidence that objects found there did not exist in, were not used in, or are earlier than in other parts of the world whose remains have yet to be investigated.

The bull-roarer had in many areas a smaller relative, called by André Schaeffner *le diable*, "the devil."[10] This is a disc, often with dentations around the rim, with two holes each side of the center, or sometimes a bone such as a knuckle bone with a hole across the center of its length, on a loop of string (see figure 1.1). There is no single name in English, for "buzzing disc" excludes the phalange or knuckle bone, and many other things might be called a "buzzer." Cajsa Lund advocated the Swedish term *snorra* (or more properly *snörra*),[11] and this, with its almost onomatopoeic sound, seems a better choice. One end of the loop is held in each hand, and the snorra is swung like a skipping rope to twist the string. An outward pull by the hands spins the snorra and, by relaxing the pull at the right instant, allows it to twist the loop again in the opposite sense. Repeated pull and release motions produce a shrill buzzing, whirring sound that was again regarded in some areas as a voice, ancestral or spiritual, protective or menacing.

Few mysteries, few rituals, are eternal. Things once secret become known, that which was sacred becomes

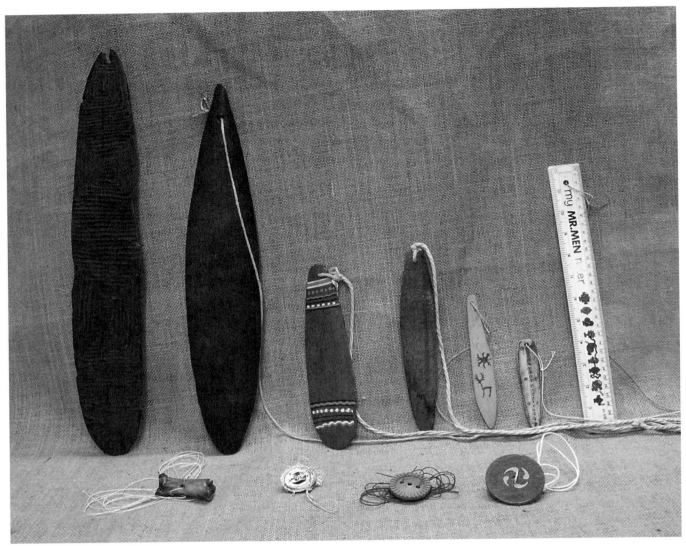

Figure 1.1. Bull-roarers (above) and Buzzers (below)

Above, L–R: *churinga*, Australia, probably Kimberley District (I 14); Papua New Guinea (II 228b); made for tourists, Queensland, Australia (V 162); West African, probably a bird-scarer (II 228a); reproduction of eleventh-century Viking, by Cajsa Lund, Sweden (IX 16); bone, Ethiopia (XII 6a); child's toy of plastic ruler, by author (XI 256a).

Below, L–R: *snörra*, pig phalange, reproducing an archaeological find, by Cajsa Lund, Sweden (IX 32); *mak-woed*, flattened Pepsi-Cola bottle top, Mu-ban-hur-dong Village, central Thailand (VI 82); green plastic coat button, by author (III 134j2); painted wood, by It's Child's Play, Newquay, England (X 256).

mundane. So it has been with the bull-roarer and the snorra. People in many areas use the bull-roarer to scare birds, using its sound and perhaps its hovering flight, which some birds might mistake as that of a hawk, to frighten birds and animals from the crops. This is a task that is often relegated to children, and so it became a child's toy, as has the snorra. Many of us have, as children, swung a ruler on a piece of string or made a snorra from a coat button or a piece of card. This has long been recognized as a classic cycle: the progression from ritual through mundane to toy. As Curt Sachs observed, many

children's toys had an origin in ritual or magic; that is why many of us study and collect musical toys, and why others collect and record children's rhymes, songs, and games.[12]

Another instrument with a voice of its own, a voice of magic, one that may date back to the beginnings of the Bronze Age, is the friction drum (see figure 1.2). Although this is a drum in the sense that there is a skin stretched over a vessel or shell, the skin is not struck; often it is not touched in any way. With a few friction drums, the skin itself is rubbed by a stick or a hand, as we

Figure 1.2. Friction Drums

Above, L–R: whirled, India (II 222); *simbomba*, external stick, Catalunya (XI 148); *ximbomba*, external stick, Murcia, Spain (XIII 100); *lion roar*, friction cord, England (I 126); *rommelpot*, external stick, reproduction, by author (IV 6).

Below, L–R: whirled geminate, China (IX 58); internal stick, Brazil (XI 8); *Waldteufel*, whirled, England (IX 128a); cock-crow, child's toy in plastic beaker, friction cord, Spain (VIII 164).

rub the skin of a tambourine with the thumb in our orchestras; with the vast majority, a stick stands in the center of the skin, or a cord passes through the skin, and the stick or the string is rubbed by the hand or by a piece of cloth or leather held in the fingers (rubbing a string with the bare hand can be painful). It is not the stick or the string that sounds but the drum that grunts or roars. The sound can be so loud that orchestrally the string friction drum is known as the "lion roar."

Henry Balfour, in what remains the most detailed and comprehensive study of the instrument, postulated an origin from the smith's bellows.[13] A simple form of bellows is a clay or wooden pot, covered by a skin with a stick or a string in the center, and a pipe leading from the base of the pot to the fire. The stick is pulled up to fill the pot with air and pushed down to drive the air into the forge, or the cord is pulled up and the skin is pushed down with the foot, again to drive the air. The sweating hands slip and slide on stick or string, and it seems as though the metal groans or cries as it flows from the ore, as a woman cries in the travail of childbirth or the gods

shout their approval of the work of the smith. Of course, this is hypothesis, but the smith has in many places been regarded as the possessor of magical powers—how else could metal be induced to flow from a stone?

There are many varieties of friction drum. The *rommelpot* in Flemish and Dutch genre paintings of the seventeenth century was a pot covered with a skin, with a stick tied into a pocket in its center. It was then most commonly a child's toy. Similar instruments were used in Italy and Spain for the "rough music," the way in which a community expressed its disapproval of the lifestyle of a neighbor. Some peoples, for example, in Brazil, reverse this pattern by placing the stick inside the drum, where it often pierces the skin, with a lateral peg through the projecting part of the stick (on the outside of the drum) preventing it from being pulled through. In many places, this type of stick friction drum has been a fertility symbol, the male stick within the female vessel being rubbed to produce its effect. The type with external stick is also often a fertility symbol, the male symbol of the stick trying to push its way into the female hollow of the drum.

String friction drums are also widespread in use, and not only in our orchestras, although they must not be confused with some plucked string instruments that we shall meet later, where it is instead the string that sounds, using a drum as an amplifier (e.g., see figure H.1). With the friction drum, the string, if pulled fast, can scream as well as roar and grunt—all sounds that can well be terrifying when used in mystic rituals. The string is most commonly outside the drumshell and may either be knotted below the skin or pass in through one hole and out through another, so that it is double.

A variant of the string friction drum, one that returns us toward the bull-roarer, is the whirled drum, a small drum whose cord is tied to a stick, called in German *Waldteufel* or "woods devil." The stick is usually smeared with rosin where the cord is tied so that the cord rubs on this to produce the sound that would otherwise be provided by the fingers. While this whirled drum is today a toy, the German name suggests the voice of spirits or demons howling from the depths of the sacred grove.

Recent publications have suggested that the locus or place may also have its own voice. Lucie Rault cites the work of French paleologists in some of the painted caves of southern France.[14] They have discovered that different parts of the caverns have their own pitch and resonance, that certain notes and overtones of those notes resonate in different parts of the cavern, and that these parts are indicated by specific markings placed on the walls of the cave. The shaman or priest (for it is difficult to think of him as a musician who "plays" the cave) must first make a sound, but need do no more than whisper in some cases, and that sound is then taken up and transmuted by the cave itself. Did Cro-Magnon man in the Aurignacian period, some 15,000 years ago, make use of these phenomena? We do not know, but at least these theories make sense of some of the groupings of figures and other details of the paintings in these caves, and once these phenomena took place—and the slightest sound in the right place would create them—it is difficult to imagine that they would not be used. We shall return to the music of the Paleolithic caves in the next section, on the lithophones or sounding stones.

Another drum, a very small one, adds or modifies a voice. If a very thin membrane, for example, goldbeater's skin or onion-skin, is fixed over a hole in a tube and that tube is then sung into, the membrane will add a buzz to the sound—in some cultures, changing the voice from human to that of a spirit or god; in other cultures, sweetening the sound; and in yet others, creating an instrument. The last of these was the origin of the kazoo bands of the years of the Great Depression and, of course, of our children's toys and their homemade substitute, the comb and paper.

Kazoos (see figure 1.3) have quite a respectable history. Marin Mersenne in 1636 illustrated the *flûte eunuque*, an instrument that was revived as the Za-Zah nearer our own time.[15] The apparent embouchure was for singing into, rather than blowing across, and fingerholes were provided mainly to make it look more like a flute, for they have no effect on the pitch, although opening them does make a slight difference to the tone quality. Tchaikovsky referred to the same instrument in his "Dance of the Mirlitons" in the *Nutcracker* ballet.

Both in Africa and in China, we find the concept of sweetening the sound. Chinese transverse flutes have a hole, midway between the embouchure or blowing hole and the topmost fingerhole, that is covered by a membrane made from the thin inner skin of the bamboo and that adds a buzz to the sound. Some Thai duct flutes have a similar hole in the side. In Africa, almost all xylophones have a hole in the side of each resonator covered with a material such as a spider's egg sac for the same purpose (see figure 1.8).

The use of the kazoo to change the voice to that of a spirit is also found in Africa, where some masks have a small tube with a membrane built in for this purpose, and it has been suggested that some ancient Greek statues of gods had something of the sort so that a hidden priest could speak for the deity.

Other ways in which instruments are used as voices are described in Interlude F, "Messengers."

Lithophones

We have discussed the use of voices in Paleolithic painted caves. What follows on from this is the suggestion in many of the same references, and in articles by Lya Dams and others, that the stalagmites and stalactites themselves were struck as instruments.[16] These curtains and columns of stone were built up over eons as calcite-filled water slowly dripped from the cavern roof and petrified. Some have been broken off short, as though struck too hard; others seem to show marks of striking below the later deposits of calcite. Many of them have what seem to be deliberate marks of color, black pigment and red ochre, as though to indicate which were the best points for sound. The black marks overlay the red, with enough calcite between the red and the black to suggest that, whatever these marks may mean, the points they indicate were of importance over long periods of time—centuries certainly, millennia perhaps.

Figure 1.3. Kazoos

Clockwise from bottom left: comb and paper (III 134 l); *Za-Zah* or *flûte eunuque*, by Matthias Barr, London (VIII 158); Chinese flute with membrane hole (I 248c); kazoos: tin, England, and plastic, Germany (VI 212 and I 24b).

Dams suggests that many of the chips and breaks appear to have been made deliberately, especially in such formations as "curtains" of folded calcite. The shorter such folds, the higher the pitches produced, so these might indicate deliberate attempts to "tune" the formations. For such details as this, there can never be any certainty, but the evidence adduced for musical purposes seems so convincing that it would be very difficult to say, at the least, that these formations could not have been used in that way. There appears to be a growing consensus that the use of music and instruments is very much older than had been thought until recently; that there is positive evidence for such use of these painted caves at least from the Late Solutrean period, about 14,000 to 17,000 BC; and that some instruments, such as flutes and whistles that we shall meet in due course, were used very much earlier, in the Aurignacian, as much as 30,000 or 40,000 years ago.

In the Ukraine, S. N. Bibikov reported a musical ensemble of mammoth bones from around 20,000 years ago.[17] Again there can never be proof, but many of the bones show undoubted signs of wear, mainly from striking but sometimes (although this is not mentioned in the English summary of Bibikov) of striations similar to those of a rasp, a type of instrument to which we shall return.

We are in a similar position with the lithophone from Ndut Lieng Krak in Vietnam, now in the Musée de l'Homme in Paris.[18] These eleven stone slabs were found while road making and are essentially undatable, although Trân Van Khê has placed them in the early Mesolithic and others have suggested a somewhat later period, in the Neolithic. Clearly they have been worked and shaped, and like any other bars, whether of stone, wood, or metal, they will produce a pitch when struck—here even perhaps a pentatonic scale—but we have no idea of how, when, why, or even if they were really used for musical performance.

We are on much surer ground when we look at the lithophones of our own time, for people still make music from stones. Going back to where we began this book, people still pick up stones from the ground to strike together to accompany music or dance—Filippo Bonanni showed children doing it in Italy in the eighteenth century, and we can surely accept this as something that has happened continually from the beginning of humanity until today.[19]

Peoples in Africa place a group of rocks of different sizes on the ground, each producing a different pitch. Peoples in northern England in the eighteenth and nineteenth centuries (and who can say how much earlier?) made instruments more elaborate than, but similar to, those of Ndut Lieng Krak. Peoples in China have for many centuries played stone chimes, now associated with Confucian rituals but known from archaeological discoveries to be very much older than Confucius's time. Peoples in many parts of the world have played the percussion boulders that are somewhat misleadingly called "rock gongs"—misleading only because they bear no resemblance to the disc of bronze that we normally call a gong.

The rock gong was first introduced to the anthropological community by Bernard Fagg in 1956.[20] He discovered a number of sites in Nigeria, many of them associated with rock paintings and painted caves (see figure 1.4). The instruments varied in size, from a hundredweight or so to massive boulders weighing several tons, with depressions showing where they had been struck

Figure 1.4.   Rock Gong

Two men (lower center) are beating the rock with stones while others sing, Mbar Village, Nigeria, 1955, *photo Bernard Fagg, courtesy Catherine Fagg.*

over long periods of time. Some would produce a single pitch; others produced a range of pitches from different points on the rock. Once the first were found and recognized, others followed fast, some because Fagg recalled seeing similar depressions on other rocks and now realized their purpose, others because, as word spread, their use, previously unrecognized as anything important, was now reported. Uses varied: many for ritual; some for signaling, with sounds that carried for several miles; many also for normal musical purposes, accompanying singing and dancing. Musical practices also varied, some being played by a single player at a time, others by groups as percussion ensembles.

After the first publication about rock gongs in *Man*, the newsletter (as it was then) of the Royal Anthropological Institute in London, many reports came from other Fellows of the Institute, some associating the rock gongs with rock slides that are often a part of women's fertility rites. Examples are now known over much of Africa and far beyond. Catherine Fagg has continued her husband's research and, as well as those from Africa, has published examples from Canada, California, Brazil, Colombia, India, Thailand, Australia, France (with medieval, Megalithic, and Paleolithic examples), and indeed much of Europe, with the suggestion that cupmarks, which are a frequently found feature of megalithic monuments of the New Stone and Bronze ages, may well be indicators of their use as rock gongs.[21] Such sites are today, at least in Britain, legally protected against damage, and anyone trying such marks to see whether they ring may well find themselves in serious trouble.

Smaller lithophones—portable slabs, as one might say—are also used in Africa, one player with a group of five or so slabs of rock of different sizes set on the ground in front of him. So far as we know at present, this pattern of lithophone seems to be confined to northern Togo in West Africa. According to Francis Bebey, every family among the Kabre people has its own set of stones, which are played to mark the agricultural seasons of the year.[22] Another use that seems restricted to one area only is the Ethiopian, where a slab, often just one, is suspended at the nodal points close to each end from a tree or other support and is used instead of a church bell. This use is reminiscent of that of the Greek and Armenian churches, especially in Muslim lands where churches are, or have been, forbidden the use of bells. There, the *semantron*, a wooden or sometimes iron bar, is suspended horizontally so that it can be struck for that purpose.

Suspended stones go back several millennia in China, and many sets have been found archaeologically in recent years, one of the most famous in the tomb of the

Marquis Yi.[23] This set of thirty-two calcareous limestone slabs covers a fully chromatic range of three and a half octaves, but the markings on their storage boxes, all dating from the fifth century BC, make it clear that they were used to play pentatonic scales. The reason for a complete chromatic set, in our terms, is that a five-note scale could then be started on any note desired. The shape of these stones is more curved than L-shaped, but the L, with the angle slightly obtuse, is the shape more commonly seen, with a suspension hole in the bottom left-hand corner of the L so that the slabs hang down with the longer side lower than the shorter. Those of the Marquis Yi were certainly used for general musical purposes, for they are associated with an enormous bell-chime, but both bells and stones came to have a special role in Confucian ritual music. This is no longer a feature of mainland Chinese life, but it survives in Taiwan and in Korea.[24] Other shapes of stone are also found in China, sometimes carved as fishes or other objects (see figure 1.5).

Stone chimes have also been used in Britain, but in only one area. It was found that stones on a certain part of Skiddaw, a mountain near Keswick in the Lake District, rang when struck, and in the late eighteenth century, the earliest of the surviving instruments was built.[25] This is in the form of a single-row diatonic xylophone covering a range of two octaves plus one note.[26] Whether there was any earlier use of these stones in unknown; it is possible, but seems unlikely, that Peter Crosthwaite, the builder of this instrument, was the first to notice their sounds. Certainly it was not the last, for another, also in the museum in Keswick, covers five chromatic octaves, and the array used in "Richardsons' Original Monstre [sic] Rock Band" in the mid-nineteenth century was even larger (as well as giving a very different meaning to the term "rock band" from that we know today), although the present whereabouts of that instrument is unknown. Nor was theirs the only such band, for Daniel Till and his sons were also well known, and, according to Blades, their instrument is preserved in the museum in Orange, New Jersey. Another is in the Horniman Museum in London, but that is a simpler version of twenty slabs, similar to those of the eighteenth century.

Percussion Bars

Basically, the *xylophone* is one or more wooden bars tuned to an acceptable pitch. It should be borne in mind that almost any bar of wood (or any other material) will produce a note of definite pitch, all the better defined if it is suspended from or resting on its nodal points, two-ninths of its length from each end.

Though one-note xylophones are fairly rare, they do exist (see figure 1.6). For example, in the Basque regions of northern Spain and southern France, the *txalaparta* is a wooden beam played, somewhat competitively, by two players who pound it with a wooden club held in each hand. The interlocking rhythms they produce are highly complex and exciting to listen to. One-note instruments are also found in Central Africa in Zaire,[27] where a single xylophone bar suspended over a resonator is, apparently, played by elephant hunters (presumably for ceremonial dance rather than to attract elephants), and in Fiji, where women lay the *lali ne meke*, a wooden bar with

Figure 1.5. Chinese Stone Chimes
L–R: two second-century BC, Han dynasty (XIII 94 and 96); more recent (XI 116).

Figure 1.6. Percussion Bars

L–R: *kidimbadimba* or *mbila*, one-note xylophone, Baluba or Basanga people, Congo (I 6); *lali ne meke*, women's instrument, Fiji (II 174); beaters for Basque *txalaparta*, Euskal Herria (XII 148).

a resonance hollow carved out on the underside, across their legs to accompany singing.

The use of two or three bars laid across the legs is found in many areas, as is a few bars laid over a pit in the ground, the pit or the space between the legs and the ground acting as a resonance chamber. A pair of wooden logs provides support for a larger number of bars. In East Africa, these logs are frequently banana stems, a fairly soft material into which it is easy to push thin sticks to hold the bars apart.[28] More elaborate is the use of a trough resonator, a built-up box or a hollowed log over which the bars are placed, to form a single resonating chamber. Such instruments are common in Southeast Asia, including in the Javanese and Balinese gamelan orchestras, where the bars are of bronze as well as wood, and also in our children's school percussion bands. The most elaborate form is that which we see in many parts of Africa, in Central America, and in all our orchestral instruments, where each bar has its own resonator, sized and tuned to match the pitch of the bar above it.

Is it justifiable to see this as a developmental sequence? There would seem to be a steady ergological sequence from the leg and pit xylophone through the log and the trough to the individually resonated. However, the fact that each type exists in various areas, to the apparent satisfaction of its community—sometimes, as in central Java, in coexistence in the same *gamelan* or orchestra—argues against such an idea: the trough is found to be the best for the wooden-barred *gambang* and bronze-barred *saron*, whereas the bronze *gender* is better

resonated with individual tubes, traditionally of wide-bore bamboo but now usually yellow-painted tin-plate.[29] The argument is reinforced in East Africa with the log xylophone that is often played by three or more players, one providing a bass part at one end, another a treble ostinato at the other end, and two players facing each other in the middle playing an elaborately interlocked melodic pattern. No other pattern of xylophone would have the space or layout to permit this.

The question is rendered more complex by theories that the xylophone originated in Southeast Asia and was carried to Africa by Indonesian traders.[30] There is no doubt at all that there was such contact, for the Indonesian influence in Madagascar is strong and there is good evidence in other parts of Africa also. But the strongest argument against such theories is the existence of all these forms of xylophone at both ends of the axis. If this was a developmental sequence, then we would expect such a sequence to be evident in only one of the areas, whereas we see it in both, and no one could seriously propose development at one end and retrogression at the other. So we are left with strong xylophone cultures in two areas, separated by the Indian Ocean, and none anywhere else in the world, for we know that the European use derived from African contact and that the Central American arose from the reconstruction of that instrument by transported African slaves.

The xylophone is widely used on the Southeast Asian mainland, in the same area as the stone instrument that we described in the previous section, and has a number of forms, the most spectacular being a horseshoe frame curving high into the air above the seated player. Horizontal forms, on trough resonators, are also common, and it is this pattern that we see repeated in Java.

In Africa south of the Sahara, the xylophone is so widespread in all its various forms that no book on African music can ignore it. It is perhaps in Mozambique, and among the peoples from that area working as contract laborers in South Africa, that the xylophone culture is at its highest, for it is there that we find the xylophone orchestras, with up to a dozen different sizes of *timbila*, from treble through alto and tenor to double bass, playing together (see figure 1.7).[31]

Each timbila has from ten to twenty bars (except the double bass, which has only three or four), depending on its part within the orchestra, lashed to a frame that has a curved bar to hold it away from the body when it is, as often happens, played on the move, suspended from a strap around the player's neck. Below each bar is a complex gourd resonator. The gourds are carefully cultivated by the makers so that there is always a selection of different sizes available, sized to suit the pitch of each bar. Cut into the sides of the spherical gourd are two holes, one of which is waxed to a matching hole in the rail that runs beneath the bars, so holding each resonator in place beneath its bar. The other hole is covered by a thin membrane held over it with wax, and over that is placed a segment of gourd to act as a trumpet and project its sound. The membrane, found on many different African instruments, adds a buzz to "sweeten" the sound, as we noted above. Its material differs from place to place and custom to custom: sometimes animal intestine, other times a bat's wing, a spider's egg sac, or, in a pinch, cigarette paper. The heads of the beaters are covered with thin strands of natural rubber, wound around and over, just as

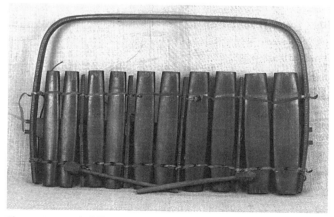

Figure 1.7. Timbila
Tswa people, Mozambique, pre-1870 (II 54).

our golf balls used to be made or as one winds a ball of wool, and they vary in size and hardness to suit the bars of each instrument. The bars themselves are made from a hardwood, although among the workers of South Africa they may be sawn-up floor boards, played with beaters covered by a piece of old tire rubber. The bars are tuned by carving away an arch below the bar, which both flattens the pitch and, by thinning the cross-section of the bar, greatly improves the tone quality.[32]

While various details will differ, this description applies to the majority of African xylophones and—without the membranes and with metal tubes instead of gourds—to our own also. The arrangements of the gourds may differ, or they may be replaced by cow horns or other hollow objects (old food cans are common in South Africa, where the traditional materials are many miles away and unobtainable locally), and the shape and design of the instruments differ, as can be seen in the illustrations in figures 1.7 and 1.8, but in general principle there are more similarities than differences.

The first indication of the xylophone in Europe appears in the sixteenth century. Holbein illustrates one in his "Dance of Death" sequence in 1538, where the skeleton supports it from a neck strap just as folk musicians have done in more recent years (see figure 1.9). Saint-Saëns, in his "Fossiles" movement in *Le carnaval des animaux*, was not the first to associate the xylophone with the rattle of dry bones! Martin Agricola illustrated one as the *Stro fidel* in 1528, with a range of three octaves, diatonic except for both B-flat and B-natural. The German name of "straw fiddle" (see figure 6.35, no. 4) arose because the bars were laid on hanks of straw, replacing the banana stems of East Africa.[33] So far as we can tell from the illustrations, the bars were simply round or square-section wooden rods, tuned just by their length. Xylophones were still being made like this, without any of the tuning or tonal subtleties of the African instruments, into the twentieth century in Europe. In Germany they sometimes retained the supports of straw, though a wooden framework padded with felt became more generally common.

The xylophone must have been a recognized instrument in central Europe, although at present our only evidence for this is the extent to which an obscure Viennese composer, Ferdinand Kauer, wrote for it in the early nineteenth century.[34] Presumably it was a folk instrument in that area, a supposition that is supported by Bálint Sárosi's description of the *facimbalom* both as an instrument in its own right and as a substitute for the local form of hammered dulcimer.[35] It was certainly this same type of instrument, with three or four rows of bars

Figure 1.8. Balo, Ghana
Back view to show the resonators and their spider's web buzzers (VII 26).

arranged with the lowest nearest to the player and the highest farthest away, totally different from our modern left-to-right layout, that was played by the Polish virtuoso Gusikow who so impressed Mendelssohn, Chopin, and Liszt in the 1830s.[36]

Figure 1.9. Renaissance Xylophone
"Death and the Old Woman," Hans Holbein, Dance of Death series, 1547.

We owe our modern xylophone to the peoples of Mexico and Guatemala, who derived it from instruments made in those areas by African slaves. There, the individual resonators, carefully tuned to match each bar, were usually made of wooden boxes, rather than gourds, and the instruments grew to a considerable size.[37] Their bars were tuned, as in Africa, by arching the undersides, producing a far better tone quality than the very chippy sound of our instruments up to the early twentieth century. J. C. Deagan of Chicago adopted these techniques and changed the layout that was usually a single row into that familiar from the piano keyboard, using metal tubes for the resonators. From his design come all our xylophones; marimbas (adopting the Central American and African name), with wider, thinner bars and lower pitch; and vibraphones, with metal bars and revolving fans in the top of each resonator tube to provide an amplitude vibrato.[38]

In Africa, a much smaller instrument commonly shares the name given to the xylophone, or something close to it. This is the *kalimba, mbira, sansa,* or *sanza*—there are many names used in the literature (see figure 1.10). The instrument consists of a series of reeds, most often today made of iron, frequently of flattened iron wire, though one still sometimes sees those made of bamboo or similar material, for example, in Cameroon. The reeds are attached to a wooden board, often the

Figure 1.10. Sansas, Mbiras, and Kalimbas

Above, L–R: East Africa (IX 44); probably Uganda (IX 46); Cameroon (VI 190); unlocated (VI 192); Shona people, Zimbabwe, traditional type with shell rattles (VI 210); modern version with bottle tops (XIII 3).

Below, L–R: by Hugh Tracey, African Music Society (I 124a); West Africa (IX 248); Karaiwanjong people, Uganda (IX 168); Chokwe people, Angola (I 204); probably South Africa (III 8); Shona people, Zimbabwe (IV 98).

upper surface of a box made either from slats of wood pegged together or by hollowing a thicker piece of wood. The reeds are bridged up by two rails and strongly tied down, normally by wire, between those rails so that they are under tension. The board or box is held between the hands, and the free ends of the reeds, held toward the player, are plucked by the two thumbs and sometimes also the forefingers.

The arrangement of the reeds differs from people to people, but a common pattern is with the longest and lowest pitched toward the middle of the row with progressively shorter reeds to each side. Some patterns, for example, the kalimba of Zimbabwe, have, as it were, an upper manual—a second series of shorter reeds above the lower, usually only to one side. Many of these instruments have buzzing or rattling elements added, either loose rings of iron around the reed between the ligature and the rail nearer the player, or fragments of seashell (now more often old bottle caps) or other rattles fixed to the board. The instruments of plain board, rather than those hollowed or on boxes, are often held inside a large half-gourd to provide added resonance, or are held against or have a smaller gourd attached for this purpose.[39]

Such instruments are, with one exception, unique to Africa, though their use has been spreading recently to "our" culture, either with imports or with instruments made in Europe and America. The sole exception is in the Caribbean, where they are also used. Much larger instruments—called, for instance, *marímbula* in Cuba—have been made there by the descendants of slaves, often using segments of old wind-up gramophone springs fixed on a resonator box large enough for the player to sit on.[40]

There is one type of instrument in our culture that is analogous with these: the musical box. Here, instead of separate reeds tied to a frame, there is a steel comb, each tooth a different length, that is placed so that the end of each tooth is within reach of pins fixed in a revolving metal cylinder or barrel. The barrel is turned by a clockwork motor, and the pins are set so that each tooth or reed is plucked at the moment required by the tune set on the barrel.

The reason that the term *reed* is used throughout this section is that, as Hugh Tracey pointed out, the tongues or *lamellae* (as they are often called) behave acoustically in exactly the same way as the free reeds of mouth organs, concertinas, reed organs, and similar instruments (see figures G.2 and G.3).[41] The tongues or "feathers" of trumps (or Jew's harps) behave similarly.[42] All are tuned in the same way, by length and mass, and all can be fine-tuned by adding additional mass to the free end of the reed.

Bells and Gongs

Bells take many forms. We can define them as vessels that are struck either with an internal or an external clapper attached to the bell, as most of ours are, or with a separate striker, as they often are in East Asia and Africa. Some bells hang from animals or in towers, some rest on the ground, some are held in the hand. All share the defining characteristic that it is the edge or rim that vibrates most strongly. This is why they can be hung from their vertex, rest on it, or be held by a handle at it, without spoiling the sound.

Gongs, on the other hand, while also vessels in the sense that if laid down flat on their face they would hold water, behave very differently, for they vibrate most strongly at the vertex or center, and they can, without degrading the sound, be hung from their rim or rest on it, as they do in the gamelan.

Bells are instruments of high antiquity. We can see small cast bells, presumably of bronze, attached to horses in Mesopotamian reliefs, and we have many small Roman bells in our museums. In China, they were casting bronze bells with such precision in the fifth century BC that they could design each bell to provide two specified pitches, depending on where they were struck.[43] Not that bronze bells were new in China at that period—their history goes back at least a thousand years earlier, and bronze was preceded by other materials such as pottery in the Neolithic period of 3000–2000 BC. The origin of the bell may be far older than that. Harry Shorto suggested that the prototype was the slit drum, for these, as we shall see in interlude F, come in all sizes, from giant, six- to ten-foot-diameter hollowed trees, to those small enough to hold in the hand.[44] He cited the long-accepted principle that the large and clumsy artifact leads to the small and neat one, and we still have many examples of wooden bells, often cattle bells, hollowed out exactly like slit drums but with swinging clappers inside.

There was a huge variety of types and shapes of bell in ancient China, some used, as everywhere else, for animals and so forth and for signaling, but many for use in musical chimes. Most of the animal bells were clapper bells, an object hanging inside the bell to strike its side when it was swung, whereas all the musical ones were struck with mallets by the players. Many of these last were narrow and pointedly oval in section. A bell that is round in section has a sustained sound, as we hear from our church towers, whereas a bell with an oval cross-section has a short sound and this is preferred for a musical chime because otherwise notes overlap each other and the melody is confused.[45] This is a detail that is still unrecognized by the designers of our carillons.

It is clear also that Chinese bell-founders knew how to tune the overtones of bells before the eighth century BC, more than two thousand years before that art was discovered in Europe. As with all idiophonic instruments, the overtones of bells are naturally inharmonic, which is why the sound sometimes seems to jangle. The overtones can be brought into harmonic relationships to avoid such jangles by adjusting the thickness of the metal at strategic points. This can be done in the casting or, more accurately, by filing or scraping the metal after it has been cast. Evidence for both methods can be seen in ancient Chinese bells, but the process was not discovered in Europe until the seventeenth century, when Jacob van Eyck, the carillonneur of Utrecht, worked with the Hémony brothers, who were bell-founders, first in Lorraine and then in Zutphen and Ghent.[46]

The carillon is our most important version of the musical chime of bells, with anything up to fifty or more bells. We have medieval illustrations from the twelfth century onward of people striking a row of bells, anything from three to a dozen or more, normally with ordinary carpenters' hammers.[47] By the seventeenth century, these had developed into much larger sets, usually hung in a church or town hall tower. They were played either from a mechanical barrel, set with pins to control which bell was struck when the barrel rotated, or by a player with a form of keyboard. The keyboard was similar to that of the harpsichord or organ, but with round rods for the keys, which were struck by the player's fist, each key controlling a tracker wire leading to one of the bells. The use of carillons has now spread around the world, and both methods of playing them are used—the barrel, or some modern computerized equivalent, to play hymns or other tunes at certain times of day, and the keyboard for recitals by a carillonneur.

This is not the only way that bells are played in towers. In Russia and some other places, one player controls a network of tracker wires with hands and feet, almost like a spider in the center of a web, as highly skilled an art as that of a carillonneur. In others, bells are simply swung or chimed to mark the time or as a summons to church. *Swinging* moves the bell so that a clapper strikes its sides as the bell swings; *chiming*, as with carillons, moves the clapper to strike the bell. A peculiarly English custom, now also heard elsewhere, is change-ringing, where each bell is numbered and the ringers permute the order of these numbers in highly complex patterns that are devised as a purely mathematical exercise. Some changes continue for many hours before the bells finally return in their courses to their starting point. It can be a matter of great triumph for a team of ringers to complete a peal that may, for example, on eight bells, involve 40,320 changes.[48]

Change-ringing as we know it today dates back only to the seventeenth century, and by that time church bells had attained their modern shapes. Some medieval bells were taller and narrower and are described by André Lehr as "sugar-loaf shape." Examples of these from the eleventh to thirteenth centuries are preserved in the Franciscan Monastery of the Flagellation in Jerusalem, from the Latin Kingdom Church of the Nativity in Bethlehem.[49] The bells that appear in the medieval manuscripts were usually a simple beehive shape (the traditional round wicker or straw beehive known as a *skep*, not the modern wooden shape). The earliest surviving European cast bronze bells larger than the Roman handbells are also mostly this shape. These date from around the eighth century AD, and the necessary technology is said to have originated in Campania in Italy (the area around Naples)—thus the origin of our term for bell scholarship: *campanology*.[50]

Before that date, European bells other than the Roman seem to have been made from folded iron sheets, exactly like the cattle bells still widely used to this day (see figure 1.11). St. Patrick's bell, preserved in the National Museum of Ireland in Dublin, was made in this way: an iron sheet forged and folded, rectangular in section, narrower at the top than at the bottom, with the sheet joined at the narrow sides by rivets.[51] Save for its age, it

is all but identical in appearance with the bell shown in figure 1.11 from a farm in Iowa. Fivos Anoyanakis describes and illustrates the manufacture of such bells and also the making of cast cattle bells.[52]

Cattle bells serve several purposes. One is for protection, both physical and mystical (see interlude A). The sound of a bell may frighten away a predator such as a wolf or an eagle, and it may also protect the animal from witchcraft and attack by elves and other evil spirits. Another purpose is for location, for the shepherd or cowherd searching for an animal in rough or wooded country will follow the sound of the bell. A third is for leadership, for if the lead animal, a bellwether, for example (the leader is often a female), carries a bell, the rest of the flock will follow. And a fourth is for pleasure and euphony. In Switzerland, among other places, a farmer will choose the bells carefully to make sure that all are in tune with each other and will derive pleasure from the musical combinations of sounds produced by the animals as they graze.

Animal bells are also often used by folk dancers. In some areas, their costumes must be very tiring to wear, for they may carry a dozen or more quite heavy bells stitched to their belts or clothing.

Similar bells were also often attached to carriages, sleighs, or horse harnesses, often for much the same reasons that they were attached to sheep and cattle. These sometimes appear in musical scores, for example by Mozart and Mahler.

They are also used domestically. Many of us have a doorbell on our house, for instance. In the days when

Figure 1.11. Iron Cattle Bells

Above, L–R: *truc*, Catalunya (XI 176); Portugal (XIII 68); small Catalan (XI 188); Germany (XII 46); Pyrenees (XIII 156); India (VII 254); perhaps Zulu (III 64a); Iowa, USA (V 64).

Below, L–R: *esquella*, Catalunya (XI 178); Switzerland (XIII 88); Yoruba, Nigeria (X 94); open-sided, Masai, Kenya (VII 98); Wiltshire, England (XIII 166).

domestic servants were plentiful, a row of bells, often differentiated by pitch, would hang in or near the servants' hall. When members of the family required a service, they would ring, and the staff would know, either by pitch or by seeing which bell was swinging, the room to which they were summoned.

A summons is one of the commonest purposes for bells: the call to church or to school, or to signal the hours of prayer. An alarm is another, whether for fire or flood or an enemy attack. Another is to tell the time, for in many parts of the world, chimes are used to signal the hours, very commonly with different, easily recognized, musical patterns to denote which quarter-hour it is.

The public use of bells has been so strongly linked with Christianity that in lands of other faiths they have sometimes been prohibited, and substitutes may be permitted instead. One common one is a bar of iron or wood, called in the Greek church a *semantron*, suspended outside the church and struck at the times for prayer. Similarly, in some places where a bell may have been too expensive or difficult to procure, a hoop of iron or a heavy piece of scrap metal may be used as a fire alarm or for other such purposes.

One of the problems of bells is their weight in relation to the pitch they produce. The Westminster chimes, broadcast worldwide by the British Broadcasting Corporation, are well known. Even the smallest of those five bells, sounding the G-sharp above middle C, weighs more than a ton, and the hour bell, known as Big Ben, sounding the E below middle C, weighs 13½ tons. When bells are needed on concert platforms or in opera houses or theaters, it is impossible to use objects of such a weight. Many shapes and materials have been tried as substitutes, the most common of which are brass tubes or, for the lowest pitches, lengths of iron drain pipe. Tubes are easy to make, cheap to buy, and can be hung in frames in chromatic sets to be played easily, but they do not sound much like real bells. The Concertgebouw Orchestra in Amsterdam has a set of rectangular iron plates that sound much better, but it would not be easy to duplicate these, for all that is known of their origin is that they were made from the armor plating of a pre–World War I British battle cruiser. Nor would it be possible to play some modern composers' bell parts on them, for these are designed for the easily accessible sets of tubes. So, for works such as Puccini's *Tosca*, Wagner's *Parsifal*, Meyerbeer's *Les Huguenots*, and Berlioz's *Symphonie Fantastique*, musicians do the best they can and hope that the future will produce something better.

Gongs are much less of a problem. Good instruments are being made today in Switzerland and elsewhere in a multiplicity of sizes, some more than three feet in diameter. Tuned gongs, demanded by some composers, are also available, so it is no longer necessary, as it was until the 1950s or so, to use those from distant lands that were seldom in tune with our scales.

It is generally believed that gongs originated in the Orient, but although they were used in China for many centuries before they appeared in our music, the Chinese themselves say that they came from the West.[53] The earliest traces are in Cretan and Greek legend: when the god Zeus was born, the young men beat on their shields to hide his infant cries and prevent his father, Chronos, from swallowing him as he had all his previous children.[54] There is a bronze disk in the museum in Heraklion, found in the Idean Cave, that portrays this scene, two young men beating each upon two gongs, between them the newborn Zeus, already a bearded adult.[55] It is thought that this disk was itself one of these gongs, and the cult site of Zeus at Dodona on the Greek mainland was well known for its gongs and bronze cauldrons, which also were beaten.

There is often confusion between such cauldrons, which are properly resting bells, and gongs. Similar resting bells, often of great size, are known in Japan. Many are alleged to be of considerable antiquity, and the largest shown in figure 1.12 bears on its side a date, equivalent to 1495 in our calendar, along with the names of the donor, the maker, and the temple for which it was made. However, doubt has been sown on such antiquity recently, and the inscriptions are said to be nineteenth-century fakes. Similarly, the Tibetan singing bells seem to be a fairly recent innovation, perhaps the invention of an acolyte with a monk's food bowl, just as we suggest later that the swannee whistle was the invention of a mischievous choir boy with his master's pitch pipe.

The presumption of the gong's antiquity in our own culture is strengthened by St. Paul's reference to it in I Corinthians 13:1 as "sounding brass" to contrast with the "tinkling cymbal"—he is not likely to have used such an analogy had he not known that the people of Corinth, a Greek city, were familiar with the gong.[56]

The use of shields as gongs, especially for processional dances, was well known among the Greeks, with the *korybantes*, and the Romans, with the *salii*. It is found elsewhere also, for example, among the Zulu of South Africa, who beat on their shields as a preliminary to battle, and in Tanzania. There is a Tanzanian wooden shield in Gothenberg's Ethnographic Museum that has a vertical slot in it—rendering it useless as a shield, but enabling it to produce two pitches when struck.[57]

The iconographic style of the Idean disk in Heraklion confirms earlier suggestions that the gong, like so many

Figure 1.12.   Resting Bells
L–R: *dobachi*, medium, Japan (III 98); *dobachi*, large, inscribed as by Wakizaka Kōji-No-Kama, Kinryūji, Japan, 1495 (II 92); *dobachi*, small, Japan (VIII 106); *inkin*, mendicant priest's bell on a handle, Japan (XI 46); singing bowl, rubbed with the beater, Tibet (XII 74).

other instruments, originated in Central Asia and spread thence east and west. It exists today in two forms. One is the flat-faced disk with a narrow everted rim that was the norm in China and that we use in our orchestras under the name of *tamtam*. The other is the disk with a deeper rim and usually a protruding central boss that is characteristic of Southeast Asia and Indonesia and that we call a *gong* orchestrally to distinguish it from the tamtam. This always produces a note of definite pitch, more precise and clearer than those with a flatter face.

The bossed gong is the central instrument of the Javanese gamelan. The largest, the *gong ageng*, is the principal instrument to which offerings are made before every performance and which is struck at the end of each long sequence of melody. Smaller gongs, both hung from frames and lying horizontally on their rims on crossed cords, punctuate the shorter melodic phrases and sound the melody themselves. *Gamelan* means no more than "ensemble" or "orchestra." It can take many forms and use many different types of instruments, but the gamelan in the sense that we have just used it, with gongs of many sizes and types and sometimes a bowed string instrument (*rebab*), a flute (*suling*), and voices, was initially the court orchestra of the rajahs. It became in due course an equivalent of our town or village band and is now played worldwide through the influence of such scholars as Jaap Kunst and Mantle Hood.[58]

Returning now to different forms of bells, one that has been used from antiquity and into our own orchestras is a special flattened form, the *cymbal*. It may be difficult when we see and hear the great clash of a pair of these instruments in our orchestras to recognize them as a form of bell, but it becomes much clearer when we examine the smaller forms of antiquity. These were often high-domed and with so little flat rim that they were little more than cup-bells. Others, such as those played by the Roman copy of a Greek dancer in figure 1.13, have a

Figure 1.13.   Roman Cymbal Player
Hand cymbals and *scabellum* (foot cymbal), *photo private collection, England.*

dome over about half the diameter, far more than our modern instruments. As well as the pair in his hands, he has a second pair in a special boot called in Rome a *scabellum*, a forerunner of the shoes of our clog dancers and tap dancers.[59]

Cymbals were also used in ancient Egypt and over much of the Near and Middle East. They are used today all over Asia, sometimes as in Turkey still (see figure A.2) and in the European Middle Ages (see figure C.1) on the ends of forked tongs, a cymbal on each branch so that they clash when the tongs are pressed together. In Myanmar (Burma), small cymbals are used as time keepers, often one fixed to a wooden block, the other held in the hand. Much of their music is punctuated with a *tak* on a wood block and a *ching* on the cymbals, coming on the first and third beats of a measure, for most of their music is in four-beat time.[60] Large instruments are used in Tibet, with very high, wide domes, and in China with very small angular domes. The Chinese cymbals were very popular in our early jazz bands, under the name of "Chinese crash," for they were designed to produce a short-lasting sound, unlike our orchestral instruments, which derive from Turkey.

We have already met the folded-iron cattle bells. A very different type of forged-iron bell is used in West and Central Africa. These again are used as time keepers and also as talking instruments, as we shall see in interlude F. Single bells are known, including small iron troughs called *atoke*, but most are double, forged together at the apex just as each bell is made by forging one curved iron sheet onto the other to form the hollow of the bell (see figure F.2).

Bells exist in many other forms, in many sizes, and for many other purposes. One of the many musical uses is the *jaltarang*, the cup chimes of India and elsewhere, a row or semicircle of tea bowls struck with a pair of light beaters. These are tuned either by being naturally of different pitches or by containing different amounts of water. Similarly, our musical glasses, usually rubbed by the player's moistened fingertips circling round the rims, were tuned either by grinding or by water. The most elaborate form of these, the glass harmonica, was said to have been invented by the American polymath Benjamin Franklin, while he was ambassador in Paris. This was a series of glass bowls, mounted concentrically on a spindle that was rotated by a pedal. The bells were set in a trough so that their rims were kept wet by water, and they were set closely enough together that the player could span them to play chords as on a keyboard instrument. Mozart wrote an *Adagio and Rondo* for the harmonica and other instruments. Acoustically, the glasses and tea bowls are bells, for like all others in this category, they are vessels whose rims vibrate when rubbed or struck.

Rattles

Rattles go far back into prehistory. Clay vessels containing pellets have been found from many early cultures, and because the vessels often replicate the shapes of natural containers such as gourds or seed pods, it is obvious that rattles of such materials that do not survive long burial in the earth must have been used in far earlier times.

So various are their forms, so many are their types, that rattles almost defy description. Even the best-known system for classifying musical instruments (for which, see the afterword on Classification of Instruments) becomes almost incoherent when dealing with them. We may define them as instruments that are shaken, but we shake them in many different ways, for instance, attaching them to horses and carriages, tying them to our legs and arms, stitching them to our clothing, leaving them out in the wind or water, placing them where our enemies may trip over them, and, of course, holding them in our hands.

Equally variable are their uses. Many are used for ritual; others for dances and other musical occasions; some for protection (see interlude A); many just for fun, especially by children; and almost all for more than one, or indeed for all, of these purposes. Many appear today in our and other peoples' orchestras and bands.

Some rattles shake against themselves, some slide to and fro, some knock together or are knocked by something else. Many are hollow, often with seeds or other pellets inside them or with a network of beads outside them. Some are scraped by something. And many combine two or more of these methods of sounding, which is why classification systems become incoherent.

Those that shake against themselves are often called *jingles*, although this term can also be used for such things as pellet bells, causing confusion, and those that are shaken to slide back and forth against their bodies include the *sistra*. There are gray areas, for example, because as the disks of the *sistrum* slide to and fro, they are striking against each other as well as against the frame. On the whole, however, we consider that the jingles are clusters of things, for example, deer hooves or nutshells that we find in Africa and in South America, or small pellet bells, as we find in India, whereas the sistrum has a set of plates or jingles that slide on bars, or bars that slide in a frame.

Figure 1.14. Jingles and Sistra

Above, L–R: one of a set of *angklung*, Java (II 170); nutshells, Brazil (V 228); two sistra, Ethiopia (VII 238 and 46); sistrum of milk-tin tops, unlocated Hispanic (XIII 132); *kacikaura*, sistrum of gourd segments, Zaria, Nigeria (VI 234).

Below, L–R: iron plate jingle, Sichuan, China (XII 112); cluster of nutshells, Amazonia (VIII 214); *kacacakai*, iron jingles, Zaria, Nigeria (VI 242); cluster of nutshells, Amazonia (VIII 212); cluster of deer hooves, Ecuador (XI 248).

The clusters of jingles are normally attached to dancers' anatomy or costumes and are seldom used as a separate instrument—they sound in response to body movement. The sistrum and the Javanese and Balinese *angklung* that is also a form of sistrum, on the other hand, are separate instruments. The anklung is made in tuned sets and is used in villages as an orchestra or gamelan instead of the sets of tuned gongs and other instruments more familiar to us. The sistrum was important in ancient Egypt and was associated with the Isis rite that was also popular in Rome in the days of the empire. It survives today in the Ethiopian Coptic Church.

Several of those that knock together or against something are described among the instruments of protection in interlude A, and comparing the appearance of the matracas in figure A.2, for example, with the jingles here, makes the difference between them clear.

Hollow or vessel rattles are much the largest group of rattles, and they take many forms (see figure 1.15). Those most familiar to us are the pellet bells and the maracas and other instruments of our Latin American dance bands. Pellet bells have a long history on horse harnesses, illustrations of which go back to ancient Mesopotamia. They were also used on carriages in Europe and America and are still seen on sleighs—so much so that as "jingle bells" they are the subject of a popular song in that context, and they are often called "sleigh bells." They are also used in groups attached to dancers'

Figure 1.15.   Vessel Rattles

Hanging, L–R: folded birchbark, Inuit people, Newfoundland, Canada (V 244); woven palm leaf, Southeast Asia (VIII 240); mule harness bells, Portugal (VI 148a); rattle drum, northern Ontario, Canada (VI 74); camel bells with pendant good-luck charm, Mongolia (V 240).

Standing, middle, L–R: rain stick (XIII 80); basket, Congo (I 98); reed box, Uganda (VI 24); Peyote rattle, Rosebud Sioux, North America (V 32); *caki buta*, reused Shelltox aerosol can, Zaria, Nigeria (VI 236); killer whale pattern, Haida people, British Columbia coast, Canada (V 68).

Below, L–R: external net, Zambia (XIII 120); baobab seed pods, Kimberley District, Western Australia (IV 120); *maracas*, Jamaica (I 108a); two baby's silver rattles and whistles, England (XII 218 and XIII 142); pellet bell, by Robert Wells, Aldbourne, England (IX 238); pellet bell, Israel (VIII 146).

legs, and they appear quite often in our orchestral music, not only in Mozart's *Sleigh Ride*, where tuned sets are required, but in many other works.

Maracas are always used in pairs and, as is normal with any paired instrument, one is always higher pitched than the other. North of the Rio Grande, similar instruments are used singly, as they are also, for example, in Brazil. Most commonly, whether single or in pairs, they are used to provide rhythm for dance music, a use that is found almost worldwide. They can also be ritual instruments, but again most often when the dance itself is part of a ritual. Shaking such instruments to provide a rhythm is not quite so easy as it looks, for unless the internal pellets—which may be seeds, pebbles, or any other such material, including birdshot—move as a coherent body against the sides of the vessel, the sound is a mush rather than a distinct rhythm. Those that have the pellets in an external net are more often twisted than shaken, sometimes holding the net of pellets still with one hand while twisting the gourd with the other; other peoples rely on inertia to hold the network still enough for the gourd to twist within the net. As with so many other instruments, the detritus of our civilization, for example, old tin cans of all sorts, reappears as vessel rattles.

Smaller vessel rattles are often grouped on straps or cords and attached to dancers' legs and arms (see figure 1.16). They take many forms—seed pods, spiders' egg cases, small deer hooves, metal pellet bells—but they are distinct from the clusters of jingles with which we began in that they are attached individually to whatever holds

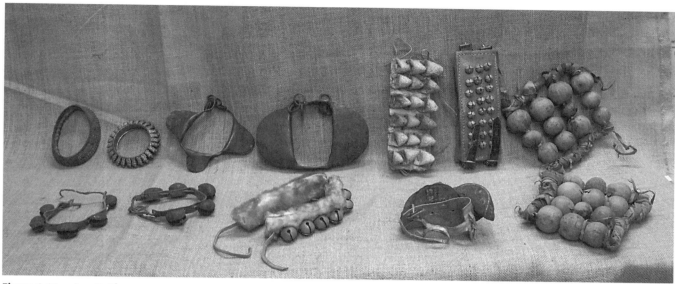

Figure 1.16. Leg Rattles

Above, L–R: silver anklet, India (I 74); silver bracelet, Israel (XII 92); brass trilobe anklet, Yoruba people, Nigeria (X 84); brass bilobe anklet, also Yoruba (X 86c); spiders' eggs on antelope leather, Zambia (I 106); pellet bells on leather straps, India (XI 234); spherical seeds on wooden sticks, South Africa (XI 200).

Below, L–R: hammered iron pellet bells on leather straps, Africa (XI 110); pellet bells on sheepskin, labeled "Made by American Indians" (V 34); folded shoe polish tins, Mbere people, Kenya (IV 110).

them and their sound is made by the seeds or pellets within them striking against their sides, rather than by shaking against each other.

Finally in this very brief survey of so large a group of instruments, we often see rattles of all sorts attached to other instruments to increase the interest of their sound. An obvious example is our tambourine, where miniature cymbals are set into slots in the side of the frame. The Caucasian *daira*, a larger frame drum than the tambourine, has rings or other jingling elements such as small pellet bells fixed to the inside of the frame, where they can be heard but not seen. The sansa, as we have already seen (figure 1.10), often has metal rings attached to the reeds or the frame, or shells or bottle tops attached to the body. Many instruments, especially in Africa, have rattles added to improve, it is often said to "sweeten," the sound.

Notes

1. A recent book (*The Origins of Music*, ed. Nils Wallin et al. [2000]) discusses some of these points, but concentrates on bird and animal song, ignoring the influence and effect of dance and of motor impulses inherent in that and other activities, and discusses, almost exclusively, vocal music rather than the use of instruments.

2. Leonard Williams, *The Dancing Chimpanzee* (1967). There are many other similar records.

3. These archaeological and other technical terms are explained in the afterword.

4. It has long been held that only *Homo sapiens* (modern humans, developing some 50,000 years ago) has the mental capacity to create art and music. More evidence appears almost daily to suggest that this may not be true and that earlier people, whether Neanderthal or even earlier, also had such capability.

5. Whereas, any inclination toward atheism or even agnosticism is the result of deliberate thought and decision.

6. The casual and accidental sounds from which *musique concrète* was created were not in themselves music. Only when a composer had manipulated and transformed them did they become music.

7. J. R. Harding, "The Bull-Roarer in History and in Antiquity," *African Music* 5:3 (1973/74): 40–42.

8. The French name, *rhombe*, comes from its shape and derives from the Greek *rhombos*; the German *Schwirrholz*, from its use: "whirring wood."

9. Otto Seewald, *Beiträge zur Kenntnis* (1934), 13–18 and Taf. 1: 5, 6, and 7.

10. André Schaeffner, *Origine des Instruments de Musique* (1936), 132.

11. In personal discussion.

12. Curt Sachs, *The History of Musical Instruments* (1940), 43.

13. Henry Balfour, "The Friction Drum," *Journal of the Royal Anthropological Institute* 37 (1907): 67–92 and plates 12–14, specifically 80–83 and plate 14.

14. Lucie Rault, *Musical Instruments* (2000), 14–24, referring to Iégor Reznikoff and Michel Dauvois, "La dimension

sonore des grottes ornées," *Bulletin de la Société Préhistorique Française* 85:8 (1988): 238–46. See also Michel Dauvois and Xavier Boutillon, "Grottes et Lithophones," in *Acoustique et Instruments Anciens* (1999), 215–23.

15. Marin Mersenne, *Harmonie Universelle* (1636), Livre Cinquiesme des Instruments à Vent, proposition IV, 229–30. The Za-Zah was registered by Matthias Barr in London in the late nineteenth or early twentieth century.

16. Lya Dams, "Palaeolithic Lithophones," *Oxford Journal of Archaeology* 4:1 (1985): 31–46; Abbé Glory, "La Grotte de Roucadour," *Bulletin de la Société Préhistorique Française* 61 (1964): 166–96, and further articles in subsequent volumes.

17. S. N. Bibikov, *The Oldest Musical Complex Made of Mammoth Bones* (1981).

18. Paul Collaer, *Südostasien* (1979), 10 and Abb. 1 and 2; Trân Van Khê, *La musique vietnamienne traditionelle* (1962), 11.

19. Filippo Bonanni, *Gabinetto armonico* (1723); all Bonanni's engravings have been reprinted, albeit much reduced in format, with new captions by Frank Ll. Harrison and Joan Rimmer in their *The Showcase of Musical Instruments* (1964), pl. 96.

20. Bernard Fagg, "The Discovery of Multiple Rock Gongs in Nigeria," *Man* (1956): 17–18; published also in *African Music* 1:3 (1956): 6–9.

21. M. C. Fagg, *Rock Music* (1997).

22. Francis Bebey, *African Music* (1975), 91.

23. Jenny F. So, ed., *Music in the Age of Confucius* (2000), 54–56; Lucie Rault, ed., *La voix du dragon* (2000), 105–7.

24. Chang Sa-hun, [*Korean Musical Instruments*] (2nd ed., 1976), p. 305 in English, and with more detail in the Korean, pp. 115–18.

25. James Blades, *Percussion Instruments and Their History* (2nd ed., 1975), 82–84.

26. *Lithos* is Greek for "stone," and *phonos* for "sound," whereas *xylon* is Greek for "wood." Thus one can speak of instruments in any material as being "in xylophone shape," but a "stone xylophone" or "metal xylophone" can only be nonsense.

27. Olga Boone, *Les xylophones du Congo Belge* (1936), 86–87.

28. Gerhard Kubik illustrates a number of such instruments in *Ostafrika* (1982), Abb. 15, 16, 24, 25, and 99–104; abb. 53 shows a simple trough xylophone. A preeminent source is again Olga Boone.

29. The quantity of literature on the gamelan is now so great that there is little point in citing any individual works. Jaap Kunst's *Music in Java* (1949; 3rd enlarged ed., 1973, ed. E. L. Heins) remains the classic text.

30. A. M. Jones's *Africa and Indonesia* (1964) is the classic text here, but should be treated with extreme caution and should be considered only in conjunction with M. D. W. Jeffreys, "Review Article: *Africa and Indonesia*," *African Music* 4:1 (1966/1967): 66–73. A more moderate text is Jaap Kunst, "A Musicological Argument for Cultural Relationship between Indonesia—Probably the Isle of Java—and Central Africa," *Proceedings of the [Royal] Musical Association* 62 (1936): 57–76.

31. See Hugh Tracey, *Chopi Musicians* (1948), diagrams 1 and 2 on pp. 89 and 97, and esp. chap. 6, pp. 118–42.

32. This tuning process was first published by Father Jones—see A. M. Jones, "Experiment with a Xylophone Key," *African Music* 3:2 (1963): 6–10—and more recently in much greater detail by Jamie Murray Linwood in "The Manufacture of Tuned Percussion Instruments" (1995).

33. Martin Agricola, *Musica instrumentalis deudsch* (1529; reprinted Leipzig, 1896; transl. William E. Hettrick, 1994), f. H iii verso (p. 118 in Leipzig, p. 60 in Hettrick).

34. R. M. Longyear, "Ferdinand Kauer's Percussion Enterprises," *GSJ* 27 (1974): 2–8.

35. Bálint Sárosi, *Die Volksmusikinstrumente Ungarns* (1967), 12–15.

36. Blades, *Percussion Instruments*, 307–8 and plate 147.

37. Vida Chenoweth, *The Marimbas of Guatemala* (1964).

38. More detail on these, and on all percussion instruments, will be found in my *Timpani and Percussion* (2002).

39. Several museums have issued detailed catalogues of these instruments. Preeminent among them are J. S. Laurenty, *Les sanza du Congo* (1962); François Borel, *Collections d'instruments de musique: Les sanza* (1986); and Gerhard Kubik, *Lamelofones do Museu Nacional de Etnologia* (2002).

40. George List, "The *Mbira* in Cartagena," *JIFMC* 20 (1968): 54–9.

41. Personal communication when I gave a talk at the African Institute in London.

42. "Jew's harp" is the oldest name in English for this instrument, followed a few years later by "Jew's trump." More recent terms such as "jaw harp" have no historical basis. A better term today is "trump" by itself.

43. Lothar von Falkenhausen, *Suspended Music* (1993). See also So, *Music in the Age of Confucius*, and Rault, *La voix du dragon*. All three are concerned with the bells found in the tomb of the Marquis Yi; von Falkenhausen also discusses their history and predecessors.

44. Prof. Harry Shorto, addressing a meeting of the Ethnomusicology Panel of the Royal Anthropological Institute in the 1960s.

45. Von Falkenhausen, *Suspended Music*, 76–77, quoting Shen Gua (1031–1095).

46. André Lehr, *The Art of the Carillon in the Low Countries* (1991).

47. For example, the York Psalter, f. 21v, dated c. 1175, with two players and fifteen bells with their note names written above them, each player with a diatonic octave, C to B, but one with B-flat and the other with B-natural. It is reproduced in many books, including my own *World of Medieval and Renaissance Musical Instruments*, plate 8, and Lehr, *Art of the Carillon*, plate 91.

48. A clear and concise account of the history and technique of change-ringing can be found in *The Sound of Bells* (1964) by Edgar C. Shepherd, a leading exponent of the craft (see pp. 19–20 on the possible numbers of changes), and even

more entertainingly if less historically in Dorothy L. Sayers's detective story *The Nine Tailors* (1934).

49. Lehr, *Art of the Carillon*, plate 104. Also illustrated in Percival Price, *Bells and Man* (1983), 96.

50. Price, *Bells and Man*, 86. However, *campana* seems to have been a Latin word of rather earlier provenance.

51. Price, *Bells and Man*, 85. Lehr shows a very similar Dutch bell from sometime in the first to third centuries, *Art of the Carillon*, plate 79.

52. Fivos Anoyanakis, *Greek Popular Musical Instruments* (Athens: National Bank of Greece, 1979)—if only all national banks would sponsor such publications!

53. The first known use of gongs in Europe was during the French Revolution, and the first time that one appeared in a score was in Gossec's *Marche Lugubre*.

54. Jaap Kunst, "A Hypothesis about the Origin of the Gong," *Ethnos* (1947): 79–85 and 147.

55. Zeus was not alone among Greek gods in achieving adult birth. Botticelli's famous painting "The Birth of Venus" shows another example.

56. See my *Musical Instruments of the Bible* (2002), 114–17 and 122–24 for more detail on this.

57. Item no. 33.11.141

58. Kunst, *Music in Java*, and Mantle Hood, *The Ethnomusicologist* (1971).

59. Illustrated in my *Timpani and Percussion*, plate 2, and in many other books.

60. John Okell told me that, when he inquired about this, he was told, "Yes, of course we have music in triple time, 1, 2, 3, –, 1, 2, 3, –," etc.

INTERLUDE A

~

Instruments of Protection

Demons hate noise. Over much of the world it is believed that noise can protect from evil. It may also be that when we are frightened, a sound—even one that we make ourselves—is a companion to hold our hand as we walk through the dark of the forest. So in Java, travelers may carry a small bamboo slit drum, partly to signal to the neighboring villages as they pass—both to show that they are not thieves traveling secretly and, from the responses, to hear where the villages are—but also to reassure themselves. So in Russia and Scandinavia, sleighs have bells, partly to make a pleasant noise and partly as protection from the witches and trolls. So, too, babies are given bells and rattles (see figure 1.15), both because the baby enjoys the sound that may keep it quiet and occupied for a while and also to keep away the fairies who might otherwise steal it for a changeling. So, too, cattle carry bells (figure 1.11), both to help locate them and also to prevent the elves from souring the milk.

Bells are particularly powerful in these respects, and so churches have bells to control the ghosts and ghouls in the churchyard as well as to call the faithful to prayer and to mark the hours. So, too, in parts of France some bells are believed to be so powerful that they can avert the summer storms that strip the fruit from the trees and flatten the crops in the fields.

It is not only bells that have this power. In Bohemia, far from the sea, the conch could drive away the tempest, as Vivaldi illustrated in his concerto *Conca*.[1] This was probably written in the 1730s, and Vivaldi is known to have had extensive connections with the Bohemian nobility, although it is unlikely that he could have written such a work if he were not familiar with the use of conch trumpets in Venice. Confirmation of the Bohemian use

is provided by Ludvík Kunz, who cites ten *Wetterhorn* (storm trumpets of shell) known to him in Bohemian collections, mostly in Pilsen and Prague.[2]

One cannot dismiss these uses as "merely superstition." When people believe in them strongly, as shown in these and many other examples, they become established uses of instruments, uses that historians cannot afford to ignore, for they are as real to those who use them as are our uses in the orchestra and anywhere else. Certainly they are as real to them as the more mundane use of instruments to protect crops from animals and other marauders.

This last type of sonic protection is even more widespread around the world. Sometimes the instruments are automatic—for example, segments of bamboo or other material hung where they will catch the wind and rattle against each other or produce sounds as the wind whistles across a hole—though these are of limited utility, for birds and animals come to pillage whether the wind is blowing or not. Ingenious devices are sometimes seen where water from a stream or rivulet fills a pivoted section of bamboo or other material, tipping its balance so that it knocks against another piece, but these again may be limited by drought or even flood.

Mostly such noisemakers require human intervention, and it is here that it becomes important to study the instrumentarium of children. Over much of the world, especially where there is no universal education, it is the children who are employed as animal scarers, and instruments that may have more serious uses in the adult world, or that once may have done so, survive among the children both for practical uses such as this and also simply as toys.

In chapter 1, we discussed the bull-roarer and the snorra (see figure 1.1), both of which survive widely in the hands of children. Rattles are commonly used, often no different from those that accompany dances and that may once have been symbols of fertility. Vessels—gourds with dried seeds within; globules of pottery with pellets within, examples of which in our museums go back to the Stone Age and that can still be bought in our shops today; old tin cans with a handful of gravel inside; coconuts; anything hollow that can contain something to rattle—all these can be and are used.

Ratchets, which once were used by watchmen in our streets, are more powerful and make a louder noise. A frame carrying thin blades of wood is swung around a handle shaped as a toothed cogwheel (see figure A.1), and if each blade is very slightly shorter than the previous one, they slip off the edge of one tooth to clack on the flat of the next in succession, providing a more continuous clatter than when there is only one blade or when all are the same length. This is an instrument that in the fields is sometimes automatic, driven by wind or a waterwheel, but more often it is held in the hand. As well as a scaring birds, it has many other uses, most familiar perhaps around the soccer field. In Britain, it was widely distributed during World War II to all air raid wardens, to be used as the signal of a gas attack, but fortunately these were never needed. These are easily recognized in collections both by their size and because there was a khaki-painted iron resonator attached to the side.

Ratchets are used occasionally orchestrally: Beethoven scored them to represent musketry in his Battle Symphony.[3] Percussionists in the pantomime or music hall use them when the comedian suddenly bends over. They are used in the synagogues at the festival of Purim, when the book of Esther is read, to drown out the name of the hated villain Haman. They have a serious use, as well, in the church. During Holy Week, the bells are silent (tradition says that they go to Rome to be blessed, although of course they do not actually leave the tower), and instead the ratchets are used. Children run about using the small ones, similar to those used in the fields, but the sexton may have something the size of a wheelbarrow or even bigger, great wooden blades like floorboards, and a cogged wheel turned with a handle like those that once were used to crank a car. The sound can be deafening, especially when more than one is used, echoing through the vaults of the church.[4]

Another instrument used as both a bird scarer and for other purposes is the clapper (see figure A.2). These in their simplest form look like oversize versions of children's castanets: a rectangular wooden plaque, tapering to a handle at one end, like a crude table-tennis paddle, with similar wooden plaques hinged to it, one on each side, with wire or cord passing through holes just below the root of the handle. Shaking it makes the outer plaques clack on the central one. These also are sometimes used in church during Holy Week, but are more often children's instruments used from door to door—a pair in the Museum of Welsh Life in St. Fagan's is labeled "egg-clappers" from Anglesey, again an Easter rite albeit quite different from that of the Roman church.

Other Easter instruments, only somewhat more elaborate in form, are the Spanish *matracas*, with wooden rods hinged to a central bar that clack against a wooden board

Figure A.1.   Cog Rattles or Ratchets

Above, L–R: Air raid warden's, 1940, England (III 246); homemade toy, England (VI 256); double-ended, Bohemia (XII 76); soccer, Swindon Football Club, England (XIII 158).

Below, L–R: farmer's iron frame, England (III 124a); Purim *gregger*, by Simon Frank, United States (XI 84); *détska rehtačka*, child's toy, Slovakia (VIII 172); of *lignum vitae*, England (IX 164); child's toy, Catalunya (XI 152); watchman's, England, eighteenth century (VIII 126); orchestral, by Hawkes, London (III 124b).

Figure A.2. Clappers, Etc.

Above, L–R: *matracas*, Catalunya (XI 172); *qaraqeb*, iron, Morocco (XIII 154); percussion sticks, Arnhem Land, Australia (II 74a); *zilli masa*, tong-cymbals, Turkey (VIII 78).

Middle, L–R: *castanyoles*, Eivissa (XI 86); spoons, England (X 120); kartal, India (XII 4); egg-clappers, England (XI 134).

Below, L–R: ivory castanets, probably France, perhaps seventeenth century (VI 252); half pair of bones, England (VII 196).

as they swing, and the Italian *tricca-ballacca*, whose two outer wooden hammers swing in a frame against a central hammer.

Clappers are also widely used for dance accompaniment, for example, Spanish castanets and their larger relatives the *castanyoles* of Ibiza, and the Indian *kartal*; to accompany other instruments or singing, such as the Australian click sticks with the didjeridu and the Moroccan iron *qaraqeb*, which are often made from old gasoline cans; and for music making by themselves, like our own bones and spoons.

Noisemakers with semiritual, semiprotective roles abound around the world. An early source that shows many kinds, most but by no means all of European origin, is Filippo Bonanni's *Gabinetto armonico* (1723), the first book on musical instruments to show as much interest in the instruments of the common people and the exotic as those of the art music of the upper classes.[5]

Notes

1. RV 163 (Fanna XI, 5). See Michael Talbot, "Vivaldi's Conch Concerto," *Informazioni e Studi Vivaldiani* 5 (1984): 66–81.

2. Ludvík Kunz, *Die Volksmusikinstrumente der Tschechoslowakei* (1974), 130–33.

3. *Wellington's Sieg oder die Schlacht bei Vittoria*, Op. 91, written originally for Mälzel's giant musical box, the Panharmonicon, and later scored for orchestra.

4. Examples can be found in all four volumes of the *Handbuch der europäischen Volksmusikinstrumente* (the only ones published before the reunification of Germany made such work impracticable): that cited above by Ludvík Kunz, the companion volume by Oskár Elschek on Slovakian instruments, that by Bálint Sárosi on Hungary, and that by Brigitte Bachmann-Geiser on the Swiss instruments.

5. All the engravings, much reduced in format, lacking the text, and with new captions, were published by Frank Ll. Harrison and Joan Rimmer as *The Showcase of Musical Instruments* (1964).

CHAPTER TWO

Drums

Trouble with Tension

Two of the five families of musical instruments suffer from problems with tension. Putting things at the most basic level with the other families, for wind instruments, all one needs is something hollow with at least one orifice into which to blow; for idiophones, something solid that is rigid enough to clang when struck; and for electrophones, a power source. But both skin instruments and string instruments need tension. When they are slack, their skins or strings can never produce a useful sound. Both need some way to tighten them and moreover to keep them at a steady and unvarying tension, because if the tension changes, so does the pitch, and they go out of tune.

Three things control their tuning: their size (diameter for drums, length for strings), their mass (the thickness, weight, and density of the skin or strings, all of which are components of mass), and the tension of skin or string (their flexibility is a major factor for tone quality but not for pitch).

Size is mainly controlled by the construction of the instrument. Only with those string instruments where one can shorten the sounding length of a string to raise its pitch, as one does on a guitar or violin, is it practicable to change the effective size in performance.[1]

The mass is controlled in production; it cannot be varied in performance.

Fortunately, there are many ways to control the tension, for all strings and drums do need to be tuned. Even the drums without a nominal fixed pitch need to be "tuned" to the optimum playing tension, and the only way left to do this is by altering the tension.

The first problem is how to do this, and the second—and more serious—is how to *keep* it done. Tuning devices that slip mean constant troubles with keeping in tune. For string instruments, the invention of the tuning peg, fitting tightly into a hole and held by friction, is comparatively recent, probably somewhere in the early years AD. The machine tuning head, a worm and cog such as we use now on guitars, is even more recent and was first devised for the double bass in the early eighteenth century; it was applied to late citterns such as English guittars in the second half of that century and to Spanish and Portuguese guitars even later. The fine-tuner, used now on the metal strings of the violin family, was probably an early-twentieth-century invention, or perhaps late nineteenth.

Until plastic drumheads were invented in the mid-twentieth century, nobody had ever found a way to keep drum-skins taut in damp weather, although the use of rope-tensioning on our military drums was a brave attempt. The theory was that as the drum-skin stretched with the increase in humidity, the rope would shrink, the one balancing the other, but it never worked really well. Rope or thong tensioning is one of the easiest ways to tension a drum-skin, but we shall meet many others, and today in our culture, and spreading elsewhere, it has mainly been replaced by rods screwing into brackets.

The next problem is how to support the tension needed for any pitch. Few materials are really rigid—almost anything will bend in time, given enough tension or weight on it. When it bends, it changes its length, becoming shorter as the two ends move nearer together. Once the length or shape changes, so does the pitch, and the instrument is out of tune. If the instrument was not straight to start with, but curved, it is all the more likely to bend further under tension. If the instrument is made of more than one piece, the area of the joint between those pieces is a natural point of weakness where tension will break the instrument apart. In later chapters, we shall see how troubles with tension have been dealt with on string instruments. Here our concern is with the drums.

Drums

With drums, the problem is mainly that skin stretches more in one direction than the other, and thus that its tension is uneven and can, over time, force a drumshell that was circular in section to become oval. This upsets the tuning and the tone, for unless the diameter is the same all the way around the shell, the pitch will be uneven and there will be a wobble or vibration in the sound.

Drums come in many shapes, types, and sizes, but in the sense that we use the word in this chapter, all are struck (the tambourine is also rubbed) and all have either one or two diaphragms, most commonly a skin, stretched over the open mouth of a vessel, across a frame, or over one or both ends of a tube.[2] We have already dealt with the friction drums and the singing membranes or kazoos in chapter 1 among the Voices; slit drums were mentioned among the Bells in chapter 1 and will be discussed further in interlude F, while the steel drums are discussed in interlude H with other newly created instruments.

The drums with a vessel as a body are called *kettledrums*, for the kettle or cauldron in which dinner was cooked—its opening covered with the skin in which dinner had lived—may well have been one of the earliest of all drums. Another possible origin for drums is the frame on which a skin was dried to cure, before it could be used as the first form of clothing. As it dries in the air, a skin tightens and, if it is securely laced to its frame, is able to sound.

Lacing a skin or drumhead to a frame, a kettle, or a drumshell, with cords or thongs passing through holes in the skin, is one way of providing that tension. Another is stitching, tucking, or lapping it onto a hoop and then lacing or otherwise attaching that hoop to the shell. Lacing the skin, with or without a hoop, using a series of thongs or cords attached to points on the shell or to another head is the method most widely seen around the world. We used rope-tensioning on our tabors from the thirteenth century to the present day. We used it on our military side drums from their first introduction in the fifteenth century until the nineteenth century or even later. We used it on our kettledrums when the nakers first appeared in the thirteenth century, and on our timpani in the fifteenth century, passing the ropes on tabors and

side drums from one head to the other, and on the kettledrums to a ring at the base of the shell. The tension of the cords or thongs can be adjusted by braces or buffs, each embracing two cords or thongs, and drawing the pairs of cords together and so tightening them, or, as elsewhere in the world, it can be done by manipulating a network of interlocking cords.

Another technique is pinning or pegging the head to the shell, but this means tightening the skin to playing tension first, often with ropes through the fringe of the skin, pinning it once it is tight enough, and then cutting away the fringe to leave a neat edge. The same applies to gluing the head. This is how the Chinese drums with nailed heads are made, as are our tambourines. The problem with pinning and gluing is that one cannot manually adjust the tension of the skin, once fixed, so the only method for control is by heat or dampness. If the skin is too tight, a little water rubbed into it will slacken it; if it is too slack, holding it to a fire, or rubbing it briskly with the hand, will tighten it—though neither method lasts for long and the process may have to be repeated often.

Combinations of pegs and thongs are widely used. Thongs pass through the head and then around pegs driven through the shell further down the body. Because the pegs stand at an acute angle to the wall of the shell, driving them further into the shell pulls the thongs a little lower, so increasing the tension of the head.

What were the earliest drums and when were they devised? We can never know. Two suggestions have been made above. Ceramic cooking pots go back only to Neolithic times, metal ones to the later Bronze and Iron ages, but hollowed wooden vessels could be far older, and nobody knows when skins were first dried by lacing them to a frame. Aborigines in Australia made a drum by beating on a rolled-up tube of bark, and a roll of dried skin could be used in the same way. One suspects that a drum in our sense, made by fitting a skin over a tube or vessel, is fairly late in human development, simply because of the technology required to make it and tension it. It may be only a few thousands of years old, ten or perhaps even less—more recent than wind instruments, even more recent than strings, and far more recent than the idiophones that, as we suggested earlier in this book, date from the dawn of humankind. If this is correct, the drums are the most recent of all the families of instruments save for the electrophones.

Today drums are found almost everywhere, although in some places only one form may be known. Among the Greenland Inuit, for example, the frame drum was the only type of instrument known.[3] In most areas, however, once any form of drum had become established, other shapes and patterns followed. Worldwide, the tubular drum is the most common.

Tubular Drums

Tubular drums vary widely in size. The shallowest, where the radius of the head is greater than the depth of the tube, are known as *frame drums* (see figure 2.1). Our example is the tambourine, but many others, such as those of the Inuit, have much shallower frames, sometimes just a twist of withies or a thin strip of wood or whalebone bent into a circle, or in Nigeria with the *sákárà*, a shallow pottery frame. Commonest, though, is the shape similar to our tambourine, a frame a few inches deep. Many frame drums have a rattling element added, for this not only enhances the sound but also tends to suppress any element of definite pitch. Sometimes the rattles are pairs of small cymbals or similar objects set into slots cut in the frame, the type most familiar to us. Alternatively, metal rings may be suspended all around the inner surface of the frame, as with the Caucasian *daira*.

Very common is the use of a snare, a strand usually of gut, running across the surface of the skin. On the *timbre* or medieval European tambourine, this ran across the outer surface, but in North Africa it is more often across the undersurface, and there it is usually a pair of snares, a single strand running to and fro and knotted through the frame at each end. The Siberian shaman's frame drum, like several others used for similar magical purposes, has cross-bars inside the frame with numerous rattles of pieces of iron and other material hanging from them to jingle and jangle.

A few frame drums have a skin on each side of the frame. The best known of these are probably the Moroccan and Portuguese *adufe*, which are often square in shape and have one or more snares, sometimes with other rattles hanging from them, running across the interior between the heads.

In a number of cultures, the frame drum is a woman's instrument. While it may also be used by men, it is often the only drum that women are permitted to use. There are many such gender restrictions in music; it is only very recently that women have been seen in our symphony orchestras (although there have long been some that were exclusively female).

I said above that the snare or other rattle may suppress, or disguise, the pitch of the drum. It is commonly stated that it is only our timpani, and a few other kettle-drums such as the Indian *tablā*, that produce notes of definite pitch, but every drum has a detectable pitch, even if in our culture we conspire to ignore it. Every orchestral drummer has at one time or another had to adjust the tension of a drum when its pitch has clashed unpleasantly with the prevailing tonality, just as every drummer carries more than one triangle for the same reason. The fact that all drums are pitched is easily proven by listening carefully to the sound of any drum and is made all the more obvious by the use of *rototoms*. These are very shallow frame drums whose tension and thus pitch are quickly changed by rotating them clockwise or counterclockwise; they are included in many drum sets. Recently Marcus de Mowbray has devised in London what he calls Tour Timps, timpani-size frame drums tuned with a pedal, and he was anticipated by Adolphe Sax in mid-nineteenth-century Paris, although his shell-less timpani were hand-tuned.[4] (The same is true of idiophones. The pitch may not always be detected as easily as with xylophones or bells, but even knocking with a knuckle on a tabletop may produce a pitch that the attentive ear can detect.)

Figure 2.1. Frame Drums

Above, L–R: rectangular, by Maruyama Sanzaemon, Japan, eighteenth century (IV 74); *adufe*, Monsanto, Portugal (VIII 148); tribal India (II 40); Morocco (VIII 74); *bendir*, Libya (VII 236); *terbang*, Java (X 206).

Below, L–R: two *sákárà*, one inverted, Nigeria (IV 190 and VI 156); *adufe*, Morocco (VIII 58); *chung*, Lucknow, India (VIII 98); *riqq*, probably Egypt (XI 226); *bendir*, Morocco (VIII 62); *mazhar*, Egypt (XI 246).

But to return to our tubular drums, most are deeper than the frame drums. Shapes vary, and we distinguish cylindrical ones (the same diameter all the way down)[5] from barrel (narrower at the ends than elsewhere), conical (narrower at one end than the other), biconical or hourglass (wider at the ends than elsewhere),[6] waisted (with less difference between the diameters of the ends and the center than true hourglass drums), and goblet (resembling a stemmed wine glass) drums. This last type (see figure 2.2) verges toward the kettledrum, for the air mass contained in the cup-shaped upper part, with a fairly narrow aperture to the stem, does strengthen the perceived pitch. This is true also with some types of hourglass drum, especially the so-called talking drums of West Africa that we shall leave until interlude F, "Messengers."

Other forms of hourglass drum are used in India and Tibet. The small wooden *damaru* is sometimes called a "monkey-drum," for it is often used by animal trainers to accompany the antics of their creatures. It is held in the hand at its waist and is played by rapidly twisting the forearm to and fro through 180 degrees so that the two pellets or knots at the ends of the cords swing to strike the heads. The cords joining head to head are fre-

quently braced into the waist, so that the pitch remains the same. If the cords are unbraced, squeezing them in the hand while playing changes the pitch, and this technique is sometimes employed by bards to accompany their narrations and by priests, often mendicants, in their recitations.

A slightly larger form of the drum has a much more musical use, for it was played as an accompaniment by dancers, often in temples. The drum was suspended from the player's shoulder and the suspension strap or cord tied around the tension cords at the waist of the drum. With a hand on the drumshell, under the tension cords, the dancer could push the drum down against the suspension strap, so tightening the tension cords and raising and lowering the pitch. As Nazir Jairazbhoy pointed out, this can be seen in a number of antique statues; he also found it surviving among folk musicians in Uttar Pradesh.[7] This type of drum is played on one head only, with a wooden beater.

Along with wooden damaru of various sizes and shapes, a different form of hourglass drum is used in Tibetan Buddhism. This one is made from the crania of two human skulls, fixed crown to crown, with skin, traditionally that of a monkey, glued across the openings. Like

Figure 2.2. Goblet and Hourglass Drums
Above, L–R: goblet drum, Myanmar (III 110); *darabukke*, Tangier, Morocco (I 214b); hourglass drum, India (X 78); *derbacka*, Berber, Morocco (X 10); *darabukke*, Israel (VII 126).
Below, L–R: two *damaru,* India (I 44a and 44b); two *thod-dar,* of human skulls, Tibet (IX 30 and I 198).

the wooden damaru, two pellets are swung against the heads on the ends of cords. The *thod-dar* is normally played with a bell (*dril-bu*) or a trumpet of human thighbone (*rkan-gling*) in the other hand (see figure 5.6), and its form and function in ritual use have been fully described by Mireille Helffer.[8]

Goblet drums are used in North Africa and the Middle East as an instrument to accompany vocal and other music, in much the same way that the *tablā* is used in India. There is not as great a control over pitch as on the Indian drums—although skilled players can produce a small range of pitches—but considerable tonal variety and interest is available from striking different parts of the drumhead in different ways. Goblet drums are also used in Myanmar (formerly Burma), various sizes being played together with drum chimes and gong chimes.

Drum chimes exist in Myanmar, Ethiopia, and West Africa, while drum orchestras are common over much of Africa. The difference between the two is that a chime consists of a number of drums of the same type, usually played by one person, whereas an orchestra has many different instruments playing together. In Myanmar, a set of narrow kettledrums, each of a different pitch, is hung round the inside of a circular bamboo framework. The player sits in the center, with each drumhead within reach, and plays elaborate tonal and melodic patterns, using the fingers rather than beaters, as is normal with any drum where the use of different tone qualities is part

of the technique. The Ethiopian drums are usually portrayed in a row, with one drummer to each drum, using a hooked stick as a beater. They are part of a ritual ensemble used in church services. The *ese* drums of the Ibo of Nigeria are a set of three or four small kettledrums, looking like small versions of a mortar for grinding grain, with a skin over the opening, plus a slightly larger open-ended tubular drum with a single head (see figure 2.3). They are tuned, each to a different pitch, by driving wedges between the fiber retaining ring and the shell. The drums are set out in a straight line and played with a bamboo beater.[9]

Other chimes are also used in Africa, often a set of smaller drums arranged around or attached to a larger mother drum. Drum orchestras are a common African accompaniment to dancing and singing. Some of them, more organized than others, we shall meet among the messengers of interlude F, but many of them give the outsider the impression that each player is doing his own thing, although the players do normally know how each one's patterns interlock with the rest of the ensemble.

Nor is Africa alone in the use of multiple drums. In New Guinea, for example, waisted drums are carried by dancers, each playing his own drum (see figure 2.4). The lizard-skin heads are tuned with beads of wax placed to eliminate unwanted overtones, and it becomes apparent when they are heard that the air column is more important to the sound than the drumhead and that they are a

Figure 2.3. *Ese* Drums
Set of *ese* drums, Ibo people, Nigeria (VII 184).

Figure 2.4.　New Guinea Drums
L–R: (IV 24); (XII 260); probably Trobriand Islands (IV 246); head not original (III 108).

form of stamping tube, an instrument that we shall meet again in the next chapter.

The extent to which the contained air inside the body of an instrument is a dominant, even predominant, characteristic will crop up again and again in this book. New Guinea drums are clearly drums, but the pitches they produce are those of the contained air column, not those of the membrane. The same is true of stamping tubes, which are nominally idiophones, and of slit drums, which again are idiophones. It may also be true of tubular bells, a type of instrument that has not yet been adequately studied. For the sound of string instruments such as violins, the area of their soundholes is an important factor, and also for that of Renaissance and Baroque lutes and guitars that had a pierced rose in their soundboards rather than the open hole that we see in classical guitars today. With the trump or Jew's harp, there is a permanent dispute between those who consider the tongue of the instrument—an idiophone—to be the more important factor and those who believe that it is the volume and shape of the air body inside the player's mouth that is the dominant, for it is that that controls the pitches produced. There is a good deal of what one might term miscegenation between the normally recognized families of instruments in our classification systems, and there is still much study to be done in this area.

Sets of drums are important in our own music, too. The military bands have their fifes and drums, groups of side drums, tenor drums, and bass drums, all of which are different sizes of the same type of tubular drum. Our pop groups and jazz bands have their drum sets, snare drum, tomtoms, and bass drum, with the addition of other drums such as the rototoms mentioned above. As in Africa and elsewhere, they have both accompanying and soloistic roles in our music. But the prime example of these functions is found in the Indian subcontinent with the tablā.

The tablā is a pair of dissimilar kettledrums: the left-hand drum, the *bāyā*, today a metal bowl, although in earlier times it was often made of pottery, and the right-hand drum, the *tablā*, a closed wooden cylindrical drum (see figure 2.5). The tablā is tuned, by hammering the wooden blocks up or down under the leather thongs, to the keynote of whatever *rāg* or melodic mode is being played. Most of the area of its head is covered by a large tuning patch of wax and other materials so that only a small ring of skin is actually played on. Nevertheless the player produces considerable tonal variety by the way in which and the exact spot on which it is played. The *bāyā*, which has only a small tuning patch, is left untuned but its pitch is continually varied in performance by pressure of the heel of the hand while it is played by the fingers. A really skilled player can adhere to the pitches of the *rāg* being accompanied, while executing complex rhythmic variants of the *tāl* or rhythmic mode.[10] When accompanying a singer or an instrument such as a *sitar*, the tablā player is the exact equivalent of the pianist accompanying a singer or an instrumentalist in our music.

The tablā is the most important and most characteristic accompanying instrument of North Indian classical music. According to legend, it derived from the barrel drum, *mrdanga*, which is held horizontally by a seated player across the knees or, when standing, from a strap over the shoulders or around the waist. The right-hand head is played similarly to the tablā and the left-hand to the bāyā. It was the deity Krishna who was said in legend to have split it in half to create the tablā. The mrdanga appears in early paintings and carvings, whereas tablā and bāyā seem to be from later times. It survives today in various versions in southern India, especially in Kerala and Sri Lanka; in northern India, it is seen more often perhaps in folk music than in classical music. The mrdanga should not be confused with the very common smaller barrel drum used in folk and casual music of all sorts, the *dholak*, a much simpler instrument that is used all over the subcontinent, without the tuning blocks and complex tuning patches of mrdanga and tablā.

Many other drums are used in India and Pakistan, among them the kettledrums *naggāra* (see figure 2.6). These were made in many sizes, the largest three feet (almost a meter) across, the smallest four to six inches (10–15 cm). The large ones were used for "gate music," bands of shawms, trumpets, and kettledrums playing atop the gateways of palaces and towns exactly as our trumpets and timpani played for royalty and nobility from Renaissance times onward. They were introduced from Persia after the Moghul conquest of India and appear in many paintings of both Persian and Indian origin.

Our kettledrums were also introduced from Central Asia and the Near East, initially the *nakers* (from the Arabic *naqqara*) that were used by the Muslims encountered during the Crusades and by the Moors in Spain (see figure 2.7). They appear in medieval manuscripts and carvings all over Europe from the thirteenth century on, two small drums hanging from the waist in front of the player's body, played with a beater in each hand. From around the fourteenth century, they were often snared, usually with a single strand of gut but sometimes with two strands crossing at right angles. Very occasionally one sees slightly larger kettledrums, either placed on the ground in front of the player or carried on the back of a servant or apprentice walking in front of him.

Our timpani arrived rather later, in the fifteenth century, from Hungary after the Turkish invasions of the Balkans. They were carried on horseback, whereas in Turkey and the East they were, and still are, played on camels. They were certainly known in Europe earlier than that, for they appear in one of the manuscripts of the *Cántigas de Santa Maria* in the 1280s, illustrating the siege of Tortosa in Syria.[11] The drums seem not to have attracted any real attention at that date, and there is no sign that any were imported so early, but beginning in

Figure 2.5.   Pair of *Tablā* with Accessories
From the player's side, *bāyā* (left) and *tablā* (right), with tuning hammer in front, India (II 144).

Figure 2.6. *Naggāra*, **Paired Kettledrums**
Above, L–R: pottery, India (VII 136); riveted iron, Jaipur, India (VIII 100).
Below: *naqqara*, copper, Egypt, inverted to show the bases (II 218b).

the mid-fifteenth century, they spread across Europe, becoming one of the emblems of regal and noble panoply and state.[12] The timpani's use, like that of the trumpets, was initially restricted to such circles, and it was not until the seventeenth century that they appeared in normal musical contexts, and not until the mid-eighteenth century were they free from all such restraints. Haydn, in the late eighteenth century, was one of the first to use them orchestrally without trumpets, and thereafter composers treated them as instruments in their own right, instead of regarding them as the bass to the trumpets.

Initially the timpani were rope-tensioned, as in the East, but metal screws, fitting into lugs fixed to the shell, appear in *The Triumph of Maximilian I* around 1500 (see figure 3.12).[13] These square-topped screws were turned with a loose key (illustrated in figure 2.9 below, between the timpani and the side drums, by Michael Praetorius in 1619). The T-handles familiar on our own hand-tuned timpani did not appear until around 1790. Retuning the drums in the course of a movement was seldom required before that date, and the inevitable clank that was produced as a loose key was moved from block to block was not serious between movements—and even that change was seldom required, as most earlier composers simply omitted the drums when one movement of a work was in a different key from others.

Not until the nineteenth century did the demand for frequent changes of pitch arise, and the first instance of single-handle tuning dates from 1812. Unfortunately no

example of this system survives. Edmund Bowles chronicles the development of mechanization in documentation and illustration to such an extent that there is no need to go into great detail here.[14]

The first successful system was that of Johann Stumpff, rotating the drum so that it screwed up and down on a central pillar. Because the sound is always better at one point on the head than another, this had its disadvantages—players could not easily reach across the drum to keep playing on that point. More useful were the various single-handle systems, the best of which was Einbigler's, developed in 1836.[15] Just as with Stumpff's system, this acted on all the tuning points equally and simultaneously, but it had the great advantage that the drum remained static and the player could continue to beat at the preferred point. While other systems were devised in both England and France, these German systems were far more widely used.

Even Einbigler's system was restrictive, because it meant that one hand would be occupied turning the handle, rather than playing. Eventually Carl Pittrich in Dresden added a pedal to the mechanism that had undergone a number of changes, in particular a great increase in weight that much improved the reliability and the stability (see figure 2.8).

Pedal timpani of systems very close to Pittrich's are still widely in use. Modern orchestras normally have a setup of four timpani, rather than the pair of drums that had been the norm from the fifteenth century (sets of

Figure 2.7. Medieval Nakers, c. 1330
Front and side views, on the nave arcade, Beverley Minster, England.

three drums came into use in the early nineteenth century), and because the timpanist has only two feet, it is not unusual to see a pair of pedals in the center flanked on each side by a single-handle drum, although today four pedals are becoming more and more usual.

Pittrich-system drums were very heavy, needing several people to move them, and even though with modern materials they are now rather lighter, many drummers required something more portable in the early twentieth century. In America, both William F. Ludwig and Cecil Strupe, who worked for the Leedy Company, designed lightweight models in the 1920s that had the advantage that they could be taken apart, the pedal mechanism separate from the drum, rendering them much more portable and much more popular with both players and those whose responsibility it was to move drums from rehearsal room to concert hall or studio. Today it is very rare to see hand-tuned timpani in any contexts save for those of the "early music" movement, where players use either surviving original timpani or modern reproductions.

Timpani, as we have said, were initially used in pairs, and the use of pairs of drums is widespread, one smaller and thus higher in pitch than the other, but otherwise identical. The same is true of many idiophones: castanets, for example, as well as claves, maracas, and African iron double bells. Frequently there is a concept of male/female contrast, although by no means always is the female higher than the male, nor is the male necessarily thought of as the dominant member of the pair. Different cultures have different ideas in such matters. Among drums, the congas, timbales, and bongos will be familiar in our Latin American music, and we shall meet the Ghanaian *ntumpani* among the messengers in interlude F. In early jazz bands, a pair of Chinese tom-toms was often used; these were replaced by the pairs of locally made tom-toms in our drum kits of the 1930s and later, although today they have multiplied in number among our pop groups.

Turning again now to the tubular drums such as our military drums, the first to come into our music was the tabor (illustrated at the lower center of figure 3.8). This

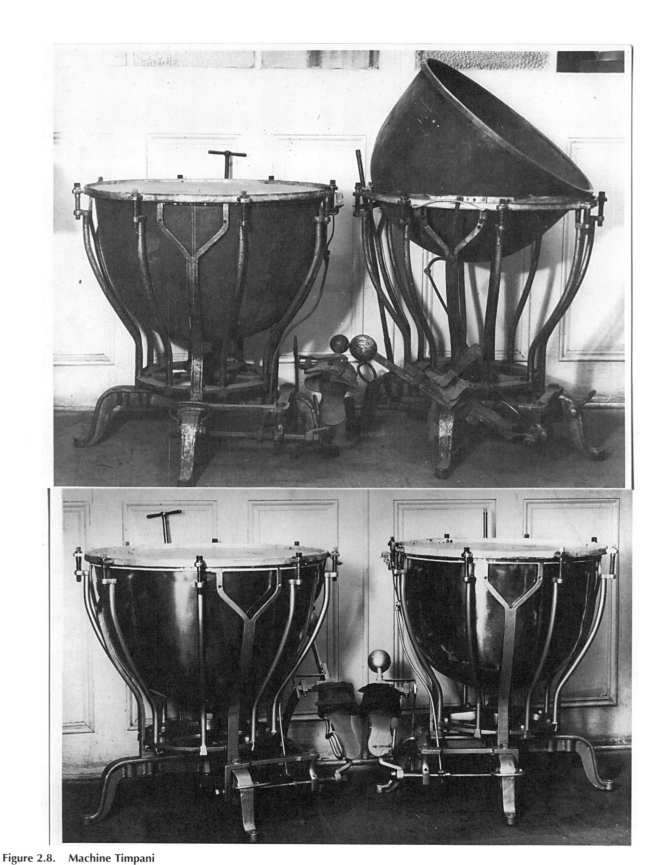

Figure 2.8. Machine Timpani

Pittrich-system, by E. Queisser, Dresden, *above,* awaiting repair; *below,* reconditioned by Len Hunt, *photos L. W. Hunt Drum Company, London, courtesy James Blades.*

was half of the original one-man band, the tabor strapped to the left shoulder and played with a beater in the right hand, the pipe played by the left hand. Pipe and tabor was the principal dance band of the Middle Ages, and it survives to this day in southern France, especially in Provence where its sound was imitated orchestrally by Bizet in his music for *L'Arlésienne*, and in much of Spain and parts of Portugal. It survives also in South America, whither it was carried by the Spanish and Portuguese, with the pipe sometimes replaced by a panpipe or some form of reed instrument.

The pipe had only three holes, one for the thumb and two for the fingers, but this sufficed for simple dance tunes because the instrument was played in the upper part of its compass, from the second to the sixth harmonic (see figure 0.1 in Explanations and Definitions for this), and three fingerholes are enough to sound the pitches of a diatonic scale between those harmonics. The range of a twelfth suffices for any normal dance tune.

The player was known as a *taborer* (a piper was a shawm or bagpipe player), for in dance music the rhythm is a more important element than the melody—so long as taborers kept the rhythm going on the drum when they stopped piping to catch their breath, or even to take a quick drink, the dance would continue. We have no evidence for what was played until the late sixteenth century, but our principal source at that date shows unequivocally that the rhythm was constant and unvarying with, always, a difference between the first beat of the bar and subsequent beats: in duple time, a quarter-note followed by two eighth-notes, and in triple time, a quarter followed by four eighths.[16] In this way, there was never any doubt about which was the first beat and therefore how the dancer should step. Very similarly, in the later Viennese waltz, the constant um-cha-cha accompaniment of bass drum and side drum provides the same rhythmic security, as does the drumming of our modern popular music of all sorts.

Pipe and tabor also sometimes provided the music for soldiers on the march, although generally then most soldiers seem to have walked at their own pace. With the rise of the mercenary companies in the last quarter of the fifteenth century, something louder and more organized was required. A larger drum, slung at the player's side (hence called the "side drum"), was introduced, and because there was now a separate piper playing the shrill transverse flute known as the fife, the drummer was able to use a beater in each hand. The earliest illustrations of this combination are both Swiss, dating from 1470 and before 1480, and the Swiss were the first mercenary soldiers, serving any power willing to pay them, as they still

do for the pope. The oldest known surviving side drum is also Swiss, dated 1575.[17] With two beaters, it becomes possible to produce the ornamental rapid and bouncing drum strokes we use today, and it is arguable that the word *drum*, and its equivalents in other languages such as the German *Trommel*, derives from these techniques, a rolled *r* following the initial consonant, as in *drrrum*, reproducing the sound of these techniques—all earlier names, such as *tabor*, have a single initial consonant, representing a plain stroke.

Because there were now two beaters, whose use requires more space on the drumhead, the snare, always present on the upper head of the tabor, dropped out of the way to the lower head, where it remains to this day and gives the side drum its alternative name of "snare drum."

The side drum was initially often very large indeed. Thoinot Arbeau describes it in 1588 as being two and a half feet in diameter and the same in depth, and there are contemporary illustrations that confirm this. By the early seventeenth century, Praetorius's illustration in figure 2.9 shows a drum just under two feet each way (his "foot"

Figure 2.9. Renaissance Timpani and Side Drums
Including timpani tuning key *(center)*, military fifes, and anvil and hammers *(Michael Praetorius*, Syntagma Musicum—De Organographia, *1619).*

was smaller than our current measure, spanning 285.36 mm, or about 11¼ inches)—he shows also that the screw tension device for the snares was already in use in Germany, although in other countries it was simply knotted and caught between the rim and head.[18] By the eighteenth century, the drum had shrunk another couple of inches, and by the mid-nineteenth had reached the size of our modern parade drums, sixteen inches each way. A smaller version, of about half the depth to make it more portable for infantry, was often then more common in Germany and France.

Up to this time, the side drum had remained rope-tensioned, just as in Praetorius's illustration, though more commonly with wide leather buffs or tug-ears to draw the tension ropes together instead of the rope ties that he shows. These ropes and buffs are still seen today, but they are often only for show, with metal screw lugs hidden underneath. Rod-tensioning, using rods with a hook at one end to go over the rim and a screw at the other end, was also a mid-nineteenth-century introduction. Double tensioning, with a screw at each end, appeared in the early twentieth century or perhaps a little before, and the modern system of lugs and screws had become universal for orchestral drums at least by the 1930s.

There have been many other sizes of drums. For orchestral use, the side drum shrank further, to fourteen inches in diameter, with the depth varying from ten to just three inches according to the sound required. These drums were also used in jazz and dance bands and became the center of the drum set, supported by a variety of other drums as can be seen in any drum set today.

For military use, in Europe the tenor drum (a term interchangeable with "field drum" in the United States) is larger than the side drum. In England, it is without a snare and is played with hard-headed felt beaters, although in Germany, where it is called *Ruhrtrommel*, it has a snare and is played with heavy side-drum sticks. Drum terminology is a minefield of imprecision and confusion, often leaving orchestral players with little option but to guess what was intended by composers from other countries. This leads to quite different sounds in performances of works such as Richard Strauss's *Till Eulenspiegel* and, even worse, Stravinsky's *L'Histoire du Soldat*.[19] It is at least commonly agreed that tenor drums are larger than normal side drums.

Larger still are bass drums. These came into Europe in the late eighteenth century from Turkey, where they are called *davul* and are played with a heavy wooden beater on one head and a light cane stick on the other, or sometimes on the shell. In the "Turkish music" that we hear in Haydn's "Military" Symphony, Mozart's *The Abduction from the Seraglio*, and Beethoven's Ninth Symphony, for example, the bass drum part is written with some note-stems upward and some downward, which indicates the survival of the Turkish technique—a beater on one head and a light switch on the other, producing an intended dum-chck alternation rather than the continual thud, thud, thud that we usually hear today.

The drums themselves were deeper from head to head than their diameter and were often known as the "long drum" for that reason. They were played, in the military bands, held by straps across the player's chest, as parade bass drums still are. Sizes more familiar to us, wider in diameter than the depth, came into use before the mid-nineteenth century, a fairly standard size being around 30 inches in diameter and 15 deep. Much larger instruments are used orchestrally today, whereas smaller sizes, initially 27 inches and later 22 inches or even smaller, were made for drum sets. The 27-inch drum was the ideal height to carry a trap-tray, on which the player could lay a selection of sticks and on which he could mount a selection of "traps," as the various wood blocks, cowbells, and other effects were called in the 1920s and '30s.[20] When it was preferred instead to mount a pair of tom-toms on the bass drum, the smaller 22-inch drum became the norm.

Drumheads for both timpani and military drums were always calfskin, or occasionally goatskin, until the 1960s when plastic heads began to appear. These new heads have a number of advantages, particularly cheapness and ease of fitting and, for the military drummer the supreme advantage, that they are not affected by humidity. Calfskin slackens as humidity rises, and it is impossible to produce a decent drum sound in the rain—but with plastic heads, the sound is the same, rain or shine. They were useful also for timpani in the earlier days of television, when the heat of the lamps was so intense that the pitch rose almost uncontrollably with skin heads, because heat tightens the skin. Because calfskin has to be prepared (a long and smelly business, albeit not as long and smelly as tanning for leather) and thinned very precisely, it has never been cheap, whereas mylar plastic is produced in sheets in a factory. And because calfskin has to be lapped or tucked onto a hoop to fit over the drumshell, this can only be done when the skin is wet, and it takes skill and practice to tuck it evenly all around so that the tension is equal in all directions. It then takes twenty-four hours to dry before it can be played. By contrast, a mylar head comes already fixed to a hoop and can be put on a drum in minutes, after which it is immediately ready to play.

The only problem with the plastic is that, for timpani, the tone quality is audibly inferior. There is a sharpness or thinness to the sound that is to some extent an advantage on the side drum and the rest of the drum set, but that many timpanists, and conductors, dislike. It seems, too, that the overtone spectrum of a plastic diaphragm is different from that of a natural material. Such a study is beyond the scope of this book, but any circular diaphragm has areas of maximal and minimal vibration, and the patterns that these areas adopt reveal the overtone spectra of any note produced.[21]

Our plastic-headed drums are not the only ones that function as diaphragms. In the Southeast Asian Bronze Age, the Dongson culture of Vietnam produced bronze facsimiles of drums. These were known in China as well, where they were awarded, much like our medals, to victorious generals. Such drums still exist among the Karen people of Myanmar and elsewhere (see figure 2.10).[22] They are cast by the lost-wax method, the skirt in several sections that are then curved to shape and soldered together, the head as a single disk. The Karen hang them from one of the pair of handles so that the head is almost vertical, and they are played much like the Turkish davul, one beater on the head and one on the shell or skirt. Other peoples hang them horizontally from all four handles. Both head and skirt are elaborately decorated with many patterns, usually with a star in the center, and many have figures standing on the head, most often a frog standing near the rim at each of the cardinal compass points, and sometimes a whole village scene, in which case they are more ornamental than musical. Similar, though more slender and sharply waisted, drums, today of brass rather than bronze, are used on the Indonesian island of Alor, and there their function has ceased to be musical but instead represents a large sum of money. In both cases, because the head functions as a diaphragm in exactly the same way as a drumhead, they should be regarded as drums and not, as they often have been, as gongs.

Skin drums are used in many more parts of the world than there is space to mention here and in individual forms, many of which will be found in the books describing the music and instruments of different parts of the world listed in the bibliography.

Notes

1. There have been attempts to alter the effective diameter of drums, with a pedal or other mechanism, but they have never worked successfully.

2. The term *membrane* is found more often in the literature than *diaphragm*, but strictly speaking "membrane" cannot be applied to the struck surface of the Burmese and Dongson bronze drums, nor to the plastic "skins" that we so often use on our drums today.

3. Personal communication in conversation with Poul Rovsing Olsen in Copenhagen. I found this hard to believe—no whistles of any sort, no melodic instruments at all—but he and other Danish ethnomusicologists had done much fieldwork in that area and he assured me that this was so.

4. A Tour Timp is illustrated in plate 38 of my *Timpani and Percussion* (2002), and one of Sax's drums in my *World of Romantic and Modern Musical Instruments* (1981), plate 94.

5. Or near enough—that a section of tree trunk will narrow slightly down its length is usually ignored.

6. "Elsewhere" because the widest or narrowest part may not be at or even near the center.

7. Personal conversation many years ago. He reported its survival in his *A Musical Journey through India* (1988); see the upper photograph on p. 48.

8. Mireille Helffer, *Mchod-rol* (1994), 232–50.

9. I owe the information on and the gift of a set of ese drums to Dr. Meki Nzewe.

10. For further information on rāg and tāl, see Nazir Jairazbhoy, *The Rāgs of North Indian Music* (1971).

11. This is the lesser known but much better illustrated version, Escorial ms. T I 1. All the miniatures were reproduced in black-and-white by José Guerrero Lovillo in *Las Cántigas* (1949), the drums appearing on his Lam. 181, illustrating cántiga 165.

12. See pp. 42–50 of my *Timpani and Percussion* for details of their introduction to Europe and for the failure of Henry VIII of England to obtain any (disproving earlier writers who misinterpreted documents to claim that he had succeeded in doing so). They seem not to have been used in England before the 1600s other than by the musicians of visiting dignitaries.

Figure 2.10. Bronze Drum
Karen people, Myanmar, *photo Tony Bingham, London.*

13. *The Triumph of Maximilian I* (1964), 115.

14. See Edmund A. Bowles, *The Timpani* (2002).

15. Both these are illustrated in my *Timpani and Percussion*, pl. 27 for Stumpff and 32 for Einbigler.

16. Thoinot Arbeau, *Orchesographie* (1588). Two dances are written out in full, with the tabor part, on pp. 30–32 and 33–37 of the 1972 facsimile version. There have been several translations of Arbeau, none of them wholly accurate, but all reproduce the same two dances. Arbeau gives the reasons for the need to distinguish the beats at great length in his discussion of the military drum beginning on p. 8.

17. In the Historisches Museum, Basel, and illustrated in James Blades, *Percussion Instruments and Their History* (2nd ed., 1975), plate 100, and in many other sources.

18. Rembrandt's famous painting *The Night Watch* shows an elaborate version of this knot very clearly, and simpler knots were still used in Britain into the eighteenth century instead of a tension screw.

19. In three recorded performances I have heard, each conducted by the composer, there are differences of sound both in drums and in specified beater types and materials.

20. For an illustration of a trap-tray setup with its traps, see plate 42 in my *Timpani and Percussion*.

21. These were first revealed by Ernst Chladni in *Entdeckungen über die Theorie des Klanges* (1787) and were applied to the timpani by Percival Kirby in *The Kettle-Drums* (1930).

22. A. J. Bernet Kempers, *The Kettledrums of Southeast Asia* (1988).

~

Musicians

Musicians have always been important to the societies in which they live, and we can tell this in our own culture from peoples' names. It is only quite recently that we have had the formality of surnames, and there is still a number of places where they do not exist in the way that they do in, say, America and Britain. In Iceland, for example, you are your father's son or daughter, Jonsson or Jonsdottir. Our society has been more male chauvinist, so we have lots of Johnsons but no Johndaughters (although we do have many people named Jones, a name that could cover either John's sons or his daughters—so many, in fact, that in Wales even today some Joneses are known also by their trade or occupation).

Because a few centuries ago there was only a fairly small number of common first names, many people were called by their trade to distinguish them from one another. So John Farmer grew the grain, John Reaper cut it, and John Carter carried it to John Miller, who ground it into flour between millstones shaped by John Stone in a frame made by John Carpenter, for John Baker to turn it into bread to be eaten on John Potter's plates in John Mason's house, with John Brewer's ale from John Cooper's barrels or the water from John Wells's wells.

We can even make some guesses at how important a trade was by how common any name was (and is). None of the people just mentioned could do their work without the tools made by John Smith, and this is why his is the most common name. (John Jones is the next most common because John was the most common first name, as mentioned above.) Musicians must have been fairly important, too, when one considers how many people one knows who have names such as Piper, Whistler, Harper, Fiddler, Horner, Drummer, and Singer today.

We have only to look back fifty years in our own society to reach the time when most people still made at least some music for themselves. Since then the transistor has reduced the radio, cassette, and CD players to pocket size and even smaller, and with the DJ replacing many musicians, many people have almost forgotten not only how to make their own music but even that they could. Our grandparents said this, too, and so did their grandparents, for with the move into the cities, there was less need for the local musician. In the city, one dance band may be enough for every thousand people, even for every ten thousand, while in the village, there was need of a band for every hundred, in the hamlet for every ten.

Musicians are and always were essential to society. They provided rhythms to help people work together in a team. Weddings and other celebrations were unthinkable without music. Legends and narratives were sung—Homer and all the bards chanted and sang, not spoke, their lays. We still sing in our bars over a beer when relaxing after a day's work, or in the barber's shop while waiting for a haircut, and it was not so long ago that muzak was played by live musicians.

In many societies, all this past history of ours is still the living present. People still haul together and dig together to the rhythms of work songs, and the sea shanty and capstan song are still alive as the sails are set and the anchor raised. The bride is brought to the groom with shawm and drum, grapes still trod to accordion or fiddle.

In the past, the court minstrel had an established place, as did the town and city waits and their equivalents such as the *Stadtpfeifer* in other languages. These organizations formed some of the earliest trade unions, or guilds as they were called in the Middle Ages. They had three main functions. One was to maintain standards among their members. Another was to protect their employment by keeping out the unqualified and the non-members, often by very strong measures that could include breaking players' arms, knocking out the teeth of brass players so that they could never play again, and similar actions. The third was looking after their members' widows and orphans, usually by apprenticing the children to other members so that they could follow their fathers' trade. As a result, the traveling player led a more precarious life, often hounded from place to place as a rogue and a vagabond, but the life was still attractive enough and the rewards sufficient that there was no lack of players. Some of these were Singers, but the majority were instrumentalists: Pipers on whistle and shawm; Harpers on harp and earlier on lyre; Fiddlers on rebec, fiddle, and violin; Drummers on pipe and tabor; even Burdens providing the drone; and many others.

The earliest methods of training had either been through the Church or by guild apprenticeship. Even in the Church, a form of apprenticeship was normal, although perhaps fairly open to entry by anybody with inclination and talent, unlike the normal apprenticeships where entry was often very strictly controlled by the guilds. There was almost a caste system. If your father was a cobbler, you probably would be, too—in some parts of Europe, not probably but certainly.

Restrictions on entry to a guild lasted longer in Germany than elsewhere, where organizations such as the trumpeters' guilds survived into the eighteenth century and others such as those for musical instrument making into modern times. Entry was often restricted to the children, and especially the orphans, of guild members, thus prohibiting the entry of others into the musical profession. Sometimes others might play as amateurs—though the trumpeters' guild, at least, was powerful enough to prevent this—but they could never play as professionals except as a Stadtpfeifer, a member of a guild of lower status. Even as amateurs, if they could not find a better amateur to teach them, they might never be able to progress beyond the stages attainable by the self-taught.

An effect of social changes in the eighteenth century that we shall discuss in interlude E on the Second Industrial Revolution was the freeing of social mobility within classes. This brought much of the guild and apprentice system to an end, even though over much of Europe the full effect of this perhaps did not take place until the latter part of that century with the French Revolution and the general upheaval all over Europe resulting from the Napoleonic Wars. With this class freedom, the cobbler's son could choose his own trade, and if he were musically inclined, he might become a musician—and not just as an amateur in the evenings when he was free from his cobbler's last, but as a professional. The result of this change was the establishment throughout Europe of many of the musical conservatories that survive to this day, where any musician of talent could be trained to professional standards. The advent of the Royal Academy of Music in London, a mid-eighteenth-century foundation, and then later the Conservatoires—Nationale in Paris and Royale in Brussels—and the similar organizations elsewhere, gave any boy or, less often, girl of musical talent a chance to embark on a musical career.

In the eighteenth century, even in England where things were much freer, the pool of available musicians was still apparently quite small, for the same names crop up again and again among the professionals in the lists of musicians appearing at the various mid- to late-century festivals throughout the country. In the nineteenth century, this changed, as it did in all other countries. Far more musicians became available, and as a result, the various concert-giving organizations did not have to pick a night when the opera was not performing to get an orchestra for their own concert.

Another change that occurred in the late eighteenth century that we shall examine in much more detail in interlude E was the demise of many princely establishments and their court orchestras. The change from private concerts to public ones had its effect on the musicians. Composers, for example, found their lives very different. Where a composer had been the *Kapelmeister* to a court—so long as he produced his weekly concert or whatever his contractual stint was, and as long as his own music, or the music that he borrowed from his friends among the other composers, was to the liking of his prince—his job and his meal ticket were secure. As the private bands began to vanish, however, he became dependent upon the whim of the public, and while it may not have been easy to satisfy one prince each week, it was very much harder to please every member of the concertgoing public. Just like today, empty seats in the hall meant lower returns at the box office. The composer could, of course, dedicate his new work to Prince this or Archduke that, and quite often such a dedication paid off in hard cash. Not always, though, and it was hardly practicable to hawk a dedication around the local aristocracy to see who would pay the most for it. Today, a composer can look to radio or the film companies for commissions or can even try Texaco to sponsor publication, and if they will not produce, try IBM or Microsoft. Beethoven could not do anything like that when he had written some string quartets.

Thus a musical career became much more precarious, even for the most eminent composers, as Mozart, for example, discovered. There was no copyright protection in those days; that meant that anyone could bring out his own arrangement of popular works. There was no performing-right system, either, so a composer would benefit from the public performance of his music only if he were putting on the concert himself, or more occasionally if someone arranged it as his benefit. The composer's only income came from commissions, for example, for a new opera; from his own performances; from grateful dedicatees; and from selling his work to a publisher. When he put on his own concerts, he took a chance on the number of tickets that would be sold on the night. If he got a good audience, fine; if not, he still had to pay for the hall, for the orchestra, and for all the printing and advertising. When he sold a work to a publisher, it was a cash sale, with no royalties on future sales. This is why we have so many stories of how fast some composers could write—they had to if they were going to eat that week.

Soloists were marginally better off. As well as playing for their faithful local public, they could tour the other cities of Europe, either hoping that their reputation had sufficiently preceded them that local impresarios would pay them to perform or putting on one concert themselves, just as young soloists put on their first public concert today, in the hope that they would make such a hit that they would then be taken up by the local concert organizers. They could also tour the courts, playing for Maria Theresa one month and for Marie Antoinette the next, and if they were lucky, this could pay off in hard cash—but more often it might be a ring or an enameled pocket watch or a jeweled snuffbox, and there were limits to the number of rings they could wear, watches they could pocket, or snuffboxes that they needed, and none of them was edible, and royal gifts are not safely salable.

Orchestral musicians were certainly better off. All these circumstances led to more concerts, and more concerts meant more work. If they could play for Beethoven one night, Schubert the next, and Haydn the night after, they had had three gigs. More concert halls set up in rivalry with each other, each with its resident orchestra. In Britain, geographically a small country, the provincial festivals proliferated, and however much the local concert would of course employ the local talent, there was always the need for stiffening from the main London bands. To this day, there are many British orchestras with proud local names that nevertheless need help from the central London pool of musicians for many of their concerts. In my career as a professional musician, there were few provincial orchestras, including those of the BBC, that I did not play in now and again. The same was true in the late eighteenth century and the nineteenth.

In the United States, the distances are so much greater that such mobility of musicians is less practicable, and thus individual cities had to form their own orchestras, depending on local sponsorship for funding that often derived from civic pride and rivalry to show that one city was better and more cultured than the next. Over much of continental Europe, the situation was different because the traditional establishments of the local opera houses demanded the existence of local orchestras.

Today things have changed somewhat. Training for professional musicians is available in almost every large city, and conservatories and schools of music are widespread. Opportunities for the amateur would-be professionals have never been wider, for if they catch the ear of a promoter, fame and fortune may be theirs almost instantly. However, it should be said that comparatively few do catch an ear in this way, and also that instant fame is seldom long-lasting. The Who may go on forever, and there must be few who have never heard of the Beatles, but for many others, it has been one hit, one almost said one strike, and out.

CHAPTER THREE

~

Flutes and Recorders

Monotone

There is a surprisingly large number of instruments that produce only one note. Few, other than signal instruments, are used alone—exceptions are the trump (see figures G.3 and G.4) and musical bow (figure G.1), whose single notes are tweaked into many pitches by human intervention. Most single-note instruments are used in groups.

One example well known to many of us is the handbell. A group of ringers each holds a bell (skilled ringers can control two in each hand) and they play tunes by each sounding their bell whenever that pitch is required in the melody.

The horn band peculiar to tsarist Russia was possible only in what was essentially a slave culture. It was cheaper and easier to provide each of a group of serfs with a horn that could produce a single note and to train them when to play it than it was to teach uneducated peasants to read music and play a proper instrument capable of a wide range of notes. The bands, when properly trained as in effect a giant human music box, had a quite wide repertoire, playing music in full harmony.[1]

A less organized ensemble occurs widely across the world with workers of various sorts. In areas where food grains, coffee beans, or other substances are ground with a mortar and pestle, for example, among the Bedouin, when one starts to pound, another will join in, producing a rhythmic antiphony, interlocking their strokes to produce patterns interesting or entertaining enough to alleviate the boredom of the tasks.

Smiths behave in similar ways, for example, among the gamelan gongsmiths of Indonesia, interlocking their strokes and producing polyphony not only rhyth-

mic but also melodic—it was not only the early acousticians of our culture, such as Pythagoras in late sixth-century BC Greece, who recognized that hammers of different weights would produce different pitches on the anvil (see figure 2.9).[2] Few smiths would produce patterns as uninteresting as those that Wagner allocated to the Nibelung.[3]

Less associated with work, more purely musical in intent, is the use of stamping tubes. These are common in those parts of the world where giant grasses such as the larger bamboos and other reeds grow to two or three inches in diameter with internodes two or three feet in length. Each tube is closed at or near the bottom by a node and open at the top, and its pitch is controlled by the length of the enclosed column of air. Groups of players, each holding one or two tubes, fit the pitches of their tubes into the melody like our handbell ringers.

Equally musical are the drum orchestras of Ethiopia and parts of West and Central Africa where each player has a single drum. Horn bands also exist in those areas, each player with an instrument of horn, ivory, gourd, or wood (see figure F.3). In West Africa a timekeeper is often used, as we have already seen and will see in more detail below, an iron bell that keeps up a constant pattern to which the other players relate their own rhythms (figure F.2).

A technique similar to that of the handbell ringers and the stamping tubes is used with end-blown flutes in several areas, for example, with the *skudučiai* in Lithuania (illustrated with the panpipes in the next section in figure 3.1) and the *mutavha* among the Venda in South Africa.[4] Each player holds a flute, sometimes two or more, and contributes their note or notes as and when required. Did this perhaps lead to the origin of the panpipe? This is a series of such tubes tied together in a raft or a bundle so that all the tubes can be played by a single player instead of requiring a group. If this hypothesis were correct, it would imply that the flute band was almost universal in the prehistory of mankind, for there are few areas that have not known the panpipe, an instrument that we shall describe in detail below.

Even in our own culture, monotonic instruments have a significant role, for who could doubt the importance of the cymbal, bass drum, and triangle in our own orchestras? All three, and similar instruments (many of them rattles), are widely used in other cultures, too.

Whistling in the Wind

That the original inspiration for the flute was the wind whistling across the end of a broken reed appears in the legends of more than one culture, including our own. It could well be true, although of course we shall never know. Without doubt the origins of the flute date back to high antiquity, and flutes of some sort were surely the earliest melodic instruments. They are likely to have been the oldest instruments of all, save for the idiophonic instruments such as the pairs of stones, bones, and sticks we discussed in the first chapter.

Bone whistles survive from Paleolithic sites dated to 40,000 BC or even earlier, and the earliest bone flutes are not so much later.[5] Because bone survives in the earth where wood, cane, and reed do not, flutes of those ephemeral materials must have been earlier still. We are frustrated by the geographical and cultural limitations of archaeology and casual discovery. We know much, and learn more all the time, of the European culture of early *Homo sapiens* simply because we have the painted caves of France and Spain and other European archaeological sites.[6] But what went on in Europe earlier than 45,000–35,000 years ago,[7] and more important, in other parts of the world, we simply do not know because either the evidence does not exist or more probably because, with archaeology a comparatively recent discipline outside Europe and America, nobody has yet found it.

If the legendary origin is correct, as it may well have been, and early people began to flute by emulating the breeze, then the earliest form was surely the same as that of the wind, the end-blown flute. This is still played today in many parts of the world as an instrument that one blows across and into the open upper end, much as we might do with a bottle, and it exists in several forms. Certainly it would seem probable that the end-blown flute with a plain cut-off end was the first and, if one could be permitted to postulate a developmental se-

quence, this might be improved by chamfering the top, shaping it to give a sharper edge, then further improved into the notch flute, then by the tongue-duct, and finally by the normal duct flute, which became our recorder. Only in very few areas do we have any evidence for the transverse or cross flute. All these instruments, and their variants, we shall meet in this chapter, a long one divided into several sections because the flute in one form or another is probably the most widespread and manifold of all the instruments there are.

The simplest end-blown flute is a tube, open at one end and closed at the other, for example, a segment of bamboo or reed closed at the bottom by the natural septum. This we have already met, used in groups, as among the Venda of South Africa and in Lithuania. We suggested above that this might have been the origin of the panpipe. It is undeniably more efficient ergonomically to tie such tubes together in a raft or bundle to form a panpipe or syrinx than it is to have a group of people, one to each tube. In the legends of our culture, the instrument was created by the Greek god Pan, who chased the beautiful river nymph Syrinx with obvious intent. The goddess Hera, taking pity on Syrinx's desire to preserve her chastity and to escape from Pan's indelicate attentions, turned her into a clump of reeds, whereupon Pan cut the reeds and made music instead of love. The instrument today is known by her name, as well as by his. The panpipe is much older than the legend, however, and is found over most of the world (see figure 3.1).

Each tube of the panpipe is usually closed at the lower end. This not only makes it easier to play but also allows the tube to be about half the length for any specific pitch than it would be if it were open ended (see "The Sounds of Science" in the afterword for the explanation of this). Some pipes have double ranks, one in front of the other, the rank nearer the player closed as usual, and that farther away almost the same length but open ended. The music then sounds in octaves, the upper octave quieter than the lower because its pipes are farther from the player's mouth. The same result can be achieved by having the farther rank stopped at the bottom and half the length of the nearer rank.

In our culture, panpipes are most commonly blown via a duct because this is easier, for children, for example, or for Papageno on stage in Mozart's *Magic Flute*. Elsewhere end-blown, blowing across the open end as one blows a bottle, is the norm. This has two advantages: one, that the pipe is much easier to make, simply cutting each pipe to the correct length; the other, that the player can introduce subtle variations of tuning by tipping the pipe so that the blowing end or embouchure is covered

Figure 3.1.   Panpipes

Above, L–R: single row, reed, Aymara people, Bolivia (V 130); double row, reed, Aymara (V 132a); double row, reed, Peru (VII 192); knife-grinder's call, bored in flat wood, Galicia, Spain (XI 94); professional musician's, metal, England (IX 114); child's toy, plastic, Germany (V 194); folk panpipe, cane, England (VII 134).

Middle, L–R: *wot*, bamboo bundle panpipe, Nathuland, Indonesia (IX 234); *rondador*, cane, zigzag arrangement, Quechua people, Ecuador (XII 138); duct-blown in wooden case, Taiwan (V 58).

Below, L–R: *nai*, bamboo on wooden frame, Romania (IV 194); flat wood, Portugal or Brazil (XII 90); *wode*, bamboo bundle panpipe, Thailand (XII 124); *skudučiai*, disjunct panpipe of wood, Lithuania (XII 278); *antara*, pottery, reproduction of pre-Columbian Peruvian by John Taylor, London (I 226).

by the lip to a greater or lesser extent, so altering the area of its aperture and lowering or raising the pitch, as we shall see in the next section. This becomes important in places such as Romania, where the panpipe *nai* is a virtuoso's instrument.

While panpipes with the pipes clumped together in a bundle are found in Oceania, especially in New Guinea (both Papua New Guinea and the Indonesian half, Irian Jaya), far more common is the raft, a row of pipes with the longest at one end and the shortest at the other. This is by no means always from left to right—while we always expect the bass to be at the left, many people are equally happy to have it on the right. Some peoples, for example, the Aymara in Bolivia, disguise this arrangement by cutting a series of reeds to the same physical length but with the natural node that closes the lower end at a different point down the tube on each pipe. An exception is the *rondador* of the Quechua in Ecuador, who prefer to arrange their pipes in a zigzag order.

With the panpipe, we have a series of tubes, each a different length and each shorter tube higher in pitch than its longer neighbor. The same effect can be achieved with a single tube by cutting off bits from the end of the tube, the pitch rising with each snip of the shears. This, of course, is not a practicable procedure if we ever want to play the lower notes again, but we can do much the same thing by boring holes along the tube and opening them in sequence from the bottom, and then covering them again with the fingers—sticking the tube back together again, as it were—when we want lower notes.

Who it was that first thought of piercing fingerholes in a single tube, instead of blowing on several tubes that each produce one note, we cannot know, but as we said above, bones with such holes survive from the Upper Paleolithic, the later periods of the Old Stone Age, and, as we also said above, flutes of cane or reed must surely be older, even though their material would not have survived as bone has done. End-blown flutes are still used in many areas (see figure 3.2), for example, in the Balkans and Turkey as the *kaval*, often a professional's and a virtuoso instrument, and in North Africa as the *nai* or *nay*. The upper end is often chamfered, shaved down by knife cuts or by rubbing on stone or materials like sandpaper to give a narrower and sharper edge that can improve the quality of the sound, imparting a brighter tone than the plain end. Reed and cane are still widely used, but so is copper or other water pipe. As we see so often here, the detritus of our modern age, waste bits of metal or plastic, are as useful as natural materials to make instruments. The only disadvantage with all end-flutes is that the player has to aim the breath accurately to impinge on the edge at the correct angle.

Some peoples have preferred to locate the sharpened edge at just one point on the circumference of the top, at the base of a notch that may be V- or U-shaped. The notch flute is somewhat easier to play than the end-blown version because it is easier to aim the air stream into the base of the notch at the correct angle to get a good sound than it is to aim it at the rim of the flute. End-blown flutes are sometimes called "rim flutes" because it is the rim that forms the sounding edge. Notch flutes, too, are widely used to this day, for example, in South America with the *qena* and in Japan with the *shakuhachi*, as well as elsewhere (see figure 3.2).

The fact that end-blown flutes are still widely used shows that ease of playing is not a prime consideration. However, it still seems possible to postulate a developmental sequence, just as those studying the earliest artifacts do with types of flint hand-axes: the flutes first with a plain edge, then with a chamfered edge, and then with a notch. One could then extend this postulated developmental sequence by moving the notch further down the tube, to become a mouth or window, and by setting a block into the head of the flute, leaving a passageway shaped to direct the air at the correct angle to the edge at the base of the mouth. The block may be the player's tongue, as it is in some areas,[8] or a piece of wood, as with our recorder (today often molded in plastic). Because there are then no problems with getting the air-stream-to-edge angle correct,

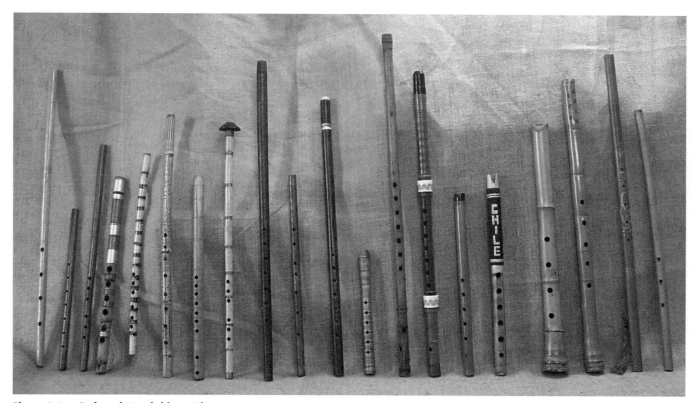

Figure 3.2.   End- and Notch-blown Flutes

L–R: End-blown flutes: *kurai*, Bashkirian Republic, Russia (XII 22); two of copper tube, Bedouin, Morocco (X 46 and XII 92); *nay*, northeastern Morocco (XII 194); with burned decoration, Morocco (VIII 46a); with incised red decoration, Tunisia (V 256); modern wooden, Turkey (XIII 26); *kaval*, cane with wooden top, Turkey (VIII 152); kaval, wood, Turkey (VI 120); kaval, brass tube, Turkey (XIII 36); kaval, plastic, as commonly used today, Turkey (XIII 28); *sopilka*, Macedonia (VII 256); kaval, Skopje, Macedonia (IV 164); and kaval, Bulgaria (VII 200). Notch-blown flutes: *qena*, Peru (IV 234); Chile (VIII 236); *shakuhachi*, Japan (I 258); *tang xiao*, Taiwan (IX 250); and *xiao*, with elaborate incised dedication to Dr. Alexandr Buchner, dated 1950 (IV 2). End-blown nose flute: Philippines (V 98).

as there are with end-blown flutes and to a lesser extent with notch flutes, the duct flute is the world's most widely distributed form of flute. If this sequence be accepted, it all happened in remote antiquity, for bone duct flutes have survived from the Neolithic period, and there is no way to tell whether such a hypothesis has any foundation in fact.

Duct flutes are almost universal around the world, and where they coexist with end flutes, they are often an amateur's instrument against the professional's end flute. For the amateur, this is partly because duct flutes are so much easier to play—to get a sound, one only has to put the end into the mouth and blow. For the professional, a more important difference is that playing accurately in tune is more practicable on the end flute than on the duct flute. As many recorder players will be aware, as one blows harder to play louder, the pitch rises. It is difficult, almost impossible, to counteract this without elaborate fingering patterns, whereas on the end and notch flutes, tipping the instrument slightly to cover or open the end compensates for this as we have already seen and as is explained in more detail in the next section. We shall return to duct flutes later.

One thing that we can say with certainty is that the transverse or cross flute—our orchestral instrument and the one we think of as *the* flute—is one of the rarest forms of all, for with a very few exceptions, to which we shall return, in earlier historical times it existed only in India and the Orient. The earliest surviving cross flutes so far known were found in the tomb of the Marquis Yi of Zeng, dating from around 400 BC.[9] These are very different from the later and the modern Chinese flutes; among other differences, their embouchure is 90 degrees around the circumference from the line of the fingerholes, and they are much shorter. While this type of flute might be indigenous to China, it seems likely, though this can only be speculation, that the transverse flute otherwise originated in India, for there it was associated with the god Krishna, and that it traveled thence to China and on to Japan. It had certainly arrived in Japan by the eighth century AD, because examples of that date are preserved in the Shôsôin at Nara.[10] In the opposite direction, the transverse flute traveled from India to Byzantium, where it arrived by the tenth or eleventh century and where we find it illustrated in church psalters of that date, and thence into Europe proper, where the earliest example so far known is a cast bronze aquamanile or water vessel of the eleventh or twelfth century now preserved in the National Museum in Budapest.[11]

It also appears sporadically in other parts of the world, with less evidence for any routes of transmission, al-though its occasional appearance in Central and South America may be linked to the voyages of the Chinese fleets.[12] One such sporadic appearance is in New Guinea, where the giant spirit flutes, up to ten feet in length, are played in pairs. They have no fingerholes (though shorter flutes three feet or so in length have a single fingerhole near the foot) and are played only in overblown harmonics, the two players alternating their notes as required. Further developments of the transverse flute will be found in a separate section.

Most of these types of flute are played by holding the *embouchure*—the playing point of the instrument—to the mouth, as that term would suggest (*bouche* is French for "mouth"). A number of peoples play instead with the nose, however. Various explanations for the choice of this technique have been given. One is that the mouth is used for mundane activities, eating, talking, and so forth, while the breath of the nose is purer, another that the breath of the nose is nearer to the soul than that of the mouth. Nose flutes are most commonly found on the islands of the Pacific. In Fiji and other parts of Oceania, they are usually quite short, with the blowing hole in the side, so close to one end that they are blown with the end of the flute held to the nose. They are made of bamboo, closed at each end and wide enough in bore to function more as vessel flutes than tubular (for which see below), so that it does not matter which fingerholes are opened or closed. In the Philippines, end-blown examples are known, closed at the top and blown through a small hole bored in the septum that closes the upper end of the tube; the other end is open, and there are fingerholes and a thumbhole. With many nose flutes, because the breath of the nose is weaker than that of the mouth, players close one nostril with a finger or thumb so as to get more force from the nostril that is open.

Can one distinguish between flutes and whistles? The answer is, not easily. One could define a whistle as a flute that produces only one note, but we have already encountered the Venda and Lithuanian flute bands in which each instrument only produces one note. Equally, we have many whistles, instruments used for signaling, that have more than one fingerhole, sometimes even two or three. So can we say that flutes are for playing music but whistles are for signaling? Again this is difficult—even though flute-type signal instruments are always called whistles—because, for example, in Africa, we have examples of instruments that one people may use for playing music but others use only for signaling. Perhaps the easiest answer is the wholly unscientific one, "I know a whistle when I see one," and to treat each instrument as we encounter it on its own merits.

Although end-blown whistles are found in many areas, the majority of whistles are duct blown, so much so that duct flutes are often called "whistle flutes." This is presumably because with a whistle one needs to be able to put it to the mouth and instantly produce a sound, without any worry about getting the angle right. What is required is a piercing sound that cuts through other noise, whether on a football field or a battlefield, and that will carry over a reasonable distance to reach the intended hearer. There are innumerable forms and shapes within the two basic categories: the vessel, where the duct leads to a hollow ball or chamber, and the tubular, where the duct leads into a tube (see figure 3.3).[13] These are also the two main categories of flutes and, as we shall

Figure 3.3. Whistles, Some with One or Two Fingerholes

Back row, L–R: coconut vessel whistle (I 206b); pottery man with horse, Ukraine (VIII 30); pitch pipe, by George Butler, London and Dublin, 1900 (III 14); Lotus Flute (swanee whistle), by S. B. Barnes, London, c. 1920 (III 16a); pottery bird whistle, Lithuania (XII 264); pottery bird whistle, by Nospelt, unlocated, 1989 (XIII 21).

Next row, L–R: horn side-by-side double whistle, England (III 28); two boatswain's calls, above British Royal Navy, below U.S. Navy with longer and straighter "gun," both by Acme, Birmingham, England (III 228a and XII 190); black pottery dog, Mexico (V 100g); metal nightingale whistle as used by drummers, England (III 114g); (in front of them): piston flute bird-warbler, Java (X 210); bone quail lure with wool-filled leather bag on which the hunter taps to drive short puffs of air into the whistle, Eivissa (XI 290).

Next row, L–R: referee's pea-whistle, "The Acme Thunderer," Birmingham (III 128b); horn hunting whistle, southern Africa (I 208); back-to-back double whistle, "The Metropolitan," Gendarmerie Nationale police whistle, by J. H. Hudson, Birmingham (III 126a); wooden samba whistle, Brazil (IX 184a); brass whistle, either Roman or Crusader period, Acre, Israel (IX 72).

Front row, L–R: folded iron skeleton pea-whistle, the sides formed by finger and thumb, England (VIII 136); pewter pea-whistle, probably by J. Dixon, England, nineteenth century (XII 128a); pottery bird, Toltec, Cuautitlan, Mexico, c. 1100–1300 (XII 286); silver whistle, by W. T., London, 1878 (XII 170); cuckoo whistle as used by drummers, by Acme, Birmingham (III 114e).

see in the next section, with flutes they must be kept separate because their acoustical behavior is very different.

Vessel whistles, and less often tubular whistles, frequently have an object within the vessel to perturb the air and produce a rolling sound. In our culture, it may originally have been a pea, for these are often called "pea-whistles." The pea was presumably squeezed through the mouth of the whistle while still soft and fresh and allowed to dry and harden so that it could not escape. Our common referee's whistle today usually has a pea of cork or plastic. The Brazilian samba whistle has a short length of wooden dowel, or even of drinking straw, to roll the sound (this is one of the many examples of a musical "whistle"—there are two fingerholes and simple melodies can be played).

A less usual way of modulating the sound is by manipulating the air outside the whistle. The boatswain's (bo's'n's) call has a long mouthpipe or duct (the "gun" in naval parlance), supported on a strip of metal (the "keel"), leading to the ball that the player holds within the hand. By moving the fingers over the mouth of the ball, the pitch can be changed quite radically and complex signals given and orders transmitted.[14] The bo's'n's call has a long history and has undergone little change in pattern or shape, certainly since the fourteenth century. We have surviving examples from the sixteenth century, the time of Henry VIII of England (several calls were found in the wreck of his warship the *Mary Rose*)[15] and of the Spanish Armada (several have been found in their wrecks, as well), and it is still used in British, American, Dutch, and other navies.[16]

Tubular whistles also use devices to render the sound more complex, the commonest of which is the use of two tubes, back-to-back within the one external tube, as with the well-known police and scout whistles.

Many whistles, especially dog and bird whistles, have a single fingerhole. Working dogs can be trained to respond to a code of two notes in different order and combination, and the cuckoo is often imitated with a two-note whistle. Another form of whistle is made of a hollow disk with a hole in the center of each face. Placing the disk between the teeth and the lips and breathing in and out with varying velocity of air-stream produces a wide range of pitches and allows one to imitate the calls of many different birds. Such whistles are also widely used by shepherds and others who have to signal instructions to working dogs. Commercial examples are made of metal; children in some places make them of fruit stones by rubbing each side on a rock until a hole is formed and then picking out the kernel.[17]

Whistles are also commonly made as toys and souvenirs, often in the form of animals, birds, or people, sometimes in grotesque combinations. These are often in pottery, and often quite roughly made, sometimes too roughly to work properly. Whistles of natural materials are also found frequently all over the world—seeds, for instance, sometimes quite large, with a hole cut in the side to form a vessel whistle. Snail shells may be used without any modification, just blowing across the opening.

While most are used for signaling, some as we suggested above are used for more than one purpose. A common one, also mentioned above, is bird imitation, and besides the cuckoo whistle, there are other more complex forms. A duct leading to a vessel containing water can imitate a nightingale with its bubbling sound, and this device, as well as being a child's toy, appears in more than one musical score. Another bird imitator is the piston whistle, a tube with a stopper that can slide up and down inside the tube. This, too, appears in our music as the "swanee whistle," but it also has a more serious use. If the stopper has graduation marks on its side so that it can be set at defined lengths, it can be used as a tuning standard, and the pitch pipe was used for many centuries before the tuning fork was invented. It continues in use with unaccompanied voices to give a starting pitch because it can provide any note, whereas the tuning fork can provide only one, and I have long suspected that the swanee whistle was invented one day by a mischievous choirboy playing around with a pitch pipe.

As well as being mouth-blown, whistles can be sounded mechanically—many will remember steam whistles on trains, for instance. A simple hunter's lure is the quail whistle, a duct whistle attached to a small bag filled with wool or such on which the hunter can tap to produce a shorter "cheep" than can easily be done by mouth. Laurence Picken found one in Afghanistan that had a small drum on which the hunter tapped to drive the air through the whistle.[18]

Almost any form of vessel or tube can be and has been used as a whistle somewhere in the world.

Vessel Flutes

Vessel flutes are often also called ocarinas, from the type most familiar to us, but they come in many other forms and shapes (see figure 3.4). The simplest, as noted in the previous section and illustrated in figure 3.3, are whistles made from large seeds or nutshells—coconuts, for example—and small gourds, with one hole for blowing across and another as a fingerhole. Vessel whistles and

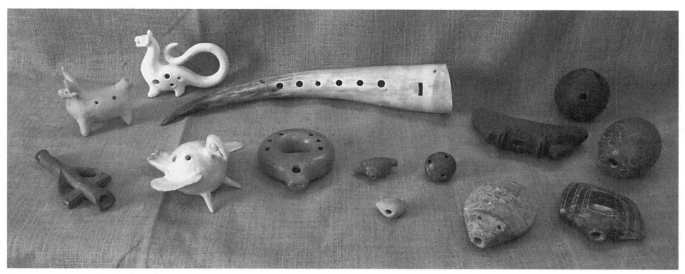

Figure 3.4. Vessel Flutes

Above, L–R: pottery cow, Russia (XII 8); pottery dragon, Israel (XIII 108); cow-horn reproduction of Renaissance tenor *gemshorn*, by Andrew Parkinson, England (VII 172, indefinite loan); coarse pottery demilune, Yaul people, East Sepik, Papua New Guinea (X 72); two incised coconuts, Kwoma and Abilam peoples, East Sepik, PNG (X 68 and X 70).

Below, L–R: anthropomorphic wood, Africa (XI 108a); reproduction pre-Columbian Mochica ceramic vulture, by John Taylor, London (I 220); reproduction pre-Columbian annular vessel flute, Ecuador (XI 212); pottery zoomorphic flute, pre-Columbian Mexico or Guatemala (VII 108a); pottery shepherd's whistle, Sarkh Kotal, Afghan Turkestan (VII 28); pottery sea urchin, pre-Columbian Guatemala (VII 108b); two vessel flutes, New Guinea, the first possibly Kuman (XII 262 and IX 198).

flutes are used in most parts of the world. All share the same characteristic that, unlike other flutes, instead of there being a tube with a column of air, there is a vessel, more or less globular, containing a body of air. As a result, they behave differently from other flutes in that the position of a fingerhole on the body makes little difference to the pitch produced when it is opened. A larger hole in one place will produce the same pitch as two or more smaller holes in other places, provided that their area is the same. What counts is the area of open hole, and in that respect the embouchure equates with fingerholes: It also is an open hole. Thus with simple edge-blown vessel flutes, the embouchure is often interchangeable with one or another fingerhole.

As soon as there is more than one hole, there are many musical possibilities. Two holes of differing diameter will produce four notes: both closed, one open, the other open, and both open. The small modern vessel flutes with four fingerholes, often seen hanging around the player's neck on a thong and first developed by John Taylor in London in the 1960s, will provide a complete scale.[19]

Two-hole vessel flutes of pottery are found in New Guinea, and wooden ones shaped rather like daggers with two side holes in bulbous or projecting wings, sometimes with a third hole at the bottom end, are common in Africa. Some peoples use these as hunting whistles, others for playing music, an example of the difficulty of separating whistles from flutes. Pre-Columbian examples from Central America, often in animal or bird shapes, are well known, and some can be seen in figure 3.4. While some have only one or two fingerholes, others have four or more.

The oldest-known vessel flutes date back to around 4000 BC in China. These were small egg- or ball-shaped vessels called *xun*, initially with one or two holes; by the third century BC, they had five holes, and by the eighteenth century AD six or more.[20] The later ones have a flattened bottom, though still more or less egg-shaped, and similar instruments with six holes, four for the fingers in front and two behind for the thumbs, are still made. It is possible that the egg shape arose as a fertility symbol, but more probably it derived from an earlier gourd or seed. Certainly it is unlikely that pottery was the first form of the instrument in China, and thus we can presume that the origin is even earlier.

Our own ocarinas (see figure 3.5) were invented in the mid-nineteenth century by Giuseppe Donati in Budrio, Italy. He devised the torpedo shape, with a wing containing the mouthpiece and duct, calling it "a little goose" (*ocarina* in Italian) from its resemblance to the

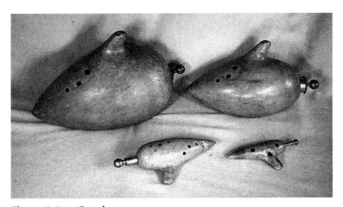

Figure 3.5. Ocarinas
The alto is missing from the set and the soprano is inverted to show the thumbholes, by Mezzetti, Budrio, Italy, *courtesy private collection.*

beak of that bird.[21] From Budrio, they spread across the world. They have been made in many materials, as well as the plain pottery that Donati employed. High-quality porcelain examples were made in Dresden by the successors to the Meissen factories; metal has often been used, as well, and today plastic. The Mezzetti brothers, who also came from Budrio, set up their workshop in Paris and they, like many others before and since, made their ocarinas in different sizes so that they could be played in ensembles. They invented the tuning plunger so that ocarinas could be tuned to play with other instruments.

The Donati system, and that developed by John Taylor, are now so common that their origins are all but forgotten, and their two fingering systems—the two rows of four fingerholes plus two thumbholes of the Italian style, and the four differently sized fingerholes of the English—are now found on serious instruments and on toys of all shapes and sizes worldwide. Both depend on the fact that it is the area of open hole that controls the pitch, and this is a factor that affects many other instruments, wind, string, and percussion (see the afterword for more detail on this).

For example, the area of their soundholes is important for the sound of violins, for it is this that tunes the resonance pitch of the body of air inside the box.[22] It is also an important factor for the sound of Renaissance and Baroque lutes and guitars that have a pierced rose in their soundboard rather than the open hole we see in classical and folk guitars today. Lynda Sayce established that this was a major factor in the switch from single to triple roses in some models of theorbo as body shapes changed in the early seventeenth century: The greater area of the pierced holes in the rose complemented the shallower bowl of the new type of body and, crucially, also the higher basic tuning in comparison with the similarly sized

bodies of the bass lutes.[23] With both bowed and plucked instruments, the pitch of the air volume contained in the body, tuned by the area of open hole as with a vessel flute, is vital to their response in performance.

For another example, it can be demonstrated easily that slit drums are affected in the same way. If one strikes the drum while progressively covering the slit with the hand, the pitch will drop as one reduces the area of open hole. This was first perceived by Raymond Clausen in his unpublished fieldwork on the island of Malekula in the New Hebrides.[24] The people he was studying and working with wanted to honor their chief with the biggest drum and the lowest note possible. They cut their tree, hauled it to the dancing ground, and hollowed it out with the biggest possible slit. To their horror, the pitch was higher than that of any of the other drums. Thus it became clear to him that the slit drum is a giant Helmholtz resonator.[25]

And as final examples, the area of open hole controls the success of cross-fingering on all woodwind instruments. It also controls the tuning of transverse and end-blown flutes (both rim-blown and notch-blown) when one covers more or less of the embouchure as one plays. Further, it applies to the hand in the bell on horns, where one is reducing the area of the open end with a hand. This is true not only for our orchestral horns, whose players in the eighteenth and early nineteenth centuries played Mozart's and others' concertos in this way, and whose modern successors habitually tune many of the notes they play with slight movements of the hand, but also for conch blowers in many parts of the world, and in Africa side-blown horns are also hand-stopped to obtain additional pitches.

So while vessel flutes are of minor importance among the musical instruments of the world, the way in which they work is of far-reaching effect on many of the other instruments described in this book.[26]

Penny Whistles and Recorders

It was Vincent Megaw who coined the term "penny whistle" for all the duct flutes of antiquity, irrespective of size or the number of fingerholes.[27] There have been attempts to make surmises about the pitches produced by and the music played on some prehistoric flutes, based on the sounds obtained by playing reconstructions of some instruments, but Dale Olsen's recent book on the flutes of South America delivers a salutary warning against such attempts.[28] He describes fingering techniques used by some players in his area that are very different from those to which we are accustomed and that, as a result, produce scales and tunings wholly unlike any that we would expect from the instruments. The lesson to learn from this is that nobody can have any idea of the musical capabilities of any instrument, especially one dependent on fingerings of any sort, be it wind or string, unless there is a player attached or available or unless one is within the culture concerned—both obviously impossible with antiquity.

An example of such an endeavor some years ago in China was reported prominently in the scientific journal *Nature*.[29] The six presumably end-blown flutes were dated to between 6300 and 5100 BC.[30] Intervals of between a wide whole tone and a minor third between some of the fingerholes of one of them are given in the article, but these intervals were produced by opening single holes in succession, and as Olsen showed, this is not necessarily a valid assumption. That is how we, and the Chinese, might play such an instrument today, but there is no way of knowing whether that technique was used in China eight thousand years ago.

Even within one's own culture and within historical times, time and changes of taste and practice can lead to misconceptions. We do not really know how our own medieval music sounded nor how any of the instruments played it, still less for any earlier periods.[31] Even the performance techniques and exact tunings used in our baroque and classical periods, little more than two hundred years ago, are debated and disputed today. Thus counting or measuring fingerholes will never tell us anything about the music, only that the culture concerned had an advanced musical system and the necessary skills to create and perform it. Beyond that, the ways that the instruments were made can tell us much about the skills involved and the quality of life in that time and place.

Instruments from antiquity are widely reported in the archaeological literature, with occasional collected summaries as in Megaw's article cited above and the special issue of *World Archaeology* that he edited.[32] Numerous instruments have been described in other journals also, especially that of the Galpin Society.

With duct flutes (see figure 3.6), as those that are often called "whistle flutes" today are properly termed,[33] the geometry of the head, the angle of the duct through the head, the width and length of the mouth, the angle of the ramp or bevel of the lip, and the shape of its sides or ears, all affect the tone quality.[34] There is no universal ideal, for each culture has its own preferences in this respect.

Most ducts are internal, but some, especially in East and Southeast Asia, are external. In Indonesia with the *suling*, the head of the instrument is closed, but one segment of the circumference is cut away for a short distance in a narrow geometric chord, and the mouth is cut in the side of the tube immediately below this. A leaf or strip of bamboo is tied around the head, fitting closely all the way around save at this cutaway point, where a narrow channel is left for the air to pass to the mouth. A similar effect is achieved in Myanmar with the *palwe* by tying a curved segment of bamboo against the head, which again forms a channel for the air.

A much more elaborate device is found in the Americas, among the Plains Indians of the north, where it is

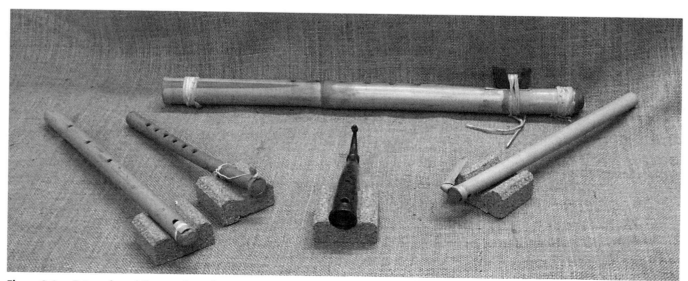

Figure 3.6. External- and Tongue-duct Flutes
Above: reproduction based on those of the Apache people, Southwest United States (V 186).
Below, L–R: *palwe*, Philippines (VII 162); *suling*, Bali (XII 52); tongue duct, India (XI 6); *suling* turned to show the mouth, Java (VI 32).

often called the Apache flute, and in earlier times in Mexico, where elaborate versions are clearly illustrated in pre-Columbian codices. Here the player blows into the end in the normal way, but a stoppage—a natural node in a cane flute, or wax or some such material in a wooden tube—directs the air out of a hole in the side of the tube. This hole is covered by a wooden block with a channel cut in its lower surface, between it and the wall of the flute, and this directs the air back into the flute through a mouth. Similar constructions are known to have existed in Asia and survive today in some of the islands of Southeast Asia.[35] This is one of the many pieces of musical evidence that lend credence to the discoveries of Gavin Menzies about circumnavigations of the world by great Chinese fleets in the 1420s.[36]

By the time we reach the European Middle Ages, the archaeological record is amplified by iconography. While it would be difficult to believe that duct flutes were not used in ancient Mesopotamia, Egypt, Greece, and Rome—cultures from which we have ample iconographical record—such instruments seem never to appear. A possible assumption is that they were regarded as instruments of the peasantry and of those people of insufficient status and importance to be figured in carvings and wall paintings. Even in the Middle Ages, it is often unclear whether an instrument is really a duct flute, for it can be difficult to determine whether a representation shows a mouth or not. Furthermore, in cases when a mouth can be distinguished, one cannot then be certain whether the instrument is a penny whistle—an instrument still commonly in use today under a wide variety of names, including those of *flageolet* and "tin whistle" (see figure 3.9)—or a recorder (see figures 3.7 and 3.8). The two differ in the number of their fingerholes.

The penny whistle (a name we will retain for the moment) usually has six fingerholes. This is by far the commonest number worldwide, although sometimes fewer and occasionally more are also seen, with or without a thumbhole that can both produce an extra pitch and also aid in the production of an upper register. The recorder, however, is distinct in always having a thumbhole plus, in its earlier form, eight fingerholes. As a result, its French name in the Renaissance and early Baroque periods was *fluste à neuf trous*, nine-hole flute. Our recorder today has only eight holes, but this is because in the high Baroque period and thereafter, the foot was made as a separate joint that could be turned so that the lowest hole could be moved to lie under either little finger, whichever hand was the lower. Until the clarinet established its two foot keys and the bassoon its A♭ key, players of all woodwinds were free to play with left hand above right, as is universal today, or with right above left.[37] So, on the early

recorder, the lowest fingerhole was duplicated and whichever was unwanted was stopped with wax, easily removed if another player wanted the reverse option.

The recorder first appears in the mid-fourteenth century. Examples have been found in Göttingen, Germany, and near Dordrecht in Holland, the former perhaps in the early 1300s and the latter certainly before 1421.[38] Brian Trowell noted the first English use of the name as 1388, and the earliest illustration I have yet found dates from 1367, also in England.[39] The bore of the Göttingen recorder was mainly cylindrical, with two localized constrictions and a considerable expansion in the foot, showing that the beneficial effects of variation in the bore were already recognized by makers. The Dordrecht recorder also has a cylindrical bore, around 0.43 inches (11 mm) in diameter and very similar to that of Göttingen (which measures about 0.46 inches/11.8 mm), but it is missing its foot. Rainer Weber suggested the possibility of a constricted foot, something we shall meet with Eastern European and other duct flutes below.[40]

Certainly by 1511, the recorder was being made in three sizes: a diskant in G, a tone higher than our alto or treble; a tenor in C; and a bass also in G. The tenor was duplicated to play both alto and tenor parts.[41] The use of a single size for both alto and tenor seems to have been common with other instruments also, for Martin Agricola, in his updated and expanded version of Sebastian Virdung's text a generation later, gives a common tuning for the middle sizes of transverse flute and fiddle as well as recorder (even though his illustrations show different sizes), calling the middle size "alto and tenor."[42] Virdung explicitly shows both ways of handing the instrument with two pictures, one with left hand above and the other with right above (see figure 3.7).

It would seem to be generally true, but not invariably so, that by the seventeenth century, the recorders that were illustrated by Michael Praetorius (see figure 3.8) and Marin Mersenne narrowed in bore from the head for some three-quarters of their length, thus improving the response and tuning of the upper octaves, and then expanded again toward the foot to around the original diameter.[43]

These instruments, like those of the previous century, were made from one piece of wood, and the tapers of their bore would have been reamed from each end. A major change came not long after 1650, beginning almost certainly in France where, at the court of Louis XIV, a group of makers radically redesigned all the woodwind instruments, probably beginning with the oboe for reasons that we shall discuss with that instrument in chapter 4. They then followed suit with the bassoon, recorder, and transverse flute, because all the instruments had to be able to work together. The principal concerns would seem to have

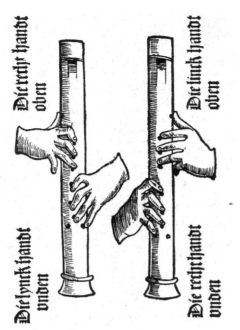

Figure 3.7. Early Renaissance Recorders
Showing the alternative fingerings of left or right hand above *(Sebastian Virdung,* Musica Getutscht, *1511).*

been those of tone quality and volume, of range or compass, and of tuning. These necessitated changes of bore design and therefore of construction, with the instruments being made in separate joints so that the bore could be worked more accurately. This meant that the body had to be thickened at strategic points, or supported with ferrules of ivory or other materials, to strengthen the sockets that received the tenons of each joint. At the same time, decorative turnings and rings were made in the wood in conformity with the aesthetic of the period, the plain undecorated shape of the earlier seventeenth century giving way to the elaborate turning of the baroque style.

The recorders were made in three separate sections: a head, a body carrying the thumbhole and all the fingerholes save for the lowest, and a foot that, because it could be turned to suit either hand, now had only a single hole for the little finger. Only on the largest sizes, where the length of the recorder demanded the use of a key to cover the lowest hole because it was beyond the reach of the unaided finger, did the earlier style survive of a key with a forked touch so that it could be reached by either hand. It seems likely that this was because its symmetrical pattern looked better, but within two generations its use was abandoned for a simpler key aimed at the right little finger. The head bore was cylindrical. The body narrowed in bore from top to bottom, and the foot continued the contracting taper of the body. This tapering of the bore had a beneficial effect both on the range and on the tun-

ing of the overblown part of the compass, bringing the upper notes much better into tune. This pattern of instrument needs little description, for it is familiar to us all today—the recorder that we still use follows the same pattern that was known to all the musicians of Europe in the late seventeenth and early eighteenth centuries.

The instrument retained its earlier name of "flute." It was still *the* flute, whereas the transverse instrument was always adjectivally qualified, in Germany usually using the Italian *flauto traverso*, whereas in France it was the *flûte d'allemagne* and in England, the equivalent, "German flute." Even as late as the early nineteenth century one still encounters "common flute" for the recorder and "German flute" for the transverse instrument.

The Renaissance recorders had been made in a wide range of sizes, from the tiny *gar klein* through the *sopranino*, which was about nine inches long (we retain here the older length measurements because we can take advantage of organ terminology where a two-foot pipe sounds middle C, a four-foot pipe the C below, and so

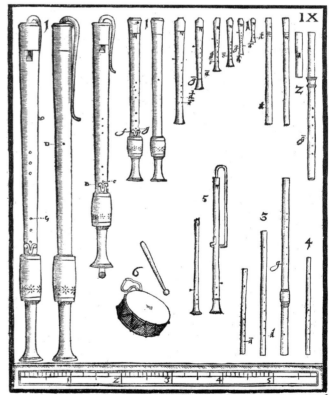

Figure 3.8. Later Renaissance Recorders
The whole set from great bass to *gar klein* (1), showing also duct flutes (2), transverse flutes (3), military fife (4), and pipes and tabor (5 and 6) *(Michael Praetorius,* Syntagma Musicum—De Organographia, *1619).*

on); the soprano or descant, with C as its lowest note at one foot; the treble or alto, around eighteen inches; and down to the great bass with a sounding length of more than six feet. With the baroque instruments, the extremes vanished (though one great bass more than eight feet long survives in Antwerp) and the range was from sopranino or piccolo, through soprano or descant, to bass. The treble or alto was now in F instead of G, as was the bass, and several intermediate sizes were introduced: the sixth flute in D, a tone above the soprano; the fourth flute, a B♭ soprano a fourth above the alto; less often a B♭ tenor fourth flute, a tone below the normal tenor in C; and much more popular, the tenor sixth flute, called in English the "voice flute," a small tenor in D.[44] It has been suggested that this last size was made so that amateurs could play music for transverse flute on the recorder, for the two instruments were at the same pitch, and the recorder was still the more popular, as well as easier to play. Equally, the small sixth flute was a potential substitute for the transverse piccolo, and there is still a good deal of controversy over whether some written piccolo parts were meant to be played on the recorder or the transverse instrument.

The one problem with the recorder, as with all duct flutes, was that it was difficult to play much louder or softer without going out of tune. As air pressure increases, the pitch rises, and whereas the transverse player could open or close the embouchure against the lip by rolling it slightly and so compensate (see the previous section and the afterword for more on this), the recorder player had no such option.

As the demand for musical expression increased in the Rococo and early Classical periods, so the use of the recorder gradually gave way to that of the transverse flute, and by the 1780s or so it had fallen out of use in professional hands. It remained an amateur's instrument for rather longer, and recorders were still being made in the early nineteenth century, although by then the flageolet was becoming far more fashionable. The recorder came back to life before the end of the nineteenth century, being revived to suit a growing interest in the sounds of early periods. The best-known protagonist of the revival was Arnold Dolmetsch in England, and he began to make reproductions of baroque instruments in 1919. His example was followed in many other countries, and the recorder, especially in the form of the plastic descant as a children's instrument, first developed by Edgar Hunt, is now ubiquitous over much of the world.[45]

While the recorder was accepted as the respectable instrument for serious music, the six-hole duct flute continued to flourish in all strata of society as a flute for all purposes—dance music, merrymaking, and whatever entertainment was desired. In the early seventeenth century, a new variety appeared, the flageolet, first recorded by Mersenne in 1636.[46] He called it one of the most pleasant and easiest to play of all the instruments then in use. It differed from other six-hole flutes in having four fingerholes in front and two holes for the thumbs at the back. It was popular in Britain also, for the diarist Samuel Pepys refers to it several times in 1667, ordering two instruments, one for himself and one for his wife from "the best maker in town," Samuel Drumbleby, and paying for lessons from Thomas Greeting, who published the first tutor for the flageolet.[47]

The flageolet came in various sizes (see figure 3.9), a particularly small instrument being designed to teach caged birds to sing the popular melodies of the day. To save the constant repetitions that were necessary for such an endeavor, makers also produced miniature barrel organs with a dozen or so small pipes and with the melodies pinned on a barrel, so allowing a machine to take over a rather boring task (a somewhat larger barrel organ is shown in figure 7.4).

The flageolet remained a popular instrument, and in the eighteenth century it is thought to have been used also instead of the piccolo. We know that when Rameau scored for piccolo in France, a transverse instrument was used, but it is thought that Mozart's piccolo parts, for example in *The Abduction from the Seraglio*, were intended for the flageolet. In the nineteenth century, it was often fitted with keywork, varying from a single key for the lowest semitone to the four keys necessary for the written F-natural, G-sharp, and B-flat, as well as the low D-sharp. Many instruments of this type were made with alternative heads, one for the transverse piccolo, the other for the flageolet, so that they could be played in either way. In the mid-century, the keywork culminated in an elaborate system based on that of the conical Boehm flute, and such instruments were often featured by soloists at promenade and similar concerts.

Pepys refers to a double flageolet, "two pipes of the same note fastened together, so that I can play on one and then echo it upon the other," and so presumably with one bore narrower than the other.[48] These are distinct from the *flûte d'accord*, which had one mouth lower than the other so that, when played with the fingers across the holes on both bores, it provided melodies in constant thirds or whatever interval was built in by the distance between the two mouths. In the late eighteenth century, the double flageolet reappeared, now for the wealthy patrons of music, the instruments elegantly made of boxwood with ivory

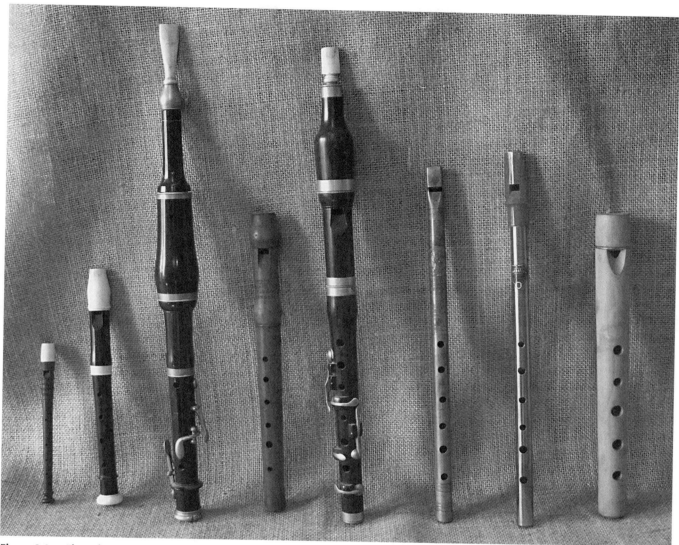

Figure 3.9. Flageolets

L–R: bird flageolet, four fingerholes and two thumbholes, reproduction of Renaissance type by Anthony Moonen, Maastricht (VIII 190); French flageolet, also with four fingerholes and two thumbholes, by F. Noblet, Paris (XIII 150); three-key French flageolet (turned to show thumbholes and key), same holes plus the keys, by J. Wallis, London (I 256); English flageolet, six fingerholes, by Improved London (IV 64); English flageolet, six fingerholes and six keys (VI 68); brass tin whistle, six fingerholes, by I&H or H&I, London (X 218a); modern tin whistle in D with plastic head, by Generation (IX 12); *flabiol*, five fingerholes, two thumbholes, and a hole for the back of the little finger, Catalunya (XI 92).

mouthpieces and silver keys, with little ivory spots set into the wood between each fingerhole to guide the correct placement of the fingers.

Single flageolets bored into the top of walking sticks were also popular with the elegant classes in the early nineteenth century. This was a period when Romanticism was all the rage, in literature and the arts in general, and an appreciation of the wonders and beauties of nature was expected of all the well educated. These were to be portrayed in watercolors, especially by genteel ladies (the use of oils was the preserve of the professional painter and watercolors were thought more suited to the amateur), or saluted by an appropriate flow of melody by the gentlemen. A cane was an accepted part of every gentleman's costume, and so a suitable instrument was built into it, ready to hand when required. Flutes and flageolets were the most common, being the easiest to play. Violins, clarinets, and occasionally oboes were also built into sticks, but more rarely because a violin must be tuned before it can be played, and both oboes and clarinets need reeds that require some preparation. Walking-stick trumpets are known as well, but their range was more limited and required more skill, so they are seldom seen.

Walking-stick flageolets seem to have been especially popular in Austria, where the flageolet was known as a *czakan*. Walking-stick flutes were known in other places also, for few musical ideas are reserved to one place or one culture. My own collection includes an English transverse piccolo, a Chinese notch flute, an East African two-hole end-blown flute, and a Slovakian *fuyara*, a short version of the six-foot-long shepherd's

flute with three fingerholes on which melodies are interspersed with cascades and flourishes of higher harmonics.

A number of eastern European duct flutes, especially those from the Slavic countries, share the characteristic of a constricted foot (see figure 3.10). The instrument is bored from the head until just before the distal end, which is then counter-bored with a narrower tool. It is possible that this idea originated with flutes of cane or

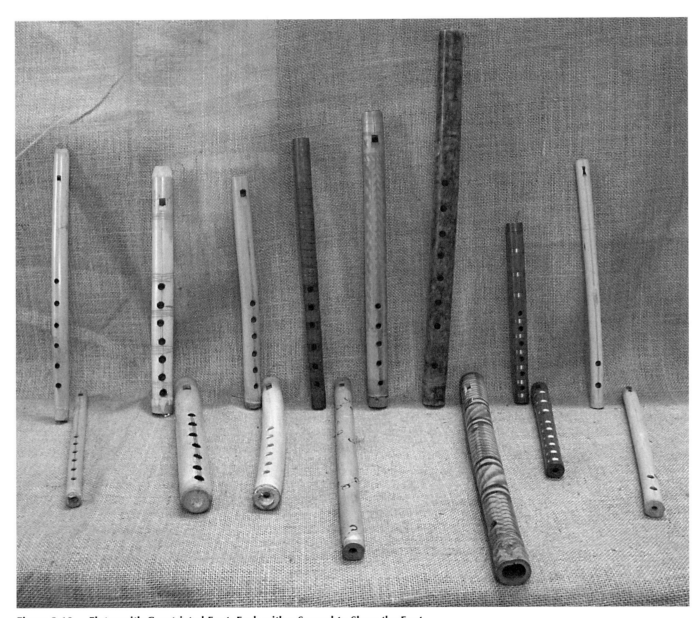

Figure 3.10.   Flutes with Constricted Foot, Each with a Second to Show the Foot

L–R: Cyprus (IV 114); Morocco, the foot closed and the lowest fingerhole acting as the constricted end (XII 204 and III 190a); Morocco, with a hole through the septum (IX 236); *fluier*, by Dimitru Tărtăreanu, Comune Vaideeni, Judeţul Vîlcea, Romania (V 152); the second anonymous (IV 192); unlocated South America (I 234a); Thailand (I 142 and V 44); pair of *čurlik-slavić*, professional quality, Bosnia or Croatia (IV 182); pair of tabor pipes, Ecuador (VI 30).

reed, with a natural bore and a smaller end-hole burned through the distal septum, examples of which are found in a number of places. The fact that some, especially in the area that was once Yugoslavia, are bound with wires, or in Romania with a spiral of brass strip, suggests that some may originally have been made in two halves, gouged out, and reunited. In Morocco, a unique form is found, apparently a seven-hole flute of reed with a stopped end, but the seventh hole is never closed in performance and functions as the constricted open end.

This constricted foot has an acoustical function, for as we saw with the recorder at the end of the seventeenth century, some narrowing of the bore extends the range and brings the upper overblown range into tune. The constricted foot achieves the same result, narrowing the bore at a strategic point.

To describe all the world's duct flutes in one chapter would be impossible, for they are one of the commonest of all instruments, certainly the commonest of all flutes. Many of us may have made them as children, tapping the bark loose from a piece of wood in the spring when the sap was rising—and most of us have bought them in plastic for our own children or grandchildren, for today we are more likely to buy the mass-produced than to make by hand. Each type differs in some respects from others, but all share in common the duct that leads (hence the name, from the Latin *ductus*, past participle of "to lead") the air through a narrow passage to the voicing edge at the base of the mouth. Usually the duct is at the front, although in Russia and some neighboring areas it is more often at the rear; this allows a more vertical position for the flute. The rear duct often goes with the constricted foot, though by no means invariably, and each also exists independently of the other.

One type that we have not mentioned so far is what might be called the "ductless duct flute." Here the head is open and empty, and it was only fairly recently that it was realized that this is an instrument in its own right and not a duct flute that had lost the block originally provided. It was Ernst Emsheimer who first published the existence of such instruments, crediting Hermann Moeck as the first who had observed them in an unpublished paper.[49] At the moment of performance, the player creates the duct with the tongue, protruding the tongue into the head of the flute and directing the jet of air to the voicing edge. The geographical range of this instrument is much wider than was at first thought (I have an example from India, shown in figure 3.6), and Cajsa Lund raises the possibility that it was widespread in antiquity.[50] We have many examples in collections of bone duct flutes from the Stone Age, and it has always been assumed that they have lost their blocks that were made from materials less durable in the earth than bone. May it not have been in many cases that there never was a block other than the player's tongue?

Transverse Flutes

We have suggested that the transverse flute may have originated in the Indian subcontinent. It would be a mistake to judge that suggestion by the small instruments of thin bamboo or other reed often seen in souvenir shops and "traditional craft" places. The serious instruments (see figure 3.11) are made of much heavier materials, usually bamboo or wood, and are often longer than our own concert flutes, much the length of our alto flute. They normally have six fingerholes, too widely spaced to be covered by the tips of the fingers—using the upper phalanges allows the hand a wider spread. These instruments can be heard today in performances of Indian classical music, and they are also used in folk music. They can be seen from earlier times in paintings and on statues, many times, as we said above, associated with the god Krishna or one of his avatars.

The early Chinese *chi* that may have derived from it was shorter, as we noted above with those from the tomb of the Marquis Yi, with the embouchure set 90 degrees away from the alignment of the fingerholes.[51] A later version, also introduced from the west through Central Asia around the second century BC or so during the Han dynasty, was similar in length but with embouchure and fingerholes aligned.[52]

Today, the Chinese flute is very different, narrower in bore than the Indian and with more holes—so many that descriptions have sometimes been badly confused. There are more holes than the player has fingers, and their positions make some of them impossible to reach. Nevertheless, one does quite often see mentions of eleven fingerholes! The true description, following down the tube from the embouchure, is first a single hole, some distance from the embouchure, that is covered with a thin membrane made from the inner skin of bamboo. This, because it is thin and delicate, is often missing from examples in museums.[53] In performance, the membrane adds a sweetening, buzzing quality to the sound, a refined version of the comb and paper of our childhood that we met in chapter 1. Then, at about the same distance from the membrane hole as that was from the embouchure, comes the first of the series of six fingerholes, followed, close to the foot of the flute, by two "vents," as holes are called that are not fingered but that control the pitch of the instrument. Close to these, but at the back of the body, are

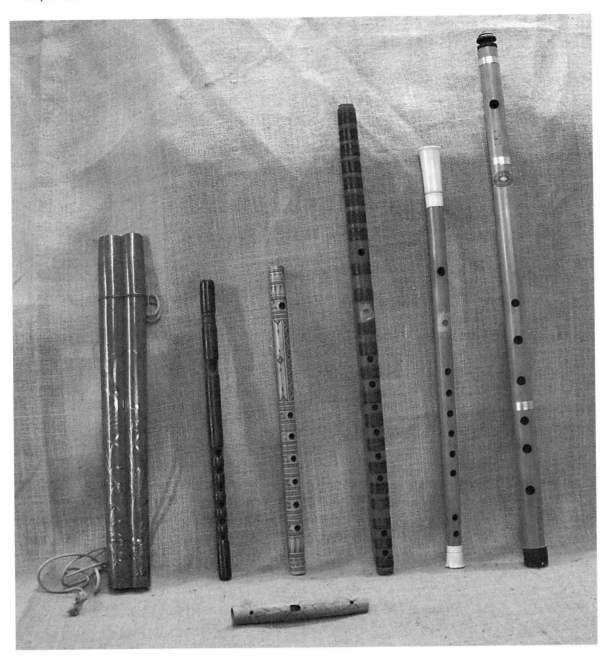

Figure 3.11. Asian Transverse Flutes

L–R: *koma-bue*, Japan, with its original lacquer case, by Jitokusai Gyokujan (the larger flute of the pair is missing) (I 236); Toradja people, Sulawesi (I 254); two *di*, China, the first missing the end ferrules of bone (I 248a), the second with ferrules of ivory (I 248a); *bansri*, India (X 228).

Foreground: off-center-embouchure flute, by F. Nopil, Samosir Island, Lake Toba, North Sumatra (XI 30).

two more holes through which should be tied a loop of silk cord that both is decorative and serves to hang the instrument when not in use. As with our own flutes, the embouchure is some distance from the top of the body, and again like ours, this is both for the sake of appearance and to help balance the instrument. The bore is closed just above the embouchure by a cork or other object. With many examples, the body is lashed with rings of waxed thread between each of the holes and at other points along its length. This version of the *dizi* is comparatively modern. Instruments of the length we know today date probably from the Song dynasty, around 1000 AD, much the same date as when the transverse flute appeared nearer Europe.

The Japanese flutes, ōteki, are similar to those earlier Chinese flutes of the Han period and are about the same length. This is as one might expect, since they seem first to have been imported between the sixth and eighth centuries AD.[54] Today their lashings of cherry bark between the holes are much thicker than those on the modern Chinese flute, and these help the player to lift the fingers from the narrowly oval fingerholes sufficiently gradually to produce an upward glissando before each note, a musical device that is often a feature of their use in the Noh theater and the ritual Gagaku court ensemble.

The Byzantine flutes of the eleventh century AD or so, when they first appeared within the borders of Europe, were much the length of the later Chinese flutes, fully that of our modern instruments.[55] The flute on the Budapest aquamanile referred to above is much shorter, but this is not surprising when one considers the difficulties of casting the flutist as a small bronze figure standing on the back of a centaur who is playing a drum. Other medieval portrayals, from those of the thirteenth-century *Cántigas de Santa Maria* onward, were presumably of wood, cylindrical externally and, we presume, also in bore.[56] Certainly this is true of the surviving Renaissance instruments, and it would be difficult to suggest that the medieval ones were different. Other than that, there is little that we can say about transverse flutes in Europe for the next couple of centuries, for their appearance is comparatively rare. They seem to have been used more in Germany than elsewhere.[57]

In the second half of the 1400s, transverse flutes appear much more widely with the rise of the Swiss and German mercenaries, who adopted them as marching instruments to such an extent that they became known as the "Swiss pipe" (*Schweizerpfeiff*, from which we get the English *fife*). These instruments were made in sets of different sizes, from diskant, the same size as our fife or B-flat or A-flat flute (terminology differs in different countries, so it is best to use both names),[58] through treble (F or E-flat flute) and tenor (which became our concert flute), to bass.[59] Flutes of these sizes are still used in our flute bands today. Few, if any, complete early sets survive, though we have a number of cases with compartments for flutes of various sizes, some of which include some of the flutes for which they were made.[60] There are many illustrations from around 1500 showing soldiers playing a flute, with similar multiple cases suspended at their side, the best known of which is probably the woodcut by Hans Burgkmair of the mounted flutists at the head of the procession in *The Triumph of Maximilian I* (see figure 3.12).[61] The use of such flutes became more common during the Renaissance, and the large number in Henry

Figure 3.12. Renaissance Transverse Flutes
The Triumph of Maximilian, c. 1520. Each player (and the standard-bearer) has a case for a set of flutes at his belt.

VIII's collection is well known.[62] There were important centers of manufacture in Italy, especially in Venice; in southern France; and in London.

There were differences in bore diameter between the flutes preserved in or associated with such cases and those flutes that we presume to have been used for "musical" rather than military purposes. We see the latter played by ladies in the well-known series of paintings, known as the *Ladies of the Half-Length*, from Antwerp around 1520, much the same date as *Maximilian's Triumph*.[63] The flute used by those ladies was a quiet domestic instrument, whereas the military flutes were necessarily shriller and louder.

The Renaissance flute was a cylindrical tube with six fingerholes, usually made from a single piece of wood, as we assume was true in the Middle Ages also. The bass flute was sometimes made in two unequal sections, the head with the embouchure separately from the body with the fingerholes.[64] It is one of the regrettable characteristics of nature that things are not always as we would wish them to be, and the overblown pitches of a cylindrically bored flute are not all well in tune. Some taper in the bore is essential for full exploitation of the potential range. This was realized in the late Renaissance and early Baroque, and flute bores were changed as a result. This is more easily recognized in the three-part flutes created, we think, first in France in the third quarter of the 1600s.

As we noted with the recorder, there was then a sudden and radical alteration of all the woodwind instruments at the court of Louis XIV of France, coming to its full fruition in 1664.[65] This revolution, for it was no less in its effects, was led by several makers and players of the Hotteterre family and their associates such as the Philidors (who were also called Danican). Their work on the oboe was taken up by contemporaries in the Netherlands such as Richard Haka and others and was gradually extended to bassoons and to flutes and recorders over the next two decades or so. Certainly by the early 1690s, perhaps a little before, the baroque flute was in use in more than one country.

How did it differ from the earlier one-piece cylindrical flute of the Renaissance? The most obvious difference is that it was made in separate joints, often with elaborately lathe-turned ferrules, and no longer the old straight cylinder of wood. There was usually a decorative head-cap, sometimes of ivory, with a link piece or decoratively turned ferrule to hold the head joint to the body, and a separate foot joint, also decoratively turned, carrying a single key, usually of silver, covering a seventh hole. The inside had also changed, for while the bore of the head joint remained cylindrical, the bore of the one-piece body joint, like that of the baroque recorder whose invention is thought to have preceded it, is inversely tapering, widest at the end nearest the head. The other major feature is the use of the key on the foot joint to produce D♯ or E♭.

The lowest note of the flute of the Baroque and early Classical periods is the d', a tone above middle C, the same as that of the old Renaissance tenor flute. Opening the holes in succession gives, approximately, a D major scale, though the F♯, always a problem note, often needs some sharpening. Chromatic notes, the sharps, naturals, and flats used in keys other than D major, were obtained by cross-fingering and half-holing, the former closing holes below the highest open hole and the latter, less satisfactorily, half-covering a hole. Closing and half-closing holes in this way alters the impedance or, in simpler terms, reduces the area of open hole and flattens the pitch (see the earlier discussion above on vessel flutes and the afterword for more detail on this).

The standard forked fingering (so called because the index and ring fingers resemble the tines of a fork) on the lower group of three holes, leaving just the middle hole open, lowers the F♯ produced by opening the two lowest holes almost to an F natural—a little extra help by rolling the embouchure toward the lip is also needed. A similar technique can lower most notes on the instrument by a semitone, except for the E produced by opening the lowest hole. The only way to play an E♭ on the six-hole flute was by half-covering the lowest hole, and it was difficult to make such a half-holed note speak clearly. An extra hole for that note at the foot, which could be opened by moving a key that otherwise held it closed, was the ideal solution. In addition, it was found that opening that key as a vent helped to bring many of the notes of the overblown range into tune.

Such flutes, revolutionary in their development and beautiful in their appearance though they are, were those of a single generation. Makers of the next generation, for example, Peter Bressan, a Frenchman who settled in London and had made such three-piece flutes in the early part of his career, went on to develop the four-piece flute that remained supreme up to the developments of Theobald Boehm in the mid-nineteenth century and that, as cheap band flutes, can still be bought today.

The one-key flute was taken up by amateurs and professionals alike, most famously by Frederick the Great of Prussia, and music was written for it by Johann Sebastian Bach and many others.

The main differences between the three-piece flute and the first of the four-piece ones are fourfold. In appearance, the ornate head-cap and joint between head and body and foot gave way to a much plainer pattern of construction, with a plain, flat cap of ivory or silver, and a gentle bulge or thickening of wood at the bottom of the head to strengthen the socket that accepted the tenon at the top of the body. Second, the diameter of the embouchure was reduced, to give the player better control (the embouchure of the ivory flute shown in figure 3.13 was later enlarged). Third, the body was divided into upper and lower body joints, the separation coming between the player's hands, between the two groups of three fingerholes. And last, internally there was a counter-taper in the foot, the bore of which now widened from around the position of the D♯ key to the end.

This division of the body had three advantages, one being that it enabled the use of a set of *corps de rechange*. There were often up to six upper-body joints, although in the later classical period only three, each differing in length by a quarter of an inch or so. The second advantage was that the use of shorter joints provided much greater ease in reaming the body. The third was that it made it more comfortable to play, because the finger-stretch on flutes long enough to play at the pitch then prevalent, a whole tone lower than today, is reduced if each half of the body can be turned to bring their fingerholes toward each hand.[66]

The use of the corps de rechange allowed players to cope with differing tuning levels, for in those days there

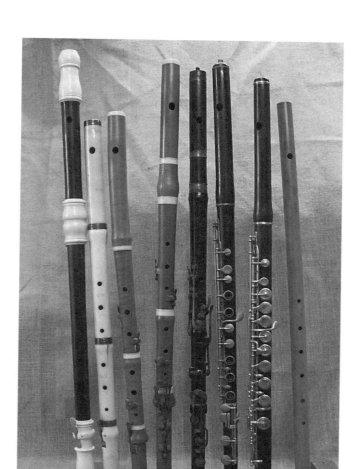

Figure 3.13. Transverse Flutes

L–R: copy of Hotteterre three-piece flute, one-key, c. 1660, by Felix Raudonikas, St. Petersburg, 1980 (VIII 188); ivory four-piece flute, one-key, by Thomas Stanesby Jr., London, c. 1750 (III 154); four-key, marked Drouet, London, but probably by Astor, c. 1820 (II 6); six-key by Richard Potter, London, c. 1790 (II 8); eight-key, by Henry Hill, late Monzani, London, 1836 (VI 150); conical Boehm system, by Cabart, Paris, c. 1890 (VII 226); cylindrical Boehm system, Montague Bros., London, late nineteenth century (XI 210); prototype of reproduction Renaissance model, by Herbert Myers for Gunter Korber, Germany, c. 1960 (IV 32).

was no recognized standard pitch, and players had to be able to play at higher or lower pitches as required.[67] It was much cheaper and more convenient to do this with a set of upper-body joints of different lengths than to have a set of different flutes. The use of the corps de rechange also allowed players, as Johann Joachim Quantz pointed out, to use a shorter joint in quiet movements, where the lower velocity of the air-stream might lead to a flatter pitch, and a longer one in the louder and brisker allegros, where the greater air velocity would sharpen the pitch, so using the different body lengths to compensate for the effect of the breath and retain the same pitch level throughout.[68]

Reaming a tapering bore is a complex process. A cylindrical bore can be drilled, for example, with a spoon bit following a smaller pilot bore, but a tapering bore needs the attention of one or more reamers to convert the cylindrical pilot bore into a taper.[69] It is not sufficient for the bore merely to be wider at one end than the other, because an even taper throughout the length will produce out-of-tune notes. For good intonation, changes of taper and often some chambering at specific points are necessary. To achieve this with long reamers in a one-piece body is difficult, but dividing the body into two sections allows for shorter reamers and therefore greater control over what is happening at the further end. It also makes it much easier to make small adjustments in the bore at any specific point necessary. Tuning can also be greatly improved by undercutting some fingerholes, widening them at the point where they reach the bore, and this, too, is more easily done with shorter joints.

The next major development was the adoption of further closed keys to eliminate the need for cross-fingering. Cross-fingering flattened the pitch but it also affected the volume and tone quality, producing a slightly quieter and more veiled sound. It was also difficult to do quickly and neatly, so that some trills—rapid alternation of two notes—could be difficult to achieve. It has been argued that the new keys may have been introduced more as shake keys ("shakes" are what trills were then called in English) than for chromatics.

Initially there were three new keys—for F♮, G♯ or A♭, and B♭—producing, with the foot key, the four-key flute. This was followed by the six-key flute, with a key for the upper C-natural and a second key for that most common of accidentals, the F-natural, so that that note could be taken by either hand. At much the same period, many players wanted to extend the range of the flute, lengthening the foot and adding two open-standing keys that could be closed to provide C♯ and middle C. The resulting eight-key flute was certainly available by the 1780s.

There was no set order for the addition of these keys, and different makers and different players adopted different combinations as they preferred. The eight-key flute, once established, remained in use throughout the nineteenth century and is still seen in some flute ensembles to this day.

This is not the place for a full history of flute development, any more than that of any other instrument, and there are many books on this subject, primarily those of Philip Bate and Ardal Powell.[70] There were many minor developments, all of them important in their day, each designed to improve facility, tone, volume, and tuning, but very often improving one of these at the expense of one or more of the others. Some of them we shall glance at in interlude E on the Second Industrial Revolution, where a further illustration will be found. Without doubt, the most important improvements of the flute in the nineteenth century were those of Theobald Boehm.

Although the new keys had considerably improved the flute, there were still inequalities of tone, and not all the keys were in their ideal position, their place sometimes being compromised to accommodate more than one function. The hole for the G♯–A♭ key in particular had to be placed in a compromised position to avoid the joint between the two hands.

Boehm's first model, the conical Boehm of 1831, had a slightly improved bore; a fingerhole for each note of the chromatic scale, all somewhat larger than those of the eight-key flute; and, the most important feature, keys on long rod axles so that the key-heads could be placed where they were wanted and their touches placed where they were most convenient to the fingers. So that the axles could travel right up the body, the old division between the two hands was abandoned. The need for separate joints for tuning had ended in the late eighteenth century with the invention of the brass tuning slide somewhere around the 1770s. This was usually housed in a separate barrel between the head and the upper-body joint, as can be seen on the eight-key flute in figure 3.13. If one pulled the tenons of a wooden flute slightly out of their sockets to lengthen the tube and flatten the pitch, this left chasms in the tube the depth of the thickness of the wood of the tenons, and did horrible things to the tuning. The thickness of a brass telescopic slide had a negligible effect in this respect, and the use of separate joints ceased to be necessary.[71] By Boehm's time, improved technology in the manufacture of reamers meant that different tapers could be set on a single reamer, removing the other main need for the division. Boehm's key mechanism, the use of long axles and ring keys, was applied by other makers to all the other woodwind instruments.

This model was followed in 1847 by the cylindrical Boehm. The body and foot reverted to the cylinder of the Renaissance, and the necessary taper, in what Boehm termed a "parabola," was placed in the head. The fingerholes were made as large as practicable and placed as nearly as possible in their correct acoustical positions. They were now too large to be covered by the fingers, and all had to be covered by plates (sometimes perforated to produce what is sometimes called the "open-key flute"). Despite some resistance and a number of short-lived rivals that provided compromises of tone and fingering between the old and the new (which we shall meet in interlude E), the 1847 Boehm swept all before it,

and in all essentials is the flute that we still use today, although there have been many adjustments and further improvements by other makers.

Leaving now the instruments of our orchestra, we return to the instruments of other cultures.

Transverse flutes are occasionally found in South America, mainly in the northern part of the continent.[72] Most have only two or three fingerholes, and one, from Suriname, has something that would better be described as a handhole: a large section of the quite short bamboo tube is cut away and the player places a hand over this area, opening it to a lesser or greater extent to produce the pitch required. A similar technique is used in New Guinea, where a short, wide-bored transverse flute has no fingerholes, the open end instead partly stopped by one hand to produce different pitches.

An unusual form of transverse flute that is found also in South America as well as in China, Southeast Asia, and parts of Oceania is that with a central embouchure. There are two varieties. One has both ends closed (as is also found with some more normal transverse flutes in South America, especially in Peru), with one to three fingerholes on each side of the embouchure, those on one side starting a little farther from the embouchure than those on the other. The other has the embouchure just off-center, each end open, and no fingerholes, opening or closing each end instead. Some, such as the Sumatran example shown in figure 3.11, use both systems. As Anthony Baines explained very clearly, the playing technique with both types depends on the fact that the longer section of tubing takes command.[73] Thus the pitch is determined by whichever fingerhole—or in the case of the holeless type, whichever end—is farthest from the embouchure. Since a stopped tube is acoustically longer than an open tube, the stopped shorter end of the holeless type is musically longer than the open longer end.

We have already mentioned the giant New Guinea flutes that are played in pairs, with interlocking fanfares of natural harmonics, and their shorter relations with a single fingerhole. Unfortunately my two examples are too large to be illustrated clearly.

Other than these, the transverse flute seems hardly to be used around the world, save where it has been introduced from our culture. One example of this is among the Toradja people on the Indonesian island of Sulawesi, whose flutes, one of which can also be seen in figure 3.11, are beautifully decorated with incised and colored patterns, but they are not native to the island. They were introduced by German missionaries and school teachers in the nineteenth century. Their beautiful decoration styles may be indigenous, but the instruments themselves are not.[74]

Harmonic Flutes

There is one variety of flutes, as distinct from whistles, that has no fingerholes: the harmonic flutes. They are blown in all the ways known for flutes—end, notch, duct, and transverse—and it is suspected that they exist over much wider areas than we yet have knowledge of, because since many consist simply of a tube, unless people are seen playing them, they may easily remain unrecognized as a musical instrument and unregarded.

The longest are the spirit flutes of New Guinea. We have above traced the origins of most of the world's transverse flutes to the Indian subcontinent, but this seems unlikely with these huge instruments, often well over six feet long, because they are so different from any other known flutes that local invention seems by far the most likely explanation. They have so wide an embouchure that the playing technique involves forming a duct with the forefinger of each hand, partly to direct the air and partly to occlude some of the hole. Both they and the shorter transverse flutes, three feet or so long and with a single fingerhole near the foot, are made from species of bamboo, and on both types the stoppers at the proximal end are so beautifully carved that they have often been collected as art objects in themselves and may be seen in many museums without the flutes of which they are an essential functional part.

While the New Guinea flutes use a simple series of harmonics with the two players alternating their notes, most—probably all—other harmonic flutes have a more complex technique, using the overtones of both the open and stopped tube, by closing the distal end with a finger. The overtones of an open tube, let us say approximately two feet long, will start on middle C and will include all the harmonic series based on that pitch. Stopping the end will sound the C an octave lower (see the afterword for the reasons for this) and sound only the odd-numbered harmonics of that note. In the musical example shown in figure 3.14, the white notes with stems pointing upward are the harmonics of the open flute; the black notes with the stems downward are those of the stopped flute. Looking at the white notes, it will be seen that there are wide gaps between the available pitches. By including the black notes, one can fill those gaps and produce a similar range to that of an open flute four feet long.

Two of the better known harmonic flutes are the Romanian *tilinca* and the Norwegian *seljefløyte* (see figure 3.15). The tilinca varies in length from two feet or less to double that and is end-blown.[75] While it was originally of cane or reed stem, it is now quite often made of a spare piece of water pipe. A wide variety of such flutes is used in Slovakia, some of reed stem, some of turned wood, and again some of convenient pieces of metal tubing, some end-blown and some duct-blown.[76] They are often used by shepherds, as in Romania. Hungarian examples are also known, and it is likely that they are or have been used over much of Europe in areas less well recorded.[77]

The Norwegian seljefløyte was traditionally an ephemeral instrument, made only in springtime from willow bark, when the bark is easily removed from the wood, but a year-round version was created by Egil Storbekken, with a plastic tube covered, for cosmetic reasons, by imitation coiled bark. It differs from other flutes in being a transversely blown duct flute. A wooden block is inserted into the end of the tube, and the distal end of the block, where the player puts the lips, is carved down to form the duct, with a mouth cut in the tube itself. It is by no means the only folk instrument that has been modernized to suit those who wish to play it in a wider context, and there are many others noted within these pages. Where and when it originated is unknown, but it must have been at least seven hundred years ago, for recently a medieval exemplar appeared. On f. 188 of the recently discovered East Anglian Macclesfield Psalter, dated to

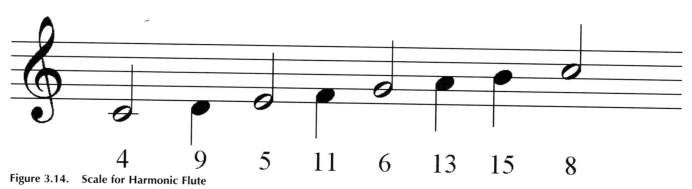

Figure 3.14. Scale for Harmonic Flute

White notes indicate the harmonics with the end open, the black notes, the harmonics with the end closed.

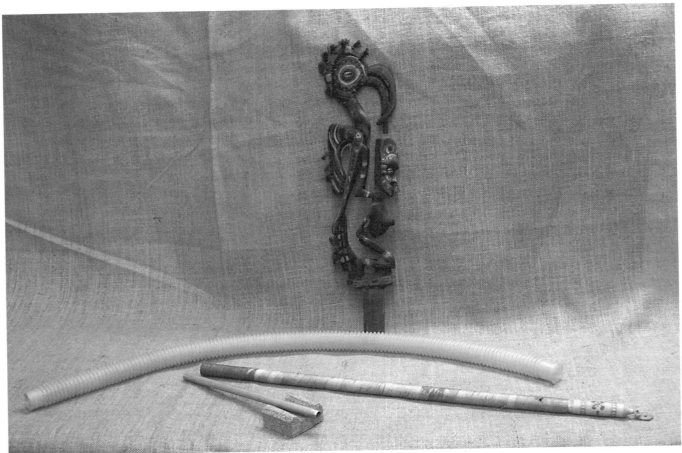

Figure 3.15. Harmonic Flutes
Top to bottom: stopper from an eight-foot-long flute, Papua New Guinea (IX 206); plastic "twirl-a-tube," United States (V 230); *seljefløyte*, by Egil Storbekken, Tolga, Norway (IX 4); *tilinca*, Romania (III 22).

1325–1335, an identical instrument is illustrated, played in exactly the same way and, so far as one can judge from an illustration of this type, made in exactly the same way.[78] Many other instruments in folk traditions will have as long a history (another example here is the trump), but it is not often that one is fortunate enough to find the evidence.

Notes

1. Johann Christian Hinrichs, *Entstehung Fortgang und Jetzige Beschaffenheit der Russische Jagdmusik* (1796), with a biography of Johann Anton Maresch, who invented this music, and measured drawings of horns, staff notation, and horn-band score.

2. Neil Sorrell of York University filmed the making of the gamelan now in York and showed the gongsmiths working in this way.

3. They first appear in *Das Rheingold* thirty-two bars before the end of Scene 2, on p. 366 in the Schott miniature score.

4. Percival Kirby devotes a whole chapter to these South African flute ensembles, which are used by other peoples as well as the Venda, in his *Musical Instruments of the Native Races of South Africa* (1934), 135–70.

5. Bird-bone and mammoth ivory flutes from Geissenklösterle in Germany have been dated to around 35,000 BC (*Current World Archaeology* 9 [2005]: 7).

6. A good recent survey is David Lewis-Williams, *The Mind in the Cave* (2002).

7. A period thought of as transitional between the Middle and Upper (or Later) Paleolithic, when modern humans seem to have coexisted with and then eliminated the Neanderthal people.

8. See Ernst Emsheimer, "Tongue Duct Flutes," *GSJ* 34 (1981): 98–105, and Cajsa Lund, "A Medieval Tongue-(Lip) and-Duct Flute," *GSJ* 34 (1981): 106–9.

9. Jenny F. So, ed., *Music in the Age of Confucius* (2000), 91–92 and 133, figs. 4.1a and 4.6; Lucie Rault, ed., *La voix du dragon* (2000), 138–39 and 277.

10. Shōsōin Office, ed., *Musical Instruments in the Shōsōin* (1967), viii, xiii, xxi, plates 22–23, 149–55.

11. Georg Kinsky, *Musikgeschichte in Bildern* [also published in several other languages at the same date] (1930), 41:2.

12. Dale A. Olsen, *Music of El Dorado* (2000); Gavin Menzies, *1421* (2002).

13. A useful recent book that describes and illustrates most British forms of whistle is Martyn Gilchrist's *Whistles* (2000).

14. In the British Royal Navy, terminology is quite strict: the instrument is the "call" and the sounds produced are the "pipes," as in the traditional "piping the side" to welcome a senior officer on board.

15. J. Gardiner, ed., *Before the Mast* (2005), 284–92.

16. I have examples of the three named in my own collection and presume that they are used in other navies also.

17. Laurence E. R. Picken cites examples of this in Turkey with apricot stones in *Folk Musical Instruments of Turkey* (1975), 376–78.

18. Laurence E. R. Picken, "An Afghan Quail-lure," *SIMP* 3 (1974): 172–75 and illus. 283–85.

19. Taylor's system is now used worldwide and comes in many sizes. One pair that he made for me were small enough that I could fit wires to make them into earrings for my wife!

20. Alan R. Thrasher, *Chinese Musical Instruments* (2000), 1–3 and 14–15.

21. An explanation that I owe to Lynda Sayce's discovery of it in an Italian etymological dictionary.

22. A detail taken up and investigated by Sir James Beament at my suggestion. See James Beament and Dennis Unwin, "The Hole Story," *Strad* 112:1132 (April 2001): 408–15.

23. Lynda Sayce, "The Development of Italianate Continuo Lutes" (2001), 75–76.

24. Personal communication. Unfortunately none of Dr. Clausen's material has ever been published, although all his field notes and recordings are now deposited in the Pitt Rivers Museum, Oxford. He was always very generous with information such as this in the days when, together with Nazir Jairazbhoy, we ran the Royal Anthropological Institute's Ethnomusicology Panel.

25. Helmholtz resonators were created by the great acoustician of that name to capture any specific pitch (see Hermann Helmholtz, *Lehre von den Tonempfindungen* [1863] or its translation *On the Sensations of Tone*, by Alexander J. Ellis ([2nd ed., 1885]). There is more than one pattern, but a common design is a spherical body, of the correct volume to resonate to the desired pitch, with a nipple projecting on one side to fit the ear, and on the other an aperture to admit the sound, fine-tuned by adjusting its area, for example, with wax: the wider the sharper, the narrower the flatter. By using such resonators, because they were tuned to any one specific pitch, Helmholtz was able to capture and identify the separate overtones inherent in the sound of any note when these were otherwise difficult to perceive or to distinguish from the sound of the fundamental. As we have seen in this chapter, the vessel flute or ocarina is in effect a Helmholtz resonator in reverse: the vessel flute emits sound, the pitch depending on the area of the fingerholes opened, whereas the Helmholtz resonator admits sound.

26. We should emphasize here that it was Raymond Clausen who first pointed out its widespread application to instruments of all sorts.

27. J. V. S. Megaw, "Penny Whistles and Prehistory," *Antiquity* 34 (1960): 6–13.

28. Olsen, *Music of El Dorado*, 26.

29. Juzhong Zhang et al., "Oldest Playable Musical Instruments Found," *Nature* 401:6751 (23 September 1999): front cover and 366–68. The title, of course, is untrue; many earlier instruments such as whistles, bull-roarers, and idiophones are known and remain playable.

30. Those are the corrected carbon dates for the site as so far excavated; the article does not say at what level within the various strata the flutes were found, nor where they should be placed within the span of 1,200 years.

31. When we performed medieval music with Musica Reservata back in the 1960s and '70s, we knew we were guessing. We hoped that we guessed right, but we could never be sure that we had.

32. *World Archaeology* 12:3 (February 1981).

33. No other term than "duct flute" will stand up to analysis. The German *Blockflöte* depends on the presence of a block, something that is absent, save temporarily, in the case of the tongue-duct flute; "whistle flute" is ambiguous because whistles can be and are sounded by other means than a duct, even though that is the commonest method in our culture; and "fipple flute" is a nonsense because there is no agreement on what is or was a fipple—see my article under that heading in *The New Grove Dictionary of Musical Instruments* (1984), 1:761. The one essential in this class of flutes is a passage or duct to lead the air to the lip or sounding edge.

34. Picken, *Folk Musical Instruments of Turkey*, 424–31.

35. Jaap Kunst, *Musicologisch Onderzoek I* (1931). See also others of his publications such as those on the music of Nias.

36. Menzies, *1421*.

37. There is one thirteen-key clarinet by Martin frères in the Edinburgh University Collection of Historical Musical Instruments built for a left-handed player, and a left-handed eight-key flute in the Bate Collection in Oxford, but such arrangements for nineteenth-century and later instruments are very rare.

38. Dietrich Hakelberg, "Some Recent Archaeo-organological Finds," *GSJ* 48 (1995): 3–12.

39. Brian Trowell, "King Henry IV, Recorder Player," *GSJ* 10 (1957): 83–84, and Jeremy Montagu, "The Crozier of William of Wykeham," *EM* 30:4 (November 2002): 541–62. See also Anthony Rowland-Jones, "Iconography in the History of the Recorder up to c. 1430," *EM* 33:4 (November 2005): 557–74, and 34:1 (February 2006): 3–27.

40. Rainer Weber, "Recorder Finds from the Middle Ages," *GSJ* 29 (1976): 35–41.

41. See Sebastian Virdung, *Musica getutscht* (1511), f. Biii verso, for the illustration of the set, and from Miii verso to the end for the tutor (the book is not paginated); in the 1993 translation by Beth Bullard, see p. 106 for the illustration and pp. 168–81 for the tutor.

42. Martin Agricola, *Musica instrumentalis deudsch* (1528).

43. This somewhat rash statement is based on measurements by Bob Marvin of instruments in Vienna ("Recorders and English Flutes in European Collections," *GSJ* 25 [1972]: 30–57) and Filadelfio Puglisi in Bologna ("The 17th-Century Recorders of the Accademia Filarmonica of Bologna," *GSJ* 34 [1981]: 33–43). The illustrations mentioned are in Michael Praetorius, *Syntagma Musicum II—De Organographia* (1619), plate 9, and Marin Mersenne, *Harmonie Universelle* (1636), Livre Cinquiesme des Instruments à Vent, 238–39.

44. The "fourth" and "sixth" are the musical intervals above the standard size of recorder, the alto in F. Thus our soprano or descant can be called a fifth flute.

45. Edgar Hunt, *The Recorder and Its Music* (1962), 141, 157. Dr. Hunt has deposited his extensive collection of such instruments in the Bate Collection in Oxford, including prototypes of a number of the instruments he designed for Messrs. Schott.

46. Mersenne, *Harmonie Universelle*, 232–37.

47. There are numerous editions of Pepys's *Diaries*, both complete and abridged, and some entries will be found in that year in almost any version.

48. Pepys, *Diaries*, entry for 20 January 1668.

49. See Ernst Emsheimer, "A Finno-Ugric Flute Type," *JIFMC* 18 (1966): 29–35, and also in his "Tongue Duct Flutes," 98–105.

50. Lund, "A Medieval Tongue-(Lip-)and-Duct Flute," 106–9.

51. It is, of course, possible that the early Indian flute was also like this. None, so far, has been found in that subcontinent of so early a date.

52. Thrasher, *Chinese Musical Instruments*, 40.

53. For those wishing to replace the membrane, it can often be bought in small paper packets from Chinese stores.

54. Shōsōin Office, *Musical Instruments in the Shōsōin*, plates 22, 23, and 149–56.

55. See, for example, Joachim Braun, "Musical Instruments in Byzantine Illuminated Manuscripts," *EM* 8:3 (July 1980): 312–27, esp. 313 and n. 35. The frequently illustrated carving of a second-century Roman soldier playing an apparent transverse flute, suggesting thus that the instrument was already known then, is almost certainly a form of the *aulos*, a reed instrument, with the reed in the socket that stands up from the body of the instrument to form the embouchure.

56. See my *World of Medieval and Renaissance Musical Instruments* (1976), plate 35, and many other sources, for f. 218v of Escorial ms. I b 2.

57. Björn R. Tammen, *Musik und Bild im Chorraum mittelalterlicher Kirchen* (2000), a study based on the Angel Choir of Cologne Cathedral, and the *Manessischen Liederhandschrift* (Heidelberg: Universitätsbibliothek, MS Palatinus Germanicus 848, c. 1340) both illustrate transverse flutes, whereas they seldom appear in manuscripts or church carvings in other countries.

58. In Britain, for example, the name derived from the lowest note, produced by closing the six fingerholes. In Germany and America, on the other hand, the name followed the pitch produced by closing those fingerholes plus the keys of the later "C-foot" extension (for which, see below), whether or not that C-foot were present. British terminology remained the same after the C-foot was introduced in the late eighteenth century because, even as late as the twentieth century, many band flutes were made without that extension, which was seldom needed in band music. Thus German and American names are a tone lower than British because a B♭ flute, for example, with a C-foot sounds A♭ as its lowest note.

59. A consort of such flutes, drawn by Urs Graf in 1523, is illustrated by Ardal Powell, *The Flute* (2002), plate 6. Powell also includes the *Cántigas* flutists (plate 4) and one of the Ladies of the Half-Length (plate 14). His book is the most recent and the most thorough study of the development of the transverse flute that we have.

60. For instance, in the Steiermärkischen Landeszeughaus in Graz, Austria—for which, see Gerhard Stradner, *Musikinstrumente in Grazer Sammlungen* (1986), 89–91 and Abb. 7–10, and Stradner, "Die Musikinstrumente im Steiermärkischen Landeszeughaus in Graz," *Veröffentlichungen des Landeszeughauses Graz* 6 (1976): 7–36.

61. *The Triumph of Maximilian I* (1964), 3.

62. Andrew Ashbee, *Records of English Court Music*, vol. 7: *1485–1558* (1993), 383–98, reprinting the two inventories of Henry VIII's musical instruments of 1542 and 1547 (London: PRO E315/160 and BL Harley Ms 1419).

63. H. Colin Slim, "Paintings of Lady Concerts," *Imago Musicae* 1 (1984): 51–73, figs. 1–4, all four of which are reproduced in many other sources.

64. See two articles by Eric Halfpenny, "Two Rare Transverse Flutes," *GSJ* 13 (1960): 38–43 and plate 7, and "A Renaissance Bass Flute," *GSJ* 23 (1970): 116 and plate 19, an X-ray of the head.

65. Bruce Haynes, *The Eloquent Oboe* (2001), 56.

66. This observation I owe to Lynda Sayce, derived from her practical experience on both three- and four-joint flutes of this period.

67. Bruce Haynes, A *History of Performing Pitch* (2002).

68. Johann Joachim Quantz's *Versuch einer Anweisung die Flöte traversiere zu spielen* (1752), available in a translation by Edward R. Reilly as *On Playing the Flute* (1966), was and remains one of the most influential treatises of the eighteenth century, covering not only flute playing but performance of music in general. The relevant passage here is chapter 16, section 8.

69. A reamer is a tapering steel tool, with its cutting edge along the side, shaped to produce the bore pattern required. See Robert Bigio and Michael Wright, "On Reaming Flutes," *GSJ* 58 (2005): 51–57.

70. Philip Bate, *The Flute* (1969); Powell, *The Flute*. See also Jeremy Montagu, *The Flute* (1990).

71. The differential coefficient of expansion between brass and wood was not then recognized, but this is why so many antique flutes have bad cracks in the head and the sockets.

72. Karl Gustav Izikowitz, *Musical and Other Sound Instruments of the South American Indians* (1935), esp. 297–303.

73. Anthony Baines, *Woodwind Instruments* (1957), 185–87.

74. Walter Kaudern, *Musical Instruments in Celebes* (The Hague, 1927), 208–9 and fig. 107.

75. Tiberiu Alexandru, *Instrumentele Muzicale ale Poporului Romîn* (Bucharest, 1956), 52–5.

76. Oskár Elschek, *Die Volksmusikinstrumente der Tschechoslowakei*, Teil 2 (1983), 121–22, 127–43, Taf. 7–8.

77. Bálint Sárosi, *Die Volksmusikinstrumente Ungarns* (1967), 69.

78. Jeremy Montagu, "Musical Instruments in the Macclesfield Psalter," *EM* 34:2 (May 2006): 189–204, esp. 201, illus. 12.

~

The Medieval Renaissance
and the First Industrial Revolution

The early Middle Ages, from the fall of the Roman Empire in the fifth century AD to the twelfth century, is a period of whose instruments we know comparatively little. Our main source of information is the iconography in liturgical manuscripts and similar works, and because most of the illustrations come from psalters, we are then bedeviled with the constant question: are these the instruments that were used then, or are they what the artists thought the instruments named in the psalms were like? And, as always, but particularly in this early medieval period, how accurate are the depictions?

We have some cross-checks. The sixth-century Alemannic lyre, tragically destroyed in Germany during World War II, closely resembled one of the instruments illustrated in the Utrecht Psalter in figure C.1;[1] it was also used as the basis for the restoration of the fragments found in the sixth-century East Anglian ship burial at Sutton Hoo. Several organs in different psalters show enough common features to suggest that they are reasonably realistic portrayals and yet are different enough from each other that they cannot be copies from a single imaginary source.[2] The long trumpets of the Utrecht Psalter also appear in enough other sources to suggest that they really did look like that, which in turn suggests that they were made of wood rather than metal. They are slightly curved and evenly conical, with bands around them as though to hold together an instrument that has been made from a piece of wood split, hollowed, and reunited, like an alphorn. The tong cymbals, a pair of small cymbals, one at the end of each branch of a pair of long tongs, also appear in a number of other psalters. The harp with its "broken" neck looks probable enough to be realistic, even if not duplicated elsewhere, as does the waisted drum, leaving only, among all the instruments we can see in that

psalter, the long-necked kithara as more problematic, for the only other evidence for that instrument is a sixth-century late Roman mosaic from Qasr el-Lebia in Libya.[3]

Other later psalters show fiddles, sometimes of rather improbable shapes, but who is to say whether what looks improbable to us seemed so in the eleventh century (that is, when the bow first appeared in Europe)? A good selection of illustrations of these was published by Werner Bachmann.[4] There is also a quite considerable number of surviving instruments: a few string instruments; a good many whistles, flutes, and horns, including the ivory horns known as *olifants*; and a number of trumps, as well as bells and rattles. All that were known to him up to the early 1970s are listed by Frederick Crane, and while some have been found since then, there has been no further comprehensive list published.[5] Some of these we have already encountered; to the rest we shall turn in due course.

Our concerns here are twofold: first, the quite sudden change among instruments as well as many other aspects of material culture that occurred in the late twelfth century and the first half of the thirteenth, and second, the medieval Industrial Revolution that powered a sudden upsurge in technology. Up to that time, instruments, like many other aspects of medieval life, had been somewhat crude. Flutes and whistles were mostly either animal or bird bones or made from woods such as elder that have an easily removed inner pith and thus a natural tube. Horns and trumpets had been animal horns or instruments made as the alphorn still is today. Fiddles and plucked instruments were hollowed out of solid blocks of wood.

Suddenly we see an entirely new instrumentarium—string instruments made as boxes or bowls from thin pieces of wood glued together; long trumpets of soldered metal sheet; reed instruments with tapering bore, so requiring

Figure C.1. Early Medieval Instruments

The Utrecht Psalter, Rheims, c. 825, f.83, *photo Utrecht University Library*.

Upper (to Psalm 149, text below), L–R: lyre, hand-drum, harp.

Lower (to Psalm 150, text on the verso), L–R: *kithara*, hand-drum, harp, long trumpets, hydraulic organ, long trumpets, lyre, tong cymbals.

the use of a lathe, some of them mouth-blown, others set into a bag so that more than one pipe could be sounded at the same time; kettledrums; and small drums called *tabors* that were played with one hand to accompany a pipe held in the other.

All of these, save perhaps the combination of pipe and tabor for which we can find no exotic evidence, came into Europe from the Near East and North Africa. Some came to us with Crusaders returning from the Holy Land, some across the Pyrenees from Iberia, where Moors, Jews, and Christians lived in a somewhat uneasy symbiosis. The sources of these instruments are clear. Many of the instruments that we suddenly see in the iconography of the thirteenth and early fourteenth centuries can be found to this day in the Muslim areas around the Mediterranean and farther eastward, and many of the European names for them are clearly of Arabic origin: *al 'ud* became our lute; *rebab* our rebec; *zamr* or *zurna* our shawm, and also *ghaita* our wait, the old English name for the shawm; *naqqara* our nakers; and *al nafir* the Spanish *añafil*, our long trumpet.

Much of the Spanish evidence comes from the manuscripts of the *Cántigas de Santa Maria*, dating from the second half of the thirteenth century.[6] Here we see many instruments played by musicians whose costumes identify them as members of each of those communities, Jews, Muslims, and Christians. From that date onward, we find the same instruments disseminated throughout Europe, along with many artifacts such as carpets and glassware that also derive from the more cultivated civilizations of the Near East and North Africa, where such other concepts as universities well predate our own.

The industrial processes that aided this proliferation have been detailed by Jean Gimpel.[7] Watermills had been known to the Romans, who used them for industrial as well as agricultural purposes, and by the eleventh century they were found on rivers all over Europe. The windmill first appeared in the twelfth century, and at much the same time tidal mills were also developed; the latter could take advantage of the regular daily surge of tides coming up and down the lower reaches of rivers, rather than being dependent on the more fitful seasonal flow of rivers. In the thirteenth century, mills were being built under bridges to take advantage of the greater power provided by the force of the water constricted between the piers. It was in the twelfth and thirteenth centuries that mills were used once again for industrial processes, as well as for grinding corn.

In the mid-thirteenth century the pole lathe first appeared, which facilitated the production of all the tapering-bored instruments such as shawms and bagpipes. Powered saws made it easier to produce the thin strips of wood essential for instruments such as lutes. The increase in mining, and the introduction of coal, made metals such as iron and copper available in far greater quantities, and brass, an amalgam of copper and zinc, became more widely used with the mining of that latter material. Hydraulic power also made possible iron and brass wire-drawing for string instruments and so made possible the invention of the keyboard instruments that came into use in the fourteenth century.

Many of these processes were invented in Europe, but it was the availability of texts from classical times that had been preserved in translations into Arabic, and the scientific writings of Persian and Arabic scholars that were translated into Latin in such centers as Toledo, that powered much of medieval thought and interest in furthering such discoveries. The result was a fundamental change in the numbers and types of musical instruments available, instruments that we can see carved on the walls of our churches and cathedrals, and in many of the psalters and other manuscripts from the thirteenth century onward that are reproduced in books and articles too numerous to list here.[8]

Notes

1. The Psalter was probably written in Rheims around 825; it is in the University Library of Utrecht, no. 32. Folio 83 illustrates both Psalms 149 and 150, above and below the text of Psalm 149.

2. All the significant ones are illustrated in Jean Perrot, *The Organ* (1971).

3. Discussed by Emmanuel Winternitz in "The Survival of the Kithara," *Journal of the Warburg and Courtauld Institutes* 24:3–4 (1961): 222–29; reprinted in his *Musical Instruments* (1967), 57–65 and plates 11–17.

4. Werner Bachmann, *The Origins of Bowing* (1969).

5. Frederick Crane, *Extant Medieval Musical Instruments* (1972).

6. Madrid: Escorial Library, mss. b I 2 and T I 1. Many of the illustrations will be found in my *World of Medieval and Renaissance Musical Instruments* (1976), and others in Tilman Seebass, *Musikdarstellung und Psalterillustration im früheren Mittelalter* (1973). Less accessibly, José Guerrero Lovillo published all the miniatures of T I 1 in facsimile (*Las Cántigas*, 1949), and Higinio Anglés the whole of b I 2 in facsimile (*La Musica de las Cántigas*, 1943–64).

7. Jean Gimpel, *The Medieval Machine* (1976).

8. See, for example, Jeremy Montagu and Gwen Montagu, *Minstrels and Angels* (1998); Gwen Montagu and Jeremy Montagu, "Beverley Minster Reconsidered," *EM* 6:3 (July 1978): 401–15; Francis W. Galpin, *Old English Instruments of Music* (1910; 4th ed., rev. R. Thurston Dart, 1975); Mary Remnant, *English Bowed Instruments* (1986). Many church guidebooks and other publications on ecclesiastical or medieval art also illustrate such instruments, but beware of confusing nomenclature and inaccurate terminology of the instruments. For reproductions from psalters and similar sources, see in particular Seebass, *Musikdarstellung und Psalterillustration*, as well as various articles of mine and others in the pages of *Early Music*.

CHAPTER FOUR

Reeds

Straws in the Wind

The dichotomy between the comparative simplicity of double reeds and the complexity of single reeds is a puzzle. The simplest double reed is a straw or other grass with one end flattened in the mouth (see figure 4.1).[1] The equivalent single reed has a tongue carefully cut out of the side of the straw near the top, with the end closed by a natural node or an artificial stopper, and so one would think it to be much more complex to devise and less likely to have occurred initially by accidental discovery. And yet the simple single reeds, often called "folk clarinets," are far more common in the world today than any simple double reeds.

The answer may lie far back in time. When both were grass or straw, and thus ephemeral since both are easily broken or so saturated by being held in the mouth that they will no longer spring open against the player's breath, perhaps the double was the more common. Today, when the more efficient hard reed and cane is used, the single reed is quite easily made, whereas the double needs careful scraping unless, in the parts of the world where such plants grow, it can be made from a tube of a different, softer type of reed or from materials such as palm leaf.

The double reed has a pair of surfaces, either thin blades of cane, as with the oboe and bassoon, or a flattened plant stem or layers of palm or other leaf, as with many exotic instruments, that beat concussively against each other when blown. The single reed has a single blade of cane or other material tied to a mouthpiece, as with the clarinet and saxophone, or a blade cut from the surface of the mouthpiece but still attached at one end,

as with many other exotic instruments, that beats percussively against the mouthpiece when blown. Both are so constructed that they lie slightly open and are forced to close, beating against each other or the mouthpiece, by the player's breath or, in the case of organs and bagpipes, by the air from a bellows or bag.

There is a third type of reed, the "free reed," so called because it does not beat against anything but swings freely to and fro through a closely fitting slot. Its behavior and use are sufficiently different from the other two that we shall devote a separate section to it.

A fourth type, a dilating reed that normally lies closed but is forced *open* by the air, is fairly rare when made from straws or other plants, but is used worldwide in the form of a player's lips. Made of straw or plant-stem, it seems to exist only as a reed whistle, rather than driving a musical instrument. The player's lips are sufficiently different from other reeds that they are better dealt with as "brass instruments," a useful common term in our culture even though many other materials besides brass are used.

Irrespective of the type of reed used, there is a further distinction, discussed in more detail in the afterword, between those reed instruments with a cylindrical bore (the inside of the tube) and those whose bore widens from top to bottom. The latter are easier to play over a wide compass because, when blown harder, the pitch jumps up (or overblows) an octave and the player can use the same, or at least similar, fingerings to produce the same pitch names an octave higher than before. The fingering for a C, for example, or any other note is much the same in each octave. However, all the archaeological or iconographic evidence that we have tells us that reed instruments of this expanding shape

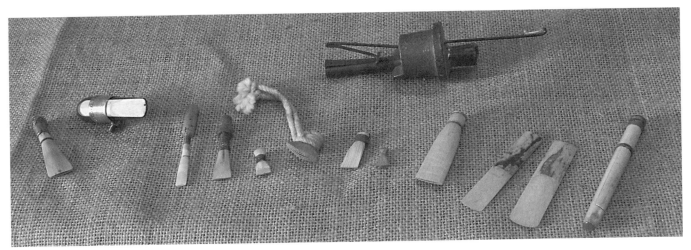

Figure 4.1. Some Reeds for Woodwinds
L–R: bassoon, single-reed mouthpiece for bassoon, oboe, Breton *bombarde*, Chinese *suona*, Burmese *hne* (multiplex), Indian *shahnai*, Egyptian *mizmar*, Chinese *guan*, clarinet, saxophone, Highland bagpipe drone.
Above: organ reed with tuning bridle.

are much later in the history of the development of instruments, presumably because such a bore is more difficult to make than a plain cylinder.

The reed instruments with cylindrical bore (it is necessary to repeat "reed instruments" because flutes behave quite differently) are difficult to overblow at all, unless helped with the speaker key found on our instruments, and when they do sound in a higher register, the pitch is a twelfth—an octave and a fifth—above the original range; thus the same note names in the higher register have very different fingerings from those in the lower register. The fingering for a C in the lower register would, with the addition of a speaker hole or key, produce a G in the upper register. On instruments without keywork, there is often a gap in the compass between the top of the fundamental register and the bottom of the overblown register, simply for lack of sufficient fingers to control enough holes to cover the whole compass. The difference between the fingering of the two bore shapes is well known to those who play both saxophone (which widens in bore) and clarinet (which is cylindrical).

The earliest evidence for instruments with expanding bore that I have so far found comes from the fifth century BC, whereas the evidence for those with cylindrical bore goes back at least two thousand years earlier, so we shall take those first. The earliest so far known is the pair of silver pipes found in the royal cemetery at Ur in Iraq, dating from around 2450 BC.[2] These, like the somewhat later Egyptian double pipes, are very narrow in bore. Francis Galpin gives the lengths as about 10½ inches, despite their fragmentary state, and the bore diameter as three-sixteenths of an inch, which suggests that they

would have had a reed of straw, perhaps a single reed like that of the Welsh pibcorn (see figure 4.13).[3] The Egyptian instruments that we see in wall paintings look longer but similarly narrow, whereas those few that have come down to us from Egypt are rather shorter, much the length of those from Ur.[4]

The earliest references to the Greek *aulos* come from Homer, recording events of around 1000 BC in verse first written down a number of centuries later, and therefore to be treated with as much caution as the identification of the biblical instruments. There has long been argument and debate on whether the aulos had double or single reeds—at least there has never been any doubt that it was indeed a cylindrical-bore reed instrument, despite the common translation, even among archaeologists (who should know better) and those who label representations of it in museums, as a "double flute." Heinz Becker cites Theophrastus (c. 300 BC) to prove that the reed was single, whereas the majority of illustrations on Greek pots clearly show that it was double.[5] There is so much definite evidence for each type of reed that we can only assume that some players used a double reed and some a single reed, perhaps in different periods or in different styles of music. What is certain is that the aulos (plural *auloi*) was a pair of pipes, held one in each hand, occasionally with the two pipes parallel so that the player could finger across both pipes with each hand (as with the single-reed double pipes to which we shall come shortly), but far more commonly held divergently so that each hand could finger only its own pipe. They were played by both men and women, frequently while dancing or processing, and players often had a strap, called the *phorbeia*, across their cheeks to support them and, presumably, prevent their distension under the air pressure.

This suggests that circular breathing, sometimes called "cheek-pumping," was used. This is a technique common in many parts of the world with all wind instruments, allowing the player to produce a continuous and uninterrupted flow of melody. It is also well known among glassblowers and those who use Bunsen burners or similar equipment with a blowpipe. One fills the cheeks with air while blowing out from the chest and then breathes in through the nose at the same time as blowing out from the cheeks, using the muscles of the cheeks instead of those of the diaphragm. Excessive use of this technique can lead to distension of the cheeks, puffing them out like balloons. The skin may stretch so much that it fails to return to shape, forming dewlaps worse than those of bloodhounds. This deformation can sometimes be seen today with players of the West African shawm (*alghaita*) and would have been abhorrent to the ancient Greeks with their emphasis on bodily perfection.

Becker suggests that the phorbeia may also have been used for the same reason that some shawm players use a pirouette or lip disc: to prevent the reeds being knocked down the player's throat by an accident while dancing.[6] This is not the only reason for the use of the pirouette, for I have been assured by players that it is necessary only for those who have lost their teeth. The one modern form of phorbeia is on the Javanese shawm (*tarompèt*), which has a curved cheek support, originally of coconut shell but now more commonly of metal (see figure 4.3).[7] Becker also points out that it is only men who are seen to use the phorbeia, never women. One reason for this may be that the women who played the auloi seem normally to have been from the lower classes of society, and so their eventual facial appearance may have been considered to be of lesser importance. It is also possible that it was only men who used circular breathing.

A very similar double pipe to the aulos, and presumably derived from it, was the Roman *tibia*, one difference being that very often the left-hand pipe was longer and had an up-curved bell on the distal end, perhaps of horn.[8] This form was referred to as the "Phrygian tibia." Later Roman examples had a form of keywork, a series of rings that could be turned to close one fingerhole and open another in a different position and so provide alternative holes. So far as we know, the rings could only be preset, not changed while playing. The alternative holes produced the equivalent, in our terms, of sharp or natural notes, and thus enabled the player to use more than one mode or key without changing instruments. A set of tibiae from Pompeii has survived with such rings.

We know nothing of the use of such cylindrical pipes with a double reed in Europe after Roman times, but they continued in the East, where they survive to this day from Turkey to Japan (see figure 4.2). The Turkish *mey*, the Armenian *baǧlama*, the Iranian *balaban*, the Chinese *guan*, the Korean *piri*, and the Japanese *hichiriki*, all have a cylindrical bore and a large double reed, the reed made from a plant stem whose proximal end has been scraped to thin it and then flattened to form two opposing faces, but without being split into two separate blades as we do with oboe and bassoon reeds. These are clearly surviving forms of the *monaulos*, a single aulos for which there is literary evidence from ancient Greece, although, as Anthony Baines pointed out, the presence of two thumbholes on the hichiriki does suggest the conflation of a double pipe, one with thumb and three fingerholes and the other with thumb and four fingerholes, onto the one body, and hence a connection with the normal paired aulos.[9]

We do not know where this type of pipe originated. It would seem unlikely that it was invented in Greece, and it is much more probable that the Greeks brought it with them as they migrated from Central Asia into Europe. Thus pipes such as the balaban and baǧlama may well be survivors of the earliest forms, though it is also possible that they traveled down the Silk Road from Greece and Rome to the Orient.

One reason for the lack of such instruments in early medieval Europe may have been the use of the shawm. This was, again, a double reed instrument, but one with a bore that widened from reed to bell. The earliest evidence for such an instrument is from the fifth century BC, among the Faliscans, one of the Etruscan peoples.[10] As always with illustrations, there are assumptions involved, but it seems improbable that anyone would make an exterior that clearly widens, with the waste of wood involved in turning down the narrower part of the body, unless the interior also followed that shape. This assumption is supported by a relief of the same period on a tomb from Chiusi, a slightly earlier pot from Vulci, a wall painting from Tarquinia, and a relief of a wedding procession, also from Chiusi.[11] A very much clearer Roman relief of the second century AD must be treated with suspicion because the player's wrist shows a break in the stone and thus it and the shawm may be the result of a later repair, but there are other Roman examples that confirm its use into the later Roman periods.[12]

Iconographic evidence is always a matter of chance—do any illustrations survive, have they been found or published, and do they show the instrument we are looking for? In this respect, post-Roman Europe was a Dark Age indeed, for there is little good iconographic material

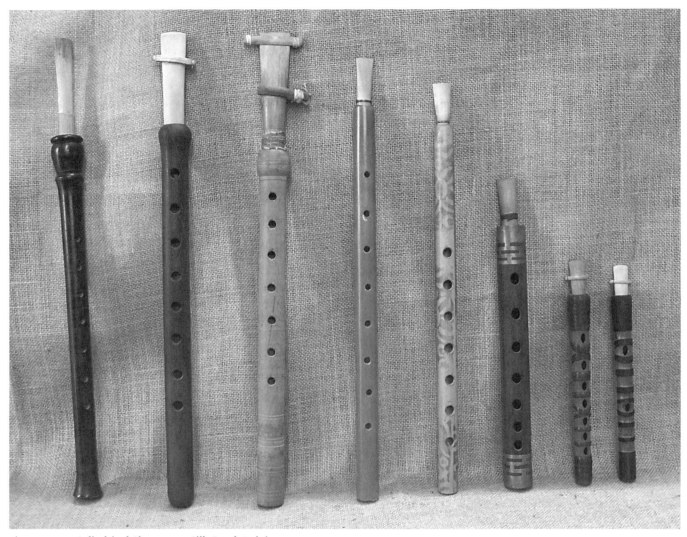

Figure 4.2. Cylindrical Shawms or Silk Road *Auloi*

L–R: *mey*, Turkey (VI 118); *bağlama*, Armenia (XIII 24); *balaban*, Iran (VIII 40); three *guanzi*, China, one of jade (VIII 176), one of decorated bamboo (VII 166b), and one of wood with decoration of low-melting-point metal (I 196); two *hichiriki*, Japan, one of bamboo (I 194) and the other of plastic, turned to show the two thumbholes (X 60).

for several centuries. There are, for that reason, gaps in our history of the shawm, but there is a good representation on a post-Sassanid silver jug from Persia of the eighth or ninth century, along with a lute and a mouth organ (both looking very Chinese), a harp, and an hourglass drum.[13]

It was in Persia and the Near East that so much of Greco-Roman culture survived, both arts and sciences, and were it not for that preservation, we should have very little Greek or Roman literature today. Certainly the shawm flourished there as it does to this day (see figure 4.3), and it was thence that it reappeared in Europe with many other instruments in the thirteenth century, as we noted in interlude C. It became the standard loud

melody instrument all over Europe, used for weddings, processions, dances, and all outdoor occasions. It was its widening bore, combined with the double reed pouched within the mouth and not held between the lips, that gave it the loud, penetrating sound, so loud that it seems to ring within the ears, and made it the ideal outdoor instrument. It became also the lead instrument for the town bands, the *Stadtpfeifer*, the city waits—our word *wait* comes from it, for one of its names in English was "wait" or "wait pipe" from the Maghribi (North African) Arabic *ghaita*. At Beverley Minster, the guild church for all the minstrels of northern England between the rivers Trent and Tweed, many musicians appear in carvings on the walls. The only two who wear swords, showing that

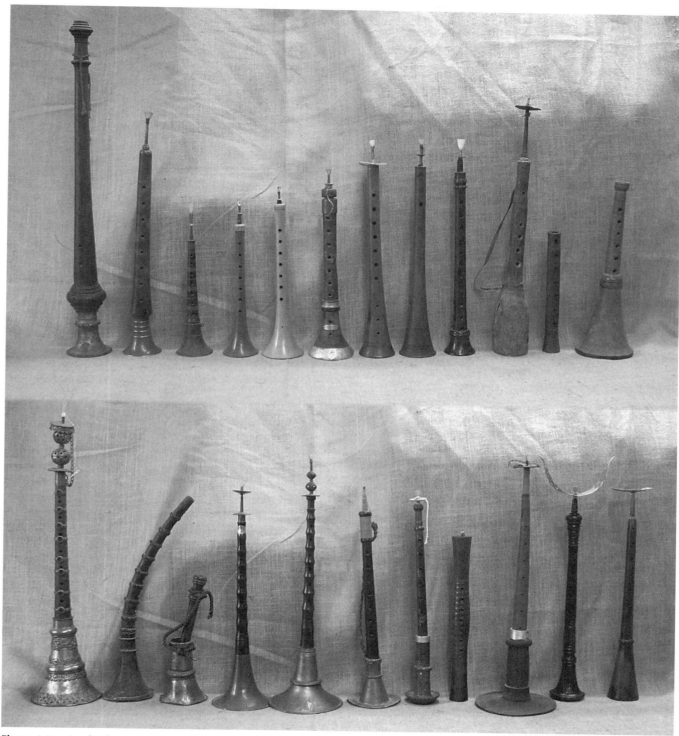

Figure 4.3. Exotic Shawms

Above, L–R: *sruti*, drone shawm, India (I 178); *shahnā'ī*, India (X 50); *horanāva*, Sri Lanka (V 188); two *zurna*, Turkey (XI 36b and 36a); *mizmar*, Assiut, Egypt (VIII 36); three Moroccan *ghaita*, the second turned to show the thumbhole, the third a quieter shawm (III 188, IX 188, and XII 294); *algaita*, Hausa, Nigeria (XII 120); *chirimía*, Oaxaca, southern Mexico, lacking its long metal staple (VII 234); *chirimía*, Isthmus of Tuantepec, Mexico, also missing its staple (V 186).

Below, L–R: *rgya-gling*, Tibet (IX 28); *mvahli*, Nepal (X 56); *hnè-galei*, Myanmar (X 54); two *suona*, one northern Chinese (VI 154) and one southern Chinese (V 190); *pī mōn*, northern Thailand (VIII 224b); *pī chawā*, Thailand (X 104); *pī klāng*, Bangkok, Thailand (VI 122); *pre-ret*, Lombok, Indonesia (IX 232); *tarompèt*, Sunda, western Java (IX 230); *serunèn*, Madura, Indonesia (XIII 160).

they were the leaders of the guilds, are the two tenor shawm or bombard players.[14]

From the Near East, it spread eastward, too, still taking its Arabic name with it, for *zurna* became *shahnāī* in India, *serunai* in Malaysia, *sona* in China, and similar names elsewhere, and its presence is taken by anthropologists as evidence for contact with Islam. In Turkey, where the shawm was the melody instrument of the Janissary bands, an important modification took place with the introduction of a forked headpiece.

The instruments of cylindrical bore are comparatively easy to make, for one can either push the central pith out of a type of wood that permits such action—elder, for example—or a hot iron or some form of drill bit can produce a central hole down any straight piece of wood, though care is needed to avoid the tool wandering offline and breaking through the side wall. A widening bore is much more difficult to produce, however. The expanding bell at the end is fairly simple, for it is within the reach of any knife, and the exterior is not too difficult to carve to shape. But the main part of the interior is much more difficult, unless one has the reamers that were described above with the transverse flutes. If so, a cylindrical pilot bore can be drilled and this can be followed by one or more reamers, with which the pilot bore can be widened progressively to the shape required. An alternative method is to use a stepped taper. This can sometimes be seen with folk instruments from communities that do not have access to complex tools: for example, a set of short bamboo or reed tubes, each stepped into the next one larger. The *phupphu* of the Nagas, a bamboo bugle with a flared bell made from a segment of gourd, was made in this way, and shawms similarly made have been seen in villages in India.[15]

The Turkish shawm that was diffused throughout the Ottoman Empire, and so is found today from Morocco to the Caucasus and into the former Yugoslavia, has a cylindrical body with an expanding bell. Inserted into the top of the bore is a wooden forked head that forms a stepped expanding bore (see figure 4.4).[16] At the top of the fork, a short cylindrical hole is bored through its head, continuing into the stem. A short metal tube is inserted into the top, the staple on the end of which the reed is set. Partway down the stem, the fork is cut away to form two tines that will go down the sides of the instrument's bore. The cutaway part is not the same length on both faces; the front, that toward the fingerholes, is cut away higher than the back, because the thumbhole is set lower than the topmost fingerhole. In this way, we have five steps, each wider than the one before: first, the metal staple that usually expands slightly in bore; then slightly wider, the bore through the head into the stem; third, the upper part of the cutout between the tines, which of course is wider from back to front than from side to side; fourth, the lower part of the cutout that, because it goes from back to front of the instrument, is even wider in that direction than before, often widening from side to side if the tines are not the same thickness from top to bottom; and fifth, the short distance past the points of the tines, which are often cut to a point from front to back and from side to side. This forked head, varying in length from an inch and a half to three or four inches, is a stepped taper and suffices to turn an instrument of cylindrical bore into one that is effectively widening—and all without the need for reamers or any such tools, for the fork can be made with any boring tool and a knife.

The shawm still has a very active existence throughout what was once the Ottoman Empire and almost everywhere to its east, certainly as far as China and Indonesia. In figure 4.3 above, we can see shawms from Turkey, Egypt, Morocco, Nigeria, India, Sri Lanka, Tibet, Nepal, Burma, Thailand, Java and other parts of Indonesia, China, and Mexico. The instrument survives also in parts of Europe, especially in the south, as

Figure 4.4. *Ghaita* **Fork**
Moroccan (III 188).

well as in the Balkans, as we can see in figure 4.5 with shawms from Macedonia; Hungary; Iberia, including Catalunya and Euskal Herria, the Basque country; and Italy and Brittany, where they are played with the bagpipes, the *zampogna* and the *biniou*, respectively, as well as a reproduction of a medieval European shawm. It is as the chanter or melody pipe of a bagpipe that the shawm survives in Britain and many other countries, and the chanter of a Scottish Highland pipe is therefore also shown in figure 4.5.

We have described above the technique of circular breathing. This method is taught to children with the aid of a glass of water and a straw, or the local equivalents. The child learns to keep the water bubbling without break or pause. This is not too difficult. What takes

much more practice is the art of keeping the pressure steady, of equalizing the air pressure from the cheeks with that of the pressure from the diaphragm as one changes constantly from the one to the other. If the air pressure drops, so inevitably does the pitch, to the detriment of the melody. This difficulty can be obviated by the use of an external reservoir such as a bag, for the bag can be filled with air from the mouth, or a pair of bellows, and a steady pressure maintained by squeezing the bag between the arm and the body.

The first recorded uses of a bagpipe have been attributed to the Roman emperor Nero and, though with less certainty, to references in two plays by Aristophanes.[17] Nero was said to have played "the aulos both with his mouth, and also with the armpit, a bag being thrown

Figure 4.5.   European Shawms

L–R: *zurla*, tenor and treble, Macedonia (IV 160 and 162); *tárogató*, modern version by József Bige, Budapest, Hungary (V 192); *ciaramella*, Italy (IX 34); *dolçaina*, Valencia, Spain (XI 100); *gralla sec*, by Xavier Auriols, Vilanova, Catalunya (XI 170); *dultzaina*, by Jose Manuel Agirre, Tolosa, Euskal Herria (XII 146); from the Franco-Spanish border near Irún, Euskal Herria (XII 94); *bombarde*, Brittany (IX 94); chanter from Highland great pipes, *piob mhór*, by P. Henderson, Glasgow, Scotland (II 216); reproduction of English medieval treble shawm by Laurence Wright, Llanfair Pwllgwyngyll, Anglesey, Wales (VII 86).

under it."[18] The second-century writer Dio Chrysostom tells us that this was to avoid the disfigurement of distended cheeks that results from the use of circular breathing. An additional advantage is that the player can sing to his own accompaniment, something that is still heard today in some areas. With the mouth-blown pipes, this is possible only in short phrases before the air in the bag runs out. The desire to sing without interruption may be one reason for the adoption of the bellows bagpipes.

Today the world of bagpipes is divided between those that have a cylindrical chanter and those with an expanding-bore chanter. The former are always quiet and are found in many parts of the world. They are also often indoor or parlor pipes such as the French court *musette*, the Northumbrian small-pipes, and the Irish *uillean* pipes. The expanding-bore pipes include all the louder bagpipes of western Europe, such as the Scottish, Spanish, Italian, Breton, and most of the other French types. We have already noted the advantage of a bag to accompany the melody with a single or multiple drone, and adding a second chanter, one can also provide a counter-melody, as on the Italian zampogna. The Irish uillean pipes have the most elaborate series of additional pipes, for as well as drones, they have the regulators. These are pipes with a series of keys that can be opened by the player's forearm while his fingers are occupied with the chanter, and so provide a range of chords. Thus they are the world's only bagpipes that can add a full and varying harmony to accompany the melody, in addition to the steady but unchanging harmony of the drones.

Oboes and Bassoons

The shawm was in one respect its own worst enemy. It was, as we said, the main melody instrument for all outdoor celebrations and processions of the Middle Ages and Renaissance, but when brought indoors, its sound was ear-splitting. In those days, this was no great problem, because the same music could be played on flutes or fiddles or other quiet instruments. It only became a problem when, in the later seventeenth century, composers began to think of the color of their music and, instead of writing music that could be played on any convenient instruments, wanted to specify the instruments and so control the sounds of the music as well as the notes.

When Lully was writing ballets for the French court of Louis XIV, he often wrote for specific groups or types of dancers, whether dressed as villagers, sailors, soldiers, or peoples from different countries, and he wrote his music to suit each group, changing the instrumentation as he thought appropriate. Some would be on strings, some on flutes (recorders then, of course), or the martial trumpets and drums, or the "oboe band" that in his early days meant shawms of different sizes. Many of these ballets were performed in the gardens of the palaces of Versailles and the courtyards of the Tuileries, which was pleasant enough in summer, but less so in winter, prompting a move indoors. And while the flutes and strings sounded fine inside, probably better than they did outdoors, the shawms were less tolerable, even though by lipping the reed, rather than keeping it pouched within the mouth cavity, the noise level could be significantly reduced. One might compare today the sound of the Indian shahnā'ī, whose players lip the reed, rendering it a pleasant indoor instrument, with that of the Chinese sona and Moroccan zurla, whose sound rings loud within the ear, or with the Highland bagpipe, to hear the difference. An additional disadvantage of the shawm was that its melodic range was somewhat limited.

As a result, the search began for a quieter *hautbois*, the French name literally "high wood" but meaning "loud wood," from which word our Old English *hoboy* and later *oboe* derive.[19] The quest was led by musicians at the French court who were both players and makers of instruments, principally members of the Hotteterre family, and the result was our oboe. There were many important differences. The reeds became longer, softer, and narrower. Whereas the lowest fingerhole of the shawm was less than halfway down the body, the fingerholes of the oboe were smaller than those of the shawm and were spread more evenly down the body, so that the distance between the lowest and the bell was much shorter. Within a generation, it became usual to replace the left-hand ring-finger hole and the right forefinger hole each with two small holes that could be opened separately to obtain the chromatic notes G♯ and F♯, or opened together for the A♮ and G♮ of the main diatonic scale. The bell, instead of opening smoothly to the end, now had an internal lip that reduced its area. And two keys were provided: the lower, the great key, normally standing open but when closed extending the range downward to middle C; and a small key, often duplicated to be played by either hand (whichever was the lower), standing closed and when opened producing E♭.[20] As a result of these changes, the range was greater, now comparing with that of the violin, the tuning was much more within the control of the player, and the sound was quieter, more eloquent, and more pleasant.

For some circles, though, the instrument was now too quiet, so an intermediate form was developed in Germany and Holland, probably for military and similar use. This version is usually known today by its German name *deutsche Schalmey*. It was long thought that it must have been a form coming developmentally between shawm and oboe, but all the evidence known today shows that it was devised later than the earliest oboes. Because most of the surviving examples are in museums—most of which are reluctant to allow their instruments to be played—little is known of its playing characteristics.

The first oboes had the three keys described—the great key and duplicated small key—but by 1800 the left-hand small key had been abandoned, for with very few exceptions everybody was playing the way in which we do now, the left hand above the right. The reed became longer and narrower almost with each decade, which means today that players of reproductions, or where possible of surviving original instruments, must experiment and produce a new pattern of reed for almost every oboe they play. The new reeds were so responsive to the player, and cross-fingering for chromatic notes was so successful, aided as it was by the duplicated fingerholes, that the oboe did not acquire the extra keys that we saw on the flute until after 1810 or so.

As with all the woodwinds, each country had its own pattern of oboe with different styles of turning, body shape, and bore shape so that the tonal character differed from place to place. Two very different types of two-key oboe from Britain can be seen in figure 4.6, both by members of the Milhouse family of makers, both dated to around 1800, one the more usual bulb-top, the other a straight-top. The latter is badly curved because boxwood, the normal material for all flutes, oboes, and clarinets of this period, is so affected by changes of humidity that it may warp. The London maker Cornelius Ward said that boxwood was more suited to a hygrometer than to a musical instrument, and as soon as more elaborate keywork was added, that might jam as the wood expanded and contracted, makers began to use more stable materials such as African blackwood. This change was aided by the commercial exploration of Africa and other countries and the importation of such woods.

While blackwood is much more stable than boxwood, it can still be affected by rapid changes of humidity, so substitutes such as ebonite (vulcanized rubber) and today various plastics, which are also much cheaper than wood, are sometimes seen. Metal has never been popular for the oboe, though the French bandmaster Pierre Auguste Sarrus introduced a whole family of metal equivalents, the sarrusophones, from treble to bass. These were short-lived, only the bass surviving for more than a generation, and even that was soon replaced by a much wider-bored version, the *contrebass-à-anche* or reed-contrabass that remained in band-instrument catalogues until very recently, for it added a sharp-attack punch to the sound of the bass tubas.

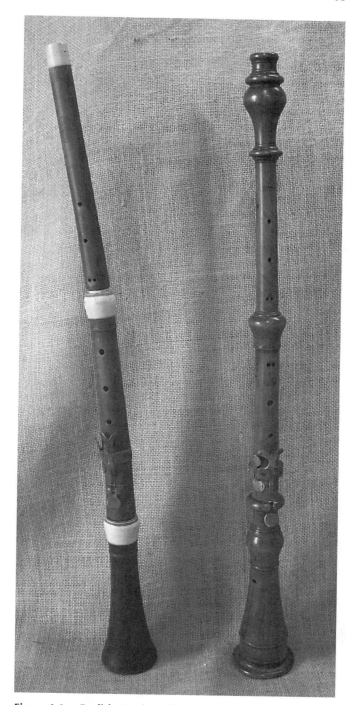

Figure 4.6. English Two-key Oboes, c. 1800
L–R: boxwood and ivory straight-top, by Richard Milhouse, Newark (XIII 140); boxwood bulb-top, by his brother William Milhouse, London (I 188).

Gradually, as musical styles became more complex and more chromatically inclined, extra keys became necessary, upward from the bottom for middle C♯, F♮ plus a vent to stabilize that note, G♯, B♭, and the upper C♮, and a speaker key to assist overblowing to the upper register.

In addition, the range was increased. The two-key oboes had two open holes on the bell that improved the sound and the tuning. One of these was now covered with a key to produce B♮ as the lowest note. Further keys were added in the 1820s to provide alternative fingerings for these chromatic notes, so that some could be taken with either hand, whichever might be the more convenient in any musical context. After Boehm had introduced his first model of flute, some of his devices such as the brille were adopted on the oboe also, as may be seen in figure 4.7.

Further developments took place in France in the second half of the nineteenth century at the hands of the Triébert family, father and son, followed by their foreman and successor, Lorée, with a series of systems culminating in the two that are mainly used today, the thumb-plate and the Conservatoire. Less common are the Barret system, which combines both thumb-plate and Conservatoire systems, and the Boehm system. The latter, because of its larger finger fingerholes, produces a rather coarser tone quality. However, it is also rather louder than the normal oboe, and that has sometimes made it popular for military bands. It is also useful for those who play other Boehm-system instruments, because its fingering is similar to that of the flute and saxophone, making it easier to put one instrument down and pick up another with only a bar or two between.

Like the Renaissance shawm and all the instruments of that period, that had come in sizes from treble to bass and more rarely contrabass, the oboe was one of a family from its earliest times. When it first appeared in France, it was accompanied by the *cromornes* (these should not be confused with the crumhorns, which we shall see below). The cromornes were a form of larger-size oboes—alto, tenor, and bass—playing the lower parts in the oboe band.[21] They were awkward to handle and, because the fingerholes were wider apart, they needed extension keys to cover them. As the oboe was further developed, the cromornes were replaced by the *oboe d'amore*, an alto in A, a third lower than the oboe, and by the *taille* or tenor oboe, a fifth lower in F. The tenor was built in two forms, one straight like the cromorne, the other curved with a widely flared metal bell, which we assume to be that known as the *oboe da caccia*.[22] All three, especially the d'amore and caccia, appear frequently in Bach's cantatas and other choral works.

The d'amore, and occasionally the taille, had a bulb bell that gave a special character to the sound. The d'amore died out, chiefly perhaps due to the extension of the oboe's range to B♭, only a semitone less than that of the d'amore. It was revived in the late nineteenth century for the performance of Bach's works and has also been scored by some modern composers.

The tenor sizes were replaced by the *cor anglais* (or English horn), which, like the caccia, was initially made with a curved body so that the player's fingers could more easily span the holes (see figure 4.8). How its name arose nobody knows, for there was never any horn of this type in England, but it has been suggested that the original name was *cor anglé* or "bent horn." Because it and the d'amore are played by the oboists, their fingering systems have always paralleled those of the oboe.

Bass oboes, later also called *hautbois baryton*, have always been available, though rare, for they tend to be large, expensive, and less efficient than the bassoons that

Figure 4.7.   Keyed Oboes

Above, L–R: ten-key, by Henry Wylde, London (215); thirteen-key Sellner system, by Stephan Koch, Vienna (210); fifteen-key, by J. T. Uhlmann, Vienna (214); sixteen-key + brille, by H. F. Meyer, Hanover (230); eight-key, by Guillaume Triébert, Paris (219).

Below, five oboes by Frédéric Triébert, Paris, L–R: eleven-key (221); système 3 (238); système 4 (236); full Barret system (239); Boehm system (237), *courtesy Bate Collection, University of Oxford.*

Figure 4.8. English Horns

L–R: *cor anglais moderne*, nine-key, by Henri Brod, Paris (249); twelve-key, by J. T. Uhlmann, Vienna (254); ten-key + brille, by Frédéric Triébert, Paris (252), *courtesy Bate Collection, University of Oxford.*

cover a similar but wider range. The German maker Heckel produced his own version of a bass oboe, called a heckelphone, wider bored than the French and therefore louder, though rather honking in tone.

The bass shawm was an unwieldy instrument, and the contrabass, more than six feet long, was even worse. A more portable version was produced, known in English as the curtal because its length was curtailed.[23] This was a single piece of wood with two parallel bores, linked together at the bottom, in effect a bass shawm folded in half in one piece of wood. Its sound was rather quieter than that of the shawm (hence the German name *Dulzian*, as in dulcet), and it, like the shawms, was made in a family; the most common size was the bass. The curtal continued in use in Spain, in all its sizes, certainly up to the end of the nineteenth century and perhaps into the early twentieth, under the name of *bajón*, as an instrument for church music.

Exactly when it was converted into the bassoon, similar in shape but made in separate joints, is still a matter of controversy, and certainly some versions of jointed curtal seem to have existed earlier than the oboe.[24] Nev-

ertheless, as we have already seen, instruments such as the cromorne were still providing a bass to the oboe before the bassoon was introduced, the earliest confirmed dates for which are in the 1670s.

As well as differences in fingerhole placement and the manufacture in separate joints, the most important difference between bass curtal and bassoon is the addition of the bell joint that extends the range from the bass C to B-flat. The bassoon is made in five separate pieces: the crook or bocal, which had also been used on the curtal, a curved metal tube that carries the reed on the narrow end; the wing or tenor joint, so called because a wing-shaped protrusion extends over the bass joint so that fingerholes can be closer together; the butt or boot that retains the old double bore, down and up through one piece of wood with a U-bend at the bottom; the long or bass joint that comes up from the boot; and at the top, the bell. The wing and the downward bore of the boot carry all the fingerholes, and the upward bore and the long joint carry two thumbholes plus keys for the thumb to cover other holes.

The bassoon is exceptional among woodwind instruments in that the normal range, comparable to that of the oboe or flute down to D, goes down to the bottom of the boot, with a lowest note G. Closing an open-standing key gives F, the equivalent of the oboe's and flute's middle C, a twelfth (an octave plus a fifth) lower. Then a series of thumbholes and keys controls the upward bore from the bottom of the boot to the bell, extending the range to the bottom B-flat.

This is why, as in figure 4.9, it is important to see both sides of a bassoon, the finger-side and the thumb-side. It is also why a bassoonist has to work far harder with the thumbs than any other woodwind player, why the upper range of a bassoon tends to be idiosyncratic, and why bassoonists have to experiment with different upper-note fingerings to find the ones that best suit any individual instrument. Like all other woodwinds, keywork began quite simply, initially with three keys: a great key to close the lowest downward hole; a lesser key for the low A♭, equivalent to the oboe's E♭; and to produce D, an open thumb key covering a hole between the thumbholes—a lower, right-hand thumbhole for E, and an upper, left-hand thumbhole for C. Closing the C hole produced B♭ from the bell. Extra keys were soon added, as on the other instruments, with the usual differences and preferences for somewhat different tone qualities from one country to another. With the advent of more complex mechanisms, two main schools developed, the French and the German.

The French system was developed by Savary in Paris, followed by Buffet, and remained close in bore design and sound to the instrument of the Classical period of

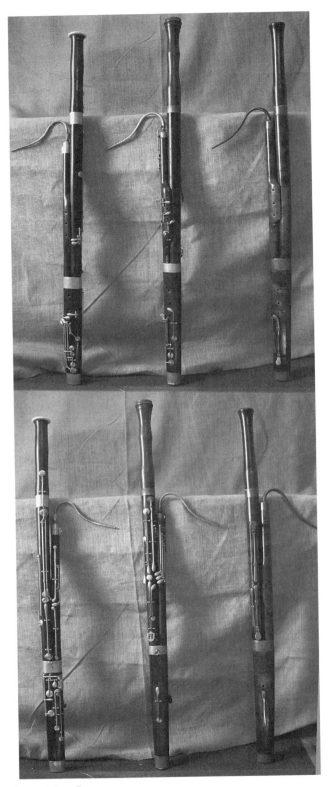

Figure 4.9. Bassoons

Finger-side (above) and thumb-side (below), L–R: German system (Almenräder), pre-1880, by Alexander, Mainz (VII 224); French system, post-1895, by Hawkes, London (II 60); six-key English, c. 1799, marked "Goulding, London," perhaps by John Hale, London (II 62).

the late eighteenth and early nineteenth centuries. Extra keys eliminated the need for many cross-fingerings, but did not prevent the instrument from retaining its sweetness of tone and characteristic differences of tonal quality in different registers. However, there were still some difficult notes that needed humoring and sometimes experimenting with different combinations of fingering to vent them clearly and reliably.

Carl Almenräder in Germany determined to eradicate the similar problems of the German-style bassoon, also in the 1820s, by moving and widening some tone holes, making some changes in the bore, and therefore having to devise a different key system, but in doing so, he produced an instrument with a much harder tone than the older bassoon and than the French. Over a number of years, and by constant tinkering with small changes in the bore, Johann Adam Heckel and his son Wilhelm, of Biebrich, gradually ameliorated this harshness and, before the end of the nineteenth century, had produced the German system that is mainly used today, even in France.[25] It is much more secure than the French system, especially in the upper register, with a far more even tone quality from top to bottom of the range. Some players consider the tone *too* even and less interesting than that of the French, so there are always some who gravitate back to the French system. Several makers in different countries experimented with a Boehm-system bassoon, but this had so open a tone and such evenness throughout the compass that it no longer sounded like a bassoon, and as a result it has never been popular.

A variant of the Boehm system was used on the contrabassophone, an instrument that was much louder than the normal contrabassoon. Double bassoons led a somewhat checkered existence from the mid-eighteenth century. Early instruments, such as that used by Handel, an instrument by Stanesby Junior of London that survives in Dublin, were an octave lower than the normal instrument with a lowest note of BB♭, but there was a later tendency to save wood, and cost, by restricting the range to bottom D or C, or even, with quart-bassoons, to E-flat or F. Tenor bassoons, sometimes called tenoroons, also existed, but while there is some repertoire for them, a more common use seems to have been for teaching children whose hands were too small to stretch to the fingerholes of a full-size bassoon. This is less necessary today with the advent of modern keywork.

Let us return now to the Renaissance. As well as the loud shawms with their widening bore, there were several double-reed instruments with a cylindrical bore and therefore a much quieter sound. One, whose name was known but was otherwise a mystery until the sole surviving example was found in the wreck of Henry VIII's warship the *Mary Rose*, was the *douçaine* or still shawm ("still" as in quiet).[26] Another was the family of crumhorns, from treble to great-bass. These were curved up at the end (*Krumm* in German).[27] Unlike many other instruments, instead of the reed being in the player's mouth, it was contained in a windcap. As a result, the player could not control the reed directly, and the instrument did not overblow to an upper register but was limited to a range of an octave plus one or two further notes. Like all reed-blown instruments of cylindrical bore, it sounded lower than an expanding-bore instrument of similar size, so that it produced a useful bass to recorders and other quiet instruments. It had a short existence, little more than a century, from around 1500. It is mentioned here partly to warn against the tendency, because it is quite easy to play and looks interesting, to extend its period of use backward into medieval ensembles and onward into those of the early baroque.

A third quiet instrument was the racket. This was a very small instrument, less than six inches high, plus its pirouette that held the reed, with a dozen or so bores, each linked at top and bottom, so that it was a long instrument with a bass range, folded up into a very compact shape. A somewhat larger descendant was occasionally made in the eighteenth century but now with an expanding bore, in effect a tightly folded bassoon, also called racket or sometimes "sausage bassoon" (therefore called *cervelat* in French, the name of a variety of sausage).

Finally, we should look at an instrument that was in effect a re-creation of the shawm, though now with a single reed lipped by the player and therefore without the loud ringing sound. This was the creation of the Belgian maker Adolphe Sax, who, on the strength of its success, was persuaded by a number of composers, among them Hector Berlioz, to move to Paris in the early 1840s. Like many other makers of the period, he named the instrument after himself, as the saxophone. Its origin seems to have been an ophicleide (we shall meet this among the serpents in chapter 5—the name is a mixture of French and Greek for "keyed snake"), played with a bass clarinet mouthpiece.[28] It was made of brass, with wide tone-holes and therefore fully keyed, for the holes are too wide to cover with the fingers.

Sax produced two families, from soprano to bass, made in alternating keys of F and C for orchestral use, and E♭ and B♭ for bands. The F and C family has been little used, though the tenor, often called the "C melody," was popular in dance bands for musicians who doubled on other instruments and did not wish to transpose cello or bas-

soon parts onto the B-flat tenor when playing arrangements that originally required those instruments.

A wooden version of the soprano saxophone was devised by Wenzel Schunda in the late nineteenth century to replace the Hungarian shawm *tárogató*, which had been banned because its sound was too exciting and led to rebellion against the Austrian rule over that country. He retained the original name but produced a quieter version of the shawm. If, however, instead of lipping the reed, one puts the lips down to its base or onto the metal ligature that holds it in place, much of the original shawm sound results, and the same is true of the saxophone. That is why I said above that Sax had re-created the shawm.

Clarinets and Other Single Reeds

At the beginning of this chapter, we said that "the simple single reeds, often called 'folk clarinets,' are far more common in the world today than any simple double reeds." This is indeed true. Wherever reeds grow, wherever cane is common, with few exceptions, these instruments exist. Nor are these the only materials. Goose quills are used as reed whistles and are also placed in the tops of instruments to generate the sound.[29] In our culture, we use metal for the reed registers of our organ pipes (which are described in chapter 7; the reed from one was illustrated above, in figure 4.1). We also used a metal single reed in the old-fashioned bulb motor horns and also in many squawkers (see figure 4.10), bird and animal lures, and children's toys, though nowadays their reeds are usually of plastic rather than metal.

The bird and animal lures had an important ritual ancestry along the Pacific Northwest coast of Canada, for the tribes there carved much larger instruments from cedar or spruce, a foot or more long, of similar types to represent the sounds of their totem animals.[30] Some are double reeds, the wood split into two halves and each half carved down at one end to leave a thin blade, with the rest of the body hollowed as a resonance chamber, in effect a giant bassoon reed. Single reeds are both single and twin—a blade in one half and the shallot (to use the organ term for the equivalent of the clarinet's mouthpiece) in the other, or a blade carved down in each half with a solid piece between, against which each blade can vibrate. All these forms are now reproduced in miniature, with plastic reeds, as modern game lures.

More common, and perhaps more interesting for us, are those that generate the sound of musical instruments (see figure 4.11). These come in two forms: the truly idioglot and the "idioglot-heterozeug."[31] With the former,

Figure 4.10. Reed Squawkers

Back row, L–R: toy bellows-blown squawk (VIII 166); plastic bulb squawk (VI 170); variable pitch warbler, Taiwan (XI 132b); "Crocodile Pipe," Fürth, Germany (XII 142); coon call, by Mallardtone, Moline, Illinois (V 138d); crow call, also by Mallardtone (V 138c); goose call, by Black Duck, Whiting, Indiana (V 138b).

Middle row, L–R: coiled children's party squawk (XII 130); the "cry" from a child's doll, England (X 198); fox call, rubber-band ribbon reed, by Burnham Bros., Marble Falls, Texas (V 138a).

Front row, L–R: Motor horn "as fitted to Rolls-Royce," c. 1920, England (III 112g); pitch pipe (A = 434 Hz) on violin mute (IV 12e); child's bicycle horn, by McDonald's Corp., made in China (XI 76).

everything is in one piece—mouthpiece, reed, and body. This is clearly the earlier form of the instrument, easily made by slicing a reed in the top of the tube and boring or burning fingerholes below. It suffers, however, from the disadvantage that no reed is permanent. Reeds soften, distort, or break, and then the instrument is useless. But with a heterozeug—the mouthpiece with its idioglot reed inserted into a separate body—when the reed suffers, the mouthpiece can be thrown away and a new one made and inserted into the body. There is then no need to replace the body as well as the reed, thus greatly reducing the time and effort required for replacement. Similar reeds are used in the drones of our Highland bagpipe and are found with most bagpipes whose chanters or drones are cylindrical in bore.

Of the many instruments of this type around the world, one of the commonest is the double pipe endemic in the Arab world (see figure 4.12). Little boys hawk these in the bazaars to tourists, and better quality ones are played by musicians. The player covers each pair of holes with a single finger, and the two parallel pipes are very slightly out of tune with each other, just enough that the resulting vibration strengthens the sound. As with the shawm, the reed is pouched in the mouth to below the end of its tongue—necessary because if the player's lip touched the tongue, it would hold it closed against the mouthpiece. A common exception to this is found in India, where the *punghi* has its mouthpieces within a gourd or coconut. These instruments are often called snake charmers' pipes, for this is one of their frequent uses.

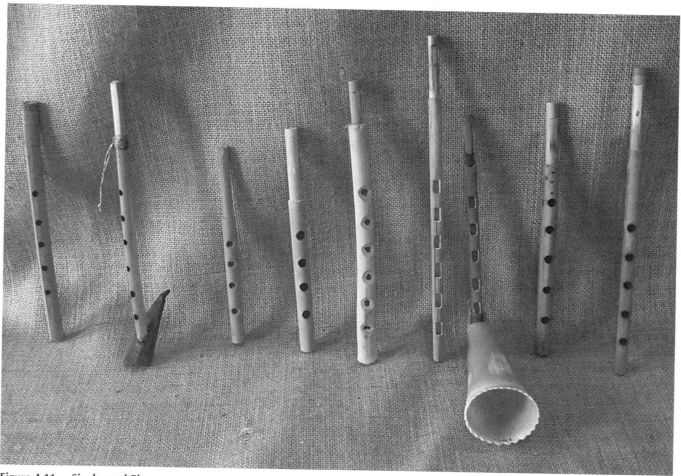

Figure 4.11. Single-reed Pipes

L–R: Crete (VIII 150); Eivissa (XI 98); Sunda, Java (IX 226); *bansi*, Padang, western Sumatra (XI 114); bagless chanter, Hungary (IX 100); two *péschtschiki* or *schaleika*, one with horn bell, Belgorod people, southern Russia (XII 86b and 86a); two single-reed pipes, Turkey (XIII 32b and 32a).

One of the instruments in figure 4.12 has had its tongues broken off to show what lies behind them. The reeds are either up-cut, cut from below and remaining attached at the top, or down-cut. The danger with the latter is that the vibration of the tongue may encourage the cut to lengthen until it eventually falls off the end, whereas the integral node at the top that closes the mouthpiece adds strength to the up-cut. The mouthpiece must be closed at the top, for if it were open, the breath would go straight down the tube rather than forcing the tongue to vibrate. The one advantage of the down-cut reed is that the player can use the lips as a bridle, to control the vibrating length of the reed and thus its pitch. The organ reed illustrated in figure 4.1 has a wire bridle so that it can be tuned by sliding it up or down the brass reed, and bagpipe drone reeds, also shown in figure 4.1, frequently have a string bridle tied around them to tune them.

The same continuous breathing that is normal on the shawm is used on these instruments as well, and for the same reasons they are often played as the chanters of a bagpipe. Figure 4.12 shows two versions of the Tunisian *zukra*, one mouth-blown and the other bag-blown.

In some other areas, for example, in Wales in older times, where the pibcorn or hornpipe survived longer than it did in England, and still in the Basque country with the *alboka*, the reeds are placed in a windcap, often made of horn. This protects the reeds from damage and keeps them dry, aiding their longevity, and the windcap functions in much the same way as the pirouette on the shawm, helping the player to keep an airtight seal around the lips while cheek-pumping. The Russian reed *rozhok* (not to be confused with the other form of rozhok that has a trumpet-type mouthpiece) has lost its reed cap, if it ever had one, but in the Balkans, where the bagpipe version may be less often used, the chanter is used by itself,

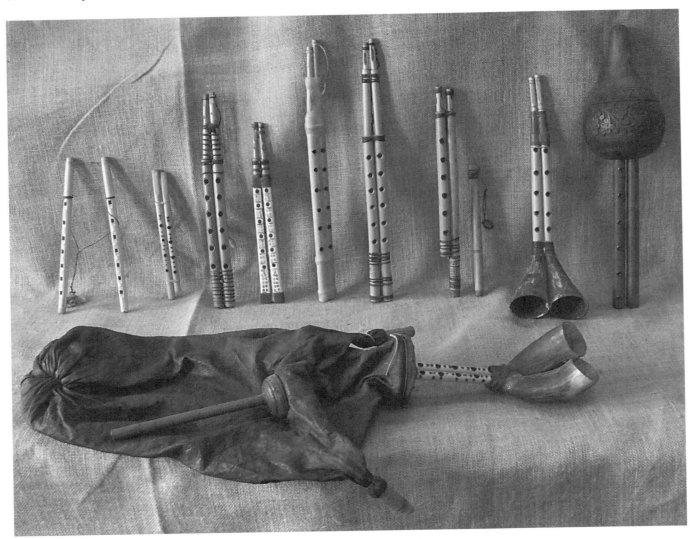

Figure 4.12. Geminate pipes

Rear, L–R: *qoshnai*, Horesm, Uzbekistan (XII 164); *reclam de xeremia*, Eivissa (XI 96); *zummāra*, Egypt (I 150a); zummāra, bird-bone pipes, probably Arabia (I 150b); zummāra, Israel (VIII 122); zummāra, with reeds broken away to show the lay (XII 134); *arghūl*, with one of its drone extensions, Egypt (I 148a); *zukra*, Tunisia (III 36); *pūnghī* with wooden wind chamber, India (VIII 42).

Foreground: bagged zukra, Tunisia (V 258).

still with its stock that is now a wooden windcap. As shown in figure 4.13, there is still often a groove at the top where it would have been tied into the bag.

In West Africa, a side-blown version is used (see figure 4.14). Here the reed is so light and flexible that it can be sounded both by blowing and sucking. In the smaller version, the *til'boro*, the player places the lips across the tube; in the larger, the *damalgo*, the reed is set into a gourd, into which the player blows, with a second gourd at the other end that has a fingerhole cut into it.

An instrument very similar to the tilboro, also leather covered but with the reed shorter and closer to the head so that it was end-blown, was described in an English in-

struction book as the "mock trumpet" in 1698.[32] The anonymous author gave the fingering for a scale with six fingerholes and a thumbhole and wrote: "Put the Trumpet in your Mouth as far as the Gilded Leather, and blow pretty strong." This is clearly the same instrument as no. 221 in the Royal Military Exhibition of 1890, which is described as

a tube of cane open at the lower end, the upper being closed by a natural joint of the cane. The tube is covered with red leather; and the reed consists of a small tongue detached from the cane itself, and shaved down to the required thickness. . . . The reed is placed on the upper

Figure 4.13. Hornpipes

Rear, L–R: *alboka*, by Leon Bilbao, Euskal Herria (XII 24); two *diple*, Istra, northern Croatia (IX 54 and IX 56); pibcorn, reproduction by Philip Bate, London (VII 122).

Foreground: reed *rozhok*, by Anatoly Zajaruzny, Kiev, Ukraine (VIII 26).

side . . . and therefore the lips could have exercised but little control over the vibrations of the tongue.[33]

This was the only known example of the early version of the *chalumeau* to survive into modern times. It was then in César Snoeck's collection, and like many of his instruments, it went to Berlin, where it was lost in World War II.[34]

We shall probably never know who first improved this instrument with a lathe-turned wooden body of more controlled diameter than the natural cane. A proper mouthpiece, similar to that of the clarinet, was added, along with a seventh fingerhole at the foot, plus two keys at the top of the body to extend the range, one at the front and one at the back. Traditionally the credit is given to Johann Christoph Denner of Nuremberg. Only seven or eight chalumeaux are known to survive, but only one of them is marked "J. C. Denner," and that is thought today to be perhaps by his younger son, Johann David, who continued to use his father's stamp with an

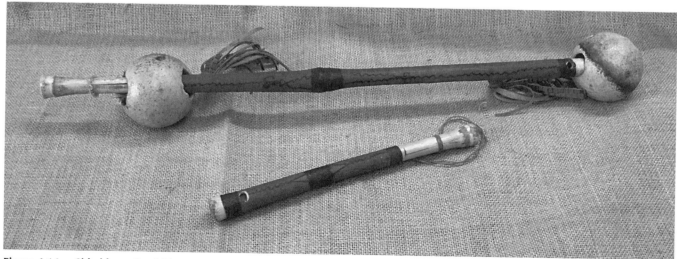

Figure 4.14. Side-blown Reed Pipes

Damalgo (VI 40b), and below, *til'boro* (VI 48), both Zaria, Nigeria.

added D.[35] However, it does seem fairly certain that it was either J. C. Denner or his elder son Jacob who extended and adapted the chalumeau to create the clarinet.

It is generally considered that the chalumeau played mainly in its fundamental register, known on the clarinet as the "chalumeau register," because the rear key is placed too low to function as a speaker and merely adds an extra note to the range. Cary Karp has suggested that it could play in either the fundamental or the overblown register, depending on the adjustment of the reed.[36] The clarinet, however, as its name suggests, was initially used mainly in the upper register where it would sound like a small trumpet, or "clarin-et"—at only 8¼ to 10 inches long (the lengths that Day and Snoeck noted) and "blown pretty strong," the mock trumpet could also have sounded in the trumpet range.

The chalumeau was much like the recorder in appearance, save for the mouthpiece and reed at the top, with the lowest fingerhole twinned for either little finger like on many later recorders. The Denner instrument has a very recorder-like foot. We know that it was made in families, because one soprano, three altos (one of them a *chalumeau d'amour* with a bulb bell), and three tenors survive. To these, Albert Rice has added what may be a bass.[37] Colin Lawson lists much music, often requiring a bass chalumeau, by composers over much of Europe (Vivaldi named it a *salmoè*) into the second half of the eighteenth century, showing that the chalumeau continued in use long after the invention of the clarinet.

The chalumeau seems to have vanished from mainstream music before the end of that century, but it continued as a folk instrument in Norway, as a simplified version of the clarinet, and was revived there by Harald Gilland in the twentieth century. Similar instruments also exist in Denmark and Finland.[38] It also reappeared elsewhere in the twentieth century and more recently as an instrument for children and folk and jazz musicians. The "schools clarinet," as the importer called the German instrument shown in figure 4.15, was designed to take children from recorder to clarinet.[39] Three others, one of them Chinese, are little more than toys. The fourth is a recently invented "folk" instrument of bamboo, from Hawaii. The fifth was popular in the 1920s and '30s for jazz and nightclub dance bands and, because it was so small, it was called the "red-hot fountain pen." Doubtless there are more today than these, so clearly the chalumeau has never really died.

There were three main differences between Denner's chalumeau and clarinet. First was the size and shape of the mouthpiece. This was considerably smaller on the clarinet than on the original chalumeau (unlike the modern chalumeaux shown in figure 4.15), with a window that is wider at the top than at the bottom, whereas the chalumeau window was much the same width throughout. Second, there was added length at the bottom of the body, with a widening bell instead of the recorder-like foot, so that the lowest note was the written F. The third and most important difference was the position and function of the two upper keys.

Which of the Denners—the father, Johann Christoph, or his elder son Jacob—invented the clarinet is not clear, and we have no dates for when either of them did so, but it must have been around 1700 or shortly afterward, because account books show that people were ordering clarinets from Jacob Denner from 1710 on. Of the clarinets said to be by the father, two in Nuremberg were lost in World War II, and others (perhaps those two also) that had been said to be his are now known to have been by the son—their maker's marks were misread. Eric Hoeprich assigned a clarinet in the collection of the University of California at Berkeley to the father, but again there has been dispute about the maker's stamp.[40]

In the same article, Hoeprich made important remarks about the position and functions of the keys. The two keys on the chalumeau were opposite each other and produced the written A and B♭ or B♮ (different authorities vary in this, so perhaps the chalumeaux also varied). Because the thumb key of the clarinet had also to act as a speaker or register key, to lift the range into the upper or overblown register, it had to be placed higher than its original position and the diameter of its hole had to be reduced. The two keys then produced the written A (opening the thumb key), B♭ (opening the front key), and B♮ (opening both). When the third key was added at the top of the bell joint, it was open-standing.[41] Closing it lowered the range to the written E, still the lowest note of the clarinet today.

The reason for the constant repetition of "the written . . ." above is that the clarinet has always been a transposing instrument, with different sizes and therefore different sounding lowest notes. The music, however, is always written with the lowest note as E, and the sound that comes out will be (to use our modern sizes) a tone lower with the B♭ clarinet, a minor third lower with the A, the written note with the C (a size not much used today), and a minor third higher with the smaller E♭. This is so that the fingering will always be the same for the same written note whichever size of clarinet is used. A further complication is that because the clarinet has a

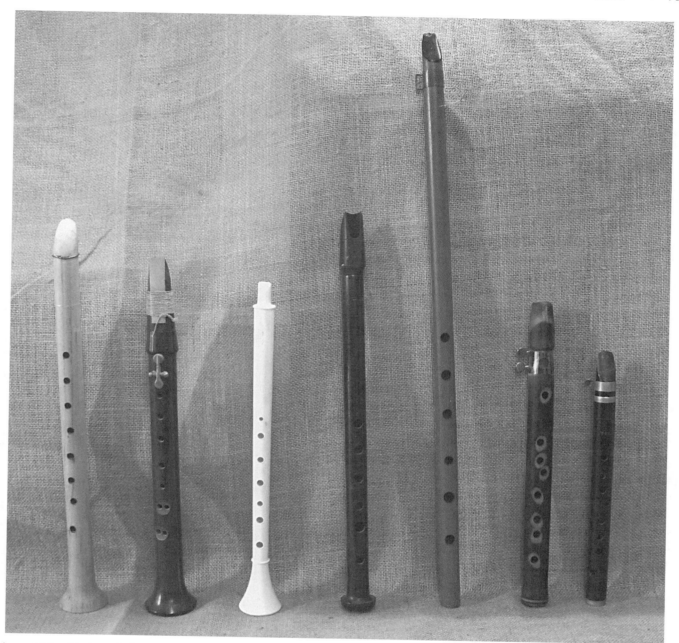

Figure 4.15. Modern *chalumeaux*

L–R: *meråker klarinet*, by Snorre Fjelldal, Trondheim, Norway (XI 78); schools clarinet, by Willy Topf, Taunus, Germany (I 166); plastic toy clarinet, by Pediwest, England (IV 60); child's clarinet, by Barnes & Mullins, London (III 224); bamboo clarinet, China (VIII 178); "Maui Xaphoon," by Brian Lee Whitman, Paia, Hawaii (XII 158); red-hot fountain pen, by Keith Prowse, London (VII 198).

cylindrical bore, it will not overblow octaves, as the recorder, flute, and oboe do, but rather twelfths, an octave plus a fifth. Therefore closing the E key will sound (on the C clarinet for simplicity) that E, but opening the speaker key at the same time sounds the B a twelfth above. Because some writers name keys for what they do in the lower register, and some by what they do in the up-

per, the safest way to name them is by both. That key is therefore the e/b' key.

Hoeprich asks, why was that key added? Many authors have written that it was to produce that overblown upper B, but that note was already available by opening both the upper keys. The answer that he gives, and it seems logical, is so that the hole sizes and placements could be altered, for the front key (instead of the speaker) to give the A, the speaker to give G♯, and both together to give B♭, as became the norm after the mid-eighteenth century. Then the e/b' key would indeed become essential to give the upper B. And thus, Hoeprich suggests, the Berkeley clarinet was indeed all made by the father and was an experimental instrument looking to a future that came into being around 1770.

A fair number of two-key clarinets survive from the first half of the eighteenth century, most of them in D, and so does a good deal of music for them in that tonality, including several concertos. The third key became common from the middle of the century, still often placed so that it could be played by the thumb of whichever hand was the lower, but already sometimes a long key at the left-hand side for the upper little finger. A fourth key for a♭/e♭" was added, between the little-finger holes. These were still duplicated for either little finger on those instruments with the e/b' key for the thumb, and the a♭/e♭" key had a forked touch so that it could be opened by either. When, by the third quarter of the century, another low key was added, this time a closed key that when opened would sound f♯/c♯", it was always placed on the left for the upper little finger beside the e/b' key, and that compelled players to decide that the left hand would be above and the right below. Thus it was the clarinet that finally convinced everybody that they should play that way.

This five-key clarinet was the norm for much of the classical period, and it remained available in makers' catalogues up to the end of the nineteenth century, and occasionally into the twentieth as a cheap instrument for military and other bands. Sometimes a sixth key was added, in England an upper shake key to make trills (then called "shakes") easier, as shown in figure 4.16 in the middle, in other parts of Europe more often a cross c♯'/g♯", as on the right-hand clarinet in that figure, along with other keys that were added in the early nineteenth century.

The five-key clarinet was the equivalent of the one-key flute and two-key oboe, the extra three keys being necessary because of the need for a speaker key to make it overblow and to cope with the complications caused because it overblew to the twelfth instead of the octave. It seems possible that this is why the clarinet was slow to be adopted as a regular member of the orchestra. It was heavier than the other instruments and more expensive, because of the extra keys, and the fingering system was less intuitive because it was different for the same note-name in each octave. And because cross-fingering was less responsive than on the other instruments, it was easier to use in tonalities neighboring its basic pitch than in distant keys. Players therefore needed one clarinet for keys with more than one flat, the B♭; another for keys

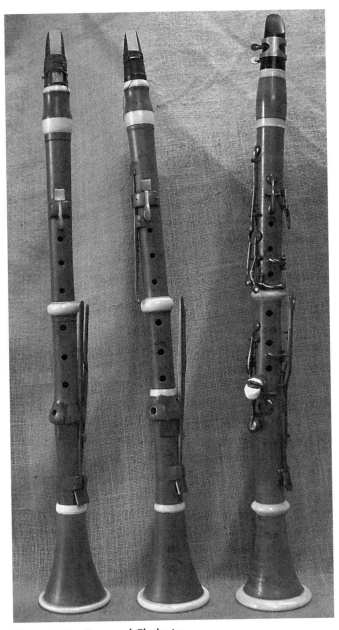

Figure 4.16. Boxwood Clarinets

L–R: five-key, by William Milhouse, London, c. 1800 (III 170); six-key, by James Wood, London, c. 1800 (VI 244); thirteen-key, by Hérouard frères, Paris, c. 1860 (VI 186).

with more than one sharp, the A; and often a third in C for that key and for the keys of F, with one flat, and G, with one sharp—making it more expensive still. As a result, players were perhaps reluctant to buy such a set, and if players did not possess them, composers, who in those days were most often writing for their own local orchestra, did not include them in their music—and, of course, if composers did not write for them, there was no inducement for players to buy them, a classic vicious circle. There were exceptions, and some courts, that of Mannheim, for example, and orchestras made good use of clarinets. They appeared more often in military bands and in opera pits than in concert orchestras, because both were always seeking novelties. The concert platform has always lagged behind the military band and the pit in accepting new instruments; today it is the recording studio, with film and television music, especially perhaps for advertising jingles which always seek new effects, that leads the way. Further keys, up to thirteen, followed in the early nineteenth century. These were no longer the older square-headed keys but were now the more "modern" rounded salt-spoon shape.

In 1810, Iwan Müller in Germany devised a new thirteen-key system, more logically arranged, and at the same time, in an influential published tutor, persuaded players to turn the mouthpiece so that the reed was placed on the lower lip, as it universally is today, instead of against the upper lip as it had always been with the chalumeau and with many early clarinets. With it against the upper lip, control of the high notes is easier but the tone is harder and a tongued staccato is impossible. On the lower lip, the tone is much warmer and rounder, tongued short notes become possible, and control of the high notes becomes a matter of practice and skill. Müller's system was further developed into the "German simple system," acquiring such devices as the brille, a pair of rings resembling a pair of spectacles (*Brille* in German). As with all systems, no two makers did things in the same way, and thus there are differences apparent between the B♭ and C instruments shown in figure 4.17. Eventually Oskar Oehler combined the German simple system with the Albert system plus his own modifications into the modern German system, used also in eastern Europe and Russia.

In Belgium in the mid-nineteenth century, Eugène Albert devised his own simple system, basing it on that of Charles and Adolphe Sax (father and son) with his own modifications, and this became the simple-system clarinet used throughout western Europe (see figure 4.18). In the meantime in France, the player Hyacinthe Klosé and the maker Auguste Buffet had in 1844 devised a more complex system, using the keywork established by Theobald Boehm on his flutes. This is always known as the Boehm system, rather inequitably to its two inventors, especially because while it uses Boehm's keywork mechanism, it does not use his acoustic system of fingerhole sizes in relation to bore diameter. Many players, especially amateurs and bandsmen, found it overly complex, and many professionals preferred the brighter sound of the Albert, which is why that system continued in use well into the twentieth century.

Even more than with other woodwind instruments, there have been many other systems, both between those described and subsequently. Each acquired its own ad-

Figure 4.17. German-system Clarinets, from Müller to Oehler

L–R: in B♭, Iwan Müller system, missing its mouthpiece, perhaps French (VII 20); in B♭, Müller system, missing both mouthpiece and barrel, by Baumgärtel, Mülhausen, Germany (IV 34); in C, elaborated German simple system, by J. Lípa, Nymburk, Czech Republic (III 200); in B♭, part-Oehler system, Russia (XI 244).

herents and each was popular for a while in one center or another, but today systems based on either the Boehm or the Oehler, according to geographical preference—but again with many modifications—are used everywhere.

Like other woodwinds, clarinets have been made in many sizes, from piccolo to double bass. Most of these have been more used in bands and studios than in orchestras, the A♭ and E♭ sopranos and the alto and bass having been particularly important to military bands, while the contrabass is more often heard today in film and television studios than in the orchestra.

One size that was particularly important in the eighteenth and early nineteenth centuries was the basset horn, an alto with a low extension to the written C. The earliest models seem to have been curved in a sickle shape, like the oboe da caccia and the early English horn, and it is possible that this is how it acquired the "horn" part of its name—"basset" being a common term for a smaller bass. Because its bore diameter was the same as on the normal clarinet, the longer tube gave a drier,

Figure 4.18.   Belgian- and French-system Clarinets, from Albert to Boehm

Pair in A and B♭, Albert or simple system, by Hawkes, London (III 222a–b); in C, simple system with two brilles, by Doré, Paris (I 38); in E♭, simple system, by Boosey, London (I 40); in B♭, Boehm system, by Mayer Marix, Paris (III 162).

rather hollow sound that attracted a number of composers, the most famous among them Mozart, who particularly associated it with his Masonic works. The friend for whom he wrote his solo clarinet music, Anton Stadler, had clarinets that also had this extension to low C, and it was for that instrument that Mozart wrote his clarinet quintet and concerto and also the obbligato parts in his late opera *La Clemenza di Tito*. It must, however, have been rare, because all printed editions of the Quintet and Concerto were bowdlerized to suit the normal clarinet.[42]

The use of the clarinet spread into many other musical areas in the nineteenth century. The high A♭ was particularly popular in Italy, and it was an Italian bandmaster who took it to Turkey where it often replaced the shawm in the Janissary bands of the Turkish army. Other sizes were popular among folk musicians in eastern Europe, and the clarinet became a leading member of klezmer and other bands. Within our own areas, it was also a leading instrument in jazz bands and in almost all forms of popular music until the electric guitar supplanted most other instruments in that area.

This spread has been aided by the clarinet's great advantage over other soprano woodwinds such as the oboe in that its cylindrical bore was much more cheaply and easily made than an expanding bore. Its reed, a single blade of cane, was also more easily and cheaply made than the double reeds of the oboe and bassoon and, because it was backed by a strong wooden, or more recently plastic, mouthpiece, it was far less likely to break in use, especially on the march. This has been such an advantage that miniature mouthpieces of similar shape have been made for the bassoon ever since the early nineteenth century (see figure 4.1), and more recently, though less often, for the oboe.

Today, good-quality reed cane is more difficult to obtain than it once was, due to greater demand, leading to premature harvesting and a lack of proper seasoning, and due also to increased atmospheric pollution. A number of artificial materials have been tried in the hope of finding a good replacement for *Arundo donax*, the best quality of which grows in southern France. While none of these has as yet been accepted by professional musicians, they have been more successful on clarinets, and also on saxophones that use a similar mouthpiece, than on the other reed instruments.

Free Reeds

Free reeds exist in two sizes, large and small (see figure G.2). With both, there is a tongue or reed that can move to and fro through a slot within a closely fitting frame, to which it is attached at one end. The frame must fit closely so that the air from the player's mouth can force the reed to move, rather than just passing round it, and to couple its vibration with its resonator. The reed is called "free" because it does not beat against anything. It moves freely up and down, above and below its frame, whereas the single reed beats against its mouthpiece and each blade of the double reed beats against the other.

The large free reeds are too big to blow and so are plucked—although blowing on them at the same time does increase and enrich their sound. They are called Jew's harps, or better "trumps," and will be described in interlude G, "Symbiosis." It is the small ones that we are concerned with here.

We know these in our culture as the reeds for mouth organs or harmonicas, concertinas, accordions, and reed organs of all sorts that were devised from the early nineteenth century on. Free reeds that had long been known in China on the mouth organ, the *sheng* (see figure 4.19), were first properly recognized in Europe in the late eighteenth century, as we shall see.

Figure 4.19.   Mouth Organs and Free-reed Horns

Above, L–R: *raj qeej*, Hmong people, Thailand (X 22b); *sheng*, China (I 172); *khāēn*, Thailand (V 54a); *angkulari*, Iban people, Sarawak (VI 138).

Below, L–R: forester's horn, Germany (with its reed cap) (IV 46); body only of Chinese sheng, lacquered wood instead of the modern metal, showing the holes for the pipes, Shanghai area (VIII 160); side-blown free-reed horn, Myanmar (VIII 226b).

Our books on acoustics usually say that the free reed can produce only a single note, but this is simply not true, except for the way that our instruments are designed. In some parts of Southeast Asia, such as Myanmar and its immediate neighbors, they also exist as a reed on instruments with fingerholes, and there they work like any other reed. Usually there are only a few fingerholes, partly because the reed is set in the side of the tube and one hand is needed to hold the tube firmly to the mouth to avoid air spillage around the sides of the tube. In Thailand, however, the *pì saw* has seven fingerholes and is played with continuous breathing, for the reed will sound both blown and sucked.[43]

Free reeds are used also on buffalo horns, with a single fingerhole in the tip to produce a second pitch. In China, similar reeds are fitted to a conch, but these may only be as toys. Köhler in London made some of his hunting horns with a free reed, both for huntsmen who were incompetent at blowing a horn properly and also to help huntsmen on days so cold that it was difficult to control the lips.[44]

The commonest use in Asia, however, is on mouth organs. These have a set of tubes, usually of bamboo, each with a free reed set into it and each with a small hole in the side of the tube. The size of each reed and the length of each tube are carefully matched, so that they will only couple, and the reed only sound, if the small hole in the side of the tube is closed by a finger; otherwise, they would all sound all the time. By covering these holes, the player can choose whether to sound single notes or chords. The reeds are held within a windchest in which all the pipes stand, or through which they all pass, so that the player's breath reaches every reed simultaneously. In Han Chinese and Japanese formal music, this windchest is a bowl, now usually of wood or metal, although originally it was a gourd. Elsewhere it is most often a wooden tube, but gourds are still used in some places such as Borneo. The reeds will sound on both blowing and drawing, but many are played only by drawing to avoid having the moist air of the breath damage the reeds. Often the pipes are arranged in a decorative order; in China, they traditionally resemble the shape of a phoenix's wings—and the sound is said to resemble the phoenix's cry. This is achieved by cutting tuning slots in the side of each tube to control its sounding length, so that what looks like a long tube may actually sound one of the higher notes.

The sheng has a continuous history in China of three thousand years or more.[45] The Japanese *shō* that derived from it goes back at least to the early centuries of our era, with two instruments surviving in the Shōsōin Depository in Nara.[46] Different forms of mouth organ are used in China by various of the minority peoples, some of them mechanically elaborate with metal pipes and keyboards.[47] One of them, the *hulusheng*, is used among the Miao, as we shall see toward the end of interlude F, to imitate the local speech patterns and so to talk, as well as for dancing.[48]

In Thailand and Laos, the mouth organ called the *khāēn* is also used for dancing, often while playing the instrument—a considerable achievement when one considers that some versions of the khāēn are more than six feet tall and that much body movement is involved, including bending deeply. The khāēn is said to be the sweetest sounding of all mouth organs because its reeds are today made of a special metal: bronze coins from the nineteenth-century reign of King Chulalongkorn Rama V. These coins are smelted and then forged until they are thin enough to be cut to size and shape. Laurence Picken provides a very detailed account of how they and the instruments are made.[49] What seems not to be recorded is what the reeds were made of before that coinage was first struck in 1887. The khāēn was an ancient instrument, perhaps as old as the Chinese sheng. By the fifth century BC, the sheng reeds were of *Arundo*

donax, separate plates with an idioglot reed cut in them, inserted into the bamboo pipes.[50] Presumably at an earlier stage they were truly idioglot, as they still are on some of the free-reed pipes with fingerholes. And presumably the same was true of the khāēn and of the many other mouth organs from this part of the world.[51] Marin Mersenne showed a khāēn in 1636, with a detailed drawing of the reed, but he did not say what it was made of.[52] Nor can one tell from the sixth- and eighth-century Persian Sassanid representations of the sheng on silver bowls and other vessels.[53]

Certainly by the time the sheng arrived in Europe in the eighteenth century, the reeds were of metal. This is when we first took a real interest in the free reed. There are traces of earlier experiments, but because descriptions are vague and no instruments survive, it is very difficult to be certain whether these were really free-reed instruments. The earliest successful uses in Europe seem to have been some special ranks in organs in the Baltic states and eastern Germany in the late eighteenth century.[54] Makers all over Europe soon began to develop what are best called "reed organs," because every maker invented his own name for his own instrument. The most important of the early ones was Grenié's *orgue expressif*, produced in Paris around 1810, which took advantage of the fact that free reeds, unlike the beating reeds used in pipe organs, could sound louder or softer with changes of air pressure without going out of tune, hence the name "expressive." Around the same time, similar developments were taking place in the United States, led by two Boston makers, Goodrich and Peaseley, both of whom were also building reed organs in the first two decades of the nineteenth century.[55]

The first harmonium, patented under that name in 1842, was invented by Alexandre Debain. It had four ranks of reeds, two at 8-foot pitch with contrasting tone qualities, one at 4-foot, and one at 16-foot, and these ranks were divided so that different stops, producing different sounds, could be used for the melody and its accompaniment.[56] In other words, it was a true rival to the pipe organ, but in a case smaller than that of an upright piano and commensurately inexpensive, for the free-reed requires no pipe. An 8-foot reed is a brass blade an inch or so long, set in a brass frame perhaps half an inch longer at each end and half an inch wider. That and a frame to carry all the reeds is all that is needed, in contrast with large wooden or metal pipes for every note on a pipe organ, as we shall see below.

A rival maker, Jacob Alexandre, produced reed organs with a percussion stop, a small hammer that struck the reed as it began to vibrate, giving a precise initiation to its sound, rather than the somewhat spongy beginning so familiar on reed organs without that device. One of his workers experimented with suction bellows, drawing the air past the reeds rather than blowing it. This was not popular in France, but he took the idea to America, where it was adopted by Mason & Hamlin, creating what is generally known as the "American organ" in contrast with the harmonium.

Thereafter reed organs were widely used in small churches and chapels throughout the world, especially in small communities and those of the nonconformist sects who could never have dreamed of affording a pipe organ. A case the size of a large upright piano could house a reed organ with a full range of stops down to 64-foot and with all the normal devices of the organs in the grandest of cathedrals. Because free reeds were cheaper than strings and did not need casework strong enough to withstand the tension that strings exert, reed organs were cheaper even than pianos. They had the further economic and practical advantages that they did not need regular tuning. They were also far more expressive and had a greater range than pianos, and so they had also a place in homes of every size, from mansion to cottage. Smaller instruments were often designed to fold into their case for easy transport. Folding harmoniums of this type were widely used for outdoor religious services of all sorts and for campfire sing-alongs.

Reed organs were eventually supplanted by the electronic organs that are described in chapter 8, although when electric keyboards were first widely introduced in the 1950s they were quite often reed organs with an amplifier built in. Even today, reed organs are still used, for they are independent of a power source, needing only the player's two feet for their air supply.

Even smaller instruments were developed, small enough to hold in the hands (see figure 4.20). The earliest, dating from 1829 in Austria, seems to have been the accordion, with melody keys on one side and one or two chord keys on the other for accompaniment (hence the name "accordion"), the two sides separated by the folding bellows. These were swiftly followed by the first concertinas, with melody buttons on each side and no chordal keys. There are many varieties, with many other names such as melodeon, bandoneon, and so on, each indicating different types of action, buttons or keys, and shapes of body. Most are divided between single-action and double-action. The single-action gives two different notes for the same button, one on push and the other on draw, usually adjacent notes such as C and D or, with chromatic instruments, C and C♯. The double-action, essential for any instrument with a piano-style keyboard for obvious reasons, sounds the same note in each direction, and therefore has either a smaller range or a greater number of buttons, but allows more freedom of action. On the other hand, the rapid alternation of push and draw of the single-action gives much greater rhythmic punch for dance music. The modern piano accordion, with a piano-style keyboard covering more than three octaves on one side, plus register buttons to add a further three octaves, and a full range of chord buttons on

Figure 4.20. Accordions Etc. and Harmonicas

Back, L–R: early accordion, by Busson, Paris (II 214); child's toy trumpet, a free reed in each "valve" case to make a one-octave mouth organ or harmonica, France (VI 56); concertina, Anglo-German system, by Metzler, London (II 204), and in front of it a concertina-reed tuner, by Louis Lachenal, London (IV 198); melodeon, by Hohner, Trossingen, Germany (XIII 78); piano accordion, the front grill removed to show the action, by Mastertone, "Foreign" (I 48).

In front: two harmonicas, the left diatonic and the right chromatic, both by Hero, China (III 52b and XII 252).

the other side to cover all keys, was developed in the early twentieth century. All were widely popular, immediately portable, and usable anywhere on land or sea for all types of music. Competitions were held, and orchestras were formed for the smaller instruments using different sizes of soprano, alto, tenor, and bass. Until the modern craze for the guitar intervened, the "squeezeboxes," as they were often called, were the favorite instrument for the wandering minstrel.

Even more popular, and smaller and cheaper yet, were the mouth-blown instruments. The simplest mouth organ or harmonica is the diatonic, like the one whose reeds are shown in figure 4.20. Like the single-action concertina, draw and blow give two adjacent notes. Chromatic harmonicas have a slider that shuts off access to one set of reeds and opens another set a semitone higher—both chromatic and diatonic are shown in the figure. As with the squeezeboxes, there is a vast range of types and sizes. The only disadvantage of the harmonica against the squeezebox is that it can produce only a melody, without chordal accompaniment. This was often overcome by street buskers with the "one-man band." A frame strapped around the head or neck would hold the harmonica to the lips, so that the hands could play a guitar or other instrument, and a set of drums and cymbals were strapped to the back and played by trackers from the feet. Nothing defeats the musician who wants to do more with an instrument than it is normally able to do.

Notes

1. When replicating this with a drinking straw, it sounds more easily if the end is cut to a point.
2. Subhi Anwar Rashid, *Mesopotamien* (1984), 46, Abb. 13 and 14.
3. Francis W. Galpin, *The Music of the Sumerians* (1936), 17, plate 4:3.
4. Hans Hickmann, *Catalogue générale des antiquités égyptiennes du Musée du Caire—Instruments de musique* (1949), 122–38, plate 85. Hickmann firmly classes them as double-reed instruments but presents no evidence for doing so.
5. Heinz Becker, *Zur Entwicklungsgeschichte der antiken und mittelalterlichen Rohrblattinstrumente* (Hamburg, 1966), 51 ff, citing Theophrastus, *Peri Phytōn Historias.*
6. Becker, *Zur Entwicklungsgeschichte*, 120–29.
7. *Tarompèt* is the name in Sunda, whence comes mine, illustrated in figure 4.3; *selomprèt* is the central Javanese name.
8. There are many illustrations of these, for example in Becker, *Zur Entwicklungsgeschichte*. One of the clearest is the relief of the Cybele priest that appears in many sources and shows the double reeds very clearly; see, for example, Günter Fleischhauer, *Etrurien und Rom* (1964), 84, Abb. 47.

9. Anthony Baines, *Woodwind Instruments* (1957), 202.
10. Becker, *Zur Entwicklungsgeschichte*, 49, Abb. 3.
11. Fleischhauer, *Etrurien und Rom*, 26, 30, 34, and 40, Abb. 4, 7, 10, and 14.
12. Fleischhauer, *Etrurien und Rom*, 72, Abb. 37. There is a much more blatant "restoration" in the Capitoline Museum in Rome, where the hands and the shawm are clearly eighteenth century.
13. Henry George Farmer, *Islam* (1966), 24–27, Abb. 7–9.
14. Gwen Montagu and Jeremy Montagu, "Beverley Minster Reconsidered," *EM* 6:3 (July 1978): 401–15, figs. 26 and 46.
15. Nazir Ali Jairazbhoy, *A Musical Journey through India* (1988), 32, photographed and recorded in a village of the Dumbu in Andhra Pradesh in 1963–1964.
16. Jeremy Montagu, "The Forked Shawm—An Ingenious Invention," *Yearbook for Traditional Music* 29 (1997): 74–79.
17. Anthony Baines, *Bagpipes* (1960), 63–64.
18. Baines, *Bagpipes*, 9, citing Dio Chrysostom, *Orat.*, lxxi.
19. The same name was used before the mid-1600s to mean the shawm and afterward to mean oboe, with a period of several decades in which it could mean either, leaving us to guess which was meant from the musical and social contexts.
20. The full story, in far greater detail, will be found in Bruce Haynes, *The Eloquent Oboe* (2001). See also Bruce Haynes and Geoffrey Burgess, *The Oboe* (2004).
21. Haynes, *Eloquent Oboe*, 37–42.
22. Names survive in music and inventories, and instruments also survive, but no instrument has a name attached nor are there illustrations with the instruments named, and therefore this has to remain an assumption.
23. It is often known today, even by writers in English, by its German name *Dulzian* or *dulcian*, even though it has a perfectly good English name, used in its historical period.
24. Maggie Kilbey, *Curtal, Dulcian, Bajón* (2002), 249–50.
25. As with all woodwinds, clear drawings of the key systems and fingering charts will be found in Baines, *Woodwind Instruments*.
26. J. Gardiner, ed., *Before the Mast* (2005), 226–49.
27. Barra Boydell, *The Crumhorn* (1982).
28. There is such an instrument in the Bate Collection in Oxford, given by Wally Horwood to prove this thesis.
29. Bálint Sárosi, *Die Volksmusikinstrumente Ungarns* (1967), 82 and 85–86.
30. F. W. Galpin, "The Whistles and Reed Instruments," *Proceedings of the Musical Association* 29 (1903): 115–38.
31. See my *Reed Instruments* (2001), 64–65, for a full discussion on this, with the reasons for introducing the new term *heterozeug*. Briefly, the reed is the same in each, an idioglot blade cut from the cane of the mouthpiece or *zeug*. With the truly idioglot, it is part of the body of the instrument, all one piece. With the idioglot-heterozeug, a similar top is set into a tube of similar material that carries the fingerholes, so that while it is still idioglot, the tongue and shallot all in one mouthpiece, the mouthpiece is not *idio-* to the instrument but

is *hetero-*, other. Detailed descriptions of many of the reed instruments illustrated and described in this chapter will be found in that catalogue.

32. Thurston Dart, "The Mock Trumpet," *GSJ* 6 (1953): 35–40.

33. C. R. Day, *Descriptive Catalogue* (1891), 110 and plate 4a.

34. C. C. Snoeck, *Catalogue* (1894), 174, no. 916.

35. See Colin Lawson, *The Chalumeau* (1981), for the clearest available information on these and of the earliest years of the clarinet. Bettina Wackernagel (*Holzblasinstrumente* [2005]) suggests that Johann David may have been the maker.

36. Personal conversation.

37. Albert R. Rice, *The Baroque Clarinet* (1992), 32–33. However, the relevant catalogue (Kurt Birsak, *Die Holzblas Instrumente* [1973], 83–94) refers to it as a *sordun*.

38. Bjørn Aksdal, *Meråker Klarinetten* (Trondheim, 1992); Mette Müller, "The Danish Skalmeje," *SIMP* 3 (1974): 164–6; anon., *Rapapallit ja Lakuttimet* (Kauhava, 1985).

39. At the price it cost me, £4 (then about $7) in the early 1960s, it was useful for that, but when the price went up and cheap plastic clarinets became available, it lost its purpose.

40. T. Eric Hoeprich, "A Three-Key Clarinet by J. C. Denner," *GSJ* 34 (1981): 21–32.

41. One of the problems of the Berkeley instrument is whether the bell-joint, which has no name on it, was also by J. C. Denner or not, and therefore whether it was he or someone else who first added that third key.

42. Colin Lawson, "The Basset Clarinet Revived," *EM* 15:4 (November 1987): 487–501.

43. Dhanit Yupho, *Thai Musical Instruments* (1960), 74–76.

44. L. C. R. Cameron, *The Hunting Horn* (c. 1905), 7–8.

45. See Jenny F. So, ed., *Music in the Age of Confucius* (2000), 95–98, and Lucie Rault, ed., *La voix du dragon* (2000), 142–43.

46. Shôsôin Office, ed., *Musical Instruments in the Shôsôin* (1967), xxi–xxii, 63–67, and plates 24–25 and 157–75.

47. Yuan Bingchang and Mao Jizeng, eds., *Zhongguo Shaoshu Minzu Yueqi Zhi* (1986), 123–34 and seven pages of unpaginated plates. The title translates as *The Musical Instruments of China's National Minorities*; there is no foreign-language summary, but the illustrations and musical examples are excellent. I am very grateful to Prof. Helen Rees for the reference and for my copy.

48. Helen Rees, *Echoes of History* (2000), 59–61.

49. L. E. R. Picken, C. J. Adkins, and T. F. Page, "The Making of a *Khāēn*," *Musica Asiatica* 4 (1984): 117–54.

50. So, *Music in the Age of Confucius*, fig. 4.3 and p. 96.

51. I am reluctant to take my Borneo and other mouth organs apart to see what the reeds are made of, other than my second khāēn, which was bought for that purpose and one of whose reeds is shown in figure G.3.

52. Marin Mersenne, *Harmonie Universelle* (1636), Livre Cinquiesme des Instruments à Vent, p. 308.

53. Farmer, *Islam*, Abb. 3 and 8.

54. Peter Williams, *A New History of the Organ* (1980), 160–61.

55. The most thorough guide through the maze of inventions and patent names is Arthur W. J. G. Ord-Hume's comprehensively illustrated *Harmonium* (1986).

56. As we noted in Explanations and Definitions at the beginning of the book, this is organ builders' terminology. The 8-foot rank of reeds produces the notes as one reads them: pressing the key for middle C sounds middle C. With a 4-foot rank, that key would sound the C an octave higher; with a 16-foot rank, an octave lower. With all three ranks drawn, all three Cs would sound simultaneously by pressing that one key. Similarly, 2-foot and 32-foot sound further octaves above and below. See chapter 7 on the organ for more detail on this. When ranks are "divided," usually around middle C, it means that one can use both halves for the same sound throughout the compass, or use the bottom half of the keyboard for one sound at the same time as the upper half for a different tone quality.

INTERLUDE D

~

The Ideal Accompaniment

If one had to select the world's most common and most effective method of accompaniment, and that most influential on the music to which it was attached, the answer would surely be the drone. This is usually, though by no means invariably, supplied by the same player as the melody so that it is also the most economical in resources. A drone is the continuous sound of that pitch most important to the melody, in our music today the tonic or keynote; in the Middle Ages, usually the *finalis*, the note to which the melody finally resolves; and in other cultures, their nearest equivalent to these.

It is probably in India that the drone is the most essential, for it pervades all Indian music, even to the extent that there is one instrument that has no other function. The *tambūrā* is a long-necked lute, looking rather like a *sitar* (see figure 6.21), but with only four, or sometimes five, strings and a plain neck without frets. It has a bridge with a surface that is wide north–south, often as much as an inch (20–25 mm), and slightly curved so that instead of the string having a sharp cutoff, as with a violin or guitar bridge, the string can vibrate against it, thus providing a characteristic sustaining quality similar to that of the brays on a harp or the *arpichordum* on the virginals. The strings are tuned to the *sa* (equivalent to the keynote or tonic of the *rāg*) and its octave, with the fifth or less often the fourth (*ma* and *pa*). There is no precise equivalent in our terminology for rāg, but mood and mode are probably closer than scale, for the scale of each rāg and its order—by no means always straight up and down—is chosen from the pitches proper to the rāg.

The importance of the drone lies in tension and release: consonances, where the melodic pitch coincides with the drone notes, are positions of rest or release, whereas dissonances create the tension that drives the

music to find again a consonance. It is one of the characteristics of music that the closer one gets to a consonance, the greater the dissonance. One could play or sing a B-natural against a C drone, which is itself close enough to be dissonant. But if one sharpens the B so that it gets closer to the C, the dissonance becomes all the greater until finally it topples over the cliff, as it were, settling with a gasp of relief on the consonance of the C.[1] One can often hear Indian musicians taking full advantage of this, especially in a slow *ālāp*, the long introduction to a performance in which the mood and the rāg are established. The player or singer will tease the audience by approaching concordance, falling away, approaching again, and falling away again, each time getting closer, until at last all is resolved and the rāg is complete.

It is easy to demonstrate that drones are also an aid to good tuning. Ask anyone to sing, unaccompanied, a major scale from a given tonic pitch, and then to sing it again, relating each note against a constant drone on that tonic—the second scale will always be better in tune than the first.

These are not the only functions of drones. Every note played or sung has attached to it a series or envelope of overtones, weak or hardly existent in the sound of a flute or a tuning fork, stronger and varying in strength and content with other instruments. That envelope is what gives each instrument its own characteristic and recognizable sound. Each note of the melody has its overtones, and so has the drone. The combination of these overtones, varying with every note played, and the ways in which they combine, reinforcing each other or detracting from each other, adds enormous richness to the sound.

Even the very presence of a drone can alter the tone quality. In Turkey and the Balkans, it is common to play

100

the *kaval*, the long end-blown or duct-blown flutes, and shorter instruments such as the Romanian *fluier* (see figures 3.2 and 3.10), with a hummed drone, known in Romania as the *ison*. It can either maintain the same pitch or shift pitch as the melody progresses, to form a harmonic bass. Both Tiberiu Alexandru and Laurence Picken have published examples of this.[2] The use of the ison alters the tone quality greatly. The sound of a flute tends to be a very pure and simple one, with very little harmonic content, but the moment one begins to hum, this changes. The tone quality becomes narrower, more reedy, with a strong hiss and the semblance, at least, of a fuller harmonic content. Just why this occurs is not clear. Picken, whose study of Turkish folk instruments is beyond compare, says only, "The possibility of producing a vocal drone while blowing depends on the throat being relaxed, which in turn has a decisive effect on the character of the air-stream and the generation of the edge-tone."[3]

The ison is an example of self-accompaniment, as is the *tambūrā*, often played by a singer as self-accompaniment, although there may be a separate player or sometimes more than one. The small harmonium, popularly called a *śruti-box*, can be used instead of a tambūrā in Indian music and may also be played either by the singer or by another musician. The sitar has drone strings built in that suffice for many players, but those brought up in a different tradition prefer to be accompanied by a tambūrā, as do players of many other Indian instruments. The *shahnā'ī* shawm is loud enough that only another, or several other, shahnā'ī can provide an effective drone. All these instruments and others discussed in this chapter we shall meet in due course or have already met.

Drones can be, and are, built into many instruments. Two obvious examples of this are the bagpipe and the hurdy-gurdy or *vielle à roue*. Once the bag was introduced, initially as we have seen as a labor-saving device, the convenience of being able to stick extra pipes into it must have been clear. All the same, though many bagpipes have them, some do not, and most commonly around the world, as in our Middle Ages, there is only one, unlike the later Scottish Highland pipe. On the hurdy-gurdy (figure 6.35), the drone strings can be lifted away from the wheel, leaving the *chanterelle* or melody string to sound alone. Nevertheless, in all those cultures where the drone is regarded as the ideal accompaniment, it is seldom silenced—it is an essential part of the music. And in some cases, it is physically inseparable; the character of the instrument is such that no drone, no instrument. Three of these we shall encounter in interlude G: the musical bow, the trump, and overtone singing.

In the European Middle Ages, many bowed and plucked string instruments were played with a drone. Sometimes there were dedicated strings for this purpose, lying beside the fingerboard rather than running over it. The player would pluck a drone string with the thumb while bowing on others, or with plucked instruments while plucking others with a plectrum in the other hand. We can see both techniques in the thirteenth-century Angel Choir of Lincoln Cathedral, on a fiddle and a citole (the fiddle is illustrated in figure 6.30). Separate drone strings were never essential, for while the melody was played on one string, other fingerboard strings could be sounded as drones. With many bowed instruments this was in fact unavoidable, for if the bridge was flat, the bow would inevitably be in contact with more than one string at a time.

The pipe and tabor, the original "one-man band," was used throughout Europe in the Middle Ages, as we have seen in chapter 2. One would not normally think of this as a drone combination, but every drum has a definite pitch, distinctly audible to those willing to hear it, and often audible to all when it produces an undesirable harmonic clash. The taborer sometimes has to adjust the tension of the drumheads or the snare to avoid such a clash, and this must have been especially important in the later Middle Ages and earlier Renaissance when the pipe and tabor were a part of larger ensembles, as was often commended.[4]

One form of tabor produced, and still produces, a much stronger drone. This was once widely used and today survives as the *txuntxun* among the Basques south of the Pyrenees, and as the *tambourin de Navarre* or *de Béarn* on the French side of the border. A wooden box, three feet long or so, has half a dozen or more strings running along its upper surface, and these are tuned, usually, to the tonic and dominant of the pipe. All are struck simultaneously by a heavy wooden beater in the rhythm required by the dance—there is no selection of one pitch or the other, for the instrument is simply a string drum, one that produces a deliberate drone.[5] The strings, like the beater, are heavy, and their sound is brightened by placing a metal staple over each string so that they are just close enough for the strings to jar against them. Like the arpichordum of the *muselaar* and the brays of the early harp, these produce a simulacrum of a harmonic spectrum that is not otherwise audible.

There is some evidence for a similar instrument, used with a small chamber ensemble, in China in the Bronze Age and later. The *zhu* was a zither with a long, narrow, trough-shaped body and a narrower neck, about the same length as the body, with no frets or other indications of any way to stop any of the five strings individually.[6] The earliest instruments, found in the tomb of the Marquis Yi at Suizhou in the province of Hubei, date from the fifth century BC, and others are known from the second century BC. Illustrations contemporary with these later examples show them being played with a stick, exactly like the txuntxun, with the player using the neck as a handle, rather than as a neck, just a way of holding the instrument. Some sticks of otherwise unknown purpose were found in Yi's tomb. These and the later illustrations suggest that the zhu was indeed a string drum, and if so, it is our earliest evidence for the use of such instruments.

The Hungarian *gardon* looks like a crudely made cello and is usually about that size. With three or four strings tuned to tonic and dominant, it is again a string drum, albeit one with a difference: It is played with rhythmic alternation between plucking one string and striking all of them with the beater. The plucking is sufficiently strong that the string slaps back on the fingerboard (which is never used as a fingerboard—the strings are not stopped but always open), an effect that Bartók imitated, especially in his quartets.[7]

String drums are also found in Indonesia, where they are made of an internode of bamboo (see figure 6.12). A narrow strip of the cortex is lifted from the surface of the bamboo and is wedged up by small pieces of stick or gourd at each end so that it stands a few millimeters proud. It is usually struck with a light stick, wound with wool or something similar to produce a better tone than a bare stick. Some instruments have two such strings with a bamboo plate wedged between them as a striking surface, usually with a hole beneath to enable the bamboo tube to resonate more effectively. Tuning can be adjusted slightly by moving the wedge pieces, although this does not seem to be taken too seriously; one has the impression that these are more drum substitutes than serious drone instruments, even though undoubtedly they do provide a drone.

A different approach to a drone is the use of an *ostinato*. This is an incessantly repeated pattern of notes and can be heard in some forms of African xylophone and other music, especially in East Africa where several musicians play on the same instrument. Those in the middle are responsible for the main melodic content, with one player at the treble end and another at the bass playing two- or three-note ostinati. While not strictly a drone, this has much the same effect and shows not only how widely drones are found but also how varied they are in their nature.

We have frequently referred to the European Middle Ages in this interlude, with bagpipes, string instruments, and pipe and tabor, and it is clear that the use of a drone was then of great importance, so much so that drones were built into organs. Some illustrations show the usual line of pipes descending in size from the bass to the treble but then with one or more long pipes at the treble end. It is a reasonable assumption that these were drone pipes, for it is improbable that players had bass keys at each end of the keyboard, especially on the small portative organs. One illustration, on one of the wings of the famous Ghent altarpiece "Adoration of the Mystic Lamb," painted by Jan van Eyck in the early 1400s, seems to show a small lever beyond the bass end of the keyboard that, when swung into position, would hold down an additional key to provide a drone.[8] We have no evidence for such a mechanism on other organs, but there would be no point in providing such pipes, especially on the portatives where weight is a serious consideration, unless there were some way to sound them.

Notes

1. This is a very simplistic explanation, derived from the chapter on "The Effect of Drones" in N. A. Jairazbhoy, *The Rāgs of North Indian Music* (1971), 65–89, and from conversations with Professor Jairazbhoy in the days when he introduced us to Indian music before he wrote that book. See his book also for full information on the Indian system of scales and tuning.

2. Tiberiu Alexandru, *Instrumentele Muzicale ale Poporului Romîn* (1956), 70 and musical examples 28 and 29, pp. 192–99; Laurence Picken, *Folk Musical Instruments of Turkey* (1975), 454 and musical example 29, pp. 400–411, showing during its course all three uses: the drone, the varying harmonic bass, and the true second part.

3. Picken, *Folk Musical Instruments of Turkey*, 399.

4. Thoinot Arbeau, *Orchesographie* (Lengres, 1588; facsimile of the 1596 edition Geneva, 1972. There are several translations into English, none of them very accurate), f. 33v.

5. Its effect can be heard in many dance movements, often called tambourin, in Rameau's operas and ballets and in keyboard music of that period.

6. Jenny F. So, ed, *Music in the Age of Confucius* (2000), 79–80; Lucie Rault, ed., *La voix du dragon* (2000), 148–49.

7. The instrument is described and illustrated, with two transcriptions typical of its use, by Bálint Sárosi, *Die Volksmusikinstrumente Ungarns* (1967), 59–63.

8. There is much literature on this painting, and it has been reproduced in many books. An article that cites many of these references and compares the painting with a real organ that survives from much the same date, is Edwin M. Ripin's "The Norrlanda Organ and the Ghent Altarpiece," SIMP 3 (1974): 193–96 and illus. 286–88.

CHAPTER FIVE

~

"Brass" Instruments: Trumpets and Horns

The use of marine shells as trumpets goes back into high antiquity, and it could well be that these are the oldest trumpets of all, for shells of suitable pattern are often washed up on beaches with the tip of the spire broken off, or a hole pierced in the side, ready-made for blowing (see figure 5.1). Any that have come down to us from antiquity are comparatively recent. Examples of the Mediterranean triton shell have been found from the late Neolithic or Chalcolithic periods (New Stone and Copper ages) in Hungary, four to five thousand years ago, and there is no reason to suppose that these were the first ever to be used.[1]

The conch is known almost everywhere within reach of the sea and, as in Hungary and other places, inland also. The main exceptions are the shores of Africa, save for Madagascar and the eastern coast as far south as Tanzania, where we will encounter the hand-stopped conch in interlude F. Why the conch is not used in West Africa (where horns of ivory, animal horn, and wood are widely used, and where large land-snail shells are used as libation vessels), in the south (where a species of seaweed is used as a trumpet), or in the north (whereas shell trumpets are used all around the rest of the Mediterranean and on the islands between, such as Crete, Cyprus, and Malta) is more puzzling, but no evidence for them nor for their use has yet been found.[2]

Shell trumpets are used for signaling, as discussed in interlude F, especially by fishermen as one would expect, but not only as foghorns, for they are used in Spain as signals of fish for sale.[3] They are also often used well inland, as, for example, with a queen conch illustrated in figure 5.1 that was used to call the hands in for meals on a farm in Iowa. They have also been important in ritual. Triton with his wreathed horn has been a common con-

cept of the gods of the sea from Greek and Roman times on. Many fragments of shells have been found at ritual sites in Minoan Crete, and there is a well-known intaglio showing a priestess blowing a conch.[4] Several complete shells, clearly used for blowing, have been found there—for example, at Phaestos and Myrtos, the latter dated to around 2300 BC—and elsewhere, as at Kition in Cyprus from around 1200 BC.[5] Conchs have been found at temple sites in what is now Israel: at Hazor from the time of King Solomon, around 900 BC; at Shiqmona and Tel Qasile, both probably from the Philistine Dagon cult (a sea god) around 1100 BC; and elsewhere.[6] One from around 700 BC was found at Nineveh and is preserved in the British Museum.[7] Traces of a ritual use survive in the modern Italian festival of Piedigrotta, where Caribbean queen conch shells, often those whose lips have been cut off to carve into cameos, are blown as general noisemakers.[8]

Pottery skeuomorphs (artificial shells),[9] almost certainly ritual instruments, have been found, in Peru from the pre-Columbian Moche people (see figure 5.7), Thailand, India, Crete, Greece, and probably elsewhere, and to copy the whole structure of the shell in pottery, as can be seen in X-ray photographs, suggests that it was an object of great importance in itself, for why otherwise go to such trouble?[10]

In India, the conch is one of the attributes of the Hindu god Vishnu and his avatar Krishna.[11] Each of Krishna's companions in the *Bhagavad-Gita* of the Hindu *Mahābhārata* had his own shell, each of a different species and each with its own name, just as the heroes of our Arthurian legends each had a named sword.[12] Krishna's own shell, the *chank* (see figure 5.6), is a heavy, white shell and, due to its mass and rigidity, has of all conchs a sound

Figure 5.1.   Horns and Conchs

Above, L–R: oxhorn used as a bugle by 48th Cambridge Boy Scouts (IV 30); mythan (buffalo) horn, Southeast Asia (XI 120); *shofar*, Casablanca, Morocco (X 202); shofar, Israel or northern Europe, nineteenth century (X 14); shofar, Israel, 1976 (III 216); shofar, Israel, Sephardic style, early twentieth century (XII 154).

Below, conchs, L–R: end-blown frog shell with fingerhole, Fiji (I 8a); side-blown baler shell, Papua New Guinea (XI 24); end-blown queen conch, used on a farm in Iowa to call the hands to meals (V 76); *horagai*, end-blown triton with copper mouthpiece, Japan (XI 44); side-blown frog shell used as a foghorn, Mafia Island, off Tanzania (IV 102); side-blown triton, Trobriand Islands (IX 212); side-blown triton, Marquesa Islands (III 68).

nearest to that of the trumpet.[13] This species is important also in Buddhism and is widely used in Tibet. That a shell as heavy as this, which according to Hornell is to be found mainly off the coast of Madras, should be worth carrying from southern India to the plateau of Tibet, emphasizes its importance, as does the elaborate silver or even gold casing into which it is often set.

These Tibetan conchs usually have an added mouthpiece, part of the elaborate casing. So too (of pewter or a similar metal) do those Bohemian conchs for averting storms described in interlude A. Japanese conchs, once war trumpets but now priestly instruments, have a mouthpiece of bamboo, metal, or lacquer. They are stopped, with the fingers rather than the hand, to produce extra pitches.[14] Conchs with pottery mouthpieces have been found in the Philippines.[15] These are all end-blown, the mouthpiece added where the apex has been removed. Also end-blown are conchs of all species in India, Europe, China, and South America, the apex removed to leave an embouchure or blowing hole in the tip.

Whether the shell is end- or side-blown is partly a matter of custom and partly of species. The common triton shell of the Pacific, and its Mediterranean and Red Sea relatives, are smooth shells and are as easily blown from the side, as they usually are in Oceania, as from the end. The frog shell is very knobbly and is therefore end-blown in Fiji, where it is known to have been a ritual instrument, whereas the triton there is always side-blown.[16] The Fijian frog shell is the only conch trumpet that has a fingerhole, drilled inside the mouth in the final whorl of the shell. Of those that I have measured, the pitch rise produced by opening it is around a minor third. Why it was used in this way is unknown—the Fijian native religion was firmly extirpated by Christian missionaries without any record. Horned helmet shells, another Oceanic species,[17] are also usually end-blown because the terminal whorls are so tightly packed that side-blowing would be impossible, and the same applies to the common Caribbean king helmets and the queen conchs.[18]

With side-blown conchs, in East Africa the bell or open mouth usually faces forward, whereas in Oceania it normally faces back so that it is more easily hand-stopped. Conchs of several species are widely used on almost all Pacific islands, many of them hand-stopped and most, other than frogs and helmets, side-blown with an embouchure pecked in the side wall of the first whorl of the shell wide enough to accept it.

Wherever horned animals exist, animal horns are blown, again a practice that presumably goes back into remote antiquity, even though our earliest historical evidence is probably the biblical story of the siege of Jericho—horn, being softer than shell, is less likely to survive archaeologically. We have earlier evidence for the use of metal trumpets, for example, those of the pharaoh Tutankhamun of around 1350 BC and the biblical account in Numbers 10 a century or two later, and it is difficult to believe that metal anticipated the natural material.[19]

The words *trumpet* and *horn* are used here interchangeably. Save for our orchestral instruments, where we all know the difference, nobody has ever produced a definition that satisfactorily distinguishes one from the other and for which one cannot immediately think of exceptions. So we shall follow common usage where it exists (alphorn, the Last Trumpet, and so forth) and for the rest use whichever word comes first to mind.

Returning to the siege of Jericho, the instrument used there was the *shofar hayovel*, the horn of a ram.[20] The shofar has been used continuously from biblical times to the present day, and in legend it will be heard from heaven as the Last Trumpet. It is still conventionally made from a ram's horn, although any other kosher animal may be used except for a cow, so that goat and antelope horns are sometimes seen in communities where sheep are scarce. The cow was forbidden because of the episode of the Golden Calf, but cow and ox horns are common enough in other cultures. Cow horns were the normal European hunting horn, certainly from the Middle Ages onward, and the ox horn (*bugle* in French) was the original bugle.

It was presumably some sort of long cow or ox horn that was the inspiration for the Danish Bronze Age *lur*, which seems to have been used in pairs (they have normally been found deposited in pairs, in lakes that became peat bogs).[21] Each member of a pair is a mirror image of the other, curving high over the players' heads, each twisted in the opposite sense to the other. There is a number of different designs, and they were clearly made over a considerable period, perhaps from before 1000 BC to around 500 BC. Their construction, cast in bronze by the lost-wax method (*cire perdue*) shows high technology, and their mouthpieces, ranging from the earliest to the last, show a clear developmental sequence.[22] The fact that the mouthpieces of the later instruments would work perfectly well in Renaissance or Baroque trumpets or in modern trombones strongly suggests an advanced musical technique. This is emphasized by the fact that some pairs have different dimensions of cup analogous to those of the Classical *cor alto* and *cor basse* French horns, facilitating higher and lower ranges.

In the days when it was more permissible to play museum instruments than it is today, recordings were published and several works were written to include lurs in concert performances. However, we know nothing at all of the musical use of these instruments in the Bronze Age, nor of their position within the culture, although the fact that they were carefully deposited in the lakes must indicate at least some importance and almost certainly some ritual connotations. Nor do we know of any earlier European horns made in this way. However, the highly skilled technology involved even in the earlier examples does make one wonder whether they might have had predecessors that have not survived or have not yet been discovered.

The Irish Bronze Age horns were rather later and rather simpler, dating from around the eighth to between the third and second centuries BC.[23] They look much more obviously like large ox horns, and the occasional discovery of large pellet bells that resemble a bull's scrotum in association with them suggests the possibility of some sort of bull cult. Where they differ most strongly from the Danish horns, and indeed from any other European examples, is that some of them are side-blown. Why this should be, we have no idea (although the advantages of side-blowing are pointed out in interlude F), but Bronze-Age Ireland joins sub-Saharan Africa, Oceania, a small part of Amazonian Brazil, and two small tribes in India as the only places in the world where horns are blown from the side.

John Coles produces evidence for contacts between Ireland and northern Europe at this period (lurs have been found, albeit rarely, in a wider area than Denmark itself, and there are some bronze horns from Germany also). He also suggests a reason for the differences in shape between the Irish and the Danish horns: the difference between two breeds of cattle, *Bos longifrons*, whose horns curve but are not twisted and so resemble the Irish horns, and *Bos primigenius*, whose horns both curve and twist and so resemble the lurs.[24]

We said above that there were no reliable distinctions between horns and trumpets. One that has often been suggested is an animal origin for horns and vegetable for trumpets. However, many appear to have originated as a combination of both. Some Irish horns look as though they might have begun as a short wooden tube thrust into a natural horn. Even more likely is that a long cane tube terminating in a horn, precisely as still exists in Madagascar, was the origin of the Etruscan *lituus*.[25]

The use of that Latin name for the instrument has long caused confusion among the Roman instruments. We have four names for these—*cornu, bucina,* and *tuba,* along with lituus—but only three instruments have been found portrayed on monuments and mosaics. There is no doubt that the cornu was the curved instrument in a G shape with a gradually expanding bore, curving over the player's head. Equally, the tuba was a long straight instrument with a cylindrical bore terminating in a narrowly conical bell. The confusion between bucina and lituus has been clarified by Renato Meucci, who has established that for the Romans they were one and the same, a bovine horn with some metal embellishments.[26]

All three were military instruments and, so far as we know from histories and illustrations, they were the only instruments the Roman armies had. There are no traces of drums nor flutes of any sort to accompany troops on the march. The Greeks, on the other hand, did use the *aulos* to accompany the march, but like the Romans, their main military instrument was the trumpet, which they called the *salpinx*.[27] This was a straight bronze instrument of cylindrical bore with a short, tulip-shaped bell. Judging from illustrations, it was around three feet long, some shorter, a few longer. No examples have as yet been found, although there are short (around 1 foot/30 cm) pottery instruments of the same shape in some museums from the Cypro-Archaic period in Cyprus.[28]

The last bronze instrument of antiquity was the Celtic *carnyx,* dating from around the early second century BC to the middle or end of the first century AD. While we have a number of representations of the carnyx, most notably the massive silver Gundestrop Cauldron in Copenhagen, which shows a procession of carnyx blowers, no complete instrument has survived. The nearest to it was one found in the River Witham, near Tattershall Ferry, Lincolnshire, in 1768.[29] This was complete—about 50 inches long, according to Piggott—save for the dragon's-head mouth of the bell. It was made of sheet bronze, rolled with a longitudinal soldered joint, in two straight sections with a telescopic joint between them, terminating at the distal end with the animal-head bell. At the player's end, there was an obliquely cut-off embouchure, very similar in pattern to that of the Dutch *midwinter-*

hoorn and the Naga *phupphu,* which allows the player to hold the instrument upward or sideways and still blow straight down the tube. This is all that we know about the carnyx, for, in the interests of science of the period, it was melted down to see what it was made of!

Around 1816, at Deskford in Banffshire, a sheet bronze head, now in the National Museum of Antiquities of Scotland in Edinburgh, was found that corresponds in all respects to the images of the bell-mouth of the carnyx, so that putting the two together, as Piggott did in one of his illustrations, we have a good idea of what we might have had. The Deskford head had a movable lower jaw and was found with a wooden tongue that was movable with springs. Such heads survive on short trumpets in the areas bordering Tibet (see figure 5.6). They were used also in nineteenth-century Europe on buccin trombones, which, instead of the normal bell joint, had a curved one that projected over the player's head (as did the bell of the carnyx) to look impressive on the march. Similar heads were also used on some upright serpents. The only other surviving fragment of a carnyx is a bell section, without the head, that was found in Dürnau.

For the next thousand years, we have very little knowledge of trumpets and horns in Europe. There are a few illustrations showing what seem to be large trumpets, often of expanding bore and sometimes bound with bands, as in figure C.1, suggesting that they may have been made like the alphorn—by splitting, hollowing, and reuniting—so needing bands to hold them together. These are usually illustrations of biblical scenes, such as Psalm 150 and the books of Daniel and the Apocalypse, and may or may not have any resemblance to anything actually used in their period.

We may assume that bovine horns continued in use as bugles, as they certainly did as drinking horns, for we can see them in the Bayeux Tapestry, illustrating the Norman conquest of England in 1066. We also know that the ivory horns called *oliphants* (because they were made from the tusk of an elephant) existed, certainly from the tenth century and perhaps earlier. We also have the legend of Roland at Roncesvaux, who blew his oliphant to call Emperor Charlemagne to his help when he was overwhelmed by the Moorish invaders—at least three oliphants survive claiming to be the one that Roland blew!

Oliphants often had a double function, as both signal horns and charter horns, to entitle the possessor to hold lands or certain rights instead of, or in addition to, a written charter.[30] One well-known example is the Horn of Ulph in York Minster.[31] Sometimes it sufficed to hold the horn, whether of ivory or ox, but others had to be blown at certain occasions.

It was not until the thirteenth century, as we said in interlude C, that the long, narrow, cylindrically bored, metal trumpet came back into use. These were not cast but were rolled up from latten (sheet brass) with a longitudinal soldered seam. The main tube was cylindrical, with a straight-sided expanding bell. They were made in sections, the joints between them sometimes being butt-soldered, supported by a knop or boss, but more usually telescopic either with the female tubing strengthened with a ferrule and the male tubing sliding into it, or again supported by a boss. Medieval illustrations are legion, most illuminated manuscripts showing one or more. Surviving examples are rare, however, a number of them almost certainly fakes. One undoubtedly genuine example was found in 1984 under the Billingsgate site in London and has been confidently dated to the fourteenth century—perhaps slightly earlier, for it had seen a good deal of use before it was lost in the Thames.[32] This instrument had no separate mouthpiece but simply a slight evasion of the tube with a ring to support the lips.

Very similar instruments are still in use in Morocco as *al nafir* (see figure 5.2) and in Nigeria and neighboring areas as *kakaki*, and there is no doubt at all that it was from North Africa that they came into Europe and, with the ancestors of the Hausa people, down into West Africa. It seems probable that, as with other instruments, they originated in Central Asia, where again they are still in use, and whence similar instruments traveled into northern India and Tibet where also they still survive. The West African and Tibetan instruments are well known, the north Indian rather less so, but examples can be found in a number of museums. More commonly in India, the instruments are evenly expanding in bore and curved, either C- or S-shaped, some of them interchangeable as either shape, for if there is a joint in the middle of the C, turning that joint through 180 degrees converts a C into an S. Some, however, are either firmly soldered into shape or made of cast metal rather than of rolled-up sheet.

A mouthpiece such as that on the Billingsgate or Moroccan and West African trumpets makes it difficult to produce more than two or three notes, quite sufficient for their purposes—in North Africa, for example, normally to signal the end of the fast at Ramadan and for military and other signals. In Nigeria, they are also used to "shout" the praises of the emir like other talking instru-

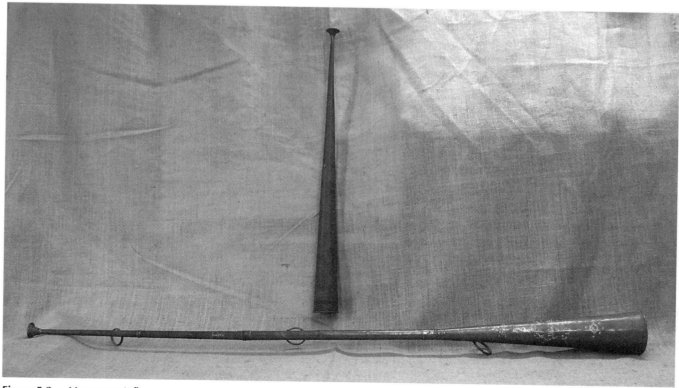

Figure 5.2.   Moroccan *Nfir*
Above: short, iron (VII 190); below: long, brass (X 128).

ments. In Europe, cup-shaped mouthpieces speedily appeared, as can be seen for example on the side wings of the great Hans Memlinc altarpiece of around 1480, now in the Royal Museum in Antwerp.[33] By this time also, trumpets were often folded for greater portability, with a U-bend added at each joint in the tubing. This was first in an S-shape (see figure 5.4), certainly by 1400, and soon after with the upper U-bend turned so that the bell-yard lay over the mouth-yard, to produce the folded shape still seen in our trumpet today.

It is often suggested (although there is considerable controversy over this) that when, as can be seen in the Memlinc painting, the player is holding the mouthpiece to the lips with the fingers, this indicates that the mouthpiece had a long stem going down into the main tubing. By drawing this out, the tube is lengthened, so producing a lower harmonic series than that of the basic tubing. It would be difficult to play rapid passages on a draw-trumpet or *trompette de menestrel* in this way, but it would certainly be practicable to play the rather slower music of a chorale, such as those that Bach sometimes wrote for a *tromba da tirarsi* (drawn trumpet). The only known surviving instrument with such a mouthpiece comes from Bach's period and is preserved in the Musical Instrument Museum in Berlin. Moving the slide from the mouthpiece to the lower U-bend made rapid movement much easier, and the trombone was certainly in existence before the end of the 1400s. Its name is the Italian augmentative of *tromba*, meaning "large trumpet." The English name was "sackbut" (with a variety of spellings and similar names in French and Spanish), from a French word meaning "draw" or "pull."

The trombone has undergone little change from that day to this, for it was a "perfect" instrument—that is, being able to play any note perfectly in tune—from the moment of its invention, simply by placing the slide in any desired position. The most important change, for which because of the possibility of later repairs we have no certain date, is the use of stockings on the legs of the slide so that only the last three or four inches of the slide are a close fit. This reduces the friction and makes the slide easier to move freely while at the same time allowing a closer fit to avoid air leakage between the inner and outer sections than would be practicable without it. Certainly by the mid-1500s, trombones were made in a family of sizes—alto, tenor, and bass—and by 1619 Michael Praetorius also shows a great-bass, an octave below the tenor, the lower register achieved by moving the back-bow with the plunger shown between the bell-joint and the next (see figure 5.3). Note that he also shows a crook (numbered 13) above the tenor trombone and next to

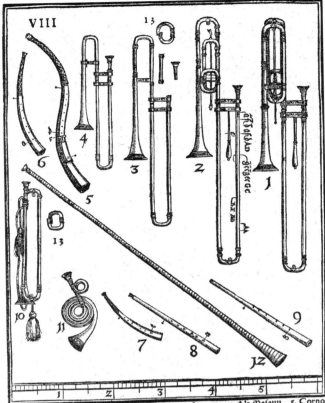

Figure 5.3.   Renaissance Brass Instruments
Bass, tenor, and alto trombones (1–4); tenor, treble, descant, straight, and mute cornetts (5–9); trumpet and whole-tone crook (10, 13); coiled trumpet (11); alphorn (12) *(Michael Praetorius, Syntagma Musicum—De Organographia, 1619).*

the trumpet, which lowers the pitch by a whole tone, and between the trombone and its mouthpiece, a shank to lower it by a semitone—the earliest evidence we have for these devices.

The handle on the slide of the bass trombone (no. 2 in figure 5.3) was necessary because the human arm is not long enough to extend a slide that length unaided. It was retained until only a few years ago, when a valve with extra tubing in the back-bow was devised that could be operated by the left thumb. This allowed the bass trombone to be made with a slide no longer than that of the tenor. The contrabass, needed for the Wagner operas, remains a problem, for even a handle will not allow the slide to extend for the full seven positions. The usual answer is a double slide, but even though the bore diameter of trombones has increased in recent years, it needs to be still wider for a good tone in the contrabass. This is usually provided by making each leg of the double slide wider than the one before, producing a somewhat unwieldy weight.

The soprano trombone has always been rare and seems first to have appeared in the eighteenth century. Up to that date, the soprano part was played by the cornett (no. 6 in figure 5.3), a wooden instrument with fingerholes and a miniature trumpet mouthpiece no larger than the cup in which an acorn sits. This was the great virtuoso instrument of the Renaissance, used for florid "divisions," as variations were then known. It, too, was one of a family, with a soprano (no. 7), a tenor (no. 5), and a bass that was not really successful. Straight cornetts (no. 8) were sometimes seen, but the curved instrument was easier to handle because the curve made it easier to cover the stretch between the fingerholes. The mute cornett was also straight but had a conical mouthpiece carved into the top of the tube that gave a much softer tone than the cup mouthpiece of the normal cornett. Both straight and mute cornetts were turned on the lathe, but this was impossible on the normal instruments because of the curved body. They had to be made by splitting a piece of wood, carving it out, and covering the body with leather, or occasionally parchment, to seal the joint. This was necessary because the glues of that period were water-soluble and thus not secure enough to seal the reunited body against air leaks.

The ensemble of cornett and trombones had a double use: to play with voices in the choir and to play at appointed hours from the tower of the church or city hall. They were therefore one of the few families of instruments that belonged both in the *instruments bas* and the *instruments haut*, the soft and loud instruments into which categories all instruments of the Middle Ages and Renaissance were divided. In the towers, they had to compete with the rattle of wheels of carts and carriages on cobbles and the shouts of the marketplace below. In the choir, they had to play as softly as required. So quiet was the cornett as a solo instrument that Marin Mersenne compares its sound to a gleam of sunshine and adds the terrifying information that players could sustain 80 "mesures" in a single breath, one achieving more than a hundred.[34]

The trumpet (no. 10 in figure 5.3), on the other hand, was initially a loud instrument, used mainly for military purposes and the hunting field (no. 11). It was used less often as an orchestral instrument in Praetorius's day, and then only for loud and jubilant choruses. By Mersenne's time, a generation later, it was provided with a mute to moderate its sound. It was not until later in the seventeenth century and early eighteenth that it became the solo instrument that we know from works such as Bach's

Brandenburg Concerto no. 2 and the many obbligato parts in his and others' music. By that time, players were ascending into the uppermost reaches of the harmonic series, to the twentieth, even the twenty-fourth harmonics (e'" and g'" above the treble stave), where the sound becomes very quiet—quiet enough to balance the other instruments of a chamber ensemble. Also, the use of the cornett had then almost died out, probably partly because it has always been a difficult instrument to play in tune but chiefly because once trumpeters had acquired the clarino technique that enabled them to play above the eighth harmonic (see figure 0.1 in Explanations and Definitions), they had a diatonic scale available. With the skill to lip their notes up or down a semitone, they could also provide the chromatic notes between the harmonics. The greatest problems, as we shall see, lay in playing the eleventh, thirteenth, and fourteenth harmonics in tune. The best players could bend them into tune most of the time, but as contemporary reviews reveal, not all the time.

Before the end of the seventeenth century, trumpeters had begun to adopt mechanical devices to fill the gaps between the lower harmonics. Purcell wrote for the "flatt trumpet," an instrument that had a short slide in the back-bow, long enough to lower the pitch by a third or so. The fact that this instrument so rarely appears in scores suggests that it was deficient either in tone or mechanically, and certainly it was difficult to play. However, a much-improved model was invented by John Hyde a century later. The English slide trumpet remained the instrument of choice for the better players there long after the invention of valves that we shall describe in interlude E, even into the early twentieth century.[35] The slide trumpet remains a natural trumpet, crooked into whichever key is needed, with the great advantage that using the slide avoids the need for bending those difficult harmonics and also provides the lower chromatic notes between the sixth and tenth harmonics. Thus a fully chromatic scale is available over much of the range with none of the degradation of tone quality that results from opening the harmonic vent-hole that is fitted on many modern so-called baroque trumpets today, such as that illustrated between the slide trumpets in figure 5.4. Some French makers also produced slide trumpets, but with the slide in the front bow.

Over most of the rest of Europe, hand-stopping had been tried, after the technique was adopted on the horn, but the trumpet bell is too small for that to work properly and the resulting sound was very poor. The key trumpet, invented around 1770, was far more successful. This had from three to five proper tone-holes covered by keys, as

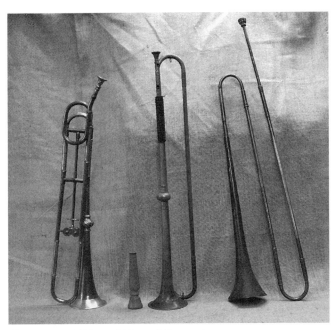

Figure 5.4. Slide and Natural Trumpets
L–R: slide trumpet, England, mid-nineteenth century (IX 24); reproduction of eighteenth-century Haas trumpet, by Meinl und Lauber, Wolfratshausen, Germany, showing its fingerholes and with its mute (IV 188); reproduction of medieval *trompette de menestrel* with its mouthpipe extended, by Peter Holmes, Colindale, England (II 116).

on a woodwind instrument. Its foremost exponent was Anton Weidinger, for whom both Haydn (in 1796) and Hummel (in 1803) wrote their concertos.[36]

The key bugle that was invented by Irish bandmaster Joseph Haliday in 1810 is a very different instrument from the key trumpet.[37] Animal horns with fingerholes go back to the Middle Ages and still survive as folk instruments in Sweden and the Baltic States (see figure 5.5),[38] but Haliday was the first to apply the same principle to the metal bugle. As we note in interlude E, the bugle's wide expanding bore is well suited to tone holes, and the instrument was immediately adopted all over Europe and in America. Its success was such that even as late as 1891, Capt. C. R. Day could write that "in agility and rapid articulation it is still preferable to any piston instrument."[39] The French maker Jean Hilaire Asté, who worked under the name of Halary, copied Haliday's instrument and in 1817 applied for a patent for a whole family of key bugles, from treble to bass, the lowest called the *ophicléide* (Greek *ophis*, "serpent," plus the French for "keyed").

The serpent had a long history, allegedly being invented by a French canon of Auxerre around 1590 to support the singing of plainsong in church. It was a sinuous wooden instrument, curving to and fro like a snake, which is how it got its name. It was much wider in bore than the cornett, with a metal crook, a metal or ivory cup mouthpiece, and six fingerholes. Because of its width of bore, and because the fingerholes had to be placed where the player could reach them rather than where they ought to be acoustically, its intonation depended much on the ear and lip of the player. Keys were added from around 1800, at first three and later any number up to thirteen, although as Reginald Morley-Pegge remarked, the more keys there were, the more out-of-tune notes were available to the less expert players.[40] Despite such remarks (and there were many even ruder in past times), the serpent was a very successful instrument in its day, with orchestral parts as late as Mendelssohn's overture to *A Midsummer Night's Dream* of 1826, and even later in English church bands, and it has achieved a notable revival today. It was an unwieldy instrument on the march, and many different patterns of upright serpent were invented, from Frichot's metal bass horn of the 1790s, through the Russian bassoon (neither Russian nor a bassoon, but a French wooden upright serpent, often with a metal bell in the shape of a serpent's head), to the ophicleide.

Of these, the ophicleide was by far the most successful, fully keyed, with a dry, woody sound, despite being made of brass. It has a wide orchestral repertoire, notably in Berlioz's *Symphonie Fantastique*, in which it punches out the "Dies Irae" theme with a precision that no modern tuba can match (a baritone is a better, though still inadequate, substitute—a tuba is too heavy). Ophicleides remained in use in many places into the end of the nineteenth century and are now being heard more and more frequently in performances on "original" instruments.

The name causes some confusion because some of the early valve tubas, built at around the same pitch, 9-foot Bb, were also known as ophicleides—they played the same part and, being closely folded with narrower bells than we see today, looked very similar.

Returning to the bugle, this has, from the eighteenth century and probably earlier, been a military instrument. It was usually made of copper—experiment has shown that the sound of copper carries farther than brass—and it was a wide-bore instrument, as we have said. Initially it was curved in a half-moon, but later it was folded once around (this was the instrument to which Haliday applied his keys). Today it is more closely folded, twice around. The postal services used a somewhat narrower-bored instrument, the *cornet de poste*. This was normally of brass, for its sound needed to carry only far enough to warn oncoming coaches or tollgates of its approach, and for convenience it was coiled in a circle, as distinct from

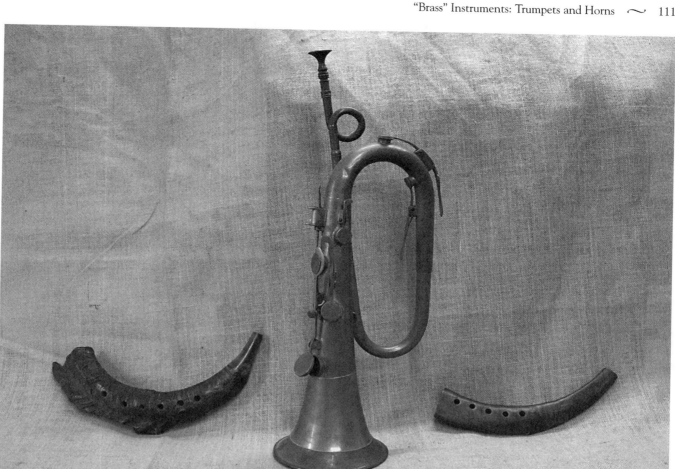

Figure 5.5.   Fingerhole Horns

L–R: Medieval fingerhole horn, reproduction by author (III 72); key bugle, reproduction of English model, Pakistan, for Paxman, London (VII 40); *bukkehorn*, Sweden or Baltic States (VI 250).

the normal straight coach horn. Both bugle and cornet rapidly acquired valves, once these had been invented, and each spawned a large family.

The flügelhorn, as the treble-valved bugle was called, had alto, tenor, baritone, bass, and eventually contrabass relatives, the lowest known as the tubas. The cornet (once valved, it dropped the rest of its name) grew only as far as the 9-foot baritone size because of its narrower bore. The names of all the instruments of both families have, over the past 150 years, descended into total confusion, complicated with a plethora of patent instruments bearing the inventor's name, such as saxhorns. The only author brave enough to sort them all out is Clifford Bevan.[41]

Briefly, each family has a treble in 4½' B♭ and a soprano in 3' E♭ and very rarely a piccolo in 2¼' B♭. Confusion starts with the 6' alto (in English, the tenor), and then becomes worse with the 9' B♭ instruments, indis-

criminately designated tenor, baritone, euphonium, and bass. The last was the first of the tubas, patented by Wieprecht and Moritz in Berlin in 1835, though the valved ophicleides seem to have been somewhat earlier. Lower tubas in 12' E♭ or F followed, sometimes called *bombardon* or similar terms that have also been used for other sizes, and then 18' BB♭ contrabasses, the largest variety normally seen today, although many makers have produced an occasional super bass, mainly for show. Because these instruments were chiefly used in the bands, military and other, the keys of E♭ and B♭ were preferred, but with the basses, we begin to get orchestral instruments, so these are also often built in C. The French tended to use an 8' C tuba, with a sufficient number of valves to obtain the same range as the 16' CC contrabass used over most of the rest of the orchestral world.

For bands on the march, the tuba is a heavy instrument to carry. Quite early on, many makers produced helicons (as always under a variety of names), instruments coiled circularly so that much of the weight could be borne on one shoulder. These had the disadvantage that the sound was projected toward the side. John Philip Sousa, bandmaster of the U.S. Marine Corps, suggested an upward-facing bell—the first sousaphone, familiarly known as the "rain-catcher." Others preferred the later forward-facing version still used today.

Brass tubing, in an inventor's hands, is as malleable as spaghetti. As a result, there is no limit to the design of these instruments, and every possible shape (and some that look impossible) has been tried. The commonest are the forward facing (even down to the tuba) and the upright (even up to the piccolo). Shapes, designs, numbers, and combinations of valves have also varied, partly to overcome the problems described in the afterword when using more than one valve at a time. Bore patterns have also varied, and our initial description of the two families of cornets and bugles is really a gross oversimplification, for there have been many in between—each, of course, with its own patent name. Even the bugle does not escape, because everywhere except in Italy and the United States, it is universally the wide-bore, expanding-bore instrument we have described. However, in those two countries alone, the bugle is a cylindrical-bore instrument—in other words, a trumpet—with a single piston to transpose the pitch, often by a fourth. For lack of space, we must leave these instruments here, but all varieties, including important variants such as *cimbasso*, essential for Italian opera, and Wagner tubas, many of them illustrated, will be found in Bevan's book.

Finally we turn to the horn and a few more instruments from other cultures.

The horn was initially a hunting instrument. We know little of its development from the animal horn before the seventeenth century, although there is plenty of evidence from the Middle Ages onward for coiled instruments that must have been made from other materials and, from around 1600, for coiled horns made of metal.[42] English hunting signals seem always to have been fairly simple, and the normal English hunting horn is a short, straight instrument, about nine inches (22.5 cm) long, whose single note can be lipped a short distance up or down—up to the mid-nineteenth century it was between twelve and fourteen inches long.

Much more elaborate calls were required in Germany and France and therefore longer, hooped or coiled horns were needed. Mersenne cites meeting huntsmen who could produce the same range as the trumpet, implying an instrument at least seven feet long, which for portability must have been coiled.[43] This may well have been

identical to no. 11 in figure 5.3, which Praetorius called a "hunting trumpet." The large horn with a single wide coil, still at trumpet pitch, was certainly in use by the middle of the seventeenth century, and by 1700, if not before, the triple-coiled horns an octave lower, at around 14' D, were in use.[44] An example of this last instrument, in 12' F of the period, sounding modern E, was made in London by William Bull at that date and called by him on his trade card a French horn. This indicates that they were known and used in England by then and that they were firmly associated with French hunting practice. An order in 1717 for twelve instruments for the Royal Buckhounds at the English court tells us that some English huntsmen played as elaborate music in the field as any German or French counterparts. Similar instruments are still used in France as the *trompe de chasse*, and they must have differed only in detail from the instruments for which Bach wrote as *corno da caccia*.

Such French and English instruments were usually made as a series of five or six stepped cylinders, each fitting into the next with a soldered joint, plus a long, gradually expanding bell joint widening into the horn's characteristic widely flared bell. In Vienna, certainly by 1725, judging from a silver pair of that date by Leichamschneider, makers could produce horns in two expanding joints, each about six and a half feet long, the first with an internal diameter of around a quarter of an inch (6 mm), expanding over that distance to around a third of an inch (8 or 9 mm), the second from that latter diameter to the bell of 9¾ inches (248 mm).[45] The reason for going into this detail is that it emphasizes the skill required and available, not only to make the horns but also to make and handle the steel mandrel on which the silver was rolled, the thickness of a knitting needle some six or seven feet long. Similar horns were built in Germany, particularly in Nuremberg.

Some horns were built so that the mouthpiece went directly into the end of the instrument, but others were designed, as in Praetorius's illustration of the *Jäger Trommet* in figure 5.3, to take a crook so that they could be played in different keys. In the eighteenth and early nineteenth centuries, it was common in England, Italy, and the German lands for horns to be provided with one or two master crooks that accepted the mouthpiece, and a number of couplers that fitted between the master crook and the horn and that could be used singly or sometimes in combinations to produce different keys. Only in France was it normal to have a crook for each key.

Players still depended on the skill of their lips to tune the poor harmonics and to produce notes outside the harmonic series. Not until the second half of the eighteenth century, after the time of the Baroque masters such as Bach and Handel, was it discovered—always said to have been by a Bohemian player, Anton Hampl—that by placing the hand inside the bell mouth and varying its position to close the bell to a greater or lesser degree, it was possible to lower the pitch by a semitone or more and thus produce nonharmonic notes with ease and much greater precision. This new style of playing led to a different manner of writing for the horn and differentiated it more sharply from the trumpet. Players, during the later eighteenth century and into the nineteenth, kept the bell always partly stopped so as to minimize the difference in volume and tone between the natural and stopped notes, aiming for as even a sound as possible throughout the range. As a result, the horn became a quiet instrument because the hand muffled the sound. This technique was maintained long after the invention of valves and among the better players and soloists, certainly up to Brahms's time and in Paris even into the twentieth century. Its revival today is only partly successful because of the need in modern concert halls to produce a louder sound and so to use a more open bell. This produces more contrast between stopped and open notes than is really compatible with the ideals of hand-horn technique.

Returning now to other cultures, we have described the use of shells, animal horns and tusks, and wood. Other materials are used also. In Tibet, trumpets of human bone, both femur and tibia, the upper and lower leg bones, are used, together with drums made of two human

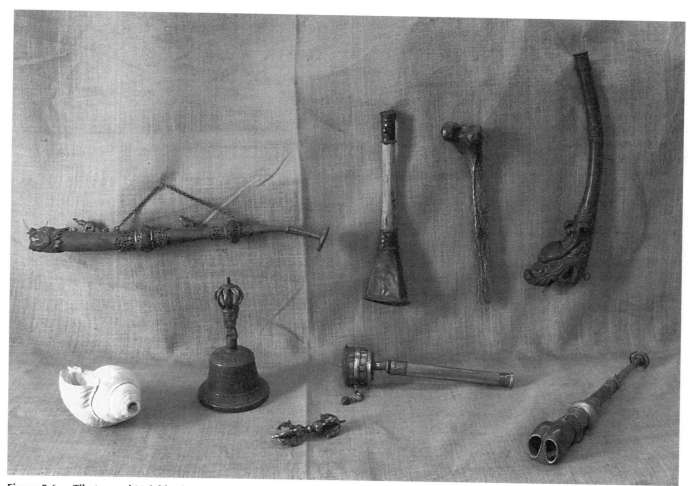

Figure 5.6. Tibetan and Neighboring Trumpets

Above, L–R: dragon-headed brass and copper, with decorations of other animals, Nepal (II 38); *rkang-gling* of human tibia with metal bell and mouthpiece sleeve, Tibet (I 162); rkang-gling of human femur, Tibet (V 236); *kang dung*, dragon-headed brass and copper, Sino-Tibetan border area (II 24).

Below, L–R: *chank*, conch, India, but used in Tibet also (III 70b); three items used with these trumpets in ritual—*dril-bu*, handbell, Tibet (VIII 218), *rdo-rje* or thunderbolt, Tibet (XII 110), and prayer wheel, Tibet (XIII 174); rkang-gling, copper and silver, shaped in imitation of a human femur for those whose status precludes the use of bone (III 142).

crania that we discussed earlier (see figure 2.2). This is not the desecration of a body as we might see it, but a reflection of the belief that the body, once left by the spirit, is no more than discarded clothing, and so may be used for any useful purpose. While such trumpets may be used in rituals, they are not regarded as suitable for the higher lamas, and for their use, metal imitations are made.[46]

Gourds are used as trumpets in East Africa, and bamboo in New Guinea and among the Naga of Assam (see figure 5.7). The New Guinea instruments are conch substitutes, as are their side-blown wooden trumpets. Whether the New Zealand wooden trumpets known as *puutorino*, referred to in interlude F, were also conch substitutes is unknown, for their use had been abandoned before written records were made, but as described in that interlude, it is thought that the fingers were moved over their figure-eight-shaped hole to vary the pitch, just as the hand is moved in the bell of a shell. A metal side-blown horn substitute is used among the Muria Gonds of India, and pottery was used in pre-Columbian Peru among the Moche people for coiled trumpets as well as for conchs. The Naga trumpets, the phupphu that we have referred to above, were developed from a straight instrument with a reed body and a segment of gourd as a bell into one with a series of short bamboo segments set into each other to form a stepped cone, to imitate the bugle calls of a neighboring military camp. Like the Celtic carnyx and the Dutch midwinterhoorn, these have an obliquely cut embouchure at the end of the tube.

We said above of the makers of our culture that trumpets and horns can be made in any conceivable shape. So, in the world as a whole, can they be from any conceivable material.

Notes

1. Nandor Kalicz, "Über die chronologische Stellung," in *Symposium über die Enstehung*, ed. B. Chropovosky (1973), 131–65.

2. J. Wilfred Jackson, *Shells as Evidence of the Migrations* (1917). His theories on migration are highly suspect, but his evidence for the use of conchs in many areas is very valuable. South African seaweed trumpets are in the Pitt Rivers Museum, Oxford, and Percival Kirby told me of his vain attempts to find one long enough to play a Mozart horn concerto. Curt Sachs records the use of conchs in Madagascar in *Les instruments de musique de Madagascar* (1938), 10–12.

3. Information from Maria Antònia Juan i Nebot, given to me along with a Mediterranean triton, *Charonia nodifera* (Lamarck), shell.

4. Arthur Evans, *The Palace of Minos* (1921–1923); regarding the intaglio, see vol. 1, fig. 222, and vol. 4, fig. 288.

5. David S. Reese, "The Late Bronze Age to Geometric Shells from Kition," part 2 of appendix 8(A) in V. Karageorghis, *Excavations at Kition 5/2* (1985), 340–71, esp. 353–64. Reese identifies the shells as *Charonia nodifera* (Lamarck), the same species as the Hungarian shell noted above.

6. Batya Bayer, "The Conch-Horn of Hazor," *Tatzlil* 3 (1963): 140–42; Amīhāi Mazār, *Tel-Qasīle* (1983).

7. Francis W. Galpin, *The Music of the Sumerians* (1936), 24 and plate 4:6.

8. In the Pitt Rivers Museum in Oxford, there are several specimens of *Strombus gigas* (Linnaeus) shells that have been used for both purposes.

9. A skeuomorph is the result of "the substitution of products of craftsmanship for components or objects of natural origin" (Laurence Picken, *Folk Musical Instruments of Turkey* [1975], 195).

Figure 5.7. Oceanic and Other Trumpets

Above, L–R: side-blown trumpet with carved decoration, Blackwater River, Papua New Guinea (IX 210); end-blown bamboo, Asmat people, Papua New Guinea (VI 4); *puutorino*, modern replica by Gray Nicol, Auckland, New Zealand (IX 8); *tuiter*, pottery, probably Bourbourg area, northern France, a children's instrument blown on St. Martin's Eve (I 222).

Below, L–R: side-blown brass horn, Muria Gonds, India (XII 152); coiled pottery, pre-Columbian Peru (XI 124); pottery conch, Mochica, pre-Columbian Peru (XI 122).

10. Jeremy Montagu, "The Conch in Prehistory," *World Archaeology* 12:3 (1981): 273–79, plates 13–16.

11. James Hornell, *The Sacred Chank of India* (1914). Hornell identifies the shell as *Turbinella pyrum* (Linnaeus).

12. Hornell quotes verses 11–19 of the *Bhagavad-Gita*, which give the names of each hero and his conch.

13. Experiment has shown that the more rigid and the more massive the material of wind instruments, the more of the energy imparted to it by the player is free to come out as sound, rather than being dissipated by vibrating the body of the instrument. When around 1950, my fellow students first had their French horns lacquered, this inhibited the vibration of the brass and the loudness was increased. A colleague, John Burton, once made a cornett from fiberglass and experimented by adding more material to the bell end. With each layer, the sound got louder until it looked like a club and sounded like a trumpet. We have already noted, in connection with drumshells, Picken's remarks to similar effect.

14. Information kindly provided by William Waterhouse from a Japanese manual, *Gyōja Nichō* (Yoshimo, 1976), 20–21.

15. An example of such a *Semifusus colosseus* (Lamarck) is in the British Museum of Natural History, London.

16. Karl Erik Larsson, "The Conch Shells of Fiji," in his *Fijian Studies* (1960), 121–47. One triton, *Charonia tritonis* (Linnaeus), in a museum in Australia, was end-blown, but it has a fingerhole and was a substitute for the frog shell *Bursa bubo* (Linnaeus).

17. *Cassis cornuta* (Linnaeus).

18. *Cassis tuberosa* (Linnaeus) and *Strombus gigas* (Linnaeus), respectively.

19. There are several descriptions of Tutankhamun's trumpets, including Hans Hickmann, *La Trompette* (1946); Lise Manniche, *Musical Instruments from the Tomb of Tut'ankhamūn* (1976) (neither is wholly correct); and my own "One of Tutankhamon's Trumpets," *GSJ* 29 (1976): 115–17, and *Journal of Egyptian Archaeology* 64 (1978): 133–34, which was based on close examination of the bronze trumpet that traveled with the exhibition of the pharaoh's treasures in the 1970s. For the biblical trumpets, see my *Musical Instruments of the Bible* (2002), 26–32.

20. Montagu, *Musical Instruments of the Bible*, 19–24 and 134–41. One should remember that what brought the walls down was all the people shouting.

21. H. C. Broholm, William P. Larsen, and Godtfred Skjerne, *The Lures of the Bronze Age* (1949), and Cajsa Lund, ed., *The Bronze Lurs* (1986).

22. There are section drawings in Broholm, Larsen, and Skjerne, *Lures of the Bronze Age*, and detailed comments in my paper "Mouthpiece Development of the Bronze Lur and Its Musical Consequences," in Lund, *Bronze Lurs*, 211–15.

23. John M. Coles, "Irish Bronze Age Horns," *Proceedings of the Prehistoric Society* 29 (1963): 326–56, and Coles, "Some Irish Horns of the Late Bronze Age," *Royal Society of Antiquaries of Ireland* 97:2 (1967): 113–17.

24. Coles, "Irish Bronze Age Horns," 347–49.

25. Curt Sachs, *History of Musical Instruments* (1940), 146, fig. 35.

26. Renato Meucci, "Roman Military Instruments," *GSJ* 42 (1989): 85–97.

27. M. L. West, *Ancient Greek Music* (1992); see p. 82 for the use of the aulos on the march and pp. 118–21 for the salpinx. The only alleged salpinx to survive is a very dubious instrument in the Boston Fine Arts Museum, with no certain provenance and differing in every respect from what we otherwise know of the instrument. See L. D. Caskey, "Archaeological Notes," *Archaeological Institute of America Bulletin* 41 (1937): 525–27.

28. There is one in the Ashmolean Museum in Oxford.

29. Stuart Piggott, "The *Carnyx* in Early Iron Age Britain," *Antiquaries Journal* 39 (1959): 19–32.

30. For charter horns in general, see Joseph C. Bridge, "Horns," *Journal of the Chester and North Wales Architectural, Archaeological and Historical Society* n.s. 11 (1905): 85–166.

31. For the Horn of Ulph, see my *World of Medieval and Renaissance Musical Instruments* (1976), 16–17 and plate 7.

32. John Webb, "The Billingsgate Trumpet," *GSJ* 41 (1988): 59–62, plates 6–10, and Graeme Lawson and Geoff Egan, "Medieval Trumpet from the City of London," *GSJ* 41 (1988): 63–66.

33. This is reproduced in many books, including my own *Medieval and Renaissance Musical Instruments*, plates VIII and IX. The instruments are discussed in detail in Jeremy Montagu, "Musical Instruments in Hans Memling's Paintings," *Early Music* 35:4 (2007), forthcoming.

34. Marin Mersenne, *Harmonie Universelle* (1636), Livre Cinquiesme des Instruments à Vent, 274, 276. Whether *mesures* meant beats or bars (measures), this is an extraordinary duration.

35. Art Brownlow, *The Last Trumpet* (1996).

36. Reine Dahlqvist, *The Keyed Trumpet* (1975).

37. Ralph T. Dudgeon, *The Keyed Bugle* (1993).

38. Magnus Bäckström, *Hornet* (1984).

39. C. R. Day, *A Descriptive Catalogue of the . . . Royal Military Exhibition* (1891), 154–55.

40. Personal conversation.

41. Clifford Bevan, *The Tuba Family* (2nd enl. ed., 2000).

42. Anthony Baines, *Brass Instruments* (1976), 138ff.

43. Mersenne, *Harmonie Universelle*, 246.

44. Reginald Morley-Pegge's *The French Horn* (1960) is still the best account of the history of the horn, although a new history by Renato Meucci and Gabriele Rocchetti, to be published by Yale University Press, is imminent. Horace Fitzpatrick's *The Horn and Horn-Playing* (London: OUP, 1970) should be treated with the greatest caution.

45. Jeremy Montagu, "On the Skill of the Nürnberg Brass Instrument Makers," *FoMRHIQ* 43 (April 1986): Comm. 722, 124–26. The use of Nürnberg (Nuremberg) instead of Vienna was sheer carelessness, for which I apologize.

46. Information given verbally by the Incarnate Lama Chime Yongdong when surveying the Tibetan instruments in the Pitt Rivers Museum, Oxford.

~

The Second Industrial Revolution

The first Industrial Revolution has been described above in interlude C. The second, which began in the seventeenth century and came to full flood in the eighteenth, led to our modern orchestras and their instruments. It was effective in two principal respects: the radical developments of mechanical technology, and the resulting changes in the makeup of society. Yet despite the fact that the latter was consequent to the former, it was the latter, the changes in society, whose influence was by far the more important.

What we now call classical music, as distinct from folk and popular music, began to take shape in Europe in the early seventeenth century, with the first adumbrations of what was to become the orchestra, and it was then mainly the prerogative of court and church.[1] The princely *cappella* was a private band, and its performances were open only to the noble family and their invited guests, although when there were outdoor celebrations, the general populace would often be able to watch and listen from afar. The church would have its choir, with or without accompanying instruments as was consonant with its customs, but while it was, of course, open to all, its musical performances were devotional, at least in theory, rather than entertainment. What little middle class there was had recourse for entertainment mainly to domestic music making.

The rise of an entrepreneurial culture in the sixteenth century, taking advantage of the great explorations and opening up trade around the world, was followed in the seventeenth century by the beginnings of the Industrial Revolution. Both of these events created a wealthy middle class that desired to share the privileges of the aristocracy and had the financial means to do so. The means were not, with rare exceptions, sufficient for the maintenance of private orchestras or other musical establishments, but did suffice, wherever enough such middle classes were gathered together, to support public performances of music in cities such as London, Paris, Hamburg, and Rome.

There are fundamental differences between court performances and public concerts. One function of court music was conspicuous consumption, to show that the prince was wealthy enough to keep a court band, all dressed in his livery. Another was much like that of the Palm Court or of the ever-present musical wallpaper in our restaurants and elsewhere today: It was a background noise to the conversation and had the virtue of allowing people to gossip slanderously about their neighbors without being overheard. There were, of course, many exceptions—courts where the prince was an ardent lover of music, even a player in his own band or a composer for it—but that did not mean that all the court, or all the prince's invited friends and hangers-on, shared his love for music. Thus even in Frederick the Great's Berlin, even in Mannheim, even in Esterházy, not everyone listened to Carl Philipp Emanuel, or Stamitz, or Haydn, as we do in our concert halls today.

With the rise of a moneyed bourgeoisie, things changed. If such people wanted to hear music, it could only be possible in a public place, for few members of the rising middle class were wealthy enough even to hire an orchestra for a private concert and so ape the aristocracy in this way. If they were going to a concert, it would be in a public hall, they would have to pay for their seats, and they would want their money's worth. They and their families would want to hear the music. The instruments had to become more numerous and, as we shall see below, they often had to grow louder, simply so that they should be audible. This need for larger bodies of musicians led to the creation of the orchestra, as distinct from the smaller bodies of instrumentalists that had preceded it.[2] Orchestras were assembled for the early theaters, for operas and concerts, for the pleasure gardens (with the added problem of the need to be audible outdoors), and for the early concert halls.

Another important element in the early history of public performance was the military band. The bands themselves were commonly the personal property of the colonel of the regiment or of the officers jointly, but their performances were inevitably public. When a regiment marches down the street with drums beating and band playing, everyone can hear it. Because the street acoustic is unfavorable for musical performance, loud instruments were essential for such ensembles, and effect and novelty were always also an important influence.

The opera, which began around 1600 initially as princely commissions, had by the middle of the seventeenth century become a public spectacle, mainly in Italy and, somewhat later, in France. This is the one form of music making for a paying public that has an earlier history than that of the concert hall. The precedence of the opera does not stop there, for in those parts of Europe where it (and cognate forms such as the *Singspiel* in Germany) were popular, it led to the establishment of the orchestra as a unified body, independent of a princely establishment. Once theaters were built for opera performances, they began to be used also as concert halls. This was partly because the musicians were paid only when they were performing so that there was a natural desire among them to perform as often as possible, but it was also because an empty theater eats money. In the centers where the opera was less established, there grew up the need for concert halls specifically designed for that purpose, and it is said that it was in London that the first public concert hall was established. An early version of the Musicians' Union built the York Buildings in 1678 as a venue for its members. The Holywell Music Room, built seventy years later in Oxford, is the world's oldest surviving concert hall still in use for that purpose.

By the second quarter of the eighteenth century, public orchestral concerts had become established over much of Europe, and also in America, though still mainly in preexisting buildings. It would be another half-century and more before most major cities acquired a hall built specifically for public concerts. In 1781 the Leipzig Gewandhaus was built, and over the next fifty or sixty years, many other cities constructed halls of similar size and importance.[3]

Once the orchestra was established in such venues, its numbers began to increase, as the composers who had previously been content with strings plus a couple of oboes and a couple of horns were now adding a pair of bassoons, followed by trumpets and drums and, by the end of the eighteenth century, flutes and clarinets and sometimes a second pair of horns. The only recourse to balance these was to increase the size of the string band. When that happened, the woodwinds were at a disadvantage, and so they had to grow louder. As they did so, they began to drown the strings, initiating a vicious circle that still plagues concert promoters today: the near impossibility of putting on a concert that will cover its cost. As the number of string players increases, the cost of putting on the concert goes up. The obvious way to cover this increased cost without pricing seats beyond what people are willing to pay is to build a larger hall to seat more paying customers. But then the orchestra has to be larger so that it can be heard, and so it goes on. This is why today some halls have become so large that from the uttermost gallery, it feels as though one is watching the orchestra through the wrong end of a telescope. Even then the hall may be, as in Berlin, receiving an annual subsidy that threatens to bankrupt the city.

An alternative to increasing the number of string instruments is to modify the instruments so that each will produce more sound. An obvious way to achieve this is to increase the string tension. This has two results: the pitch rises and, only too often, the instrument collapses. The history of musical pitch is one of inexorable rise.[4] Between 1670 and 1870, the pitch of each note name rose by about a minor third, the A that the orchestra tunes to going from around 392 Hz to around 452 Hz (from the equivalent of modern pitch G to B♭). There have been many attempts to bring it down to where singers can reach their higher notes without overstraining their voices, the most successful being the introduction of the French *diapason normal* in 1858 at A = 435 Hz and Henry Wood's London Promenade concerts in 1895 at A = 439, followed by the international convention in 1939 that established our modern concert pitch of A = 440, all about a whole tone higher than in 1670.[5] Despite this, many orchestras are today playing higher again in the vain search for greater brilliance, gradually working their way back up toward the old high pitch.

String instruments were threatening to collapse by the end of the eighteenth century, by which time pitch had risen by about a semitone, from 392 Hz to between 409 and 415. The solution was the radical reconstruction that we shall describe in more detail at the end of chapter 6 when discussing the violin. Briefly, this involved resetting and realigning the joint between the neck and the body, plus lengthening the neck, thereby increasing the tension of the strings and making them louder still. To withstand the pressure of that tension, the internal bass bar had to be heavier and the sound post thicker.

Since it was normally neither feasible financially to increase the number of wind players nor desirable musically to have two playing in unison, the answer was to modify them also to produce more sound.[6] This was more necessary with flutes than with the other woodwinds, because of their acoustical nature in anything but the highest registers, where their shrillness allows them to cut through. Some modification of the bore already described had helped, especially widening the foot joint so that the taper was reversed, expanding from the position of the D♯ hole to the end. The first step was to widen the embouchure again, back toward what it had been in the early Baroque with the three-piece flute, as we can see on the ivory one-key flute in figure 3.13.

The next recourse was to try to widen the fingerholes, so that each would vent more sound, but this tended to upset the tuning unless they could be moved to a different position—difficult within the span of the hand—or unless the player could modify the playing technique sufficiently to force the instrument into tune. Charles Nicholson achieved this in the early 1820s in London by enlarging some of the fingerholes, first moderately and then more widely, while pulling the resulting sharper pitches into tune by the strength of his lip and embouchure control. Some of his contemporaries criticized the powerful sound he emitted, saying that it sounded more like a trumpet than a flute, though others praised it. Many of his rivals, less strong in lip or skilled in control, complained that his flutes were impossible to play in tune. Nevertheless, many were made and sold (see figure E.1).

It was Nicholson's powerful sound that inspired Theobald Boehm—because he was unable to rival it on a normal flute—to produce his systems that we have described above in chapter 3 on the transverse flute and illustrated in figure 3.13.[7] Nor was Boehm the only maker who tried to evolve new ways of combining wider holes and playing in tune. Abel Siccama, in 1842, widened some holes and moved the two ring-finger holes farther down the tube to obviate their consequent sharpness, adding a key to cover each, with its touch piece in the normal position so that it could be reached by the finger. There were many other attempts to produce designs with greater power but without the complexity of the first Boehm system.

Figure E.1. Keyed Flutes

L–R: eight-key, Nicholson wide-hole model, by Clementi, London (I 244); German Reform system, by G. Mollenhauer, Cassel (VIII 128); Siccama's "Diatonic Flute," by Chappell, London (IV 202); Pratten's "Perfected Flute," one of many different models using that name, by Boosey, London (VI 18); Carte's 1851 system, the "Council Prize Flute," by Rudall, Rose, Carte, London (III 192); Carte's 1867 system, by Rudall, Rose, Carte, London (VII 218).

Nevertheless, it was Boehm's mechanism, designed and made initially due to his skill as a goldsmith but then produced commercially by many other makers thanks to the great mechanical improvements of the Industrial Revolution, that proved most successful. Even his rivals frequently adopted his long rod axles that conveyed the motion of a finger so easily from one end of the flute to the other. The older lever keys had been adequate on the earlier flutes, but they were limited in effective length. A key that is too long between finger and axle, or between axle and head, can never be positive in its motion. When too long between finger and axle, it is liable to bend and is limited in its arc of movement. When too long between axle and head, the problem is more serious because it is difficult for the spring to produce enough pressure to seal the hole against air leakage without being too heavy for rapid movement in fast music. A rod axle, however, with its touch pieces and keys set at right angles to the axle, could have a short movement between the finger and the axle and, because it was the axle that was long, not the lever, an equally short movement between the axle and the keyhead. What was more, because of devices such as Boehm's clutch and the use of tubular axles, it was possible for one rod to move inside another and for more than one key to be carried on the same axle. Even without that modification, the axles could lie close enough together to allow neighboring fingers to control keys where they were needed, as may be seen on modern instruments today. It was this keywork of Boehm's, and the many adaptations of it, that allowed the construction of all the modern woodwind systems.

Boehm's second model, the 1847 cylindrical Boehm, met strong resistance in his native land because some players thought the tone too open and because it required a new fingering system that some were reluctant to learn. The German Reform Flute, a modification of the old eight-key flute, nevertheless depended greatly on Boehm's mechanism, with rings and rod axles over much of the body, even though there were still long keys toward the head for vents to tune the upper register. It was Boehm's mechanism, too, that enabled Richard Carte to produce his 1851 system, which endeavored to retain much of the earlier fingering on Boehm's design of body, and later Carte's more successful 1867 system. This remained popular in Britain into the twentieth century.

In France makers had concentrated first on improving the older model and then on perfecting the Boehm systems. A number of features on the later Boehm flutes were devised by his licensees in Paris and then adopted by Boehm himself as well as by other makers.

With brass instruments, the developments of mechanical technology were perhaps more important, for it was these that allowed all the instruments to play chromatically. Previously this had been possible only on the trombone, the slide trumpet over part of its range, and, more quietly than was now desirable, on the hand-stopped horn. All three of these are described in chapter 5. It was these developments that also permitted the creation of all the instruments of the brass band and of the orchestral basses.

The initial attempts to gain chromaticism were made by a carefully placed fingerhole and by keys. The use of a fingerhole as a harmonic vent produced a subsidiary harmonic series, and this seems to have been occasionally popular with posthorns, whose players could then extend a short flourish with a few extra notes. It met with limited success on more serious brass instruments, due probably to the deterioration of tone quality that results, as can be heard from many imitation "baroque" trumpeters today. They use this method because they have not succeeded in re-creating the *clarino* technique of the seventeenth and eighteenth centuries safely enough to satisfy conductors and recording companies.[8] This consisted not only of ascending into the higher reaches of the harmonic series, from the sixteenth to the twenty-fourth overtones, but also in having the skill and strength to pull the eleventh (halfway between F and F♯), the thirteenth (a flat A), and the fourteenth (a very flat B♭) into tune with their lips.

The use of keys met with more success initially. Kölbel's *Amorschall*, for example, a French horn with some form of keywork, had a considerable reputation in St. Petersburg and elsewhere in the third quarter of the eighteenth century. Much more successful, even though the player has to tread carefully to equalize the tone and volume of the vented and natural notes, was Anton Weidinger's keyed trumpet, for which both Haydn and Hummel wrote concertos, both of which are still in the repertoire and occasionally played today on reproductions of the instrument originally intended.[9] That instrument and Joseph Haliday's keyed bugle of 1810, the ancestor of many keyed brass basses, are described in chapter 5.

The wider, conical bore of the keyed bugle is well suited to venting by side keys, and it was successfully mastered by many players throughout Europe and America, though mainly in military bands and in the more popular musical ensembles, especially by soloists, whereas the narrower-bored keyed trumpet seems to have been used seldom much beyond Austria and southern Germany and in some Italian opera orchestras.[10]

It was not until well after the invention of valves, initially in Prussia, that the chromatic brass instruments other than the slide trombone, valve trumpet, and valve horn became accepted orchestrally. One wonders whether this was due to some form of snobbishness. The bugle, in military circles, was the instrument of the plebeian infantry, very different from the trumpet of the aristocratic cavalry. Was this one reason why the keyed and valved bugles were not adopted into the orchestra, even though the keyed bugle's larger offshoots such as the ophicleide were (partly for lack of any alternative) admitted in the bass? Or was it merely that the early valves worked better on the narrower-bored orchestral instruments?

Not that valves worked all that well in the early days. Valves have to overcome a number of problems, as makers know only too well even today. First, they must move fluently and return rapidly to their initial position when released. This requires an easy fit and a strong spring, but if the fit is too easy, air will leak around the sides and ruin the sound. If the spring is too heavy, it will take too much effort to move it, whereas if it is too light, it returns slowly—but if it returns too quickly, it will bounce before settling, again ruining the sound. The ports, or channels through the valve, must be as nearly as possible the same diameter as the main tubing, but if the valve is too wide, it will be too heavy to move easily, and if it is long enough to allow each row of ports to be clear of the next, it will take too much time to move. If the ports are too close together, the tubing of one will constrict the next, something that is still often seen today—looking through one port will show a small bump in the tubing where the next port fits too closely to it and constricts its diameter. The valve must also be keyed into position so that it cannot twist within the casing and move its ports out of alignment with the main tubing, but such keys in their grooves can add a further element of friction and so stiffen and slow the movement. Finally, it must be made of, or at least plated with, metals that will not wear away with the constant friction, so again causing leaks. Modern makers claim to have overcome all these problems, but they were already making the same claim in the 1870s, and it was not true then, either. As always, there is still room for improvement.

The first valves were invented by a horn player, Heinrich Stölzel, who applied for a Prussian patent for them in December 1814, granted in the following October.[11] This was a narrow cylindrical piston (see figure E.2), adaptations of which, known by his name, were still being made for cheap brass instruments, especially cornets, into the early twentieth century. It differed from the later types of piston valve by using the bottom of the piston as part of the air passage, and it suffered tonally from the narrowness of its bore and sharp bends in the air column.

The idea of valves seems to have spread rapidly, for in 1816 Friedrich Blühmel, having initially accused Stölzel of stealing his ideas, was experimenting with a rotary valve, and by 1818 he had patented a piston box valve. This was square, rather than cylindrical, and had the advantage of being short-stroke, meaning that it took less time to move—an advantage that was taken

Figure E.2.   Valves for Brass Instruments
L–R: Stölzel piston, Berliner piston, Périnet piston, rotary valve rotor.

up with a cylindrical piston by Wilhelm Wieprecht in 1833, whose model was pirated by Adolphe Sax. Although Stölzel and Blühmel worked together to improve the box valve, it soon fell out of fashion, perhaps due to its greater friction than the cylindrical valve but probably mainly due to greater difficulties in accurate manufacture. A cylindrical valve can be finished and polished on a lathe, but there is no equivalent tool for something square or rectangular.

Other valve types followed rapidly, with Blühmel's first successful rotary valve in 1828, followed by Riedl's in 1835. The latter is essentially the same as that used on horns and many other instruments today. One reason for its popularity is its shorter, and therefore faster, movement, needing merely to rotate 90 degrees within its casing. A quite different type was the double-piston valve first devised by Friedrich Sattler in Vienna in 1821. Instead of one piston with ports through it to let air both into and out of the auxiliary tubing, this has two small pistons side by side, one letting air into the auxiliary tubing and the other letting air back out again. Despite its seemingly greater complexity, it is still used on horns in Vienna today, and a very similar valve was widely used in Belgium on instruments of all sorts under the name of *système belge*.

Wieprecht's wide-bore, short-stroke piston, usually known as *Berliner Pumpen*, gained popularity for several reasons. The advantages of its short stroke were mentioned above. Its wider bore avoided constrictions in the tubing, as did its layout, keeping all the tubing in the same vertical plane, making it easier to design the instrument. The long-stroke piston valves had three levels of tubing: from the top, first the port that led the air into the auxiliary, then the port to run through into the main tubing, and then the port out of the auxiliary. Wieprecht's pistons, on the other hand, had only two levels, with two ports side by side in each. Sax adopted them for many of his instruments, but without troubling to acquire a license from Wieprecht for doing so, leading to one of the many lawsuits that plagued his career.

Hector Berlioz, one of the French musicians who had persuaded Sax to move his manufactory to Paris around 1840, much preferred these valves, which he called *cylindres*, to the *pistons*, meaning either Stölzel's or François Périnet's valves.[12] Périnet produced his piston, intermediate in bore between Stölzel's and Wieprecht's, in 1838, and it remains widely used on all types of brass instruments other than horns and some heavy basses today. Thus in less than a generation, all the valve types surviving today were created.

There were many others, some of them variants of these mentioned, different models of piston or rotor, and others of quite different construction. There must have been something in the air that suggested that the time for valves had come, for there is nothing to suggest that any of the German systems were known in America when Nathan Adams invented his twin-vane system in Lowell, Massachusetts, in 1825. He also invented a rotary valve perhaps a year earlier or the same year, and examples of both his models are preserved on the USS *Constitution*, where he had served as bandmaster during the War of 1812.[13] There is no space here to describe these or any of the many other types of valve, most of them short-lived, which are often rare and treasured objects in collections. Many are described and illustrated in all the books on brass instruments.[14]

Valves, as soon as they were invented, were applied to all the brass instruments—even to trombones, which were fully chromatic already. Valve trombones had three advantages over the slide instrument: they could be played by anyone who already had a brass-playing technique, without the need for learning the more difficult system of slide positions; they took up less space, an important consideration in cramped quarters such as theater pits; and they were easier to handle in military bands on parade, on the march, and on horseback.[15]

For trumpets, the adoption of valves meant that they were now chromatic throughout their range, whereas after the demise of the clarino technique of the Baroque, they had been limited—in those countries that ignored the slide trumpet—to a range from the second harmonic to the twelfth (see figure 0.1 in Explanations and Definitions) and thus to common chords plus the supertonic (the ninth harmonic, written D) in the upper octave and a risky upper fourth (the eleventh harmonic that needed to be lipped down to F or up to F♯).

For the horn, valves meant that players could draw their hand further out of the bell and so produce a louder sound, while still producing the full range of notes that had been available only to the skilled handhorn player but were now to be available to all.

The use of valves also permitted the introduction of the whole families of valved cornets and bugles that are the basis of our brass and military bands and the lower registers of the orchestra today.

When did this happen? With horns and trumpets probably immediately, though evidence is scanty. Stölzel's application for a patent mentions trumpet and bugle as well as horn, and Blühmel's adds trombone. The first musical work that we can be sure was played on a valve horn was Schubert's song "Auf dem Strom" (D. 943) with horn obbligato, written in March 1828 for Josef Rudolf Lewy.[16] It is known that both he and his brother, Eduard Constantin Lewy, gave recitals on valve horns in 1827, and that Eduard was the fourth horn player at the first performance of Beethoven's Ninth Symphony in 1824.[17] Whether he played that famous solo in the slow movement with the valves or the hand, we do not know. As W. F. H. Blandford pointed out, there is nothing very difficult in it as a handhorn part.[18] There is, incidentally, no problem about the solo being for the fourth horn; it is only modern usage that calls it this. To Beethoven, it was the second horn of the second pair, and the *cor basse* or second player was usually a soloist, because he had the wider range in his technique. In this instance, the first pair is pitched in B♭ basso and the second pair is in E♭, and the latter is the required tonality at that point in the movement.

As for the valved bugles and cornets, their introduction followed the social changes to amateur and municipal music making consequent on the Industrial Revolution.

Town bands have a long and distinguished history in Europe, starting with the medieval city waits and *Stadtpfeifer* that, like the guilds of minstrels somewhat earlier, seem to have dwindled away by the middle of the eighteenth century, though surviving in some areas into the nineteenth century. Even outside the towns, there were always some musicians around, either residents who had acquired the skill but worked mainly at some trade or agricultural pursuit, or wandering minstrels—how else could there be village dances, wedding parties, and all the other occasions where music has traditionally been expected? One source for such musicians ever since music became an essential part of military life has been the retired army bandsman, including, and perhaps more importantly than those of the well-known regiments, the bands of the local militias. Another, certainly in Britain, has been the church.

During the Commonwealth in mid-seventeenth-century England, organs were abolished in many, perhaps all, churches. After the Restoration of the monarchy in 1660, when the use of less austere musical settings again became permissible, there was often no money, especially in the smaller parishes, for a new organ, and singers might have been accompanied by instruments. John Playford in 1658 published the second edition of A *Breif Introduction To the Skill of Musick*, in which were included "the Tunes of the Psalmes as they are commonly sung in Parish-Churches with the Bass set under each Tune, By which they may be Play'd and Sung to the *Organ, Virginals, Theorbo-Lute* or *BASS-VIOL*."[19] In the seventh edition of 1674, Playford says, "I refer you to my large Book lately published in Folio [in 1671] Entituled, *Psalmes and Hymns in Solemn Musick of Four Parts*, in which is 47 several Tunes, with the *Bass* under each *Common-Tune*, as proper to sing to Organ, Theorbo, or Bass-Viol." Even earlier, in 1599, Richard Allison published his *Psalmes of David in Meter* with written-out accompaniments for lute, orpharion, cittern, and bass viol.[20] Nicholas Temperly cites Benjamin Hely's *Compleat violist or an introduction to yͤ art of playing on yͤ bass viol* of 1699, which includes "a collection of psalm tunes set to the viol, as they are now in use in churches where there are organs," as being perhaps the earliest record, but these earlier references show clearly that Hely had been anticipated by a century, and longer still elsewhere in Europe.[21]

Many parish records from the middle of the eighteenth century show purchases of instruments and accessories such as reeds and strings,[22] and church bands survived in Britain, as in many other countries, into the end of the nineteenth century, as we know from the novels of Thomas Hardy and others. The same players would be available for local dances and other such occasions. Many churches hold instruments surviving from such bands (sometimes today deposited for safety in local or other museums), and in America a special genre of cello survives, the so-called church basses.

There was certainly an upsurge of civilian bands throughout Europe at the end of the Napoleonic Wars, just as happened later in the United States after the end of the Civil War. Large numbers of soldiers were immediately redundant, and many were thrown on to the streets with no homes and no jobs (as happened again in 1919, in 1945, and to a lesser extent after the Korean and Vietnam wars). Those who had a skill useful in civilian life were the lucky ones, and many ex-service musicians formed their own peripatetic bands. Four other factors came together at this point. One was the increasing number of industries employing large numbers of workers. Another was the beginnings of the great conurbations, villages becoming towns, towns becoming cities. Another was the introduction, first, of the keyed bugles and basses, and then of the valved cornets and bugles. And a fourth was the mechanization of musical instrument making.

Earlier instrument making had normally consisted of a master with perhaps a partner and an apprentice or two, making each instrument themselves, though perhaps buying small wares such as keys from an independent maker. There is good evidence that John Hale was a key maker to the woodwind trade in London from the 1770s,[23] and half a century earlier the Dutch makers Hendrik and Frederik Richters had their keys made by the silversmith Hildebrand van Flory, a family connection.[24] Lute makers were doing this in the early sixteenth century with pegs, ribs, and even soundboards with pre-cut roses,[25] and it seems likely that such practices were widespread throughout the music trade. By the end of the eighteenth century, and perhaps earlier, flute makers, for example, were turning each joint in batches and then assembling completed instruments.

In the 1820s there were beginning to be small factories, and in the 1840s Adolphe Sax was one of the first to establish a major factory in Europe, with large workshops filled with rows of work benches, producing instruments in bulk.[26] Steam power was a common element in such factories in many countries, with rows of machines powered by belts from wheels on long axles running the length of the workshop, and there are many photographs surviving of such shops, both in Europe and the United States.[27]

There were many reasons for the concept of the works band, including the perceived moral effect of music among philanthropic mill and mine owners, the local pride and solidarity engendered by a band, and the desire for a spare-time occupation among people working fixed hours in an urban environment rather than from dawn to dusk as individuals in the countryside. All these were combined with the availability of a wide variety of instruments at cheaper prices.[28]

In many cases, a factory or mill owner would buy instruments for the band, and in others he would stand as guarantor for their costs, because the creation of the band was to his advantage, both for the reasons given above and for the prestige the band would give his business.

Equally it was worthwhile for the new instrument manufacturers to give credit to bands for the purchase of their instruments, for it meant quantity sales and, in the later days of band competitions, prestige that it was their instruments that had been played by a prize-winning band.

One reason for the popularity of brass instruments in such bands was that they were interchangeable. A player of one could change to another, as experience showed a preference for a different voice, from soprano to bass, or as need within the band dictated, for all worked on the same principle: three valves (two in the earlier days) arranged in the same way and, once standardized, the first lowering the pitch by a tone, the second by a semitone, and the third by a tone and a half, and all were sounded by a cup mouthpiece. The only difficulty would be changing from a small mouthpiece to a larger or vice versa, and with goodwill a week or two of practice would overcome that. There was no such standardization among the reed woodwinds. Oboists, clarinetists, and bassoonists, although all reed players, require different techniques with different types or sizes of reed; furthermore, oboes and bassoons have always been among the most expensive instruments with difficult and expensive reeds. Flutists have a very different embouchure technique from the other woodwinds, but flute bands, arranged similarly to brasses from piccolo to bass, were also popular, again because of the ease of changing from one part to another.

As a result, the brass band movement became widespread in Britain, with the further advantage that music for all the instruments was written in treble clef and suitably transposed, so that there was no need to learn a new clef if one changed from one instrument to another, and it spawned a considerable industry of its own, with journals and music published for its members, as well as encouraging the expansion of instrument making.

In the United States, a national tragedy coincided with the establishment of musical instrument factories. The Civil War led to an enormous expansion of military bands, some created with the new armies, others the result of town bands joining the army as a unit.[29] After the war, many such bands returned to civil life and became, as in Europe, a valued feature of municipal life, again leading to a considerable industry, much of which still survives. Town, school, and college bands, like much amateur music making, were greatly reduced in numbers by the introduction of mass entertainment in the second half of the twentieth century, with the rapid growth of preference for listening to or watching others do things from the comfort of one's own home or the local cinemas, rather than doing it for oneself. Nevertheless, bands

still flourish in many places throughout America and Europe, and the amateur band movement is still in surprisingly good health. For example, in Austria, in the Tyrol alone, there are still almost five hundred local bands to this day, and much the same is true in many other parts of the world.[30] The constituent instrumentation may not be the same as in our culture, but a band of musicians is an essential element of life in the overwhelming majority of world cultures, even if it consists of just a shawm and drum or whatever the local equivalent may be.

Where our influence has been strong worldwide is with the military band. These became much more formalized in their constituent parts in the first half of the nineteenth century. Each national war ministry laid down specific numbers of each instrument. This led to the invention of several new instruments because, as the brass proliferated with the introduction of the new keyed and valved types, the woodwinds, which could not compete in volume, were at a disadvantage. As we have seen, the orchestral oboe, bassoon, and clarinet underwent similar development to that of the flute, but neither oboe nor bassoon was loud enough for military use, and also, as armies found themselves active in tropical countries with the rush of many European nations to acquire overseas empires, they were not robust enough to withstand extremes of climate. This led to the invention of metal equivalents.

Adolphe Sax reinvented the shawm when he created the saxophone, a wide-bore, reed-blown instrument. Pierre Auguste Sarrus tried to rival him by inventing the sarrusophone as a family of brass oboe-type instruments, going down to bassoon size. He was successful initially—chiefly for political reasons, since Sax was disliked by many influential people in Paris, both for being too pushy and as a Belgian interloper—but Sarrus's instruments are forgotten today like many others of this epoch. Charles Mahillon's wider-bore *contrebasse à anche*, a form of brass contrabassoon, was more useful than the contrabass sarrusophone, so much so that it can still be found in band instrument catalogues; it gives a sharper bite in the bass than the tuba, which can sound rather woofy.

In the United States, several special forms of instrument were designed specifically for the bands, including "over-the-shoulder" brass instruments, with their bells projecting backward to be more audible for the troops marching behind, and the whole series of sousaphones, designed for the great Marine Corps bandmaster John Philip Sousa, to replace the older helicon basses, as we have seen in chapter 5 on the "brass" instruments.[31]

Today, national differences between one style of military band and another have largely been ironed out, and almost wherever in the world a state visit may occur, the visiting sovereign or president is likely to be greeted with a very familiar lineup playing the visiting and local national anthems.

Notes

1. Jonathan Wainwright and Peter Holman, eds, *From Renaissance to Baroque* (2005).

2. John Spitzer and Neal Zaslaw, *The Birth of the Orchestra* (2004).

3. These dates are drawn from the various editions of *The Oxford Companion to Music* from those edited by Percy A. Scholes (1938–1947), through that of Denis Arnold (1983) to that of Alison Latham (2002).

4. Bruce Haynes, *A History of Performing Pitch* (2002). The subject is far more complex than our very brief description here, as reference to this exemplary study will show.

5. Dr. George Cathcart, an ear and throat specialist, subsidized the first of those Promenade concerts on the condition that Wood and his orchestra would adopt the lower pitch. See Henry J. Wood, *My Life of Music* (1938), 93.

6. The slight variation of pitch that is almost inevitable between two players in unison becomes audible and obtrusive, whereas with strings the greater number of players covers this, as does the incessant vibrato universally used since the early twentieth century.

7. Theobald Boehm, *Die Flöte und das Flötenspiel* (1871; 1908 translation as *The Flute and Flute-Playing*, trans. Dayton C. Miller, translator's note p. 8, quoting a letter from Boehm to Broadwood. See also Richard S. Rockstro, *A Treatise on . . . the Flute* (2nd ed., 1928), specifically in this context, paragraph 580. This is a thorough and entertaining history, if somewhat controversial.

8. There are some players who have achieved this skill, but it is always risky, and many conductors and especially recording companies for whom a duff note can mean a whole new (and very expensive) recording session, insist on safety first and the use of harmonic vents.

9. Reine Dahlqvist, *The Keyed Trumpet* (1975). There are several recordings available of the keyed trumpet.

10. Ralph Dudgeon, *The Keyed Bugle* (1993).

11. Herbert Heyde, *Das Ventilblasinstrument* (1987), 14. Further information here also derives from this book, which remains the most comprehensive study of the origins of the valve, albeit ignoring all inventions and developments outside the German-speaking lands.

12. Hector Berlioz, *Traité d'Instrumentation et d'Orchestration* (1844; 2nd ed., 1880s, reprint, 1970), 185 while discussing the horn, and 191 with the trumpet.

13. Robert E. Eliason, "Early American Valves for Brass Instruments," *GSJ* 23 (1970): 86–96.

14. For example, Anthony Baines, *Brass Instruments* (1976); Baines, *European and American Musical Instruments* (1966); Philip Bate, *The Trumpet and Trombone* (1966); Reginald Morley-Pegge, *The French Horn* (1960), in addition to other texts already cited here. Many of these books have been reissued recently. A new and up-to-date series is pending from Yale University Press, although so far only the volume on trombone has appeared.

15. Most of the stories are true of musically ignorant colonels insisting that all the trombonists move their slides uniformly, irrespective of the different parts they were playing.

16. Otto Erich Deutsch, *Schubert* (1951), 460–61.

17. Morley-Pegge, *French Horn*, 108.

18. W. F. H. Blandford, "The Fourth Horn in the 'Choral Symphony,'" *Musical Times* 983 (January 1925): 29–32; 984 (February 1925): 124–29; 985 (March 1925): 221–23.

19. John Playford, *A Breif Introduction To the Skill of Musick* (2nd ed., 1658), 49. This text may also have appeared in the first edition of 1654, but there seems to be no surviving copy in England in which one could check.

20. My thanks to Dr. Lynda Sayce for this source.

21. Nicholas Temperley, *The Music of the English Parish Church* (1979), 148.

22. K. H. MacDermott, *The Old Church Gallery Minstrels* (1948). Temperley's first reference for these (*Music of the English Parish Church*, p. 149, table 7) is for 1742, in Youlgrave, Derbyshire, "For hairing the bow of the viols, 8d.," followed by six entries for bassoons in various churches, starting in 1748.

23. Many woodwind instruments marked with other names have keys stamped IH on the underside. One speculation is that this was Hale's way of indicating that he had made the whole instrument and had then sold it on for others to stamp their own name in more visible places. This practice of makers selling unmarked instruments for dealers to add their names was widespread in the later nineteenth century and is still common today.

24. Jan Bouterse, *Dutch Woodwind Instruments* (2005), 463.

25. Again, information that I owe to Lynda Sayce.

26. Malou Haine, *Adolphe Sax* (1980); illustrations of part of the factory in 1848 are on p. 124 and in 1860 on p. 129.

27. Many such photographs have appeared in issues of the *Newsletter of the American Musical Instrument Society*.

28. Much of the early history of the band movement in Britain, with emphasis on brass, will be found in Trevor Herbert, ed., *Bands* (1991). Entertaining information and background can be obtained from Algernon S. Rose, *Talks with Bandsmen* (1894).

29. Margaret Hindle Hazen and Robert M. Hazen, *The Music Men* (1987).

30. Erich Egg and Wolfgang Pfaundler, *Das Grosse Tiroler Blasmusikbuch* (1979).

31. Many of these are illustrated in Hazen and Hazen, *Music Men*, e.g., p. 95 for the "rain-catcher" and pp. 93 and 135 for the "over-the-shoulder."

CHAPTER SIX

~

String Instruments

From Bows to Lyres, Harps, and Lutes

The mouth-resonated musical bow is an instrument symbiotic with the player (see interlude G). One of its problems is that while the player's buccal cavities are efficient musically and provide a wide range of pitches and sonorities, they are not very efficient as a resonator and the amount of sound produced is small, enough for the player and any hearers gathered close around but little more. A gourd or similar object, attached to the bow stave and normally using whatever ligature braces the string to link the string to the gourd as well as to the bow stave, is far more resonant and produces a much louder sound. The gourd is open at the back, the opposite side to the bow stave, and different overtones can be selected by moving that opening against the player's chest to open or close it to a greater or lesser extent. The result is not usually as wide a musical range as with the mouth, but enough for at least some melodic movement.

While one normally calls such an instrument a "gourd bow," any hollow object can be used as the resonator. In Brazil the *birimbão* (see figure G.1) usually has a coconut shell, often gaily painted, and the player has a small rattle of woven basketry on a finger of the hand holding the tapping stick to add an extra accompaniment. Wherever musical bows are used, children may use an old tin can as a resonator, for worldwide the detritus of our throwaway culture is used to make instruments.[1] Still, gourds are the most common, and in South Africa among the Swazi, Zulu, and Xhosa, they are often as big as a pumpkin.

Henry Balfour illustrated a wide range of gourd bows as well as mouth bows, many from Africa, a few from South America, and a number from Asia.[2] As we discuss later in interlude G, there has long been debate over whether any of the South American bows are indigenous, or whether they derive from Africans. It seems probable, in our present state of knowledge, that they originated either from those made from remembered practice by African slaves or their descendants or, before the advent of Columbus and his successors, from the chance contacts, for which there is considerable evidence, between Africa and South America in earlier times—the geographical bulges of two continents are close enough together for fishermen and others to have been blown from one to the other. There is much evidence that is becoming increasingly accepted of contacts also via the Chinese exploratory and trading voyages of the early fifteenth century and perhaps even earlier.[3] However, it must be accepted that so far nobody has adduced any evidence for string instruments in any pre-Columbian South American iconography.

A number of the Southeast Asian instruments are not strictly bows at all, for the stave may be rigid, sometimes with a tuning peg or some other projection that will hold the string away from the stave at one end, with a curved termination at the other. Such instruments are verging toward the stick zither. This has a rigid stick as the body with one or more strings running along or above it, parallel with its surface. It can sometimes be difficult to define the border between such bows and zithers, but two examples that are clearly on the stick-zither side are simple forms found in tribal India and East Africa. The former has small sticks standing upright on the stick body and projecting toward the string, held in place with wax, so that they may be used as frets on which to stop the string. A similar effect is achieved in East Africa with a board on edge, where the wood can be cut away between the frets. In both areas, a gourd is used for a resonator, as with the bow. But we should return to the gourd bows from which we have digressed; we shall return to zithers of all sorts later, where both these examples are shown in figure 6.11.

There are a few bows where a second string has been used, but on the whole adding more strings to one's bow has not been successful without considerable modification. Such modification has gone in two directions—to the pluriarc ("many bows") and to the bow harp—but the development of a few instruments has, as it were, stuck in midstream. The bow has become rigid, more strings have been acquired, but the resonator has remained attached to the middle of the bow instead of, as with the pluriarc and the bow harp, migrating to one end. One example is the *wuj* of Kafiristan (see figure 6.1), where a short and rigid arc stands on a large, waisted, skin-covered resonator.[4] Another is the Kru "harp" of Liberia, a stick forked like a Y, sometimes with a third stick closing the open side to form a triangle, with the stem of the Y sitting in a gourd.[5] There are other va-

rieties, but, like these two, they are fairly rare. They are often called harps, but the term is not strictly accurate, for the strings do not pass to the resonator—the most accurate term might be "harps that are not harps."

With the pluriarc, there is a common resonator, a bowl or more frequently a box, from which several flexible sticks—the "bows"—project, each one carrying its own string, the other end of which is tied to the end of the resonator. Examples of such instruments have been collected almost exclusively from Central Africa, mainly in the area that used to be called the Congo.[6] The pluriarc is not the most efficient of instruments. Neither the bow staves nor the strings are usually very strong, so the string tension is low and, as a result, so is the volume. It has long been a hypothesis that in search of greater musical efficiency, the two outermost bow staves might have become rigid and that a wooden bar, or yoke, linking the two staves might have carried the strings from the bows in between, and so, in replacing them, have created the lyre. There is no evidence for this whatsoever (particu-

Figure 6.1.   Harps and Pluriarc
L–R: ivory bow harp, Congo (II 34); pluriarc, Congo (XI 68); *wuj*, Kafiristan (VIII 52).

larly as we shall shortly suggest another source as the origin for the East African lyre), but speculations of this sort are always fascinating.

The other route for the development of the multistring bow is toward the bow harp. Here, the bow stave becomes rigid and the bowl of the resonator is built onto its end, open side upward, looking somewhat like a giant spoon with a crescent-shaped handle. In most cases, a skin covers the open face of the resonator to form a soundboard or "belly." A series of strings is attached to the stave, one after the other along its length, with the other end of each string passing through the belly and toggled beneath it, often passing through a wooden spine as an extra support to avoid tearing the skin. This is a far more successful solution than the pluriarc, and while bow harps are found over much of Africa, they have been used also in many other parts of the world. Again, there is no evidence for such a developmental sequence, but this is because we are dependent on evidence from either archaeology or iconography. The materials from which string instruments are made, all vegetable in origin, do not easily survive long burial in the earth. Iconography such as we would need is a very recent invention, not more than five millennia old in Egypt and Mesopotamia, from periods when lyres and bow harps were already fully developed, and fewer centuries than that in sub-Saharan Africa.

There are three basic forms: the simple bow harp, with a gently curved neck; the arched harp, where the neck curves more sharply and comes over the resonator to form something akin to the letter C; and the angle harp, where the neck forms an acute angle as it leaves the resonator, somewhat like the symbol <.

Both bow harps and angle harps are found in Africa, the bow harps rather more commonly and the angle harps among the Azande, for example. Both were used in ancient Egypt and Mesopotamia as we shall see later in the section on harps.

The arched harp was used in India in ancient times and can be seen in the iconography of that area.[7] It survives in Myanmar as the *saùng gauk*.[8] The instrument suffers, however, from two inherent problems. If the strings are placed too far up the arch, their tension will be enough to bend the arch toward the resonator, so shortening the distance between them and throwing the strings out of tune. Thus, graceful as the arched neck appears, in Myanmar, for instance, much of the length of the arch is purely decorative, and none the worse for that, but this is one reason why the strings occupy only a part of the arch. The other reason is that a string that is vertical to its resonator acts as a frequency-doubler,

sounding an octave higher than one would expect for its length, tension, and mass.[9] If the string were too high on the arch, there would be a risk of this occurring.

On the whole, the angle harp has been more widely used than the arched harp. It is still played in the Caucasus and other parts of Central Asia.[10] It was used in earlier times in China and Japan and survives still in Korea along with many other instruments associated with Confucian ritual.[11]

There is one further instrument that also must surely owe its existence to the bow, and that is the first of the lutes. Here, instead of a curved or angled neck with a resonator attached to the end, the neck is straight. As with the bow harp, the resonator has moved to the end of the stave, again with the opening facing the string instead of behind, and again with a skin belly covering that opening. Where the lute differs from the harp is not just that the neck is straight but, much more important typologically, that all the strings run along the neck and then run parallel with the belly, instead of diving into it, and all end at the same point on its length, rather than ending one by one along the belly.

The simplest lutes are the spike lutes, both plucked and bowed (see figure 6.27 for the latter), and it is these that are closest to the gourd bow. The string is attached to each end of the spike, and its vibration is transmitted to the belly of the resonator by a bridge, an object only just too large to merely bridge the space between belly and string. The downward pressure of the string keeps the bridge wedged in place—if it were the exact height of the space it would fall out and it would not transmit the vibrations efficiently. A gourd bow, if its stick were rigid and straight and the gourd upturned and its opening covered with skin, would then be a spike lute. From this, all our guitars, lutes, and fiddles derive.

We shall look below to each of the instruments whose descent from the gourd bow we have traced in this short introduction, but we should pause briefly to consider whether we have been justified in such a process.

Today this developmental approach is unfashionable in musicological circles, and yet it holds true among archaeologists, who can see how one type of stone tool leads to another, just as the paleontologists can look at fossil bones to see how one species led to another. I believe that developmental sequences such as the above—and such as we met with end-blown flutes progressing into notch flutes and thence into duct flutes—are justified. There is not, however, nor can there ever be, any evidence. Such developments occurred, if they occurred at all, long before there was any written record, far too long ago, as we have said, for any archaeological evidence to survive in the earth.

So, accept them if you will, ignore them if you prefer. The one thing without doubt is that each type of instrument existed. Whether sequentially or independently, we shall never know—we can, as so often, only guess.

Lyres

It would be difficult to say which has been the more important in the world's musical history: the lyre or the harp. Some peoples have preferred the one and some the other.

There are fundamental organological differences between the two instruments, although their musical use may be very similar. The lyre has a body and two arms that rise from it to a crossbar, the yoke, where the upper ends of the strings are attached. The strings run parallel with the soundboard, and their sounding lengths all terminate at the bridge so that with many types of lyre they are all the same length. The exceptions are the asymmetric lyres, which have arms of different lengths. One end of the yoke is then higher than the other, and thus each string is a different length, those from the higher end longer than those from the lower.

The harp, on the other hand, has a body and a neck, the latter, as we discussed above, rising from one end of the body either in a curve or at an angle. The strings come down to the body from the arm, each a different length, and terminate at different points along the length of the soundboard of the body. Instead of being parallel to the soundboard, they are, when viewed from the end of the body, vertical to it. With some harps, as we shall see in the next section, there is a forepillar between the distal ends of the neck and the body, to hold the two apart.

A frustration with the lyre is that we first encounter it as a highly developed instrument in early historical contexts. Superbly constructed and beautifully decorated examples from around 2450 BC were found in the royal graves at Ur in Mesopotamia, the city whence Abraham journeyed into biblical history, allegedly some three or four centuries later. These are massive instruments with a large wooden soundbox, at least eight and perhaps as many as a dozen strings, and a great bull's head rising from one end of the soundbox, or in one case a ram standing in a thicket. Many were decorated with semiprecious stones and gold, one even was covered with silver. A stone plaque from Nippur a century earlier shows a similar instrument, as do seals and other carvings from the same area.

Where did these come from and what did earlier types look like? We have no idea. There seems to be no evidence at all for anything earlier, but here, as so often, we are in the hands of the archaeologists. We can see only what they have found—what remains in the ground is hidden from us.

From this period on, the lyre seems to have continued in use among the Sumerians, at first with little change, and then in the Babylonian period a thousand or so years later, without the bull's head and joined by a rather smaller and more portable model. A thousand years later still, in Sennacherib's Nineveh, the lyre was clearly smaller and simpler, and several models of harp had gained the ascendancy.[12]

To the east, lyres seem to have been unknown in India, where the harp was preeminent, and to the west, while it was known in Egypt, especially around 1500 BC, it was far less popular than the harp. One similar in type to the Babylonian examples mentioned above survives in the Egyptian Antiquities Museum in Cairo, along with two closer to the Semitic asymmetric type, to which we will come shortly, and two other asymmetric lyres are in the Louvre in Paris.[13] The two in the Louvre and one in Cairo are all dated to the reign of Pharaoh Thutmose III (1504–1450 BC).

The two areas most closely associated with the lyre are ancient Israel and Greece. In the former, it was the legendary archetypal string instrument (e.g., Genesis 4:21, where the Hebrew *kinnor* is commonly mistranslated as a harp) and was also the instrument of the psalmist King David.[14] It is in Israel, at Megiddo, that we find what may be the first illustration of a lyre, scratched on a paving stone before 3000 BC. The problem is that the scratched picture is by no means clear. Martin West and Batja Bayer regard it as a lyre, Joachim Braun as a harp—it could well be either.[15] If it is a harp, there is undoubtedly a forepillar, as on the Cycladic harps. On the other hand, if it is a lyre, it is asymmetric and the yoke, the crossbar, is curved. Whichever it is, it is somewhat impressionistic, but Bernhard Aign convincingly illustrates its congruence with the Cycladic harps that we shall encounter in the next section.[16] Again whichever it is, Dr. Bayer suggests that it may well be the earliest representation of any string instrument anywhere. Later lyres in Israel are definite enough, both from the text of the Bible and from illustrations ranging in date from before 2000 BC (similar to the Sumerian from Ur) to the sixth century AD, and today on modern Israeli coins.[17]

In Greek legend, it was Hermes, the messenger of the gods, who found the shell of a dead tortoise, covered the opening with oxhide as a belly, fitted arms and a crossbar or yoke, and attached seven strings of sheep-gut.[18] Apollo took the lyre from him, and it became his musical emblem. How far back such a legend extends into time is always a historian's problem, for the source that we quoted from is late, probably from the sixth century BC. Nevertheless, it gives us solid and useful information, as do a number of Homeric references. The body of the lyre, known in the Homeric period as the *phorminx*, was a bowl, traditionally made, as it is frequently illustrated on Greek pots, from the upper carapace of a tortoise (hence the alternative name of *chelys*, Greek for "tortoise"; see figure 6.2). Some examples seem to show that the whole carapace was used, upper and lower parts together, but this still leaves gaps where the animal's head, legs, and tail projected that would need to be covered to produce a good resonating cavity. Many illustrations show the whole opening of the bowl to be skin-covered. The strings were already sheep's gut—the material conventionally used from that period up to the present day on many varieties of stringed instrument—and were, according to Homer, well-twisted, as indeed they still are today.[19]

There were three types of Greek lyre, the simplest of which we have just described. This was called *lyra* (the name *phorminx* seems to have died out from general use after the early Homeric period). The second was a more elegant variety, still with a tortoiseshell body but with much longer, gracefully curved arms, called a *barbitos*. The third was the elaborate box-bodied instrument, the *kithara*, that was especially associated with Apollo and seems to have been the choice of the professional bards and musicians. By contrast, the lyra was the instrument of amateurs, especially for after-dinner songs, and of the

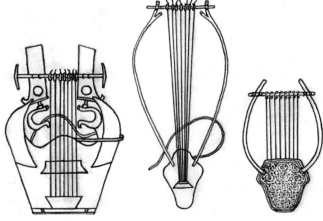

Figure 6.2. Greek Lyres
L–R: *kithara*, wooden-bodied concert lyre; *barbiton*, larger tortoiseshell lyre; *chelys*, small tortoiseshell lyre shown from the back, *drawn by Margaret Hauser.*

hetaira, the women who provided entertainment of various sorts. As with the lute in Elizabethan England, every well-brought-up lad was expected to be able to play the lyra and take his turn with a song, and there are many Greek pots showing young men being taught this art. There is a vast amount of literature, both ancient Greek and modern, on the construction and use of all three varieties, to such an extent that it is unnecessary to go into further detail here,[20] save for two other matters: a detail of shape and the means of string attachment.

We have referred above to symmetric and asymmetric lyres. On a symmetric lyre, each of the two arms extends the same distance above the body of the lyre and the two, if extended to a vertex below the body, would form two sides of an isosceles triangle. Thus all the strings were the same length and their pitch could differ only by varying tension (if carried to extreme that could deform the instrument) or mass. One of the problems of gut strings is that as the mass (in this context, inevitably controlled by the thickness) increases, the flexibility and thus the response of the string decreases. One way of avoiding this was by using what has become known as "high-twist gut."[21] Thus Homer's use of the phrase "well-twisted" makes one wonder whether this was already known at so early a period in European musical history.

With the asymmetric lyre, on the other hand, the arm farther from the player is longer than the nearer one. As a result, the strings are unequal in length, and their pitch could be differentiated in this way, either solely or in combination with the other two factors, mass and tension, depending on the proportions of the instrument.

So far as we know, the modern idea of a tuning peg, a piece of wood with the string twined round it that would pierce the yoke and that could be turned to wind the string more or less, and so to tighten or slacken it, was unknown in antiquity. On the Sumerian lyres we have already met and the larger Ethiopian lyre yet to come, each string was wound around both the yoke and a small wooden bar that could then be used as a lever to help wind it further for tuning. An alternative method was to twine the string around a strip of animal skin and then to wind that around the bar of the yoke; this grips the yoke sufficiently to hold the tension, but can be turned to raise or lower the pitch for tuning. Both these methods can be seen on pots and other Greek illustrations, and both seem to be described in texts, although a problem is that the general word *kollopes* is used indiscriminantly for both.

The final problem in this area is with the larger lyre, the kithara, whose yoke has a round knob at each end. Was this turned to tighten or slacken all the strings simultaneously and thus transpose the pitch up or down a tone or so? Anyone who has tried to use such a method on any string instrument will know that it does not work—some strings stretch more or less than others. On the other hand, for a quick retuning, with one or two strings then touched up as necessary, it might be useful. Much ink has been spilled over the small elements within the curves of the arms of the kithara—are they some form of mechanism or not, and if so, for what purpose?

And finally in this discussion of the Greek instruments, might there be any truth in the legendary origin, their invention by Hermes? Here we can categorically say no. There is no doubt that the lyre was known in Crete long before it was known in Greece and that the Mycenaean Greeks acquired it, probably along with much else, from the Minoan culture of that island. What we would dearly like to know is what happened to it in Greece between the end of the Mycenaean period and the earliest portrayals on the Geometric-style pots of the early Classical period, a gap of some hundreds of years while the Dorians were completing their overthrow of the Mycenaean culture. We can see lyres during this interregnum on some of the islands between Greece and the Anatolian mainland, but none in Greece.[22]

From Greece, the lyre was passed to the Romans and to the Hellenistic culture of Ptolemaic Egypt and the surrounding area. Thence, it would seem probable, the lyre, in its lighter lyra or chelys form, traveled up the Nile to the Meroitic people of the Sudan, where it still survives today, as it does in Uganda and Ethiopia and even down into South Africa, under the name (among others) of *kissar* (see figure 6.3). The tortoiseshell has

Figure 6.3. Lyres

L–R: *beganna*, Ethiopia (I 46); *kissar*, Uganda (II 32a); *hearp*, Anglo-Saxon, small-size reproduction by George Higgs, Faversham, England (VII 170).

been replaced by a segment of gourd, usually rather less than hemispherical, or occasionally by hollowed wood, and the belly of oxhide has been replaced by one most commonly of snakeskin. This is sometimes nailed in place, but it is more usually attached by innumerable cords to a small patch of animal skin at the back. The strings, still of twisted gut (though unlikely to be sheep, more probably of goat or various types of antelope), are attached to the yoke by kollopes of twisted cloth rather than animal skin. With these differences, the instrument is still clearly that that Hermes may or may not have invented.

Of less certain origin is the much larger *beganna* of Ethiopia. This has a body of hollowed wood—sometimes bowl shaped, sometimes box—and long arms, fully as long as those of the barbitos, with a yoke that may be integral with the arms, as seen in figure 6.3, or pegged together from separate pieces of wood. The strings are wound around both the yoke and the small wooden levers that we have described on the Sumerian lyre and the Greek kithara, and which are also found on some late Israelite mosaics. The Ethiopian monarchy legendarily traced its origin to the descendants of the Queen of Sheba and King Solomon. It has been suggested, purely hypothetically, that this much larger form of Ethiopian lyre might derive from the kinnor, the lyre of Solomon's father, David the Psalmist.

It was probably from Byzantium, the capital of the Eastern Roman Empire, that the Germanic lyre derived, for many of the Byzantine Imperial Guards came from the German tribes. Only one example of such a lyre has come down to us into modern times, the so-called Allemanic lyre of the sixth century AD, but that, tragically, was destroyed by the aerial bombardment of Berlin during World War II. It was, however, used as the model for the reconstruction of the lyre fragments found in the English Sutton Hoo ship burial of the seventh century, and this may still be seen in the British Museum. There are also many portrayals of similar lyres in medieval manuscripts throughout Europe from the eighth to the eleventh centuries (e.g., see figure C.1).[23]

Lyres were also bowed in the Middle Ages—as soon as the bow was invented, it was applied to almost any plucked instrument whose shape was suitable, including the long and narrow lyre from around 1000 AD.[24] Lyres appear then to have been made as a shallow, flat box, the arms integral with the body, and on the bowed instruments with a neck, dividing the open space between the arms into two sections, allowing the player to stop the strings, as on a fiddle, and thus shorten their length to obtain different pitches.

On the plucked lyre, the notes that can be played are, at least in theory, limited to the number of strings. The player can pluck them one or more at a time, or can strum across them all (there is good evidence for both techniques) either with the fingers or with a *plectrum*, a slip of wood, bone, ivory, horn, or quill used to pluck the strings. We can see on Greek pots the player with a plectrum in one hand and with the fingers of the other hand outspread against the strings. This is clearly a strumming technique, sweeping the plectrum across all the strings, but damping those strings that the player does not want to sound with the fingers, just as one does with the bars of an autoharp (see figure 6.13). We can also see, on other pots, the forefinger and thumb of the left hand pinching together, showing that some players would pluck with the plectrum in one hand and with the fingers of the other. Both techniques are used today in Africa. What is less certain on Greek pots, but used today in Africa, is sometimes pinching one string to stop it, or pressing it against the yoke, to shorten its sounding length and raise the pitch.[25] What seems to have been a wholly new practice in the eleventh century was the use of a fingerboard to change the pitch of any or all of the strings.

Later medieval bowed lyres became, once again, rather more lyre-shaped, shorter and wider, but still with a fingerboard. We have examples in the Chapter House of Westminster Abbey in London, painted between 1390 and 1404, and in the stained glass of the Beauchamp Chapel in Warwick, which can be dated almost precisely to 1447.[26] These last clearly are precursors of the Welsh *crwth*, an instrument that survived into the nineteenth century and whose use has occasionally been revived today (see figure 6.4).

The crwth, as we know it from surviving late-eighteenth-century and early-nineteenth-century examples, borrowed a number of features from the baroque violin, including the wedged fingerboard (see figure 6.31). Four strings that could be stopped ran over the fingerboard, and there were two bourdon or drone strings alongside the fingerboard that could be either bowed or plucked with the thumb of the fingering hand to provide a drone. The bridge was unusual, for it was set at an angle across the belly so that each string was a different length. It had one long foot that passed through one of the soundholes to rest on the back, and one short foot resting on the belly.[27] We shall encounter other fiddles with a similar arrangement.

There was also a Nordic form of the bowed lyre, known under a variety of names, among them, *tallharpa* in Swedish, *jouhikantele* in Finnish, and *nares-jux* among

The harp, on the other hand, is still very much with us in many parts of the world.

Harps

Of the various types of harp mentioned above, that least common today is the arched harp, for its only significant survival is in Myanmar, whither it traveled from Sumeria via India. The Sumerian evidence, which appears to be scanty, is a relief on a single fragment from a stone vessel of around 3000–2500 BC.[29] It is of particular interest because it shows the arm arching over the resonator and the spare ends of the strings hanging down beyond the arm as today in Myanmar, whereas the Indian examples illustrated by Claudie Marcel-Dubois, Walter Kaufmann, Muriel Williamson, and Judith Becker show a rather shorter, and mostly thicker, arm, nearer to that of the bow harp.[30] The Burmese *saùng gauk* is one of the most beautiful instruments to look at (see figure 6.5), and its sound is also immensely attractive.[31]

There was a wide variety of bow harps in ancient Egypt, ranging in shape from a shallow curve, like the African instruments illustrated in figure 6.6 and usually held up on the player's shoulder, to C-shaped, and in size from quite small to those standing higher than the player.[32] The carvings and wall paintings show early examples of the association of blindness with instrumental performance, for which there is good historical evidence throughout the ages. The instruments chosen are usually those that work well when played alone, without other

Figure 6.4. Bowed Lyres
Crwthau, fifteenth century, Beauchamp Chapel, St. Mary's Church, Warwick, England, *photo Axel Poignant.*

the Ostyaks and Khants of Yakutia in Siberia.[28] The last is plucked rather than bowed. None of these instruments has a fingerboard, and the Finnish and Swedish players stopped the melody string with the backs of the fingers, holding the nearer arm of the instrument and raising a finger from it toward that string; the other strings were drones. Today, save among some revivalist folk groups, these bowed lyres are extinct, and the only areas in which the lyre now survives are eastern and southern Africa.

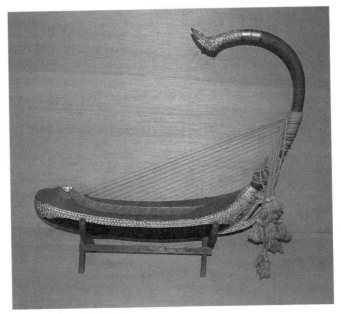

Figure 6.5. Arched Harp
Saùng gauk, Myanmar (Burma), *photo Tony Bingham, London.*

accompaniment, save perhaps the player's voice. Most often, they are those where each element to be touched has a fixed position, so that the distances to and from each are the more easily remembered by the hands. As well as in ancient Egypt, the harp was widely chosen in Wales and Ireland, where we have many references to blind harpers, because the distance from one string to another is fixed, just like the keys of our piano, another common and more recent choice. The best known, because of its frequent portrayal in late Renaissance and Baroque paintings in the hands of blind beggars, was the hurdy-gurdy or *vielle à roue* (see figures 6.34 and 6.35), for here again the positions of the keys are fixed, as is that of the crank that turns the wheel to rub the strings.

Bow harps pervade Central and East Africa, all recognizably derivative from ancient Egypt.[33] One of particular interest is the *ennanga* of Uganda.[34] This has a thick belly of leather, tensioned by innumerable thongs to a pad of leather on the back of the resonator, just like the lyre from the same area that we have already encoun-

tered and similarly, though with rather thinner thongs, to the Ugandan drums we met above. Each tuning peg pierces the neck, and each string passes over the point of its peg and around the back of the neck to the stem of the peg. The string is then secured around the peg, rather than through it as our tuning pegs are. Immediately below each peg is a ring of banana fiber covered with lizard skin and prevented from sliding down the neck by a small wooden wedge. The string rests against this ring as it passes down to the belly, and when it is plucked, it jars against the ring, adding a buzz to the sound exactly as with the brays on our medieval harps and on the Basque *txuntxun*, and with the *arpicordum* on the Flemish *muselaar*, one of the two forms of virginals. The added buzz is widely liked and desired in Africa, but so far as I know the ennanga is the only African instrument that produces it with brays. Most commonly on string instruments, the buzzers are added metal rings on a strip or leaf of thin metal terminating in a spike that is driven into the end of the neck. On sansas (mbiras or kalimbas), as

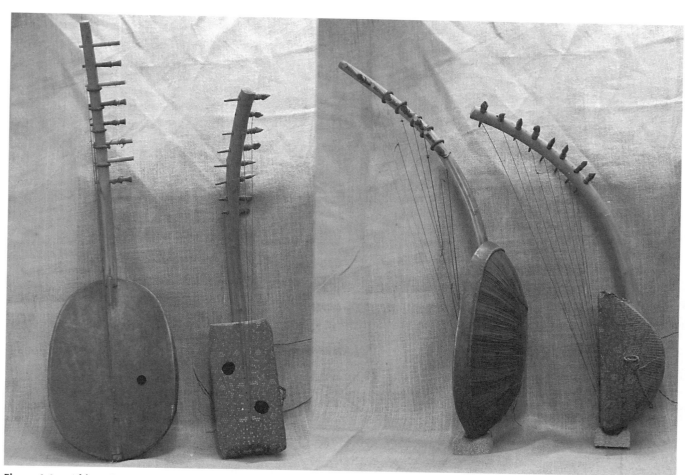

Figure 6.6. African Bow Harps
L–R: *ennanga*, Uganda (X 24); Ruwenzori Mountains, Congo (IX 6).

we have seen in chapter 1, the buzzers may be placed around the reeds or tongues themselves, or around an added metal bar, or attached to the resonator box. With xylophones, the buzzers are miniature kazoos. Whatever the method, the universal aim, as with the European bray, is to add "sweetness," the impression of greater harmonic content, and interest to the sound.

The angle harp is unusual in that some peoples play it one way up and some the other, and even more unusual in that both techniques can be seen in the same culture, as some of the reliefs at Nineveh reveal.[35] One type has the resonator held horizontally with the arm projecting vertically at the far end—very clearly an "arm," because the terminal at the upper end is usually shaped like a hand. The strings are plucked with a large plectrum and so produce a stronger sound than when played with the fingers. The other type is plucked by the fingers and held with the resonator upward against or beside the chest, with the arm projecting forward from the lower end, unlike European instruments whose arm or neck is always above the resonator. In only one of Subhi Anwar Rashid's plates do both appear together.[36] One has a slight impression that the horizontally held and plectrum-played instrument may have been mainly used outdoors, and the vertically held and finger-plucked harp indoors, or at least in more intimate settings. Another difference between the two types is that, in one, the vertical arm forms a right angle with the horizontal resonator, whereas with the other, the upward resonator forms an acute angle with the horizontal arm (hence the term "angle harp," for the resonator and arm meet at a defined angle, in contrast with the bow harp, where the union is curved). This contrasts with the Egyptian angle harps, as on the British Museum model and the late example illustrated by Hans Hickmann, where although the resonator is held upward, it forms a right angle with the arm.[37]

It was the angle harp that became the ancestor of our instruments. Even in its original simple form that survives, for example, in the Caucasus and Central Africa, it was a successful instrument, but as with the arched harp, there is one major problem: the joint between the neck and the soundbox or resonator can never be wholly rigid. As one tunes it, tightening the strings pulls the neck, however slightly, toward the soundbox. So, as one string is brought into tune, the increased tension of that string pulls the neck forward and slackens the other strings. The art of tuning such a harp is thus difficult to achieve. The solution—the addition of a rigid forepillar to hold the end of the neck and the end of the soundbox apart—may be obvious to us, but with two exceptions, it

seems to have taken millennia to arrive and was not invented until somewhere around AD 800. Our first evidence for it is in the Utrecht Psalter, written in Rheims in northern France about 825 (see figure C.1).

The first exception comes from the Early Cycladic period in the Cycladic Islands, between Greece and Turkey. We know practically nothing of that culture, dating from about 3200–2100 BC, more than a thousand years earlier than the Minoan and Mycenaean cultures of Crete and mainland Greece, save for the marble figurines and other artifacts they left in their tombs.[38] Ten of these figurines are of harpists, figures seated on a stool or a well-made chair, with a harp held on the knee (see figure 6.7). In each case, there is a large and solid forepillar, although in one the forepillar is broken off, leaving only a round mark on the end of the resonator to show that it was similar to all the others.[39] In all the examples where the upper part of the forepillar survives (two are broken off), there is a duck's bill projecting forward from the pillar just below the joint with the neck.[40] In every case, the base of the forepillar is curved back to slot into the front of the end of the resonator. It has sometimes been suggested that this forepillar merely represents the outermost string, especially as the players' hands are often grasping it, but both the duck-bill and the way the forepillar goes into the fore-edge of the soundbox make this highly improbable.

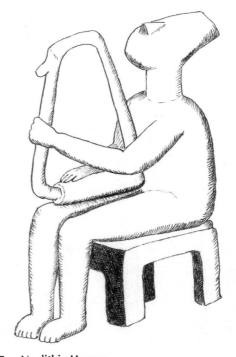

Figure 6.7.   Neolithic Harper
From marble statuettes, c. 3000 BC, Cycladic Islands, Aegean Sea, *drawn by Sarah Montagu.*

The other ancient forepillar that we see illustrated on some Greek pots is much later, toward the end of the fourth century BC. A few illustrations show angle harps with the resonator upward, and sometimes these have a forepillar that is much lighter than the Cycladic, but effective nonetheless. The resonator swells in size toward the bass strings and curves right over the horizontal neck, so that there is no constructional problem in fitting a forepillar between the two.[41] This is sometimes a simple rod, but is most commonly a standing bird. Martin West describes another type seen in this period as a "spindle harp," for the resonator, which on this type is usually but not invariably on the far side of the instrument from the player, is wider in its center than at either top or bottom.[42] Illustrations show that these late Greek harps were mainly women's instruments.

What is so puzzling is why or how a device as useful as the forepillar should have appeared twice in history, some two thousand years apart, and then have been forgotten, not only between those two occasions but again after the second time for a further millennium or so. Perhaps ethnomusicological and archaeological research in the Caucasus could produce an answer, for in Georgia today we can find small angle harps both with and without a forepillar. Two of those illustrated in the *Atlas of Musical Instruments* are traditional instruments and are without forepillar; two are "improved" models with a forepillar, and two are "improved" models without one.[43] Similar instruments are seen in Abkhazia (with forepillar) and Ossetia (without).[44]

Once it was finally reinvented around the ninth century, however, the forepillar has never been forgotten in Europe. The earlier illustrations from this period, mostly from psalters, are fairly schematic, for the lyre was still the more important instrument and, to confuse us, was called the *hearp* in Early English. It is not really until the late thirteenth century that, with rather more surviving sources, we can recognize two distinct types of harp and, with the aid of apparently greater artistic realism, assess their musical viability.

One is a light instrument with a gently curved neck usually carrying T-shaped tuning pegs, much like those used on fiddles and other instruments, with a forepillar also gently curved, the two usually meeting with an animal-head finial.[45] The soundbox swells out to form a curved shoulder that is pierced with one or more soundholes, which are often filled with wooden tracery similar to that in church windows. It is normally assumed that what we see is like a Picasso picture and that what looks like a swelling from front to back is actually half of one from side to side, so that we are seeing in profile what is re-

ally part of the front view. This type of harp is illustrated in many psalters, bibles, and other such texts, and it would appear to be the ancestor of the well-known Gothic harp that is widely illustrated from around 1400 on.

The other is a much heavier form of harp, with a massive curved forepillar, a strongly arched neck, and a large box resonator that widens from the treble to the bass. This instrument first appears in 1270 in the Angel Choir of Lincoln Cathedral (see figure 6.8), and it is instantly recognizable as the ancestor of what is today called the Irish harp or *clarsach*. We do not know whether it actually originated in East Anglia or some other place in contact with that English area and then eventually passed to Ireland, or whether it was imported from Ireland—all we can say is that its earliest illustrations are East Anglian. Certainly there were harps in Ireland by then, but all the Irish illustrations so far discovered are of a much simpler instrument, smaller and often almost square in outline, rather than triangular. There were by then harps in Wales, too, but of these we have only descriptions saying that they also were simpler instruments with a skin belly on the soundbox and horsehair strings.

Whether the Lincoln harp had metal strings, like the later Irish instruments, we do not know. The large blocks we can see on its soundboard may well have been brays—they look much too large to be belly pins. The bray was a small L-shaped piece of wood whose longer arm pinned the string into its hole in the belly, with the other, shorter arm just touching the string close to the soundboard so that it buzzed against it. This

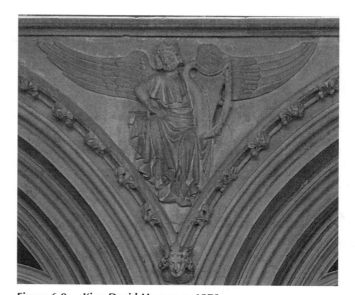

Figure 6.8. King David Harper, c. 1270
The earliest known illustration of what was later known as the Irish harp, Angel Choir, Lincoln Cathedral, England, *photo Nicholas Bennett*.

seems to strengthen the overtones of the string, enriching the sound and making it louder, just as in Uganda.

The soundbox of the fifteenth-century Irish harp was carved out of a solid block of wood, normally willow, from the back, so that the front and sides were integral, with a plate of different wood inserted into the gap at the back. We have several surviving examples in Dublin (at Trinity College and elsewhere) and Edinburgh (the Queen Mary and Lamont harps) from which we can garner this information.[46] There are many contemporary references and descriptions to tell us that the strings were of metal wire, often silver, sometimes gold, and that the players plucked them with their fingernails—the player who offended a patron with his lyrics might have his nails broken, leading to an enforced vacation without pay until they grew again. The Gothic harp, used over all the rest of Europe, was much more lightly constructed, with its graceful slender body and gut strings.

Both grew in size, the Gothic perhaps more so than the Irish, and the resonator of the Gothic was, certainly by the end of the sixteenth century and perhaps earlier, built up from slats like a box, with a belly of softwood such as spruce. In Italy, a second rank of strings was provided to render the instrument more extensively chromatic. The neck was cut away in a step so that the second set of tuning pins was inset below the first, allowing the two ranks to run side by side to the soundboard without confusion. It is usually assumed that the earlier harps were tuned diatonically, and when the player wished to change key, it would be necessary to tune one or more strings in each octave from natural to sharp or flat or vice versa. There is evidence that some harps already had a few alternative notes, for example, both B-natural and B-flat to play both hard and soft hexachords, but the new *arpa doppia* or double harp had a string for each semitone over most of its range. The double ranks were necessary because a single rank of twelve notes to the octave would spread an octave outside the span of a player's hand and place the bass notes beyond the reach of the player's arms unless the instrument had a very small range.

The diatonic Renaissance harp was carried overseas by the colonizers of the New World and survives today in a very active folk tradition in Central America. The soundbox has been increased in size, but we can still see two pin feet projecting from the base of the soundbox, seen also in surviving instruments of the Renaissance. Playing technique seems to have changed, because the American instruments are often carried up on the player's shoulder, with the resonator almost parallel with the ground, and are played in that position while the player walks along, something for which we have no evidence in the European Renaissance. Also, a second player often drums on the soundbox to provide a rhythmic accompaniment.

By around 1600, again in Italy, a third rank was introduced, creating the triple harp.[47] This had the diatonic notes duplicated in the two outer ranks and the chromatic notes in the middle rank between them.[48]

The triple harp became one of the standard harps for the Baroque period, the instrument for which Handel wrote his concerto, for example, and it survived long after that in Wales, even into the twentieth century, when it all but died out. It was revived just in time for Nansi Richards-Jones, the last player who had been taught its traditional techniques, to pass them on to players who were beginning to play it, both as a folk tradition and for early-music performance. She emphasized the importance of what she had been taught: to strike the harp low on the strings, close to the soundboard—very different from the modern technique on the pedal harp.[49] She described also the advantage of the two diatonic ranks being tuned in unison. This allowed a rapid reiteration of notes that is difficult to achieve on the pedal harp because plucking a single string in overly quick repetition causes a confusing jumble, due to the new pluck on a string killing the sound of the previous one, often with a jarring sound when the vibration of the first pluck is too rudely interrupted (unlike the piano, a harp has no dampers to limit the vibration of its strings). Alternating two strings allows each to ring properly.

The triple harp, however, was expensive to maintain, due to the great number of strings, which have never been cheap to buy, and the diatonic harp therefore continued in use wherever the musical contexts permitted. Players became adept at stopping a string against the neck with a finger or thumb when necessary, to shorten its length sufficiently to raise the pitch by a semitone. This change of tuning could be more easily achieved by turning a metal hook to bear on the string at the correct point, and the hook harp was certainly in use before the end of the seventeenth century. The number of hooks on surviving instruments varies, and it was probably unusual to find a complete set allowing for every possible chromatic note, such as we see on some modern folk harps today.

It was necessary to have a hand free from playing to move a hook, and when from the mid-eighteenth century onward composers began to demand greater freedom to change key in the course of the music, some quicker form of mechanism became essential. Many experimental systems were developed, initially mainly in the southern German states, but the first really successful system was that normally attributed to Jean-Henri Nadermann in Paris, introduced in the mid-1770s. This was described in detail in the great French *Encyclopédie*.[50]

Nadermann's mechanism provided a *crochet*, a small hook, for each string. When the appropriate pedal was depressed, the crochets for each E-flat string, for example, drew the string in toward the neck so that its vibrating length was shortened by pulling it against a small bridge, as may be seen in the detail drawing, top right, in figure 6.9. The inherent inefficiency of this method was both that of converting the movement of the mechanism along the neck into a lateral movement to pull the crochet sideways toward the neck, and the resulting distortion of the string, as well as its somewhat inadequate cutoff on the bridge.

The Cousineaus, father and son, also in Paris, surmounted these problems before the end of the decade by providing a pair of *béquilles* or small crutches, one each side of each string, that rotated to grip the string between them and stop its sounding length. Its efficiency depended on each béquille rotating equally, the one from north to east, as it were, and the other from south to west, so as to grip the string between them with equal force and firmness. The second Cousineau system was a somewhat impractical design with two rows of pedals.

More successful was Sébastien Erard's system of the late 1780s (see figure 6.10), essentially that of our harp today. Erard devised a rotor with two fixed pins, between which the string passed. When the pedal was depressed, the rotor turned so that the *fourchette*, or little fork

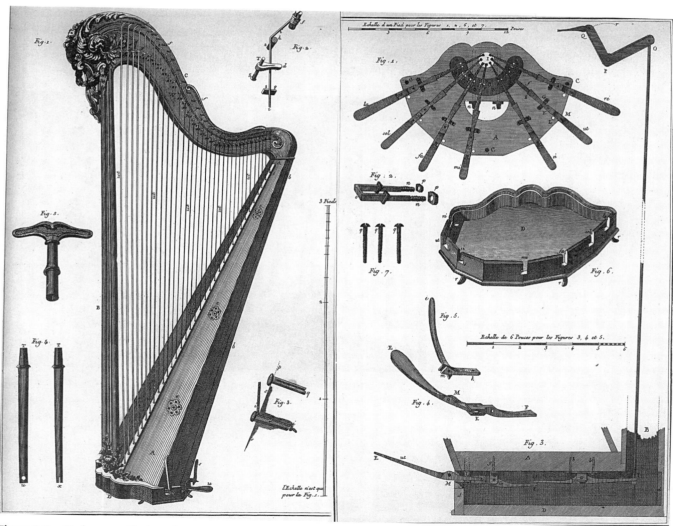

Figure 6.9.   Nadermann Single-action Harp
Fig. 2 is the *crochet* that draws each string to a bridge to raise the pitch by a semitone (*Diderot et d'Alembert*, Encyclopédie, Paris, c. 1770).

formed by the two pins, turned with it and gripped the string firmly between the pins, thereby shortening its sounding length.

With all three of these systems, there was a pedal for each note of the diatonic scale. One pedal controlled the mechanism for all the C strings, another for all the F strings, and so on. An eighth pedal often controlled a louver or shutter that opened or closed the soundholes cut in the back of the body, so as to give greater control of volume. It is a characteristic of plucked strings that the act of plucking allows much less variation of dynamic than hammering—this was the basic reason for the piano's ultimate domination over the harpsichord—so that a mechanical means of varying the loudness was desirable. The harp was tuned to flat keys, usually E♭, so that, as far as possible, notes would retain the same name whether the pedal were up or down, A♭ becoming A♮, C becoming C♯, and so forth. As the pedal was depressed, it was moved slightly sideways to slip into a notch, thus locking it in position until moving it back released it.

As music became increasingly chromatic, this had its limitations: for example C♭ could only be obtained by shifting B♭ to B♮, and there was then no B♭ available. Erard, who had moved from Paris to London in 1792 to avoid the Terror of the French Revolution, fitted a second row of fourchettes at the correct distance below the original rank, as in figure 6.10, and a second notch for each pedal, creating the modern double-action harp in 1810.[51] This was now tuned, as harps are still today, in C♭ so that each string produced the flat when the pedal was up, the natural when it was depressed and moved sideways into the first notch, and the sharp when further depressed and moved into the second notch.

Models of harps have changed over the years to provide greater strength to withstand the heavier strings and higher tension that provide greater volume. The two earlier models of Nadermann and Cousineau are instantly recognizable from the large curved volute at the far end of the neck overhanging the forepillar. Each had its mechanism passing through the neck. Erard not only

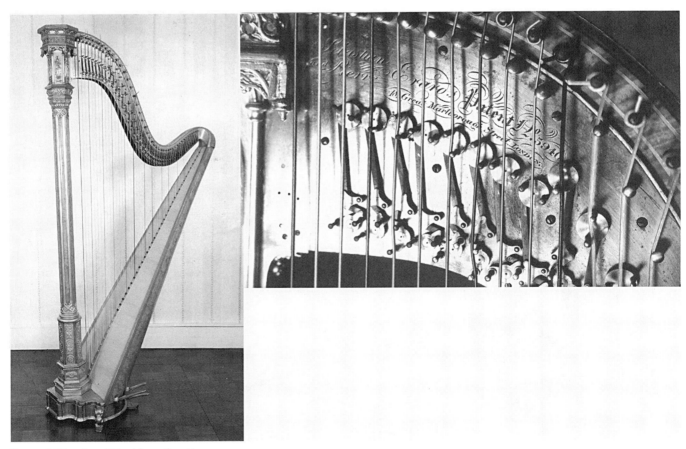

Figure 6.10. Erard Double-action Harp
With detail of the mechanism, Sébastian Erard, London, post-1810, *courtesy Clive Morley Harps and Morley Galleries.*

strengthened the neck by laminating it but also fitted the mechanism below the neck, between brass plates bolted to it, and he strengthened the body. Erard's own earlier pattern is called the "Grecian," with a capital at the top of the forepillar supported by winged figures reminiscent of the caryatids on one of the temples on the Acropolis in Athens. The Gothic harp was somewhat larger and stronger, and the capital of the forepillar was decorated in ways similar to that of church architecture. The harp today has further increased in power, usually with a body that swells toward the bass to provide a larger air body for resonance, and with a laminated soundboard to withstand a further increase of string tension. The mechanism has been rendered more efficient, but it remains recognizably that of Erard.

Erard's harp was not without its rivals, in addition to its many copiers and competitors. The most important of the rivals was the double harp of Gustave Lyon, introduced in 1894. This followed the earlier model of the Italian arpa doppia, with a second set of wrest pins in an inset step in the neck. The "white" notes of the piano were tuned by the upper row of pins, the "black" notes, placed in their usual sequence of twos and threes, from the lower. The two ranks of strings crossed in a shallow X, so allowing each hand access to each rank, much like the seventeenth-century Spanish double harp that had been another of the Baroque forms.

The two firms, both in Paris, cemented their rivalry by commissioning works from the two leading French composers of the day. Erard commissioned Maurice Ravel to compose his Introduction and Allegro for pedal harp and chamber ensemble; Lyon asked Claude Debussy to provide his *Danses Sacrées et Profanes* for double harp and strings. Today the latter is played always on the pedal harp, for the double harp failed to overcome its rival, even in later years when the American offshoot, Lyon and Healey, produced a more elaborate model with two separate necks rising from the same resonator, and two forepillars in a giant X.

Throughout all these modifications to the concert harp and the harp of the amateur wealthy enough to possess one, the simpler instruments continued in active use.[52] The hook harp remained popular in German lands, and Bálint Sárosi describes and illustrates a Hungarian version with a simple pedal mechanism connected by external cables to the hooks, whereas on the French pedal harps all the mechanism was by steel rods passing inside the body to the neck.[53] There is an example in the Néprajzi (Ethnographic) Museum in Budapest.

The traditional Irish harp survived into the eighteenth century. A wholly new model was devised by John Egan in Dublin around 1815. His "Royal Portable Irish Harp" was a copy of the Erard harp, but small enough to stand on a table or stool. Pedals were therefore impracticable and instead Egan fitted *ditals*, or finger-levers, into the forepillar to control the fourchettes on the neck. This was only single-action, but that was all that was required for domestic music, the use for which it was designed. It differed radically from the traditional Irish instrument in that its body was constructed similarly to Erard's harps with a spruce or such wood front and a curved back made from thin slats, not hewn from a solid block of willow.

The creation of the modern Celtic folk harp or clarsach follows that pattern, although the body is normally built as a four-sided box from slats, shaped like that of the old Irish and Scottish instruments. There are no fourchettes or other internal mechanisms, but instead a brass blade is provided for each string that can be turned against it to shorten its sounding length, just like the old hooks. A few makers today are producing the traditional model, but the cost in time and labor of carving it out is against it, as is the proper technique of plucking the high-tension brass strings with the fingernails, a technique wholly foreign to players trained on the pedal harp or who are moving to a pseudo-folk tradition from instruments such as the guitar. Thus the market is small and the true bell-like sound of the Celtic harp is seldom heard today. However, the Historical Harp Society of Ireland is now actively reviving these instruments and encouraging beginners to start on them so that they do not need to unlearn techniques from gut-strung harps. For economy, the bodies are often made from slats, but in all other respects they follow the traditional pattern rather than that of the modern folk harp.

There was around 1800 a whole gallimaufry of small amateur instruments devised by makers such as Edward Light and Angelo Ventura under names such as "harp lute," "harp guitar," "dital harp," and other combinations including the word "harp." These tended to have a body with strings running parallel to the soundboard, so that none of them were really harps but were in fact guitars with open basses. Some of the strings ran over a guitar-style fingerboard and the basses ran up across a gap to a neck that terminated with a small pillar on the far side. Some of these basses had ditals or other levers to change the pitch of the "harp" strings, which were intended to be plucked to accompany whatever was being played on the melody strings along the fingerboard. They were pretty instruments that had a vogue in the salons of the fashionable in the first quarter of the nineteenth century, and they often appear in the sale rooms today.

Zithers

We need, here, to define the word *zither*.[54] It is any instrument that consists simply of one or more strings and a string-bearer (e.g., a stick, bar, board, or box; see figure 6.11). Any resonator, such as a gourd or a box, must be detachable while still leaving the instrument viable. Thus our piano, for example, would be classified as a board zither because one could take everything away except for the soundboard and the strings and there would still be an instrument there. Equally with the hammered dulcimer, classified as a box zither, one could remove the sides and the bottom, and there would still be a board zither. On the other hand, if you took away the body from a guitar, there would be no instrument left, just a neck with some strings dangling in the air. The only type of zither where this definition is questionable is the tube zither, because the resonator is the inside of the tube, and this cannot be removed.

The most elaborate of the stick zithers, both musically and in construction, is the North Indian *vīnā*, of which there are several distinct types. The reason for the digression above, defining the zither, is that the South Indian *vīnā* is quite different from the North Indian one. The North Indian, also sometimes called *bīn*, is a stick zither with two large gourd resonators, one near each end, that can be removed, still leaving the stick intact with its strings. The South Indian *vīnā*, however, is a lute, an instrument with a neck and an integral resonator, usually made from half a large gourd with a wooden belly that, like that of the guitar, cannot be removed without destroying the instrument.

Here another digression is necessary. The Indian subcontinent is musically divided into the south, that is, the southern part of India, and the north, which includes the nations of Pakistan and Bangladesh, as well as the northern part of India.[55] The instruments of the north were heavily influenced by the Moghul invasion from Persia,

Figure 6.11.   Stick, Bar, Raft, and Tube Zithers
L–R: bar zither, Tonga people, Zimbabwe (IV 90); stick zither, tribal India, probably Khandda people, Ghamsarh District, east coast (VII 76a); two idiochord raft zithers, back view to show the rattle compartments, Nigeria (VI 230), and front view, also Nigeria (I 144b); *valiha*, tube zither, with both idiochord and heterochord strings, and bone and cloth decoration, Madagascar (V 154).

whereas the Carnatic or southern instruments have, to a great extent, escaped that influence, but may have later been influenced by the North Indian derivatives of the Persian.

The vīnā is a good example of this. The North Indian vīnā has remained much as it was in pre-Moghul times, but is now to a great extent relegated to the role of a folk instrument and to some other traditional usages. It was replaced in the new rulers' court by a more fashionable instrument, the Persian *setar* (meaning "three strings"), an instrument widely used in slightly different forms from the Turkish dominions in the Balkans (the *saz*) to Afghanistan (the *dutar*, "two strings") and beyond (see figure 6.20), including much that was the southern part of the Soviet Union. In India, it gradually became Indianized, changing its name mildly to *sitar*, remaining always a lute with a long neck and an integral resonator, but acquiring accessories from the vīnā such as drone strings and, eventually, sympathetic strings. These are extra strings of wire that not only add a silvery shimmer to the sound of its main strings when they vibrate in sympathy with them, but can also be plucked to add an extra stratum of accompanying sound. The curved metal frets on the neck, which allow the main strings to be pulled to one side to add ornamental and expressive glissandi, are a comparatively recent device (see figure 6.21). Some of these developments were seen in the south as advantageous, but there was no desire to abandon the traditional vīnā in favor of the upstart and foreign sitar. So the vīnā changed and acquired those characteristics that were seen as advantageous, such as the lute resonator, but retained others, such as the traditional styles of frets, that were preferred.

Stick zithers are common in many areas, as are bar zithers, being, as it were, a board on edge. We have already met the simplest of stick zithers, the musical bow, in the introduction to this chapter (see also interlude G), but true stick zithers, as may be seen in figure 6.11, are rather more complex and often have posts standing up as frets, as here, against which the string can be stopped. Both the Indian stick zither here and the Zimbabwean bar zither have drones, as well as frets.

The Malagasy tube zither is more complex still. The original form of the *valiha* that was brought from the islands of Indonesia was a simple instrument with idiochord bamboo strings raised from the cortex or bark of the tube. Madagascar has been one the world's cultural melting pots, an Arab trading center for centuries, and for many years ruled by the French. Thus the valiha has sometimes acquired the four strings of the violin (one of the pegs is missing from the example in figure 6.11) and

also the bone and velvet ornamentation more characteristic of Arab taste than the French.

A further type of zither is the raft zither, and this also is known in many areas, although it is only in West Africa, so far as I know, that it sometimes combines the zither with a shallow woven basket at the back, filled with seeds or other pellets to provide that extra rattle or buzz so loved in Africa. Both idiochord and heterochord versions are known, the idiochord, as in figure 6.11, having the strings raised from the plant stems that form the raft. It is interesting that the Nigerians have found the same solution that we have with the piano: if a string is wound with something, its mass is increased and its pitch lowered. On the piano, copper wire is wrapped around the steel core; here, a strip of leaf or grass is wound around the plant string to increase its mass. Some of the strings in the figure are broken, something that happens easily with so delicate a material. What is curious is that even where, as in some areas, both heterochord and idiochord types are found, a heterochord string seems never to be attached to an otherwise idiochordal instrument to replace a broken string. So far, nobody has produced an indigenous explanation for such reluctance to repair an otherwise viable instrument.

Another type of zither that seems to appear only in Africa, especially in East Africa, is the trough zither. This is usually a piece of wood hollowed out by removing most of its upper surface and much of its thickness, save for the rim. The strings run across the trough formed in this way and are bridged up by the rim at each end. On the *inanga* from Rwanda illustrated in figure 6.12, the string is one continuous length, running back and forth. The loops around the series of points at each end generate sufficient tension and friction for each length of string to hold its own pitch.

The two commonest forms of zither are the board zither and the box zither. These are closely related because the box zither is simply a board with added sides and bottom. There are intermediary forms, for example, boards with a side but no bottom, as in the Hungarian *citera* in figure 6.12 and our piano that lost the planks that closed its bottom not long after 1800 (we shall describe our stringed keyboard instruments in a separate section below even though they are all technically box or board zithers). One should also add that many board zithers do have an auxiliary box, for they are often placed on or in a gourd or other container to act as a temporary box to add resonance.

The better examples of this type of citera, one of the many different types used in Hungary, have a horse's head at the top of each section, instead of simple

Fret?

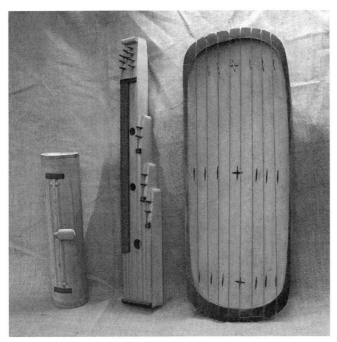

Figure 6.12.   Tube, Box, and Trough Zithers
L–R: bamboo tube zither, used as a string drum, Borneo (VIII 220); *citera*, open-bottomed box zither, Hungary (III 194); *inanga*, trough zither, baTutsi people, Rwanda (IV 78).

scrolls.[56] The open drone strings are tuned in unison with the lowest note—to its octave (the first subsidiary section), a fifth higher (the next), and the double octave (the shortest). The fretting on the fingerboard is chromatic, but note that the flat seventh (in C the B-flat) is on the front row, the natural behind. This is because, if the lowest note is C, the keynote of the instrument is F. A similar arrangement is often seen on other zithers, among them the Appalachian dulcimer.

The simplest, and presumably the earliest, of all the "board" zithers uses the ground as a board. The ground zither may be just that, sticks pushed into the ground with one or more strings running between them, but more often a small pit is dug and a board placed across it as a resonator.

Box zithers are widespread in our culture (see figure 6.13). One of the best-known is the Salzburg or Tyrolean zither, which has four strings running over a fretted fingerboard, with accompanying strings lying to one side. A number of others are similar in arrangement, mostly but not exclusively Central European in origin, although made today in many other areas. One in particular deserves a glance, for this is the only negatively arranged instrument. The autoharp has the normal fretted fingerboard plus accompanying strings arranged in groups, each of which represents a standard chord. Across these groups lies a series of bars, each marked with the name of a chord. The player depresses the relevant bar and sweeps the plectrum across all the strings, but only those for the specified chord will sound. This is because the bar, instead of sounding the desired chord, *prevents* all the other chords from response by damping them with felt pads glued on its underside. On all other instruments, one plays the notes required—only on the autoharp does one "unplay" the extraneous notes.

Many zithers are without the fretted fingerboard and just have each string tuned to a different pitch. Others—the Appalachian dulcimer, for example—reverse the arrangement and have just the fretted fingerboard. The origins of the latter seem to lie in Scandinavia, where the *psalmodikon* and earlier instruments such as the *langeleik* and *langspil* were popular, often, as the name for the first suggests, for accompanying psalms and other religious melodies in a domestic or small school setting. Some of the instruments of this type, for example the *épinette des vosges*, acquired bourdon (drone) strings, and it becomes difficult to distinguish some of those with a greater quantity of strings from the Central European zither. We see this with many different instruments, two distinct types gradually merging as each acquires more of the characteristics of the other.

An unfretted zither, the psaltery, is frequently seen in the medieval angelic bands.[57] Like so many medieval instruments, it derived from the Muslim lands, where the *qanun* is still widely used; one of the medieval names, *canon*, shows the connection. The qanun today is a more complex instrument with multiple courses and, at the head of each course, a series of four or more metal flaps that, when lifted under the string, shorten its length sufficiently to raise the pitch by around a quarter-tone, to allow for the microtonal tunings popular in the Ottoman culture.

The psaltery was a box zither, sometimes triangular or trapezoid but more often with two parallel sides and two widening sides, one or both curved, as in figure 6.13, to allow for differential string lengths. Sometimes the body was harp-shaped, and in the earlier medieval periods, it may be difficult to be certain whether one is looking at a harp or a harp-psaltery, but when the area behind the strings is a different color from the background, one normally assumes that this represents a soundboard and that the instrument is therefore a harp-psaltery. While one occasionally sees the strings plucked with the fingers, the normal technique was to use a quill plectrum in each hand.

Just as the lyre was the instrument of the gods in ancient Greek legend, so in the Nordic *Kalevala* the *kantele*, a triangular wing-shaped psaltery, was the first of instruments. It is still a popular folk instrument today and is widely taught in schools, especially in Finland.

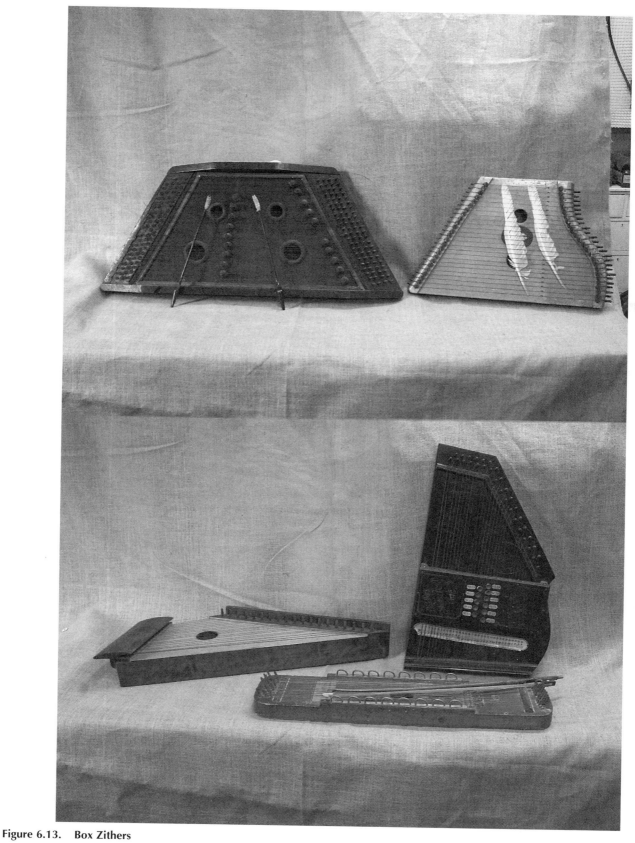

Figure 6.13. Box Zithers

Above, L–R: hammered dulcimer with beaters, England (IV 72); psaltery with quill plectra, England, 1891 (II 202).

Below, L–R: *kantele*, finger-plucked, Finland (III 88); autoharp, plectrum-plucked, by Müller, Germany (VI 220); in front: ukelin and bow, United States (V 22).

Sometime around the mid-sixteenth century, people began to strike the strings of the psaltery with light hammers instead of plucking them, so creating the hammered dulcimer (because its strings are plucked rather than struck, the Appalachian dulcimer is actually a form of psaltery rather than a dulcimer). There is still debate whether the Persian *santur* derives from our dulcimer or the process was the other way around—both seem to have appeared at much the same date. Certainly the Chinese *yangqin* comes from either one or the other, for its name means "foreign zither." The dulcimer became a popular instrument in the nineteenth century and still has a considerable following. It was only in Hungary, however, that it became a recognized concert instrument.

The *cimbalom* had long been a popular folk instrument, accompanying bands of fiddles and *tárogató* (the folk shawm that we have already met) with arpeggios of broken chords and its own melody line.[58] It was then quite similar in appearance to the English dulcimer illustrated in figure 6.13, but it was "modernized" by Jozsef Schunda around 1870 in Budapest, made much heavier, provided with legs instead of being hung around the player's neck or placed on a light stand, and given a damper pedal so that notes could be stopped instead of ringing on or having to be stopped by the side of the player's hand. It appears in music by Hungarian composers such as Bartók and Kodály, and also by Stravinsky, among others. It also remains a staple instrument of Gypsy and other bands. The cimbalom has multiple stringing, three or four wire strings to each course.

Because strings are never cheap, some simple instruments were made for village use in Hungary with wooden bars instead of strings, with the bars arranged in the same order as the strings of the cimbalom.[59] One would presume that this *facimbalom* ("wooden cimbalom") and its arrangement of bars was the origin of the old European four-row xylophone that had the same arrangement, with several notes duplicated. This was the standard form of the xylophone in the nineteenth century and early twentieth over the whole of Central Europe.

A few zithers are played by bowing. Some are quite narrow boxes so that the bow can be tipped to attack different strings. An unusual form, the ukelin, was popularized by mail order in the United States in the first half of the twentieth century. This has melody strings that are each bridged by the hoops at the side, plus sets of strings tuned to different chords. The melody strings are bowed by tipping the bow from hoop to hoop while the left hand plucks the accompanying chords—something easier to do than to describe.

One zither that is very different musically is the string drum. There are several forms of this. In Indonesia, there are thick bamboo internodes with one or more idiochordal strings raised from the cortex, often with a bamboo plate attached to the string or strings with a resonance hole beneath it (see figure 6.12). Two others we met in interlude D, the Basque *txuntxun*, which was known in France as the *tambourin de béarn* from the Baroque period to the present and also appears over a wider area in a number of late medieval manuscript illuminations, and the Hungarian *gardon*.

Let us now turn to the east. We have already mentioned the Chinese yangqin, but the *qin* are a large family with relatives elsewhere in the Far East. All seem to have originated in China, and all are long and narrow in shape. Most have a curved upper surface like a segment of a tube and are therefore often called "half-tube zithers," and some, for example, the Korean *kayagum* and the Japanese *koto*, are also slightly curved lengthwise. Both these and the Chinese *zheng* have a set of silk strings running along the upper surface (the number varies from one type to another within each family) whose pitch is determined not by their full length but by the position under each string of a movable bridge that can be adjusted to alter the mode or scale. The bridge is shaped rather like the wishbone of a chicken, two legs forming an arch with a projection from the crown of the arch to support the string, high enough that finger pressure on that part of the string behind the bridge can produce a vibrato. In each of these countries, the respective instrument has a similar role to the piano with us and is used both solo and to accompany other instruments.

In China, the classic qin has sometimes been called "the poet's lute," even though it is a zither, not a lute. It has been associated with Confucius, with philosophers, and with the highest class of classical music. Unlike the zheng, it has no bridges, save for the ridge at each end, so that the strings must differ in mass to be tuned to different pitches. Along the soundboard is a series of inlaid spots of ivory, mother-of-pearl, or other material, and these spots mark the places at which, if the string is touched lightly there, different harmonics will sound. The playing technique alternates the full tone of the plucked string and the lighter ringing sound of harmonics. The music is written in elaborate letter-tablature, far more elaborate than that used on our lute, also an instrument that usually plays from tablature rather than from staff notation.

Most Western lute tablatures have a set of lines, each representing one of the strings, and show, by letters or numbers on each line, at which fret each string should be stopped, with note stems above to mark the duration of each note, using the same conventional flags as staff notation at the top of each stem for eighth, sixteenth, and other notes. The qin tablature shows the Chinese equivalents of these, but it also shows the way in which the string should be plucked, whether plain or with vibrato, and the many other features that control musical style, tone quality, and all the other qualities that contribute to musical performance. Thus when a Chinese musician plays music from the time of Confucius, we can hear almost exactly how it was played in that period, the fifth century BC, whereas when one of our lutenists plays the music of John Dowland, only four centuries old, we can hear the same notes and rhythms that he played, but all the other aspects of performance are the interpretation of the modern player rather than of the composer.

Stringed Keyboards

There are four ways of sounding a string from a keyboard: rubbing, touching, plucking, and hitting. While the earliest history is still fairly obscure, this seems to have been the order of invention.

Rubbing

The earliest form, dating from the eleventh or twelfth century or perhaps a little earlier, was played by two people. One turned the wheel with a crank set into the end of the body, the other turned knobs, each of which rotated a blade upward to press against the strings and so define their sounding length. This was before the keyboard, as we know it, had been invented. There were

usually two or three strings that all sounded together, each blade stopping them all simultaneously. The instrument was called an *organistrum*, perhaps because it played in *organum*, the term for music moving in block chords, as the organ also did at this time. The organistrum had descendants, the thirteenth-century symphony and the later *vielle à roue* or hurdy-gurdy (see figure 6.35), but these, although they had keyboards, we shall leave until the end of this chapter when we discuss the bowed lutes.

Other than on these instruments, rubbing is the rarest and least successful method of producing a sound on stringed keyboards, along with a host of other attempts to produce a sustained sound.[60] Rubbing has usually involved a series of wheels to which the required strings are pulled by trackers from the keys and, judging by its lack of survival—only one such instrument is still in existence—it probably proved expensive, mechanically unreliable, and unstable in tuning.[61]

Touching

Touching the string is the simplest method. A metal blade or tangent on the far end of the key rises to touch the string with just sufficient impetus to make it vibrate. So long as the contact between tangent and string is maintained—this is why it is called "touching" rather than "hitting"—the string will sound until its vibration dies away. The tangent establishes the sounding length of the string, from the tangent to the bridge. The clavichord (see figure 6.14) works in this way, and when the key is released, the string's vibration is stopped by strips of cloth around its opposite end from the bridge. Because the player's finger is on one end of the key and the tangent is on the other, there is a feeling of intimacy and

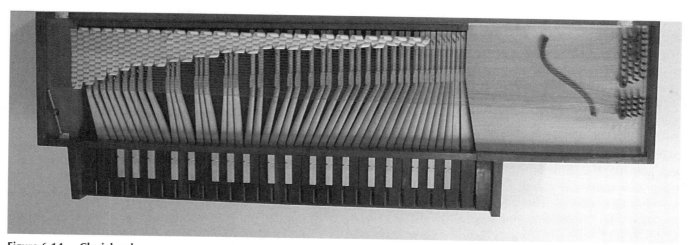

Figure 6.14. Clavichord
German seventeenth-century type, by John Rawson, London (VIII 14).

of contact with the music unlike that with any other keyboard instrument. By using a subtle vertical vibrato on the key, it is possible to make a slight swell in the loudness as well as a pitch vibrato on the notes—the *bebung* that was praised as a means of expression by many eighteenth-century musicians.

Partly because of its mechanical simplicity, and therefore low cost; partly because of its quietness (it has been, exaggeratedly, described as the only instrument that one occupant of a double bed can play without disturbing the other); partly because of its portability; and perhaps chiefly because of the necessity of accuracy and clarity of touch required to produce a good tone, the clavichord has always been a favorite practice instrument. Instead of playing in a cold church and paying someone to pump the bellows, organists could play in the warmth and comfort of their homes, reproducing the use of two manuals by placing one clavichord on top of another, and even going to the extent of adding a pedal clavichord. Both Mozart and Chopin are said to have carried clavichords for practice on long coach journeys.

It is arguable that its origin lay in the monochord. This was the standard teaching instrument from antiquity onward: a single string (hence its name, *mono* = "one", *chord* = "string") running over a marked surface, with a movable bridge that could be slid from mark to mark to produce any required pitch. Inevitably its movement was slow, plucking the string with a plectrum at one point, then moving the bridge accurately to the next point and plucking again. But with a set of keys and tangents to touch the string at each required point, the movement could be almost instantaneous. Precisely such an instrument is illustrated in a British Library manuscript from the fifteenth century.[62] With a single string, its ability to play music would be very limited, but with more strings it would succeed, as shown in the windows of the Beauchamp Chapel in Warwick of 1447.[63] This instrument appears to have six strings and twenty-six keys, giving a range of two or three octaves, depending on whether it was fully chromatic or not.

Because the tangent fixes the vibrating length of the string, it is possible for several tangents to share a pair of strings (clavichords seem always to have had double courses, with the strings for each note in pairs), each tangent stopping the string at the desired point, a semitone apart. This limits the chords that one can play because only the tangent with the shortest string length, that nearest the bridge, will sound, but since the major third in this period was regarded as a discord (see the afterword's section on "Scales and Music" for the reasons for this), four or five tangents sharing a string was an acceptable number, as is shown in the first detailed description of keyboard instruments, Henri-Arnaut de Zwolle's manuscript of around 1440.[64]

As musical styles elaborated, "fretting," as such sharing of strings was called, became less acceptable, and by the late seventeenth century no more than three notes were shared, as in figure 6.14. Through the eighteenth century, pair-wise fretting was common, confusingly termed "fret-free," for nobody needed to play together two notes a semitone apart. Careful fingering was needed for some trills and graces, but neat fingering is always essential on the clavichord—hence its value for practice. Larger instruments, wholly fret-free with a string for each key, were certainly available before 1700 for those who could afford them and were willing to spend the extra tuning time. One of the advantages of the fretted instruments is that one needs to tune only one of the shared notes—if one was in tune, the others had to be because they used the same string. Another is reduced tension on the casework and load on the bridge, leading to freer tone.

The clavichord remained popular for domestic use throughout the eighteenth century, but it was eventually supplanted by the introduction of the small square piano, and its use died out in the early nineteenth century. By the end of that century, however, its revival had begun, and it is now available from many makers, as with the instrument shown in figure 6.14.

Plucking

The action of plucking a string is slightly more complex. The plectrum must pass the string, plucking as it goes, and then return so that it may pluck again. If the plectrum is fixed in its holder, it will pluck the string a second time as it descends, something that is musically undesirable. So the plectrum, traditionally a small piece of quill, or sometimes of leather, is fixed in a tongue that pivots so that the quill may slide unobtrusively past the string as it falls back. A spring, traditionally of hog-bristle, pushes it back upright, ready to pluck again. It is also undesirable that the string should be allowed to ring on and overlap the following notes, so a small cloth flag is provided that will stop the vibration of the string when the key is released. If all this is fixed rigidly to the key, it is less efficient, and so the whole apparatus—quill, tongue, and damper—is placed at the top of a slip of wood that jumps up from the end of the key and is therefore called a "jack." A jackrail runs above each row of jacks to prevent them from jumping right out.

The chief of the family of instruments that works in this way is the harpsichord, which first appears around 1425 and can be seen in that same window in the

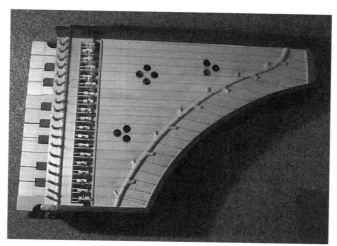

Figure 6.15. Harpsichord
Replica of one of the earliest known illustrations, fifteenth century, by Richard Shann, Glan-y-gors, Wales (VIII 34).

Beauchamp chapel, and in Arnaut's manuscript as replicated in figure 6.15. Smaller instruments, rectangular in shape, or sometimes pentagonal but then usually in a rectangular case, were also popular. These were called *virginals* in English and Flemish, *épinette* in French, and *spinetto* in Italian.

Terminology is a perpetual problem, for "virginals" was also used for the harpsichord in sixteenth-century England and "spinet" in English was used for a rather different eighteenth-century instrument (and has been commonly misused in more modern times for the square piano). To be specific, the clavichord was also called "manichord" and similar names (confirming the derivation from the monochord), with close equivalents in other European languages, except for German where it was called *Klavier*.[65] The harpsichord, the large wing-shaped instrument (*Flügel*, "wing," in German), was the *arpicembalo* or just *cembalo* in Italian—the latter term also used in Germany, where it was also called *Instrument*—and *clavecin* in French. The virginals was usually, as we have said, rectangular, with the keyboard to the left side of the front (top in figure 6.16), and the later spinet roughly triangular (bottom in the drawing), sometimes called "leg-of-mutton" shape.

The strings of the virginals run parallel with the long sides, running across the keyboard, with both bridges on the soundboard. The strings of the spinet, by contrast, run away from the keyboard, parallel with the straight side, and one bridge is on the soundboard, the other on the wrest plank. The spinet is really just a small, domestic-size harpsichord. There was also a special Flemish form of virginals, the *muselaar*, that had the keyboard toward the right-hand end (in the middle of figure 6.16) so

that the strings were plucked nearer to the middle of their length, thereby producing a different tone quality because that plucking position eliminates the even-numbered harmonics.[66]

The virginals was essentially a domestic instrument. With a few exceptions, it was only in Flanders that it had more than one keyboard. There, a small 4' instrument was often provided that was stored in a recess in the long side but could be taken out and placed on top of the main instrument. The jackrail was then removed so that the jacks of the mother could also push up the jacks of the child through holes cut in its bottom board. In this way, one hand on the mother's keyboard could play both instruments in octaves, plucking both the mother's 8' strings and making the child's jacks pluck its 4' strings, while the other hand played the child's keyboard, so playing in just the upper octave and allowing a contrast of sound. Equally, one could play with both hands on one keyboard or on the other.

The harpsichord was the main keyboard instrument, other than the organ, for public performance. In the fifteenth century, the instrument seems to have been quite small, as in figure 6.15, although whether it was as small

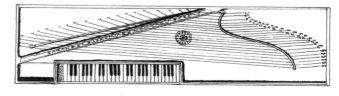

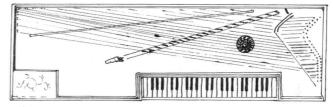

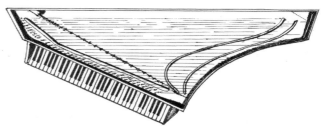

Figure 6.16. Virginals, Muselaar, and Spinet
Top to bottom: virginals with jackrail covering the jacks close to the back-bridge; muselaar with jacks well away from the back-bridge, both with both bridges on the soundboard and both seventeenth-century type; leg-of-mutton spinet, eighteenth-century type with back-bridge on the wrest plank and bridge and hitch-pin rail on the soundboard, *drawn by Sarah Montagu.*

as some medieval illustrations suggest, barely a couple of feet long, we do not know.[67] The only known surviving fifteenth-century instrument is an upright harpsichord, or *clavicytherium*, probably southern German of around 1480, in the Royal College of Music in London.[68] Most other early surviving harpsichords are Italian. These were lightly built instruments, often of cypress wood, and were normally provided with an outer case constructed so that it could be played either in its case or slid out and laid on a table. The earliest seem to have been single-strung, one string for each note, but later instruments most commonly had two sets of strings, either both at the same 8' pitch or one 8' and one 4', an octave higher. Because the sound of a string differs quite perceptibly according to where it is plucked, the two 8' strings had a slightly different tone quality even though the two rows of jacks, one for the front 8' and the other for the back 8', were only an inch or so apart.

The second most important school of harpsichord making was the Flemish, primarily centered on Antwerp. Here the most influential dynasty of makers, which was established in 1579 and survived until 1706, was the Ruckers family and their descendants the Couchet family.[69] Initially they mainly produced virginals (only one harpsichord by Hans Ruckers, the first generation, survives), but they went on to build what became the most desirable harpsichords of their time.

The Ruckers instruments followed the German tradition, whence the family originated, with much heavier cases than the Italian and therefore without a separate outer case. Most of the earlier instruments had one 8' and one 4' rank and were still single manual. The first double-manual harpsichords, with one keyboard above and behind the other, appeared before the end of the sixteenth century, but these were very different from what we think of as a double-manual today. Essentially they were two harpsichords in one, pitched a fourth apart, the upper manual shifted to the right so that the F keys of the lower manual plucked the same strings as the C keys a fourth lower on the upper manual. There is still much argument over the reasons for this arrangement, for while it provides an easy way to transpose, this was something that all keyboard players were trained to do, and transpositions of a fourth or a fifth are among the easiest. Nevertheless, these were the only double-manual harpsichords that the Ruckers dynasty was willing to produce. When their harpsichords were updated in the next century, as many were, the keyboards were realigned into what became the normal pattern, and the instruments were thus altered into what are called "expressive doubles." Only one Ruckers survives (in Edinburgh) in its original transposing setup, although some allegedly contemporary Spanish instruments have recently come to light, for the Ruckers model was copied over much of Europe.[70]

The expressive double became the norm from the early 1640s.[71] With an 8' and a 4' on one manual and another 8' on the other, plus the option of coupling the manuals together for the fullest sound, as well as the additional effects of a buff and a lute stop, the late seventeenth- and eighteenth-century harpsichords had a wide range of contrasting sounds available. The two 8's now contrasted more strongly because, with the 4' jacks between them, their plucking points were farther apart.[72] The buff stop was a wooden batten carrying a row of pads of buff leather that could be slid sideways so that the buffs touched the strings and dulled the sound—in Germany, this was called the lute stop. The English lute stop was very different. An extra row of jacks plucked one of the 8' ranks very close to the nut (the bridge on the wrest plank), producing a very bright sharp sound (the Germans called it the *nazard*). To provide even greater contrast, some makers used hard leather plectra on one of the 8' ranks, producing a different sound from the normal crow quill on the other.

As time went on, individual national styles became much more clearly differentiated. Arrangements of which manuals controlled which strings, and how one manual could be coupled with the other, varied from place to place. German instruments in particular grew more complex, occasionally adding 2' and 16' ranks and so, with everything coupled, being able to sound four octaves together.

English instruments were often provided with a pedal-controlled machine stop, analogous to an organist's presets, whereby the player could produce sudden changes of sonority without moving a hand from the keys. A second pedal controlled a swell, an inner lid that opened to let out more sound. This was developed to compete with the piano, which, unlike the harpsichord, could get gradually louder or softer—the harpsichord could do so only in steps by adding or subtracting registers. The main effect of the swell, though, was to make the sound quieter, for even when it was open, some of the sound was obscured, and far more when it was closed.

In France, there was a craze for Flemish instruments. Despite the fact that the French makers were among the best (more of their instruments are copied today than any others), unless an instrument was by Ruckers or Couchet, it was little esteemed. One solution was to rip the soundboards from Flemish virginals by those makers and install them in new harpsichords. Another was out-and-out forgery. But, of course, nobody wanted a Flemish harpsichord in original condition. The range was too small, C/E to c''', and it had to be expressive. The C/E is the indication for the short octave. It was seldom that players required all the chromatic notes in the bass, so the E key sounded C, the F key its own note, the F♯ sounded D, the G itself, and the G♯ sounded E. This is why much early music has quite extraordinary finger-stretches in the bass—one could cover a tenth or more within what would be the normal span of an octave.

The use of short octaves went on for a surprisingly long time. As the range of instruments was increased, the G/B replaced the C/E. A fully chromatic range, F' to e''', became standard only by the second quarter of the eighteenth century. The short octave must have been known still later—if only on organs, where it saved a great deal of metal for pipes in the bass—into the nineteenth century, because one of Beethoven's last piano sonatas, no. 31, op. 110, in A-flat, uses the sequence of notes obtained by playing straight up the keys of the short octave as a fugue subject in its last movement.

The process of enlargement was called *ravalement*, and it was a fairly major operation. A new keyboard was needed, and the case had to be rebuilt, the soundboard and wrest plank extended, along with the jack guides (the slots in which the jacks move up and down), new ornamental papers printed to line the inside of the case if it was still to look like a Ruckers, the soundboard repainted, for many are beautifully decorated, and so on. The same process was applied to the older, originally French instruments that were updated.

The harpsichord remained the main keyboard instrument rather longer than is generally realized, in Austria as late as 1790 or so, presumably partly for reasons of cost—not everybody could, or even wanted to, replace a good harpsichord with a newfangled piano. Certainly some of Mozart's earlier keyboard concertos were catalogued by his father and elsewhere as being for the harpsichord—the E-flat Concerto, K.271, of 1777 is the first that seems likely to have been composed for the piano, and even that is titled "per il clavicembalo."[73]

Hitting or, More Politely, Hammering

Keyboards with hammers appeared as early as those with plectra. Arnaut de Zwolle's treatise shows four types of jack with his harpsichord, three with plectra and one that hammered. The last, he said, was particularly appropriate for the *dulce melos*. This was a rectangular keyboard version of the dulcimer with a series of bridges to divide the strings into separate lengths. Dulcimers like Arnaut's appear in a few Italian paintings and carvings of the fifteenth century, and some modern instruments, such as the Hungarian *cimbalom*, also divide their strings to get more than one note from each string.

The dulcimer faces the same problem as the drum: that the action of creating the sound also stifles it. If the

hammer remains on the string, or the beater on the drumhead, for more than a very small fraction of a second, it mutes the sound of the string or skin and produces a thud rather than the desired ring. The solution is the relaxed wrist—the player learns to spring the hammer or beater away as fast as, or even faster than, it went on. But a mechanical equivalent of the relaxed wrist is very difficult to achieve with a mechanism from a keyboard, and this is probably why the keyboard dulce melos met with little or no success and why Arnaut's hammer action was not, or was seldom, applied to the harpsichord for another 250 years. One of the few exceptions was the eighteenth-century *pantaleon*, in effect a dulcimer with a keyboard.[74] This came despite the fact that the great advantage of hammering is that one can hit gently or strongly, producing quiet or loud sounds, whereas plucking gently or strongly makes only a slight difference—although quite enough that skilled harpsichordists can demonstrate phrasing through their touch on the keys.

The mechanical equivalent of the relaxed wrist is the escapement, and this was invented by Bartolomeo Cristofori in Florence shortly before 1700 when he produced his *gravicembalo col piano e forte* (harpsichord with soft and loud).[75] The essentials for a piano action—in addition to all the basic apparatus of keyboard, strings, dampers to stop the strings from sounding longer than desired, framework, and so forth—are hammers that will fly freely from the key and a check that will catch the hammers as they fall back and prevent them from bouncing up again and having a second whack at the strings. If the hammer is rigidly attached to the key, it cannot fly, and so an intermediate lever is necessary. A block toward the end of the key pushes up the second or intermediate lever but disengages or escapes from it just before it reaches the height of its travel. The second lever then both flips up the hammer and also accelerates its speed of travel so that it strikes the string with greater impetus than it otherwise would. As the hammer falls back, it was held by crossed threads, as on Cristofori's first action that we know only from drawings by a contemporary reporter, or by a lever poised to catch it, as on the three surviving Cristofori pianos. Meanwhile the far end of the key has pushed up the damper, which falls back to stop the vibration of the strings only when the key is released.

While the modern piano action is vastly more complicated, this is still approximately what happens. There have been many refinements over the three centuries since 1700, but an interesting point is that it was more than half a century after Cristofori's time before all his essential devices had come into general use. In the meanwhile, makers had compromised, simplified, economized, and otherwise bowdlerized the original pattern to produce actions that were less efficient than the original. These avoided the complication of the intermediate lever, relying, on English instruments, on a block or other device to stop the key immediately after a rod mounted on it had struck the hammer, and on German and Austrian pianos, on a similar block or *Prelleiste* to catch the back end of the hammer and so flip it up at the strings.[76]

The original pianos were the same size and shape as the harpsichords: the same shape as, and only a little smaller than, our grand piano. This took up too much floor space for ordinary domestic use, however. This led to the introduction of upright pianos, and the earliest uprights were upright indeed, for they were grands bent 90 degrees behind the keyboard, so that what would normally have extended five or six feet forward now soared up toward the ceiling. There were four disadvantages to these uprights. One was that they were inherently unstable and therefore had to stand against a wall. Following from this, another disadvantage was that players had to have their back to the rest of the family or the audience. The third was that the instruments were large and awk-

ward to carry upstairs to the main living room, which was then normally above the ground-level rooms. The fourth, and most serious, was that the hammers tended to dwell on the strings so that there was no "relaxed wrist."

The solution was the square piano (see figure 6.17), initially no larger, and little more expensive, than the clavichord. This was invented by Johann Christoph Zumpe in 1766 in London and immediately became popular all over Europe, remaining the preferred domestic piano in America almost up to the end of the nineteenth century.

While to our ears the sound of the square seems barely adequate for domestic use, even the earliest models were used for chamber music and for concertos with a small band of players. Johann Christian Bach, the youngest son of Johann Sebastian, settled in London and gave regular concerts with the Zumpe pianos there, though also using grands for larger occasions. As a result, while the harpsichord remained the more important instrument on the continent of Europe, in Britain the piano took the lead.

One disadvantage of the early piano was that it was quieter than the harpsichord. This was chiefly due to the

Figure 6.17.   Square Piano
By Frederick Beck, London, 1786, *photo Tony Bingham, London.*

fact that the normal string gauges for a harpsichord are ideal for plucking but are too light to respond properly to hammering. However, if heavier strings are fitted and tuned to the same pitches, the strain on the casework is such that the instrument is torn apart. In addition, the gap between the soundboard and the wrest plank, where the tuning or wrest pins are fitted, tries to close. There has to be a gap, because otherwise the hammers and dampers could not get to the strings. This had not been a problem with the harpsichord because the gap had been filled with what was in effect a wooden bar made up of the jack-guides, the slots through which the jacks rose. Early attempts to stabilize the piano were a series of iron hoops that spanned the gap, holding the two sides apart, or metal rods running from the wrest plank to a metal plate holding the hitchpin rail at the far end. Various patterns of iron frames followed, with one part screwed to the wrest plank and another to the tail of the instrument, but it was not until Alpheus Babcock of Boston invented the full iron frame, made in a single casting for a square in 1825, that success was achieved. He was followed by Jonas Chickering, also of Boston, in 1843 with a frame for a grand, and then by many other makers and models, culminating in instruments such as the modern grand (see figure 6.18).

Meanwhile string technology had been improving. If iron or brass wire is too thick, it becomes stiff and reluctant to produce a good sound, but if two thinner strings are twisted together, they retain their flexibility while achieving the same mass as a thicker string. Such strings can be found on early square pianos, thus compensating for the short length in the bass compelled by the small dimensions of the instrument. Similar strings were used on grands also, followed by strings with an open-coiled overwinding to increase their mass even more and so provide the heavier strings required for hammering. Eventually the close-coiled covering was devised that is used today.

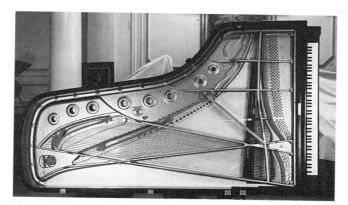

Figure 6.18. Modern Grand Piano
Courtesy Messrs. Steinway, London.

The hammers of Cristofori's pianos were made of glued-up rolls of layers of parchment, so that they were both firm and elastic, with a pad of soft doeskin leather to strike the strings. These were followed with other makers by wooden hammers with a leather cover, first with the hard surface on the outside and later turned over so that the softer inner surface of the leather struck the string, both of which were less elastic and thus with harder tone quality than Cristofori's. As strings became heavier, so perforce did the hammers, and a better cover was sought. This was found by the French maker Henri Pape, who cut up felt hats to make the hammers for his pianos, and felt is universally used today.[77]

Actions were also improving, with the makers of each nation superseding each other. The Stein, Streicher, and Walter pianos were preferred in Vienna in Mozart's time. Haydn, when he visited London, was impressed with Broadwood's pianos and took one home. Thomas Broadwood gave an improved model to Beethoven when his deafness progressed to the point where he could no longer hear the Austrian instruments, and this was eventually replaced by a still more powerful Austrian instrument.[78] Actions became heavier with the desire for greater power, to the extent that the rapid reiteration of notes became difficult. This was overcome by Erard of Paris with his double escapement. Instead of the hammer falling all the way back to the check, there was an intermediate stage that held the hammer partway back, even after the finger had left the key, supported by a spring to keep it nearer the string for a short while, ready to fly back when notes had to be rapidly repeated. Associated levers allowed the escapement hopper also to reset in an intermediate position instead of falling all the way back. This device is still present on our pianos.

Dampers became heavier, but still by no means as heavy as they are today. One reason that there is so little pedaling marked in the original editions of Chopin's music is that the dampers of his piano did not cut short the sound as our dampers do. The tone rang on enough, even after the damper fell back, that he could obtain the singing legato for which his playing was so famous without using the damper lift that our pianists have to employ today in his music. His tuner on his London visits, Alfred Hipkins of Broadwoods, recorded that he disliked the heavy actions of the English grands and played his London recitals on a square piano.

These were still produced in the mid-nineteenth century, even though by that time the upright had become more common because makers were producing lower models. Around 1800, John Isaac Hawkins of Philadelphia produced the first American low upright, in effect turning the soundboard of the old high upright upside-down, so that instead of reaching to the ceiling it reached to the floor, just as our uprights do today. This meant that bass strings had to be shorter than before, but the lack of tonal quality was overcome by introducing heavier covered strings for the bass. It was at this period that the American instrument-making trade came into being. Previously the main source of instruments of all sorts had been by importing from Europe, although there was already a nascent indigenous industry for woodwinds and brass. With the Napoleonic Wars and the naval blockades, followed by the resulting War of 1812, imports were severely restricted. American piano and other makers multiplied and produced many important developments, not least the iron frames already mentioned.

Piano technology progressed on both sides of the Atlantic, with the various nineteenth-century international exhibitions acting as a spur, as one maker saw what another was producing, until by about 1880 the piano was more or less in its modern state. For music written before that time, purists today, under the influence of the Early Music movement, will often prefer to use a reconditioned piano of the appropriate period or, as makers get to grips with the reproduction of late classical and romantic instruments, with newly made copies of older instruments. While playing Brahms on a modern piano by a maker such as Bösendorfer will produce much the sounds that Brahms would have heard, this is not true of Chopin, and still less of Beethoven. Many modern writers have complained that Beethoven's piano writing sounds muddy and confused in the bass, but this is not Beethoven's fault. The bass parts are clear enough on pianos of his own time; the fault is that of the modern instruments.

Since the second half of the twentieth century or so, piano sound has, to many ears, been degraded by the search for increased brilliance. String tensions have increased to such an extent that, especially in the treble, strings have become as rigid as bars with the resulting obtrusive presence of nonharmonic overtones that jangle in one's ears and a tone quality reminiscent of that of the xylophone.

It was also around 1880 that the Early Music movement began, promoting the performance of music of earlier times on the instruments for which it had been intended. Alfred Hipkins gave concerts on harpsichord and virginals, as did other scholars in Germany and Austria. The movement really took off when a Swiss player, Arnold Dolmetsch, who had settled in London, began to produce clavichords, as well as recorders and viols. His first clavichord, now in the Bate Collection in Oxford, was built in 1894 and was much praised by George Bernard Shaw. Since that date, makers of clavichords and harpsichords have sprung up everywhere.

Initially the harpsichords suffered from the feeling that the improvements that had been good for pianos must also be good for harpsichords, so that iron frames and heavy strings were combined with a row of pedals to save taking a hand from the keyboard to change registrations.[79] The Boston makers Frank Hubbard and William Dowd led a revolution to learn from the accumulated wisdom of three centuries of harpsichord making by returning to the models and practices of the historical periods (although the modern plastic Delrin quill lacks the brilliance of the original crow feather).[80] Nowadays the so-called plucking piano has fallen into disrepute, but one has to hope that some at least survive in usable condition, because there is a considerable early-twentieth-century repertoire of works, by composers such as de Falla, Poulenc, and Frank Martin, that require the facilities of instruments such as those made by Pleyel, who was one of the leaders in the revival harpsichord.

Plucked Lutes

As we suggested in interlude E discussing tension, the strings wage a constant battle with the body of every stringed instrument: The body is trying to keep the two ends of the strings apart, and the strings are trying to fold the body up. The simplest way to overcome this among the lutes—a technical term covering all those stringed instruments that combine a neck with a body or resonator—is the "spiked lute," a type that is or has been widespread wherever around the world stringed instruments are used.

At one end of the neck, there is usually some way to adjust the tension for tuning. At the other, there is just a knot or some other way to attach the strings. Partway along, usually toward the bottom, the neck passes straight through a resonator or body, like a spike through a ball. With this arrangement, there is no strain on the body and the utmost that the strings can do with their tension is to curve the neck somewhat, which does no harm. Either the strings lie closely enough to the neck that they can be pressed against it, even if there is a slight curve, or else they are stopped just by placing the fingers against them, in midair as it were.

An obvious ancestor of the spiked lute is the gourd-resonated musical bow, for if the bow stave becomes rigid and passes through the resonator, rather than being attached to it and removable, we have a spiked lute. Such instruments can be either plucked or bowed; the latter are called "spiked fiddles" and will be covered in the next section.

The simplest way of adjusting the string tension—and, judging by the absence of any sign of tuning pegs or similar devices on Mesopotamian and other early reliefs, the earliest—is by either tying the string around the neck or, more probably, attaching the upper end of the string to a leather thong and tying that around the neck.[81] This system survives on instruments from West Africa, as shown in figure 6.19, and is surprisingly successful—one would expect the thong to slip, but it seems to hold reasonably well. Some way of adjusting tension is essential, because a string will sound only when it is tight, and when more than one string is used on an instrument, their pitches must agree with each other, either at the same pitch or at some interval that is musically useful within the culture.

The West African instruments referred to and illustrated in figure 6.19 are found from Nigeria up into the Manding area of the West African bulge. Along with the *gnibri* of the North African Maghrib, they are a variant of the spiked lute that may be called "half-spiked," for the neck does not pierce the distal end of the resonator: It passes through the upper end of the resonator and under the upper part of the belly, commonly of skin, sometimes being laced through the skin to hold it more firmly, and ends under the resonator hole cut in the belly, where the

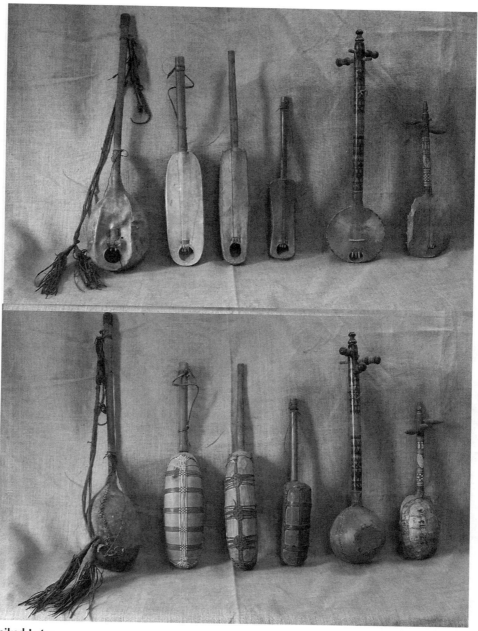

Figure 6.19. Half-spiked Lutes

Front and back; L–R: *garaya*, skin body, Hausa people, Nigeria (III 58); three wooden-bodied lutes, West Africa (the precise location could be determined by the patterning of thongs on the back) (VII 248, II 42b, and II 42a); *gnibri*, the back a reused pudding basin, pre-1938, Morocco (VII 246); gnibri, the back a tortoise shell, Morocco (X 36).

strings can be tied to its end. The West African instruments traditionally had strings of twisted horsehair, as in those shown, but they and the gnibri, like so many other instruments today, are now more often strung in monofilament nylon. Its common availability as fishing line has been a boon to instrument makers worldwide, especially wherever its somewhat inferior tone quality is less important than its ease of application and, often, longevity.

Typologically, most spiked lutes belong to the category of long-necked lutes: those with a neck as long as, or more usually longer than, the body. Outstandingly so are the Chinese *sanxian* (see figure 6.22) and its Japanese derivative, the *shamisen*. Both have very small box bodies, six inches or so wide, the former with snakeskin and the latter with catskin bellies and backs, on the end of a neck around a yard long. Strings on both are traditionally of silk.

Although larger-bodied spike lutes do exist, when a larger soundbox is required for greater resonance, it seems to have been more usual to build the body onto the neck, rather than to use the spike form. This has been especially true in eastern, central, and southern Asia, from Turkey with its European offshoots from the days of the Ottoman Empire, through the Caucasus and the southern states of what was once the Soviet Union,

to the northern parts of the Indian subcontinent and the western parts of China. Under such names as *saz, tar, tanbur, rebab, buzuk,* and their variants, long-necked lutes with a variety of body shapes abound.

Most, though by no means all, are wire-strung and played with a plectrum, a small piece of convenient material to pluck the strings. The belly may be either wood or skin. The choice often depends on the prevailing climate, both because persistent damp makes a skin belly slack and because climate affects the availability of the most suitable woods, such as the close-grained members of one of the coniferous tree families. One of the simplest body shapes is the narrow pear- or almond-shape of the tanbur, saz, and dutar found from Turkey and the Balkans through the Central Asian republics whose names end with -stan (see figure 6.20).[82] Traditionally the body was shaped from a block of wood, using a draw-knife for the exterior and an adze and gouge for the interior. Laurence Picken describes and illustrates the technique in detail, with X-radiographs, and cites the example of an adze-made saz with body walls no more than two millimeters thick.[83] More recently, some makers have built up the body from thin slats of wood, a process that Picken also describes and illustrates. Examples of each can be seen in figure 6.20.

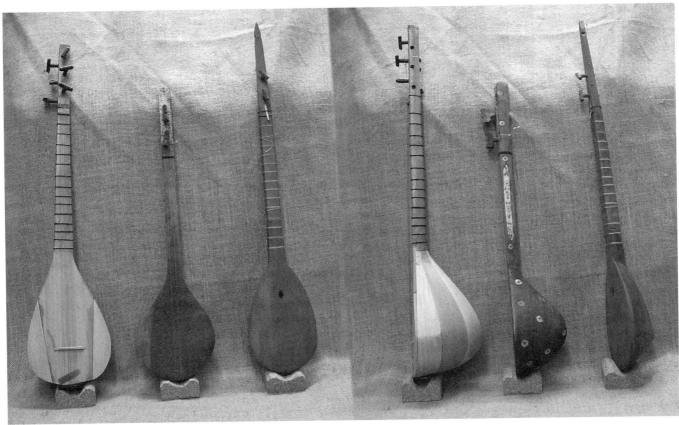

Figure 6.20. Saz Types
Facing and profile; L–R: *saz*, carvel bodied, Turkey (IX 36); *dutar*, Afghanistan (VIII 54); *cift telli*, solid bodied, Turkey (VI 72).

The center of the belly is a thin piece of coniferous wood with, in Turkey, narrow wings of a different wood. The neck is mortised into the stem of the body in a long V-shape to maximize the glue area and has small T-shaped tuning pegs at the upper end. The number of strings varies from place to place, with two or three either single or double courses being a common arrangement.[84] The Afghan *dutar*, as its name indicates (*du* = "two," *tar* = "strings"), originally had two strings, initially of gut, later of steel wire. However, names persist but instruments change, and today the dutar has fourteen strings, many of them sympathetic, in a synthesis made to suit modern playing conditions with a different Afghan instrument, the *rubab*.[85] Similarly, as we saw above with the zithers, the Indian sitar changed from a three-string instrument to the version with many extra strings, both drones and sympathetics, that we have today in North Indian classical music. The sitar, like the South Indian vīnā, differs from the instruments we have been discussing by having a large gourd as a resonator, cut in half to make the body, with a wooden plate fitted as a belly (see figure 6.21).

The term *belly*, for the soundboard on the front of the instrument, derives from our anthropomorphic terminology for instruments such as the violin. Once one has the head, neck, shoulders, and back, the front is obviously the belly. This has sometimes caused confusion on instruments with a rounded back such as the sitar, because a rounded belly is also only too often part of the human frame! Nevertheless, on instruments, the belly is always at the front, immediately under the strings, and an alternative name for the soundboard.

There are many other body shapes found on long-necked lutes, including the figure-eight front view of the

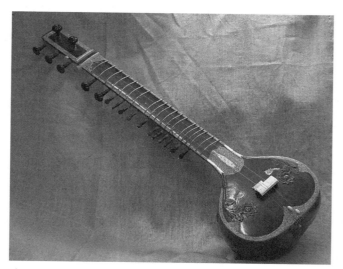

Figure 6.21.   Sitar
By Modern Musical Instruments Mfg. Co-op, Delhi, India (XI 142).

Persian and Caucasian tar, the triangular body of the Russian *balalaika*, the winged resonators seen among the Uzbeks and Tajiks, and what one might almost describe as spade-shaped in other parts of what was the southern Soviet Union, sometimes straight-sided and sometimes curvilinear.

We note a recent European derivative of the saz, the *bouzouki*, in interlude H. Another of a rather earlier date was the Italian *colascione*. This had a small body, more half-pear than almond-shape, a long neck, and, according to Mersenne in 1636, either two or three single strings.[86] The fretting seems not to have been fully chromatic.

Most of the instruments we have been considering so far have frets along the neck at preselected points. While some today have metal frets inset into the front surface of the neck, like our guitar or mandolin, many have strands of gut, occasionally of wire or today of nylon, tied around the neck, allowing the fret to be moved to adjust the tuning, or to alter the scale or mode from one system to another. The function of a fret is not, or at least not wholly, to tell the player where to place the fingers for any particular note, but primarily to give the sounds a brighter tone. Anyone who plays the violin will know that there is a considerable difference between the ringing sound of an open-string note and the sound of a fingered note. This is because the nut at the top of the neck provides a sharp cutoff to the vibrating string length, whereas the fleshy finger stopping the string on the fingerboard gives a slightly fuzzy cutoff. The use of a fret means that every note has that same ring as the open string because the fret provides that same sharp cutoff. This is why most players stop the string immediately behind a fret, rather than on top of it. A few instruments, of which the sitar is the prime example, have specially designed frets, a curved bar across which the player can pull the string sideways to alter its tension and produce a glissando or slide to a different pitch, often of a fifth or more.

It is said that the Arabic *'ud* did not have frets (it has none today), but so many early treatises on that instrument describe the fretting positions along the neck that they must have been there originally. One would guess that the frets survived at least to the thirteenth century, because this is when *al 'ud* was introduced into Europe, and the European lute, whose name is a transliteration of the Arabic, has always been fretted. Why the use of frets should later have been abandoned in the Arab world is unknown, although one possibility is that, as their scales became more and more complex, with intermediate microtonal notes as well as the normal separation of sharps from flats (to use our terminology for a distinction between the semitone above and the semitone below any note), there were simply too many frets and it became difficult to distinguish, or fit the fingers, between them. A more likely reason is that the frets had to be abandoned when *glissandi*, sliding from one pitch to another, became an important part of the repertoire, for sliding up or down a fretted neck produces a chromatic scale, not a glissando. The 'ud seems originally to have had four courses, and by the ninth century, according to Al-Kindi, the two lower were of gut and the two upper of silk; Ziryab claimed to have added a fifth string earlier in that century, and today there are normally six, usually five double and one single.[87] They were, and still are, plucked with a plectrum, as are the strings of the 'ud's derivatives throughout what was once the Ottoman Empire.

With the 'ud and the lute, we have reached the short-necked lutes, instruments whose neck is as short as or shorter than the body, or in our terms whose neck-to-body joint comes at the twelfth fret or earlier (see figure 6.22). Many instruments have shorter necks still, and there is a very wide variety of types, including many, especially among the bowed variety, that are carved from a single piece of wood, neck and body together.

As with the long-necked instruments, evidence for such instruments in Europe before the twelfth century is very scanty. There are lyres and harps and a variety of forms of psaltery in abundance, but very few plucked lutes, despite already a fairly plentiful supply of bowed ones. We are, of course, dependent on what artists, almost exclusively in religious contexts such as psalters and church carvings, chose to illustrate. It is quite possible that this is wholly misleading, that there were such instruments in use, perhaps in secular music, but so many of these illustrations seem to show ordinary people making music that it does look very much as though lutes of any sort were first introduced into Europe as fiddles (something that did not happen until around 1000) and were only plucked by those lacking a bow or the skill to use one.

There are a very few exceptions. The Utrecht Psalter, written in Rheims around 825 (see figure C.1), shows an instrument with a very small, lyre-shaped body with a long neck whose only parallel is on a Roman mosaic in Libya.[88] The Stuttgart Psalter from Paris at very much the same date shows a plucked instrument with a very long body whose only known parallel is played today among the Berber of southern Morocco, and there is a number of instruments with long necks in several tenth-century Spanish Mozarabic manuscripts of the Book of Daniel.[89] These last are contemporary with our earliest European illustrations of fiddles.

Our lute arrived in Europe with what we described in interlude C as the Medieval Renaissance, in the late twelfth and early thirteenth centuries, from the Arab lands to the south and the east. It was already well established in those areas and seems likely to have originated where so many other instruments appear to have begun, between the Aral and Caspian seas, and to have spread thence east and west. The Chinese acknowledge that their version, the *pipa*, came from the west, and it was well developed there before the eighth century AD. Elaborately decorated versions of it from that date survive as the Japanese *biwa* in the Shōsōin Repository in Nara.[90] One early Persian representation is on a Sassanid silver vessel of the sixth century in Tehran, along with a shawm, tong cymbals, and Chinese mouth organ, the last showing how wide cultural contacts then were.[91]

When the lute arrived in Europe, it is said to have had four double courses, although a Sicilian manuscript of the late twelfth century shows five single strings,[92] and the mid-thirteenth-century Spanish *Cántigas* shows nine strings that may, perhaps, have been grouped 2, 3, 2, 2.[93] By the late fifteenth century, Tinctoris tells us that in Germany there were five courses, occasionally six; that each, save for the highest, might be tuned in octaves rather than unison; and that the strings were plucked either with the fingers or with a quill plectrum.[94] There is music surviving in the Italian Pesaro manuscript from the same period for a seven-course lute.

A Flemish treatise of around 1440 tells us precisely how to build a lute, with its dimensions and proportions, but says nothing about the stringing.[95] This instrument was quite small, with a body that was similar to pear-shape but was short enough and deep enough to be almost hemispherical, shorter than the instruments we have already referred to in illustrations, and much deeper from belly to back than the Chinese or Japanese. The back was built up from thin strips of wood, like the Persian instruments, gluing them edge-to-edge on a mold and probably, like the Persian and many later European lutes, with strips of parchment glued internally along the joints to strengthen them. The Chinese and Japanese instruments, on the other hand, have a shallow body carved out from a solid block of wood. They and the Persian instruments have a peg-box and head that curves back from the line of the neck. The European instruments, certainly from the *Cántigas* onward, have the peg-box turned sharply back, almost at a right angle, making the construction stronger, allowing it to withstand the strain of the strings rather better and, on larger-bodied instruments, bringing the tuning pegs into easier reach of the hand.

Our lute initially shared one important characteristic with the oriental instrument: it was played with a

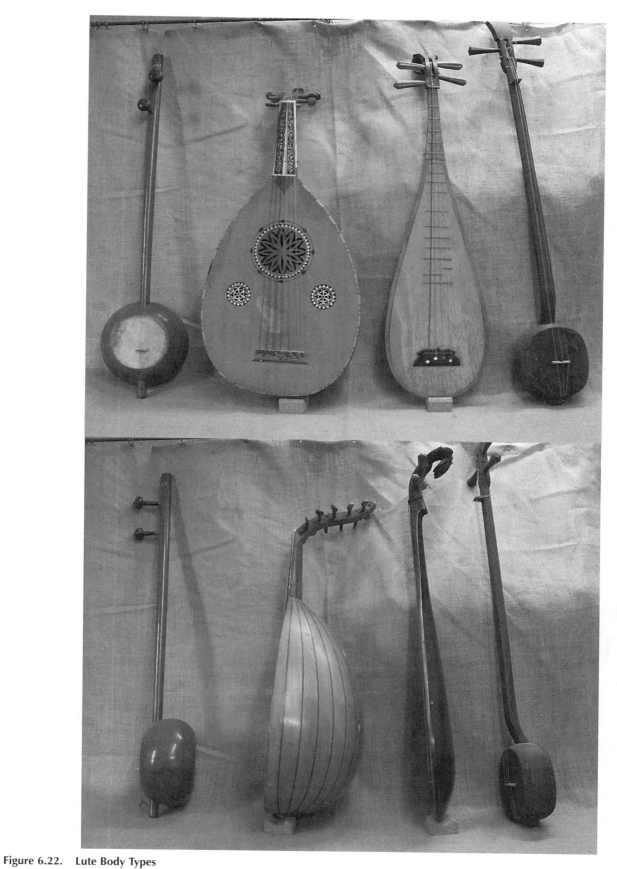

Figure 6.22. Lute Body Types

Facing and profile; L–R: drone lute *ramsagar*, Bina, Delhi, India (VIII 198); *'ud*, Tangier, Morocco (II 58); *pipa*, China (VII 92); *sanxian*, China (II 26).

plectrum. This means that, save for occasional strummed chords, it was essentially a melodic instrument. Tinctoris's statement, therefore, that by his time (the 1480s or so) fingers were also used to pluck the strings, implies a major change, for when playing with the fingers, one can pluck several nonadjacent strings at the same time, making it much easier to play polyphonically. Thus the lute adopted the role that it held into the nineteenth century of being both a melodic and a harmonic instrument. It could accompany its own melody with harmony, and it could be used as an accompanying instrument, to provide the harmonies for a voice or for other instruments. It was not long after this that it increased in body size and, by virtue of the resulting increase in string length, and through improved string-making technology, extended its practicable range downward to the low G, the so-called *gamma-ut* that gave rise to our word *gamut*, often regarded in its

time as the basic pitch that all others sprang from, an octave and a half below middle C (see figure 6.23).

The lute, with its rounded back formed from a number of very thin strips of wood, is a delicate and fairly expensive instrument. It is not surprising, therefore, that less expensive instruments with flat or only slightly vaulted backs were also popular. Tinctoris refers to three of them: the *viola*, used by the Spanish and Italians; the *guiterra* or *ghiterne*, which he says was invented by the Catalans; and the *cetula*, also an Italian instrument, which was strung with wire instead of gut.

The first of these, the viola, better known to us by its Spanish name as the *vihuela*, was tuned like the lute with six courses of gut strings, and, as with the lute, the belly was pierced with a tracery rose cut into the wood. In Spain, it was commonly used instead of the lute, playing the same repertoire, perhaps because, being flat-backed and shaped rather like a guitar, it was so clearly

Figure 6.23. Family of Lutes
L–R: treble, alto, tenor, and bass, based on those of Vvendelio Venere, Padua, late sixteenth century, by Ivo Magherini, *photo Ivo Magherini, courtesy Lynda Sayce.*

different from the Moorish lute at a time when the Moors were being expelled in the *Reconquista*. Its use died out in Spain before the end of the 1500s, although it still exists in parts of South America, whither it was taken by the Spanish invaders. Its name, however, survived to mean the guitar into the next century in Spain, and still survives—though as *viola*—in Portugal for the guitar, whereas *guitarra* refers there to a later version of the cittern, to which we shall return. As we note in several places here, instruments change name and shape with bewildering facility, something that we shall encounter again with the vihuela/viola name.

Tinctoris's second instrument, the guiterra, had a rounded back, but the early guitar of the next century, which took its name, was often flat-backed like the vihuela, but smaller, shallower-bodied, and with only four courses. The round-backed guiterra had already a long history before Tinctoris's time, for it was widely used in the Middle Ages under its other name of ghiterne, or in English gittern, and can often be seen in medieval manuscript illuminations. It is still with us, for it was the origin of those small round-backed instruments, looking rather like miniature lutes, that are sometimes called *pandurina* and *mandore* and developed into the various forms of mandolin, some of them quite small-bodied and gut-strung, others with wider bodies, deeper backs, and wire-strung such as the Neapolitan, the only type to survive at all widely at the present day.[96] The medieval gittern had a flat-backed rival, the *citole*, which was probably wire-strung and often had points, sometimes in a trefoil shape, at each corner of the body, a pattern often referred to as "holly-leaf."[97]

Tinctoris's third instrument, the cetula, with its wire strings and wooden or later metal frets, became in the next century as important an instrument over much of Europe as the lute. In English, it was known as the cittern. It became a widely popular instrument throughout the Renaissance, especially for casual music making, not only because of its cheaper flat-backed body but also because it was wire strung. The lute was at a disadvantage there because its gut strings were far more expensive than wire and were often imported, involving customs duties in addition to the initial cost. Iron wire, however, because of its industrial importance, was much cheaper and more likely to be available locally. In addition, gut strings are affected by changes of humidity and break easily, especially the very thin trebles. Thus if taverns and barbershops were expected to have an instrument hanging on the wall, ready for anyone who wanted to sing, it is not surprising that it was more often a cittern than a lute.[98] The cittern was also well established in serious music making and has a considerable repertoire in published music.

The early history of the guitar is so well recorded that there is little need to go into great detail here.[99] It had initially four courses of strings, and a fifth was soon added, before 1600. This arrangement lasted well into the eighteenth century, for up to then all tutors and known music are for four or five courses. A sixth course was added before 1780.[100] From around 1800, the instrument was simplified to the six single strings we know today. During the course of the nineteenth century, the body was greatly improved, initially by José Pagés, who redesigned the strutting on the underside of the belly, and the instrument reached essentially its modern form as the classical guitar at the hands of Antonio de Torres Jurado.[101]

There has been some confusion between two seventeenth-century types: the ordinary guitar, and the *chitarra battente* or plectrum guitar. The former was gut-strung as usual and the latter wire-strung. Because most chitarre battente have a slightly vaulted back, usually made from strips of wood glued side-by-side, there has been a tendency to apply that name to all guitars of that shape, but many ordinary guitars were also built in that way. Equally, both had a circular soundhole that was filled with a rose very elaborately cut from parchment, though today the guitar's soundhole is left open. The sure way to tell them apart is that gut strings are tied to a bridge glued to the belly, whereas wire strings pass over a freestanding bridge, held in place by the tension of the strings, to pins fixed in the bottom rib of the body. This is both because the greater tension of the wire strings would rip a glued bridge from its place and because it is not possible to knot wire strings on the bridge like gut ones—they break at the knot. Also, the ordinary guitars had gut frets tied around the neck, which wire strings would cut, so the chitarra battente had metal frets inset into the fingerboard, as all guitars do today.

The further developments, with all the various modern forms of folk and popular guitars, including the many electric (amplified acoustic) and electronic types (solid-bodied with built-in electronics), are beyond the scope of a book of this size, as are the many smaller versions such as the Portuguese *machete* that, in the islands of the Pacific, was transmuted into the ukulele and spread thence to the rest of the world.

There was, around 1800 and for a generation or so afterward, a rash of what one might call oddities. Some were the result of the French *Empire* fashion and its flirtation with neoclassicism, leading to instruments built to simulate ancient Greek lyres but with a guitar fingerboard running up the center. Others were those crosses between guitars and harps described above among the harps, with extra bass strings running from a short harp-like neck supported by a side pillar.

There was also, beginning in the second half of the eighteenth century, a resurgence of the cittern, under the misleading name of guitar or more commonly guittar. The English guittar was wire-strung like the old cittern, but with a deeper body and shorter neck. Initially it had normal tuning pegs, but later a brass screw mechanism was devised, turned with the winding key of a pocket watch, a far more efficient tuning mechanism for wire strings than friction pegs.[102] In Germany, it was called the *cither* (leading to potential confusion with the zither), in France the *cistre*. In Sicily, it was a mandolin variant that is still commonly seen as the flat-backed mandolin. In Spain, it became the rather smaller *bandurria*, and in Portugal, whither it was taken by English in-

volved with the Port trade, it is still a very popular instrument as the guitarra (see figure 6.24). There the watch key has been replaced with a fanlike arrangement of knurled knobs.[103] Extended versions, with a longer crooked neck carrying bass strings, were known in France as the *archicistre*.

And this brings us back to the lute, for that instrument, in addition to its role as a soloist, had always been a first choice for accompaniment, initially for singers and later for instrumental groups. With the rise of harmonic music in the sixteenth century, the idea of a melodic line supported by lower voices in chordal harmony (as distinct from the older practice of polyphony, independent melodic strands all worked together into a whole), there grew up the need for instruments to provide such chordal harmony, known as continuo, to support or replace the lower voices. Lutes had grown larger, to tenor and bass

Figure 6.24. Flat-backed Lutes

L–R: *guitarra*, by Manuel Pereira, Lisbon, Portugal (VII 142); *bandurria*, by Roca, Valencia (XII 6); flat-backed mandolin, by Catania Carmelo, Sicily (V 168).

sizes, but there is a limit to the size of lute body that can be handled with any ease. More important, with the quality of gut strings then available, the sound of thick bass strings that could be carried on any manageable body size was rather dull. The solution, claimed as his own invention in 1594 by an Italian lutenist named Piccinini (although there is evidence for some such device a decade or so earlier) was an extended neck to carry separate bass strings.[104] The chitarrone or theorbo and the archlute, as well as the many other extended-neck lutes, varied in size and arrangement, from about four or five feet long to the full-size theorbo that extends a full six and a half feet (see figure 6.25).

Instruments such as these, and the other patterns of extended-bass lute, were standard continuo instruments throughout the Baroque period, from the "New Music" of Caccini of 1600 and that of Monteverdi certainly through to Corelli's and Handel's time in the early eighteenth century, and even into the nineteenth. Today they have been revived and are frequently seen on our concert platforms and in our opera pits in historically informed performances of music.

Finally in this section on the plucked necked instruments, we return to a spiked lute of another culture and its influence on our own. There has long been debate on whether the banjo derived from the ancestral memory of an African instrument or was simply a small drum with a stick thrust diametrically through it. Whichever is the truth is of little moment. What is undoubtedly true is that the banjo originated on the Southern slave plantations of the United States. Its cheapness, with wire strings and simple body, and its power of sound—a well-tensioned drum head makes an excellent resonator and is easily repaired or replaced—led to its increasing popularity. As a result, the practice grew of making banjo equivalents of other instruments, so that the early twentieth century saw guitar-banjos, mandolin-banjos, ukulele-banjos (also called banjoleles), and others, each with the stringing of the first half of the name and the body and construction of the second.

In the late nineteenth and early twentieth centuries, banjo and mandolin were the instruments of choice for casual music making and for concert use in music halls and such places. Banjo and mandolin ensembles were also widely popular. Today both have been replaced by the ubiquitous, and even cheaper, factory-made guitars, while the banjo and mandolin orchestras have been replaced by the electric guitars of our popular music.

Bowed Lutes aka Fiddles

There have been many attempts to trace the origin of the fiddle bow. The most convincing, now generally accepted, is Werner Bachmann's, assigning it to Central Asia, where a number of other instruments seem to have originated.[105] Thence it spread both east and west. We still have no firm date for its invention, for we depend on written evidence that is scanty, and on iconography that in an Islamic area is even scantier. However, al-Fārābī, a Persian scholar who was born in Central Asia, refers to bowing before 950; there is a Spanish Mozarabic manuscript of the Apocalypse of St. John from around 920 showing bowed instruments; a Japanese *biwa* from around 950 in the Shōsōin repository has an illustration on its soundboard of a fiddle; and from 1000 or so on, there are many Byzantine illustrations and more early Spanish and other sources.[106] So wide a geographic distribution by the first half of the tenth century suggests an origin certainly before 900, perhaps as early as around 800.[107] While the original form may have been a roughened grass stem, as some evidence suggests, by the tenth century it was already as it is today: a wooden stick with horsehair bowstrings, although there is a vast array of different types and shapes of stick. Some are so curved as to be C-shaped and are grasped near the middle of the curve, others appear almost flat with the hand in what we would consider a normal position, and there are many other shapes in between.

With the bow's invention, the string instruments at last joined the wind and the human voice in the ability to sustain a singing line, leaving only the percussion and those strings that remained plucked as instruments that depended on rapid reiteration of notes for a sustained sound.

At one time or another, almost every form of string instrument has been used with a bow, either handheld or,

Figure 6.25. Alto Lute and Theorbo
Back and front; the alto based on Vvendelio Venere, Padua, 1592, the theorbo on Magno Dieffopruchar, Venice, 1608, both by David Van Edwards, *photo David Van Edwards, courtesy Lynda Sayce and David Van Edwards.*

like the wheels of the hurdy-gurdy and some keyboard instruments, mechanically operated.

Although horsehair, when viewed under a lens, has a roughened surface, this alone is insufficient to grip a string and make it sound. Some substance, commonly a form of resin, has to be applied to the hair. Our violinists carry a block of purified rosin that they apply to the bow as and when required. Many exotic fiddles have a lump of resin stuck to the body of the instrument that the player can rub the bow against as often as needed while still playing.

Bowing a string is not the continuous process that we hear as its sound, but rather one that can be described as "stick and slip."[108] The hair sticks to the string until the tension of the string overcomes the grip of the hair. At that point, it slips back to where the hair can grip it again, a process of sawtooth or zigzag movement so rapid that the sound produced seems continuous to the ear.

Most players prefer to have the bowhair in a flat ribbon, either gripped in a device to hold it so, as on our violins, or tensioned and flattened by the fingers of the bowing hand. However, some, for example, Dalmatian *gusle* players, braid the hair as they do the horsehair that forms the string of their one-string fiddle.

The advantage of a single string is that regardless of the body shape of the fiddle, the bow can always access the string. When there is more than one string, the bow (or, as in Java, the instrument) must be tipped so that it can reach whichever string is required. When, in the European Middle Ages, there were from three to five strings, only one was normally a melody string or *chanterelle*—the others were used as drone or *bourdon* strings, either played by the bow or plucked with the thumb of the other hand as can be seen on a number of medieval carvings (see figure 6.30).

Note that, by using "the other hand" in the previous sentence, we have deliberately avoided the use of "left hand," as it would be with us today, for illustrations make it clear that players pleased themselves whether they played left- or right-handed, as they often still do in other cultures today. Nowadays, one player in a symphony orchestra with the bow going the opposite way to everyone else would often be unacceptable, although, as with the British Allegri String Quartet for many years, it could have its advantage in such an ensemble, with all four instruments facing the audience.

While it may be that some bowstrings were tensioned by the natural spring of the wood, many early bows were loose-haired and tensioned by the hand, as they still are in other parts of the world. In our culture, the first mechanical device to tension the hair was the fixed frog, a piece of wood glued to the stick at the handle end to hold the hair away from the stick—something that is always necessary with a straight or slightly curved stick, unless as in India the player uses his fingers, to avoid the wood of the stick coming into contact with the instrument's strings (see figure 6.26). It would seem probable that this was preceded by sticks that were naturally forked, with a stub to attach the hair, or were carved with a thicker piece at that end, a practice that survived at least to the sixteenth century in England and probably elsewhere.[109] The separate but fixed frog was certainly in use before 1463, for such a bow, with a straight stick, survives with the *violeta* of St. Caterina de' Vigri, who died in that year.[110]

The next development was the clip-in frog, a piece of wood that could be placed between the stick and the hair but was removable. It did not allow any alteration of hair tension, save by finger pressure on the hair or by changing to a deeper frog, but this was overcome by the adoption, probably in the late seventeenth century, of the *crémaillère*, a metal bridle fixed to the frog that could be slipped into notches on the top of the bowstick, so allowing the frog to be drawn back from notch to notch to tighten the hair.

The screw frog that we use today, and that other cultures such as the Chinese have recently adopted, was invented sometime not long before 1700.[111] This has a screw in the end of the stick that passes through a lug in

Figure 6.26.   Fiddle Bow Frogs
L–R: Chinese bent bamboo, Indian cloth-wrapped, Mexican inserted block, Yugoslavian fiddle peg, Renaissance clip-in, Norwegian crémaillère (bridle and notch), modern screw.

the base of the frog, drawing it backward or forward in a slot in the underside of the stick. There is one bow attributed to Antonio Stradivari with a screw frog.[112] By the 1750s, screw frogs were the norm.

The hair must be held away from the stick at the point as well as at the handle end, so straight sticks and those that were gently outwardly curved must also have a projection at the point. Patterns vary, and in our culture various terms are used such as "slipper," "swan's bill," "pike head," and so forth, on early types in the European Baroque.[113] As bowing became more forceful in the eighteenth century and there was greater risk of the stick hitting the strings, heads were deepened in a variety of forms, and the stick was strengthened by providing an inward camber to cope with the strain of tighter hair. Two makers are credited with the development of the bow into its modern form, François Tourte in Paris and John Dodd in London, both by about 1785. Of the two, Tourte is regarded by players today as the greater master. To the reasons for these later changes we shall return with the history of the violin.

The Chinese bow mentioned just now is unusual. It is a bamboo stick, bent at each end to hold the hair away from the stick, thus obviating the need for a nut of any sort. The *erhu*, the most important form of fiddle (there are several others, all with *hu* as the latter part of their names), most commonly has two strings tuned a fifth apart.[114] The bowhair passes between these strings, unlike that of any other fiddle, so that the player tips the bow down to play one string and up to play the other. When there are four strings, these are tuned to the same two pitches and the bow has two bands of hairs, one band passing between the strings of each pair. Today, such bows are often fitted with a screw frog and, for those with two bands of hair, a double frog with two screws.[115]

These instruments are spike fiddles (see figure 6.27), the neck passing through a tubular wooden body, usually hexagonal in section—other Chinese types have cylindrical bodies, often of bamboo. Spike fiddles of this sort are widely used elsewhere, for example, in East Africa. In Java, the *rebab* has a body shaped like the heart on the ace of hearts and a closed back, and the spike may be complex rather than a single stick of wood or, sometimes, of ivory. The Bedouin fiddle called the *rabāba* and the Egyptian *rabab al-mughanni* or "poet's fiddle," which has two strings, also have complex spikes, a wooden neck with a metal spike extending it through the body and resting on the ground. Body shapes vary widely according to cultural preference. Round is probably in the majority, taking advantage of natural substances such as bamboo, coconut shells, and gourds, today even of tin

cans, but square or squarish is common. The Ethiopian *masenqo* is unusual in setting its square body at an angle as a diamond shape. The southern Moroccan Berber rebab is also unusual for a one-string fiddle in setting its peg not from back to front but from side to side, so that the string runs diagonally from the end of the peg to the circular resonator, which is also unusual in that it has a snare running across it like that of a drum.

Skin is a common material for bellies, being always available, whereas thin plates of suitable wood may be harder to come by. This is true also of solid-bodied fiddles that are even stronger than the spiked lutes, whether bowed or plucked, in resisting the impulse to fold up under the pull of the strings. Despite the effort necessary to hollow out the body, they are a widespread form of fiddle. Many, like the Indian *sarinda* and *sarangi* and the Moroccan *rebab andaluz*, are made of a single piece of wood hollowed out to form the body, with a skin over all or much of the front. The sarinda is a folk instrument usually with three or four strings, but the sarangi is an urban instrument with four playing strings and a large number of sympathetic strings to add a silvery shimmer to the sound—one does sometimes see, as in figure 6.27, sarindas that have acquired sympathetic strings like those of the sarangi. The sarangi has in the past often had a somewhat dubious reputation, for it was often used to accompany dancers who extended their incomes in less respectable occupations. In recent years, however, through its use by the great virtuoso Ram Narayan, it has become accepted as a major solo instrument.

The rebab andaluz has that name for two reasons: first, to distinguish it from the other forms of rebab in North Africa, the Arab and the Berber; second, because it was taken back to Morocco after the *Reconquista* when the Moors were expelled from Andalusia and the rest of Spain in the fifteenth century. It had been widely used in Spain, appearing, for example, among many other instruments in the thirteenth-century *Cántigas de Santa Maria* and surviving there even after the expulsion. Ian Woodfield describes the Kingdom of Aragon as the main area within which the use of the rebab remained endemic.[116] This, centered in Aragon itself in north-eastern Spain, covered a much wider area, from southern France down to Pays Valencia and beyond in Spain, through the Balearic Isles and Sardinia, over to the Kingdom of Naples in Italy and to Sicily, an area of influence that, as we shall see before the end of this chapter, was of great importance in the history of bowed instruments in Europe.

In our culture, solid bodies (see figure 6.28) survived into the seventeenth century, despite the invention in

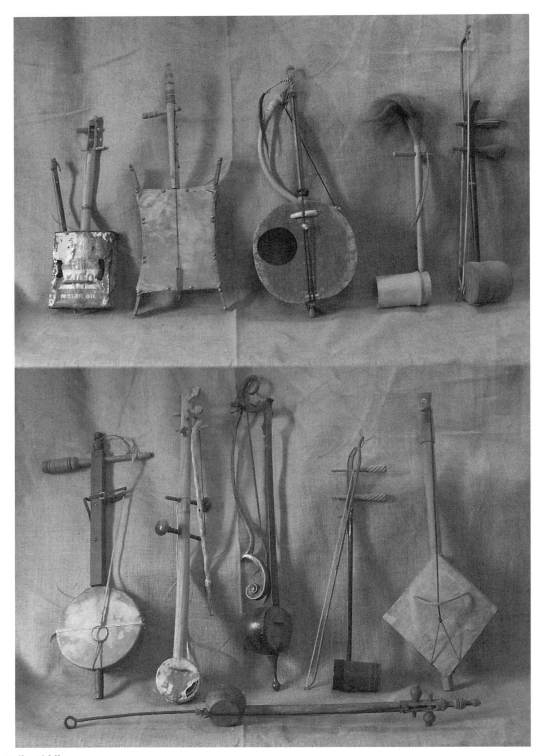

Figure 6.27. Spike Fiddles

Above, L–R: *rabāb* and bow, the body a reused Shell oil can, Morocco (VIII 200); *rabāba*, Bedouin, Syria (V 36); *goge* and bow (the large soundhole allows the gourd body to double as a collecting box in performance), Niger (VIII 48); *sese* and bow (broken), tubular wooden body and colobus monkey-tail decoration, Botswana (III 234); *banhu* and bow, tubular bamboo body, the bowhair passing between the strings, Beijing, China (III 56).

Below, L–R: Berber *rebab*, body a wooden ring, skin-covered on both faces, southern Morocco (X 6); *rāvanhattā* and bow, coconut body, two bowed strings (from the larger pegs) and five sympathetic strings (from the smaller pegs at the top), India (VIII 182); rebab, elaborately carved scroll and bow, smoothed coconut body, Indonesia, probably Flores (XI 136); *erhu* and bow, hexagonal wooden body, bowhair between the strings, China (II 28); *masenqo*, by A. Butisian, the body a square wooden frame, skin-covered on each face, Ethiopia (X 38).

Lying flat at the bottom: *kemengeh* or *rabāb al-mughannī*, coconut body, Egypt, 19th century (VI 254).

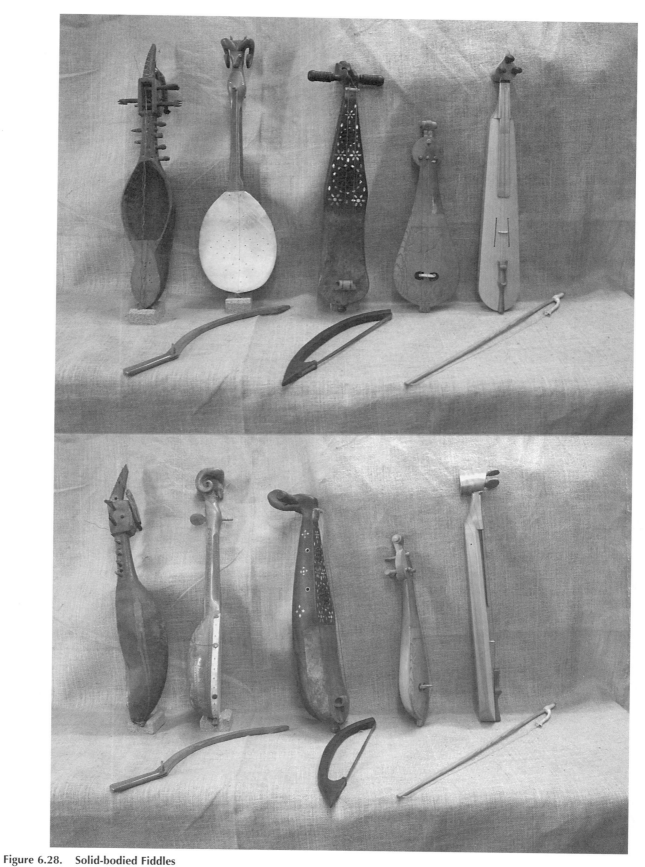

Figure 6.28. Solid-bodied Fiddles

Full-face and profile views, L–R: *sarinda*, India (VIII 108); *gusle* and bow, Yugoslavia (IX 92); *rebab andaluz* and bow, Morocco (IX 190); Greek island *lira*, Crete (II 50); *karadeniz kemençe* and bow, Turkey (IX 10).

the Middle Ages of instruments with a separate neck set into the top of the body. The earliest European form was the *rebec*, an instrument that resembles a pear sliced in half. It was the European version of the Andalusian rebab (as we noted above, *rebab* is a word that is applied to many instruments, all of which have in common a skin belly),[117] the main difference being a wooden belly instead of skin. It appears as a plucked instrument in some early illustrations, for example, on the porticos of twelfth-century Romanesque churches in Spain and southern France, even if more frequently as a bowed one. Occasionally we can see it plucked with a plectrum, and then we can be sure that it really was plucked, but very often we see it just held in the hand by the Elders of the Apocalypse, and we are then left to wonder whether the sculptor simply left out the bow. It

survived in Russia as the *gudok* into the nineteenth century, and to this day in Poland and the Balkans and, as the *lira*, in the Greek islands.

Flat-backed instruments also existed, such as the sixteenth-century fiddle shown in figure 6.29, which was found in a disused well in Płock in central Poland.[118] This is nearer to the violin shape, and we simply do not have the evidence to know whether such instruments were crudely made copies of violins, like those made to this day in Mexico and elsewhere, or had evolved in this form from the medieval fiddle. The Płock fiddle has neck and body all in the same piece of wood. The two fiddles of much the same date found in the wreck of Henry VIII's warship the *Mary Rose* had solid bodies but appear to have had separate necks,[119] whereas the Mexican "violin" illustrated in figure 6.29 with the replica of the

Figure 6.29. Polish and Mexican Fiddles
Replica of sixteenth-century fiddle from Płock, Poland, by Andrzej Kuczkowski (XI 112); folk ?violin,? Tarahumara people, Togno Village, Chihuahua, Mexico (V 18).

Płock fiddle was made like a violin, with back, belly, and separate ribs and neck by a folk musician in Chihuahua.

Save for St. Caterina's violeta—which was carved, neck and body, from the solid—no medieval fiddles survive, so we do not know whether these were also carved or made of separate pieces. The earliest fiddles were large spade-shaped instruments (those played with the C-shaped bows in the tenth century). Thereafter, oval instruments with three, or sometimes five, strings appear, followed in the twelfth century by rebecs. Larger fiddles, often played downward on or between the knees, also appear in the late twelfth century, usually in figure-eight shape, sometimes as narrow as an Appalachian dulcimer but normally much wider than that. By the fourteenth century, a much more solid oval instrument was adopted for playing at the shoulder, sometimes almost an oblong in shape—as it were, a rectangle with rounded corners. When one says "at the shoulder," this was not the position of the modern violin but usually held against the point of the shoulder or the upper chest rather than on top of the shoulder and under the chin. Because painters were not as yet using perspective and sculptors could not risk an instrument projecting into the air, we do not know whether these fiddles were held outward or really were, as we often see them, held flat against the body.

Fiddles were often very large, larger than a modern viola, as in the Angel Choir at Lincoln Cathedral (see figure 6.30). This is a particularly interesting carving because it shows that the ribs of the fiddle curve inward so that the belly and the back overhang them. It is one of those illustrations that does make one wonder whether all such instruments were carved from the solid or

Figure 6.30. Medieval Fiddle
With the thumb plucking a bourdon string, Angel Choir, Lincoln Cathedral, England, c. 1270, *photo Leslie Hare.*

whether belly, back, and ribs were separate pieces. The playing technique is also interesting because the left thumb is tucked under one of the five strings, in a position to pluck it as a rhythmic drone to accompany the melody.[120] This is an anticipation of the Italian *lira da braccio* of the Renaissance, also a large instrument, which had two bourdon strings lying off the fingerboard to be used as drones (see no. 5 in figure 6.32).

The lira da braccio was a fiddle used as a musical equivalent of Apollo's lyre in scholarly circles, in a period when an awareness of the Greek and Roman classics was coming back into the European culture, around 1500. In the period that we have just been discussing, the twelfth to fourteenth centuries, the lyre itself was still very much alive, mainly as a bowed instrument as we noted above. It appears in a number of twelfth-century medieval manuscripts, usually in the hands of King David in psalters, but it can also be seen in the early-fourteenth-century wall paintings of Westminster Abbey Chapter House.[121] It can be seen, too, in the windows of the Beauchamp Chapel at Warwick dated to 1447 (see figure 6.4).

The lyre's use continued in Britain into the eighteenth century as the Welsh *crwth*, which, like the lira da braccio, had two bourdon strings off the fingerboard. We have already discussed the crwth's bridge, with one foot on the belly as usual and the other, longer foot standing through one of the soundholes on to the back. This arrangement is by no means unique. The Płock fiddle had a similar bridge, and the Greek island lira (see figure 6.28) achieves the same result by having a soundpost that stands in a soundhole between one foot of the bridge and the back of the body.

While the lira da braccio was used for what one might call upper-class music, the rebec thrived at all levels of society as the fiddle for dance music. At a date not long before 1500, certainly in the north of Italy, an improved model was devised—perhaps in Ferrara, for it is in the Palazzo of Ludovico el Moro there that we have the earliest portrayal so far discovered of a violin, painted around 1505 probably by Benvenuto Tisi, who was known as "Il Garofalo." This violin combined the three strings of the rebec with a more resonant sound box, modeled somewhat as a miniature version of the body of the lira. Perhaps, though we can never know for certain, this shape was deliberately chosen as an attempt to upgrade the status of the instrument, making it look like the more respectable lira. But certainly the sound was stronger and rounder than the rather nasal quality of the rebec.

The new instrument was called the *violino*, a diminutive of viola (*-ino* connotes small, whereas *-one* is an augmentative, meaning large, as in *violone* or *trombone*), because the first size of the instrument was the treble *viola da braccio* or arm fiddle family, as distinct from *viole da gamba* or leg fiddles, the family of viols. The viols were already in existence and were always played held downward, resting between the knees or ankles according to size, whereas the violin, as we call it in English, was held upward on the arm. It quite rapidly acquired a family of larger relatives, tenor and bass, for they appear in a wall painting in Saronno, north of Milan, by Gaudenzio Ferrari in the 1530s; a slightly earlier painting of his in Vercelli, further to the west, dated 1529, was long believed to be the first portrayal of a violin.[122]

We know very little of the early development of the violin family, but it does seem clear that they were regarded as of a lower class than the viols and were perhaps principally used for dance music for their first century or so. It was the makers in Cremona, initially Andrea Amati (1511 or earlier to around 1580), who brought the violin to its full fruition, followed by makers in Brescia, preeminently Gasparo da Sàlo (1540–1609).

Amati's earliest surviving violin is dated 1564 and is now in the Ashmolean Museum in Oxford. By that time, the instrument must already have become more respectable, for it is one of a set of thirty-eight instruments, violins of two sizes, violas (a tenor is also in the Ashmolean), and basses (the bass violin was later modified slightly into the cello) made for Charles IX of France.[123] As Charles Beare points out, he must by then have been making violins for some time and have already established a high reputation if his instruments were to be ordered by the king of France.[124] These were already four-string instruments, as they are today, but David Boyden mentions two three-string violins, allegedly by Amati, dating from the 1540s, and suggests that it is even possible that he was the maker of the violin portrayed by Ferrari in 1529.[125] Certainly the extensive shading on the belly of that instrument suggests the high arching characteristic of Amati's work.

By the time of Amati's death, da Sàlo was fully active and making instruments of comparable quality in Brescia, as were his successor Maggini and, in Cremona, Amati's son Girolamo. With Amati's grandson Nicolò, Cremona once again became the more important center, for it was he who taught Guarneri, Rugeri, Rogeri, perhaps Stainer, and above all Stradivari. Jacob Stainer (c. 1617–1683) worked in Absam, near Innsbruck in the Austrian Tyrol, and his violins followed the high-arched Amati model and were even more sought after, especially in central and northern Europe, than the Cremonese. This style of violin dominated European taste throughout the eighteenth century and is still frequently seen in later copies.

While in his lifetime Antonio Stradivari (c. 1644–1737) was already recognized as a great master, it was not until after the social changes we discussed in interlude E that his flatter model gained the preeminence that it retains to this day. The reasons for this are those of tone color and projection. The higher-arched violins have a sweetness and a sound sometimes compared with that of the flute, whereas the less highly arched Stradivarius model has a reedier sound, sometimes compared with the oboe, that has a far greater projection (see figure 6.31). This fulfilled the needs of violinists as orchestras became larger toward the end of the eighteenth century.

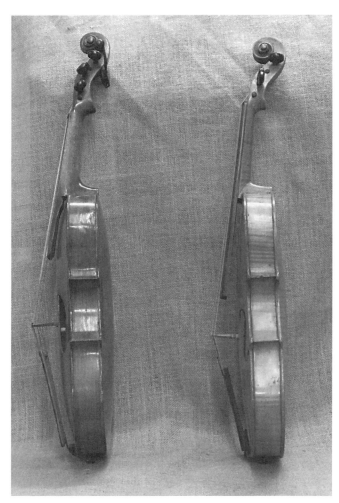

Figure 6.31. Violins in Profile

L–R: *Hardanger fele*, with the short, straight neck and wedge under the fingerboard of a Baroque violin, and even higher arching of belly and back than the Amati model, Norway, probably by Johannes Bårdsen Tveit, Samnanger, early nineteenth century (X 298); modern violin, with the longer, canted back neck introduced around 1800, and the less arched belly and back of a Stradivarius copy, Germany, early twentieth century (II 148a).

With the creation of the new large concert halls, replacing the older and more intimate music rooms, and around the beginning of the nineteenth century the introduction of keyed woodwind, valved brasses, trombones, and percussion instruments, even this was insufficient, and all the members of the violin family were drastically remodeled. The greater string tension, resulting from the general rise in pitch that we have already discussed, was tearing violins apart. To overcome this, almost all existing instruments were reconstructed, leaving us with a bare handful of instruments, a couple of Strads, one or two Stainers, and so on, still as they were made by their masters.[126]

There are four main parts of the violin, viola, 'cello, and double bass: the belly, the back, the ribs that hold these two apart, and the neck. At the top end of the neck is the scroll and pegbox that carries the four tuning pegs, and along the neck runs the fingerboard against which the player stops the strings. On the belly stands the bridge that holds the strings up to keep them clear of the belly and transmits their vibrations to the wood of the belly and thence to the air inside the box. Two holes are carved through the belly to let the sound out, traditionally in an *f* shape, although older fiddles more often had C-shaped, D-shaped, or crescent-moon holes. The nicks that represent the crossbar of the *f* mark the point where the bridge is best placed (on older violins, it was often placed lower down). Along the underside of the belly the bass-bar is glued and helps to transmit the vibrations of the bridge along the wood of the belly and acts as a girder to strengthen it. It is called the bass-bar because it stands under the bass foot of the bridge, the side the lowest string passes over. Under the treble foot of the bridge stands the soundpost that transmits vibrations to the back and also acts as a pillar to support the belly under the pressure of the strings on the bridge.

Inside the body, there may be small blocks in each corner to strengthen the glue joints of the ribs (the ribs are made in sections: on each side, there are two outward curves for the upper and lower bouts and an inward curve for the middle bout or waist), and there are linings along the upper and lower edges of the ribs to give a slightly wider surface as a gluing area to attach the belly and back. Inside the bottom end of the body is a block into which the end-button is set—the tailpiece that holds the lower end of the strings is attached to this button by a strong piece of gut, or today often wire. Inside the upper end of the body is another block through which two or three nails were burned into the end of the neck to hold it in place.

This last point is where many older instruments failed, because the increased tension of the strings ripped the neck from the body. So this was one of the first changes. A new neck was made with an integral block, and the ribs were mortised into this instead of it just being nailed through them. At the same time, the neck's angle was changed—its upper surface had been parallel with the line of the top of the ribs. Now the neck was canted back to produce a stronger angle, just as one leans back on a rope to take the strain of a heavy load. The old neck had had a wedge between it and the fingerboard because, since the strings slant upward from the nut at the top of the fingerboard to the bridge, it was necessary for the fingerboard to slant upward also—otherwise it would have been difficult to stop the strings against it in the higher positions. This wedge was now no longer needed. And at the same time as these changes, the neck was lengthened a little. This had the advantage of increasing the string tension again and so making the instrument louder.

This further increase of string tension necessitated internal strengthening also, with a stronger girder and pillar. The bass-bar was made thicker and was greatly lengthened, running now almost the whole length of the belly, and the soundpost was also made thicker. At the same time, the fingerboard was lengthened because composers were expecting players to climb higher in their range. This had already happened to some extent, as is clear when comparing the ranges of a Corelli sonata with the works of Mozart, and those with Beethoven.

Now, when did all this happen? To some extent, we don't know. It seems probable that the cello may have been the leader in this. Certainly in the eighteenth century cellists were expected to play farther up the fingerboard than violinists, and it seems possible that their instruments were strengthened in this way before violins were. Certainly it did not all happen at once. Beethoven's orchestras, which straddled the end of the eighteenth and the beginning of the nineteenth centuries, would have had a mix of old and new instruments, but by the time of his Ninth Symphony, first performed in 1824, surely all or almost all would have been converted. By this time, too, all the players would have been using something like the Tourte model bow.

These changes altered not only the construction of the instruments but also the sound that they produced—after all, that was the main purpose of the operation. As a result, nobody now living has heard the sound of a Stradivarius or an Amati—what we hear is an amalgam of the work of the master with that of the reconstructor, one of the leaders in which was Jean-Baptiste Vuillaume (1798–1875), who established his workshop in Paris in 1828 and became one of the leading violin dealers of his time and also made, or commissioned, instruments based on those of all the great makers of the past.

Since then, the violin family has undergone little change save in string materials. These also affect the sound. Strings at first were of twisted sheep's gut. The bottom string, G on the violin, octaves of C on violas and cellos, was covered with an overwinding of silver wire from the mid-seventeenth century on, followed in due course by the next string. The wire E-string, the highest on the violin, came into use around the beginning of the twentieth century and was quickly adopted because it was far less likely to break than the very thin gut string that preceded it. Some of the greatest players of that century, Fritz Kreisler, for example, refused to use it because of a dislike of its whining tone quality. Various synthetic materials have now replaced gut on all the strings, usually with a metal overwind, and many players are using wire throughout, once again for the sake of a louder sound and longevity in use, despite its harsher sound.

The violin remains the leading member of the family, but there are and have been many others. In the eighteenth century, there was a small violin, the violino piccolo, tuned a third or so higher than the normal size. It is difficult to identify, because it is identical in size with the smaller violins made for the use of children. A half-size violin tuned to normal violin pitches is a child's instrument; the same instrument with thinner strings tuned up a third is a piccolo such as Bach demands in his *Brandenburg Concerto no. 1*. There is a tendency to say that such an instrument by a great maker must be a piccolo, and one by a run-of-the-mill maker is a child's, but if Count This or Prince That ordered a violin for his child, he would naturally go to the same maker as he did for himself. Only the stringing or the tuning could give us the answer, and neither of these survives from the eighteenth century, so labeling any small violin as a piccolo in a museum is an act of hope.

Violas initially came in three sizes—contralto, alto, and tenor—all three tuned the same, a fifth lower than the violin. Tenor violas such as the Ashmolean Amati have a wonderful sound, but few survive because of the crippling stretch required to play them—most have been cut down to a more reasonable size.[127] Most today are of the two smaller sizes. There have been attempts to improve the sound by increasing the depth of the body, but this tends to make the sound tubby.

The bass violin, once it had acquired its fourth string, was tuned with B-flat as its lowest note, but it was not long before it came up a tone to its modern tuning, the period in which this happened varying from country to country. Certainly by the eighteenth century all violoncellos were as they are today. What took much

longer to be established was the way in which they were supported. Some early pictures show the cello supported on a small stool, but more usually it was held between the player's calves. A tail-spike appears intermittently but was not finally adopted universally until the end of the nineteenth century.

The ways in which instruments are held affect the technique with which they are played. The violin chin-rest was invented, so he claimed, by Louis Spohr in 1820. Before that time, the violin was sometimes gripped between the chin and the shoulder, but was just as often rested against the shoulder or upper chest. As a result, much of the weight was taken by the left thumb and this, plus the lack of a firm grip, makes a great difference to the way in which one shifts from one position to another up and down the fingerboard, something not fully realized by most players in early music ensembles today. They tend to retain the habit of gripping with the chin that they had learned in their early years on modern instruments. Equally, on the cello, the support given by the legs is different from that given by a spike, and this again affects the way in which one shifts positions.

Vibrato, rocking the finger slightly as one holds a note, is also a fairly modern concept. There is no doubt that it was used as an expressive ornament in the eighteenth century, and on the viol a century earlier, but the constant wide vibrato used today on all notes was a twentieth-century invention. It has the great advantage that it covers the very slight differences of tuning inevitable when a number of people are playing the same part in unison.[128]

The double bass has led a more checkered life than any other member of the family. In much music before the middle of the eighteenth century, we cannot be certain whether the indication "Bassi" implied double basses or not, and therefore whether it was just cellos or the composer expected instruments an octave lower—and if so, whether he got them would depend on whether an orchestra had them. There are instruments surviving by the great Brescian makers of the sixteenth century, but their history is much obscured by confusion with great bass viols, to which we shall come shortly.

Certainly one of the oldest surviving basses had three strings, but others had five, or even six, like viols. The three-string bass, with a lowest note around the A, a third below the cellos' C, was still being used throughout Europe into the nineteenth century, but four-string instruments were already in some use in the seventeenth century and common in the eighteenth. Because of the much greater stretch along the fingerboard, tuning is normally in fourths, instead of the fifths used by all other members of the family, with (on four strings) E as the lowest note, a sixth below the cello. Composers before Beethoven did not normally differentiate their bass parts, assuming that bass players would play an octave below the cellos as far as they could, perhaps simplifying the more rapid parts where they became too hectic for the wider stretch, and putting up an octave any passages requiring notes below the A or the E. Mahler, at the end of the nineteenth century, was one of the first to demand a low C-string, so that basses would always be an octave below the cellos, and a number of five-string basses have been built or adapted, and many others have had an extension added to take the E-string down to C.

There have been many other members of the family over the years—too many to mention here—though one is of especial interest, the Norwegian folk violin, the *Hardanger fele*. This has retained until very recently all the characteristics of an Amati or Stainer baroque violin, as may be seen in figure 6.31, maintaining the highly arched belly and back, the straight neck and the wedge between it and the fingerboard, with the addition of a set of sympathetic strings. Modern Harding fiddles, those made in the last twenty or thirty years, have followed the pattern of modern and reconstructed violins.

The Hardanger fele is the last survivor of a group of instruments that used sympathetic strings to increase resonance. The first reference to this practice comes from Tinctoris around 1487, who says that the Germans added sympathetic strings to the lute.[129] Several sixteenth- and seventeenth-century instruments, both bowed and plucked, adopted such strings.[130] A well-known member of the group was the *viola d'amore*, usually built with a rather flamboyant body, with six or seven strings and the same number of sympathetic strings. A number of eighteenth-century composers wrote for it, and there was an attempt to revive it in the twentieth century. Another member was the *baryton*, a form of bass viol whose sympathetic strings were accessible through the back of the neck so that they could be plucked for accompaniment to the bowed strings as well as sounding sympathetically.[131] Haydn wrote works for it because it was a favorite of his employer, Count Esterhazy.

The violin is also widely used in other cultures, often replacing, for example, the rebab in North Africa, and has been adopted as their own by musicians in India and elsewhere. In those cultures, it is usually held downward on the lap or knees by musicians sitting, as is usual there, on the ground. In Myanmar, a version of the violin is used that, while recognizably a violin, still looks like a Burmese instrument. Elsewhere other makers have produced their own variants on the normal pattern, either

through lack of professional violin-making skills, as in the otherwise excellently made Mexican variant shown in figure 6.29, or, as in some parts of Europe, combining the technology of some other suitable object, such as a clog or wooden shoe, with that of the violin.

We come at last to what was for two centuries the most important family of bowed string instruments of our own culture: the viols or, as they are properly termed, the *viole da gamba* (see figure 6.32). The violin family was termed the *viole da brazza*, "arm fiddles," because, as we said above, their most important members were held on the arm. The viols were held on or between the legs and were therefore *da gamba*. They were invented, as Woodfield has established, in Valencia in the southern part of the Spanish kingdom of Aragon, not long before 1470, by applying the bow of the rebab to the vihuela that, as its names indicate, was played in three ways: the *vihuela de mano*, with the basic technique, plucked by the fingers; the *vihuela de péndola*, plucked with a plectrum; and the *vihuela de arco*, played with the bow of the rebab.[132] This technique of bowing the vihuela spread throughout the Kingdom of Aragon, which, as we said earlier,

1. 2. 3. Violn de Gamba. 4. Viol Baftarda. 5. Italiänische. Lyra de bracio.

Figure 6.32. *Viole da Gamba*

Illustration from Michael Praetorius, *Syntagma Musicum—De Organographia* (1619).

extended across the Western Mediterranean to Italy, aided by the fact that members of the Borgia family, who had been bishops of Valencia, had become popes in Rome, first Calixtus III and later Alexander VI.

Initially the vihuelas were interchangeable, plucked or bowed as the player preferred, and even when bowed still had the guitar-type bridge, glued to the soundboard, so that all the strings were in the same flat plane. This was a severe limitation on performance because while the fingers, or a plectrum, could dip between the strings and choose which to pluck, the bow was limited to either the lowest or highest, unless it played chordally across all six. Illustrations show that before 1500 the raised bridge, free-standing on the belly and held in place by the tension of the strings, was already in use in Italy.[133] Thereafter the viol spread widely in Italy, especially, like the violins, through the d'Este family of Ferrara, one of whom married Pope Alexander VI's daughter, Lucrezia Borgia.

The two families, violins and viols, are wholly distinct from each other, save that both have bodies and necks and are played with a bow. The major differences between them are set out in the following table and described in more detail below:

Viola da Gamba	Viola da Braccio
large developed first	small developed first
flattish body	arched body
ribs and plates level	ribs inset from plates
six strings	three, later four, strings
strings tuned 4, 4, 3, 4, 4	strings tuned 5, 5, 5
fingerboard fretted	fingerboard unfretted
bowed underhand	bowed overhand
up-bow stronger	down-bow stronger
used for vocal and chamber music	used for dances
characteristically quiet	characteristically loud
used in ensemble	often used solo
introvert	extrovert

All the evidence we have shows that the two families were independent, invented in different places and for different purposes, and have always been built and played quite differently, as the table shows. The two plates of the violin, belly and back, were carved out from wooden wedges or blocks to achieve their arched shape, whereas the early viols had both belly and back made from flat sheets of wood, the belly being bent by heat to make a smoothly curved, shallow arch, and the back left flat but bent inward at a slight angle toward the top so that the upper part of the body was shallower than the lower; this

made it more comfortable to hold with the upper part against the player's chest. The ribs of violins are set into the plates so that they are overhung by the plates, whereas the plates of the viols were set level with the ribs. The viols have always had six strings, which were tuned like those of the vihuela and the lute, whereas the violin, like its predecessors the rebec and the lira da braccio, was tuned in fifths. Again like the vihuela, the viols had frets tied around the neck, whereas the violin, like the rebec and lira, did not. And finally, the players of each held their bows differently, the viols with the hand below the hair with the palm facing upward, the violin with the hand above the stick and the palm downward. As a result, the stronger stroke of the viol bow was the push, the up-bow, whereas the stronger stroke of the violin bow was the pull, the down-bow.

The viols were primarily ensemble instruments, with alto, tenor, and bass, and occasionally a great bass, although by the middle of the seventeenth century a small-size bass, the "division viol," was used alone, save for an accompanying bass line, especially for playing divisions, as improvisations and variations were then known.[134] Over the following century, the full-size bass also became a solo instrument, especially in France with virtuosi such as Marin Marais, often by then with a seventh string. By that time, its use as an ensemble instrument had largely died out, save for private use in old-fashioned households.

The rise of the violin band, with the establishment of the Vingt-quatre Violons du Roi at the French court and their imitations at other courts, such as the Twenty-four Violins of Charles II of England following the restoration of the monarchy there in 1660, had swept all before them.[135] It was such violin bands that led to the creation of the orchestra that was based on the group of violins playing with more than one to each part.[136] In such combinations, the ensemble of viols, with a single player to each part, had no role to play. Save as a solo instrument, with players such as Carl Friedrich Abel, who was playing the viol in London until 1787, the use of the viols dwindled by the middle of the eighteenth century, with rare exceptions, and were not commonly heard again until their resurrection by Arnold Dolmetsch at the end of the nineteenth century.

Today viols have regained their place both as a chamber ensemble and for solo performance with many early music groups, for the homogeneity of their sound when heard together has a quality that no other group of instruments can rival, and they have a repertoire of wonderful music from the sixteenth and seventeenth centuries that can be played in no other way.

A very different instrument, one that seldom played with other instruments, has much less chance of revival. This is the *tromba marina* (see figure 6.33), an instrument whose name has never been satisfactorily explained, for while it could and did sound like a distant trumpet, nobody in their senses would take a long trapezoidal wooden box with one (occasionally more) strings out to sea. Something like it had existed in the Middle Ages, a long narrow box usually held upward with the lower end up in the air, but we have no idea how that instrument was played, except that it was bowed. By the Renaissance, when it seems to have been quite widely used in Germany as the *Trumscheit* and *Nonnengeige* ("nuns' fiddle"), the tromba marina was played with the lower end on the ground and with its own peculiar technique.[137] It was bowed at the upper end of the string and fingered below the bow, unlike all other bowed instruments. The string was not stopped against the fingerboard but was touched lightly by the finger at selected points so that it sounded only the natural harmonics of the string's fundamental, thus playing the same notes as a natural trumpet. Its bridge was also peculiar to itself, for one foot rested firmly on the soundboard but the other was a fraction shorter and therefore buzzed against the belly, or more usually against a small plate of ivory or hardwood set into the belly, and it was this added snarl that made it sound remarkably like a trumpet. The instrument survived into the eighteenth century, and by that time many had acquired a large number of wire sympathetic strings set inside the body to add greater resonance to the sound.

Finally we return to that group of instruments that were bowed quite differently, the player rotating a wheel to rub against the strings instead of a bow. The earliest form, the organistrum, was described at the beginning of the section on keyboard instruments. By the thirteenth century, this had shrunk considerably, to a small rectangular box easily managed by one player, with a row of keys along the upper edge, each of which moved a tangent sideways to stop the string at the desired point (see figure 6.34). By then it was called the symphony, and judging by the frequency of its appearance in medieval manuscripts and carvings, it must have been widely used.

It was used, too, in the early Baroque, for Michael Praetorius illustrates, on a plate of miscellaneous instruments, two versions that he calls "peasant's fiddles" (on the left in figure 6.35), the one above, with the conventional key-box, shown open so that the tangents can be seen, stopping the two strings that run inside the box, with two drone strings running outside the box. By this time, it was called the *vielle à roue* (wheeled fiddle) in French and hurdy-gurdy in English. It was often used by blind beggars because it was easy to play without being able to see it—with one hand on the crank and the other on the keys, it could be played by feel. There are many paintings showing this use, which continued into the nineteenth century. The instrument is still played in

Figure 6.33. *Tromba Marina*
Played by Canon Francis W. Galpin, *courtesy Brian Galpin, photographer unknown.*

Figure 6.34. **Symphony**
St. Mary, Tewkesbury, Gloucestershire, England, c. 1340.

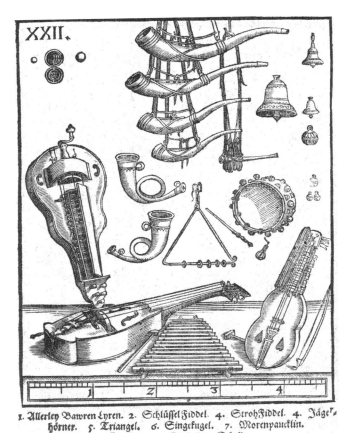

1. Allerley Bawren Lyren. 2. Schlüssel Fiddel. 4. Stroh Fiddel. 4. Jäger
hörner. 5. Triangel. 6. Singekugel. 7. Morenpaucklin.
8. Glocken 9. Cimbeln : Schellen.

Figure 6.35. Hurdy-gurdies and Other Instruments
Hurdy-gurdy (*middle left*); wheeled fiddle (*bottom left*); keyed fiddle (*bottom right*); plus xylophone (*Strohfidel* in German), triangle, tambourine with pellet bells as well as jingles; other bells and pellet bells, and hunting horns (*Michael Praetorius*, Syntagma Musicum—De Organographia, *1619).*

parts of France, where it coexists with the bagpipe whose sound it resembles, for both play a melody accompanied by drones, and in Germany, Poland, and Hungary.

Praetorius's second model has a normal fingerboard, a version that has not otherwise survived, but he also shows a variant, in the opposite corner, that he calls a "keyed fiddle," combining a bow with the keys and tangents instead of a wheel. This remains a popular folk instrument in Sweden, where it is called the *nyckelharpa* and is still actively played.[138]

Despite the supremacy of the violin, there are still many other fiddles in use around the world, some like the rebab in North Africa played side-by-side with the violin, but others independently like the nyckelharpa. The *talharpa* or bowed lyre still exists in Finland,[139] though whether the Welsh bowed lyre, the crwth, will successfully be revived is uncertain. Simpler instruments were also in use until very recently, for example, by street

buskers in our own culture, among them a variety of what were called "jap fiddles" in the early twentieth century, one-string fiddles, some of them with a simple cigar-box style resonator. Others, often called phonofiddles, were more elaborate with resonance horns, made by Strohviols and rival firms (see figure 6.36).[140]

These last were simplified versions, made for buskers and amateurs, of fully fledged members of the violin family, from violin to double bass, that were used extensively in the early recording studios in the pre-electric days. With only one microphone to be shared by soloist and orchestra, ordinary violins had little chance of being heard against wind instruments and voices, so these instruments, with a diaphragm similar to that of the old wind-up gramophone leading to a large metal horn, were the instruments of choice.

While the jap fiddle and Strohviols may be little heard today, the musical saw is still going strong, sometimes struck with a hammer but more often bowed. Some were ordinary carpenters' saws, usually with the teeth ground away for safety, but others were specially made for the purpose. Bowing on the edge of the blade makes it vibrate, and flexing the blade with the other hand makes it produce different pitches.

Nor is the saw the only nonstring instrument that is bowed. In the studios today, percussion players are expected to bow cymbals and gongs to produce strange sounds for all sorts of special effects. Nobody has yet devised a way of getting the hair of a bow onto a drumhead, but it is surprising what a superball can do. This is a child's toy of a plastic that will bounce much higher than an ordinary rubber ball and so confound those physicists who state that no dropped ball can bounce higher than its original position. Drummers fix one on the end of a piece of stiff wire and then rub it across a drumhead, producing an astonishing range of sounds, especially when used on pedal timpani whose skin-tension can be varied at the same time.

Notes

1. Not just instruments; copper telephone wires have been popular as necklaces and bracelets, and their glass insulators can be knapped into excellent "flint" tools and weapons. There are many other examples of reuse.

2. See Henry Balfour, *The Natural History of the Musical Bow* (1899).

3. See Gavin Menzies, *1421* (2002).

4. Thomas Alvad, "The Kafir Harp," *Man* (October 1954): 151–54.

5. Gerhard Kubik, *Westafrika* (1989), Taf. 180.

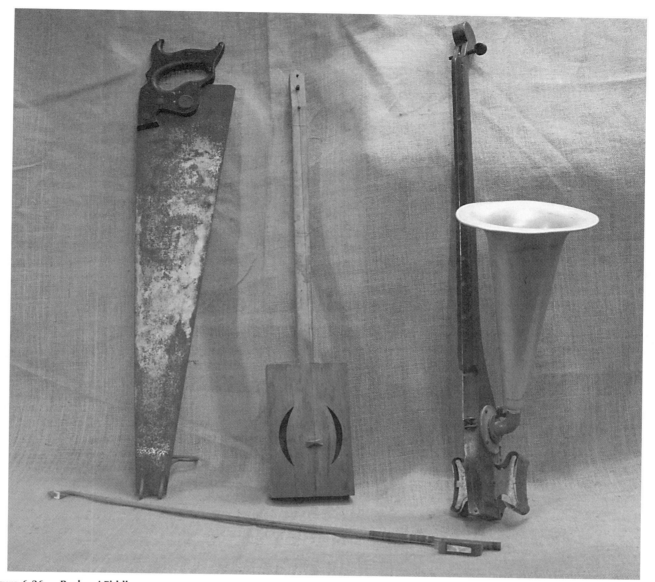

Figure 6.36. Buskers' Fiddles

L–R: musical saw, by Jérôme Thibouville-Lamy (VI 10); jap fiddle (I 54); Stroh fiddle, by Strohviols, London (XIII 138).

6. With the Congo, we have today the same terminological problem as with India, and there is no way to tell which modern national name should be used, for any tribal style will often ignore national boundaries. What was called the Belgian Congo in the nineteenth and early twentieth centuries is now several discrete nations, and before the nineteenth-century Europeans marked that space out so arbitrarily on the map, its cultural area had an even wider geographical spread. Many of the tribes and peoples in what was to become the Congo also live in what are now neighboring countries (hence much of the modern warfare endemic in that area). Even "Central Africa" is a fairly vague term, also covering parts of Angola, the eastern parts of the various West African states, and the western parts of some of the East African nations. The great variety of such instruments may be seen in

the illustration fascicle of J. S. Laurenty, *Les cordophones du Congo Belge et du Ruanda-Urundi* (1960). For other types of instruments, the other volumes in that series by Laurenty and by his predecessor at the Musée du Congo Belge, Olga Boone; all appear in our bibliography.

7. Claudie Marcel-Dubois, *Les instruments de musique de l'Inde ancienne* (1941).

8. Muriel C. Williamson, "The Iconography of Arched Harps in Burma," in *Music and Tradition*, ed. D. R. Widdess and R. F. Wolpert (1981), 209–28.

9. C. J. Atkins et al., "Frequency-Doubling Chordophones," *Musica Asiatica* 3 (1981): 1–9.

10. K. Vertkov, G. Blagodatov, and E. Yazovitskaya, *Atlas of Musical Instruments of the Peoples Inhabiting the USSR* (2nd ed., 1975), figs. 477–82, 504, and 523.

11. Chang Sa-Hun, *Korean Musical Instruments* (1976), pp. 99–100 in Korean and p. 302 in the English summary; Shōsōin Office, ed., *Musical Instruments in the Shōsōin* (1967), pp. vii and xi in English, plates 6 and 94–111. See also "Harp," *The New Grove Dictionary of Musical Instruments*, ed. Stanley Sadie (1984), 2:158, fig. 30.

12. Illustrations of all the types mentioned so far will be found in Subhi Anwar Rashid, *Mesopotamien* (1984), and examples of the lyres from Ur are preserved in the British Museum in London, the University of Pennsylvania Museum in Philadelphia, and, we hope still, the Iraq Museum in Baghdad.

13. Hans Hickmann, *Catalogue générale des antiquités égyptiennes du Musée du Caire—Instruments de musique* (1949), 154–56 and plates 93–95; Christiane Ziegler, *Catalogue des instruments de musique égyptiens* (1979), 118–21.

14. Jeremy Montagu, *Musical Instruments of the Bible* (Lanham, 2002), 11–15.

15. M. L. West, *Ancient Greek Music* (1992), 49; Bathyah Bayer, *The Material Relics of Music in Ancient Palestine* (1963), 26–27; Joachim Braun, *Music in Ancient Israel/Palestine* (2002), 58–61 and figs. 2.6a–b and 2.7a. Professor Braun's book was originally published as *Die Musikkultur Altisraels/Palästinas* (1999), but the illustrations in the translation are more numerous and better (and differently numbered and arranged), and therefore it is that version which is cited here.

16. Bernhard Aign, *Die Geschichte der Musikinstrumente des Ägäischen Raumes* (1963), 379.

17. Braun, *Music in Ancient Israel/Palestine*, table 2, pp. xxxii–xxxvi. Note that his no. 16, the origin of that on the modern Israeli half-shekel coin, is generally considered to be a fake.

18. Martha Maas and Jane McIntosh Snyder, *Stringed Instruments of Ancient Greece* (1989), 36, quoting *Hymni Homerici* 4.41–54 (the *Homeric Hymn to Hermes*).

19. Homer, *Odyssey* 21.48.

20. The three works cited above by West, Maas and Snyder, and Aign cover the field thoroughly, and each has a copious bibliography.

21. Djilda Abbott and Ephraim Segerman, "Strings in the 16th and 17th Centuries," *GSJ* 27 (1974): 48–73; there are also many other relevant articles by the latter author.

22. Aign and Maas and Snyder illustrate and describe many examples.

23. Other examples include plates 1, 2, and 6 in my *World of Medieval and Renaissance Musical Instruments* (1976), hereafter *Medieval & Renaissance*, from the Utrecht and other Psalters, dating from the seventh and eleventh centuries. Plate 3 there shows the reconstructed Sutton Hoo lyre, referred to here.

24. See Montagu, *Medieval & Renaissance*, plate 4, and more especially, Tilman Seebass, *Musikdarstellung und Psalterillustration im früheren Mittelalter* (1973), 23–33, a special and very detailed study of the manuscript (Paris: BN, fonds lat. 1118) from which my and his plates Taf 1 and 10 have come.

25. This would imply a change from one mode to another, a practice that as far as we know was foreign to Greek musical style and that, along with the Greek modes, are subjects beyond the scope of this book. But if it can be done in Africa today, it would be rash to say that it could not have been done in ancient Greece.

26. Jeremy Montagu, "The Restored Chapter House Wall Paintings in Westminster Abbey," *EM* 16:2 (May 1988): 239–49, esp. figs. 16, 21, and 22. For Warwick, see Montagu, *Medieval & Renaissance*, plates 54 and 55.

27. Nicholas Bessaraboff, *Ancient European Musical Instruments* (1941), 314–17, fig. 58, and plate 10:291. His plate 8:225 shows the Allemanic lyre mentioned above.

28. Otto Andersson, *The Bowed-Harp* (1930); Vertkov, Blagodatov, and Yazovitskaya, *Atlas of Musical Instruments*, 228 and figs. 734–35.

29. Rashid, *Mesopotamien*, 56; Francis W. Galpin, *The Music of the Sumerians* (1936), plates 5:1 and 5:2; Judith Becker, "The Migration of the Arched Harp," *GSJ* 20 (1967): 17–23, fig. 7. Dating of this vessel differs from one authority to another, hence the spread in the text, as does its present location, Galpin assigning it to Istanbul and Rashid to Chicago. Much of Canon Galpin's text should be regarded with some caution.

30. Marcel-Dubois, *Les instruments de musique*; Walter Kaufmann, *Altindien* (1981); Williamson, "Iconography of Arched Harps"; Becker, "Migration of the Arched Harp."

31. Muriel Williamson's two articles on its construction are very detailed: "The Construction and Decoration of One Burmese Harp," *Selected Reports* 1:2 (1968): 46–76; "Supplement," *Selected Reports in Ethnomusicology* 2:2 (1975): 111–16.

32. The full range is illustrated in Hans Hickmann, *Ägypten* (1961), with too many relevant plates to enumerate.

33. Bo Lawergren's survey of their acoustics, "Acoustics and Evolution of Arched Harps," *GSJ* 34 (1981): 110–29, is interesting and instructive.

34. Margaret Trowell and K. P. Wachsmann, *Tribal Crafts of Uganda* (1953), 393–99, plates 93A, 112, and 113.

35. Rashid, *Mesopotamien*, Abb. 141, 145–47, 151–52.

36. Rashid, *Mesopotamien*, Abb. 151. Note that there is a small section of stone missing, including the vertical arm, which has led to frequent misinterpretation of this figure. The spare end of the strings, cascading in a curve from the absent arm, have been joined to the playing part of the strings in many drawings of this relief, producing a fictitious form of dulcimer that never existed.

37. R. D. Anderson, *Catalogue of Egyptian Antiquities in the British Museum* (1976), 2, fig. 3; Hickmann, *Ägypten*, Abb. 98. Anderson shows a number of surviving harps on pp. 72–86, including a tomb model in excellent condition (pp. 82–86) that may give a more accurate impression of what the real instruments looked like than their reconstructions.

38. Maas and Snyder, *Stringed Instruments of Ancient Greece*, 1 and plate 1. Aign's Abb. 4 in *Die Geschichte der Musikinstrumente*, based on the figurine in the Metropolitan Museum, New York, is not very accurately drawn. The best source is Martin van Schaik, *The Marble Harp Players from the Cyclades* (1998); nine of the harpists are illustrated with detailed de-

scriptions and references. For the Cycladic culture in general, see J. Lesley Fitton, *Cycladic Art* (1989).

39. Schaik, *Marble Harp Players*, fig. 10; Athens Archaeological Museum 8833.

40. Schaik discusses this element and the importance of the aquatic bird in Greek religion and music in his article "The Divine Bird," *Imago Musicae* 18/19 (2001/2002): 11–33.

41. Maas and Snyder, *Stringed Instruments of Ancient Greece*, 163, figs. 14 and 15; West, *Ancient Greek Music*, plates 17 and 21; Max Wegner, *Griechenland* (1963), Abb. 22; Schaik, "The Divine Bird," figs. 3–5 and 13–14, all dating from between 350 BC and 300 BC.

42. West, *Ancient Greek Music*, 72 and plate 22; Maas and Snyder, *Stringed Instruments of Ancient Greece*, 164, figs. 16 and 17, and p. 161, fig. 11b and detail, for one with the spindle on the near side, against the player's body.

43. Vertkov, Blagodatov, and Yazovitskaya, *Atlas of Musical Instruments*, figs. 477–82. These are described in detail (in Russian) on pp. 128–29 and briefly in English on pp. 217–18.

44. Ibid., figs. 504 and 523, respectively.

45. E.g., Schaik, "The Divine Bird," fig. 15; Montagu, *Medieval & Renaissance*, plates 8, II, IV, 21.

46. Robert Bruce Armstrong, *Musical Instruments* (1904); Joan Rimmer, *The Irish Harp* (1969); Joan Rimmer, "The Morphology of the Irish Harp," *GSJ* 17 (1964): 39–49.

47. Marin Mersenne, *Harmonie Universelle* (1636), Livre Quatriesme des Instruments, 216: "la Harpe à trois rangs a esté inventée il y a trente ou quarante ans par le sieur Luc Antoine Eustache Gentil-homme Neapolitain." Thirty or forty years before 1636 takes us back to around 1600.

48. Joan Rimmer, "The Morphology of the Triple Harp," *GSJ* 18 (1965): 90–103.

49. In a BBC broadcast interview of Nansi Richards-Jones by Joan Rimmer many years ago.

50. Minkoff has published a facsimile, much reduced in size, of *Art du Faiseur d'Instruments de Musique et Lutherie* (1785), from *L'Encyclopédie Méthodique*. Although the text of this 1972 reprint edition (pp. 36–42) is from one of the later versions of the *Encyclopédie* and describes two different Cousineau systems, the accompanying illustrations (plates 2–4 in the second sequence of numbers) that are described in detail on pp. 144–46, appear to derive from a different version of the *Encyclopédie* and show that of Nadermann.

51. British Patent 3332 of May 2, 1810.

52. Mozart's Concerto for Flute and Harp was written for such an amateur, presumably, from its date of 1778, playing either a Nadermann- or Cousineau-style instrument. Jane Austen writes of another in *Mansfield Park*, and many other examples could be adduced.

53. Bálint Sárosi, *Die Volksmusikinstrumente Ungarns* (1967), 62–64 and plate 4b.

54. See the afterword for more detail on the classification of instruments. The standard text on zithers as a whole is Tobias Norlind, *Systematik der Saiteninstrumente*, vol. 1: *Geschichte der Zither* (1936).

55. Because the north was a single cultural area before the divisions that followed World War II and the freedom from British domination, all references to India and to North India must be understood as applying equally to India, Pakistan, and Bangladesh unless we use the phrase "India proper." It is impossible to say that any one instrument or any one musical style originated in an area now covered by any one of the modern states. One cannot tell from which of these nations any museum instruments may have derived, unless either they carry a maker's name and address or a collector has recorded not merely where they were obtained but where they originated.

56. Sárosi, *Die Volksmusikinstrumente Ungarns*, 30–46.

57. All the books cited above illustrating medieval instruments will show many psalteries, including all the shapes described here.

58. Sárosi, *Die Volksmusikinstrumente Ungarns*, 41–46.

59. Sárosi, *Die Volksmusikinstrumente Ungarns*, 12–14.

60. See "Sostenente Piano," *The New Grove Dictionary of Musical Instruments*, 3:419–22.

61. Michael Praetorius, *Syntagma Musicum II—De Organographia* (1619), plate 3, for an illustration of the Nuremberg Geigenwerk. A similar instrument by Raymondo Truchado survives in the Brussels Museum of Musical Instruments, for which see F. J. De Hen, "The Truchado Instrument," in *Keyboard Instruments*, ed. Edwin M. Ripin (1971), 19–26 and plates 32–34.

62. Joannis Gallici, *Liber Notabilis Musicae*, British Library, Add. Ms. 22315, f. 15, illustrated in my *Medieval & Renaissance*, plate 42. The earliest picture of a clavichord so far noted is dated to around 1400; see Edmund A. Bowles, "A Checklist of Fifteenth-Century Representations of Stringed Keyboard Instruments," in *Keyboard Instruments*, ed. Edwin M. Ripin (1971), 11–17, plate 15b.

63. Plate 45 in my *Medieval & Renaissance*.

64. G. Le Cerf and E.-R. Labande, *Les Traités d'Henri-Arnaut de Zwolle* (1932), ff 129 and 129v, both reproduced in my *Medieval & Renaissance*, plates 43 and 44.

65. As in J. S. Bach's *Das Wohltemperierte Klavier* or *Well-Tempered Clavichord*, the 48 preludes and fugues designed to show the advantages of "well-tempering" as a means of playing all keys in the same temperament.

66. A string vibrates as a whole, but also, for its overtones, in sections, with all the even-numbered harmonics having a node, or area of minimum vibration, in the center of the length. If the string is plucked at or near that point, there cannot be a node there, and therefore those overtones are absent. To remedy this to some extent, a device called the *arpicordum* was provided, a wooden batten with a series of brass brays that could be slid to rest against the string and add that same extra vibration that we have seen on the harp and other instruments.

67. Bowles, "Checklist of Fifteenth-Century Representations," 11–16 and plates 1–31. The plates include all the drawings of Arnaut de Zwolle.

68. Elizabeth Wells, ed., *Keyboard Instruments* (2000), 18–26.

69. Donald H. Boalch, *Makers of the Harpsichord and Clavichord* (3rd ed., 1995).

70. Andreas E. Beurmann, "Iberian Discoveries," *EM* (May 1999): 183–208. Considerable doubt has been cast on the authenticity of these instruments; see John Koster, "A Contemporary Example of Harpsichord Forgery," *EM* (February 2000): 91–97.

71. John Koster, "A Netherlandish Harpsichord of 1658 Reexamined," *GSJ* 53 (2000): 119n8.

72. This was the French setup. In England, the two 8's were next to each other and the 4' jacks were farthest from the player.

73. Observations that I owe to Michael Cole.

74. See Michael Cole, *The Pianoforte in the Classical Era* (1998), 24–39, for a description of this instrument, its antecedents, and its successors.

75. The most detailed description of Cristofori's pianos is Stewart Pollens, *The Early Pianoforte* (1995). Pollens also prints all the relevant parts of Arnaut's treatise with a clear English translation and interpretation and cites the evidence for earlier Italian pianos.

76. Clear drawings and descriptions of all these actions will be found in Cole, *Pianoforte*.

77. Alfred Dolge, *Pianos and Their Makers* (1911), illustrates many patterns of hammer and of piano actions and frames.

78. It was John Broadwood, the founder of the firm, who supplied Haydn with a piano, and his son Thomas who presented one to Beethoven. See Michael Cole, *Broadwood Square Pianos* (2005), 161–62.

79. Wolfgang Joachim Zuckermann, *The Modern Harpsichord* (1969).

80. Frank Hubbard, *Three Centuries of Harpsichord Making* (1965).

81. Books in the Musikgeschichte in Bildern series, already frequently referred to here, include a number of relevant illustrations. A particularly useful text for the first part of this section is Richard G. Campbell, *Zur Typologie der Schalenlangshalslaute* (1968), Abb. 1–14.

82. Many illustrations will be found under the names of the various republics in the pages of Vertkov, Blagodatov, and Yazovitskaya, *Atlas of Musical Instruments*.

83. Laurence Picken, *Folk Musical Instruments of Turkey* (1975), 208ff.

84. A course is a set of one or more strings tuned to the same pitch, sometimes in octaves, and treated in performance as a single string. Our mandolins, twelve-string guitars, and early music lutes all have double courses.

85. John Baily, *Music of Afghanistan* (1988), and his "Recent Changes in the Dutār of Herat," *Asian Music* 8:1 (1976): 29–64. Baily's photographs of all three versions and the rubab can be seen in my "The Creation of New Instruments," *GSJ* 59 (2006): 3–11.

86. Mersenne, *Harmonie Universelle*, Livre Second, 99–100.

87. Henry George Farmer, *Studies in Oriental Musical Instruments* (1939), 89–92; for the use of frets, 45–68.

88. Emmanuel Winternitz, "The Survival of the Kithara," *Journal of the Warburg and Courtauld Institutes* 24:3–4 (1961): 222–29; reprinted in his *Musical Instruments* (1967), 57–65. Plate 17 includes the Libyan mosaic.

89. See Montagu, *Medieval & Renaissance*, plate 5, and Seebass, *Musikdarstellung und Psalterillustration im früheren Mittelalter*, Abb. 93 for the Stuttgart Psalter, and Abb. 123 and 124 in the latter for some Mozarabic examples.

90. Shōsōin Office, *Musical Instruments in the Shōsōin*, plates 7–16 and 112–23. There is doubtless much detail in the Japanese text (41–48), but only a very brief English summary on p. vii and plate captions on pp. xii–xiii and xviii–xix.

91. Henry George Farmer, *Islam* (1966), Abb. 3 and 4 and text figure on p. 18.

92. Seebass, *Musikdarstellung und Psalterillustration im früheren Mittelalter*, Abb. 18 from the Cappella Palatina Palermo.

93. Montagu, *Medieval & Renaissance*, plate 20.

94. Anthony Baines, "Fifteenth-Century Instruments in Tinctoris's *De Inventione et Usu Musicae*," *GSJ* 3 (1950): 19–26.

95. Le Cerf and Labande, *Les Traités d'Henri-Arnaut de Zwolle*, 32–34, plate 15.

96. For the best elucidation of all the early forms and their nomenclature, see James Tyler and Paul Sparks, *The Early Mandolin* (1989).

97. These two names had often been confused until Laurence Wright proved all previous writers wrong, including me, in *GSJ* 30 (1977): 8–42, with his article "The Medieval Gittern and Citole: A Case of Mistaken Identity." Previously they had normally been reversed, the citole called the gittern and the gittern the citole.

98. It is often said that the reason for the preference was that the lute took time to tune whenever it was needed, whereas wire strings hold their pitch better, and the cittern was therefore always ready to play. However, I am assured by Lynda Sayce, an experienced player of both instruments, that the cittern is the more difficult to tune and that wire strings tend to creep in pitch more than gut. So it would seem that cheapness is the more probable reason, combined perhaps with the propensity of the lute's treble string to have broken where it hung.

99. See James Tyler, *The Early Guitar* (1980).

100. Tyler, *Early Guitar*, 55.

101. Harvey Turnbull, *The Guitar from the Renaissance to the Present Day* (1974).

102. See the comment above from Dr. Sayce. The difficulty of tuning wire strings accurately with normal pegs is one of the main problems with the cittern. This, too, is why modern violins have adjusters for wire strings.

103. Probably because the guitarra was played by people of all classes of society, and because even among the upper classes, pocket watches, and their keys, went out of fashion.

104. Lynda Sayce, "The Development of Italianate Continuo Lutes" (2001), 1–2.

105. Werner Bachmann, *The Origins of Bowing* (1969).

106. Bachmann, *Origins of Bowing*, 25, plates 1, 13, and others. For the biwa, see also Shōsōin Office, *Musical Instruments in the Shōsōin*, plate 116.

107. Reference to Picken's fourth Postscript on Diffusion and its time scale (Picken, *Folk Musical Instruments of Turkey*, 579–609) would suggest a date up to a millennium earlier, but that would take us into a period from which we have much Central Asian iconography and could expect to see pictorial evidence, of which there is none. One might suggest that transmission times by the first millennium AD were faster than in antiquity, due to the proliferation of trade routes, and that for safety we should date the invention of the bow to a period anywhere from around AD 500 on and certainly before 850.

108. Murray Campbell and Clive Greated, *The Musician's Guide to Acoustics* (1987), 213–14.

109. A crudely carved bow of this type was found in the wreck of the *Mary Rose*, which sank in 1545. See J. Gardiner, ed., *Before the Mast* (2005), 248–49 and figs. 5.24 and 5.25.

110. Marco Tiella, "The Violeta of S. Caterina de' Vigri," *GSJ* 28 (1975): 60–70.

111. David D. Boyden, *The History of Violin Playing* (1965), illustrates (plate 29) and describes (pp. 206–9) all three types, and on the same plate shows a bow with a screw frog dated 1694.

112. Boyden, *History of Violin Playing*, plate 28. See also Boyden's article "The Violin Bow in the 18th Century," *Early Music* 8:2 (April 1980): 199–212. Some of his conclusions were disputed by Julian H. Clark, "Bows—A Maker's Response," *Early Music* 8:4 (October 1980): 503–5.

113. Boyden illustrates many of these and the following types in both the above sources.

114. Bachmann (*Origins of Bowing*, 49) points out that *hu* equates with "barbarian" and was employed by the Chinese especially for the tribes of Central Asia, thus strengthening the supposition that the use of the bow derived from that area.

115. Colin Huehns, "Experimental and Traditional *Huqin*," *GSJ* 56 (2003): 61–68, esp. figs. 12–14 in the color section.

116. Ian Woodfield, *The Early History of the Viol* (1984), 15ff.

117. A point made in conversation by John Baily.

118. Ewa Dahlig, "A Sixteenth-Century Polish Folk Fiddle from Płock," *GSJ* 47 (1994): 111–22.

119. Mary Anne Alburger, "Bowed String Instruments," in J. Gardiner, ed., *Before the Mast*, 242–49.

120. This was very successfully done by John Sothcott in one of our Musica Reservata broadcasts (18 May 1971)—these are all preserved at the British Library Sound Archive.

121. Jeremy Montagu, "The Restored Chapter House Wall Paintings," *Early Music* 16:2 (May 1988): 239–51.

122. Emanuel Winternitz, "Early Violins in Paintings," in his *Musical Instruments and Their Symbolism* (1967), 99–109 and plates 38–41. The previous article in the same volume, "The Lira da Braccio," pp. 86–98 and plates 30–37, also by Winternitz, describes and illustrates the lira da braccio.

123. Boyden, *History of Violin Playing*, 35–36.

124. "Amati," *The New Grove Dictionary of Musical Instruments*, 1:53–55.

125. Boyden, *History of Violin Playing*, 19.

126. The Ashmolean Amatis had suffered this treatment but were put back into a putative "original" state.

127. Max Gilbert, a leading London viola player who had such an instrument and made a marvelous sound on it, told me that he spent a fortune with osteopaths for the sake of its tone quality.

128. Players may, and hotly do, deny this as a reason for it, but if, as I once did when conducting some baroque music, one asks players, even some good professionals, to play without vibrato, the truth of my statement may become painfully apparent.

129. Baines, "Fifteenth-Century Instruments," 22.

130. See, for example, Terence Pamplin, "The Influence of the Bandora," *GSJ* 53 (2000): 221–32.

131. Terence Pamplin, "The Baroque Baryton" (2001), and in due course, now that Pamplin has died, a book by Carol A. Gartrell based on her researches and this doctoral thesis for which she was the supervisor.

132. Woodfield, *Early History of the Viol*, 61 and plate 38, the earliest illustration he had found, dated c. 1473.

133. Woodfield, *Early History of the Viol*, plate 53, dated 1497.

134. Christopher Simpson, *The Division Violist; or, The Art of Playing Extempore upon a Ground* (2nd rev. ed., 1665).

135. Peter Holman, *Four and Twenty Fiddlers* (1993).

136. John Spitzer and Neal Zaslaw, *The Birth of the Orchestra* (2004).

137. Cecil Adkins and Alis Dickinson, *A Trumpet by Any Other Name* (1991).

138. Jan Ling, *Nyckelharpan* (1967), in Swedish with an abbreviated English translation, illustrates many types.

139. Andersson, *Bowed-Harp*.

140. Alison Rabinovici, "Augustus Stroh's Phonographic Violin," *GSJ* 58 (2005): 100–123. See also Julian Pilling, "Fiddles with Horns," *GSJ* 28 (1975): 86–92.

INTERLUDE F

~

Messengers

As we have seen, there are some instruments that have their own voices, and these voices may carry a message, as with the bull-roarer, for example. This can not only speak as an ancestor or a god but can also warn those who are not initiates to run before they see something that only an initiate is permitted to see and live. There are others that can convey a message of far greater precision. Some are very familiar to us. One, mechanical and general rather than personal, is the set of bells that tells us the time to within a quarter of an hour. Bells convey other messages, too: that it's time to come to church; or, with a slower tolling, that someone has died; or that this is an occasion for festivity and rejoicing, either general and national, or locally a wedding; or just that some bell-ringers are having fun; or for a school full of children and teachers, that work is over for today.

Bells are used, too, to signal location and for identification. An animal with a bell is much easier to find than one without, and in many areas, farmers pick their bells carefully by pitch so that they can recognize the bells of their own animals and not find, after following a bell, that the animal attached belongs to someone else. But animal bells have other functions as well and will be discussed in greater detail below.

Some instruments are used for conversations without any great import of meaning. An alphorn (see figure 5.3) can be heard from pasture to pasture, and often from a high pasture to the farm in the valley below. Its use may be no more significant than that the players are still alive and that no accident has befallen them or their herds or flocks, or, from one player to another, the whiling away of time by blowing tunes to each other. Another use for the instrument is to entertain the animals. The late great folk music scholar A. L. Lloyd once played a recording he had made in Romania, which started with the clangor of sheep bells as the animals milled in fright from some disturbance. As the shepherd began to play the *bucium*, the alphorn of that area, gradually the sound of the bells dwindled as the sheep became pacified by the sound of the horn, until at last all was still. Not, perhaps, so impressive as the Orpheus legend, where the wild animals came to hear his voice and his lyre, but an example of the universal usage among shepherds, cowboys, and other animal herders, who know well the use of music to calm their flocks and herds.

The use of the alphorn, a long trumpet of hollowed wood, is not confined to the Alps of Switzerland and Austria. Wherever there are high mountains, people have found that long trumpets, anything from three to twelve feet in length, are the ideal instruments. The sound travels well and is often amplified by echoes. Most such instruments are made by cutting a young tree, splitting it lengthways, hollowing out each half, reuniting it, and then covering it with a close sleeve of coiled bark or other material so that it does not leak down the sides. In some areas, for example, the Altiplano of South America, a form of reed or cane is used for the *trutruca*, and in other places, such as Tibet, metal is found. In Romania both metal and wooden alphorns exist.

Nor are alphorns confined to the mountains, for in at least two areas, very similar instruments are used in the marshes of the lowlands: the *ligawka* in eastern Poland and western Russia is one, and the *midwinterhoorn* in the eastern Netherlands, in the Twente district, is another.[1] Because there is no shortage of water in those areas, these lowland horns are usually left uncovered, without the usual spiral of bark, and this is one way they can be recognized and distinguished from the highland horns. A few circles of twisted withy to hold them together, or often today metal bands, is all that is required, for they can be dropped in the nearest ditch (traditionally in the Netherlands down a well, a process that has several ritual connotations, especially for fertility rites) so that the wood swells and seals the seam between the two halves. The midwinterhoorn, like the Swiss alphorn, is used more often today in folkloric festivals than for its original purposes as a signal or ritual instrument, but most players are still aware of, and when playing are conscious of, the older significance both of the instrument itself and of the calls that are blown upon it.[2]

The Dutch instrument furnishes an interesting example of how traditions can be damaged by overenthusiastic experts in folklore. Traditionally the midwinterhoorn was always made, usually by clog makers, by cutting a tree and hollowing it out, a laborious task that took some days.[3] In the 1920s, stovepipe makers adapted their techniques of rolling and seaming *blik*, as their tin-plated steel was known, to the horn, imitating the curved bell by diagonally soldered joints. Such instruments could be made quickly and cheaply and became widely popular in the Twente. When after World War II there was interest in reviving folk arts and other aspects of national life, the folklorists banned these instruments of blik from their festivals and competitions, insisting on a revival of the wooden form. Thus what had become a folk instrument was abolished by folklorists in the interest of reviving an outmoded model. Music and instruments develop in all cultures, not only in the Twente, and folklorists and other ethnomusicologists can no more stem the tide than can we on the beach beside the sea.

The use of an instrument as a summons is widespread around the globe. The church bell and the factory hooter are not alone, and almost any instrument may perform this role. So, too, is an instrument as a warning, and in our culture it was traditionally the bells that had that task, as a static signal for fire and many other crises and fitted as a mobile signal to ambulances and police cars, although more recently we hear the siren. In Britain, no church bell rang from 1940 until all danger of German invasion had passed, for while sirens frequently warned of the approach of the Luftwaffe for air bombardments, it was the bells that would warn of paratroops or seaborne attack.

For mobile warnings of approach, it is often horns and trumpets that have the edge, whether the motor horn (see figure 4.10) or the older coach horn. Many postal services still use the posthorn as an emblem, for the post, as a royal or state service, had priority over all other traffic on the roads and free passage through toll gates and

other obstacles. The posthorn was a signal for other coaches to clear the way and for gates to open. Its use was adopted by other traffic also, and codes of signals evolved in addition to blowing melodies to entertain the passengers.[4] Different models appeared, with the shorter tandem horn ostensibly for two-horse carriages (this is the instrument, usually in 2½' A-flat, that the "Posthorn Gallop" is played on today) and the full-length coach horn in 4½' B-flat, often coiled in a circle in Continental Europe, for the four-in-hand.

Foghorns are usually now mechanical, but the fisherman can still use a seashell, a conch trumpet.[5] War parties in New Guinea used rhythmic codes on their conch trumpets to signal as they returned how many heads they had taken, or lost.[6] More advanced codes were used on conchs in Malekula in the New Hebrides to signal, for example, what type of pig, and how many, had been killed for the *maki* ceremony.[7] This was done by hand-stopping, moving the hand in the mouth of the triton shell to occlude its opening to a greater or lesser extent, exactly as eighteenth-century French horn players did to perform the concertos of Mozart. Closing the bell flattens the pitch, and opening it sharpens it, for one is reducing or increasing the area of open hole, as we discussed in chapter 3, among the vessel flutes. The same hand-stopping technique is used by ferrymen in Kenya, as a signal to start and stop hauling, and by fishers on Mafia Island off Tanzania, opposite the Ufiji River delta, who use it as a foghorn (see figure 5.1).[8]

Jeffrey Nussbaum of the Historic Brass Society has told me that hand-stopping is used on conchs by Steve Torre, a jazz trombonist in the United States.[9] There is pictorial evidence for hand-stopping on short horns in an eighth-century manuscript in the British Library.[10] It could be that the technique survived among folk musicians, perhaps even to the extent that Hampl's use on the horn in the mid-eighteenth century was not so new a discovery as historians have always thought. The conch will be described in more detail below.

For the ultimate use of instruments to talk—really talking in words rather than just using a signal code—we have to look to Africa where, because the languages are usually tonal, an instrument can be used for real speech. Let us take, as an example, the word *musician*. If it were a word in one of these languages, it would have one meaning when pronounced *mùsícián* (low pitch, high pitch, low pitch) and would mean something quite different if pronounced *músìcián*, different again as *músíciàn*, and so on. By reproducing the rhythm of that word and whichever pitch-pattern is relevant, that word can be "spoken" by an instrument. Of course, there will be a number of other words with the same rhythmic and pitch sequence, but one copes with this by redundancy, repetition, and extension: the musician, the tall musician, the tall stout musician, the tall stout musician with a beard, the tall stout musician with a beard and glasses, the tall stout musician with a beard and glasses who is visiting us, and so forth until the meaning narrows down to only one person, or one thing or whatever else the subject may be. When, as in some languages, there are more than two tones, for instance, *mùsícîân* (low, high, middle, as we often say that word in English), then one may need less redundancy to convey the meaning.[11]

With such a language, almost any instrument can be used, depending on the circumstances. The sound of the big slit drums, and also the large paired drums called *ntumpan* in Ghana, carries for miles, as does that of the horn. The Nigerian and Ghanaian hourglass-shaped drums (see figure F.1) or any paired drums are excellent for fairly local use, as are the iron double bells. So is ordinary labial whistling, for example, in the Canary Islands where it has been elaborated into a complex code.

The pitch of a slit drum depends upon several factors, primarily the volume of the cavity and the area of the opening. Some woods are denser than others and produce different pitches when struck. The thickness of the lip on which the drum is struck also affects the pitch, and one way to produce two tones is to have the lip on each side of different thickness. The point that one strikes along the side can also make a difference. It was Raymond Clausen—during his fieldwork in Malekula, where giant slit drums, often resembling a huge phallus, stand upright around the dancing ground—who pointed out the importance of the area of the slit: the greater the area of open hole, the higher the pitch, as we saw above in chapter 3. Thus both the wood of the drum and the air that it contains are relevant factors.

Not all slit drums stand upright—most are recumbent, often on legs, as with some African examples that resemble in appearance the vaulting horse we see in gymnastic displays, but sometimes resting on pieces of wood to hold them off the ground or slung by ropes from supports. In many areas, the slit drum is of high status, sometimes sacred, and often it has its own house to protect it and shield it from casual or improper gaze. Frequently they are decorated, in New Guinea often with a crocodile's head at one end and its tail at the other. There is a wide variety of shapes and sizes; some can be the size of a canoe, and others fit in the palm of the hand. We meet a number in the course of this book, and others may be seen in my book on percussion instruments.[12]

Figure F.1. Talking Drums
L–R: two-tone slit drum, Congo (VII 90); *donno*, pressure drum, Ghana (VIII 18); *kalangu*, pressure drum, Nigeria (V 206).

The Ghanaian ntumpan resemble the tops of huge wineglasses, a large body with a short narrow stem at the bottom. This shape couples the resonance of the contained air with that of the drum skin, which aids their sound to carry great distances. Paired drums are used in many other areas, but any drums can be used, depending on the distance that one wants the message to carry, including the drums of a dance band. I have heard a friend called to take his turn at the drums by the colleague who was playing at that moment. This use, too, is common with the hourglass-shaped drums, so often used for speech that they are called "talking drums," the Nigerian *kalangu*, the Ghanaian *donno*, and the other drums of that shape. These have a skin over each end and a multitude of thongs to brace the skin that go straight from head to head. With the drum held under the arm, squeezing those thongs into the narrow waist of the drum with the upper arm pulls the heads down the shell, increasing their tension and raising their pitch, and so the drum can talk. When the master drummer of a band is using one of these drums, as well as keeping a part in the rhythm of the ensemble, he can talk to the dancers, entertaining all those present by interpolating comments on the news of the day, the expertise of the dancers, or any other subjects, just as a good master of ceremonies or a square dance caller can do in any other culture.

An essential part in such African bands is played by the double bell, for an ensemble of drums often needs a steady ostinato that each player can set his own rhythm against. In European music of the late Middle Ages and early Renaissance, polyphony was a common practice, quite separate strands of music, skillfully interwoven to make a musical whole. In Africa, especially with drum ensembles, polyrhythm is used in the same way, separate rhythmic patterns that interweave to make a musical whole. A great help to this is an iron bell playing a steady repetitive pattern such as the one that Father A. M. Jones recognized and called the standard pattern: *kón-kó-lò-kón-kón-kó-lò*, where the *kó* is half the length of the *kón* or the *lò*.[13] In our terms, the high-pitch *kón* and the low-pitch *lò* would be quarter-notes, and the high-pitch *kó* eighth-notes.

But this is not the only use of such bells. They can talk as well. One of those illustrated in figure F.2 was made by

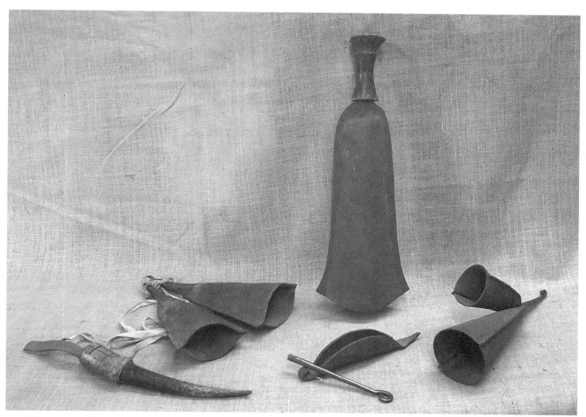

Figure F.2.   African Forged Iron Bells

Rear, L–R: *kuge*, double bell, with striker, *kahon mahiri*, by Sarkin Kugen Kano Husaini, Kano, Nigeria (VI 158); single bell, Congo (II 240); double bell, back-to-back, Ghana (VII 68).

Foreground: *atoke*, Togo (VIII 10).

Sarkin Kugen Kano Husaini, bell maker to the emir of Kano. He made two *kuge* at the command of the Emir Alhaji Mohammed Sanusi for the durbar of 1956 at Kaduma. One he kept for his own use to "shout" the praises of the emir and also for general messages, just as we might have a town crier; the other he sold to me with its striker, the *kahon mahiri*, of white oryx horn. But while our town crier rings his bell to attract attention, he has to use his voice to shout his message. The *sarki* can do it all with the bell.[14]

These bells are forged from iron, the apex of one linked to the apex of the other by an integral curved iron bar. Each bell is an elongated U in plan and a narrow oval in section, made by placing one curved iron U-shaped plate on another and hammer-welding the edges together to form the bell. In Ghana, the smaller bell rests on the back of the larger, usually with a much greater difference in size between the two from those that are side-by-side—there always is some difference in size, of course, to obtain the two pitches. Single bells are also used, either similar in shape or, in some areas, a trough-shaped piece of iron. It was these that were replaced by a hoe blade in Afro-Cuban music and in other parts of the New World when their music was re-created by those who had been abducted and taken as slaves across the seas.

Side-blown horns of almost any material are ubiquitous in sub-Saharan Africa (see figure F.3). There are several advantages in blowing a horn through a hole in its side. For one thing, the whole of the air column is resonated—horns behave quite differently from flutes

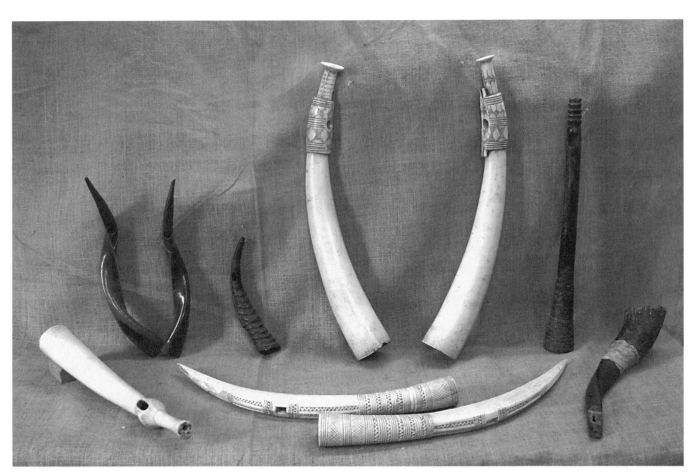

Figure F.3. African Side-blown Horns

Above, L–R: pair of blackbuck horns, Uganda (III 74); antelope horn, the embouchure on the flat face of the horn as is normal for the Zulu (X 296); pair of ivory horns, male and female, embouchure on the concave side as is the most common, with fingerhole in the tip, Mangbetu people, northeast Congo (III 182); wooden horn, Kariba area, Zimbabwe (VI 124).

Below, L–R: ivory horn, Nile-Congo watershed, northern Congo, showing the fingerhole in the tip (I 154); pair of ivory horns, perhaps votive, with embouchure on the convex curve as is normal with the Ibo people, Nigeria (III 76); compound horn, antelope above and cow below, joined with a leather sleeve, unfinished, the embouchure partly cut, the tip removed but the fingerhole not yet bored, Luo people, Kenya (IV 100).

in this respect.[15] Another advantage is that a large and heavy horn—some ivory horns from the Congo are more than six feet in length—can be easier to hold sideways than projecting straight forward.[16] The third, and in this context perhaps the most important, is that if the embouchure, the blowing hole, is in the side, a fingerhole can be bored longitudinally through the narrow end. By opening and closing that hole, two different pitches can be obtained. Examination of museum examples makes it clear that the interval between those pitches is important to some peoples. The distance between the fingerhole and the embouchure does not affect the pitch,[17] but the diameter of the hole does—again, the greater the area of the open hole, the higher the pitch obtained—and there are many side-blown horns in collections with the fingerhole bushed, narrowed with a lining of some material. Others no doubt have been widened but it is more difficult to ascertain whether that was done initially in boring the hole, or subsequently to alter its tuning.

Hand-stopping is used on horns as well as on conchs, sometimes as an alternative to a fingerhole but also often in addition to it. Side-blowing makes it easy to reach the distal end with the hand so as to stop it, whereas with end-blowing it could be out of reach. If a language uses more than two tones, then hand-stopping as well as opening a fingerhole can provide a variety of pitches.

African horns are made from many materials. Ivory is always the most distinctive, often the most prestigious and reserved for the chief, but the horns of all horned animals are used, sometimes deliberately paired so that one curves or twists one way and the other in the opposite direction. Gourd is common, especially in East Africa, and wood is often seen. Some horns are complex, among the Luo of Kenya, for instance, where one horn is inserted into another, usually with the joint covered with a leather sleeve to keep it airtight. Gourd horns are also often made in this way in Uganda, built up with sections of different diameter and shape.[18] By no means all African horns are side-blown; many are blown from the end. Where horns are side-blown, the position of the embouchure is sometimes characteristic of a people or an area. Most crescent-shaped horns are blown on the concave side, but the Ibo of Nigeria usually blow on the convex side and the Zulu on the flat side.

Horns, like all the instruments considered in this interlude, are blown in many parts of the world, perhaps everywhere save among the peoples of the Arctic Circle and, it is always said, in the Americas. The conch was widely used in Central and South America, but animal horns not at all. Those who explain the lack of horns in

North America by the absence of cattle before the arrival of the Europeans forget the buffalo. Are their horns not suitable for blowing?[19] This is a musical puzzle for which we have no answer. Another puzzle is the absence of ivory horns in India. Indian elephants have tusks, and their ivory is used for almost every imaginable purpose except for blowing. Why? We do not know.

Another instrument that is often used for talking is the trump or Jew's harp. This we shall meet in more detail in interlude G on symbiosis, but we should note here that it is quite widely used for speech, especially for lovemaking. The sound is quiet, and a lover outside a hut may use it to convey sweet messages to the beloved within, unheard from neighboring huts. What makes it easier to believe is that one obtains the different notes on the trump by varying the shape of the mouth, as one does while pronouncing the various vowels, *a*, *e*, *i*, *o*, and *u*.

Another instrument said to have been a talker is the New Zealand *puutorino* (see figure 5.7). This cigar-shaped wooden instrument is said by various writers to have been an end-blown flute or a trumpet, and by others, a speech-substitute. Moving the fingers over the figure-eight-shaped mouth halfway down the tube varies the pitch—the far end is almost closed, only a pinhole remaining open. The traditional Maori use of the instrument had died out before it was properly studied, and we only have early travelers' reports to go by, but Dr. T. Barrow of the Bernice Bishop Museum wrote, "We do know that the *putorino* was talked into and that actual words could be heard by the skilled listener."[20]

The need for "a skilled listener" is not unusual for all such instruments. Not every African can understand "drum language," and the lover with the trump may well hope that only his intended hearer can understand what he is saying and not her parents or siblings.

The other area best known for a tonal language is China, but there seems to be much less general use of instruments for talking than there is in Africa, perhaps because, with more pitches employed, it might become too complex for general use. One example of its use was described by Hu Jiaxun among the Miao people, but there it is restricted to the use of one instrument, a mouth organ—the *lusheng*—that, with a pentatonic scale, can imitate the complex tonal system of the Miao language.[21] There seem to be traces of other talking instruments in China, but so far little research has been done on this subject in that country and, as far as is known at present, the use today is found only among the minorities and not among the Han themselves.[22]

It is not only instruments that talk in this way. As well as drum language, there is also what one might call "vowel language," the use of the voice to talk but without whole words, for consonants cannot carry for miles across peaks and valleys, but high-pitched vowels can. An example, in English for simplicity, might be "[H]ow are [y]ou?" with a reply "O[k]ay a[nd] [y]ou?" Such calls, sometimes semi-sung, sometimes yodeled, are widely used, especially in areas without a tonal language that would allow an instrument to be used instead. As well as for communication from person to person, such calls are also used to summon animals. Hog-calling is well known in the United States and certainly used to be the subject of competitions at country fairs and like occasions. Nor is this practice confined to America, nor—and this is where we come full circle in this chapter—to the voice. Many peoples use instruments to summon their animals and workers, almost any instrument whose sound will carry well across the pastures and through the woods.

Is this talking or is it signaling? Is there a difference between them? The infantry bugle, the cavalry trumpet, the naval boatswain's call—these surely are signals, a series of pitches, each sequence conveying a specific meaning, but without any semantic content. Many have verbal phrases attached: "Come to the cookhouse door," "Time to rest," "Rise and shine," and so forth, but these are attached only by custom and usage—the words have no syllabic or melodic connection to the notes. The use of instruments as animal calls does frequently have such connection. Anyone who has trained an animal knows that while the words of each command are important, the melodic contour in which they are expressed has often as much meaning to the animal as the verbal content of the phrase. It is that melodic contour, often one integral to the language used, that can be expressed instrumentally.[23]

Notes

1. Piotr Dahlig, "Ligawka mazowiecko-podlaska," *Muzyka* 32:4 (1987): 75–110.

2. Everhard Jans, *Het Midwinterhoorn Blazen* (1977).

3. Jeremy Montagu, "The Construction of the Midwinterhoorn", *GSJ* 28 (1975): 71–80.

4. "An Old Guard" [Köhler, probably J. A.], *The Coach Horn* (1878?; 3rd ed., 1888).

5. *Conch* comes from the Greek word for "shell," and thus the common term "conch shell" is tautologous and should be avoided.

6. Signal codes were recorded by E. W. P. Chinnery ("Further Notes on the Wooden Kipi Trumpet and Conch Shell by the Natives of Papua") and W. N. Beaver ("A Further Note on the Use of the Wooden Trumpet in Papua") and published in *Man* 1917:55 and 1916:16, respectively. These were rhythmic only, and neither author gave any indication of the use of different pitches.

7. Personal communication from Dr. Raymond Clausen.

8. Personal communications from Sir Kenneth Oakley (letters dated February 2 and February 16, 1967), who had heard conchs blown by ferry crews in Kenya at the Mtwapi and Kilifi hand-hauled ferries between Mombasa and Gedi, and who stated clearly that hand-stopping was used there on side-blown *Bursa bubo* (Linnaeus) conchs as a signal to begin and finish hauling. The information regarding Mafia Island came from Mr. de Keller, who sold me my example from that island illustrated in figure 5.1.

9. Personal communication (email dated April 21, 2003).

10. BL Cotton Vespasian A.i., f. 30, illustrated in my *World of Medieval and Renaissance Musical Instruments* (1976), plate 2.

11. The best explanation of the whole system will be found in Father J. A. Carrington's *Talking Drums of Africa* (1949).

12. Jeremy Montagu, *Timpani and Percussion* (2002).

13. A. M. Jones, *Studies in African Music* (1959).

14. The kuge and much of the information was provided through the kindness of the Madauchi Ibrahim Bagudu of Zaria, Nigeria, unfortunately without pitch indications. Nor do David Ames and Anthony King provide tonal patterns, even though their book, *Glossary of Hausa Music* (1971), where much further information may be found, is entitled a glossary.

15. This can be demonstrated easily by experiment with a series of tubes, each having a hole in the side at different positions. Wherever along the side of the instrument the hole may be, trumpeting, blowing into the hole through vibrating lips, produces the same pitch, whereas fluting, blowing across the hole, produces a different pitch for each position of the hole.

16. See Jean-Sébastien Laurenty, *La Systématique des Aérophones de l'Afrique Centrale* (1974), for examples of such large ivory horns and many others.

17. This is another difference between trumpeting and fluting—when blowing as a flute, the distance between fingerhole and embouchure does affect the pitches obtained—and is also easily demonstrated by placing a stopper with a hole through it in the tubes mentioned above.

18. Margaret Trowell and K. P. Wachsmann, *Tribal Crafts of Uganda* (London, 1953), 348–51, pls. 82–3.

19. The National Bison Association's website (www.bison-central.com) lists "signals" as one of the uses of the horns (and rattles from the scrotum as well as drums from the hide, the latter a well-known use) among the by-products of the bison, but unfortunately gives no references for this, nor whether this use of the horn was traditional or modern. My thanks to Jim Matheson, the association's assistant director.

20. Letter dated November 11, 1966.

21. Hu Jiaxun, "Miao *Lusheng* Speech," *Journal of Music in China* 1 (1999): 39–54 (translated by Cui Yanzhi from "Qianxibei Miaozu lusheng 'yu' xianxiang tanxi," *Musicology in China*, supplementary issue [1997]: 20–26).

22. This information on the tonal use of language in China, and the previous reference, I owe to Prof. Helen Rees of the University of California, Los Angeles. Further research on this use of speech in music in China, as yet unpublished, has been carried out by Yang Xian-Ming, showing that its use is much more widespread than has generally been recognized (personal communications). It should perhaps be stated that a Han Chinese linguist whom I have consulted denies the possibility of its use in that language. Nevertheless, Yang's research goes a long way to suggest that it was almost certainly used there in the past.

23. Many languages have their own melodic contour built in. One shepherd in Wales told me that he had come from Yorkshire and had had to learn Welsh so that the dogs would understand him.

~

CHAPTER SEVEN

Pipe Organs

Only two instruments have had royal titles. The lute was called the "Queen of Instruments All," and the organ has long been called the "King of Instruments." However, when it first appeared, in Alexandria in Hellenistic Egypt around 250 BC, the organ was then only a princeling. It was small, and its range, though unknown, was probably not much more than an octave. We do know that its air pressure was provided and stabilized by water, that it was invented by a hydraulic engineer called Ktesibios, that just like our organs today it had keys that controlled sliders to admit the air to the pipes, and that those keys were sprung so that the sliders moved back to shut off the air as soon as each key was released.[1]

The growth of its popularity was rapid and by the first century AD, hydraulic organs were available with several ranks of pipes, the selection of which was controlled by stops. The Romans used the organ both for general musical purposes and also to accompany gladiatorial contests in the arena, with the suggestion that the fighters timed their strokes to the music of the organ (or that the organist matched his music to the fight, as our circus bandmasters keep time to the horses).[2] We have Roman mosaics of gladiators in the amphitheater, showing the organ accompanied by a standing trumpeter and two seated horn players, apparently all playing together, but we have no description at all of what they played, and little, if any, evidence that they really were an ensemble.

Both this use in the amphitheater and written descriptions make it clear that the hydraulic organ was a loud and powerful instrument. The drawing at the foot of figure C.1 shows the tanks for the water, the wind chest, and the bellows, plied by four pumpers. The illustration is inaccurate in some details: it appears to be two organs in one, and of course there were really far more pipes,

with the keyboard on the players' side. It was probably drawn by someone with only a rather vague memory of how the organ looked, but it does give an idea of what the *hydraulis* was like.

The pneumatic organ, one that simply had bellows and a wind chest without the added power of a weight of water to pressure the air, was a much quieter instrument, but otherwise similar, again with sprung keys and, in at least one case, the ability to choose between ranks of pipes. This we know from one surviving Roman instrument, dated AD 228, found in the ruins of a guild clubroom in Aquincum, the Roman suburb outside Budapest.[3] It had four ranks of thirteen pipes, three ranks stopped and one open. Regrettably these were all in so fragmentary a state (the building had been destroyed by fire and the organ buried in the debris) that there is no way to establish the original range or tuning.

An organ is a highly complex combination of comparatively simple mechanisms. A rank, or row, of pipes stands on a wind chest. Each rank produces a different sound, but let us start with the simplest: a principal or *diapason* that with a speaking length of 8 feet (from the mouth to the top, not counting the foot below the mouth that is there to guide the air) would sound the C two octaves below middle C.

A row of these pipes, each a little shorter than the last, will match the keyboard of an organ with a range, just as an example, of five octaves from that C. Going up to three octaves above middle C, there will be sixty-one pipes in that rank, known as the 8-foot, with speaking lengths from 8 feet to 3 inches. We can see something very similar arranged as the front of many church organs (we will come shortly to the device that allows the pipes to be displayed in a decorative order, rather than in one diagonal sequence). Behind that rank will be other ranks with different types or sizes of pipe.

The foot of each pipe stands in a hole in a board, and below this is another board with corresponding holes that forms the top of the upper half of the wind chest. Between these boards, running from one side of the organ to the other, is a row of sliders, one below each rank, with holes spaced in them so that normally there is a blank piece of wood below each pipe of the rank, but when the slider is pulled out, its holes match the holes above and below to let the air through. These sliders are controlled by the stop knobs, usually to each side of the keyboard, and when a stop is pulled out, the slider moves out also. In this way, the organist can control which ranks will sound.

Below the lower board is a series of channels running from front to back, each channel or groove corresponding to one key. When a key is depressed, it pulls down a pallet in the bottom of the groove that opens it to the wind chest, into which the air has been pushed by a set of bellows. When the finger is lifted, a spring closes the pallet and the air is shut off. So if the key for the D a tone above middle C is depressed, the air goes into that D's channel, and if the diapason stop is drawn, then that D of that rank will sound. If another stop is also drawn, for example, the 4-foot diapason, then the D an octave higher will sound as well.

On the better organs, there were two sets of bellows, the lower set operated by the blower or blowers to fill the upper set, which is controlled by a lead weight (on the hydraulics system, by the weight of the water). This is to avoid changes of air pressure, and therefore of pitch (as we saw with recorder and flute); because the upper set is controlled by a weight rather than by the blowers, the air from it is always at a steady pressure. This is the very simplest system—the mechanism can become far more complicated than this, as we shall see.

In fact, the early medieval organs were simpler still. The use of sprung keys had been forgotten, and so had the use of stops. On a simple organ with just one row of pipes, the sliders were in the front instead of keys. The player pulled out a slider, and the pipe above it sounded; to stop it, he had to push the slider back in again. This made playing slow and allowed him to sound no more than two notes at a time, one with each hand.

Winchester Cathedral had an enormous organ by around 960.[4] There were forty sliders, operated by two players, just as we see in figure C.1, and each slider had ten holes, with above each slider ten pipes. In other words, there were forty "keys" and ten ranks of pipes. Each rank of pipes would have produced a different sound, probably some of them different pitches as well to form chords. And all ten pipes on each "key" all sounded at once! This was a system called *Blockwerk* and seems to have been common in the early Middle Ages before stops were reinvented in the fourteenth century. The noise must have been horrendous—so loud that, as we are told, people stopped their ears when they got too close—for there were twelve bellows above and fourteen below, blown by seventy men; we do not know whether these were twenty-six independent bellows or the lower fourteen drove air into the twelve above.

There are numerous medieval illustrations of smaller organs from the tenth to early thirteenth centuries that show similar sliders. The pipes on these early organs were all the same diameter, as they are at Aquincum and as they were on the organ in the Church of the Nativity in Bethlehem. These latter are preserved in the Studium Biblicum Franciscanum Museum of the Convent of the Flagellation in Jerusalem and are thought to date to the eleventh-century Latin Kingdom.[5] The speaking length of the longest of the surviving 220 or so pipes is around 23½ inches (60 cm) and the shortest 6⅔ inch (17 cm), suggesting that the lowest note may have been middle C (although, of course, there may have been longer pipes that were not found). The pipes are of bronze (a few are of a considerably lighter white metal), and all were made by rolling them around a mandrel with a soldered overlap.[6]

By the mid- to late thirteenth century, organ building had progressed. Keys were sprung once again, and we have many illustrations of a small organ—so small that it could be carried while it was played and is therefore today called a *portative* (see figure 7.1).

Figure 7.1. Portative Organ
Pre-1350, St. Mary the Virgin Church, Adderbury, Oxfordshire.

A rather larger organ, which was certainly known by the early fourteenth century, could be carried around and then placed in position to be played, and is called the *positive*. Like the portative, it was built initially with the longest pipes at one end and the shortest at the other, but by the fifteenth century a major development had taken place: the invention of what organists call the "roller board." This is a wooden rod with a projection on the side at each end. A rod from the key, called a "tracker," pushes up the projection at one end so that the board rotates. As it does so, the projection at the other end pushes up another tracker, which opens the pallet below the appropriate pipe.

The importance of this invention is that it was no longer necessary to have the pipe standing immediately above the key, because, as can be seen in figure 7.2, the roller from the lowest key could go to the pipe in the center of the organ, that from the next to the pipe to its left, that from the next lowest to the pipe to the right of center, and so on. In this way, organs could be built in a decorative pattern still familiar to us today. A further and more practical advantage is that the weight of the organ is distributed evenly, instead of the left side being far heavier than the right—an important factor when designing the casework, and especially when fixing the organ on a church wall. Henri-Arnaut de Zwolle's treatise of 1440 is very detailed, describing and illustrating much of the construction of organs; their pipes; stops, which had now been reinvented so that organists could again choose which ranks would sound; and their bellows.[7]

From this time on, organs grew more and more complex, with added keyboards or manuals, pedal boards, and far more stops and thus available tone colors, but in principle they still worked in the same way. Many organs are built like this today, in the neoclassical movement that began around 1930 in Germany, to escape from the great wash of sound made possible by the inventions of the nineteenth and earlier twentieth centuries, and to recreate the organs of the Baroque for which Johann Sebastian Bach and his contemporaries wrote what is still regarded as the center of the organist's repertoire in Germany and the Netherlands.

These Baroque organs were built on the *Werkprinzip*. The organ is divided into discrete sections or *Werke*, using the German terms with the approximate English equivalents: the *Brustwerk*, the *Hauptwerk* (together the English Great) and later the *Oberwerk*, the *Rückpositif* (English Chair or Choir), and the *Pedal* (the same in English). Each had its own keyboard and each its own tonal characteristics. The Rückpositif was a complete small organ and was behind the organist's back (*Rück* = "back") or bench (hence the English Chair), visible in figure 7.2 in front of the balcony rail. The Brustwerk was immediately in front of him, the Hauptwerk above it, and the Oberwerk above that (*Brust* = "breast," *Haupt* = "high," and *Ober* = "above"). The pedal pipes were in the towers to each side and were controlled by a keyboard played by the organist's feet.

Save for the vastly increased number of registers and pipes, there is nothing in such eighteenth-century organs that would have been new to Arnaut nor to the early-sixteenth-century organist of Malmö. Everything still worked by trackers, roller boards, and similar devices.[8] There was direct mechanical contact between the player's finger on the key and the pallet that let the air into the pipe. The only real problems were possible limits to the number of mechanical linkages and, more seriously, that if a large number of stops were drawn, the weight on the key of that number of pallets to be opened, against their springs and the air pressure, made playing a greater physical effort. This effort was overcome by the invention in the early nineteenth century of the pneumatic lever.

Figure 7.2. Organ

Sixteenth century and later, Malmö, Sweden. The positive organ hangs from the balcony rail and thus conceals the manuals.

This was a small bellows or "motor," as organists call it, that was operated by a tracker from the key but that then sent a puff of air down a tube to open the pallet, replacing all further trackers and other mechanical linkages. The only weight on the key was that of the initial tracker to the motor, and playing became much less effort. The great French organ builder Aristide Cavaillé-Coll applied this system to many organs, and with the full development of the tubular-pneumatic action, adopted by Henry Willis in England, much larger organs with higher wind pressure became practicable and, because the tubes could be of any required length, it became possible to scatter the pipework around the church wherever it could most conveniently be placed. Willis put the pedal pipes of London's St. Paul's Cathedral in one gallery of the dome and part of the Great in another. It was organs of these types, some of the largest of which were built in the United States, that made possible the music of Liszt, Reger, Franck, Saint-Saëns, Widor, and other composers for the Romantic organ. With the application of electromagnets to the pneumatic motors, further separation became possible, and the "console," as the organist's desk with the keyboards and stops is called, could be far away from the organ itself, connected with a long umbilical cord full of electric cables (see figure 7.3).

One of the impulses toward the development of the neoclassical organ was, as we said, the desire to re-create the organ of the Baroque, but another was a preference for the direct physical contact and immediate response of the tracker action rather than the slightly spongy feel of the keys and the delay of the pneumatic systems. It took time for the impulse of the air to move down the tube, so organists had to play ahead of the choir or orchestra. Even the electro-pneumatic action was not instantaneous, and the separation of organ from organist compounded the problem, for if the console was placed in the choir and the organ at the other end of the church, the sound of the organ took time to arrive at the choir. If the notes of the organ were to be simultaneous with those of the choir, the organist had to play even further ahead.

The German *Werkprinzip* was not the only style of seventeenth- and eighteenth-century organ building. English organs were much simpler, and pedals were nonexistent save sometimes for pull-downs, wires that would pull down the keys of the lowest octave of the manual so that they could be played with either hand or foot. Many organs were destroyed by the Puritans during the Cromwellian Interregnum of 1649–1660, and it was only in the larger town churches that they had been replaced before the nineteenth century. In village churches, the church band, of whatever instruments could be gathered

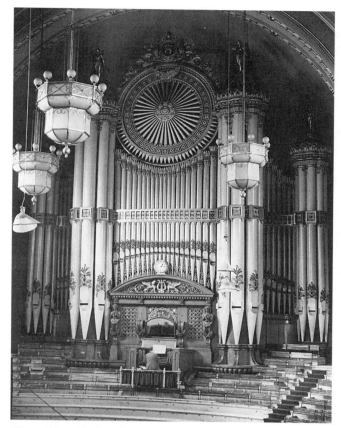

Figure 7.3. Modern Organ
Leeds Town Hall, Yorkshire. Built Gray & Davidson, 1857, pneumatic lever action with four manuals, 6,500 pipes down to open 32'; rebuilt, converted to tubular pneumatic and fifth manual added Abbot & Smith, 1898; rebuilt again, converted to electro-pneumatic with detached console (not shown here), Wood & Wordsworth, 1972, *photo* Yorkshire Post, *courtesy Leodis, www.leodis.net.*

together, or sometimes a barrel organ, were the common accompaniment to services.

In France, organs were as large as those in Germany, but operated on a different principle of choruses, contrasting individual solo registers or small combinations with the *plein jeu* of different types of flue pipes and the *grand jeu* of the full organ, adding the reed stops. The shape and patterns of French pipes differed from the German, and so their tonal characteristics differed as well. Also dissimilar were the ways in which stops were used in combination.[9] One reason that we do not hear French Baroque organ music, which was quite differently conceived from that of Bach, as often as the German is that outside France there are far fewer organs with the appropriate pipe patterns and registrations. In addition, French composers left very specific and detailed instructions of how the music was to be played, with complex *agréments* or ornamentation that tend to put off those players who have not studied such matters in depth.

Another major disparity between these national styles is that the French composers tended to indicate on their music the registrations—the specific combinations of stops—that should be used, whereas the Germans usually left these indications of color to the player's choice. As a result, we have a much better idea of the actual sound of the music of D'Anglebert, Couperin, Corrette, and their contemporaries than we have of that of Buxtehude and Bach. For the latter composers, we have the notes, but often we have little idea of whether the sound resembled that of a string quartet or of a full orchestra or, at the whim of the player, of either or both.

In Spain, it was common to divide the organ, with half on each side of the choir. A special feature was the use of horizontal reed pipes, often powerful trumpet stops, projecting forward instead of standing upright.

One Spanish invention was adopted throughout the world: the swell box. A characteristic of the organ is that its sound is terraced. Each rank is voiced to a specific volume, controlled by the air pressure. If the air pressure is increased, the sound gets louder but the pitch also gets sharper, something that of course is undesirable. On the other hand, if some of the registers are enclosed in a box whose sides can be opened, the volume can be varied without affecting the pitch. This is the principle of the swell. The organist can, by using a pedal, open louvers in the box and so alter the amount of sound.

Reed pipes were known in Arnaut's day, and by the seventeenth century a considerable number were available. The reed, as we saw above, is a blade of brass, fitting over a shallot (very like a clarinet or saxophone reed on its mouthpiece), with a bridle of iron wire on the reed that can be moved to control its pitch (see figure 4.1). The pipes on a reed stop act only as resonators, affecting the tone rather than the pitch, though the length and shape of the pipes, and thus internal volume, must be appropriate to the pitch.

The resonator is designed and voiced, like the pipes of all the flue stops except the diapasons, so that the sound approximates to that of some other instrument, deliberately resembling them quite closely on the large cinema organs such as the Wurlitzers of the first half of the twentieth century. Furthermore, each "voice" is provided in a number of sizes. We mentioned above the 8-foot, which speaks at the written pitch, and the 4-foot an octave above. Each rank is named for the nominal length of the written C two octaves below middle C. If the organist plays middle C with a 16-foot stop drawn, he hears that note an octave lower than written; with the 32-foot, those very large pipes at each side in figure 7.3, it would be an octave lower again. With a 4-foot stop, the organist hears the C below middle; on a 2⅔-foot, the G above

that. Pipes are named either by their length or by their effect, so that the last in the previous sentence is also called a "quint," from the Latin for "fifth," the G being a fifth above C (one counts both ends, so C-D-E-F-G equals five). The quint is normally a twelfth higher than written, an octave plus a fifth, as this produces a less muddy sound than would an actual fifth. Similarly the 2-foot register is also called a fifteenth.

The organ is unique among instruments in being able to sound a large number of notes by pressing a single key. It can play a melody on a single rank, of course, but it can also produce a swath of sound by drawing half a dozen or more stops—especially as some stops, called "mixtures," open a combination of several ranks of pipes. A large organ in full cry can produce a glorious sound, but to the players of other, simpler, single-voiced instruments, it does sometimes seem to have a poor signal-to-noise ratio. There is so much going on that it can be very difficult to hear the music through the uproar! This, as we said, was one of the reasons for the neoclassical movement, and it is also the reason why quite small positive organs remain popular.

A special form of very small organ had only reeds. This was the regal, which often had tiny resonators, the whole thing sometimes so small that keyboard, reeds, and bellows could all be folded up into the shape of a large book—hence called a bible regal. Regals had a sharp, snarling sound similar to that of crumhorns and rackets and were often built into larger organs. The bible regal was re-created in the nineteenth century with free reeds as very small harmoniums.

The barrel organ was a mechanical instrument, used in churches and other places where an organist was not available. It worked on a similar principle to a music box, although it was normally much larger. A wooden barrel had pins placed in it that tripped levers set below the pipes to open their pallets. The "player" turned a crank that both rotated the barrel and operated the bellows, so that all was contained in the same case. Barrel organs varied in size.[10] Some were very small indeed, perhaps contained in a clock case to play at certain hours—even smaller ones were placed in decorative birdcages to imitate canaries or linnets, or were used to teach caged birds to sing. Slightly larger ones, such as that in figure 7.4, were often domestic instruments, early precursors of record players, with the barrels pinned with popular tunes of the day, whereas church barrels were pinned with hymns and psalm tunes. Even larger ones were used in music halls, and Beethoven's "Battle" Symphony was originally written for one of the largest, which had a number of orchestral instruments built into it.

Early barrel organs are important research tools because they reproduce the music as it was played in their

Figure 7.4.   Barrel Organ
Front board removed to show the barrel and bellows, and between them the pipes, by Flight & Robson, London, c. 1825 (Bate Collection 958), *courtesy Bate Collection, University of Oxford.*

own day. A well-pinned barrel can be the nearest thing we have to a recording of Handel or Mozart playing their own music, and it is especially important for the study of aspects of performance practice such as ornamentation and, in the Baroque period, the very common use of *notes inégales*—playing unevenly notes that were written evenly, the contemporary equivalent of swinging it slightly.[11]

Barrels are not the only device for mechanical organs. Many fairground and similar organs use "books" made from perforated cardboard and have extra effects such as drums and bell-plates built in. A special variety of such organs existed in America, known as *calliopes*. These were operated by high-pressure steam, rather than air, in effect a series of tuned steamboat whistles, and their sound was much louder as a result.

Organs are extremely expensive instruments. That in figure 7.3 has 6,500 pipes, from the 32-foot down to the smaller ones, and pipe metal, a mixture of tin and lead, has never been cheap. What is more, the nominal 32-foot measure is only the speaking length, from the mouth to the top, but there must also be another two or three feet of metal for the conical foot on which it stands, and if the lowest note on the keyboard or manual is lower than the C two octaves below middle C, then the pipe must be even longer. When one adds the cost of all the mechanisms, plus the time it takes to make everything and install it and the maintenance and tuning required, it is not surprising that reed organs were used in small chapels and that electronic instruments have become popular even in large churches and halls. To these last we shall turn in the next chapter.

Notes

1. Jean Perrot, *The Organ* (1971), devotes pages 5–22 to the endeavor to establish the identity and date of the inventor, and 23–42 to the mechanism of his invention. Much here on the early history is derived from the following pages of his book.

2. Perrot, *The Organ*, 50, quoting the *Satyricon* of Petronius.

3. Melinda Kaba, *Die Römische Orgel von Aquincum* (1976), describes and illustrates the instrument in great detail.

4. Perrot, *The Organ*, 229–32.

5. I saw them and measured some in 1984; see my "The Oldest Organ in Christendom," *FoMRHIQ* 35 (April 1984): Comm. 534, 51–52. This chapter has been expanded with some more information and measurements of forty-nine of the pipes on my website, jeremymontagu.co.uk.

6. The one fragment of pipe that I was allowed to bring back and have analyzed was 95.6 percent copper, 2.3 percent tin, and 1.2 percent lead, with the usual slight traces of other metals. Unfortunately this mixture is so typical of bronze that it is of no help in dating the pipes.

7. The manuscript of the treatise is Paris: B.N. ms. Latin 7295. A translation with facsimile was published by G. Le Cerf and E.-R. Labande as *Les Traités d'Henri-Arnaut de Zwolle* (1932; reprinted 1972).

8. Every book on the organ has numerous drawings of the mechanisms involved.

9. Full details of each style will be found in Peter Williams, *The European Organ* (1966), as well as other sources.

10. Arthur W. J. G. Ord-Hume, *Barrel Organ* (London, 1978) illustrates a wide range of instruments, with many details of the mechanism.

11. David Fuller, *Mechanical Musical Instruments* (1974).

~

Symbiosis

Almost all musical instruments require some human intervention, but in only a few of them do the cavities of the human body form a part of the sound chain. Two of those few are the trump or Jew's harp and the simplest form of the musical bow, the mouth bow. With each, the player uses the mouth cavity to resonate overtones of the fundamental provided by the instrument and to produce music that is a sequence of these overtones or harmonics.

It has long been accepted that the musical bow is the earliest of string instruments. In Greek legend, it was Apollo, the sun god, who was inspired by the twang of his sister Diana's bowstring as the divine huntress's arrow sped from the bow. In India, the bow was invented by Shiva, again a god. In Japanese legend, when the sun goddess Amaterasu had hidden herself in a cave, plunging all into Stygian gloom, it was the music played on a group of bows that tempted her to come forth from the cave, and thus restore light to the world. These legends, and many more, are cited by Henry Balfour in what is still the most comprehensive survey of the instrument, *The Natural History of the Musical Bow* (1899).

Such legends are surely true in essence, that the bow was the earliest of the string instruments, but what we can never know is whether the archer's bow inspired the musician's or the musician's use of a bow led to the archer's. The most common playing technique is to tap the string with a light stick, and while this could have been an arrow from the archer's quiver, equally it could have been a stick in the hand of a musician who, seeing a target, launched the first arrow.

The ground bow is a flexible stave with one end planted in the earth and a string running from the upper end to a plate of wood or bark over a resonating hole in the ground. In the same way, it could have inspired the

snare, and equally easily the hunter's snare could have inspired the ground bow.

In neither case shall we ever know the answer, for the archer's bow must date back to the Mesolithic or even to late Paleolithic times, when the first arrowheads appear in the archaeological record. The ground bow may be even earlier.

The archer's bow is simply a wooden stave, flexible enough to be bent, yet rigid enough and strong enough always to resist such a bend and to try to revert to the straight. It is normally thinned somewhat toward the two ends, and this is true of the musical bow also. Balfour cites, as his first example, the bow of the Damara people of southwestern Africa, which, when Francis Galton was traveling in that area around 1850, was still being used for both purposes.[1] A hunter would

> while away his spare time in strumming upon his improvised instrument. . . . When required for music, all that is done is to add a little string bracing towards, but not at the centre of the bow, drawing the bow string to the bow. This not only tightens the bow-string and raises the notes producible, but also divides it into two unequal lengths giving different notes, which can be elicited by tapping rhythmically with a small stick.[2]

This account describes the technique used on a wide variety of mouth bows. Most have a string braced and divided in this way, although some use either a knuckle or a small stick to stop an undivided string close to one end, far enough from the end to raise the pitch by one note. A few combine both techniques, to provide a third fundamental and thus a fuller sequence of available overtones.

The player holds the bow between the lips or against the teeth, or sometimes the string between the slightly parted lips. By altering the mouth shape as one does when forming the different vowels, while moving the tongue to alter the mouth capacity, overtones of the fundamental are produced that are mainly drawn from the harmonic series. C. J. Adkins has shown that in the case of the trump, some of the overtones are nonharmonic, and it would seem probable that this applies also to the bow, even though that instrument has not yet been studied in the same scientific detail.[3]

Because this series is available from any fundamental, when the bow is braced off the center of the string, then by tapping one half of the string with the striking stick, one obtains the overtones of, for example, C and on the other half those of D or whatever the equivalents may be in the local scale system. The same is achieved when the string is stopped near one end, and either gives enough notes for any simple melody.

The mouth bow is widely known from Africa, and many reports have been published, in addition to Balfour's particularly those by Percival Kirby and David Rycroft.[4] Shapes and patterns vary, mostly sticking fairly closely to the archer's pattern. In East Africa, a somewhat elaborated model is found, with a rigid cylindrical central section six inches or so in length, sometimes twice that or even more, and thinned arms. The arm at each end is only a quarter of an inch or so thick, continuing the line of the outermost part of the cylinder. Very commonly one arm is more bent than the

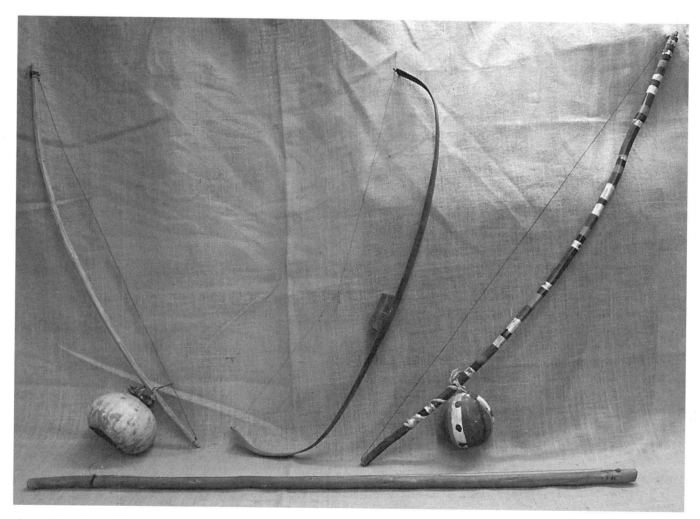

Figure G.1. Musical Bows

Above, L–R: gourd bow, Tonga people, Zimbabwe or Zambia (IV 88); mouth bow, Macorecon people, Zimbabwe (VII 188); *birimbão*, gourd bow, Brazil (VII 244).

Below: *lesiba*, blown mouth bow, Teyateyanang, Basutoland (X 110).

other. A complex variant of this is the three-part bow, the central cylinder with a hole bored in each end to receive a flexible arm.

The normal material for the stave is wood, although cane is sometimes seen. With those bows that were both archer's and musician's, the string material would normally be gut or sinew. For bows of strictly musical purpose, more fragile materials were often used, such as reed and other vegetable materials. Since the advent of commercial materials, wire has often replaced those natural materials that require more preparation, as has common string and, more recently, monofilament nylon.

Most bows are tapped with a light stick. Few, if any, have the string plucked, for this would be a less effective method of performance. Some have notches cut in the bow-stave, usually near one end, and these are rasped with a stick. Rasping the stave makes it vibrate, and that vibration is in turn passed to the string. The sound is then a combination of a musical rasp and of the bow-string and its overtones. More rarely, the string is rubbed, as Rycroft recorded.[5]

Some bows are blown, but this seems confined today to the *lesiba* of the Xhosa people and the *!gora* of the Korana, both of South Africa.[6] Balfour, in a long and detailed paper, quoted travelers' reports from as early as 1704, from the much wider area over which this type of bow was then distributed.[7] These blown bows have a string that is attached to the stave at one end but at the other is attached to a strip of quill fixed to the other end of the stave. The player blows forcefully on this quill, and that makes the string vibrate.[8] These are the only known mouth-blown bows, although Balfour draws an analogy with the flat blades of grass that children blow between their thumbs, while pointing out that these latter are not resonated by the mouth to produce more musical sounds.[9] The only other aeolian bows are those attached to kites that are known from India and were widely used in China.

The ordinary mouth-resonated musical bow is by no means confined to Africa, even if it survives there more widely than elsewhere. Examples are known from India, Melanesia, and Polynesia. These are sometimes differently shaped, the stave a flat wooden lath, thin enough across the width to be flexible. The fact that in many other areas gourd-resonated bows are known suggests that mouth bows may well once have existed there as well. One problem with the mouth bow is that the sound is very quiet; it is an instrument primarily designed for the player's own enjoyment. Another is that if players wish to sing to their own accompaniment, they are then reduced to the two, or at most three, fundamentals of the bowstring, as evinced in a number of Rycroft's recordings

where singing alternates with wider-ranging playing. The use of a gourd or other resonator solves both these problems, and the use of the gourd bow is more widespread today than that of the mouth bow. We have already discussed the gourd bow at the beginning of chapter 6.

Meanwhile, there is one problem that we should at least outline, and this is the vexed question of whether any string instruments existed in the Americas before the arrival of Christopher Columbus. There have been no archaeological discoveries of string instruments on the continent, nor has any evidence been adduced for their existence in any of the ancient cultures. Illustrations of many instruments appear in the Mexican codices, and many others on Mochica pots, but none of them are stringed.

The peoples of North America were certainly archers long before the Europeans arrived, for arrowheads have been found there from much earlier periods. And yet it is normally held that there were no string instruments known in pre-Columbian times, and certainly there is no evidence for their presence. The Brazilian gourd-resonated bow, the *birimbão*, is believed to derive from those made by African slaves. There is a very simple bowed tube zither known from the North American Plains, referred to as the "Apache fiddle," but nobody has ever produced any definitive evidence for its origin or date.[10] It would seem surprising that if there were archers, there were no musical bows, but at present no more can be said.

The bow is not a difficult instrument to make, though a suitable piece of wood has to be found, cut, and shaped, and a string of some material must be obtained and prepared. With the advent of trading stores, it may well often have been easier to pay a few cents for a ready-made instrument that would play the same music. The musical resemblance between the mouth bow and the trump was noted by several of the early travelers, who would describe an instrument that was new to their readers in terms of one that was already familiar to them. One German writer cited by Balfour even referred to the bow as "die Maultrommel," using the German name for the trump.[11]

This was our second example above of a symbiotic instrument: the trump or Jew's harp. The common English name is a stumbling block, and nobody knows its origin.[12] The modern form, in our culture, has a metal frame (the shape varies, as may be seen in figure G.4) with two parallel arms that lie closely to each side of a flexible steel tongue that functions as a reed. The closeness is acoustically important, to ensure that the vibration of the reed is coupled to that of the player's mouth cavity. One end of the reed is fixed rigidly to the back of the frame and the other is turned up in a right angle so that it may be plucked with a finger. The end is usually rolled over, or at least bent, so as not to scratch the finger. The instrument is played with the frame against the teeth, and as the reed is plucked, the overtones of its sound are selected and amplified by movement of the tongue and alteration of the mouth capacity, exactly as with the musical bow. The sound of the reed provides a constant drone just as does that of the bowstring.

Where the trump originated is unknown, but the relationship between it and the mouth organ in Southeast Asia is so clear that one would suggest with some confidence that it is likely to have been somewhere in that area. Both instruments will function only if, fitting closely in a frame, there is a reed that is free to vibrate to and fro within that frame. The pitch of each reed depends on its length and its mass, and it is quite common to see the free end of the reed loaded to increase its mass and so lower the pitch. Those for the mouth organs are small enough to respond to blowing by the player's mouth. The trumps are too large for this to work and therefore they are plucked, but just by looking at them one can see that they are the same. Some are of bamboo, and others, like those in figure G.2, are cut in a piece of thin metal sheet. All these are idioglottal, the reed or tongue being from the same piece of bamboo or metal as the frame. Heteroglot-

tal trumps and mouth organ reeds are also known from the same area, again very similar in shape.

In many areas, the trump was used for magical purposes, especially love magic, as we have already seen in interlude F. It is believed that it can speak, and certainly in some traditions both players and hearers purport to hear and understand the words it sounds as well as the music. It is also used for dance music and, particularly in Indonesia, in groups somewhat orchestrally.

Geneviève Dournon-Taurelle and John Wright, in their *Les guimbardes du musée de l'homme* (1978), go into far greater morphological and typological detail than we have space for here. It will probably suffice here to introduce three main types: the flat, mainly idioglottal examples such as those characteristic of East and Southeast Asia, made usually of bamboo, metal, bone, or ivory (see figure G.3); those partly circular in section from New Guinea and other parts of Oceania, mainly Melanesia, always of bamboo; and those of metal, always heteroglot, a metal frame, most commonly iron, with an inserted reed, most commonly steel, used from India and western Siberia through to Europe and, subsequently, beyond.

The simplest of these are the Melanesian.[13] These are made by slicing a section of bamboo longitudinally, usually retaining part of the node at what will become the

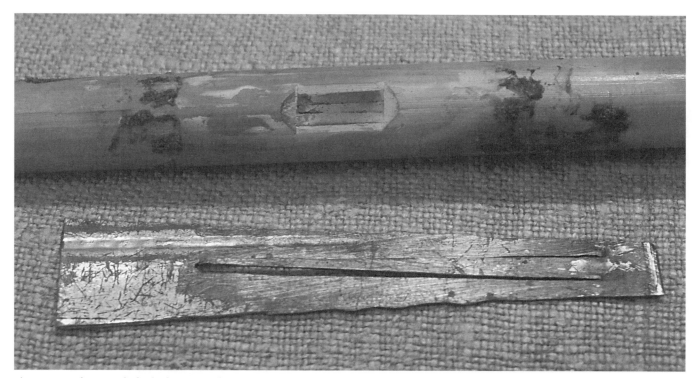

Figure G.2. Blown and Plucked Free Reeds
Above: detail of mouth organ *khāēn* reed, Thailand (V 54b).
Below: trump, Philippines (V 198).

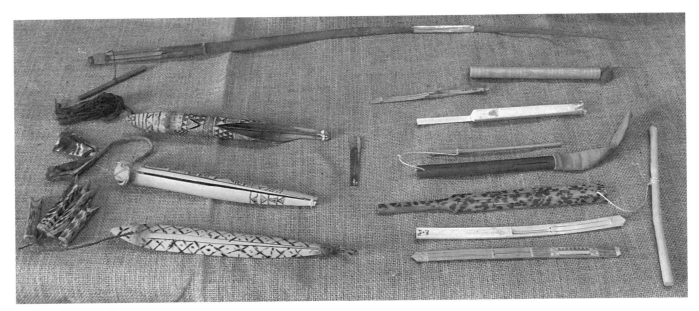

Figure G.3. Idioglot Trumps

All bamboo unless otherwise stated.

Left column, front to back: with rattles on the pulling cord, Papua New Guinea (XI 118); by Michael (then a child), Gumini, Central Highlands, Papua New Guinea (V 158); by Simon Mana, inverted to show the underside, also Gumini (VIII 138); Malay style but said to be New Guinea (the long tail was repaired while in use) (IX 194).

Center: brass, Philippines, shown in detail in figure G.2 (V 198).

Right column, front to back: two *kubing*, one inverted to show the underside, T'Boli people, Mindanao, Philippines (X 290 and 292); *geng-gong* with pulling stick, Bali-Aga, Tenganan, Bali (XI 230); *rinding*, with pulling stick and cloth case, Bali (VI 34b); *bambaro*, guinea corn, children's substitute for the iron bambaro in figure G.4, Zaria, Nigeria (VI 238); Thailand, with decorated bamboo case (VIII 228).

hinge end, and forming the body into a long, narrow oval, coming to a point at the distal end. A narrow tongue is cut or abraded down the centerline of the body, usually stopping just short of the pointed end. That end is separated into two points, which are tied together with thin cord to aid structural stability. The cord is knotted between the points to hold them far enough apart to allow the reed to vibrate freely, yet close enough together for acoustical linkage.[14] A hole or projection at the hinge end has a cord attached and the player holds this cord, partly to jerk the hinge but also as a measure of length so as to knock on the reed at the correct position and aid its vibration. The instruments may look clumsy to our eyes, although they are often elaborately decorated with incised and stained, or burned, patterns, but in skilled hands they are as efficient as most other patterns.

The flat East and Southeast Asian variety also differs from the trump that we use by being plucked at the hinge end rather than at the free end of the tongue. This is done either by plucking directly with the finger on the body at that end or again by jerking a cord tied through a hole at that end. Many such instruments are very carefully made, with inserts of thin bamboo in the body, at each side of the reed, that can be adjusted to control the width of the gap between the reed and the frame.

The third type, with an iron frame, is seen in Nepal and the Indian subcontinent in general. It has been suggested that it traveled thence into Europe, where it was known by late Roman times.[15] Medieval examples are common in collections and show that the instrument was known and used throughout Europe (see figure G.4). An important center of manufacture was, and remains, in the Austrian Tyrol, centered on the town of Molln.[16] It was produced there, in England, and in Italy for export and trade over wide areas.[17] This European form of the instrument was generally adopted in Africa, where there is no known indigenous form. It was a common article of trade goods from the sixteenth century on, carried there to exchange for gold, ivory, and other products. It became a cheap and ready-made substitute for the musical bow, whose music it could play and whose use it could supplant. Instruments copying the European were then made by African blacksmiths, especially in the western areas such as Nigeria.

In Mongolia and Siberia, there is a tradition of flat, idioglottal instruments, often made from bone and similar materials, but today they have adopted variants of the European model, often somewhat larger and heavier than the norm and of much better quality than most others save perhaps the Norwegian, whose handmade trumps have a well-deserved reputation for excellence. In these

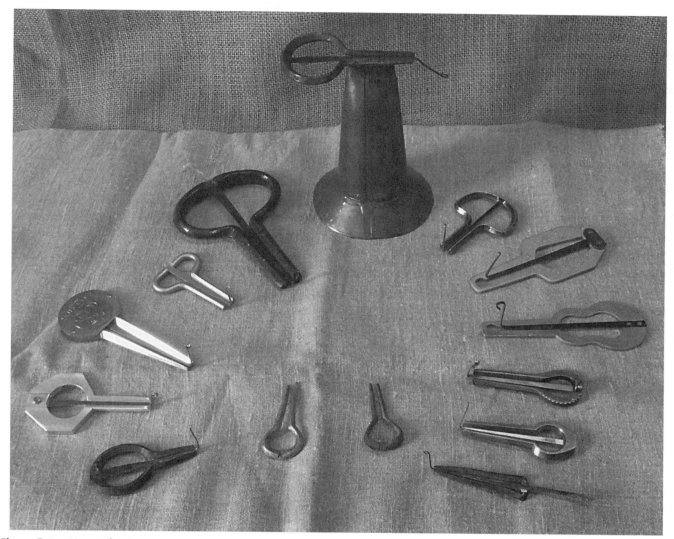

Figure G.4. Heteroglot Trumps

Clockwise from bottom left: *bambaro*, iron, Zaria, Nigeria (VI 202b); *kubiz*, aluminum with steel reed, by Magroupor Ravil Hanifovich, Bashkirian Republic, Russia (XII 20); *khomus*, steel, by Revo Chemchoyev, Borogon, Sakha Republic, Russia (XII 28); *Maultrommel* in A, steel, by Friedrich Schlütter, Zelle-Mehlis, Germany (IX 84); iron, English style, Chile (X 200); Phono-Harp, iron on tin-plate resonator, by M. Troman, Birmingham, England (X 12); Maultrommel, by Karl Schwarz, Molln, Austria (I 34); *scacciate i pensieri*, Italy (VI 184); *guimbarde*, "Modèle Far West," by CBS Masterwork, France (VI 168); *munnharpe* in F, iron, by Bjørgulv Straume, Valle, Norway (XII 210); munnharpe in E, bronze, by Jakob Lavoll, Norway (XII 186); iron, Afghanistan (VIII 206a).

Center: two English medieval trumps, bronze (XII 70), and wrought iron (XII 72), found in the mud of the Thames, London, each missing its reed.

areas, there is a strong tradition now of skilled craftsmen making individual instruments to order. Elsewhere in Europe and the United States, although individual craftsmen do exist, there seems to be more emphasis on mass production, excellent for the amateur and for the increasing popularity of the instrument, which has begun to appear once again on the concert platform and frequently in the studios, but less suited to the virtuoso.

In many areas, trumps are made with more than one tongue, as in Taiwan, or several trumps may be used, as among the Naxi in Yunnan and Sichuan in southwest China, where three are held to the mouth together.[18] The *Aura*, which Heinrich Scheibler claimed to have invented in the early nineteenth century, was an extreme form of this, with up to a dozen trumps clamped together so that the player could modulate from one key to another. Karl Eulenstein, one of the greatest nineteenth-century virtuosi on the instrument, used a set of at least sixteen, picking them up one by one as required by the music he was playing.[19]

We said just now that the trump was used in Africa as a substitute for the musical bow, but there are some areas that have produced a substitute for the trump. One is in New Guinea, where, among the Tifalmin, often as a boy's plaything, a beetle may be held against the mouth. Its wings buzz furiously to produce the fundamental pitch that is varied by altering the mouth capacity.[20]

Lajos Vargyas described a Mongolian trump substitute to the Nineteenth Conference of the International Folk Music Council in Ostend in 1967, introducing for the first time to many of us the phenomenon now usually known as overtone or multivoice singing.[21] The musician sounds a vocal drone and, by manipulation of the tongue and vocal tracts, also sounds the overtones of that drone. A detailed study of the techniques employed to achieve this, and the acoustical phenomena involved, by one eminent performer, Trân Quang Hai, has been published by the Institut de la Voix in Limoges.[22]

The multivoice singing technique has long been widespread in the eastern parts of what was once the Soviet Union, especially among the Tuva, the Bashkir, and their neighbors, areas where the use of trumps is strong, and there are numerous recordings of its use. Trân and his followers have taught many people in our culture how to do it, and it is beginning to be heard with some frequency in our own music. The basic technique is not difficult to acquire—it consists of humming (but with open lips) a sound similar to "ill" or "ell" at the back of the mouth, with the tongue curled up toward the roof. Far more difficult and the result of long practice (it has been suggested not all of it good for the physical well-being) is to produce a clear, flexible, singing overtone sound with a minimum of obtrusive drone.[23]

A rather different technique is cultivated in some parts of Tibet. Here the drone, instead of being generated at the back of the mouth, comes, it would seem, from the depth of the stomach—although in practice probably no lower than the base of the throat—resembling the sound of the long trumpets so widely used in that culture. To see and hear a group of monks producing these eerie sounds, accompanied by cymbals and alternating with the long trumpets, is indeed impressive, but how the overtones are produced, I cannot say.[24]

A more overt use of the vocal tracts with an instrument is humming while one plays. This is how horn players produce chords, for example, in Weber's *Concertino*: one note is played, another is hummed, and a third, sometimes a fourth, just appear as resultant tones. For instance, playing the fifth harmonic, the written E, and humming the third, the G, will produce the second harmonic, C, as a difference tone $(5 - 3)$ and the eighth, the upper C, as a summation tone $(5 + 3)$. This use of humming is by no means restricted to the harmonic series. It is also one of

the ways by which modern wind players produce special effects called for by various modern composers. As we have already seen in interlude D, this is how Turkish and Balkan, especially Bulgarian and Romanian, flutists produce a drone to accompany their instrument.

These are all examples of a close symbiosis between the player and the instrument—the one cannot be divorced from the other, for in these last cases the player has become the instrument.

We said at the beginning of this interlude that with only a few instruments does the human body provide part of the sound chain, but this may be because conventional scientific acoustical analysis of instrumental sound concentrates solely upon the instrument. Instruments are usually divorced from the player, generating the sound by mechanical means in order to keep it as constant as possible, well separated from the vagaries of a musician's input. But this is not how instruments are played. Every teacher knows that the player's posture, and thus the access to the player's inner spaces and organs, has a very considerable impact on the sound produced.

To take just one very clear example, when a trumpeter fills the lungs and then holds that posture and that lung expansion with the muscles of the chest as the lungs slowly empty of air, this will produce a far brighter and stronger sound than when the chest is allowed to fall as the lungs empty, despite playing at the same dynamic level. The air cavities of the chest are providing resonance chambers for the sound, even though that sound is being generated far above, at the contact point between lips and mouthpiece.

The trumpet is not alone in this. Although my experience has been in teaching brass instruments, I am told by others that it applies also to woodwinds and strings. Clearly, this is one of the many reasons why no two players ever sound the same, even if one hands the same instrument to another, and thus why, as we just said, no mechanically induced acoustical experiment can ever tell us the truth about any instrument. With wind instruments, as with the voice, it is all the parts of the vocal tract, from the diaphragm up to the cavities of the sinus, that affect the sound, and perhaps it is even the covering of those cavities. We do not know to what extent the hardness or softness of the bones, or their thickness or the thickness of their fleshy covering, affects the sound produced within them.

With other instruments, the subtleties of the musculature affect even the slightest motions and the sounds that result from them. I know as a player that this applies to percussion instruments. A momentary relaxation of the wrists as the cymbals come together greatly improves the sound,[25] just as relaxation in the arms, wrists, and fingers in the grip on the beaters of all drums and other instruments is essential for good tone quality. Every player of every instrument is, at least to some extent, symbiotic with it, and no scientific explanation for this has yet been satisfactory. Obviously skill is involved, but so may be the body, and very certainly the spirit.

Notes

1. Henry Balfour, *Natural History of the Musical Bow*, 5–8, citing Francis Galton, *Travels in S. Africa* (1851), and other authors.

2. Balfour, *Natural History of the Musical Bow*, 5.

3. C. J. Adkins, "Investigation of the Sound-Producing Mechanism of the Jew's Harp," *Journal of the Acoustical Society of America* 55:3 (March 1974): 667–70.

4. Percival Kirby, *The Musical Instruments of the Native Races of South Africa* (1934); David Rycroft, *Zulu, Swazi en Xhosa* (1969).

5. David Rycroft, "Friction Chordophones in South-Eastern Africa," *GSJ* 19 (1966): 84–100.

6. Kirby devotes a whole chapter to descriptions and photographs of these instruments, *Musical Instruments*, 171–92.

7. Henry Balfour, "The Goura," *Journal of the Royal Anthropological Institute* 32 (1902): 156–76 and plates 12–14.

8. How he at the same time alters the mouth shape to produce different pitches I do not know. Neither Rycroft nor I was able to get any sound out of his or my examples when we experimented with them together, and that inhibited investigation.

9. Balfour, "Goura," 170–71.

10. David P. McAllester, "An Apache Fiddle," *Ethno-Musicology Newsletter* 8 (September 1956): 1–5.

11. Oscar Baumann, *Eine Africanische Tropen-Insel* (1888), 99.

12. "Jews trump" is the oldest English name, according to the *Oxford English Dictionary*, in a reference to the rates of Customs charges from 1545. Very recently, in his article "Jue harpes, Jue trumpes, 1481," in *JIJHS* 2 (2005): 7–10, Michael Wright has pushed the first reference more than fifty years earlier. Various writers have pretended that "jaws" is the original term, into which "Jews" has been modified by folk etymology, but there is no lexical justification for this; the earlier name is "Jews," but why nobody knows. Frederick Crane has rightly suggested in an editorial (*Vierundzwanzigsteljahrschrift* 4 [1994]: 5–7) that in these days when people are liable to take offense from perfectly ordinary, or traditional, language, the instrument would be better referred to as the trump *tout court*.

13. Hans Fischer, *Schallgeräte in Ozeanien* (1958), translated by Philip W. Holzknecht as *Sound-Producing Instruments in Oceania*, ed. Don Niles (rev. ed., 1986—the first edition

should be avoided), 27–29 (in the translation, 47–52) and figs. 107–113.

14. Dournon-Taurelle and Wright, *Les guimbardes*, 45–50, figs. VII, 1–5, and 14.

15. Dournon-Taurelle and Wright illustrate Gallo-Roman examples (*Les guimbardes*, 103). These will also be found in *Le Carnyx et la Lyre* (1993), 20–21, nos. 3–7.

16. Karl M. Klier, *Volkstümliche Musikinstrumente in den Alpen* (1956), 71–77.

17. The English centers of Birmingham and Sheffield are well known. For a major center in Italy from the sixteenth century to the late nineteenth, see Alberto Lovatto, "The Production of Trumps in Valsesia," *JIJHS* 1 (2004): 4–17.

18. Helen Rees, *Echoes of History* (2000), 62–64 and track 6 on the accompanying CD.

19. Leonard Fox, *The Jew's Harp* (1988), contains a translation of Scheibler's original article from the *Allgemeine musikalische Zeitung* 30 (24 July 1816), as "The Aura," 87–95, and also Wilhelm Ludwig Schmidt's booklet in praise of the instrument (printed in Quedlinburg in 1840), as "The Aura or Mouth-Harmonica Presented as a Musical Instrument," 97–152. Fox also provides a translation of Klier's chapter on the trump from *Volkstümliche Musikinstrumente in den Alpen* on pp. 65–83 and Fanny Roodenfels's edition of the autobiography of her father, Karl Eulenstein, on pp. 160–211.

20. This was described, with a recording, by Prof. Anthony Forge at a meeting of the Ethnomusicology Panel of the Royal Anthropological Institute in London in the early 1960s and, according to Gilbert Rouget (in Dournon-Taurelle and Wright, *Les guimbardes*, 6), by B. Juillerat at a seminar of the Département d'Ethnomusicologie in Paris in 1971.

21. Lajos Vargyas, "Performing Styles in Mongolian Chant," *JIFMC* 20 (1968): 70–72.

22. Institut de la Voix, *Le chant diphonique* (1989).

23. A recently published study by Mark van Tongeren, *Overtone Singing* (2002), goes into this technique in considerable detail, describing its use in many parts of the world, including by composers such as Stockhausen, with many references to recordings, and it includes a CD of folk use and demonstrations of how it is done.

24. So often in any research, descriptions depend on being able to do something oneself, and I have tried this without success, just as neither David Rycroft nor I was able to get any sound out of our !gora. The technique was first brought to general notice by David Lewiston with his recording *Tibetan Buddhism: Tantras of Gyütö: Mahakala* (Nonesuch Records, 1973), recorded in the Gyütö Tantric College, Dalhousie, Himachal Pradesh.

25. This I learned, standing next to Harry Eastwood in the Royal Philharmonic under Sir Thomas Beecham. "Why do you get so much better a sound from cymbals than I?" I asked him. "You just do it like this," he replied—leaving me to work out what "this" was.

CHAPTER EIGHT

~

Electrophones

The music of the spheres, the song of the stars in their courses, the quires of angels, the idea of music above and beyond that of humanity has inspired many generations. But could it ever be heard? Lev Termen came close in 1920 when he waved a hand at an alarm system controller and music appeared from nowhere, music that soared and swooped from the ether itself.[1]

His *theremin* was the first successful electronic musical instrument, working from hand capacitance and feedback, just as a microphone produces a howl when it comes too close to a loudspeaker. Its only problems were that because pitch was controlled by the distance of the hand from the rod that stood up from the machine, changes of pitch were almost inevitably continuous and sliding, and it was difficult to judge where to place the hand precisely for any specific pitch. That the theremin was monophonic was no hindrance to its success—the same is true of all our wind instruments and many others—and a number of composers wrote for it as a solo voice, accompanied by orchestra or other instruments. It can still be heard today (it has been a popular instrument for amateur construction), but as a serious instrument, it was soon overtaken by a host of other inventions.

The most successful of these is Maurice Martenot's *ondes martenot* that combines the use of a keyboard, so that notes can be separated, with the use of the "ruban," a ring on a tape, that allows the player to add the glissandi that remain one of the characteristics of this type of instrument. These characteristics have been exploited very successfully by Olivier Messiaen, whose wife, Yvonne Loriod, was one of the leading virtuosi on the ondes, and by many other composers.

There were other instruments of similar types, none of which has survived into general use. Even the ondes is comparatively rarely seen and heard today beyond the recording studios, where there is always demand for different voices. On the whole, the electronic movement went in two directions. One was amplification, not only of the guitar but of many other instruments, even of the piano, with, for example, the Neo-Bechstein, which could be made far louder than an ordinary piano. The other was toward keyboard instruments that might substitute for the pipe organ with better sounds, closer to those of the real thing than those of the reed organ.

There has been a vast range of this second group. The best known of the earlier machines was probably the Hammond organ, which used toothed wheels to generate the sound electronically. A later development was in crystals that would vibrate at a permanently fixed rate, as they do in watches and clocks, and whose vibrations could then be divided electronically to produce all desired pitches, combined with controls that would add harmonic frequencies to imitate the sounds of other instruments or of the various registers of the pipe organ. All suffered from the basic problem that electronic sounds are generated differently from those of a pipe organ. However close they came in tone quality, something that can be achieved by judicious mixtures of harmonics into the envelope of sound, none of the notes began in the same ways as those of pipes.

The way a note begins is one of its most important characteristics, something that only became recognized with the advent of the wire or tape recorder. When experimenters recorded the sound of different instruments, snipped off the beginning of each note and then played the resulting sounds, even experienced musicians found it difficult to identify which instrument was being played to them. Apparently it is much more the initial transients that our ear recognizes than the later elements of the sound, and it is precisely these initial transients that are the most difficult to imitate electronically.

Electronic instruments changed radically with the advent of the synthesizer and then with the computer. The first synthesizer was the invention of Robert Moog. With it, the tone quality of almost any instrument could be produced with the turn of a knob, and initially we were regaled with demonstrations of imitation, though always suffering from that same problem of the initiation of the note. The next stage was incorporating the sampler, taking an individual note of an instrument as a sample, and then replicating it over a range as wide as, or even wider than, the original instrument could produce. Here there were greater problems because, for example, middle C on a French horn has a subtly different tone quality from the C above or below because their envelopes of overtones differ. A sampled middle C raised or lowered by an octave does not show those differences. This is another reason why electronic instruments never sound quite like the real thing. However, while both synthesizers and sampler-synthesizers were and remain useful for imitating other instruments, they were far more successful musically when they were used to create their own sounds. Here and especially with the advent of computerization, the potential of such instruments is limited only by the imagination of the player.

It is also the computer that has enabled the electronic organ to begin to compete more successfully with the pipe organ, as the technology improves. Some have incorporated recordings of real organs, and others have become better at analyzing and then reproducing true organ sound from their own resources. There is still much resistance to such competition from many organists, but one has to accept that there are advantages both in cost and in space. We noted some of the cost factors in chapter 7, and it is worth remembering, too, the amount of space that so many pipes and so much mechanism takes up. The internal complexity of the better computer electronic machines means that the cost saving is not as great as it was with the Hammond and with many simpler and cheaper purely electronic devices, but the sound today is nearer to the real thing than it was twenty or forty years ago.

Many instruments have been modified electronically. Initially this was, and often still is, just by attaching a microphone and plugging that and a loudspeaker into an amplifier, but that is simply amplification. A more effective method is fitting transducers under each string, but even this was initially only amplification, as with the Neo-Bechstein piano and early electric guitars. Some instruments respond to such treatment more easily than others. A flute, for example, can have a microphone instead of the normal stopper at the top of the bore, but it is more difficult to decide the best position for a microphone on other wind instruments. But experiments in this area are taking place in many parts of the world, for example with the 'ud and the saz in Turkey, as well as in our own culture.

Only when more elaborate circuitry, and often computerization, is involved do instruments become truly electronic, but once this happens, as with the synthesizers and the MIDI, there is no limit to what can be achieved. How much can be achieved by one person, live in performance, remains to be seen. At present, much of this sort of development can only be achieved by preparation, presetting effects; by recording, playback with electronic modification and so forth; or by team effort, one person playing and another manipulating the sound. One would think that to play, for example, a violin or a clarinet and simultaneously vary or multiply all or any constituents of its and any other sounds electronically for oneself, as one plays in public, would be impossible, but who knows what the future and advancing skills and equipment will bring?

Even in static societies, instruments and music are modified over time, and such modification increases rapidly after contact with the musics of other cultures, especially when those other cultures are seen to be "superior" or more fashionable than the traditional. The availability of the transistor radio and the cassette player, and with them our popular music and its styles, has had exponential effects on traditional musics worldwide. Our own culture is dynamic, rather than static, and musical styles and sounds in all genres have changed so much over the past fifty years, even more in the past twenty, that nobody can foretell what even the next decade will bring.

One can see such changes in the past, for example, the thirteenth-century Medieval Renaissance; the great changes in the early Baroque three centuries later, in the years between 1600 and 1670 or so; then those consequent on the Industrial Revolution only a century and a half later, between 1750 and 1800; and those from the mid-nineteenth century to the first half of the twentieth, the time scale always contracting. Not one of the instruments still in use when I entered the musical profession in 1950 was still unchanged in the orchestra twenty years later, and since then change has been more rapid still, and over almost all cultures in the world. We can look to the future only in anticipation and fascination to see what changes it will bring to all instruments, traditionally acoustic, recently electronic, and whatever the next technological development will be. Of one thing experience teaches us to be certain: that there will be further technological developments and that these will fascinate our children and our grandchildren as much as those detailed in these pages have fascinated us.

Note

1. Gleb Anfilov, *Physics and Music* (1966), 140–45.

INTERLUDE H

~

Newly Created, Recognized, or Discovered Instruments

Newly Created

What is a "new" instrument? Sometimes this is easily answered. The Moog synthesizer was something completely new, an entirely new concept in the creation of musical sounds. So were the *theremin* and the *ondes martenot* as well as a number of other electronic instruments. So were the steel drums of Trinidad. But was the electric guitar a new instrument? Initially it was an acoustic guitar with a microphone attached, feeding into an amplifier. When the microphone had been built in and changed to electronic pickups, the solid body replacing the acoustic one, and all the various attachments to the amplifier had been devised, had it then become new?[1] Or was it only modified, changed, or adapted, so that it could enjoy a new life?

The steel drums were an improvement on the use of brake drums and any other pieces of scrap metal, and it was certainly a new "invention" when Winston Simon found that by controlling the size of the dents in a garbage can he could tune them to specific pitches.[2] Each pan is a gong chime on a single body. Each marked-out area, separated from the next by heavily punched lines in the metal, is the equivalent of a single kettle of a Javanese *bonang*, but what gives the pans their unique sound is the leakage of vibrations across those lines. While each area, domed up by hammering from below, has its own pitch, enough vibration is shared by contiguous areas for them to produce the characteristic shimmer.

Other instruments changed as they traveled from one culture to another. The Greek *bouzouki*, so popular in nightclubs in urban Greece and today widely used elsewhere, is a conflation of the Neapolitan mandolin with the *saz*, a common instrument in Greece when that country was part of the Ottoman Empire. The bouzouki retained the original long neck of the saz but replaced its own small almond-shaped body with the mandolin's larger body, along with its characteristic multirib vaulted back, large end-clasp, scratch-plates on the belly, and change of belly angle at the bridge position, and added the mandolin's four double courses of strings with their machine tuning pegs. Was the bouzouki then a new instrument? Certainly it was new in the estimation of its users and hearers, for now it was a Greek instrument.

Another instrument that has been modified as it moved from one culture to another is the *didjeridu*, once the instrument solely of some tribes of the Australian aborigines, but now available in music and other shops everywhere. The didjeridu was and remains a ritual instrument in its own culture, used also for social music and dance. Traditionally it was the only melodic instrument within that culture, and it has therefore developed an extremely advanced and complex technique.[3] The basic method is that of the trumpet, though with everted rather than incurled lips. In addition to blowing the fundamental pitch, at least the first overtone is sounded, but on a wooden tube somewhat unevenly hollowed by natural agencies such as termites, these overtones are not harmonic. The player will also hum, sing, or speak down the tube while blowing, so that chords and other resultants are heard. All the while he maintains a continuous sound by the use of cheek-pumping. He accompanies this, if no second player with click sticks is available, by tapping highly complex rhythms on the side of the tube with a stick. The wooden instrument is the most common form, but bamboo is also used, the nodes knocked out with a fire-stick, and narrow-bore plastic drainpipe, two inches or so in diameter, was at one time a common substitute, just as the glass insulators from telegraph wires were a popular material for Aboriginal flint-knapping.

Now that the didjeridu is so widely used in our culture, new uses have been found for it in our own music. The instrument has often been adapted with a machine-bored wooden tube, nicely painted to look "authentic," and with instruction books suitably simplified for our capabilities, although few if any of our players have mastered all the subtleties to be heard in the hands of its traditional masters. Some of our players have even added key-covered fingerholes. Has this made it a new instrument? New to us, yes, but as an instrument, probably not.

How many of these changes could be regarded as an "invention"? Robert Moog's certainly was, as were Lev Termen's and Maurice Martenot's (for which, see chapter 8). We shall, in this interlude, meet this question again and again. When the Patent Office grants a patent, it is because it accepts the device as new, indeed an "invention." When these are modifications of bore or keywork to already existing wind instruments, are the results a new instrument or are they a new way of playing an old one? Adolphe Sax was granted many patents, but most, even the saxophone as we said in chapter 4, were for modifications to bore shape and mechanism.

These are all interesting questions in themselves, but they lead to a much more important one: Why are new instruments created? For the guitar, first, to make more sound and then the freedom to play in the new and then innovative musical styles of rock, then pop, and now many others. With the saxophone, according to Sax, to bring the quality of a string sound to the military band. For Moog, it was for the ability to create wholly new sounds, as had Termen and Martenot before him, and also to synthesize and imitate the sounds of other instruments, and then, with the addition of the sampler, to record sounds of any sort and manipulate them once again to create new sounds. We can guess that the Greek *kithara*, the big concert lyre, was created to produce something more expressive and also impressive, for the professional singer, than the simple tortoiseshell *lyra*.

Rubbing strings with a bow, undeniably an invention, allowed the sound of string instruments to be sustained, and to approach more nearly the qualities of the human voice. This has long been an ideal for instruments. Almost every new instrument within historical times has been compared to the human voice. Certainly this was true of the oboe, and of the clarinet, and of many others before and since.

The invention of the modern form of keyboard, we have already suggested, was for convenience, to save sliding the bridge of the monochord and to enable an instant shift from one pitch to another. Its adoption by the organist allowed the player, as discussed in chapter 7, to move more quickly from note to note than by pushing in and pulling out sliders, and permitted the use of harmony. Here we have the transference of a new invention to improve a preexisting instrument, just as elements of Theobald Boehm's keywork, invented for his first model flute, were transferred to all other woodwind instruments.

We know why Boehm invented his new flutes: again, first, to produce a greater sound, then adding his keywork to enable players to get their fingers around his new flutes, and with his second model, to improve the tuning and eradicate any inequalities of tone quality on his first model.

We know why the valves were invented for brass instruments: to provide them with a fully diatonic, and then chromatic, scale. The valves, certainly, were an invention, but how "new" were the instruments to which they were attached? And did such "new" inventions always meet acceptance? The valve horn may have been new, but the use of the valves, rather than the hand in the bell, was felt by many people, both players and hearers, to destroy its musical qualities—an attitude that persisted certainly to Brahms's time, as can be perceived by seeing the way in which he wrote for the instrument. Even later, the handhorn was taught in the Conservatoire in Paris into the twentieth century. John Hyde's late-eighteenth-century invention of the slide trumpet was preferred to the valve trumpet in England for a hundred years or more for much of the repertoire. The valved cornet was used for most new music that required the use of valves.

Many newly invented instruments will be found in these pages, and there are many others also,[4] as well as many where one is by no means sure whether the invention constitutes an instrument in its own right. An example of this is the MIDI system. Does this addition to an instrument, allowing it to reproduce other instruments as well as its own characteristics, constitute a new instrument?

What about new playing techniques? Is tapping on the strings of an electric guitar, instead of plucking them, creating a new instrument? Or multiphonics on woodwind instruments, produced by the adoption of unorthodox fingerings and other methods?[5] Did the *ison*, adding the hummed drone to a flute, create a new instrument? All three created new sounds.

Clearly there is no uniformity in the whys and wherefores of invention (and many more examples could be adduced), but the commonest seem to have been to improve the sound, to extend the repertoire and/or the range, and certainly in recent times, to create new sounds.

Newly Recognized

Instruments have been newly recognized when we have recently realized that an instrument that we thought behaved in a certain way actually behaves quite differently. An example of this is the whole family of plucked drums, those instruments that have a skin-covered resonator with a string rising vertically from the skin. These are found principally, perhaps exclusively, in India, with the *ananda lahari* and *gopi yantra* and similar folk instruments (see figure H.1). All are variable in pitch. Of those illustrated, if the player pushes together the wooden wishbones of the gopi yantra, the string tension is increased, raising its pitch. With the ananda lahari, pulling on the small drum, here a brass pot, that holds the free end of the string, has the same effect. Both are thus melodic instruments, moving from one pitch to another by those glides so familiar and important in Indian vocal music.

In the past, these had been regarded as a form of friction drum, but whereas rubbing the stick or string makes the drum growl or roar through the vibration of the drumhead, here it is obviously the string that sounds and the drum is no more than a resonator, just as with the banjo. On the banjo, the string is parallel with the drumskin; with these, it is vertical, which has the acoustic effect of doubling the frequency, so permitting a string of quite moderate tension to sound in a musically useful range.[6] Much larger instruments, similar to the ananda lahari but usually made of pottery, are also used, especially by village musicians in southern India. The gopi yantra is often used by bards to accompany their sung and chanted narratives.

Newly Discovered

Something that is only just beginning to be recognized as an instrument is the human body itself. At the beginning of this book, we postulated that clapping the hands inspired the use of sticks and stones that are both louder and less painful for extended performance. But handclapping persists everywhere as an accompaniment or even as the music itself, and it is by no means always the flat clap—cupping the hands to different degrees produces different pitches, controlled by the differing volume of enclosed air. Body-clapping is also common in some areas—there are ancient Greek pots showing lines of dancers slapping their posteriors.[7] This is not a practice that has died out.

Margaret Kartomi has described the techniques used in Aceh, on the northwest coast of Sumatra, as "the peak of body percussion technique."[8] A wide range of different

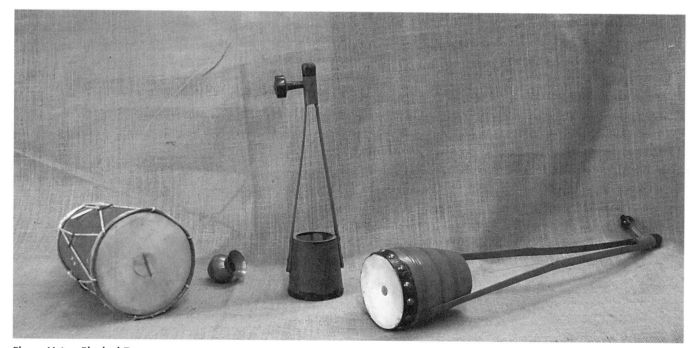

Figure H.1. Plucked Drums
L–R: *ananda lahari* (VI 156); two *gopi yantra* (VII 258a–b), all from India.

techniques is used there, the most resonant being slaps by men on the lower chest, amplified by deep breathing to expand the lungs (women slap the upper chest instead, a less resonant area). They also slap all other parts of the body within reach. Lucy Durán suggested that the finger-snapping techniques and stamps of flamenco dancers were even more elaborate.[9] Doubtless, as this subject receives further study, many other examples will come to light.

Professor Kartomi suggested that foot-stamping might be regarded as "quasi body-percussion," and here again further study and discussion will determine whether it can be regarded as true body percussion or an extension thereof.[10] We must be aware, though, of instruments played by stamping on them with the feet, for example, the Andaman Island shields.[11] If bare feet on the ground are included as body percussion, can we also include the extension provided by the use of prepared footwear, for example in tap dancing and clog dancing? Or the Roman *scabellum* shown in figure 1.13? Since at the time of writing this subject was presented at a conference only months ago, one could regard this as wholly newly discovered, and certainly it is an excitingly new area to investigate and discuss.

We have already described two recently discovered instruments, both so simple that they have been overlooked. One was the harmonic flute *tilinca*, often just any old bit of tubing (see figure 3.15) and therefore recognized only when an ethnomusicologist such as Tiberiu Alexandru found it in use. The other was the tongue-duct flute (see figure 3.6), about which Ernst Emsheimer and Cajsa Lund have published, whereas previously it seemed just to be a broken instrument lacking its block or duct.

Doubtless there are many more undiscovered instruments out there, for it is seldom that a new book on instruments or on other cultures appears that does not in-

clude something we have never seen before. Nor, as one of my grandchildren taught me, are there any bounds on the ingenuity of humanity.[12]

Notes

1. Whether such changes altered the classification position (for which see the afterword) of electric guitars from chordophone to electrophone was disputed between Hugh Davies and myself. He believed that such instruments had been sufficiently changed that they should now be treated as electrophones, whereas I believed that they remained chordophones, because their sound was generated by plucking a string.

2. Peter Seeger, *Steel Drums* (1961), 3. Jeffrey Thomas's account ("Steel Band/Pan" in *Encyclopedia of Percussion*, ed. John H. Beck [1995], 297–331) is more complex, but "Spree" Simon still receives a credit as *an*, if not *the*, inventor.

3. Trevor A. Jones, "The Didjeridu," *Studies in Music* 1 (1967): 23–55; 2 (1968): 111.

4. Further examples will be found in my article "The Creation of New Instruments," GSJ 59 (2006): 3–11.

5. Bruno Bartolozzi, *New Sounds for Woodwind* (London, 1967, 2nd ed. 1982).

6. C. J. Adkins et al., "Frequency-Doubling Chordophones," *Musica Asiatica* 3 (1981): 1–9; Laurence E. R. Picken, "The 'Plucked' Drums," *Musica Asiatica* 3 (1981): 29–33.

7. Curt Sachs, *Geist und Werden der Musikinstrumente* (1929), Taf. 1, Abb. 3.

8. In the keynote paper "On the Cusp of Music and Dance: The Art of Body Percussion as a Cross-cultural Phenomenon and Expression of Identity and Social Change in Aceh, Indonesia," presented to the British Forum for Ethnomusicology Conference, London, April 2005.

9. In a verbal comment after the presentation of Kartomi's paper.

10. In conversation after her paper.

11. Sachs, *Geist und Werden*, Taf. 1, Abb. 4.

12. Jeremy Montagu, "The Eliphone," GSJ 51 (1998): 196–97, describing the musical use of a plastic triangular binding-strip.

AFTERWORD

~

Archaeology and Other -ologies

"The proper study of mankind is man," said Alexander Pope, and "study of" is as good a translation of *-ology* as any other.[1] Such study began in Europe in the sixteenth and seventeenth centuries and led to the Renaissance. In Italy, *accademie* were established, with similar bodies in France and Germany, and in Britain with the Royal Society, founded in 1662.[2] Today that society is purely for science as we understand the word today, but at that time "science," as its name indicates, was taken to cover all aspects of knowledge.[3]

Initially, and in some respects for long after, musical instruments were regarded as curiosities, something to display in a cabinet with no interest in their function or capability. However, with the beginnings of the scientific approach, the remnants of earlier times began to be recognized as the evidence of the work and culture of our ancestors and predecessors and to be regarded as antiquities. Thus what we now call archaeology came into being even before that term was first so called,[4] as the study of antiquities and of antiquity itself. Equally the exotica brought back by the early explorers as souvenirs and curiosities began to be recognized as the work of people not unlike ourselves, and this was the start of anthropology.

The antiquaries, as archaeologists were then called, came to realize that the material relics of earlier times were not all coeval, that some were earlier than others. Prehistory had to be divided into discrete parts—a process that has continued to the present day, for new discoveries continually result in the need for new categories and the redistribution of old ones.

Briefly, prehistoric time was divided into four great periods: the Paleolithic, Neolithic, Bronze, and Iron ages. Between the Paleolithic and Neolithic—that is, the Old and New Stone—ages, the Mesolithic, or Middle Stone Age, led an uneasy existence, sometimes being recognized in its own right, sometimes being absorbed into either or both of its neighbors. Even today there is no general agreement for the dating of these ages, and even where there is agreement, they vary widely in different parts of the world. The earliest hominids, the ancestors of humanity, date from anything between four million and two million years ago, and the earliest dates for *Homo sapiens*, modern man, are anywhere around 100,000 to 90,000 years in the past, still in the Paleolithic period, arriving in Europe about 50,000 years ago. The Bronze Age started in different parts of the world between 5000 and 2000 BC. Between these two ages came the Neolithic, which is even more difficult to date because authorities are divided as to what defines that period: was it the invention of pottery, the start of agriculture, or the establishment of towns and cities? There is no agreement, and all three happened at different times in different places.

Between the Neolithic and Bronze ages was then inserted the Chalcolithic. This was a period when native metal was not smelted and alloyed with tin to make bronze but was treated, as in Central and South America, as though it were a stone and hammered into a desired shape, giving that era the name Chalcolithic, or Copper-Stone, Age. Even less persistent than the Mesolithic was the Eolithic, or Dawn of Stone, Age. This is where the accidental tools resulting from our initial stone clappers in our first chapter might have belonged, a time before our ancestors had learned to chip stone into a desired tool pattern, but when they were able to recognize the utility of a sharp edge if one by chance should come to hand.

Each of these periods was subdivided, and most of these subdivisions are known by the name of the find-spot where their characteristic patterns of artifacts were first recognized. Neanderthal, a valley in Germany, is one of the best known, giving its name to a species of genus *Homo* earlier than *Homo sapiens*, one that was thought to be without any art or music, although new discoveries are changing that perception. Because the earlier antiquaries and archaeologists were working in Europe, most of these divisions have European names. This is inevitably now leading to resentment as the science of archaeology spreads to areas where people lived and worked much earlier. Humanity spread across the world from Africa long before Europe was first colonized, and even longer before the first arrivals crossed into the Americas. We can expect to see changes in these terms.

European scholars in the seventeenth and eighteenth centuries began to study the peoples of areas that explorers were beginning to open up. Many books were published with illustrations of people, their tools, and the flora and fauna discovered during these explorations, and this is why we can see musical instruments from exotic lands in the pages of Michael Praetorius's *Syntagma Musicum* and in other works. The antiquaries among such scholars regarded those peoples who were still in a premetallic culture as living representatives and equivalents of the European Paleolithic and Neolithic peoples. This approach gradually became less fashionable, and when such peoples were studied for their own sakes, anthropology, the study of humanity, became recognized as a science in its own right. The difference between anthropology and ethnography (from *anthropos*, Greek for "humankind," and *ethnos*, Greek for "a people" or "a tribe") is today mainly one of approach, ethnography studying the material culture, and anthropology the sociology and the way in which people lived. *Ethnology* had been an older term that was replaced by *anthropology*.

Within the study of the material culture of other peoples came that subdiscipline of their musical instruments and music. Initially, the leaders in this, in the nineteenth century, were German, and the field was called *Vergleichende Musikwissenschaft*, the German *-wissenschaft* being roughly the equivalent of our *-ology*. *Vergleichende* means "comparative," and so in English the study of exotic music was first called "comparative musicology." As with the idea that primitive people living in a lithic culture were the living fossils of our remote ancestors, this approach also became unfashionable, because all music should be studied in its own right rather than compared with other musics. In 1950 Jaap Kunst therefore coined the term *Ethnomusicology*. At much the same time, *primitive* became a taboo word, not merely as politically incorrect but also as factually false, for there was little if anything that was primitive in most such cultures.

Today, we are beginning to look askance at *ethnomusicology* as a term, partly because we are all *ethnē*; partly because the Greeks used that word often with a suggestion of "foreign," whereas ethnomusicology is now recognized as an approach to studying all types of music, ours, theirs, and anyone else's; and partly because *ethnic* has often come to imply cheap, nasty, and fake when applied to goods in our shops or food in our restaurants. The term *World Music* has been taken by a movement involved in music in schools, along with the casual use and mixture of exotic musics into our culture, and ours into theirs. In addition, ethnomusicologists (to continue the use of the word for the present) came to realize that they study the whole field of music, whereas the musicologists study only that very small fraction that originated in Europe. Thus there is a growing movement for the ethnomusicologists to take over the term *musicology* and leave those who study Bach and Beethoven to find themselves some more local term, such as *endomusicology*.

Classification of Instruments

Before a large mass of material can be described in any scientific manner, it must be sorted into coherent groups. This process is called *classification* and is done by gathering objects that share similar characteristics into piles, as it were, and then grouping piles into heaps, and heaps into mounds, and so forth. On the whole, this works better than separating the mass into divisions, those divisions into sections, and so on, and the process of gathering has become the accepted scientific method.[5] The first question, always, is that of criteria: how shall we sort them?

There is an almost infinite number of ways. One can classify by materials, as the Chinese did before 2000 BC, putting together into one group all those instruments with strings, into another all those of stone, then all those with skins, and then all those of bamboo; other materials such as clay and metal were introduced later. Another method is by use, and this is a way that is often used around the world within any one community: for example, all those that accompany dancing, those for singing, those played by women, those of hunters, others used by boys before they are initiated, and so forth. Playing position is another system often used: all that are held vertically, or all held horizontally, those played resting on the ground, and so on. Color is used in some places—brown, red, or white, for instance. One could also use size, although that is not very useful, grouping instruments in three- or six-inch steps, perhaps. One could even classify alphabetically, all those whose name begins with the letter G, and so on. All these and many more are classification systems, and many of them are in use around the world. The subject of classification and its history as a whole is a fascinating one, and Margaret Kartomi's survey is by far the best available.[6]

The essential factor, though, in any scientific system, as is normally the concern in our culture, is that each instrument must have only one possible place, and this is why none of the above systems can be satisfactory outside its own culture or area. Using the first letter of the name can work in only one language. The way an instrument is held may vary from culture to culture, and indeed from player to player. Using color would break down very quickly with us where, for instance, the first clarinets were pale brown wood, then had ivory mounts added that were white or cream in color, or were even made wholly of ivory, then were commonly of blackwood and also often made of metal, either brass or silver, and now you can buy clarinets of artificial materials in all the colors of the rainbow. Classification by use can work only within one culture, even only in a part of that culture, and fails as soon as instruments can be used both for dance music and to accompany song. It can seldom be exported to another tribe or group because what one people use for one purpose, the next may use for an entirely different purpose. Nor can material be useful when flutes can be made of reed, wood, bone, ivory, glass, china, metal, plastic, or any other material. Hence the Hornbostel and Sachs system, which is based on the sounding material—the object itself; a membrane, or more properly a diaphragm; a string; or the air—has been generally adopted today as the only possible cross-cultural system that can be applied worldwide.[7] Because it is a numeric system, it can be free of cultural or linguistic bias, as we shall show below.

The Hornbostel and Sachs (more easily H-S) system, first published in 1914, grew out of one proposed by Victor-Charles Mahillon in 1880.[8] That, in its turn, derived from the Hindu system of the Nātyaśāstra, attributed to the sage Bharata who lived around the beginning of the Christian era.[9] This may have been the codification of something even older and divides instruments into "stretched" (strings), "covered" (drums), "hollow" (winds), and "solid" (the nonskin percussion). Mahillon translated these, with words rooted in Greek, as *chordophones, membranophones, aerophones,* and *autophones,* respectively.[10] Hornbostel and Sachs accepted the first three of Mahillon's terms, but preferred *idio-*

phones to *autophones.*[11] To these, Canon Galpin added *electrophones* in 1937.[12]

With all systems, including H-S, there are anomalies and problems. Some of these John Burton and I tried to address in 1971.[13] Our proposed system was based on the Linnean, introduced by Swedish botanist Carl von Linné from 1735, and today the universal basis (with a good deal of subsequent modification) for the classification of all the natural species of the animal and vegetable kingdoms.[14] It seemed to us more logical, and in particular much easier, for adding newly discovered types of instruments and coping with hybrids, and it aroused some interest. However, much influenced by Laurence Picken's remarks,[15] I decided that one is better off with a system that people will use than suggesting one that they won't. In addition, the H-S system has the overwhelming advantage that it is culture-free.

Every system that is based on the names of instruments carries with it a load of cultural connotations, even bias, because within each culture, the names are culture specific. If one uses "guitar" as a type name, then everyone has an immediate mental picture of Elvis Presley, the Beatles, the Who, Andrés Segovia, Julian Bream, or whoever your favorite may be, and of the instruments that we saw in their hands. If that name is then applied as a type name to an African, Chinese, Japanese, or whatever culture's instrument, all those people will be insulted and will immediately, and not surprisingly, take considerable umbrage. If instead one uses "321.322" as a name, everybody can be happy. I can explain what that is in English, using as my verbal example a guitar, while others can do so in their own languages with a verbal example that fits that number in their own instrumentarium. Similarly, so long as we all refer to "121.2," it does not matter whether, in our own language, we call it a trump, a *vargan,* a *guimbarde,* a *Maultrommel,* a *genggong,* a Jew's harp, or anything else.

One other style of system that deserves a mention is the pictorial or schematic, the best known being Oskár Elschek's *Zeichen* and Mantle Hood's *organograms.*[16] The main problem with these and other similar systems that depend on the precise placement, direction, and length of lines on a little drawing is that they need a very steady hand, rulers, set squares, and a fine-pointed pen, as well as, until one is very accustomed to them, frequent reference to the manual to remind oneself of what each little squiggle means and precisely where it should be placed. With the now universal use of computers, they would also require very elaborate graphics programs to succeed.

I must admit that the similar problem of remembering the meaning of a string of numbers is one of the difficulties with the Hornbostel and Sachs, to which we now return. Each of the great families—idiophones, membranophones, chordophones, and aerophones—bears a number, 1 to 4, respectively (plus 5 for Galpin's electrophones), with successive numbers for lower criteria. To elaborate with an example, 1 is for idiophone, 11 for struck idiophone, and 111 for directly struck idiophone. That is a difficult term, but the verbal definition clarifies it: "that the player can apply clearly defined strokes and that the instrument itself is equipped for this kind of percussion," in contrast with 112 for indirectly struck idiophones, for which "the intention of the instrument is to yield clusters of sounds or noises, and not to let individual strokes be perceived," in other words, rattles and such things.[17] Narrowing the classification further, then follows 111.1, for concussion idiophones or clappers, two sonorous objects directly struck together, as distinct from 111.2, percussion idiophones, where one sonorous object is directly struck with or against a nonsonorous object, whether the hand, a beater, the ground, or anything else. Further figures are added for shape: 111.11, sticks; 111.12, plaques; 111.13, troughs; 111.14, vessels. Within the last, we have 111.141 for castanets and 111.142 for cymbals, to which I added 111.143 for bells after acquiring a pair of Nigerian double-bells that are struck concussively against each other.

Looking at it in this way makes it appear to be a divisive system, rather than the cumulative type that we said was preferable above, and so initially I took it to be. However, Nazir Ali Jairazbhoy's brilliant "Explication" resolves any such doubts, and with the use of trees, similar to those that Burton and I used in our appendix 3, he shows that it is indeed a cumulative system.[18]

One must remember that Hornbostel and Sachs subtitled their publication *Ein Versuch*, a trial or an experiment, and they expected it to result in discussion with their colleagues and gradual improvement and elaboration. That this did not happen to any significant extent is probably due to the date of publication, coinciding with the beginning of World War I, when most people had other things to think of for the next four years. As a result, there has never been a concerted effort to fill some of its gaps, nor to overcome the basic problem of any numerical system: that one can extend it longitudinally as far as one wishes, as it becomes expedient to define smaller groups with fewer characteristics in common, but it is impossible to extend it laterally because there is nothing between 1 and 2 save for a subdivision of 1. This can cause problems when introducing a newly discovered or newly recognized type of instrument.

For example, many string instruments have a neck that runs right through the body, projecting at the lower end (we have encountered above many such instruments under the names of spike lutes, spike fiddles, etc.), and many have a separate neck that is attached to the top of the body, like our guitars and violins. There is an intermediate stage, however: the half-spike lute or fiddle, where the neck enters the body but stops partway down and neither is attached to the upper end of the body nor projects through the bottom. Here we need a number between 321.31, spike lutes, and 321.32, necked lutes, but none is available. The ideal solution would be to move the necked instruments to 321.33, but unless every organologist, worldwide, would agree to this, it is not a really helpful suggestion. Therefore I must use 321.33 for the half-spike lutes.

Because new instruments are invented and others are recognized, I have found it useful to introduce other new numbers or modifications. The first, to take them in their numerical order, is to move the slit drum from percussion tubes (111.231) to 111.242.3, a subsection of bells, because the equivalence between wooden bells and slit drums can easily be shown, as it was here, or even to their own section of 111.243. Next, we need a new section within gongs for those with a divided surface to cover the West Indian steel drums, 111.241.12, for each is an individual multiple gong; when they are used in sets, as they usually are, then it becomes 111.241.22. Another shape of percussion vessel is the trough, 111.243, or if slit drums take that number, then 111.244. The rock gong, even though we have seen it to be possibly prehistoric in origin, was unknown in 1914 and comes at the end of the directly struck percussion as 111.25.

A shape of shaken idiophone that they forgot, though they must have heard it in the theater often enough, is the great sheet of metal shaken for thunder, so 112.14 is needed for the sheet rattle or thunder sheet. They marked "(individual) friction plaques" as being unknown, but the musical saw is an example, just as sandpaper blocks are friction sticks. Returning to the theater, the wind machine, cloth over a rotating barrel, is a friction sheet, so again we have a new number, 134.

As we saw in chapter 2 with the bronze drums of the Karen and the Dongson and other instruments, thin sheets of nonelastic materials behave in exactly the same way as stretched membranes, and therefore we need either to change the name *membranophone* to *diaphragmaphone* or, and probably better, to add the two italicized words to their definition of *membranophones*: "The sound is excited by tightly-stretched membranes *or diaphragms*."

This implies that we need to fit the bronze drums in somewhere, and because shape is a criterion and into none of those listed will they fit, we are probably best off with their own section, 211.27.

Two earlier definitions are invalid. The first, of 211.211, single-skin cylindrical drums, says that a second skin that is there only as part of the lacing device to attach the main skin and that is not used for beating, does not count as a skin. However, it should count, because it does affect the sound, whether it is struck or not. The obvious example is our side-drum or snare-drum. Nobody beats on the lower head, but the drum would not work without it, because there would be nothing for the snares to vibrate against. And therefore the word *usable* must be deleted from the definition of 211.212, double-skin drums—any drum with two skins, usable or not, belongs here. More arguable is the definition of 211.211.2, closed cylindrical drums. To my mind, if the drum is a vessel, whether cauldron-shape (kettledrums) or saucepan-shape (closed cylindrical), it should be a kettledrum. It will behave in the same way acoustically whatever the shape of the vessel, whether it is "bowl- or dish-shaped" or "tubular," and if one looks at the range of shapes that have been used for our timpani over the centuries, it is clear that they all belong together. Finally among the membranes, as we have seen in interlude H, the plucked drums are quite different from the friction drums and are string instruments; therefore, 22 must become 33. (It is probably safer to leave 22 as a blank with the note "plucked drums, now 33" than to move up the present 23 to fill the gap.)

Save for that and the new 321.33 for half-spike lutes, the only other change among the chordophones is the new 322.212.3 for harps with strings in two or more parallel planes for the Renaissance arpa doppia and the Welsh triple harp. 322.212.1 was for a single plane of strings, and 322.212.2 for two planes crossing each other like the Lyon double harp, but they forgot the triple harp.

There are far more serious problems among the aerophones, so serious that John Burton and I found it impossible to resolve them. That was the main reason we designed our own system. To start with, there is a basic division between the "free aerophones—The vibrating air is not confined by the instrument" and the "wind instruments proper—The vibrating air is confined within the instrument itself." But this could apply to string instruments also, for instance. The violin depends for much of its sound on the vibrating air confined within the instrument. With the exception of the flutes, it is not the air that generates the sound but the reed or the lips. The air amplifies the sound, the length or volume of the air column or body affecting its pitch, as it does with a slit drum, for instance, but it does not generate the sound.

The other main problem is that while most of the "free aerophones" are defined as "idiophonic interruptive idiophones or reeds," the definitions for many of them also cover the reeds that are used in normal reed instruments. An oboe or bassoon reed is a concussion reed, and so on. And then, if I may say so without disrespect to two scholars of far greater stature and knowledge than I, it was stupid to divide 422, "reedpipes," by whether they had double reeds (oboes) or single reeds (clarinets) when (1) it is the shape of the bore, cylindrical or expanding, that affects the sound and acoustical behavior, not the type of reed; (2) many of the examples can be, and are, played with either type of reed; and (3) upon arrival of an unknown instrument in a museum, any curator can see whether the bore is cylindrical or expanding but may have no way of telling what sort of reed used to be stuck into the end of it.

The only answer is to leave things as they are and make the best of them, with the usual few necessary additions. The first is 412.15 for the instruments that Canon Galpin and Henry Balfour called "retreating reeds."[19] Second, there is a minor error under 412.22. The bull-roarer does turn on its axis, but the whirring disk and the ventilating fan rotate in their own plane, like sirens, and therefore must move up one into 412.21.

The first of the "wind instruments proper," 42, are the "edge instruments or flutes," 421—which leaves us with the problem of Picken's "edgetone instruments that are not flutes," such as those double disks, with a central hole passing through both sides of the disk, that one places between the lips and teeth. These are made from tinplate, bottle tops, or fruit-stones and are sometimes called "widgeon whistles" or "labial whistles," and one plays them by breathing in and out through the hole. We should follow Picken and assign them the number 420.1.[20]

No separate number is assigned to the notch flute, but it is sufficiently distinct from the end-blown flute with a plain edge that it should have its own section. One would like it to follow the end-blown flute (421.11), but 421.12 is already occupied by side-blown flutes and 421.13 by vessel flutes, so it seems better to give it 421.14 than to shift everything else.

Duct flutes are divided between those with an external duct, 421.21, and those with an internal duct,

421.22. The H-S system suggests including with the latter those Native American flutes that have an internal *and* an external duct, but they are so different that it seems better to give them their own designation as 421.23. And if duct flutes with a stopped end without fingerholes are 421.221.31, then those Moroccan flutes that *do* have fingerholes, the lowest of which is not fingered but provides a side-hole substitute for the open end, should be 421.221.32.

The reed instruments we have to leave as they are, despite the comments above, but among the reedpipes with free reeds, 422.3, we might place the side-blown horns that use a free reed rather than the player's lips in a group of their own since they have only a single hole in the apex (like many African side-blown horns) rather than the number of fingerholes that those of bamboo or cane possess, and call them 422.33.

With trumpets, one has to ask, what is a "natural trumpet"? In H-S, it is an instrument "without extra devices to alter pitch." If a fingerhole is an "extra device to alter pitch," however, we need to recognize that not all conch trumpets are natural, as we saw above from Fiji, and that many, perhaps even most, African side-blown horns have a hole in the tip for that purpose.

We also have to delete the word *throughout* in the definition of 423.231, valve bugles: "The tube is conical throughout." The inventor who can produce a conical tuning slide will make a fortune. And as Arthur Benade pointed out, today it is the horn whose tubing is predominantly cylindrical and the trumpet that is predominantly conical, but if we keep the H-S numbers and names and forget those definitions, which apply only to our own orchestral instruments, do we with our own instruments know what is a horn and what is a trumpet.[21]

It was precisely such additions, amendments, and discussions that Hornbostel and Sachs were expecting when they published their *Systematik* as *Ein Versuch*. They expected, too, that we and others would expand their categories to cater for the finer and more precise definitions. For example, several of their categories go down to 9 figures, and with suffixes to show how the instruments are played to even more; others have no more than three figures. This is not because those are simpler categories but because it is left to us to do some of the work of classification, to look at those groups of instruments and to see the smaller piles and heaps for which they have given us only the mounds. They provided, in their introduction, an example of how this might be done among the members of the xylophone family. There is still much for future generations to do in this area.

Scales and Music

However many instruments we have, we cannot produce music until we decide what notes they can or should play. There is an infinite number of potential notes in the octave, and every musical culture has to decide which of them to use. Almost all peoples of the world do recognize the octave, even if only as the difference between what men sing and what women sing. We speak of "singing in unison," but when men and women sing unisons together, they are not true unisons (*unison* means "as one"). They are singing the same note-name, but at that distance apart that we call the *octave* (from the Latin for "eight," because we have eight notes when we go from A up through the alphabet to G and then to the next A), the women an octave higher than the men.[22]

Other peoples have different numbers of steps to the octave. Five steps, a pentatonic scale (from the Greek *penta*, "five"), is very common (four is much less usual and three very rare). One often sees references to *the* pentatonic scale, meaning the equivalent of the five black notes of our piano, and something like this is not unusual in many parts of the world, although which note you start on makes a big difference to the order of different sized steps, whether you start on F♯, C♯, or any other note. This is not the only pentatonic scale, however, because the widths of the five steps vary quite considerably from one people to another. In some places, the steps are nearly equal, for instance, in Java where they have two different scales, one of which, *slendro*, has five steps that vary only slightly in size.

To measure intervals we use a unit called the "cent," our equivalent of the millimeter and equally artificial but equally useful. There are 100 cents in an equal-tempered semitone (any one of the steps from note to adjacent note, white or black, of our piano) and 1,200 in an octave.[23] Five equal steps would each cover 240 cents, but while three of the steps in the slendro scale are usually around that size, one is usually wider, up to about 260 cents, and another rather narrower, perhaps as little as 220 cents.[24] Since 10 cents (one tenth of a semitone) is usually reckoned to be the smallest interval that most people can perceive, the difference of 20 cents, and usually less, between the average step and the wider or the narrower step of the slendro, is very little. The other Javanese scale, *pelog*, has seven steps—although they often use only five, or occasionally six, of these—but these seven unequal steps are very different from our unequal seven steps. They are different, too, from the steps of some other heptatonic (Greek *hepta* = "seven") scales of the Southeast Asian mainland, where, as in parts of Central Africa, one finds equi-heptatonic scales, seven equal steps.

Our heptatonic major scale is unequal, with steps of two sizes, whole tones from C to D, D to E, F to G, G to A, and A to B, with semitones, only half as wide, from E to F and B to C—a scale with seven equal steps sounds very different.

Many other heptatonic scales exist, or have existed in the past, using all sorts of intervals. Ellis was the first to publish precise measurements of exotic scales.[25] Since then, many other sets of measurements have been published in the ethnomusicological literature, sometimes as the basis for equally exotic hypotheses.[26] The one thing that all the measurements have in common is that while an equi-heptatonic scale has steps of 171 cents each, if some steps are going to be narrower than that, others must be wider if all are going to fit into a 1,200-cent octave. Thus if on our piano we want to keep to our conventional seven steps, some of which are to be whole tones, we cannot have more than five of them, and the others must be semitones. If all steps were whole tones, we could fit only six of them into the octave, a hexatonic scale (Greek *hexa* = "six"), as Debussy did when he wrote music using the whole-tone scale, six steps to the octave (C, D, E, F#, G#, A#, C, if one starts on C).

The 100-cent semitone and 200-cent whole-tone steps of our current equal-tempered scale are a very modern convention. They were first devised between 1550 and 1600 by a number of theorists, but they were used only sporadically thereafter until the mid-nineteenth century. In our modern orchestras and choirs, they are used only when the presence of a piano or other modern keyboard instrument, or the performance of atonal music, makes them necessary.[27]

Every musical culture has its preferences and its own conceptions of the ideal of being "in tune." Ours is a pure consonance with the absence of beats, those vibrations that are heard when two people playing the same note are slightly out of tune and that are also heard when two or more different notes of the harmonic series are played together but again slightly out of tune. This absence of beats can only be achieved by using a scale made up precisely of those intervals of the harmonic series that correspond to the notes of a scale. A more complete series can be seen in figure 0.1 in Explanations and Definitions; here we include only those useful for this purpose (see figure AW.1). It will be noticed that three harmonics are missing here, numbers 11, 13, and 14. These do not fit our preferred series of pitches, as we have noted previously. The pitches that they would represent can be determined from the others: if G is a fifth up from the lower C, F is a fifth down from the upper C, and so on.

If we start a scale on the eighth harmonic, where the notes of the series come close enough together to do so, we can build a scale with "natural" steps and produce chords with beautifully pure intervals.[28] This works very well melodically and harmonically with voices, for example in a church choir, and with any instrument whose pitches were not preestablished by a tuner and then fixed. It cannot work on, for example, a keyboard instrument that has been tuned to these "pure" or "natural" intervals starting on C, because the moment one wishes to change key from C major (in which it sounds lovely), one immediately strikes a problem. If we use the numbers of each harmonic as the integers of a ratio, it becomes obvious that the ratio 10:9 must be smaller than 9:8, and so we have two different sizes of whole tone: from C to D, a major tone of 204 cents, and from D to E, a minor tone of 182 cents. If our scale is to begin major tone, minor tone, semitone, as the harmonic series provides, we cannot start it on D on a keyboard that has been tuned to C because the first step, D to E, has been fixed by the tuner as a minor tone whereas we now want a major tone.

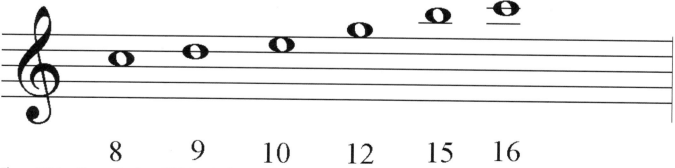

Figure AW.1. Harmonics from Which to Make a Musical Scale

This had already been recognized as a problem in ancient Greece, where the philosopher and mathematician Pythagoras came up with the logical solution of having only one size of whole tone, the major tone of 9:8 that measures 204 cents. However, the interval of a pure major third, C to E, 10:8 or 5:4, measures 386 cents, the sum of the two different whole tones, the major tone (204 cents) plus the minor tone (182 cents). Pythagoras's two major tones, 204 + 204 cents, produced a horrible third of 408 cents, wildly sharp. The sevenths were also very sharp, but, for melodic use, a sharp leading note, the base for the last step of the scale, was rather liked because it pushed the music on toward the keynote.

This process, changing the tuning of one or more notes of the scale to produce more practical results, is called tempering, so this example is known as the Pythagorean temperament. Once the use of the organ became common in church choirs, from the ninth century on, the Pythagorean temperament had perforce to be adopted, and its use spread into instrumental music also, with the invention of the string keyboards, such as the harpsichord, in the early 1400s.

The major third was regarded as a dissonance in the Middle Ages, and this was because in the Pythagorean temperament, at 408 cents, it was indeed dissonant. This had not mattered in ancient Greece, where they did not use harmony as we do, but in the Middle Ages it did matter. When harmonic theory progressed to the stage where it wanted to use the third, the Pythagorean temperament had to be abandoned so that one with a better third could be adopted in its place. Nobody, though, wanted to go back to two different whole tones, for keyboard instruments were by then in use everywhere, and therefore a new size of whole tone was constructed, dividing a pure major third (386 cents) in half, taking its average or mean. This is why it is called the meantone temperament.

This is not the place to go into the full history of European temperament, nor into the mathematical problems behind it. It may suffice to say that the problems are inherent in Nature because our pure, beat-free intervals do not add up as we would wish them to do. A fifth, C to G or the ratio 3:2, measures 702 cents; an octave, C to C, 2:1, measures 1,200 cents. And so if we pile fifth upon fifth, C to G, G to D, D to A, and so on, we shall never return to C, only, after the necessary twelve steps, to B♯, 24 cents higher than C. The major third measures, as we have said, 386 cents, and piling three of them on top of each other, C to E, E to G♯, and G♯ to C, give us only 1,158 cents, woefully flat of the octave, 42 cents short. As we try to tune our instruments, the better in tune the

thirds are, the worse the fifths become, and vice versa. The history of temperament since the late fifteenth century has been that of compromise: to make the fifths as pure as possible without rendering the thirds intolerable.

Our modern equal temperament has fifths that are almost pure (700 cents instead of 702) and thirds that are not quite as bad as Pythagorean (400 instead of 408) but still quite nasty, a lot worse than pure (386). The thirds are bad enough that organs were still tuned in meantone in the 1850s, albeit a meantone that was a better compromise than the one that had been first devised in 1523.[29] Harpsichords and pianos have sounds that die away fairly quickly, so that the built-in pulsations of the equal-tempered third are no worse than unpleasant. Because the organ can sustain a chord almost indefinitely, however, those thirds were intolerable to a musician's ear, hence the adherence to a form of meantone or other unequal (often called irregular) temperament.

Even though meantone had been improved over the centuries by making the thirds slightly wider than pure and thus improving the fifths, as composers became more adventurous and wanted to change key more often during the course of a piece of music, if they had started in a key where the note between A and G was tuned to G♯, they might need to have an A♭ instead. The resulting chord was so out of tune that the beats between the E♭ and the G♯ were so fast that they howled like a wolf. And so some keyboards had the G♯/A♭ key cut across its middle and provided with two strings or pipes, so that one could be tuned to each note. The same might be done to D♯/E♭ because these four notes were the worst affected by meantone. For the same reason, all the flutes that Johann Joachim Quantz built for himself and for his royal master, Frederick the Great, had two keys on the foot joint, instead of the more usual one, one for E♭ and the other for D♯.[30] A number of other makers followed his example. Both Pythagorean and meantone scales, because of the way they are constructed, have to have two different sizes of semitone, with the result that sharps and flats, normally just one note on the keyboard, are not the same as each other. In meantone, the difference between them is the 42 cents that we met a few lines above.

Other makers and players went much further. Vicentino's *arcicembalo* of 1555 divided every key, some more than once, so that every interval might be in tune on that harpsichord. There have been modern equivalents with thirty or more keys to the octave, such as the Janko piano, but these like the arcicembalo, as well as being expensive, tend to tax the player's memory to an excessive extent, trying to remember which key went with which other key to be in tune in any particular context. Pianists and organists today (few of whom tune their own instruments) put up with equal temperament, and most other musicians, save when playing with piano or organ, keep as well in tune as they can with their colleagues, keeping intervals as pure as possible by making notes a little sharper or a little flatter, as may be needed, than they would be in equal temperament on the piano.

String players can move a finger very slightly up or down a fingerboard, and singers have no problem with it, but wind players have to fudge things by lipping the pitch a little up or down. This is why it is a mistake to make wind instruments too rigidly "in tune," even though that might make things easier for beginners. They need to be flexible enough to allow for a little variation in this way.

One effect of equal temperament was the loss of color in music. With earlier temperaments, each key was slightly different in its intervals. Even without having perfect pitch, one could tell a difference between the keys; some were brighter, some were darker, and composers would often choose a key accordingly. This was certainly true in the various meantone temperaments, and it remained so in what are called the irregular temperaments, as may be heard in works such as Bach's *Well-Tempered Clavichord*, where the music in each of the preludes and fugues suits the character of each key.[31] This is also the origin of the numerous theories and conceptions of color in music—a difference of tuning produced a perception of a different color and led to the invention of the color organ that Scriabin included in some of his music. It was a purely subjective perception, though, for few composers ever agreed in assigning the same color to the same key.

With our own scale so firmly fixed to the harmonic series and our musical harmony so heavily biased toward thirds, fourths, and fifths, it is difficult for us to comprehend the musics of those other peoples who do not hear things that way. And yet, around the world, it is only in the Indian subcontinent that we hear music akin to our own. There, tuning is even more precise than ours, for they commonly work against a drone as we have already discussed. In their theoretical basis for scales, dividing the octave into 22 *srutis*, they have a similar concept to our major and minor tones, with some whole tones larger than others.[32]

But India is the exception. In most other cultures, the fifth and third simply do not exist. This is a permanent puzzle for musical psychologists. The sounds of the natural harmonics are all around us. If one listens with care to any musical note one can hear at least a few overtones, and for most instruments, these are the notes of the harmonic series (but not with percussion—and especially not for the idiophones, for most of their overtones are inharmonic). In Africa, all the pitches produced by the musical bow are those of the harmonic series, and yet this has had little effect on their music. Why this should be, we do not know, but this, and the preference for monody over harmony, are the main reasons that so many musics sound so strange to us, and ours, of course, to them.

The Sounds of Science

The main problem with most of our published studies of musical acoustics is that—apart from the excellent explanations of how sound waves behave and the basic facts about instruments such as the larger or longer, the lower-pitched—the major part of the information is *post hoc*. The books explain what has happened when sounds are made on known instruments, not necessarily what will happen or might happen with an instrument that has not been seen or studied before. Thus the behavior of many instruments from cultures other than our own remains unexplained because they are not instruments that the acousticians have encountered, and they have no theoretical, or *propter hoc*, basis upon which to form any opinions.

We shall not try here to cover all these lacunae, partly for reasons of space, but chiefly because many of the problems have yet to be studied and the answers remain unknown, though we shall be forced to enumerate some, at least, of the anomalies. We shall also try to explain simply and untechnically the basis of how instruments work, at least insofar as we need to do so to amplify or elucidate remarks in our text.

Let us begin with flutes, all those instruments that one sounds by blowing across a hole, as children do with a bottle or pen top, or for that matter a whistle or a recorder. If, as well as a pen top, one has an open-ended tube of the same length and diameter, that tube will sound about an octave higher than the pen top. Leaving aside all the technicalities (these can be found in any book on musical sound),[33] the sound has to go to the bottom of the pen top and then back up again to the top to escape and thus travels twice as far as it does from one end of the open tube to the other, equating with a tube twice as long and so an octave lower. It is not *exactly* an octave, because the air column has an impetus of its own and continues for a very short distance beyond the open end of the tube, just as, when a car brakes suddenly, we are forced forward in our seats because we have an impetus independent of that of the car. This, on the instrument, is called "end correction." If the tube were doubled in length, the end correction would also double, whereas that of the pen top remains single. So to produce an exact octave, the length of the end correction has to be taken into account as well as that of the tube.

Advantage is taken of this octave difference between stopped and open tubes by organ builders. As we have seen, many organ pipes are duct flutes. The pipe for the C below the bass stave, two octaves below middle C, must be eight feet long and organists therefore call it the 8-foot C; the C an octave lower is the 16-foot, and so on. Since these are the speaking lengths, from the lip to the end, one also needs another foot or more in length for the pipe to stand on. Pipe metal is expensive, and when one remembers that one needs a pipe for each note of each rank of pipes, or stop, the cost mounts up very rapidly. Replacing the 16-foot ranks with stopped 8-foot pipes represents a considerable saving of cost, as well as of space, and replacing the 32-foot with stopped 16s and the 64-foot with stopped 32s saves even more.

There is a difference of tone quality due to the different harmonic content. A stopped pipe loses its even-numbered harmonics, or at least greatly weakens them. However, the savings in cost and space far outweigh this, and the different tone qualities are themselves advantageous in creating different combinations of sounds.

As we observed with the panpipe in chapter 3, a player can tip the top of the instrument against the lower lip, so slightly covering it, reducing its aperture and thus slightly altering the pitch. This is because, all other things being equal, the wider the aperture, the higher the pitch produced, and the narrower the lower. This is also one of the ways organ pipes are tuned. The tuner has a set of solid and hollow cones. Inserting a solid cone into the end of the pipe opens it slightly and sharpens the pitch; placing the hollow cone over the end constricts it slightly and flattens the pitch. We described this effect of the area of the open hole, here the end of the organ pipe, in chapter 3's discussion of vessel flutes.

Turning to the reed instruments, a woodwind instrument of cylindrical bore that is reed driven (flutes behave quite differently) will function as what organists call a "stopped tube." It sounds an octave lower than a flute of the same length, and when overblown (blowing harder, increasing the airspeed, so that the pitch jumps up to the next overtone), it sounds a twelfth, an octave and a fifth, above the fundamental, or lowest note. A reed-blown tube that widens from the reed to the bell, often called a conical bore or conoidal (conoidal because it widens conically rather than being exactly a cone), however, overblows to the octave and while its fundamental sounds

lower than that of the flute of the same length, it is not as much lower as that of the cylindrical tube.

To take practical examples, if one had a flute, an oboe, a soprano saxophone, and a clarinet all with the same length of bore (in other words ignoring the length of the flute from the cork to the top of the head), the clarinet would sound an octave lower than the flute, and the oboe and the saxophone would sound much the same as each other (the saxophone has a wider bore that makes some difference) and a little lower than the flute. The reason that the oboe and saxophone are lower than the flute is that, although one may refer to them as being of conical or conoidal bore, this is not strictly true; a cone comes to a point and these do not, because there has to be room for a mouthpiece or a reed and staple. The explanation seems to be that when they are blown, the cone or conoid completes itself partway down the player's gullet and that this, rather than the body of the instrument, is the true length; the pitch would be the same as that of a flute of that same length.

We shall return shortly to what happens next on "our" instruments, but we must emphasize here that the type of reed has nothing whatever to do with this behavior; it is solely a matter of the shape of the bore: the saxophone, with its clarinet-like mouthpiece and single reed, behaves in exactly the same way as the oboe with its double reed; both oboes and bassoons may be, and sometimes are, played with special single-reed mouthpieces adapted to their size (see figure 4.1) without this having any different effect on their musical behavior.

The problem, with which we started this afterword, is that the above statements do not always hold true with instruments from other cultures. We have, for example, already met the forked shawm, where a mainly cylindrical body is rendered acoustically conoidal by the use of a series of short cylinders, each a bit larger than the previous, so producing a stepped cone. So why does this not happen with the instrument we called in chapter 4 by one of its more common names, the *zummāra*? Here, too, we have a mainly cylindrical body, with at least two smaller-diameter steps, and yet it behaves cylindrically, rather than conically. Even more perturbing, if a cylinder is long enough in relation to its bore, it seems to forget that it is a cylinder and starts to overblow octaves, not twelfths. This can easily be demonstrated with lengths of plastic tubing of suitable diameters to accept reeds or mouthpieces, and most of us have heard hosepipe trumpets demonstrated in this way.

Trumpets and horns are also types of reed instrument, for the player's lips are functioning as a dilating or retreating reed. The reeds on oboes, clarinets, and bassoons stand open in their position of rest. As the player blows, they close, and then bounce open, due to their natural elasticity; the frequency with which they do this, closing and opening, controls the sound.[34] The player's lips, on the other hand, start from a closed position and are forced apart by the airstream, bouncing closed again by the action of the buccinator muscles of the mouth.[35] Other examples of a dilating reed are ephemeral instruments such as grass or reed stems with longitudinal slits that open and close when the player—often with these instruments, a child—blows into the end of the stem. Thus one would expect trumpets and horns to behave in a similar fashion to the other reed instruments, but when one looks at alphorns, for example, they all behave in much the same way whether the bore expands, as it does on the well-known Swiss instruments, or is almost entirely narrowly cylindrical, as on the Scandinavian ones. Some help is given to these by the short conical termination of the bell (like that of a hosepipe trumpet when one puts a kitchen funnel into the end), but more seems to come from the determination and strength of the player's lips that force it to behave in the way intended.

The fourth type of reed is the free reed, where a blade of metal or cane vibrates freely to and fro in a close-fitting slot. Most books say that the free reed can produce only one pitch, and this is true of the way in which we use it, but in other parts of the world, mostly in Southeast Asia, it is used on a tube with fingerholes, where it behaves exactly like any other reed because it is designed to couple to the air column of the instrument just as are double and single reeds.

When fingerholes are opened on a tube, starting with that farthest from the mouthpiece, the length of tubing beyond that hole is effectively cut off and the air column is shortened to that extent. The pitch therefore goes up because the longer the air column, other things being equal, the lower the pitch; the shorter the air column, the higher. The extent to which the pitch rises will depend on the position of the hole on the tube, and especially on the relative diameters of the fingerhole and the instrument's bore. If the hole is as wide as the bore, it is almost totally effective in cutting off the tubing below. However, this is seldom useful in practice because the hole may then be too wide to be stopped securely with the finger. It also means placing the holes in their correct acoustical positions to produce the desired scale, and they are then almost certain to be too far apart for the fingers to reach them. So the best design for woodwinds without keywork (by far the most common around the world, and true for ours as well until the mid-nineteenth century) is to compromise and to position the holes

along the tube where they will best suit the player's hand, and then tune the notes produced by adjusting the diameters of the holes.

Basic string acoustics are rather simpler. The pitch depends on the length, mass, and tension of a string: the longer, the lower; the greater the mass, the lower; the tighter the tension, the higher. Ideally an instrument with several strings would have them all at around the same tension. This can improve tone quality (the best sound, in our culture, is said to be produced by strings that are near the breaking point, but they must not be so near that they break too often) and also prevent distortion of the body of the instrument, for if the strings at one end or on one side are tighter than those at the other, the body will twist under the strain. However, this does not often work out in practice, even if most instruments come as near to the ideal as possible.

If all strings are also to be the same length, as they are on a violin or guitar, they must differ in mass, and a glance at any such instrument shows that they do. There are different ways of achieving this. There are limits to the thickness of a gut or metal string; too thick a gut string would be so stiff that it would produce a dull thud; too thick a metal string, and it would be halfway to the bar of a glockenspiel or orchestral bells. Twisting a gut string more tightly makes it more flexible and therefore better sounding. Taking a thinner string and loading it with something to increase its mass is a better solution, and this is why we have covered strings in the bass of all our instruments.

If some strings can be longer than others, this makes design easier, but not as much as one might hope. If two strings of the same mass and tension are to be tuned an octave apart, one must be twice the length of the other. A piano made that way would stretch the whole width of the concert platform. So varying the length alone can seldom be a useful answer. Again compromise is used, varying both length and mass, as one can see on the piano or harp and, regrettably since it eventually damages the body of the instrument, also with some variation of tension.

If one touches a string lightly at its midpoint, it vibrates in two halves, sounding an octave above the basic pitch; touching it one-third of the way along makes it vibrate in three parts, sounding a twelfth above the fundamental. These ratios, 2:1, 3:1, and so on, are those also of the harmonic series, and of the frequencies produced.

A few string instruments are played in this way. Our *tromba marina* works entirely in this manner. The small studs set into the soundboard of the Chinese *qin* show where to put the finger to obtain these harmonics. Their use is a common effect on our violin and other instruments. Woodwinds also work similarly; a small hole opened on the body of the instrument will encourage the air column to break into parts in very much the same way as does a string. Partly opening the thumbhole of a recorder, "pinching" it, opening the speaker key on a clarinet, and so forth, help the instrument to overblow to a higher harmonic without having to blow harder and thus play louder.

With trumpets and horns, when the air column is long enough, altering the lip tension (there is never-ending debate on just how this is done) persuades the air column to break into sections, and so to sound different members of this series of harmonics or overtones (there is dispute, too, over whether they really are harmonics, but in practice it is the various members of that series that are sounded). This is how natural horns and trumpets, those without valves and slides, were played in the Baroque and Classical periods. They are still played like this today, for though there are gaps between the harmonics, these are filled by lengthening the air column by the valves or a slide. Thus depressing a valve that opens access to a tube long enough to lower the pitch by a whole tone, or extending the slide of a trombone by the same amount, produces a harmonic series a tone lower than that of the instrument in its natural state. So, taking the trumpet, built in B-flat, as an example, depressing the second valve produces the harmonic series of A; depressing the first valve, the series of A♭; the third valve, or first and second together (but see below), the series of G; the second and third, of F♯; the first and third, of F; and all three, of E (all written a whole tone higher because the trumpet is treated as a transposing instrument, with the B-flat written as C).

But, and it is a big but, there is a problem here. The first-valve tubing is designed to be long enough to lower a B♭ tube by a whole tone, the second-valve tubing by a semitone. Once the first valve is depressed, the tubing is no longer about four feet, six inches long; it is around five feet, three inches. The second-valve tubing is not long enough to lower that by a semitone—it needs another half-inch or so. And it gets worse when the third valve is brought into action. This is why the better models of trumpets have rings or triggers to push out the valve tuning slides while one plays. This can be designed quite easily with the trumpet, though with more difficulty with the German orchestral trumpet because that is held differently. It is not practicable on the horn, nor on the instruments that are held vertically like the tuba. This is why some models of upright instruments have a fourth valve, to avoid the combination of first

and third. However, the temptation then is to use the fourth valve in combination with the others, to fill the gap between, for example, the E we noted above for all three, and the bottom B♭. This makes things even worse. For this reason, the better models of tuba have complicated extra lengths of tubing on the valves such as the compensating system designed by David Blaikley for Distin and Boosey that automatically adds extra lengths of tubing to correct the pitch when more than one valve is depressed at a time.[36] Likewise, this is why Adolphe Sax, followed by some other makers, designed instruments with independent valves, to avoid the use of more than one valve at a time—some of them with independent tubing and bell for each valve, resulting in players looking as though they were surrounded by a nest of snakes raising their heads in the air.[37] Horn players can compensate by moving the hand in the bell, as they did on the handhorn.

Percussion acoustics are rather more complex. Skins and plates behave in very much the same way. There is little difference between a tightened drum-skin and a diaphragm of metal or other material. The bronze drums of Southeast Asia are indeed drums, not gongs as they are sometimes called—the circular metal plate behaves exactly like a skin drumhead. The overtones of all drums are inharmonic. When any instrument is played, if one listens carefully, one can hear the overtones in its sound; this is particularly easy on the Indian sitar, where one can detect as many as sixteen harmonics in the sound. Where these overtones are harmonic, the sound is enriched by them, and it is the different strengths of the overtones that give each instrument its characteristic sound. Where they are not harmonic but are inharmonic, the sound can jangle or jar.

With many members of the percussion family, there are ways to cheat their natural behavior, by varying the thickness in different places of a bar or bell, for instance (we have all heard bells where this has not been done, with a jarring sound as a result). Using an air column or air body as a resonator can help also, as with members of the xylophone family and with kettledrums such as our timpani. Many percussion instruments, with the exception of bells, have a short enough sound that this inharmonicity does not matter too much. However, the modern piano, whose string tension has increased enormously in the past fifty years in the interest of producing a louder sound, suffers very badly in this respect. While the overtones of a string are normally harmonic or not far off, those of a bar are not, and the strings of the piano, especially in the upper range, are so tight that their acoustic behavior is closer to that of bars than of strings. That is why the sound of the piano can jangle in the ear when one listens closely.

The best instruments are built empirically. "Perfect" designs, for example, woodwinds with an exactly even taper, are always out of tune, for it is essential to modify a "perfect" bore to allow for the quirks of nature. This is where the success of the best makers exists—the knowledge gained by experience of precisely where and how much to modify a bore that is theoretically perfect but out of tune in practice. Few really good instruments are the result of theoretical or scientific design; almost all require the extra cuts of the knife, the twist of the reamer, the tap of the hammer. Similarly, few good concert halls have been the result of the architects' acoustical studies; most have required tweaking before working well enough to satisfy musicians and audiences. For both, instruments and halls alike, the work of the experienced craftsman reigns supreme.

One final thought. The instrument that is built to be perfectly in tune is always a pig to play. "In tune" is always a matter of context. As we saw in the previous section on scales, these are always a compromise. Unless one were playing alone with only a "perfectly in tune" keyboard instrument as accompaniment, every note would need to be bent, even if only very slightly, to be "in tune" with whatever notes and harmonies other instruments, or for that matter voices, are sounding. The instrument that is "perfectly in tune" does not bend easily and is far more difficult to play than one that is designed to be a little flexible. And even the keyboard instruments are never perfectly in tune; octaves at the extreme top and bottom need to be stretched a little if they are to sound in tune. A keyboard that is tuned only against an electronic meter, however exact it may appear on the screen, will always sound out of tune to the human ear. The only true judge *is* the human ear, and it is essential to be flexible if one wishes to be really "in tune."

Notes

1. Alexander Pope, *Essay on Man*, Epistle 2 (1734). *Logos* is more literally "discourse," and thus *-ology* is perhaps better as "teaching," but one cannot teach unless first one should study.
2. The Royal Society began around 1650 with debates and experiments in Wadham College, Oxford, with the encouragement of the warden, John Wilkins, and participants such as Christopher Wren, Robert Boyle, Robert Hooke, and John Locke.
3. *Scientia*, Latin for "knowing," "discerning."
4. From the Greek *archaio*, "ancient."

5. As the "ordering of organisms into taxa on the basis of their similarity" (Ernst Mayr, *The Growth of Biological Thought* [1982], 185).
6. Margaret J. Kartomi, *On Concepts and Classification of Musical Instruments* (1990). See also my review of it and of two other works on classification in GSJ 49 (1996): 214–20.
7. Erich M. von Hornbostel and Curt Sachs, "Systematik der Musikinstrumente," *Zeitschrift für Ethnologie*, Jahrg. 1914, Heft 4/5 (1914): 553–90. This was translated into English by Anthony Baines and Klaus P. Wachsmann in "Classification of Musical Instruments," GSJ 14 (1961): 3–29. Other translations have also been published: in Finnish by Timo Leisiö ("Soittenten Luokitusjärjestelmä," *Musiikki* 1–4 [1974]: 1–73, with useful sketches); in Catalan by Maria-Antònia Juan i Nebot ("Classificació d'instruments musicals," *Fulls de Treball de Carrutxa*, segona època 2 [1994]: 89–108); in Castilian, again by Maria-Antònia Juan i Nebot ("Versión castellana de la Clasificación," *Nassarre, Revista Aragonesa de Musicología* 14:1 [1998]: 365–87); and in Italian by Febo Guizzi ("Sistematica degli Strumenti Musicali," in his *Gli strumenti della musica popolare in Italia* [2002], 409–82), and doubtless others that I have not as yet encountered into other languages. There have also been numerous adaptations, expansions, and other variants.
8. Victor-Charles Mahillon, *Catalogue descriptif et analytique* (1880). This is the first volume of five that Mahillon compiled for the Brussels Conservatoire Museum. All five were reprinted in 1978.
9. Kartomi, *On Concepts and Classification*, 58.
10. The suffix *-phone* means "sound"; the first half of each word means "string," "skin," "air," and "self-," respectively.
11. The Greek *autos* means "self," whereas *idios* is stronger, meaning peculiarly to oneself. Kartomi, *On Concepts and Classification*, 137–38, gives the various other names, mostly Latin-based, that have been used in Europe since the early Middle Ages.
12. Francis W. Galpin, *A Textbook of European Musical Instruments* (1937), 27–36.
13. Jeremy Montagu and John Burton, "A Proposed New Classification System," *Ethnomusicology* 15:1 (January 1971): 49–70.
14. Kartomi, *On Concepts and Classification*, 183–84.
15. See Laurence E. R. Picken, *Folk Musical Instruments of Turkey* (1975), 557–609, esp. 560–62.
16. Oskár Elschek, "Typologische Arbeitsverfahren bei Volksmusikinstrumenten," SIMP 1 (1969): 23–40; Mantle Hood, *The Ethnomusicologist* (1971), 144–96. See also Kartomi, *On Concepts and Classification*, 204–9 and 184–86, respectively.
17. Baines and Wachsmann, "Classification of Musical Instruments," 14, 15.
18. Nazir Ali Jairazbhoy, "An Explication of the Hornbostel-Sachs," in *Selected Reports in Ethnomusicology 8: Issues in Organology*, ed. Sue Carole DeVale (1990), 81–104.
19. F. W. Galpin, "The Whistles and Reed Instruments of the American Indians of the North-West Coast," *Proceedings of the Musical Association* 29 (1903): 115–38. So far as I know,

Balfour never referred to these in print, but they appear on his labels in the Pitt Rivers Museum, Oxford. Examples there are stalks of plants such as rice with vertical slits in the sides. When blown from one end of the stalk, the slits dilate under the air pressure, opening and closing. It is arguable that the human lips function in a similar fashion with a brass instrument—the air forces them to open from a closed position, the opposite movement from a double reed of cane, where the air pressure forces them to close from an open position, as was pointed out by Murray Campbell and Clive Greated in *The Musician's Guide to Acoustics* (1987), 306–8.

20. Picken, *Folk Musical Instruments of Turkey*, 376–80. Incidentally, Picken calls the retreating reeds "multiple slit-reeds" (p. 349) and regards them as 412.11 (concussion reeds), despite their opposite movement from other concussion reeds.

21. Arthur H. Benade, *Horns, Strings and Harmony* (1960), 192.

22. Why do we normally speak of one note being higher or lower in pitch than another? Is it because on a string instrument "higher" notes are further up the fingerboard? That's not the case on a cello—the "higher" notes are nearer the floor. On a woodwind instrument, yes (not on a bassoon, though, nor on a transverse flute). Certainly not on a keyboard; they are "righter" or "lefter." Singers "feel" notes "on the mask," behind the skin of the face, and there certainly "higher" notes are higher, but this seems to be a fairly recently expressed concept. On paper, yes, further up the page as it sits on a music desk, but this is only since scales were written down in the way we write them in staff notation within our culture, that is, since the late thirteenth century or so; other cultures think differently. In parts of Africa, some notes are bigger than others—look at the bars of a xylophone, the lengths of the strings on a harp, the sizes of animal horns or tusks, or the diameter of drums, and it becomes logical that "lower" notes are "bigger." Even to us, a bass voice can sound "bigger" than a tenor.

23. Cents were devised by Alexander J. Ellis and published in his "Tonometrical Observations on Some Existing Non-harmonic Musical Scales," *Proceedings of the Royal Society* 234:37 (1885): 3680–85. They were explained in great detail in appendix 20, section C, to his translation of Hermann Helmholtz's *Lehre von den Tonempfindungen* (1863), entitled *On the Sensations of Tone* (1875; 2nd ed., 1885).

24. This last step must of necessity be narrower, for since there are 1,200 cents in the octave, if one step is to be wider than the average, another must be narrower. In practice this is not always true, because in Java they stretch the octaves in the treble, just as we do when tuning the piano—1,220 can sound better in tune than 1200! It is what we hear that counts, not what the machine measures.

25. Ellis was the first person to provide exact measurements of scales in the modern manner, using the set of fifty to seventy tuning forks to cover an octave, as he describes in section B of his appendix 20 to Helmholtz, *Lehre von den Tonempfindungen*. Before his time, from the days of the ancient Greeks and per-

haps earlier, the standard tool was the monochord, a string of known length and pitch stretched over a soundbox, on which, by moving a bridge along a measured scale, in the sense of a ruler, one can alter the pitch and read off the length. This was much less accurate than Ellis's forks, for neither the string nor the rule were always wholly true, and distortion near the ends of the rule is almost inevitable. The results could be expressed in measurements or, more usually, by ratios, but these are really only useful when they are simple, such as the 9:8 against 10:9 as in figure AW.1. Once the figures get much larger than this, it becomes difficult to recognize which of two groups of numbers is the greater. The monochord was the only tool most of us had for measuring pitch until electronic gadgets such as the Stroboconn and the Melograph were invented in the middle of the twentieth century and until the now ubiquitous Japanese electronic tuners became common toward its end.

26. Comparison of tunings of xylophones was one of the bases of Father A. M. Jones's theories of the connections between Africa and Indonesia, referred to in chapter 1 when we were discussing xylophones. One major criticism of his work was that he did not allow for the fact that the pitch of wooden bars varies as the wood dries out in the atmosphere of our museums and that, as the result of age and poor storage, many of the lumps of wax added for tuning had dropped off and gotten lost.

27. To investigate the subject further, J. Murray Barbour's *Tunings and Temperaments* (1951) is a good place to start, as are the articles on "Temperament" in *The New Grove Dictionary of Music and Musicians* (2nd ed., 2001) and *The New Grove Dictionary of Musical Instruments* (1984). An article of mine on my website, www.jeremymontagu.co.uk, "Tuning and Temperament and Why We Have to Do It," goes into a little more technical detail than this afterword and gives a number of differently tempered scales with all the cents figures. For non-European scales, Alain Daniélou's *Introduction to the Study of Musical Scales* (1943) is useful, but note that he uses *savarts* instead of cents to express intervals, a French system of larger units, and therefore less useful because they often need to be divided with decimal points.

28. For simplicity, we are dealing here only with what is called a "diatonic major scale," represented by the white notes on the piano from C to C. We have other scales, for example, a minor scale, again the white notes on the piano but going from A to A. The other most important scale in our music is the chromatic scale, using all the notes, both white and black, between any two notes of the same letter name. It is that equal-tempered scale that is essential for atonal music, deriving from the theories of Arnold Schoenberg, in which there is no concept of major or minor keys, because, since all steps are equal, there is no feeling of tonality (i.e., of any particular key).

29. The first meantone was devised by Pietro Aron in 1523 and is usually known either by his name or as "quarter-comma meantone," because the fifths were made wider than pure by 6 cents, a quarter of the 24-cent (Pythagorean) comma produced

by piling up the fifths from C to B♯. Sixth-comma is a better compromise, as are some of the irregular temperaments such as Werckmeister's, for which see the sources cited above in note 27.

30. Johann Joachim Quantz, *Versuch einer Anweisung die Flöte traversiere zu spielen* (1752; trans. and ed. Edward R. Reilly as *On Playing the Flute* [1966]), 31 and 40–42.

31. "Well-tempering" was a very different conception from "equal tempering." See, for example, John Barnes, "Bach's Keyboard Temperament," *EM* 7:2 (April 1979): 236–49, and the related correspondence in succeeding issues. There have been several subsequent articles in that journal, some more convincing than others.

32. N. A. Jairazbhoy, *The Rāgs of North Indian Music* (1971), 34–36.

33. Two good ones are Campbell and Greated, *Musician's Guide to Acoustics*, and Arthur H. Benade, *Fundamentals of Musical Acoustics* (1976).

34. The way in which they do this, and the importance of this frequency matching the air column inside the instruments, are all matters too technical for a book of this nature and are discussed in great detail in all the standard books on acoustics.

35. Campbell and Greated, *Musician's Guide to Acoustics*, 306–8.

36. British patent no. 4618 of 1878.

37. French patents nos. 14608 and 75861 of 1862 and 1867. A number of these are illustrated in Malou Haine and Ignace de Keyser, *Catalogue des Instruments Sax* (1980), 49 and 176–86.

Bibliography

Abbreviations

CNRS	Centre National de la Recherche Scientifique
CUP	Cambridge University Press
DVfM	Deutscher Verlag für Musik
EM	*Early Music*
FoMRHIQ	*Fellowship of Makers & Researchers of Historical Instruments Quarterly*
GSJ	*Galpin Society Journal*
JAMIS	*Journal of the American Musical Instrument Society*
JIFMC	*Journal of the International Folk Music Council*
JIJHS	*Journal of the International Jew's Harp Society*
OUP	Oxford University Press
SIMP	*Studia instrumentorum musicae popularis*
YUP	Yale University Press

Bibliography

Abbott, Djilda, and Ephraim Segerman. "Strings in the 16th and 17th Centuries." *GSJ* 27 (1974): 48–73.

Adkins, C. J. "Investigation of the Sound-Producing Mechanism of the Jew's Harp." *Journal of the Acoustical Society of America* 55:3 (March 1974): 667–70.

Adkins, C. J., R. C. Williamson, J. W. Flowers, and L. E. R. Picken. "Frequency-Doubling Chordophones." *Musica Asiatica* 3 (1981): 1–9.

Adkins, Cecil, and Alis Dickinson. *A Trumpet by Any Other Name: A History of the Trumpet Marine*. Buren, the Netherlands: Frits Knuf, 1991.

Agricola, Martin. *Musica instrumentalis deudsch*. Wittemberg: Georg Rhaw, 1529. Reprint, Leipzig: Breitkopf und Härtel, 1896. Trans. William E. Hettrick, Cambridge: CUP, 1994.

Aign, Bernhard. *Die Geschichte der Musikinstrumente des Ägäischen Raumes bis um 700 vor Christus*. Frankfurt am Main: J. W. Goethe-Universität, 1963.

Aksdal, Bjørn. *Meråker Klarinetten*. Trondheim: Ringve Museum, 1992.

Alburger, Mary Anne. "Bowed String Instruments." In J. Gardiner, ed., *Before the Mast: Life and Death aboard the Mary Rose*, 242–49. Archaeology of the Mary Rose, vol. 4. Portsmouth, England: Mary Rose Trust, 2005.

Alexandru, Tiberiu. *Instrumentele Muzicale ale Poporului Romîn*. Bucharest: Stat Pentru Literatură și Artă, 1956.

Alfonso X el Sábio. *Cántigas de Santa Maria*. Escorial Library (Madrid), Mss. b I 2 and T I 1.

Allison, Richard. *The Psalmes of David in Meter, the plaine Song beeing the common tunne to be sung and plaide upon the Lute, Orpharyon, Citterne or Base Violl, severally or altogether . . . .* London: Thomas Morley, 1599. Facsimile, London: Brian Jordan in association with Scolar Press, 1980.

Alvad, Thomas. "The Kafir Harp." *Man* (October 1954): 151–54.

Ames, David W., and Anthony V. King. *Glossary of Hausa Music and Its Social Contexts*. Evanston, Ill.: Northwestern University Press, 1971.

Anderson, R. D. *Catalogue of Egyptian Antiquities in the British Museum*. Vol. 3, *Musical Instruments*. London: British Museum, 1976.

Andersson, Otto. *The Bowed-Harp: A Study in the History of Early Musical Instruments*, trans. Kathleen Schlesinger. London: William Reeves, 1930.

Anfilov, Gleb. *Physics and Music*, trans. Boris Kuznetsov. Moscow: MIR, 1966.

Anglés, Higinio. *La Musica de las Cántigas de Santa Maria del Rey Alfonso el Sábio: Facsimil, Transcripción y estudio critico*. Barcelona: Biblioteca Central, 1943–1964.

Anoyanakis, Fivos. *Greek Popular Musical Instruments*. Athens: National Bank of Greece, 1979.

Arbeau, Thoinot. *Orchesographie: Metode et teorie en forme de discours et tablature pour apprendre a dancer, ...* Lengres: Iehan des Preyz, 1588. Facsimile of the 1596 edition, Geneva: Minkoff, 1972.

Armstrong, Robert Bruce. *Musical Instruments: The Irish and the Highland Harps.* Edinburgh: David Douglas, 1904. Facsimile, Shannon: Irish University Press, 1969.

Arnold, Denis, ed. *The New Oxford Companion to Music.* Oxford: OUP, 1983.

Art du Faiseur d'Instruments de Musique et Lutherie: Extrait de L'Encyclopédie Méthodique Arts et Métiers Mécaniques. Paris: 1785. Reprint, Geneva: Minkoff, 1972.

Ashbee, Andrew. *Records of English Court Music,* vol. 7: *1485–1558.* Aldershot: Scolar Press, 1993.

Bachmann, Werner. *The Origins of Bowing and the Development of Bowed Instruments up to the Thirteenth Century,* trans. Norma Deane. London: OUP, 1969.

Bachmann-Geiser, Brigitte. *Die Volksmusikinstrumente der Schweiz.* Handbuch der europäischen Volksmusikinstrumente 1:4. Leipzig: DVfM, 1981.

Bäckström, Magnus. *Hornet—skogens instrument.* Falun: Dalarnas Museum, 1984.

Baily, John. *Music of Afghanistan: Professional Musicians in the City of Herat.* Cambridge: CUP, 1988.

———. "Recent Changes in the Dutār of Herat." *Asian Music* 8:1 (1976): 29–64.

Baines, Anthony. *Bagpipes.* Oxford: Pitt Rivers Museum, 1960.

———. *Brass Instruments: Their History and Development.* London: Faber, 1976.

———. *European and American Musical Instruments.* London: B. T. Batsford, 1966.

———. "Fifteenth-Century Instruments in Tinctoris's *De Inventione et Usu Musicae.*" *GSJ* 3 (1950): 19–26.

———. *Woodwind Instruments and Their History.* London: Faber, 1957 et seq.

Baines, Anthony, and Klaus P. Wachsmann. "Classification of Musical Instruments." *GSJ* 14 (1961): 3–29.

Balfour, Henry. "The Friction Drum." *Journal of the Royal Anthropological Institute* 37 (1907): 67–92 and plates 12–14.

———. "The *Goura,* a Stringed-Wind Musical Instrument of the Bushmen and Hottentots." *Journal of the Royal Anthropological Institute* 32 (1902): 156–76 and plates 12–14.

———. *The Natural History of the Musical Bow: A Chapter in the Developmental History of Stringed Instruments of Music.* Oxford: Clarendon Press, 1899.

Barbour, J. Murray. *Tunings and Temperaments: A Historical Survey.* East Lansing: Michigan State University Press, 1951. Reprint, New York: Da Capo, 1972.

Barnes, John. "Bach's Keyboard Temperament: Internal Evidence from the *Well-Tempered Clavier.*" *EM* 7:2 (April 1979): 236–49.

Bartolozzi, Bruno. *New Sounds for Woodwind.* 2nd ed. London: OUP, 1967.

Bate, Philip. *The Flute: A Study of Its History, Development and Construction.* London: Ernest Benn, 1969.

———. *The Trumpet and Trombone.* London: Ernest Benn, 1966.

Baumann, Oscar. *Eine Africanische Tropen-Insel, Fernando Póo und die Bube.* Vienna: E. Hölzel, 1888.

Bayer, Batja. "The Conch-Horn of Hazor." *Tatzlil* 3 (1963): 140–42.

——— [Bathyah]. *The Material Relics of Music in Ancient Palestine and Its Environs.* Tel Aviv: Israel Music Institute, 1963.

Beament, James, and Dennis Unwin. "The Hole Story." *Strad* 112:1132 (April 2001): 408–15.

Beaver, W. N. "A Further Note on the Use of the Wooden Trumpet in Papua." *Man* (1916): 16.

Bebey, Francis. *African Music: A People's Art,* trans. Josephine Bennett. London: Harrap, 1975.

Becker, Heinz. *Zur Entwicklungsgeschichte der antiken und mittelalterlichen Rohrblattinstrumente.* Hamburg: Hans Sikorski, 1966.

Becker, Judith. "The Migration of the Arched Harp from India to Burma." *GSJ* 20 (1967): 17–23.

Benade, Arthur H. *Fundamentals of Musical Acoustics.* New York: OUP, 1976.

———. *Horns, Strings and Harmony.* Garden City, N.Y.: Anchor Books, Doubleday, 1960.

Berlioz, Hector. *Traité d'instrumentation et d'orchestration.* Paris: Henri Lemoine, 1844. Reprint of 1880s 2nd ed., Farnborough: Gregg Press, 1970.

Bessaraboff, Nicholas. *Ancient European Musical Instruments.* Cambridge, Mass.: Harvard University Press for the Museum of Fine Arts, Boston, 1941.

Beurmann, Andreas E. "Iberian Discoveries: Six Spanish 17th-Century Harpsichords." *EM* 27:2 (May 1999): 183–208.

Bevan, Clifford. *The Tuba Family.* 2nd enl. ed. Winchester: Piccolo Press, 2000.

Bibikov, S. N. *The Oldest Musical Complex Made of Mammoth Bones* [in Russian with English and French summaries]. Kiev: Institute of Archaeology, Academy of Science, Ukrainian SSR, 1981.

Bigio, Robert, and Michael Wright. "On Reaming Flutes." *GSJ* 58 (2005): 51–57.

Birsak, Kurt. *Die Holzblas Instrumente im Salzburger Museum Carolino Augusteum.* Salzburg: Carolino Augusteum Museum, 1973.

Blades, James. *Percussion Instruments and Their History.* 2nd ed. London: Faber, 1975.

Blandford, W. F. H. "The Fourth Horn in the 'Choral Symphony.'" *Musical Times* 983 (January 1925): 29–32; 984 (February 1925): 124–29; 985 (March 1925): 221–23.

Boalch, Donald H. *Makers of the Harpsichord and Clavichord, 1440–1840.* 3rd ed., ed. Charles Mould. Oxford: OUP, 1995.

Boehm, Theobald. *Die Flöte und das Flötenspiel, in akustische, technischer und artistischer Beziehung.* Munich: Joseph Aibl, 1871. Translated by Dayton C. Miller as *The Flute and Flute-Playing in Acoustical, Technical, and Artistic Aspects.* Cleveland, Ohio: Dayton C. Miller, 1908; reprint of 1922 2nd ed., New York: Dover, 1964.

Bonanni, Filippo. *Gabinetto armonico.* Rome: Nella stamperaìia di G. Placho, 1723.

Boone, Olga. *Les tambours du Congo Belge et du Ruanda-Urundi.* Tervuren: Musée du Congo Belge, 1951.

———. *Les xylophones du Congo Belge.* Tervuren: Musée du Congo Belge, 1936.

Borel, François. *Collections d'instruments de musique: Les sanza.* Neuchâtel: Musée d'Ethnographie, 1986.

Bouterse, Jan. *Dutch Woodwind Instruments and Their Makers, 1660–1760.* Utrecht: Koninklijke Vereniging voor Nederlandse Muziekgeschiedenis, 2005.

Bowles, Edmund A. "A Checklist of Fifteenth-Century Representations of Stringed Keyboard Instruments." In *Keyboard Instruments: Studies in Keyboard Organology,* ed. Edwin M. Ripin, 11–16 and plates 1–31. Edinburgh: Edinburgh University Press, 1971. Reprint, New York: Dover, 1977.

———. *The Timpani: A History in Pictures and Documents.* Hillsdale, N.Y.: Pendragon, 2002.

Boydell, Barra. *The Crumhorn and Other Renaissance Windcap Instruments: A Contribution to Renaissance Organology.* Buren, the Netherlands: Frits Knuf, 1982.

Boyden, David D. *The History of Violin Playing from Its Origins to 1761 and Its Relationship to the Violin and Violin Music.* London: OUP, 1965.

———. "The Violin Bow in the 18th Century." *EM* 8:2 (April 1980): 199–212.

Braun, Joachim. *Music in Ancient Israel/Palestine.* Grand Rapids, Mich.: William B. Eerdman, 2002.

———. "Musical Instruments in Byzantine Illuminated Manuscripts." *EM* 8:3 (July 1980): 312–27.

Bridge, Joseph C. "Horns." *Journal of the Chester and North Wales Architectural, Archaeological and Historical Society* n.s. 11 (1905): 85–166.

Broholm, H. C., William P. Larsen, and Godtfred Skjerne. *The Lures of the Bronze Age: An Archaeological, Technical, and Musicological Investigation.* Copenhagen: Gyldendal, 1949.

Brownlow, Art. *The Last Trumpet: A History of the English Slide Trumpet.* Stuyvesant, N.Y.: Pendragon Press, 1996.

Cameron, L. C. R. *The Hunting Horn: What to Blow and How to Blow It.* London: Köhler & Son, c. 1905. Reprint, London: Swaine Adeney Brigg, 1950.

Campbell, Murray, and Clive Greated. *The Musician's Guide to Acoustics.* London: Dent, 1987.

Campbell, Richard G. *Zur Typologie der Schalenlangshalslaute.* Strasbourg: Heitz, 1968.

Carnyx et la Lyre, Le [exhibition catalogue]. Besançon: Musée des Beaux-Arts et Archeologie; Orléans: Musée Historique et Archeologique de l'Orleanais; Évreux: Musée de l'Ancien Eveche, 1993.

Carrington, J. A. *Talking Drums of Africa.* London: Carey Kingsgate Press, 1949. Reprint, New York: Negro Universities Press, 1969.

Caskey, L. D. "Archaeological Notes: Recent Acquisitions of the Museum of Fine Arts, Boston." *Archaeological Institute of America Bulletin* 41 (1937): 525–27.

Chang, Sa-hun. *Korean Musical Instruments* [in Korean with English summary]. 2nd ed. Seoul: Seoul National University, 1976.

Chenoweth, Vida. *The Marimbas of Guatemala.* Lexington: University of Kentucky Press, 1964.

Chinnery, E. W. P. "Further Notes on the Wooden Kipi Trumpet and Conch Shell by the Natives of Papua." *Man* (1917): 55.

Chladni, Ernst Florens Friedrich. *Entdeckungen über die Theorie des Klanges.* Leipzig: Wiedmann, 1787.

Clark, Julian H. "Bows—A Maker's Response." *EM* 8:4 (October 1980): 503–5.

Cole, Michael. *Broadwood Square Pianos.* Cheltenham, England: Tatchley Books, 2005.

———. *The Pianoforte in the Classical Era.* Oxford: Clarendon Press, 1998.

Coles, John M. "Irish Bronze Age Horns and Their Relations with Northern Europe." *Proceedings of the Prehistoric Society* 29 (1963): 326–56.

———. "Some Irish Horns of the Late Bronze Age." *Royal Society of Antiquaries of Ireland* 97:2 (1967): 113–17.

Collaer, Paul. *Südostasien.* Musikgeschichte in Bildern 1:3. Leipzig: DVfM, 1979.

Crane, Frederick. *Extant Medieval Musical Instruments: A Provisional Catalogue by Types.* Iowa City: University of Iowa Press, 1972.

———, ed. *Vierundzwanzigsteljahrschrift der Internationalen Maultrommelvirtuosengenossenschaft* 4 (1994).

Dahlig, Ewa. "A Sixteenth-Century Polish Folk Fiddle from Płock.'" *GSJ* 47 (1994): 111–22.

Dahlig, Piotr. "Ligawka mazowiecko-podlaska w świetle źródeł współczesnych." *Muzyka* 32:4 (1987): 75–110.

Dahlqvist, Reine. *The Keyed Trumpet and Its Greatest Virtuoso, Anton Weidinger.* Nashville, Tenn.: Brass Press, 1975.

Dams, Lya. "Palaeolithic Lithophones: Descriptions and Comparisons." *Oxford Journal of Archaeology* 4:1 (1985): 31–46.

Daniélou, Alain. *Introduction to the Study of Musical Scales.* London: India Society, 1943.

Dart, R. Thurston. "The Mock Trumpet." *GSJ* 6 (1953): 35–40.

Dauvois, Michel, and Xavier Boutillon. "Grottes et Lithophones." In *Acoustique et instruments anciens: Colloque organisé par la Société Française d'Acoustique et la cité de la musique, 17 et 18 novembre 1998,* 215–23. Paris: N.p., 1999.

Day, C. R. *A Descriptive Catalogue of the Musical Instruments recently exhibited at the Royal Military Exhibition, London, 1890.* London: Eyre & Spottiswoode, 1891.

De Hen, F. J. "The Truchado Instrument: A Geigenwerk?" In *Keyboard Instruments: Studies in Keyboard Organology,* ed. Edwin M. Ripin, 19–26 and plates 32–34. Edinburgh: Edinburgh University Press, 1971. Reprint, New York: Dover, 1977.

Deutsch, Otto Erich. *Schubert: Thematic Catalogue of All His Works in Chronological Order.* London: J. M. Dent, 1951.

Dolge, Alfred. *Pianos and Their Makers.* Covina, Calif.: Covina Publishing, 1911. Reprint, New York: Dover, 1972.

Dournon-Taurelle, Geneviève, and John Wright. *Les guimbardes du musée de l'homme.* Paris: Institut d'Ethnologie, 1978.

Dudgeon, Ralph. *The Keyed Bugle.* Metuchen, N.J.: Scarecrow Press, 1993.

Egg, Erich, and Wolfgang Pfaundler. *Das Grosse Tiroler Blasmusikbuch mit Ehrentafel der Tiroler Blasmusikkapellen.* Vienna: Fritz Molden, 1979.

Eliason, Robert E. "Early American Valves for Brass Instruments." *GSJ* 23 (1970): 86–96.

Ellis, Alexander J. "Tonometrical Observations on Some Existing Non-harmonic Musical Scales." *Proceedings of the Royal Society* 234:37 (1885): 368–85.

Elschek, Oskár. *Die Volksmusikinstrumente der Tschechoslowakei, Teil 2.* Handbuch der europäischen Volksmusikinstrumente 1:2. Leipzig: DVfM, 1983.

———. "Typologische Arbeitsverfahren bei Volksmusikinstrumenten." *SIMP* 1 (1969): 23–40.

Emsheimer, Ernst. "A Finno-Ugric Flute Type." *JIFMC* 18 (1966): 29–35

———. "Tongue Duct Flutes: Correction of an Error." *GSJ* 34 (1981): 98–105.

Evans, Arthur. *The Palace of Minos.* 4 vols. London: Macmillan, 1921–1935.

Fagg, Bernard. "The Discovery of Multiple Rock Gongs in Nigeria." *Man* (1956): 17–18. Also published in *African Music* 1:3 (1956): 6–9.

Fagg, M. C. *Rock Music.* Oxford: Pitt Rivers Museum, 1997.

Farmer, Henry George. *Islam.* Musikgeschichte in Bildern 3:2. Leipzig: DVfM, 1966.

———. *Studies in Oriental Musical Instruments: Second Series.* Glasgow: Civic Press, 1939.

Fischer, Hans. *Schallgeräte in Ozeanien: Bau und Spieltechnik—Verbreitung un Funktion.* Strasbourg: P. H. Heitz, 1958. Translated by Philip W. Holzknecht as *Sound-Producing Instruments in Oceania,* ed. Don Niles. Rev. ed. Boroko, Papua New Guinea: Institute of Papua New Guinea Studies, 1986.

Fitton, J. Lesley. *Cycladic Art.* London: British Museum Press, 1989.

Fleischhauer, Günter. *Etrurien und Rom.* Musikgeschichte in Bildern 2:5. Leipzig: DVfM, 1964.

Fox, Leonard. *The Jew's Harp: A Comprehensive Anthology.* Lewisburg, Pa.: Bucknell University Press, 1988.

Fuller, David. *Mechanical Musical Instruments as a Source for the Study of Notes Inégales.* Cleveland Heights, Ohio: Divisions, 1974.

Gallici, Joannis. *Liber Notabilis Musicae.* British Library, Add. ms. 22315.

Galpin, Francis W. *The Music of the Sumerians and Their Immediate Successors the Babylonians and Assyrians.* Cambridge: CUP, 1936. Reprint, Strasbourg: Heitz, 1955.

———. *Old English Instruments of Music, Their History and Character.* London: Methuen, 1910. 4th ed., rev. R. Thurston Dart, 1975.

———. *A Textbook of European Musical Instruments.* London: Williams & Norgate, 1937.

———. "The Whistles and Reed Instruments of the American Indians of the North-West Coast." *Proceedings of the Musical Association* 29 (1903): 115–38.

Gardiner, J., ed. *Before the Mast: Life and Death aboard the* Mary Rose. Archaeology of the *Mary Rose,* vol. 4. Portsmouth: Mary Rose Trust, 2005.

Gilchrist, Martyn. *Whistles.* Princes Risborough, England: Shire, 2000.

Gimpel, Jean. *The Medieval Machine: The Industrial Revolution of the Middle Ages.* 2nd ed. Aldershot, England: Wildwood House, 1988.

Glory, Abbé. "La Grotte de Roucadour." *Bulletin de la Société Préhistorique Française* 61 (1964): 166–69. [See also his further articles in subsequent volumes.]

Guerrero Lovillo, José. *Las cántigas: Estudio arqueológico de sus miniaturas.* Madrid: Instituto Diego Velázquez, 1949.

Guizzi, Febo. *Gli strumenti della musica popolare in Italia.* Lucca: Libreria Musicale Italiana, 2002.

Haine, Malou. *Adolphe Sax (1814–1894): Sa vie, son œuvre et ses instruments de musique.* Brussels: Éditions de l'Université de Bruxelles, 1980.

Haine, Malou, and Ignace de Keyser. *Catalogue des instruments Sax au Musée Instrumental de Bruxelles.* Brussels: Musée Instrumental, 1980.

Hakelberg, Dietrich. "Some Recent Archaeo-organological Finds in Germany." *GSJ* 48 (1995): 3–12.

Halfpenny, Eric. "A Renaissance Bass Flute." *GSJ* 23 (1970): 116.

———. "Two Rare Transverse Flutes." *GSJ* 13 (1960): 38–43.

Harding, J. R. "The Bull-Roarer in History and in Antiquity." *African Music* 5:3 (1973/1974): 40–42.

Harrison, Frank Ll., and Joan Rimmer. *The Showcase of Musical Instruments.* New York: Dover, 1964.

Haynes, Bruce. *The Eloquent Oboe: A History of the Hautboy from 1640 to 1760.* Oxford: OUP, 2001.

———. *A History of Performing Pitch: The Story of "A."* Lanham, Md.: Scarecrow Press, 2002.

Haynes, Bruce, and Geoffrey Burgess. *The Oboe.* New Haven, Conn.: YUP, 2004.

Hazen, Margaret Hindle, and Robert M. Hazen. *The Music Men: An Illustrated History of Brass Bands in America, 1800–1920.* Washington: Smithsonian Institution Press, 1987.

Helffer, Mireille. *Mchod-rol: Les instruments de la musique tibétaine.* Paris: CNRS, 1994.

Helmholtz, Hermann. *Lehre von den Tonempfindungen als physiologische Grundlage für die Theorie der Musik.* Brunswick: F. Vieweg und Sohn, 1863. Translated by Alexander J. Ellis as *On the Sensations of Tone as a Physiological Basis for the Theory of Music.* London: Longman, Green, 1875. Reprint of the 1885 2nd ed., New York: Dover, 1954.

Herbert, Trevor, ed. *Bands: The Brass Band Movement in the 19th and 20th Centuries.* Milton Keynes, England: Open University Press, 1991.

Heyde, Herbert. *Das Ventilblasinstrument.* Leipzig: DVfM, 1987.

Hickmann, Hans. *Ägypten.* Musikgeschichte in Bildern 2:1. Leipzig: DVfM, 1961.

———. *Catalogue général des antiquités égyptiennes du Musée du Caire—Instruments de musique.* Cairo: Institut Français d'Archéologie Orientale, 1949.

———. *La trompette dans l'Égypte ancienne.* Cairo: Institut Français d'Archéologie Orientale, 1946.

Hinrichs, Johann Christian. *Entstehung Fortgang und Jetzige Beschaffenheit der Russische Jagdmusik.* St. Petersburg, Russia: J. D. Gerstenberg, 1796. Facsimile, Leipzig: Zentralantiquariat der DDR for Bärenreiter, Kassel, 1974.

Hoeprich, T. Eric. "A Three-Key Clarinet by J. C. Denner." *GSJ* 34 (1981): 21–32.

Holman, Peter. *Four and Twenty Fiddlers: The Violin at the English Court, 1540–1690.* Oxford: Clarendon Press, 1993.

Hood, Mantle. *The Ethnomusicologist.* New York: McGraw-Hill, 1971.

Hornbostel, Erich M. von, and Curt Sachs. "Systematik der Musikinstrumente: Ein Versuch." *Zeitschrift für Ethnologie,* Jahrg. 1914, Heft 4/5 (1914): 553–590. Translated by Anthony Baines and Klaus P. Wachsmann as "Classification of Musical Instruments." *GSJ* 14 (1961): 3–29.

Hornell, James. *The Sacred Chank of India: A Monograph of the Indian Conch* (Turbinella pyrum). Madras Fisheries Bulletin 7. Madras: Government Press, 1914.

Hu Jiaxun. "Miao *Lusheng* Speech of Northwestern Guizhou and Its Musical Presentation." *Journal of Music in China* 1 (1999): 39–54. Translated by Yanzhi Cui from "Qianxibei Miaozu lusheng 'yu' xianxiang tanxi." *Musicology in China,* suppl. issue (1997): 20–26.

Hubbard, Frank. *Three Centuries of Harpsichord Making.* Cambridge, Mass.: Harvard University Press, 1965.

Huehns, Colin. "Experimental and Traditional *Huqin:* The *Sanhu* and *Erxianzi.*" *GSJ* 56 (2003): 61–68.

Hunt, Edgar. *The Recorder and Its Music.* London: Herbert Jenkins, 1962.

Institut de la Voix. *Le Chant Diphonique.* Dossier no. 1. Limoges: Institut de la Voix, 1989.

Izikowitz, Karl Gustav. *Musical and Other Sound Instruments of the South American Indians: A Comparative Ethnographical Study.* Göteborg, Sweden: Elanders, 1935.

Jackson, J. Wilfred. *Shells as Evidence of the Migrations of Early Cultures.* Manchester, England: Manchester University Press, 1917.

Jairazbhoy, Nazir Ali. "An Explication of the Hornbostel-Sachs Instrument Classification System." *Selected Reports in Ethnomusicology* 8 (1990): 81–104.

———. *A Musical Journey through India, 1963–1964.* Los Angeles: University of California, Department of Ethnomusicology, 1988.

———. *The Rāgs of North Indian Music: Their Structure and Evolution.* London: Faber, 1971.

Jans, Everhard. *Het Midwinterhoorn Blazen.* Enschede: Twents-Gelderse Uitgeverij Witkam, 1977.

Jeffreys, M. D. W. "Review Article: Africa and Indonesia." *African Music* 4:1 (1966/1967): 66–73.

Jones, A. M. *Africa and Indonesia: The Evidence of the Xylophone and Other Musical and Cultural Factors.* Leiden, the Netherlands: E. J. Brill, 1964.

———. "Experiment with a Xylophone Key." *African Music* 3:2 (1963): 6–10.

———. *Studies in African Music.* Oxford: OUP, 1959.

Jones, Trevor A. "The Didjeridu: Some Comparisons of Its Typology and Musical Functions with Similar Instruments throughout the World." *Studies in Music* 1 (1967): 23–55; 2 (1968): 111.

Juan i Nebot, Maria-Antònia. "Classificació d'instruments musicals, segons Erich von Hornbostel i Curt Sachs." *Fulls de Treball de Carrutxa,* segona època 2 (1994): 89–108.

———. "Versión castellana de la Clasificación de instrumentos musicales según Erich von Hornbostel y Curt Sachs (*Galpin Society Journal* XIV, 1961)." *Nassarre, Revista Aragonesa de Musicología* 14:1 (1998): 365–87.

Kaba, Melinda. *Die Römische Orgel von Aquincum (3. Jahrhundert).* Budapest: Akadémiai Kiadó, 1976.

Kalicz, Nandor. "Über die chronologische Stellung der Balaton-Gruppe in Ungarn." In *Symposium über die Enstehung und Chronologie der Badener Kultur,* ed. B. Chropovosky, 131–65. Bratislava: Slovenskej Akadémie Vied, 1973.

Kartomi, Margaret J. *On Concepts and Classification of Musical Instruments.* Chicago: University of Chicago Press, 1990.

Kaudern, Walter. *Musical Instruments in Celebes.* Ethnographical Studies in Celebes, vol. 3. The Hague: Martinus Nijhoff, 1927.

Kaufmann, Walter. *Altindien.* Musikgeschichte in Bildern 2:8. Leipzig: DVfM, 1981.

Kempers, A. J. Bernet. *The Kettledrums of Southeast Asia: A Bronze Age World and Its Aftermath.* Rotterdam: A. A. Balkema, 1988.

Kilbey, Maggie. *Curtal, Dulcian, Bajón: A History of the Precursor to the Bassoon.* St. Albans, England: M. Kilbey, 2002.

Kinsky, Georg. *Musikgeschichte in Bildern.* Leipzig: Breitkopf und Härtel, 1930. Published in English as *A History of Music in Pictures.* London: J. M. Dent and Sons; New York: E. P. Dutton & Co., 1930. [Editions in other languages are available as well.]

Kirby, Percival. *The Kettle-Drums.* London: OUP, 1930.

———. *The Musical Instruments of the Native Races of South Africa.* London: OUP, 1934.

Klier, Karl M. *Volkstümliche Musikinstrumente in den Alpen.* Kassel: Bärenreiter, 1956.

[Köhler, probably J. A.; attributed to "An Old Guard"]. *The Coach Horn: What to Blow and How to Blow It.* London: Köhler & Sons, 1878? 3rd ed., 1888. Reprint, London: Swaine Adeney Brigg, 1907– .

Koster, John. "A Contemporary Example of Harpsichord Forgery." *EM* (February 2000): 91–97.

———. "A Netherlandish Harpsichord of 1658 Re-examined." *GSJ* 53 (2000): 117–39.

Kubik, Gerhard. *Lamelofones do Museu Nacional de Etnologia.* Lisbon: Ministério da Cultura, 2002.

———. *Ostafrika.* Musikgeschichte in Bildern 1:10. Leipzig: DVfM, 1982.

———. *Westafrika*. Musikgeschichte in Bildern 1:11. Leipzig: DVfM, 1989.

Kunst, Jaap. "A Hypothesis about the Origin of the Gong." *Ethnos* (1947): 79–85, 147.

———. *Music in Java: Its History, Its Theory, and Its Technique*. The Hague: Martinus Nijhoff, 1949. 3rd enl. ed., ed. E. L. Heins. The Hague: Martinus Nijhoff, 1973.

———. "A Musicological Argument for Cultural Relationship between Indonesia—Probably the Isle of Java—and Central Africa." *Proceedings of the Musical Association* 62 (1936): 57–76.

———. *Musicologisch Onderzoek I: Over Zeldzame Fluiten en Veel-stemmige Muziek in het Ngada- en Nageh-Gebied (West-Flores)*. Batavia: Koninklijk Bataviaasch Genootschap van Kunsten en Wetenschappen, 1931.

Kunz, Ludvík. *Die Volksmusikinstrumente der Tschechoslowakei, Teil 1*. Handbuch der europäischen Volksmusikinstrumente 1:2. Leipzig: DVfM, 1974.

Larsson, Karl Erik. "The Conch Shells of Fiji." *Etnologiska Studier* 25 (1960): 121–47.

Latham, Alison, ed. *The Oxford Companion to Music*. Oxford: OUP, 2002.

Laurenty, Jean-Sébastien. *La systématique des aérophones de l'Afrique Centrale*. Tervuren: Musée Royal de l'Afrique Centrale, 1974.

———. *Les cordophones du Congo Belge et du Ruanda-Urundi*. Tervuren: Musée Royal du Congo Belge, 1960.

———. *Les sanza du Congo*. Tervuren: Musée Royal de l'Afrique Centrale, 1962.

———. *Les tambours à fente de l'Afrique Centrale*. Tervuren: Musée Royal de l'Afrique Centrale, 1968.

Lawergren, Bo. "Acoustics and Evolution of Arched Harps." *GSJ* 34 (1981): 110–29.

Lawson, Colin. "The Basset Clarinet Revived." *EM* 15:4 (November 1987): 487–501.

———. *The Chalumeau in Eighteenth-Century Music*. Ann Arbor, Mich.: UMI Research Press, 1981.

Lawson, Graeme, and Geoff Egan. "Medieval Trumpet from the City of London." *GSJ* 41 (1988): 63–66.

Le Cerf, G., and E.-R. Labande. *Les traités d'Henri-Arnaut de Zwolle et de divers anonymes (MS. B. N. Latin 7295)*. Paris: Auguste Picard, 1932. Reprint, Kassel: Bärenreiter, 1972.

Lehr, André. *The Art of the Carillon in the Low Countries*. Tielt, Belgium: Lannoo, 1991.

Leisiö, Timo. "Soitinten Luokitusjärjestelmä, Erich M. von Hornbostel ja Curt Sachs." *Musiikki* 1–4 (1974): 1–73.

Lewis-Williams, David. *The Mind in the Cave*. London: Thames & Hudson, 2002.

Lindley, Mark. *Lutes, Viols and Temperaments*. Cambridge: CUP, 1984.

Ling, Jan. *Nyckelharpan: Studier i ett folkligt musikinstrument*. Stockholm: P. A. Norstedt, 1967.

Linwood, Jamie Murray. "The Manufacture of Tuned Percussion Instruments in Indonesia and Africa—A Selective Study." Ph.D. thesis, London Guildhall University, 1995.

List, George. "The *Mbira* in Cartagena." *JIFMC* 20 (1968): 54–59.

Longyear, R. M. "Ferdinand Kauer's Percussion Enterprises." *GSJ* 27 (1974): 2–8.

Lovatto, Alberto. "The Production of Trumps in Valsesia (Piedmont, Italy)." *JIJHS* 1 (2004): 4–17.

Lund, Cajsa, ed., *The Bronze Lurs*, vol. 2 of *Second Conference of the ICTM Study Group on Music Archaeology*. Stockholm: Royal Swedish Academy of Music, 1986.

———. "A Medieval Tongue-(Lip-)and-Duct Flute." *GSJ* 34 (1981): 106–9.

Maas, Martha, and Jane McIntosh Snyder. *Stringed Instruments of Ancient Greece*. New Haven, Conn.: YUP, 1989.

MacDermott, K. H. *The Old Church Gallery Minstrels*. London: S. P. C. K., 1948.

Mahillon, Victor-Charles. *Catalogue Descriptif & Analytique du Musée Instrumental du Conservatoire Royal de Bruxelles, Précédé d'un essai de classification méthodique de tous les instruments anciens et modernes*. Gand: C. Annoot-Braeckman, 1880. Reprint, Brussels: Les Amis de la Musique, 1978.

Mannessischer Handschrift. Heidelberg University Library, MS Palatinus Germanicus 848, c. 1340.

Manniche, Lise. *Musical Instruments from the Tomb of Tut'ankhamūn*. Oxford: Griffith Institute, 1976.

Marcel-Dubois, Claudie. *Les instruments de musique de l'Inde ancienne*. Paris: Presses Universitaires de France, 1941.

Marvin, Bob. "Recorders and English Flutes in European Collections." *GSJ* 25 (1972): 30–57.

Mayr, Ernst. *The Growth of Biological Thought: Diversity, Evolution, and Inheritance*. Cambridge, Mass.: Belknap Press, 1982.

Mazār, Amīhāi. *Tel-Qasīle*. Tel Aviv: Mūsēiōn Ha'Āretz, 1983.

McAllester, David P. "An Apache Fiddle." *Ethno-Musicology Newsletter* 8 (September 1956): 1–5.

Megaw, J. V. S. "Penny Whistles and Prehistory." *Antiquity* 34 (1960): 6–13.

Menzies, Gavin. *1421: The Year China Discovered the World*. London: Bantam Press, 2002.

Mersenne, Marin. *Harmonie Universelle, contenant la Théorie et la Pratique de la Musique*. Paris: Sebastien Cramoisy, 1636. Facsimile, Paris: CNRS, 1963. [There is no reliable English translation of Mersenne.]

Meucci, Renato. "Roman Military Instruments and the *Lituus*." *GSJ* 42 (1989): 85–97.

Montagu, Gwen, and Jeremy Montagu. "Beverley Minster Reconsidered." *EM* 6:3 (July 1978): 401–15.

Montagu, Jeremy. "The Conch in Prehistory: Pottery, Stone, and Natural." *World Archaeology* 12:3 (1981): 273–79 and plates 11–18.

———. "The Construction of the Midwinterhoorn." *GSJ* 28 (1975): 71–80.

———. "The Creation of New Instruments." *GSJ* 59 (2006): 3–11.

———. "The Crozier of William of Wykeham." *EM* 30:4 (November 2002): 541–62.

———. "The Eliphone—A Retreating Reed." *GSJ* 51 (1998): 196–97.

———. *The Flute*. Princes Risborough, England: Shire, 1990.

———. "The Forked Shawm—An Ingenious Invention." *Yearbook for Traditional Music* 29 (1997): 74–79.

———. "Mouthpiece Development of the Bronze Lur and Its Musical Consequences." In *The Bronze Lurs*, ed. Cajsa Lund, 211–15. Stockholm: Royal Swedish Academy of Music, 1986.

———. "Musical Instruments in Hans Memling's Paintings." *Early Music* 35:4 (2007), forthcoming.

———. Instruments in the Macclesfield Psalter." *EM* 34:2 (May 2006): 189–204.

———. *Musical Instruments of the Bible*. Lanham, Md.: Scarecrow Press, 2002.

———. "The Oldest Organ in Christendom." *FoMRHIQ* 35 (April 1984): Comm. 534, 51–52.

———. "On the Skill of the Nürnberg Brass Instrument Makers—A Tribute." *FoMRHIQ* 43 (April 1986): Comm. 722, 124–26.

———. "One of Tutankhamon's Trumpets." *GSJ* 29 (1976): 115–17. Reprinted in *Journal of Egyptian Archaeology* 64 (1978): 133–34.

———. *Reed Instruments: The Montagu Collection, an Annotated Catalogue*. Lanham, Md.: Scarecrow Press, 2001.

———. "The Restored Chapter House Wall Paintings in Westminster Abbey." *EM* 16:2 (May 1988): 239–51.

———. *Timpani and Percussion*. New Haven, Conn.: YUP, 2002.

———. *The World of Medieval and Renaissance Musical Instruments*. Newton Abbot, England: David & Charles; Woodstock, N.Y.: Overlook, 1976.

———. *The World of Romantic and Modern Musical Instruments*. Newton Abbot, England: David & Charles; Woodstock, N.Y.: Overlook, 1981.

Montagu, Jeremy, and John Burton. "A Proposed New Classification System for Musical Instruments." *Ethnomusicology* 15:1 (January 1971): 49–70.

Montagu, Jeremy, and Gwen Montagu. *Minstrels and Angels: Carvings of Musicians in Medieval English Churches*. Berkeley, Calif.: Fallen Leaf Press, 1998.

Morley-Pegge, Reginald. *The French Horn*. London: Ernest Benn, 1960.

Müller, Mette. "The Danish Skalmeje." *SIMP* 3 (1974): 164–66.

The New Grove Dictionary of Music and Musicians, ed. Stanley Sadie. 2nd ed. London: Macmillan, 2001.

The New Grove Dictionary of Musical Instruments, ed. Stanley Sadie. London: Macmillan, 1984.

Norlind, Tobias. *Systematik der Saiteninstrumente*. Vol. 1, *Geschichte der Zither*. Stockholm: Musikhistorisches Museum, 1936.

Olsen, Dale A. *Music of El Dorado: The Ethnomusicology of Ancient South American Cultures*. Gainesville: University Press of Florida, 2002.

Ord-Hume, Arthur W. J. G. *Barrel Organ: The Story of the Mechanical Organ and Its Repair*. London: Allen & Unwin, 1978.

———. *Harmonium: The History of the Reed Organ and Its Makers*. Newton Abbot, England: David & Charles, 1986.

Pamplin, Terence. "The Baroque Baryton: The Origin and Development in the 17th Century of a Solo, Self-accompanying, Bowed and Plucked Instrument Played from Tablature." Ph.D. thesis, Kingston University, 2001.

———. "The Influence of the Bandora on the Origin of the Baroque Baryton." *GSJ* 53 (2000): 221–32.

Perrot, Jean. *The Organ from Its Invention in the Hellenistic Period to the End of the Thirteenth Century*, trans. Norma Deane. London: OUP, 1971.

Picken, Laurence E. R. "An Afghan Quail-Lure of Typological and Acoustic Interest." *SIMP* 3 (1974): 172–75 and illus. 283–85.

———. *Folk Musical Instruments of Turkey*. London: OUP, 1975.

———. "The 'Plucked' Drums: *Gopi Yantra* and *Ananda Lahari*." *Musica Asiatica* 3 (1981): 29–33.

Picken, L. E. R., C. J. Adkins, and T. F. Page. "The Making of a *Khāēn*: The Free-Reed Mouth-Organ of North-East Thailand." *Musica Asiatica* 4 (1984): 117–54.

Piggott, Stuart. "The *Carnyx* in Early Iron Age Britain." *Antiquaries Journal* 39 (1959): 19–32.

Pilling, Julian. "Fiddles with Horns." *GSJ* 28 (1975): 86–92.

Playford, John. *A Breif Introduction To the Skill of Musick: for Song and Viol. In two Books. First book contains the Grounds and Rules of Musick for Song. Second Book, Directions for the Playing on the Viol de Gambo, and also on the Treble-Violin*. 2nd ed. London: Printed by W. Godbid, for John Playford, 1658.

Pollens, Stewart. *The Early Pianoforte*. Cambridge: CUP, 1995.

Powell, Ardal. *The Flute*. New Haven, Conn.: YUP, 2002.

Praetorius, Michael. *Syntagma Musicum II—De Organographia*. Braunschweig: Elias Holwein, 1619. Facsimile, Kassel: Bärenreiter, 1958. Translated and edited by David Z. Crookes. Oxford: Clarendon Press, 1986.

Price, Percival. *Bells and Man*. Oxford: OUP, 1983.

Puglisi, Filadelfio. "The 17th-Century Recorders of the Accademia Filarmonica of Bologna." *GSJ* 34 (1981): 33–43.

Quantz, Johann Joachim. *Versuch einer Anweisung die Flöte traversiere zu spielen*. Berlin: Johann Friedrich Boss, 1752. Translated and edited by Edward R. Reilly as *On Playing the Flute*. London: Faber, 1966.

Rabinovici, Alison. "Augustus Stroh's Phonographic Violin, a Journey: Victorian London, Australia, Transylvania." *GSJ* 58 (2005): 100–123.

Rapapallit ja Lakuttimet. Kauhava: Kansanmusiiki-instituutin, 1985.

Rashid, Subhi Anwar. *Mesopotamien*. Musikgeschichte in Bildern 2:2. Leipzig: DVfM, 1984.

Rault, Lucie, ed. *La voix du dragon: Trésors archéologiques et art campanaire de la Chine ancienne*. Paris: Musée de la Musique, 2000.

———. *Musical Instruments: A Worldwide Survey of Traditional Music-Making*. London: Thames & Hudson, 2000.

Rees, Helen. *Echoes of History: Naxi Music in Modern China*. Oxford: OUP, 2000.

Reese, David S. "The Late Bronze Age to Geometric Shells from Kition." In V. Karageorghis, *Excavations at Kition*, vol. 5, part 2, pp. 340–71 [part 2 of appendix 8(A)]. Nicosia, Cyprus: Department of Antiquities, 1985.

Remnant, Mary. *English Bowed Instruments from Anglo-Saxon to Tudor Times*. Oxford: Clarendon Press, 1986.

Reznikoff, Iégor, and Michel Dauvois. "La dimension sonore des grottes ornées." *Bulletin de la Société Préhistorique Française* 85:8 (1988): 238–46.

Rice, Albert R. *The Baroque Clarinet*. Oxford: Clarendon Press, 1992.

Rimmer, Joan. *The Irish Harp*. Cork, Ireland: Mercier Press, 1969.

———. "The Morphology of the Irish Harp." *GSJ* 17 (1964): 39–49.

———. "The Morphology of the Triple Harp." *GSJ* 18 (1965): 90–103.

Ripin, Edwin M. "The Norrlanda Organ and the Ghent Altarpiece." *SIMP* 3 (1974): 193–96 and illus. 286–88.

Rockstro, Richard S. *A Treatise on the Construction, the History and the Practice of the Flute, Including a Sketch of the Elements of Acoustics*. London: Rudall, Carte, 1890. Reprint of the 1928 2nd ed., London: Musica Rara, 1967.

Rose, Algernon S. *Talks with Bandsmen*. London: William Ryder & Son, 1894. Reprint, London: Tony Bingham, 1995.

Rowland-Jones, Anthony. "Iconography in the History of the Recorder up to c. 1430." *EM* 33:4 (November 2005): 557–74; 34:1 (February 2006): 3–27.

Rycroft, David. "Friction Chordophones in South-Eastern Africa." *GSJ* 19 (1966): 84–100.

———. *Zulu, Swazi en Xhosa instrumentale en vocale muziek*. Tervuren: Koninklijk Museum voor Midden-Afrika, in conjunction with Belgische Radio en Televisie, 1969.

Sachs, Curt. *Geist und Werden der Musikinstrumente, von Curt Sachs . . . Mit 48 lichtdrucktafeln*. Berlin: D. Reimer, 1929. Reprint, Hilversum: Frits Knuf, 1965.

———. *The History of Musical Instruments*. New York: W. W. Norton, 1940.

———. *Les instruments de musique de Madagascar*. Paris: Institut d'Ethnologie, 1938.

Sárosi, Bálint. *Die Volksmusikinstrumente Ungarns*. Handbuch der europäischen Volksmusikinstrumente 1:1. Leipzig: DVfM, 1967.

Sayce, Lynda. "The Development of Italianate Continuo Lutes." Ph.D. thesis, Open University, 2001.

Sayers, Dorothy L. *The Nine Tailors*. London: Gollancz, 1934.

Schaeffner, André. *Origine des instruments de musique: Introduction ethnologique à l'histoire de la musique instrumentale*. Paris: Payot, 1936. Reprint, Paris: Mouton, 1968.

Schaik, Martin van. "The Divine Bird: The Meaning and Development of the Water Bird Embellishment on Musical Instruments in Ancient Greece." *Imago Musicae* 18/19 (2001/2002): 11–33.

———. *The Marble Harp Players from the Cyclades*. Utrecht, the Netherlands: Dutch Study Group on Music Archaeology (NWM), 1998.

Scholes, Percy A., ed. *The Oxford Companion to Music*. 10 editions. London: OUP, 1938–1970.

Seebass, Tilman. *Musikdarstellung und Psalterillustration im früheren Mittelalter*. Bern: Francke Verlag, 1973.

Seeger, Peter. *Steel Drums: How to Play Them and Make Them*. New York: Oak, 1961.

Seewald, Otto. *Beiträge zur Kenntnis der Steinzeitlichen Musikinstrumente Europas*. Vienna: Anton Schroll, 1934.

Shepherd, Edgar C. *The Sound of Bells*. London: Record Books, 1964.

Shōsōin Office, ed. (Kenzo Hayashi, Shigeo Kishibe, Ryōichi Taki, and Sukehiro Shiba). *Musical Instruments in the Shōsōin*. Tokyo: Nihon Keizai Shimbun Sha, 1967.

Simpson, Christopher. *The Division Violist; or, The Art of Playing Extempore upon a Ground*. 2nd rev. ed. London: Henry Brome, 1665. Facsimile, London: J. Curwen, 1955.

Slim, H. Colin. "Paintings of Lady Concerts and the Transmission of 'Jouissance vous donneray.'" *Imago Musicae* 1 (1984): 51–73 and figs. 1–4.

Snoeck, C. C. *Catalogue de la collection d'instruments de musique anciens ou curieux*. Gand: J. Vuylsteke, 1894. Facsimile, Ghent: Guy Rooryck, 1999.

So, Jenny F., ed. *Music in the Age of Confucius*. Washington: Freer Gallery of Art and Arthur M. Sackler Gallery, Smithsonian Institution, 2000.

Spitzer, John, and Neal Zaslaw. *The Birth of the Orchestra: History of an Institution, 1650–1815*. New York: OUP, 2004.

Stradner, Gerhard. "Die Musikinstrumente im Steiermärkischen Landeszeughaus in Graz." *Veröffentlichungen des Landeszeughauses Graz* 6 (1976): 7–36.

———. *Musikinstrumente in Grazer Sammlungen*. Tabulae Musicae Austriacae, Bd XI. Vienna: Verlag der Österreichischen Akademie der Wissenschaften, 1986.

Tabourot, Jean. See Arbeau, Thoinot.

Talbot, Michael. "Vivaldi's Conch Concerto." *Informazioni e Studi Vivaldiani* 5 (1984): 66–81.

Tammen, Björn R. *Musik und Bild im Chorraum mittelalterlicher Kirchen, 1100–1500*. Berlin: Dietrich Reimer Verlag, 2000.

Temperley, Nicholas. *The Music of the English Parish Church*. Cambridge: CUP, 1979.

Thomas, Jeffrey. "Steel Band/Pan." In *Encyclopedia of Percussion*, ed. John H. Beck, 297–331. New York: Garland, 1995.

Thrasher, Alan R. *Chinese Musical Instruments*. Hong Kong: OUP, 2000.

Tiella, Marco. "The Violeta of S. Caterina de' Vigri." *GSJ* 28 (1975): 60–70.

Tongeren, Mark C. van. *Overtone Singing: Physics and Metaphysics of Harmonics in East and West*. Amsterdam: Fusica, 2002.

Tracey, Hugh. *Chopi Musicians: Their Music, Poetry, and Instruments*. Oxford: International African Institute, 1948.

Trân Van Khê. *La musique vietnamienne traditionelle*. Paris: Presses Universitaires de France, 1962.

The Triumph of Maximilian I: 137 Woodcuts by Hans Burgkmair and Others. New York: Dover, 1964.

Trowell, Brian. "King Henry IV, Recorder Player." *GSJ* 10 (1957): 83–84.

Trowell, Margaret, and K. P. Wachsmann. *Tribal Crafts of Uganda*. London: OUP, 1953.

Turnbull, Harvey. *The Guitar from the Renaissance to the Present Day*. London: Batsford, 1974.

Tyler, James. *The Early Guitar: A History and Handbook*. London: OUP, 1980.

Tyler, James, and Paul Sparks. *The Early Mandolin: The Mandolino and the Neapolitan Mandoline*. Oxford: Clarendon Press, 1989.

Utrecht Psalter. University of Utrecht Library, Ms. no. 32, c. 825.

Vargyas, Lajos. "Performing Styles in Mongolian Chant." *JIFMC* 20 (1968): 70–72.

Vertkov, K., G. Blagodatov, and E. Yazovitskaya. *Atlas of Musical Instruments of the Peoples Inhabiting the USSR* [in Russian with English summaries (2nd ed. only)]. 2nd ed. Moscow: State Publishers, 1975.

Virdung, Sebastian. *Musica getutscht*. Basel: Michael Furter, 1511. Trans. and ed. Beth Bullard. Cambridge: CUP, 1993.

Von Falkenhausen, Lothar. *Suspended Music: Chime Bells in the Culture of Bronze Age China*. Berkeley: University of California Press, 1993.

Wackernagel, Bettina. *Holzblasinstrumente Bayerisches Nationalmuseum München*. Tutzing: Hans Schneider, 2005.

Wainwright, Jonathan, and Peter Holman, eds. *From Renaissance to Baroque: Changes in Instruments and Instrumental Music in the Seventeenth Century*. Aldershot, England: Ashgate, 2005.

Wallin, Nils, Björn Merker, and Steven Brown, eds. *The Origins of Music*. Cambridge, Mass.: MIT Press, 2000.

Webb, John. "The Billingsgate Trumpet." *GSJ* 41 (1988): 59–62 and plates 6–10.

Weber, Rainer. "Recorder Finds from the Middle Ages, and Results of Their Reconstruction." *GSJ* 29 (1976): 35–41.

Wegner, Max. *Griechenland*. Musikgeschichte in Bilden 2:4. Leipzig: DVfM, 1963.

Wells, Elizabeth, ed. *Keyboard Instruments*. London: Royal College of Music, 2000.

West, M. L. *Ancient Greek Music*. Oxford: Clarendon Press, 1992.

Widdess, D. R., and R. F. Wolpert, ed. *Music and Tradition: Essays on Asian and Other Musics Presented to Laurence Picken*. Cambridge: CUP, 1981.

Williams, Leonard. *The Dancing Chimpanzee: A Study of the Origins of Primitive Music*. London: André Deutsch, 1967.

Williams, Peter. *The European Organ, 1450–1850*. London: B. T. Batsford, 1966.

———. *A New History of the Organ*. London: Faber, 1980.

Williamson, Muriel C. "The Construction and Decoration of One Burmese Harp." *Selected Reports* 1:2 (1968): 46–76.

———. "The Construction and Decoration of One Burmese Harp: Supplement." *Selected Reports in Ethnomusicology* 2:2 (1975): 111–16.

———. "The Iconography of Arched Harps in Burma." In *Music and Tradition: Essays on Asian and Other Musics Presented to Laurence Picken*, ed. D. R. Widdess and R. F. Wolpert, 209–28. Cambridge: CUP, 1981.

Winternitz, Emanuel. "Early Violins in Paintings by Gaudenzio Ferrari and His School." In Emanuel Winternitz, *Musical Instruments and Their Symbolism in Western Art*, 99–109 and plates 38–41. London: Faber, 1967.

———. "The Lira da Braccio." In Emanuel Winternitz, *Musical Instruments and Their Symbolism in Western Art*, 86–98 and plates 30–37. London: Faber, 1967.

———. "The Survival of the Kithara and the Evolution of the English Cittern: A Study in Morphology." *Journal of the Warburg and Courtauld Institutes* 24:3–4 (1961): 222–29. Reprinted in Emanuel Winternitz, *Musical Instruments and Their Symbolism in Western Art*, 57–65 and plates 12–17.

Wood, Henry J. *My Life of Music*. London: Victor Gollancz, 1938.

Woodfield, Ian. *The Early History of the Viol*. Cambridge: CUP, 1984.

Wright, Laurence. "The Medieval Gittern and Citole: A Case of Mistaken Identity." *GSJ* 30 (1977): 8–42.

Wright, Michael. "Jue harpes, Jue trumpes, 1481." *JIJHS* 2 (2004): 7–10.

Yuan Bingchang and Mao Jizeng, eds. *Zhongguo Shaoshu Minzu Yueqi Zhi*. Beijing: Xin Shijie Chubanshe, 1986. Reprint, Taiwan: Musical China, 1988.

Yupho, Dhanit. *Thai Musical Instruments*, trans. David Morton. Bangkok: Department of Fine Arts, 1960.

Zhang, Juzhong, Garmann Harbottle, Changsui Wang, and Zhaochen Kong. "Oldest Playable Musical Instruments Found at Jiahu Early Neolithic Site in China." *Nature* 401:6751 (23 September 1999): front cover and 366–68.

Ziegler, Christiane. *Catalogue des instruments de musique égyptiens*. Paris: Éditions de la Réunion des Musées Nationaux, 1979.

Zuckermann, Wolfgang Joachim. *The Modern Harpsichord: Twentieth-Century Instruments and Their Makers*. New York: October House, 1969.

Index of Instruments and Accessories

Page numbers in italic refer to figures.

accordion, 97
adufe, 29
aeolian bows, 196
aerophones, acoustics, 217–19; classified, 213–14
alboka, 87, 89
Alemannic lyre, 70, 131
alghaita, 75, 77
Alor, bronze drums, 81
alphorn, 106, *108*, 180, 219; construction, 180; lowland, 180–81; Romania, 180
American organ, 97
Amorschall, 119
ananda lahari, 207
angklung, 19, 20
angkulari, 95
angle harp. *See* harp
animal lures, 85, 86
animal scarer, 24
antara, 46
anthropomorphic terminology, 155
anvil, *37*, 44
Apache, fiddle, 196; flute, 117
Appalachian dulcimer, 142, 144
arched harp. *See* harp
archicistre, 160
archlute, 161
arcicembalo, 216
area of open hole, 32, 51, 52
arghūl, 88
arpa doppia, 136, 139
arpicembalo, 147
arpichordum, 101, 133, 177n66
atoke, 18, *183*
aulos, 74–75, 106

Aura, 199
autoharp, *143*
automatic instruments, 24

babies' bells and rattles, 24
bağlama, 75, *76*
bagpipe, 79–80, 87; drones, 101; reeds, 86, 87
bajón, 83
balaban, 75, *76*
balalaika, 155
balo, *12*
bambaro, *198*, 199
bandoneon, 97
bands: brass, 123; church, 110, 122; civilian, 122; competitions, 122; flute, Lithuania, 44; flute, Venda, 44; horn, Africa, 44; horn, Russia, 44; Janissary, 78, 94; klezmer, 94; military, 117, 123; one-man, 37, 98; town, 121, 123; violin, 172; works, 122–23
bandurria, *160*
banhu, *164*
banjos, 161
bansi, 87
bansri, 60
barbitos, 129
baritone, 110, 111
bark drum, 65
barrel organ, 56, 192–93
baryton, 171
bass drum, 38
bass horn, 110
bass oboe, 83
bass shawm, 83
bass violin, 170. *See also* cello
basset horn, 93–94

"Bassi," 170
bassoon, 83–84; double (contra), 84; keys, 83; parts of, 83; range, 83; systems, 83–84
bāyā, 32, 33
beetle, 200
beganna, 130, 131
bells, 14–16, 180; animal, 14, 15, 24, 180; change-ringing, 14–15; defined, 14; domestic, 15–16; forged iron, 18, 44, 183–84; hand, 44; as musical chimes, 14, 47; powers of, 24; resting, 16, 17; as signals, 181; singing, 16, 17; slit drum as prototype, 14; substitutes for, 16; tubular, 16, 70; tuning overtones, 14; weight of, 16; with two pitches, 14. See also pellet bells
"belly," 155
bendir, 29
béquilles, 137
bīn, 140
biniou, 79
bird lures, 50, 85, 86
bird-scarer, 4, 24, 25
birimbão, 125, 195, 196
biwa, 156
Blockwerk, 189
boatswain's call, 49, 50
bombard, 78
bombarde, 79
bombardon, 111
bonang, 205
bones, 26
bore, of reed instruments contrasted, 73–74, 218
bouzouki, 205
bow, 161–63; Chinese, 163; frog, 162–63; hair, 162; how held, 172; point, 163; tensioned, 162; Tourte, 163, 169
bow harp. See harp
bowing, 162–63, 206; brass instruments, acoustics, 218–19; crooks and shanks, earliest, 108; developments of mechanical technology, 119; harmonic vent, 109, 119; left- or right-handed, 162; malleable as spaghetti, 112; mouthpiece shapes, 105, 107; origins of, 161; percussion players, 174; popularity of in bands, 123; terminology for, xiv. See also individual instruments; valves
brays, 101, 133, 135
brille, 93
broken reed, 45
bronze drums, 39
buccin trombones, 106
bucina, 106
bucium, 180
buffalo horns, 185
bugle, 105, 112
bugle, 110, 112; bamboo, Naga, 78, 106, 113. See also key bugle
bukkehorn, 111
bull-roarer, 3, 4, 180
buskers, 98, 174

buzuk, 154
buzzers, 4, 6, 11, 12, 13, 133
buzzing disc, 3

caki buta, 20
calliopes, 193
cane instruments, 57–58
canon, 142
carillon, 14
carnyx, 106
castanets, 26
castanyoles, 26
cattle bells, 14, 15, 24
cello, 170; leader in modification, 169
cembalo, 147
cervelat, 85
cetula, 158, 159
chalumeau, 89–90, 91; d'amour, 90; bass, 90; keys, 90; mouthpiece, 90
change-ringing, 14–15
chank, 103–4, 113
charter horns, 106
cheek-pumping, 75, 79, 87, 205
chelys, 129
chi, 59
children's instruments, 4, 5, 24, 85, 196
chirimía, 77
chitarra battente, 159
chitarrone, 161
chordophones, acoustics, 219; classification, 212
chung, 29
church bass, 122
churinga, 4
ciaramella, 79
cift telli, 154
cimbalom, 144, 149
cimbasso, 112
circular breathing, 75, 79, 87, 205
cistre, 160
citera, 141
cither, 160
citole, 159
cittern, 159
clappers, 25, 26
clarinet, 90, 91–94; bore, 94, keys, 90–92, mouthpiece, 90; mouthpiece, position, 93; reed, 94; sizes, 93; slow to be adopted, 92; systems, 93, 94; transposing instrument, 90
clarino technique, 109, 119, 121
clarsach, 135–36, 139
clavecin, 147
claves, 1
clavichord, 145–46; fretting, 146; names for, 147; revived, 152
clavicytherium, 148
click sticks, 1, 26, 205

clog violin, 171
coach horn, 181
cock-crow, 5
cog-rattles, *25*
colascione, 155
color organ, 217
comb and paper, *7*
common flute, 55
concertina, 97
conch, 24, 112, 103, *104–5*, 181; absence from Africa, 103; added mouthpiece, 104; fingerhole, 104; hand-stopping, 181; pottery skeuomorphs, 103, *114*; protection against storms, 32; substitutes, 113; uses, 181
constricted foot, 118, 124–25
contained air, as a dominant, 32
contrabassoon, 84
contrabassophone, 84
contrebass-à-anche, 81, 123
cor anglais, 82, 83
cor anglais moderne, 83
cornet, 111, 206
cornet de poste, 110
cornett, *108*, 109
corno da caccia, 112
cornu, 106
corps de rechange, 62–63
crémaillère, 162
crochet, 137
cromornes, 82, 83
crook, 108
crumhorns, 85
crwth, 131, *132*, 167, 174
čurlik-slavić, 58
curtal, 83
cylindrical and widening bores contrasted, 73–74, 218
cymbals, *17–18*; Chinese crash, 18; on tongs, 18, 70, *71*
czakan, 58

daira, 21, 29
damalgo, 88, 89
damaru, 30
darabukke, 30
davul, 38, 39
derbacka, 30
detritus of our modern age, *20*, 47, *164*, 205
détska rehtačka, *25*
deutsche Schalmey, 81
dholak, 32
di, 60
diable, 3
didjeridu, *1*, *26*, 205–6
diple, 89
 dital harp, 139
division viol, 172
dizi, 60

dobachi, *17*
dolçaina, 79
Dongson drums, 81
donno, *182*, *183*
Dordrecht recorder, 118
double bass, 170–71
double bassoon, 84
double bells, *183–84*
double harp. *See* harp
double pipes, 86
douçaine, 85
draw-trumpet, 108
dril-bu, 31, *113*
drones, 100–102; importance in India, 100
drums, in general, defined, 28; all pitched, 29; barrel, 30, 33; bouncing strokes, 37; chimes, 31, 93; frame, 28–29; goblet, 31; heads, 38–39; hourglass, 30–31, 113, 183; kettle, 33–35; orchestras, 31, 44; origin, 28, 65; pellet, 30; shaman's, 29; tensioning, 27–28, 38; terminology imprecise, 38; tubular, 28–33, 37–38; tubular, shapes of, 28, 29; waisted, 31, *32*; snares, 29, 32, 37; woman's instrument, 29. *See also* individual instruments; friction drums; plucked drums; steel drums
drums, in "our" culture. *See* individual instruments
duct flutes. *See* flutes, duct-blown
dulce melos, 149
dulcimer, hammer, 11, 140, *142*, 144, 149
dultzaina, 79
Dulzian, 83
dutar, 141, *154*, 155

egg-clappers, 25, *26*
electric guitar, 205, 206
electronic amplification, 202, 203, 205
electronic organs, 202–3; initiation of notes, 202
embouchure, 48
English horn, 82, 83
ennanga, *133*
épinette, 147
épinette des vosges, 142
erhu, 163, *164*
ese, *31*
esquella, 15
euphonium, 111

facimbalom, 11, 144
fiddles, 161–74; belly material, 166; Mexico, *166*; Norway, 171; solid-bodied, 163–64, *165–66*; spiked, 163, *164*. *See also* bowing; keyed fiddle
fiddles, medieval, 70, 166–67; how held, 167; Lincoln Cathedral, *167*; *Mary Rose*, 166; Płock, *166*, 167
field drum, 38
fife, *37*, 61
fine-tuner, 27
fingerhole brass, 104, 109, 110, *111*

flabiol, 57
flageolet, 56–57, 58; alternative heads, 56; bird, 56; double, 56; keywork, 56
flat-backed mandolin, *160*
flatt trumpet, 109
flauto traverso, 55
Flügel, 147
flugel horn, 111
fluier, 58, 101
fluste à neuf trous, 54
flûte d'accord, 56
flûte d'allemagne, 55
flûte eunuque, 6, 7
flutes, 44–65; acoustics, 217–18; as recorder, 55; bone, Paleolithic, 45, 46; China, prehistoric, 53; distinction from whistles, 48; harmonic, 65–66; nose-blown, 47, 48; notch-blown, 47
flutes, cross. See flutes, transverse
flutes, duct-blown, 48, 52–59; constricted foot, 54, 58–59; developmental sequence, 47; external duct, 53; external plus internal duct, 54; geometry of the head, 53; position of duct, 59; problematic fingering techniques, 52–53; rear duct, 59; tongue-duct, 53, 59; with added membrane, 6; with hummed drone, 151. See also flageolet; recorder
flutes, endblown, 44, 45–47; chamfering the end, 45, 47; developmental sequence, 45; materials, 47; playing accurately in tune, 48; with hummed drone, 150–51
flutes, transverse, 48, 59, 60–61, 62, 63, 64–66, *118*; adoption of closed keys, 63; Baroque vs. Renaissance, 62; Boehm system, conical, 63, 64, 118; Boehm system, cylindrical, 63, 64, 119; bore in Baroque, 62; bore in the Renaissance, 61; central embouchure, 64; China, development in, 59–60; cross-fingering, 62; earliest surviving, 48; electronic, 203; first appearance in Europe, 48, 61; hand-stopping, 64; Indian origin, 48; modification in nineteenth century, 118–19; New Guinea spirit flutes, 48, 65; one-key, 62; Quantz keys, 216; rarity in world, 48; Reform flute, *118*, 119; sizes, Medieval, 61, systems, 118–19; three-piece vs. four-piece, 62; tuning slide, 64; upper-body joints, advantages of, 62; with added membrane, 6, 59
flutes, vessel, 50, *51–52*; acoustic behavior, 51; ocarinas, 51–52; oldest known, 51
foghorns, 181
forked shawm, 78
forepillar, 134–35
fourchette, 137
free reed instruments, 13, 73, 94–95, 96, 97–98, *197*; acoustics, 219; defined, 94; reed organs, 96–97; reed organs, percussion stop, 96. See also mouth organs.
frequency-doubler, 127, 207
frets, 155–56, 172
friction drum, 4, 5–6, 207
fuyara, 58

gambang, 10
gamelan, 10, 17, 19; gongsmiths, 44
gar klein, 55
garaya, 153
gardon, 102, 144
gemshorn, *51*
gender, 10
genggong, 198, 211
German flute, 55
ghaita, 76, 77
ghiterne, 158, 159
gittern, 159
glass harmonica, 18
gnibri, 153
goge, 164
gong ageng, 17
gongs, 16–17; defined, 14; earliest traces, 17; orchestral, 17; shields as, 16; smiths, 44
gopi yantra, 207
!*gora*, 195, 196
gourd bow. See musical bow
gralla sec, 79
grass stems, flattened, 196
gravicembalo col piano e forte, 149
gregger, 25
ground bow. See musical bow
guan, 75, 76
gudok, 166
guimbarde, 199, 211
guitar, 27, 159, 161, 211; electric, 205, 206
guittar, 27, 160
guitarra, 62, 159, *160*
guiterra, 158, 159
gusle, 162, *165*

half-spiked lutes. See lutes
hammer dulcimer. See dulcimer
Hammond organ, 202
handbells, 44
hand-stopping: on conches, 52, 181; on flutes, 139–40; on horns, 52, 113, 121, 181, 185, 206, 209; on trumpets, 109
Hardanger fele, 168, 171
harmonic vent-hole, 109, 119
harmonica, 97, 98
harmonium, 96–97, 101
harp: angle harp, 127, 134; arched harp, 127, *132*; bow harp, *126*, 127, 132–33; contrasted with lyre, 128
harp, pillar harp, 134–39; Baroque, 136, 139; brays, 101, 133; Cycladic, *134*; double, 136, 139; gothic, 136; hook, 136, 139; hook, external pedal mechanism, 139; Irish, *135–36*, 139; medieval, 133, 135–36; modern folk, 139; pedal, *137–38*, 139; pedal, tuning, 138; Renaissance, 136; Renaissance, transmitted abroad, 136; triple, 136; Welsh, 135, 136; with blind musicians, 306

harp guitar, 139, 160
harp lute, 139, 160
harp-psaltery, 142
harpsichord, *146*, 147–49; mechanism, 146; names for, 147; national styles, 148; *ravalement*, 149; revival, 152; split keys, 216; stops, 148; transposing, 148
hautbois, 80
hautbois baryton, 82
hearp, *130*, 135
heckelphone, 83
helicon, 112
Helmholtz resonator, 52
heterozeug reeds, 85–86
hichiriki, 75, 76
highland pipe, 79, 80
high-twist gut, 129, 219
hnè-galei, 77
hoboy, 80
hoe blade, 184
horagai, *104*
horanāva, 77
horn: animal origin, 106; distinction from trumpet, 105; free-reed, 95; hand-stopping, 52, 185, 208, 209; Irish Bronze Age, 105; materials, 113, 185; materials, buffalo, 185; materials, ivory absent from India, 185; motor, 85, 86, 181; side blown, 105, 113, *184*–85; side blown, advantages of, 184–5
horn, orchestral, 112–13; chords, xv, 200; construction, 112; crooks, 112; French, 112; hand-stopping, 52, 113, 121, 181, 206; hunting instrument, 112, *174*; hunting instrument, with free reed, 95; valve horn, 206
horn, worldwide, animal, *104*, 105–6, *184*; metal substitutes, 113; with fingerholes, 110, *111*
horn band: African, 44; Russian, 44
Horn of Ulph, 106
hornpipe, 87
horsehair, 135, 153, 161, 162
hulusheng, 96, 185
hummed drone, 101
hurdy-gurdy, 15, 101, 173, *174*; with blind beggars, 133, 173
hydraulis, 188

idioglot reeds, 85–86
idiophones, acoustics, 220; classified, 212; all pitched, 29
inanga, *141*
inkin, *17*
Instrument, 147
instruments bas and *haut*, 109
instruments: best built empirically, 221; compared with human voice, 206; flexibility important, 221; inclusivity, 2; modified over time, 203; began, 1

jacks, 146
Jäger Trommet, 112

jaltarang, 18
jap fiddles, *174*
"jaw harp," 22n42
Jews harp. *See* trump
jingles, 18
jouhikantele, 131

kacacakai, *19*
kacikaura, *19*
kahon mahiri, *183*, *184*
kakaki, 107
kalangu, *182*, *183*
kalimba, 12–13, 21, 133
kantele, *142*
karadeniz kemençe, *165*
Karen drums, 81
kartal, 26
kaval, *47*; with *ison*, 101
kayagum, 144
kazoo, 6, *7*, 134
kemengeh, *164*
keyboard, invention, 206
key bugle, 110, *111*, 119
key trumpet, 109–10, 119
keyed fiddle, *174*
keys, lever inadequate, 118–19
khāēn, 95, 96, *197*
khomus, 199
kidimbadimba, *10*
kinnor, 128, 131
kissar, *130*–31
kithara, 70, *71*, 129, 206
Klavier, 147
knuckle bone, 3
kollopes, 129
koma-bue, 60
koto, 144
Kru "harp," 126
kubing, *198*
kubiz, 199
kuge, *183*, *184*
kurai, *47*

lali ne meke, 9, *10*
langeleik, *142*
langspil, *142*
lesiba, *195*, *196*
ligawka, 180
lion roar, 5
lira, Greek island, *165*, *166*, *167*
lira da braccio, *167*; tuning, 172
lithophone, 6–9
lituus, 106
long drum, 38

long-necked lutes. *See* lutes, plucked worldwide
Lotus flute, 49
lur, 105
lusheng, 185
lutes in Europe, 156–58, 160–61; as accompanist, 160; construction, 156; extended, 161; introduction into Europe, 156; playing technique, 158; tablature, 144–45
lutes, bowed. *See* fiddles
lutes, plucked worldwide, 152–56; body shapes, 155; half-spiked, *153*; long-necked, *154–55, 157*; long-necked, medieval, 156; short-necked, 156–57, 158–61; spiked, 127, 152–54, 161
lyra, 129
lyre, *71*, 126, 128–30, 131, 135; Alemannic, 70, 131; bowed, 131, *132*, 167, 174; contrasted with harp, 128; Greek, 128–29, 131; legendary origin, 128, 130; playing techniques, 131; symmetric and asymmetric, 129
lyre guitars, 159

machete, 159
machine tuning, 27
mak-woed, 4
mammoth bones, 7
mandolin, 159, 161, 205
mandore, 159
manichord, 147
maracas, 20
marimba, 12
marímbula, 13
masenqo, 163, 164
matracas, 19, 25, 26
maui xaphoon, 91
Maultrommel, 196, 199
mazhar, 29
mbila, 10
mbira, 12–13, 21, 133
mechanical instruments, 14, 33
melodeon, 97
membrane, 6, 11, 59
membranophones: acoustics, 220; classified, 212–13
meråker klarinet, 91
mey, 75, 76
MIDI, 203, 206
midwinterhoorn, 106, 180–81
military instruments, Greek and Roman, 106
mirliton, 1–12, 26
mizmar, 77
mock trumpet, 88
monaulos, 75
monkey-drum, 30
monochord, 146
monofilament nylon, 154
mortar and pestle, 1, 44
mother and child, 147

motor horns, 85, 86, 181
mouth bow. *See* musical bow, mouth bow
mouth organs, 95, 96, 97, 98; relationship with trump, 197
mrdanga, 32
munnharpe, 199
muselaar, 101, 133, *147*
musette, 167
musical bow: aeolian, 196; gourd bow, 125, 152, *195*, 196; ground bow, 194
musical bow, mouth bow, 125, 194–95, 96; distribution, 196; legendary origins, 194; overtones, non-harmonic, 195; playing technique, 194–95, 196
musical box, 13
musical glasses, 18
musical saw, *174*, 212
mutavha, 44
mvahli, 77
mylar heads, 38–39

al nafir, 107
naggāra, 32, 34
nai, 46, 99
nakers, 28, 32, 35
naqqara, 32, 34
nares-jux, 131
nay, 47
negative instrument, 142
nfir, 107
noise-makers, 2, 26
Nonnengeige, 173
nose flute, 102
ntumpan, 182, 183
nyckelharpa, 174

oboe, 80, *81*, *82*, 83; fingerholes, 80; keys, 80, 81–82; reeds, 80, 81; sizes, 82; systems, 82
oboe d'amore, 82
oboe da caccia, 82
ocarinas, 51–*52*
oliphants, 106
ondes martenot, 202
one-note instruments, 44–45
ophicleide, 85, 110, 120; valved, 111
organ, *190*, *191*; abolished in Commonwealth, 122; Aquincum, 188, 189; barrel, 56, 192–93; Bethlehem, 189; *Blockwerk*, 189; drones, 102; English, 191; expensive, 193; fairground, 193; free reeds, 96; French, 191; Germany and the Netherlands, 190; hydraulic, *71*, 188; invention, 188; mechanisms, 188–89; neo-classical, 190, 191; pneumatic, 188–93; pneumatic lever, 190–91; portatives, *189*; positive, *190*; reed, 87, 192; reed organs, 96–97; regal, 192; registration, 192; roller board, 190; Roman, 188; signal-to-noise ratio, 192; sliders instead of keys, 189; Spanish, 192; split keys, 216; swell box, 192; tuning the pipes, 218;

Werkprinzip, 190; Winchester Cathedral, 189. *See also* electronic organs
organistrum, 145, 173
orgue expressif, 96
ōteki, 61
"over-the-shoulder" brass, 123

paired instruments, 20
palwe, 53
pandurina, 159
panpipes, 44, 45–46
pans, 205
pantaleon, 149
parlor pipes, 80
pedal harp. *See* harp
pellet bells, 19, *20, 21,* 174
penny whistle, 52; number of fingerholes, 54
péschtschiki, 87
phonofiddles, 174
phorbeia, 75
phorminx, 129
phupphu, 78, 106, 113
pī chawā, 77
pī klāng, 77
pī mōn, 77
pì saw, 95
piano, 140, 141, 149–50, *151,* 152; action, 149, 151; dampers, 151; double escapement, 151; escapement, 149; hammers, 151; inharmonicity of overtones, 220–21; Janko, 216; Neo-Bechstein, 202, 203; quieter than harpsichord, 151; sound degraded, 152; square, *150;* strain on the casework, 151; strings, 151; upright, 150, 152; with blind musicians, 133
piano accordion, 97
pibcorn, 74, 87, 89
piccolo parts, for transverse or recorder, 56
piob mhór, 79
pipa, 156, *157*
pipe and tabor, 37, *55,* 101
piri, 75
pirouette, 75
pitch pipe, 50
plastic drainpipe, 205
plectrum, 131, *142,* 146
Płock fiddle, *166,* 167
plucked drums, *207*
plucking piano, 152
pluriarc, *126*
"poet's lute," 144
posthorn, 110, 119, 181
preret, 77
psalmodikon, 142
psaltery, *142*
pūnghī, 86, 88
puutorino, 113, *114,* 185

qanun, 142
qaraqeb, 26
qena, 47
qin, 144, 219. *See also* yangqin
qoshnai, 88
quail lure, 105

rabāb, 164
rabab al-mughanni, 163, *164*
rababa, 163, *164*
racket, 85
rain-catcher, 112
rain stick, *20*
raj qeej, 95
ramsagar, 157
ratchets, 25
rattles, 18, *19, 21,* 24, 25; cluster, 18–19; external net, 20; paired, 20; sliding, 18–19; vessel, 19
rāvanhattā, 164
reaming a bore, 136–37
rebab, 17, 154, 163, *164*
rebab andaluz, 163, 165, 166, 171
rebec, 166, 167; tuning, 172
rdo-rje, 113
reclam de xeremia, 76
recorder, 54–55, 56; as the flute, 55; bore in Baroque, 54–55; bore in Renaissance, 54; constricted foot, 54; difficult to determine in iconography, 54; Dordrecht, 54; first appearance, 54; Göttingen, 54; intonation problems, 56; number of fingerholes, 54; revival, 56; sizes in Baroque, 56; sizes in Renaissance, 54, 55–56; which hand above, 54
red-hot fountain pen, 90, *91*
reed cane, 94
reed-contrabass, 81
reed instruments, acoustics, 218; bore contrasted, 73–74, 218; Northwest coast of Canada, 85
reeds, *74;* dilating, 73, 218; double and single contrasted, 73, 218; retreating, 213; types, 73
reeds, free. *See* free reed instruments
reed pipe origin, 75
Reform Flute, *118,* 202–3
regals, 192
resting bells, 16, *17*
rgya-gling, 77
rhombe, 21n8
rhombos, 3
rinding, 198
riqq, 29
rkan-gling, 31, 113
rock gong, 8
rommelpot, 5
rondador, 46
rosin, 162
rototoms, 29

rozhok, 87, 89
rubab, 155
Ruhrtrommel, 38
Russian bassoon, 110

sackbut, 108; and cornett, 109
sákárà, 29
salmoè, 90
salpinx, 106
Salzburg zither, 142
samplers, 203
sandpaper blocks, 212
sansa, 12–13, 21, 133
santur, 144
sanxian, 154, 157
sarangi, 163
sarinda, 163, 165
saron, 10
sarrusophones, 81, 123
saùng gauk, 127, 132
sausage bassoon, 85
saxophone, 85, 123, 206
saz, 141, 154, 205; electronic, 203
scabellum, 17, 18
scacciate i pensieri, 199
schaleika, 87
schools clarinet, 90
Schweizerpfeiff, 61
Schwirrholz, 21n8
seaweed trumpet, 103
seljefløyte, 65, 66
semantron, 8, 16
serpent, 110; upright, 106, 110
serunai, 78
serunèn, 77
sese, 164
setar, 141
shahnā'ī, 77, 78, 80, 101
shakuhachi, 47
shamisen, 154
shawms, cylindrical bore 74–75, 76; expanding bore, 75–76,
    77, 78–79, 180; forked, 78; loudness, 170; stepped, 78;
    still, 178
shell trumpets. See conch
sheng, 94, 95, 96
shields, Andaman, 208; as gongs, 16
shō, 96
shofar, 104, 105
short-necked lutes. See lutes, plucked worldwide
side-blown horns. See horns
side drum, 37–38
simbomba, 5
singing bowls, Tibet, 17, 44
single reed instruments, 85–86, 87, 88–89; double and single
    contrasted, 73, 218; reeds, 85; reeds, idioglot, 85–86

sistrum, 18–19
sitar, 101, 141, 155, 220
skudučiai, 44, 46
sleigh bells, 19, 24. See also pellet bells
slide trumpet, 109, 206
slit drums, 14, 24, 52, 182; area of aperture, 32, 52
small-pipes, 80
snake charmers' pipes, 86
snares, 29, 32, 37
snorra, 3–4
sopilka, 47
sousaphone, 112, 123
spiked fiddles. See fiddles
spiked lutes. See lutes, plucked worldwide
spinet, 147
spinetto, 147
spoons, 26
square piano, 150
squawkers, 85, 86
squeeze-boxes, 98
sruti, 77
śruti-box, 101
stamping tubes, 32, 44
steel drums, 205
stepped cone, 164
stick and slip, 162
still shawm, 85
stone chimes, 8, 9. See also lithophone; rock gong
stopped pipes, 218
string drum, 102, 141, 144; bamboo, 102, 144
string instruments: acoustics, 219, in Americas, 125, 196;
    classification, 212; modification of, 117–18; terminology
    of, xiii–xiv; with drone, 101. See also fiddles; lutes
stringed keyboards, methods of sounding, 145; hitting,
    149–52; plucking, 146–49; rubbing, 145; touching, 145–46
strings, behavior, 219; materials, 153–54, 156, 159, 161, 170;
    overwound, 141, 151, 170
Stro fidel, 11, 174
Stroh fiddle, 174
suling, 17, 53
suona, 77, 78, 80
superball, 174
swanee whistle, 16, 49, 50
sympathetic strings, 141, 171, 173
symphony, 173
synthesizers, 203
syrinx. See panpipe

tablā, 32, 33
tabor, 28, 35–37, 55
taille, 82
talharpa, 131, 174
talking drums, 181–82, 183
talking instruments, 107, 181–85
tambourin de Navarre or Béarn, 101, 144

tambourine, 21, 28, 29, *174*

tambūrā, 100, 101

tamtam, 17

tanbur, 154

tandem horn, 181

tangents, 145–46

tang xiao, 47

tar, 154, 155

tárogató, 85, *79*, 144

tarompèt, 75, *77*

tenor drum, 38

tenoroon, 84

tension, 27

theorbo, *161*; rose area, 52

theremin, 202

thod-dar, 30–31

thundersheet, 212

tibia, 75

til'boro, 88, 89

tilinca, 65, 66

timbila, *11*

timbre, 29

timpani, 32–35, 36, *37*; played with a superball, 174; pedal, 34–35, 174; shell-less, 29; tensioning, 28, 34; tuning, 34

tin whistle, *57*

tomtoms, 35

tong cymbals, 18, 70, *71*

Tour timps, 29

toys, children's, 4, 5, 24, 85

transverse flute. *See* flute, transverse

tricca-ballacca, 26

triple harp, 136

tromba da tirarsi, 108

tromba marina, 173, 219

trombone, *108–9*; buccin, 106; and cornett, 109; valve, 121

trompe de chasse, 112

trompette de menestrel, 108, *110*

trough zither, *141*

truc, 15

trump, 13, 32, 94, 196, *197–99*, 211; for talking, 185, 197; overtones non-harmonic, 195; relationship with mouthorgan, 197; substitutes for, 200; typology around the world, 198–9

trumpets, orchestral, 108, *109–10*; "Baroque," 109; Billingsgate, 107; folded shape, 108; hand-stopping, 109; medieval, long, 70, 107; medieval, wide, *71*, 106; mute, 109, *110*; slide, 109, *110*, 206; triggers, 220; with sliding mouthpiece, 108. *See also* key trumpet

trumpets, worldwide: C- or S-shaped in India, 107; distinction from horns, 105; materials (bamboo, bone, gourd, and wood), 113; mouthpiece shape, 105, 107; Roman, 106, 188; Tibet, bone, 113; vegetable origin, 106

Trumscheit, 173

trutruca, 180

tuba, 106

tuba, 110; family, 111

tubular bells, 16, 32

tuiter, *114*

tuning, control of, 27, 100, 152–53

tuning peg, 27, 129, 153

tuning slide, conical, 214; on flutes, 64

"Turkish music," 79

twirl-a-tube, 66

txalaparta, 9, *10*

txuntxun, 101, 133, 144

Tyrolean zither, 142

'*ud*, 155–56, *157*; electronic, 203

uillean pipes, 80

ukelin, *142*, 144

ukulele, 159

undercutting fingerholes, 137

valiha, *140*, 141

valves, *120*; *Berliner Pumpen*, 120; combination problems, 220; compensating, 220; double-piston, 120; effect of, 220; independent, 220; invention, 119–21; piston, 120, 121; problems of, 120; rotary, 120, 121; *système belge*, 120; twin-vane, 121

vargan, 211

vibraphone, 12

vielle à roue, 101, 133, 173

vihuela, 158, 171

vihuela de arco, 171

vīnā, 140–41, 155

viola, 158, 159

viola, 170

viola d'amore, 171

viola da braccio or *da brazza*, 168, 172

viole da gamba. *See* viols

violeta, 162, 167

violin, 167, *168–72*; chin-rest, 170; construction, 172; distinct from viols, 172; how held, 170; in early recording studios, 174; in other cultures, 171; modification, 169; mute, 86; origin in Italy, 167–68; parts of, 169; strings, 170; tone and projection, 168; tuning, 172; vibrato, 170

violino piccolo, 170

violoncello. *See* cello

viols, 168, *171–72*; construction, 172; development in Italy, 172; distinct from violins, 172; origin in Spain, 171; tuning, 172

virginals, *147*, Flemish, 147, 148

voice flute, 56

Wagner tuba, 112

wait pipe, 76

Waldteufel, 5, 6

walking stick instruments, 57–58

watch-key tuning, 160

Wetterhorn, 24

whistles, 49, 50; bone, Paleolithic, 45; buccal, 50; distinction from flutes, 48; nightingale, 50; pea-whistles, 50; piston, 50; police, 50; quail, 50; requirement of, 49; samba, 50; slide, 50; widgeon, 213
wind instruments: mistake to make "in tune," 217; terminology of, xiii
wind machine, 212
windcap, 87
wode, 46
woods, stability of, 81
woodwind, acoustics, 218, 219; metal, 123; modification, 118–19; radical alteration in 1600s, 62; which hand above, 54
wot, 46
wuj, 126

xiao, 47
ximbomba, 5
xun, 51

xylophones, 9–12, 102; beaters, 11; four-row, 1–22, 144; in Europe, 11–12, 174; leg, 10, log, 10; one-note, 9, 10; orchestras, 11; resonators, 6, 11, 12, 134; trough, 10

yangqin, 144

zampogna, 79, 167
za-zah, 6, 7
zheng, 144
zhu, 101–2
zilli masa, 26
zithers, defined, 140; bar, 140, 141; board, 140, 141, 142; bowed, 142, 144; box, 141, 142–44; ground, 142; half-tube, 144; raft zither, 140, 141; stick zither, 125, 140–41; trough, 141; tube zither, 140, 141
zukra, 87, 88
zummāra, 88, 218
zurla, 79, 80
zurna, 77, 78

Index of Places and Peoples

Abkharzia, 135

Aceh, 207

Afghanistan, 50, 141, 154

Africa, 3, 6, 8, 10, 11, 12, 14, 18, 21, 31, 48, 51, 52, 103, 105, 127, 131, 133, 181–85, 195; Central, 18, 126, 133, 134; East, 10, 102, 113, 125, 133, 163, 195; North, 29, 31, 47, 76, 107, 153, 163, 171, 174; Southern, 194; West, 18, 30, 31, 75, 88, 107, 141, 153. *See also* individual countries; South Africa

Africa and Indonesia, 10

Alor, 39

Americas: pre-Columbian, 51, 54, 103, 265, 125, 196; Central, 10–19, 48, 110, 136, 185; South, 3, 18, 37, 47, 48, 52, 64, 140, 125, 180, 185

Andaman Islands, 208

Anglesey, 25

Apache people, fiddle, 275; flute, 54

Aquincum, 188, 189

Arab peoples, 32, 86, 155–56

Aragon, Kingdom of, 163, 171

Armenia, 75

Armenian church, 8, 16

Asia, 18, 54, 95; Central, 17, 59, 75, 107, 127, 154, 161; East, 14, 53; South-East, 10, 17, 39, 53, 54, 64, 95, 125, 196, 198. *See also* individual countries

Assam, 113

Australia, 1, 3, 8, 26, 28, 205

Austria, 58, 97, 149, 168

Aymara people, 46

Azande people, 127

Babylon, 128

Bali, 10, 19

Balkans, 33, 47, 79, 87, 100, 141, 154, 166

Baltic states, 96, 110

Bangladesh, 140. *See also* India

Bashkir, 200

Basque region. *See* Euskal Herria

Beduin people, 44, 163

Bethlehem, 189

Berber people, 156, 163

Bohemia, 24, 104

Bolivia, 46

Borneo, 96

Brazil, 5, 8, 20, 50, 105, 125, 196

Brittany, 79, 80

Burma. *See* Myanmar

Byzantium, 48, 61, 131, 161

Cameroon, 12

Canada, 8; Northwest Coast, 85

Canary Islands, 182

Caribbean, 13

Catalunya, 79

Caucasus, 21, 29, 78, 127, 134, 135, 154, 155

Celebes. *See* Sulawesi

Ceylon. *See* Sri Lanka

China, 6, 8–9, 14, 16, 17, 18, 28, 39, 48, 51, 53, 59–60, 64, 75, 78, 94, 95, 96, 101, 127, 144, 154, 156, 163, 185, 196, 199, 210

Colombia, 8

Congo, 126, 185; defined, 175n6

Crete, 16, 103, 130, 134

Cuba, 13, 184

Cyprus, 103, 106

Dalmatia, 162

Damara people, 194

Denmark, 90, 105

Dongson culture, 39

Dordrecht, 54

Ecuador, 46

Egypt, 18, 19, 74, 78, 127, 128, 130, 132, 133, 134, 163, 188

England, 8, 9, 14, 129, 147, 181, 209
Ethiopia, 8, 19, 31, 44, 131, 163
Etruria, 75, 106
Europe, 11
Euskal Herria, 9, 79, 87, 101, 133, 144

Faliscan people, 75
Fiji, 9, 48, 104
Finland, 90, 131, 142
Flanders, 5, 14, 133, 147, 148
France, 3, 6, 8, 24, 80, 82, 84, 93, 94, 137–38, 148, 160, 166,
    172, 174

Georgia, 135
Germany, 6, 81, 96, 131, 139, 148, 160
Ghana, 182, 183, 184
Göttingen, 54
Greece, 166, 167, 205
Greece, ancient, 3, 6, 16, 44, 45, 74–75, 103, 106, 128–29,
    131, 135, 194, 205, 208, 216
Greek church, 8, 16
Greenland, 28–29
Guatemala, 12

Hausa people, 107
Hawaii, 90
Holland. See The Netherlands
Hungary, 33, 48, 65, 79, 85, 102, 103, 139, 141, 144

Iberia, 72, 79. See also Portugal; Spain
Ibiza, 25
Ibo people, 31, 185
Iceland, 41
India, 8, 18, 25, 30, 32, 48, 59, 78, 86, 100, 103, 105, 107,
    113, 125, 132, 140, 154, 155, 163, 194, 196, 198, 207,
    217; defined, 140, 177n55; ivory horns in, 185
Indonesia, 17, 53, 154, 78, 102, 141, 144, 197. See also
    individual islands
Inuit people, 28–29
Iran, 75, 155. See also Persia
Iraq, 74
Ireland, 80, 105, 133, 135–36, 139
Israel, 103, 128. See also Jerusalem
Italy, 5, 7, 15, 26, 79, 80, 103, 136, 148, 155, 163, 167–68,
    172, 209. See also Rome

Japan, 16, 47, 48, 61, 75, 96, 104, 127, 144, 154, 156, 161,
    194
Java, 10, 17, 19, 24, 75, 78, 163, 214
Jerusalem, Latin Kingdom, 15, 189

Kabre people, 8
Kafiristan, 126
Kano, 184
Karen people, 39

Kenya, 181, 185
Kerala, 32
Korana people, 196
Korea, 9, 75, 127, 144
Kru people, 126

Laos, 96
Liberia, 126
Libya, Qasr el-Lebia, 70, 156
Lithuania, 44
Luo people, 185

Macedonia, 79
Madagascar, 10, 106, 141
Mafia Island, 181
Magdalenean sites, 3, 6–7
Maghrib, 76, 153
Malaysia, 78
Malekula, 52, 181, 182
Malta, 103
Manding, 153
Melanesia, 196, 197–98
Mesopotamia, 14, 19, 127, 128, 153
Mexico, 12, 54, 78, 166, 196
Miao people, 96, 185
Middle East, 31
Moche people, 103, 113, 196
Molln, 198
Mongolia, 198, 200
Morocco, 26, 29, 59, 78, 107, 156, 163
Mozambique, 11
Muria Gonds (people), 113
Myanmar, 18, 31, 39, 53, 78, 95, 127, 132, 171

Naga people, 78, 106, 113
Naxi people, 199
Neanderthal, 210
Nepal, 78, 198
The Netherlands, 5, 81, 180–81
New Guinea, 3, 31, 46, 48, 51, 64, 65, 113, 181, 182, 200
New Hebrides, 52, 181
New Zealand, 113, 185
Nigeria, 8, 29, 31, 78, 107, 141, 153, 182, 183–84, 198
Nineveh, 128, 134
Northumbria, 80
Norway, 65, 90, 171, 198

Oceania, 46, 48, 64, 104, 105. See also individual islands
Ossetia, 135
Ottoman Empire, 78, 142, 154, 156, 205

Pakistan, 140. See also India
Persia, 76, 141, 144, 156. See also Iran
Peru, 64, 103, 113, 275
Philippines, 48, 104

Poland, 166, 180
Polynesia, 196
Portugal, 27, 29, 37, 159, 160
Provence, 37

Quechua people, 46

Romania, 46, 59, 65, 101, 180
Rome, 161, 163
Rome, ancient, 14, 16, 18, 72, 75, 76, 79, 101, 106, 156, 188
Russia, 14, 24, 44, 59, 87, 154, 155, 166, 180
Rwanda, 141

Salzburg, 142
Sassanid people, 76, 96, 156
Scandinavia, 24, 142. *See also* individual countries
Scotland, 79, 80
Siberia, 29, 132, 198
Sicily, 160
Silk Road, 75
Slovakia, 58, 65
South Africa, 11, 44, 125, 130, 196
Soviet Union. *See* individual states; Russia
Spain, 5, 25, 37, 80, 83, 103, 158, 159, 160, 161, 163, 166
Sri Lanka, 32, 78
Sudan, 130
Sulawesi, 64
Sumatra, 64, 207
Sumeria, 128, 132
Surinam, 64
Swazi people, 125
Sweden, 110, 131, 174
Switzerland, 15, 16, 37, 180

Taiwan, 9, 199
Tajikistan, 155
Tanzania, 16, 181
Thailand, 6, 8, 78, 95, 96, 103
Tibet, 16, 18, 30–31, 78, 104, 107, 113, 200
Tifalmin people, 200
Togo, 8
Toradja people, 64
Trinidad, 205
Tunisia, 87
Turkey, 18, 33, 38, 39, 47, 75, 78, 94, 100–101, 154, 203
Tuva people, 200
Tyrol, 123, 142, 168

Uganda, 130, 133, 185
Ukraine, 7
United States of America, 8, 20, 43, 53–54, 96, 103, 121, 122, 123, 139, 144, 150, 161, 181, 185, 186, 193; instrument-making trade, 152
Ur, 74, 128
Uzbekistan, 155

Venda people, 44
Vietnam, 7, 39

Wales, 74, 87, 131, 133, 135, 136, 167, 174; sobriquets, 41

Xhosa people, 125, 196

Yakutsia, 132
Yugoslavia, 59, 78

Zaire, 9
Zimbabwe, 13, 141
Zulu people, 16, 125, 185

General Index

Page numbers in italic refer to figures. Authors' names are only listed here when they appear in the main text.

Abel, Carl Friedrich, 172
accademie, 209
Acme, *49*
acoustical analysis, fallacies of, 200
acoustics, brass, 218–19; fingerholes, 219; flutes, 217–18;
    percussion, 220; problems with, 217; reed instruments,
    218; string instruments, 219
Adams, Nathan, 121
Adkins, Cecil J., 195
aerophones, acoustics, 217–19; defined/classified, 213–14
Africa and Indonesia, 10
Agirre, Jose Manuel, 79
Agricola, Martin, 11, 54
Aign, Bernhard, 128
Albert, Eugène, 93, *94*
Alexander VI, Pope, 172
Alexander, Gebr., 84
Alexandre, Jacob, 96
Alexandru, Tiberiu, 101
al-Fārābī, 161
Al-Kindi, 156
Allegri String Quartet, 162
Allison, Richard, 122
Almenräder, Carl, 84
Amati, Andrea, 168, 170, 171; his model preferred, *168*
Amati, Girolamo, 168
Amati, Nicolo, 168
Amaterasu, 194
animal calling, 186
animal lures, 85, 86
animal scarer, 33
Anoyanakis, Fivos, 15
anthropology, contrasted with ethnography, 210
anthropomorphic terminology, 155
Apocalypse, Elders of the, 166

Apollo, 129, 167, 194
Arabic names for instruments, 72, 78
Arbeau, Thoinot, 37
archaeology, limitations of, 45
area of open hole, 32, 51, 52
Aristophanes, 79
Armada, Spanish, 50
Arnaut de Zwolle, Henri, 146, 147, 149, 156, 190, 192
Asté, Jean Hilaire, 110
Astor, 63
Atlas of Musical Instruments, 135
Auriols, Xavier, 79

Babcock, Alpheus, 151
Bach, Johann Christian, 150
Bach, Johann Sebastian, 108, 112, 113, 190, 192; *Brandenburg
    Concerto no. 1*, 170; *Brandenburg Concerto no. 2*, 109; *Well-
    Tempered Clavichord*, 217
Bachmann, Werner, 70, 161
Baines, Anthony, 64, 75
Balfour, Henry, 5, 125, 194, 196, 213
bands. *See* Index of Instruments and Accessories
bards, 41
Barnes & Mullins, *91*
Barnes, S. B., *49*
Barr, Matthias, *7*
Barret, Apollon Marie Rose, *82*
Barrow, Dr. T., 185
Bartók, Béla, 102, 144
Bate, Philip, 63, 89
Baumgärtel, 93
Bayer, Bathja, 128
Bayeux tapestry, 106
Beare, Charles, 168
Beauchamp Chapel, Warwick, 131, *132*, 146, 147, 167

beats, 215
Bebey, Francis, 8
bebung, 146
Beck, Fredeick, *150*
Becker, Heinz, 74, 75
Becker, Judith, 132
Beethoven, Ludwig van, 151, 169; *Battle Symphony*, 25, 192; *Ninth Symphony*, 38, 121; *Piano Sonata* in A flat, no. 31, op. 110, 149; piano writing, 152; violin range, 169
Behm, Theobald, 62, 118; mechanism, *63*, *64*, *82*, *93*, *94*, 206
bellows, smith's, 5
"belly," 155
Berlioz, Hector, 85, 121; *Symphonie Fantastique*, 16, 110
Bethlehem, 41, 415
Bevan, Clifford, 111, 112
Beverley Minster, Yorkshire, *35*, 76–78
Bharata, 211
Bibikov, S. N., 7
Big Ben, 16
Bige, József, *79*
Bilbao, Leon, 89
Bina, *157*
bird lures, 86, 105, 181
bird scarer, 10, 33, 35
birds, caged, teaching, 56
Bizet, Georges., *L'Arlésienne*, 37
Black Duck, 86
blackwood, 81
Blades, James, 9
Blaikley, David, 220
Blandford, W. F. H., 121
blindness and music, 132–33, 173
Blockwerk, 415
Blühmel, Friedrich, 120, 121
bodily perfection, ancient Greece, 75
body percussion, 207–8
Bonanni, Filippo, 7, 26
Boosey, *94*
bore, of reed instruments contrasted, 158–59
Borgia family, 172; Pope Alexander VI, 172; Lucrezia, 172
Bos longifrons and *primigenius*, 105
Bösendorfer, 152
bourgeoisie, rise of, 116
bowing, 162–63, 206; left- or right-handed, 162; origins of, 161; percussion players, 174
Bowles, Edmund, 34
boxwood, 81
Boyden, David, 168
Brahms, Johannes, 113, 152, 206
brass, malleable as spaghetti, 112
Braun, Joachim, 128
Bressan, Peter, 62
Broadwood, John and Thomas, 151
Brod, Henri, 83
buffalo horns, 185

Buffet, Auguste, 83, 93
Bull, William, 112
Burgkmair, Hans, 61
Burnham Bros., 86
Burton, John, 211
buskers, *174*, 226
Busson, 97
Butisian, A., *164*
Butler, George, *49*
Buxtehude, Dietrich, 192

Cabart, *63*
Caccini, Giulio, 161
Calixtus III, Pope, 172
campanology, 15
Cántigas de Santa Maria, 33, 72, 61, 156, 163
capella, a private band, 116
Carmelo, Catania, *160*
Carte, Richard, *118*, 119
Cavaillé-Coll, Aristide, 191
caves, Palaeolithic, 3, 6, 7
cents, 214
change-ringing, 40
changes in society, 116
Chappell, *118*
Charles II, King, 172
Charles IX, King, 168
charter horns, 106
cheek-pumping, 75, 79, 87, 205
Chemchoyev, Revo, *199*
Chickering, Jonas, 151
children's instruments, 4, 5, 24, 85, 196
Chinese fleets, voyages of, 48, 54, 125
Chopin, Frederick, 146, 151, 152
chordophones, acoustics, 219; classification, 212
chromatic scales, xv
circular breathing, 75, 79, 87, 205
clarino technique, 109, 119, 121
classical music, taking shape, 116
classification, cultural connotations, 211; Chinese, 210; Hindu, 211 Linnean, 211; Mahillon, 211; Montagu-Burton, 211; pictorial or schematic, 211; systems of, 210–14
classification, Hornbostel and Sachs, 211, 212–14; aerophones, 213–14; chordophones, 212; idiophones, 212; membranophones, 212–13
Clausen, Raymond, 52, 182
Clementi, *118*
clog dancers, 18, 208
Coles, John, 105
color in music, 217
composers affected by social change, 42–43
Concertgebouw Orchestra, 16
concert halls, 117; design, 221
Confucian ritual, 8, 9

Confucius, 8, 144, 145
conservatoires, 42
constricted foot, 118, 124–25
contained air, as a dominant, 32
continuo, 160
copper vs. brass, 110
copyright, lack of, 43
Corelli, Archangelo, 161, 169
Corinthians, Epistle to, 16
Corrette, Michel, 192
Couchet family, 148
Couperin, Louis, 192
court music, function of, 116
Cousineau, Georges, and Jacques-Georges, 137, 138
Crane, Frederick, 70
Cristofori, Bartolomeo, 149, 151
Crosthwaite, Peter, 9
cross-fingering, 62, 63
cylindrical and widening bores contrasted, 73–74, 218

Dams, Lya, 6–7
dance, inherent in nature, 1
D'Anglebert, Jean-Henri, 192
da Sàlo, Gasparo, 168, 393
David, King, 128
Day, C. R., 90, 110
Deagan, J. C., 12
Debain, Alexandre, 96
Debussy, Claude, 215; *Danses Sacrées et Profanes*, 139
Denner, Jacob, 90
Denner, Johann Christoph, 89, 90
Denner, Johann David, 89
d'Este family of Ferrara, 172
detritus of our modern age, 20, 47, *164*, 205
developmental sequence, 10, 45, 47, 127
diatonic scales, xv
Dio Chrysostom, 80
Dionysian mysteries, 3
Dodd, John, 163
Dolmetsch, Arnold, 56, 152, 172
Donati, Giuseppe, 51–52
Doré, *94*
Dournon-Taurelle, Geneviève, 197
Dowd, William, 152
Dowland, John, 145
drone, 100–102; aid to good tuning, 100
Drumbleby, Samuel, 56
Durán, Lucy, 208

Early Music movement, 152
Easter rites, 25
ebonite, 81
Edwards, David Van, *161*
Egan, John, 139
Einbigler, Johann, 34

electric versus electronic, 205
Ellis, Alexander J., 215
Elschek, Oskár, 211
empirical design, 221
Emsheimer, Ernst, 59
Encycloplédie, 137
end correction, 218
endomusicology, 210
entrepreneurial culture, rise of, 116
Erard, Sébastien, 137–38, 151
Esterhazy, Count, 171
ethnography, contrasted with anthropology, 210
ethnomusicology, 210
Eulenstein, Karl, 199
Eyck, Jacob van, 14
Eyck, Jan van, *Adoration of the Mystic Lamb*, 102

Fagg, Bernard, 8
Fagg, Catherine, 8
Falla, Manuel de, 152
Ferrari, Gaudenzio, 168
fertility rites and symbols, 5, 8, 25
fingerholes, effects of, 219; undercutting, 137
fingering techniques, problematic, 52–53
Fjelldal, Snorre, *91*
flamenco dancers, 208
Flight & Robson, *193*
flint knappers, 1
Flory, Hildebrand van, 122
folklorists, over-enthusiastic, 181
Franck, César, 191
Frank, Simon, *25*
Franklin, Benjamin, 18
Frederick the Great, 62, 216
frequency-doubler, 127, 207
frets, 155–56, 172
Frichot, Louis Alexandre, 110
frustration in studies of early times, 3

Galpin, Francis W., 74, *173*, 211, 213
Galpin Society Journal, 53
Galton, Francis, 194
gamut, 158
Garofalo, Il, (Benvenuto Tisi), 167
gate music, 32
Gilland, Harald, 90
Gimpel, Jean, 72
gladiators, 188
Goodrich, Ebenezer, 96
Goulding, 84
Gray & Davidson, *191*
Greeting, Thomas, 56
Grenié, Gabriel-Joseph, 96
Guarneri, Andrea, 168
guilds, 41–42

Gundestrop Cauldron, 106
Gusikow, 12
Gyokujan, Jitokusai, 60

Haka, Richard, 62
Halary, 110
Hale, John, 84, 122
Haliday, Joseph, 110, 119
hammering versus plucking, 149
Hampl, Anton Joseph, 113, 181
Handel, George Frideric, 84, 113, 161; *Harp Concerto*, 136;
    "recording," 193
hand-clapping, 207
Hanifovich, Magroupor Ravil, *199*
Hardy, Thomas, 122
harmonic series, 215; absence of in other cultures, 217
harmonic vent-hole, 109, 119
Hawkes, *25, 84, 94*
Hawkins, John Isaac, 152
Haydn, Franz Joseph, 34, 151, 171; *Military Symphony*, 38;
    Trumpet Concerto, 110, 119
Heckel, Johann Adam, and Wilhelm, 83, 84
Hely, Benjamin, 122
Helffer, Mireille, 31
Helmholtz resonator, 52
Hémony brothers, 14
Henderson, Peter, *79*
Henry VIII, King, 50, 61, 85, 166
Hermes, 129, 130
Hérouard frères, *92*
hetaira, 129
hetero-, explained, xiv
Hickmann, Hans, 134
Higgs, George, 6.3
"higher and lower," 222n22
high-twist gut, 129, 219
Hill, Henry, 63
Hipkins, Alfred, 151, 152
Hoeprich, Eric, 90, 91
hog-calling, 186
Hohner, *97*
Holbein, Hans, 11, *12*
Holmes, Peter, *110*
Holy Week, 25
Homer, 41, 74, 129
hominids, 209
Homo Neanderthal, 210
Homo sapiens, 209
Hood, Mantle, 17, 211
Hornbostel, Carl Moritz von, and Sachs, system, 211–14
Hornell, James, 104
horsehair, 135, 153, 161, 162
Hotteterre family, 62, 63, 80
Hu Jiaxun, 185
Hubbard, Frank, 152

Hudson, J. H., *49*
human body, 207–8
human voice, 206
hummed drone, 101
Hummel, Johann Nepomuk, *Trumpet Concerto*, 110, 119
Hunt, Edgar, 56
Husaini, Sarkin Kugen Kano, *183, 184*
Hyde, John, 109, 206

iconography, medieval, reliability of, 70, 156
idio-, explained, xiv
idiophones, acoustics, 220; all pitched, 67; defined/classified,
    212
"in tune," 221
Indonesian traders, 1–19
industrial processes, 72
industrial revolution, 116
initial transients, 202
initiation rites, 3
instrument-making, industrialization of, 122
instrumentarium, medieval change in, 70–72
instruments, inclusivity, 3; modified over time, 203; origins
    of, 1–2
Isis rite, 19
ison, 101, 206

Jairazbhoy, Nazir Ali, 30, 212
Janissary bands, 78, 94
Janko, Paul von, 216
Jericho, siege of, 105
Jones, Fr. A. M., 183

Kalevala, The, 142
Karp, Cary, 90
Kartomi, Margaret, 207–8, 211
Kauer, Ferdinand, 11
Kaufmann, Walter, 132
Keith Prowse, *91*
Kirby, Percival, 195
klezmer, 94
Klosé, Hyacinthe, 93
Koch, Stephan, *82*
Kodály, Zoltán, 144
Koenig, *Posthorn Gallop*, 181
Köhler, John, 95
Kölbel, Ferdinand, 119
kon-ko-lo, 183
korybantes, 16
Kreisler, Fritz, 170
Krishna, 32, 48, 103
Ktesibios, 412
Kuczkowski, Andrzej, *166*
Kunst, Jaap, 17, 210
Kunz, Ludvík, 24

Lachenal, Louis, 97
Ladies of the Half-Length, 61
Last Trumpet, 105
Lavoll, *199*
Lawson, Colin, 90
Leedy, 35
Lehr, André, 15
Leichamschneider, Johann, 112
Lewy, E. C., and J. R., 121
Light, Edward, 139
Lincoln Cathedral, 101, *135*, 167
Linné, Carl von, 211
Lípa, J., *93*
Liszt, Franz, 191
Lloyd, A. L., 180
Lorée, François, 82
Loriod, Yvonne, 202
Louis XIV, King, 54, 62, 80
Ludovico el Moro, 167
Ludwig, William F., 35
Lully, Jean-Baptiste, 80
Lund, Cajsa, 3, 5, 59
Lyon, Gustave, 139
Lyon and Healey, 139

Macclesfield Psalter, 65
Magdalenean sites, 3
Maggini, Gio Paolo, 168
Magherini, Ivo, *158*
Mahabhārata, 103
Mahillon, Charles, 123
Mahillon, Victor-Charles, 211
Mahler, Gustav, 171
male/female contrast of instruments, 35
Mallardtone, 86
Mana, Simon, *198*
Marais, Marin, 172
Marcel-Dubois, Claudie, 132
Marix, Mayer, *94*
Martenot, Maurice, 202, 206
Martin, Frank, 152
Mary Rose, 50, 85, 166
masks, Africa, 6
Mason & Hamlin, 97
master drummer, 183
mechanical technology, development of, 119
Megaw, Vincent, 52, 53
Meinl und Lauber, *110*
membranophone, acoustics, 220; defined/classified, 212–13
Memlinc, Hans, 108
Mendelssohn-Bartholdy, Felix, *Midsummer Night's Dream Overture*, 110
Menzies, Gavin, 48, 54
mercenaries, 37, 61
Mersenne, Marin, 6, 54, 56, 96, 109, 112, 155

Messiaen, Olivier, 202
Metzler, 97
Meucci, Renato, 106
Meyer, Heinrich Friedrich, *82*
Meyerbeer, Giacomo, *Les Huguenots*, 16
Mezzetti brothers, *52*
Michael, *198*
Milhouse, Richard and William, *81*, *92*
military instruments, Greek and Roman, 106
minstrels, 41, 121
Modern Musical Instruments Mfg. Co-op, *155*
Moeck, Hermann, 59
Moghul conquest of India, 32, 140
Mollenhauer, Gustav, *118*
monofilament nylon, 154
Montague Bros., 63
Monteverdi, Claudio, 161
Moog, Robert, 203, 206
Moonen, Anthony, *57*
Moritz, Johann Gottfried, 111
Morley-Pegge, Reginald, 110
Mowbray, Marcus de, 29
Mozarabic manuscripts, 156, 161
Mozart, Wolfgang Amadeus, 146, 151; *Adagio and Rondo*, 18; Clarinet Quintet and Concerto, 94; harpsichord concertos, 149; *Il Seraglio*, 38, 56; *La Clemenza di Tito*, 94; *Magic Flute*, 45; Masonic works, 94; Piano Concerto in E flat, K.271, 149; "recording," 193; *Sleigh Ride*, 20; violin range, 169
Müller, *142*
Müller, Iwan, *93*
multiphonics, 206
multivoice singing, 200
music, definition of, 1–2; home-made, 41
musical instrument making, mechanization of, 211–12
musical notes, terminology, xiv
musical pitch, history of, 117
"musical sound," 2
musicians, affected by social changes, 42–43; availability of, 121; as names, 41; essential to society, 41, 121; sources for, 121–221; training, 42
Myers, Herbert, 63

Nadermann, Jean-Henri, *137*, 138
names by trade, 41
Nara, Shōsōin Repository, 48, 96, 156, 161
Nātyaśāstra, 211
Neanderthal, 210
Nero, Emperor, 79
"New Music," 161
Nicol, Gray, *113*
Nicholson, Charles, *118*
Noblet, F., *57*
noise as protection, 24
Nopil, F., 60

notes inégales, 193
Nussbaum, Jeffrey, 181

octave, steps to the, 214
Oehler, Oskar, 93
Olsen, Dale, 52–53
one-man band, 98
opera, 117
orchestra, creation of, 117, 172; growth of, 117
organum, 145
ostinato, 102
"our" music, etc., 2
Ottoman Empire, 78, 142, 154, 156, 205
overblowing, 220
overtones, xiv, 100, 220
overtone singing, 200

Pagés, José, 159
painted caves, 6, 7, 8
Pan, in legend, 45
Pape, Henri, 151
Parkinson, Andrew, 51
Patent Office, 206
Peaseley, Arthur Merrill, 96
Pediwest, 91
Pepys, Samuel, 56
Pereira, Manuel, 160
performing rights, 43
Périnet, François, 120, 121
Philidor family, 62
Piccinini, Alessandro, 161
piccolo parts, for transverse or recorder, 56
Picken, Laurence, 50, 96, 101, 154, 211, 213
Piedigrotta festival, 103
Piggott, Stuart, 106
Pittrich, Carl, 34, 36
player's posture, 200
Playford, John, 122
Pleyel, 152
plucking vs. hammering, 149
polyrhythmy, 183
Pope, Alexander, 209
Potter, Richard, 63
Poulenc, Francis, 152
Powell, Ardal, 63
Praetorius, Michael, 34, 37, 54, 55, 108, 112, 173, 174, 210
pre-Columbian, 51, 54, 103, 265, 125, 196
prehistoric time, periods of, 209–10
Pratten, Robert Sidney, 118
"primitive," a taboo word, 210
Puccini, Giacomo, Tosca, 16
Purcell, Henry, 109
Purim, 25
Pythagoras, hammer weights, 44; temperament, 216

Quantz, Johann Joachim, 63, 216
Queisser, E., 36

rāg, 100
Ram Narayan, 163
Rameau, Jean-Philippe, 56
Rashid, Subhi Anwar, 134
Raudonikas, Felix, 63
Rault, Lucy, 6
ravalement, 149
Ravel, Maurice, Introduction and Allegro, 139
Rawson, John, 145
reaming a bore, 63
reed cane, 192–93
Reger, Max, 191
relaxation, bodily, 200–201
relaxed wrist, 149, 200
religion, instinctive, 1
resin, 162
resonance chambers of the body, 200
resultants, xv
rhythmic counterpoint, 1
Rice, Albert, 90
Richards-Jones, Nansi, 136
Richardsons' Rock Band, 9
Richters, Hendrik and Frederik, 122
Riedl, Josef Felix, 120
Roca, 160
Rogeri, Giovanni Battista, 168
rosin, 162
"rough music," 5
Royal Academy of Music, 42
Royal Military Exhibition, 88
The Royal Society, 209
Ruckers family, 148
Rudall, Rose, Carte, 118
Rugeri, Francesco, 168
Rycroft, David, 195, 196

Sachs, Curt, 4; and Hornbostel system, 211–14
St. Patrick, 15
St. Paul, 16
Sta. Caterina de' Vigri, 162, 167
Saint-Saëns, Camille, 191; Carnival of the Animals, 11
salii, 16
Sanusi, Emir Alhaji Mohammed, 184
Sanzaemon, Maruyama, 29
Sárosi, Bálint, 11, 139
Sarrus, Pierre Auguste, 81, 123
Sattler, Friedrich, 120
Savary, Jean Nicholas, 83
Sax, Adolphe, 29, 85, 93, 120, 121, 122, 123, 206, 220
Sax, Charles, 193
Sayce, Lynda, 52

scales, 214; equal-tempered, 215; harmonic or just, 215, *219*; heptatonic, 214–15; hexatonic, 215; India, 217; *pelog*, 214; pentatonic, 214; *slendro*, 214; wholetone, 215. *See also* temperament
Schaeffner, André, 3
Scheibler, Heinrich, 199
Schlütter, Friedrich, *199*
Schubert, Franz, *Auf dem Strom*, 121
Schunda, Jozsef, 144
Schunda, Wenzel, 85
Schwarz, Karl, *199*
Scriabin, Alexander Nicolyevich, 217
Sellner, Josef, *82*
shaman, 66
Shann, Richard, *146*
Shaw, George Bernard, 152
Sheba, Queen of, 131
Shiva, 194
short octave, 148–49
Shorto, Harry, 14
Shōsōin Depository, 48, 96, 156, 161
Siccama, Abel, *118*
Silk Road, 75
Simon, Winston, 205
smiths, 1, 5, 44
Smythe, Ethel, *Concerto for violin and horn*, xv
Snoeck, César, 89, 90
society, changes in, 42–43, 116
Solomon, King, 131
song, inherent in nature, 1
sound as protector, 32
Sousa, John Philip, 112, 123
Spohr, Louis, 170
srutis, 217
Stadler, Anton, 94
Stadtpfeifer, 41, 42, 76, 121
Stainer, Jacob, 168, 171
stalagmites and stalactites, 6–7
standard pattern, 93, 183
Stanesby, Thomas, Junior, *63*, 84
statues, Greek, 6
Stein family, 151
Steinway, *151*
stepped cone, 78
stick and slip, 162
Stölzel, Heinrich, *120*, 121
Stone Ages, knowledge of, 3
stopped pipes, 218
Storbekken, Egil, 65, 66
Stradivari, Antonio, 163, 168; his model preferred, *168*
Straume, Bjørgulv, *199*
Strauss, Richard, *Till Eulenspiegel*, 38
Stravinsky, Igor, 144; *L'Histoire du Soldat*, 38
street buskers, 98

Streicher, Nanette, 151
Strohviols, *174*
Strupe, Cecil, 35
Stumpff, Johann, 34
Stuttgart Psalter, 156
Swiss mercenaries, 37, 61
sympathetic strings, 141, 171, 173
Syrinx, 45

tablature, 144
talking instruments, 107, 181–85; need for a skilled listener, 185
tap-dancers, 18, 208
Tărtăreanu, Dimitru, *58*
Taylor, John, 46, *51*, 52
Tchaikovsky, Piotr Il'yich, *The Nutcracker*, 6
temperament, 216–17; equal, 215, 216; equal, loss of color, 217; irregular, 217; meantone, 216; Pythagorean, 216
Temperly, Nicholas, 122
tension, 27
tension and release, 100
Termen, Lev, 202, 206
Theophrastus, 74
Thibouville-Lamy, Jérôme, *174*
third a dissonant interval, 216
Thutmosis III, Pharaoh, 128
Till, Daniel, 9
Tinctoris, Johannes, 156, 158, 159, 171
Tisi, Benvenuto, 167
tonal languages, 181–82; China, 185; need for a skilled listener, 185
Topf, Willy, *91*
Torre, Steve, 181
Torres Jurado, Antonio de, 159
Tourte, François, 163, 169
toys, children's, 4, 5, 24, 85
Tracey, Hugh, *13*
Trân Quang Hai, 200
Trân Van Khê, 7
Triébert, Guillaume and Frédéric, *82*, *83*
The Triumph of Maximilian I, 34, 61
Troman, M., *199*
Trowell, Brian, 54
tuning, control of, 61–62, 100, 153
"Turkish music," 38
Tutankamun, Pharaoh, 105
Tveit, Johannes Bårdsen, *168*
Twenty-four Violins, 172

Uhlmann, Johann Tobias, *82*, *83*
undercutting fingerholes, 63
unisons, 214
Utrecht Psalter, 70, *71*, 134, 156, 188

Vargyas, Lajos, 200
Ventura, Angelo, 139
Vergleichende Musikwissenschaft, 210
Vertkov, K., et al., 135
vibrato on string instruments, 170
Vicentino, Nicola, 216
Vingt-quatre Violons du Roi, 172
Virdung, Sebastian, 54, *55*
Vivaldi, Antonio, 90; *Conca*, 24
vowel language, 186
Vuillaume, Jean-Baptiste, 169

Wagner, Richard, *Parsifal*, 16; *The Ring*, 44, 108
waits, 41, 76, 121
Wallis, Joseph, *57*
Walter, Anton, 151
waltz, Viennese, 37
Ward, Cornelius, 81
water mills, 72
Weber, Carl Maria von, *Concertino*, xv, 200
Weber, Rainer, 54
Weidinger, Anton, 204, 110
Wells, Robert, *20*
West, Martin, 128, 135
"Western music," 2
Westminster Abbey, Chapter House, 131, 167

Westminster chimes, 16
Whitman, Brian Lee, *91*
Widor, Charles-Marie, 191
Wieprecht, Wilhelm, 111, *120*, 121
Williamson, Muriel, 132
Willis, Henry, 191
Winchester Cathedral, 189
Wood, Sir Henry, 117
Wood, James, *92*
Woodfield, Ian, 163, 171
woods, stability of, 81
work songs, 41
World Archaeology, 53
World Music, 210
Wright, John, 197
Wright, Laurence, *79*
Wylde, Henry, *82*

Yi, Marquis of Zeng, 9, 48, 59, 102
yodel, 186

Zajaruzny, Anatoly, 89
Zeus, 3; birth of, 16
Ziryab, 156
Zumpe, Johann Christoph, 150

~

About the Author

Jeremy Montagu has published a number of books on musical instruments, including *Musical Instruments of the Bible* (Scarecrow Press, 2002), *Reed Instruments: The Montagu Collection, an Annotated Catalogue* (Scarecrow Press, 2001), *Percussion Instruments* (Yale University Press, 2002), *Minstrels and Angels: Carvings of Musicians in Medieval English Churches*, with his late wife, Gwen (Scarecrow Press, 1998), and others that can be seen on his website, www.jeremymontagu.co.uk. He has also written many articles in journals such as the *Galpin Society Journal* and *Early Music*, as well as entries in several encyclopedias, including the New Grove dictionaries and all the instrument articles in *The Oxford Illustrated Encyclopedia of the Arts* and the 2002 edition of *The Oxford Companion to Music*. He owns one of the largest private collections of musical instruments in the world, many of which are illustrated here. Now retired, he was the curator of the Bate Collection of Musical Instruments and lecturer in the University of Oxford. He has also been a visiting lecturer in a number of other universities. He is the president of the Galpin Society for Musical Instruments and a Fellow of the Society of Antiquaries of London. He is also a past president of the European Seminar in Ethnomusicology.